Gardening by Mail: A Source Book

Barbara J. Barton

A directory of mail-order resources for gardeners in the United States and Canada, including seed companies, nurseries, suppliers of all garden necessaries and ornaments, horticultural and plant societies, magazines, libraries, and a list of useful books on plants and gardening.

EVERYTHING FOR THE GARDEN AND GARDENER

Tusker Press
1987

Published by Tusker Press
P. O. Box 1338
Sebastopol, CA 95473
(707) 829-9189

Programming by Nancy D. H. Jacobsen
BobRed Co.
P. O. Box 229
Forest Knolls, CA 94933
(415) 488-9279

Dedicated to my parents, Hildor & Marguerite Barton, and to my aunt, Margit Barton McNulty; they thought I could do anything, made it possible, and it worked!

Library of Congress Cataloging–in–Publication Data

Barton, Barbara J.
Gardening by mail 2.

Includes bibliographies and indexes.
1. Gardening – United States – Directories.
2. Horticulture – United States – Directories.
3. Gardening – Canada – Directories. 4. Horticulture – Canada – Directories. 5. Mail–order business – United – States – Directories. 6. Mail–order business – Canada – Directories. I. Title.

SB450.953.U6B36 1987 635'.029'47 87–25558
ISBN 0–937633–02–X (pbk.)

PRINTING: 7 6 5 4 3 2 1

Loving thanks to Cathleen Daly for the drawing of roses on the title page.

TABLE OF CONTENTS

Introduction

- i **Introduction**
- ii **Important Information For Using This Source Book**
- iv **State, Provincial And Country Abbreviations Used In The Tables And Indexes**

Listings

- A **Plant And Seed Sources** — Listed Alphabetically
- B **Garden Suppliers And Services** — Listed Alphabetically
- C **Professional Societies And Trade Associations** — and Umbrella Groups — Listed Alphabetically
- D **Horticultural Societies** — and Plant Societies — Listed Alphabetically
- E **Magazines** — Horticultural Magazines Available on Subscription — Listed Alphabetically by Title
- F **Libraries** — Horticultural Libraries — Listed by State or Province
- G **Books** — List of Useful Horticultural Books

Indexes

- H **Plant Sources Index** — Plant and Seed Sources Indexed by Plant Specialties
- J **Geographical Index** — Plant and Seed Sources Indexed by Location
- K **Product Sources Index** — Garden Suppliers and Services Indexed by Specialty and Location
- L **Society Index** — Horticultural Societies Indexed by Plants or Special Interests
- M **Magazine Index** — Society and Subscription Magazines Indexed by Title

Practical Matters

- I Found You in Gardening by Mail — A Catalog and Information Request Form
- Record of Catalog Orders and Requests
- Reader Feedback
- Request for Listing in Next Edition or Update of Current Listing
- Order form for Gardening by Mail
- Updates to Gardening by Mail
- Last Minute Changes and Corrections

Table of the Symbols and Abbreviations Used in this Book
Appears Inside the Front and Back Covers and on the Bookmark

Introduction

Dear Gardener:

I don't know how you fell in love with growing things, but I came home from work one day and found a Wayside Gardens catalog in the mail. It was as fatal and irresistible as Cupid's dart — soon I was carrying seed catalogs to read on the bus, rushing to second–hand book stores in my lunch hour, always trying to learn more.

As this insatiable habit was developing, one of my greatest frustrations was that there seemed to be no *easy* way to find out everything I wanted to know. If I saw a lovely plant in a book or a garden, where could I get one to try to grow myself? Surely there must be wonderful gardening magazines, but few were listed in periodical directories and there were very few on newsstands — what did *real* gardeners do? Where were there plant and horticultural societies? Would they allow *me* to join? Where might I find a horticultural library to browse in? Even though I'm a reference librarian myself, it all seemed to be so difficult! Only *old* gardeners knew — and it took them years to find out.

When suddenly I had the time and the opportunity, I decided to "whip together" the *ideal* reference book for people like me — one full of sources of seeds, plants and supplies, societies to join, libraries to haunt, magazines to curl up with, and a list of good introductory books on plants and practical gardening, some "good reads", and books of inspiring pictures to feast the imagination.

My mind began to spin with grandiose ideas — I'd index the sources in many ways to make the book even more useful. I'd describe what was in their catalogs, if you could visit them and when they were open, if the nurseries had display gardens to go and see, and list them by location so that I could plan trips to include lots of horticultural high spots! I'd mention their shipping seasons, whether they sold wholesale to the trade, what their minimum order was, if they shipped to buyers overseas, and if they listed their plants by botanical name. Every day I thought of some new tidbit of information that the gardeners of North American just had to be told!

Now nearly four years later, and the second edition nearly finished, I'm *much wiser.* Putting together the "ideal" reference book is nearly impossible; it is *very* difficult to get thousands of people to send in information in a standard format, and the information is only current on the *day* they send it in! Many were cooperative, a few uncooperative, and some will return their questionnaires or send their catalogs months after the book goes to press. I learned all of this last time, and this time plan to keep the book current with updates until a new edition is published in about two years.

Reaction to **Gardening By Mail** was *very* exciting — a number of good reviews, and many wonderful letters from readers. Pretty heady stuff to a green-as-grass writer with a file of three rejection slips! One agent told me that the book was "so dry and dull that I cannot imagine a book market for it." I was crushed, but stubbornly thought that there *must* be other people like me out there *somewhere,* and Tusker Press came into being. Imagine my joy when the first enthusiastic letter came addressed to "Reader Feedback"! These letters were the best part of my mail all year, and encouraged me to do it all again: they are *always* opened first. There **are** lots of people out there like me!

It's been a busy but very happy time for me: I've finally moved to the country to an old house and garden in Sonoma County. Next to "Saskatoon, Saskatchewan", "*moved to the country*" has to be the most beautiful phrase in any language! My garden is almost derelict, but has lovely trees and a stream, and will provide a lifetime of work and pleasant living for me and my beloved pets.

Again, I owe thanks to Jim Robertson for giving me a perfect cover design, and to my gardening friends and readers for suggestions for improvements and additions. Thanks also to the companies which allowed me to use the charming drawings from their catalogs which add so much. Effusive thanks go to Georgie March, whose accurate typing and sharp proofreading eye will be much appreciated by readers; her humor and willingness to throw the ball for my dog, Alice, were much appreciated here at World Headquarters.

As before, most thanks of all go to my old friend Nancy Jacobsen, who has devised even greater feats of programming, and while I don't panic quite as often, her humor and friendship are enduring pleasures.

This book is meant to be useful, not permanent, so I encourage you to mark it up all you want!

Barbara

Barbara Barton

Sebastopol
September, 1987

Important Information For Using This Source Book

Who's Listed – Almost every mail order garden business I could locate and find enough information about by my cut-off date. In all but the few cases noted, everyone listed has received from one to three requests for information. For those who didn't reply or who didn't send their catalog, the notes give what I know about their specialties: I did not "make up" any information – in each case I give you **all** the information I could gather from every source I could find. This will provide you with enough information to contact them and ask for more. Some companies listed last time resisted multiple pleas for information and have been dropped because I'm not sure they're still in business. All names I found after the cut–off date were a heartbreak – but I may list them in the quarterly updates (see Practical Matters at the end of the book).

Addresses – Where I know it, I have given both the mailing address and the location of the business (these are sometimes the same). Please use the first address given for inquiries by mail. Where the location of the business has a different "town" address from the post office, this is given in parentheses after the "street" address.

Call Ahead Or By Appointment Only – Many of these businesses are run by one person, who sometimes has a full time job elsewhere or has to run the errands of us ordinary folk. Please honor their requests that you contact them before coming to visit, and don't try to visit those companies which don't welcome visitors – if they don't have a sales location, or give other information on how to visit, they may NOT be open to visitors – you should call to find out. Some of the businesses are strictly mail–order and not set up to welcome visitors.

Retail And Wholesale – It is common for businesses to sell multiple items at a declining cost per item; many also sell "wholesale to the trade" (those who buy the merchandise for resale or other business uses). Do not inquire about buying wholesale unless you qualify – it's best to send your inquiry on business letterhead.

Payment To Other Countries – I have tried to indicate where you may pay with International Reply Coupons, available at most Post Offices, or International Money Orders, available at larger Post Offices (ask for Form 6701 in the U.S.). Some overseas businesses ask for U.S. Notes, as changing checks sometimes costs more than the amount of the check. Others will accept U.S. personal checks, and will inform you of the proper amount to send. You can sometimes charge to your credit card, which automatically takes care of foreign exchange. I have also indicated where I could how much Canadians should send to the U.S. to take into account the dollar difference. They should check with their Post Office or banks about other forms of payment. Except as noted, all prices not in U.S. or Canadian dollars are in the currency of the country where the business or organization is located.

Self-addressed Stamped Envelopes — Always send a business-sized envelope (10 inch or 27 cm.) as your SASE — most of the lists will not fit into anything smaller. Also note if the business has requested more than the usual first class postage — the list may well be too heavy for one stamp.

Plant And Agricultural Regulations — You should check with local agricultural authorities to see if seeds, bulbs or plants from other countries may be imported, and what permits may be needed. Agricultural regulations in the United States have discouraged many Canadian companies from shipping plants and seeds south. I have tried to indicate where companies say they cannot ship due to regulations. This listing indicates where companies will ship (USA/CAN/OV) — it makes no sense to request catalogs from businesses which will not ship to your area. Companies are justified in charging a fee for the preparation of export papers. In some cases, endangered plants are protected by international treaty — ethical companies indicate the sources of their wild–collected seeds and plants.

Botanical And Common Names — When I have seen the catalog, I try to indicate where botanical names are used. The catalogs are not always consistent, and I have not checked to see that the names are up to date. It is common that herbs, fruits and vegetables are listed only by common and cultivar names, and many popular garden plants are listed by their cultivar names, frequently without botanical names. I have used the term "collectors' list" to indicate plant lists which assume knowledgeable buyers, and have brief or no plant descriptions.

Trade Names — In the Product Sources Index, I have indexed trade names as Registered Trade Marks (R) or Trade Marks (TM).

Notes On Catalogs — The notes are based on study of the catalog — where I have received no reply or no catalog, the notes are necessarily very brief. I have used the expressions "nice, good, wide, broad, or huge selection" and so forth to indicate the breadth of selection offered, not as a quality judgment on what's offered. I tried to cram as much information as I could into limited space — including items I was unable to index in the eight specialties. Unless otherwise indicated, companies ship all year. There is so much of interest in these notes, that you should never use this book without a pencil in your hand, so that you can highlight items of special interest.

Buying By Mail Order — I'm delighted, as I'm sure you will be, by all of the wonderful things we can buy for gardens through the mail. Naturally, I have not been able to buy from many of the businesses listed, as my purse is too tiny! I'd suggest that you place a small order first, and judge each company by its service and products. The Mail Order Association of Nurserymen, Inc. publishes guidelines for ordering, but the principles are based on common sense and caution — there are more honest businesses than bad ones.

Ordering Catalogs/Literature — One thing that businesses like to know is where their customers heard about them. Being included in **Gardening by Mail** costs listees only a catalog, postage, and a few minutes to fill out a questionnaire, but I'd be happy for them to know that it has been worth their efforts. It would also encourage those who didn't reply, or replied minimally, to take the time to respond fully in the future.

To let people know that you heard about them through this book, I have included an order/request form for catalogs, literature and information in the Practical Matters section of this book. If you don't use the form, please tell them you heard about them in **Gardening by Mail.**

Please keep in mind that catalogs and postage are expensive to small businesses, and request only catalogs for merchandise that you would truly be interested in. An avalanche of requests could be considered more torture than benefit to a one–person business; please be patient and considerate of the effort that goes into offering something special and operating without much help.

Errors and Omissions — Thanks to Georgie March, proofreading standards have improved by light–years. I'd love to be able to blame errors, bad jokes and oversights on her. However, corrections and improvements go to her credit — errors, mistakes and bad jokes are mine alone. Maria Callas complained that the critics only mentioned the few wrong notes she sang, not all the right ones!

State, Provincial and Country Abbreviations Used in Tables and Indexes

U.S. and Canada

AB	Alberta, Canada
AK	Alaska
AL	Alabama
AR	Arkansas
AZ	Arizona
BC	British Columbia, Canada
CA	California
CO	Colorado
CT	Connecticut
DC	District of Columbia
DE	Delaware
FL	Florida
GA	Georgia
HI	Hawaii
IA	Iowa
ID	Idaho
IL	Illinois
IN	Indiana
KS	Kansas
KY	Kentucky
LA	Louisiana
MA	Massachusetts
MB	Manitoba, Canada
MD	Maryland
ME	Maine
MI	Michigan
MN	Minnesota
MO	Missouri
MS	Mississippi
MT	Montana
NB	New Brunswick, Canada
NC	North Carolina
ND	North Dakota
NE	Nebraska
NF	Newfoundland, Canada
NH	New Hampshire
NJ	New Jersey
NM	New Mexico
NS	Nova Scotia, Canada
NV	Nevada
NY	New York
OH	Ohio
OK	Oklahoma
ON	Ontario, Canada
OR	Oregon
PA	Pennsylvania
PE	Prince Edward Island, Canada
PQ	Province of Quebec, Canada

U.S. and Canada (continued)

PR	Puerto Rico
RI	Rhode Island
SC	South Carolina
SD	South Dakota
SK	Saskatchewan, Canada
TN	Tennessee
TX	Texas
UT	Utah
VA	Virginia
VT	Vermont
WA	Washington
WI	Wisconsin
WV	West Virginia
WY	Wyoming

Overseas

Au	Australia
En	England *
Ge	Germany
In	India
Ne	New Zealand
Sc	Scotland *
So	South Africa
Sw	Switzerland
Wa	Wales *

* also UK in some listings

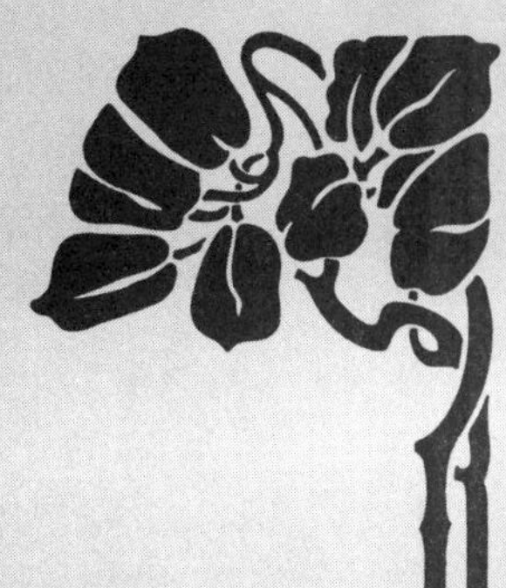

Plant and Seed Sources

Plant and seed sources are listed alphabetically. Former names and alternative names used as marketing codes are cross-indexed to the main listing. Their specialties (Plants, Seeds, Supplies, Books, Bulbs) are indicated at the top of the notes on catalogs.

For display gardens or other exhibits, the months given are the best time to visit to see plants in bloom or fruit. Check to see if you can visit at other times of the year.

See index section for:

H. Plant Sources Index: An index of plant and seed sources by plant specialties.

J. Geographical Index: An index of plant and seed sources by location. United States and Canadian sources are listed by state or province. Overseas sources are listed by country. Within each primary location, sources are listed alphabetically by city or post office. Symbols indicate which sources have nurseries or shops and which sell by mail order only.

Be sure to check the Changes and Corrections List at the end of the book (see Practical Matters). This list is updated with each printing.

Plant and seed sources found too late to include in this edition, as well as changes and deletions to current listings, will be listed in our quarterly updates (see Practical Matters).

Other Sources of Seeds and Plants

In addition to the sources listed, harder-to-find plants can sometimes be found in the seed exchanges and plant sales of horticultural societies or botanical gardens. You can also place an advertisement in the "plants wanted" section of many society magazines.

Many societies provide members with lists of specialist nurseries, and there is a list of "plant finding source books" in the Books section.

Finally, many gardeners are very generous with seeds and cuttings of their plants when properly asked — be you likewise!

A Table of the Symbols and Abbreviations Used in this Book
Appears Inside the Front and Back Covers and On the Bookmark

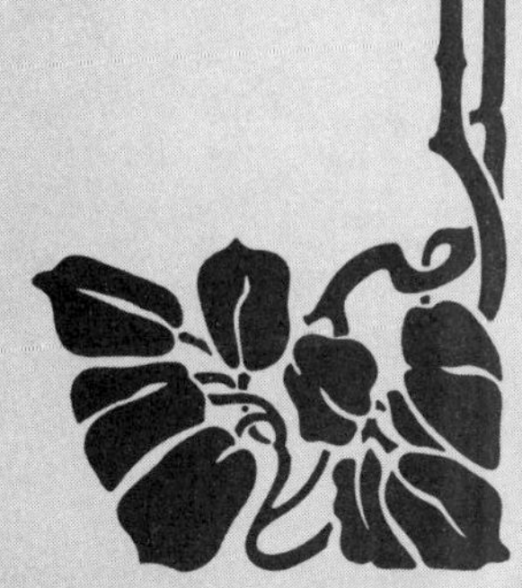

For Explanations of Abbreviations/Codes Used in Listings See Bookmark or Inside Covers

A & P Orchids
Peters Road
Swansea, MA 02777
(617) 675-1717
Penny & Azhar Mustafa

PLANTS
Small **orchid** nursery offers a list of hybrids written in orchidese, but welcome to collectors, I'm sure. Among the plants unfamiliar to me are hawkinsara, brownara and cattleytonia. Plants available in several sizes and seedling flats. (1985)
Catalog: Free, R&W, CAN, SS:4-10, $20m
Nursery: All Year, Daily, By Appointment Only
Garden: Winter-Spring, By Appointment Only

Abbey Gardens
4620 Carpinteria Ave.
Carpinteria, CA 90313
(805) 684-5112 or 1595 TO/CC $20m
Tom Loehman & Lem Higgs

PLANTS BOOKS
Color catalog offers a broad selection of **cacti and succulents** to hobbyists and collectors: some plants briefly described. I don't know why, but I can't look at a cactus catalog without wanting one of everything -- they are very fascinating plants! They also sell books. (1968)
Catalog: $2, R&W, CAN/OV, SS:3-11, $10m, bn
Nursery: All Year, Daily
Garden: March-Oct, Daily

Abundant Life Seed Foundation
P. O. Box 771
1029 Lawrence
Port Townsend, WA 98368
(206) 385-5660 or 7192 TO/CC $20m
Non-Profit Foundation

SEEDS BOOKS
"A non-profit educational foundation ... raising and collecting open-pollinated cultivars without chemicals." Offers a wide choice of seeds: **vegetables, Northwestern native plants, Native American grains, garden flowers** and books on many garden subjects. Bulk prices available. (1975)
Catalog: $1, CAN/OV, bn/cn
Nursery: All Year, M-F
Garden: Growing Area, M-F, Call Ahead

Adamgrove
Route 1, Box 246
California, MO 65018
Eric & Bob Tankesley-Clarke

PLANTS
Catalog offers a huge selection of bearded, beardless, Siberian, arilbred and species **iris**: all well described and with some cultural information. Also offers a somewhat smaller selection of **daylilies**, both diploid and tetraploid. Have taken over the business of David B. Sindt. (1983)
Catalog: $1d, MO, CAN/OV, SS:7-9, HYB
Garden: April-July, By Appointment Only

Adams County Nursery, Inc.
P. O. Box 108
Aspers, PA 17304
(717) 677-8105
Phillip Baugher

PLANTS
Catalog offers a broad variety of **fruit** -- apples, pears, peaches and nectarines, sweet and sour cherries, plums and apricots, on a variety of rootstocks for various growing conditions, for both home gardeners and large commercial growers. Informative color catalog. (1905)
Catalog: R&W, SS:Spring,Fall
Nursery: All Year, M-F: March-May, Sa
Garden: All Year, M-F

Adventure in Cold Climate Gardening

See Solar Green, Ltd.

Ahrens Strawberry Nursery
R. R. 1
Huntingburg, IN 47542
(812) 683-3055 TO/CC $25m
Philip C. Ahrens

PLANTS BOOKS SUPPLIES
Informative color catalog offers 35 varieties of **strawberries** and other berries, grapes, dwarf fruit trees, asparagus and rhubarb, as well as specialized supplies for the commercial strawberry grower. They also sell cookbooks for fruit growers. (1930)
Catalog: Free, R&W, SS:10-7, $10m
Nursery: Oct-July, M-F

Air Expose
4703 Leffingwell St.
Houston, TX 77026
George Haynes, III

PLANTS
Offers a good selection of **hibiscus**, both sub-tropical and hardy: described only by color of flowers.
Catalog: Long SASE, R&W, CAN/OV, $25m, HYB
Nursery: April-Oct, after 4 pm Weekdays

Aitken's Salmon Creek Garden
608 N. W. 119th St.
Vancouver, WA 98685
(206) 573-4472 TO $10m
Terry & Barbara Aitken

PLANTS
"Hybridize and sell all varieties of bearded **iris** in addition to a small selection of Japanese iris, Siberians, Pacific Coast Natives and a few species iris": plants very briefly described. (1978)
Catalog: $1d, R&W, CAN, SS:7-9, $10m, HYB
Nursery: April-June, Evenings & Weekends, Call Ahead
Garden: April-June, Evenings & Weekends, Call Ahead

Sherwood Akin's Greenhouses

See Sherwood's Greenhouses

Akkerdraai Seeds

See C 'n C Protea

Alberta Nurseries & Seed Company
P. O. Box 20
Bowden, AB, Canada T0M 0K0
(403) 224-3544
Ed Berggren

PLANTS SEEDS
Offers **vegetable and flower seeds** in the U.S. and Canada and general nursery stock in Canada. Varieties are specially selected for short season climates.
Catalog: Free($2 USA), R&W, USA, SS:4-5
Nursery: All Year, M-F

Alberts & Merkel Bros., Inc.
2210 S. Federal Highway
Boynton Beach, FL 33435
(305) 732-2071
J. L. Merkel

PLANTS
Specializes in **orchids, bromeliads and other tropical foliage plants.** Issues three catalogs at $1 each: orchids, bromeliads or other tropical plants. (1890)
Catalog: See Notes, CAN/OV
Nursery: All Year, M-Sa
Garden: All Year, Greenhouse

Alfrey -- Peter Pepper Seeds
P. O. Box 415
Knoxville, TN 37901
H. W. Alfrey

SEEDS
List of **unusual and hot peppers, also okra, luffa and castor beans** as a deterrent to moles: plants briefly described, some photographs. Also have a **pepper tomato** which looks like a bell pepper, but is hollow for stuffing.
Catalog: Long SASE, MO, CAN/OV

Alice's Violet Room
Route 6, Box 233
Waynesville, MO 65583
(314) 336-4763
Alice Pittman

PLANTS SUPPLIES
List features **African violets** from many well-known hybridizers, both recent and older favorites, including trailers, miniatures and semi-miniatures: a broad selection, plants briefly described. Also offers potting soil. (1980)
Catalog: Long SASE, SS: 5-6,9-11, $3m
Nursery: All Year, Daily, Call Ahead
Garden: All Year, Daily, Call Ahead

Allen Company
P. O. Box 1577
Salisbury, MD 21801
(301) 742-7122 TO/CC $15m
Richard & Nancy Allen

PLANTS
Color catalog of **strawberries, asparagus, raspberries, blueberries** and a **thornless blackberry**: plants are well described with growing suggestions. Check with your local agricultural authorities about ordering these plants from out of state -- some states have strict regulations. (1885)
Catalog: Free, R&W, SS:11-6, $15m
Nursery: Jan-May, M-F, By Appointment Only

Allen, Sterling & Lothrop
191 U.S. Route 1
Falmouth, ME 04105
(207) 781-4142 TO/CC
Shirley Brannigan

SEEDS SUPPLIES
Catalog offers a good selection of **short-season vegetable seeds**, annual and perennial flowers: all well described with cultural suggestions. They also sell **growing and greenhouse supplies, fertilizers and supplies** for basket-making! Basket-making classes are offered in Falmouth. (1911)
Catalog: Free, R&W
Nursery: All Year, M-Sa

Arthur Eames Allgrove
P. O. Box 459
Wilmington, MA 01887
(617) 658-4869
Arthur E. Allgrove

PLANTS SUPPLIES
Selection of **carnivorous and 'woodsy' terrarium plants** and collections of plants for 'partridge berry bowls' -- sound charming, don't they? Also several booklets by the proprietor on terrarium growing, grapevine and moss baskets and wreaths to be decorated by the buyer. (1932)
Catalog: $.50, SS:10-4, $15m, cn/bn
Nursery: May-Sept, Sa, Call Ahead

Allwood Bros. (Hassocks) Ltd.
Mill Nursery
Hassocks, W. Sussex, England BN6 9NB
Hassocks 4229
W. Rickaby

SEEDS
This firm is famous for its hybrid **dianthus and carnations**. Catalog lists the seed of 39 species and hybrids. Also offers a special plant support for for taller growing carnations. (1911)
Catalog: Free, R&W, OV, HYB, cn/bn
Nursery: All Year, M-F

For Explanations of Abbreviations/Codes Used In Listings See Bookmark or Inside Covers

Alpen Gardens
173 Lawrence Lane
Kalispell, MT 59901
(406) 257-2540 TO
Bill & Lois McClaren

PLANTS
"Specializing in early varieties, new introductions and cream-of-the-crop **dahlias.**" Collectors' list gives brief description of each plant and stars their "cream-of-the-crop" choices. (1979)
Catalog: Free, MO, CAN/OV, SS:AY, HYB
Nursery: All Year, Daily, Call Ahead
Garden: Aug-Sept, Growing Area, Call Ahead

Alpenflora Gardens
17985 40th Avenue
Surrey, BC, Canada V3S 4N8
(604) 576-2464
C. & H. Fischer

PLANTS
A broad selection of **rock garden and alpine plants**, perennials and miniature shrubs, shipped to the U.S. in "eighteen-packs" of the buyer's choice. Plants not described, listed only by botanical name.
Catalog: $2, R&W, USA, SS:W, $75m, bn
Nursery: All Year, Daily

Alpina Research & Montane Garden
Route 2, Box 265 B
Asheville, NC 28805
Majella Larochelle & Vee Sharp

SEEDS
Another project of the inexhaustible Majella Larochelle is a new botanical garden in North Carolina. They will publish a rare plant seed list once a year, and will trade or accept donations of plants or seeds of rare perennials, trees and shrubs. Definitely for love, not-for-profit! (1975)
Catalog: Long SASE, MO, CAN/OV, bn

Alpine Gardens & Calico Shop
2201 6th Street
Monroe, WI 53566
(608) 325-3824 TO $20m
Charlotte Keleher

PLANTS
A broad selection of **sedums, sempervivums and jovibarbas** and other alpine plants: listed only by botanical name with no plant descriptions. All are grown outside all year in Wisconsin, so they're very hardy. (1976)
Catalog: $1, R&W, SS:4-10, $20m, HYB
Nursery: March-Oct, Daily, Call Ahead
Garden: May-June, Daily, Call Ahead

Alpine Plants
P. O. Box 245
695 Wolf St. (Kings Beach)
Tahoe Vista, CA 95732
(916) 546-5518 TO/CC $15m
Andrea Kincaid & Brent Thrams

PLANTS
A nice selection of **alpine and rock garden plants and Western mountain native plants** for landscape use: all well described with suggestions for use, with charming illustrations. They also sell lovely posters and note cards of wild and garden flowers. (1978)
Catalog: $1, R&W, CAN/OV, SS:3-6,9-12, $15m
Nursery: Jan-Nov, Daily, Call Ahead

Alpine Valley Gardens
2627 Calistoga Rd.
Santa Rosa, CA 95404
(707) 539-1749
Wilbur & Dorothy Sloat

PLANTS SEEDS
A small family nursery offers over 500 named **daylilies** in limited quantities for the gardener wanting named and newer hybrids; new varieties added every year. Also **alstroemeria** seeds from a "grandparents" patch of Ligtu hybrids (mixed colors). Plants very briefly described. (1979)
Catalog: Long SASE, CAN, SS:AY, $10m
Nursery: All Year, Daily, Call Ahead
Garden: June-July, Daily, Call Ahead

Alston Seed Growers
Littleton, NC 27850
Clifton C. Alston

SEEDS
"Rare old time **non-hybrid corn**", several varieties and an "**everlasting old** garden tomato which has volunteered for over 100 years in a few old Southern gardens." Also **moon and stars watermelon, and 'bushel' gourds.** (1975)
Catalog: $1, R&W, MO, CAN, SS:11-4

Altman Specialty Plants
553 Buena Creek Rd.
San Marcos, CA 92069
(619) 744-8191 TO/CC $15m
Deena & Ken Altman

PLANTS BOOKS SUPPLIES
Their "Catalog of Unusual Succulents" is just that – offers a broad selection of **cacti and succulents**, as well as bonsai pots and books on cacti and succulents. Plants briefly described, many illustrated in color or black and white. (1974)
Catalog: $1, R&W, MO, SS:3-12, $15m, bn

Amaryllis, Inc.
P. O. Box 318
1452 Glenmore Ave.
Baton Rouge, LA 70821
(504) 924-5560 or 4521 TO/CC $15m
Ed Beckham

PLANTS SEEDS BULBS
Offers a broad variety of named hybrid and species **amaryllis**, as well as a few other bulbs – Lycoris radiata, habranthus and agapanthus and daylily seedlings: very brief descriptions. Also offers daylily and amaryllis seed; seed list not seen. (1942)
Catalog: $1(2 IRC), R&W, CAN/OV, SS:9-5, $15m, HYB
Nursery: All Year, Call Ahead

American Bamboo Company
345 W. Second Street
Dayton, OH 45402
Todd Mumma

PLANTS
Sells rhizomes of **bamboo** hardy in Northern climes – Phyllostachys bissettii and others. In 1987 they were selling P. angusta, P. aurea, P. aureosulcata, P. duscis, P. nigra cv. Henon, P. nidularia and P. viridis cv. Robert Young. Availability list issued in January. (1956)
Catalog: Free, MO, CAN, SS:4, $8m, bn

American Daylily & Perennials
P. O. Box 7008
The Woodlands, TX 77380
(713) 351-1466 TO/CC $20m
R. J. Roberson

PLANTS
Color catalog of **daylilies, cannas and Louisiana iris**: most illustrated and all well described. They also offer liriope and Ardesia japonica as groundcovers. Locals can attend their annual Bloom Festival at the growing ground. Sales are mail order only. (1976)
Catalog: $3d(7 IRC), R&W, CAN/OV, SS:3-6,9-10, $20m, HYB

Ames' Orchard and Nursery
6 East Elm Street
Fayetteville, AR 72703
(501) 443-0282
Guy & Carolyn Ames

PLANTS
Small nursery specializes in disease and insect-resistant **fruit stock**: antique apples, hardy blueberries, thornless blackberries, strawberries and raspberries, grapes and peaches: each well described in an informative catalog. Apples also sold in combinations. (1983)
Catalog: 2 FCS, R&W, MO, SS:11-4

Anderson Iris Gardens
22179 Keather Ave. N.
Forest Lake, MN 55025
(612) 433-5268
Sharol Longaker

PLANTS
Offers a broad selection of **tall bearded iris and herbaceous peonies**: all plants are briefly described. Some iris are their own introductions, many are recent award winners. (1978)
Catalog: Free, SS:7-10, HYB
Nursery: May-Oct, Daily
Garden: May-June, Daily

Angel Seed Company
P. O. Box 100
Garden City, MI 48135-0100
(313) 722-3616
Angeline Civello

SEEDS BOOKS SUPPLIES
Offers a nice selection of **vegetable and herb seeds**, including European vegetables. Also offers **wildflowers, perennials and everlastings**, some gardening books and supplies and a few recipes.
Catalog: $1d, R&W, MO, CAN, $10m

Angelwood Nursery
12839 McKee School Rd.
Woodburn, OR 97071
(503) 634-2233
Frank & Ilse Batson

PLANTS
A good selection of **ivy** cultivars, about 100 types, listed by shape of leaf or type: no plant descriptions, but there's general information on ivy classifications in their leaflet. There are over 200 cultivars on display at the nursery, an official AIS Standard Reference Collection. (1979)
Catalog: Free, R&W, CAN/OV, SS:AY, $20m
Nursery: All Year, M-Sa, Call Ahead
Garden: All Year, Growing Area, Call Ahead

The Angraecum House
P. O. Box 976
Grass Valley, CA 95945
(916) 273-9426
Fred Hillerman

PLANTS BOOKS
Specialist in **species and hybrid orchids** from Africa and Madagascar. Offers a cultural manual for $4.50 and "Introduction to Cultivated Angraecoid Orchids of Madagascar" for $32.95 postpaid and autographed.
Catalog: Free

Antique Rose Emporium
Route 5, Box 143
Brenham, TX 77833
(409) 836-9051 TO/CC $10m
Mike Shoup

PLANTS
Color/b&w catalog offers a broad selection of **old garden roses**: each well described, with a good deal of historical and cultural information. Roses grown on their own roots, selected for fragrance and long bloom in Zones 6 and above. (1983)
Catalog: $2, R&W, CAN, SS:1-5, $10m
Nursery: All Year, Tu-Su
Garden: Spring & Fall, Tu-Su

Antonelli Brothers
2545 Capitola Rd.
Santa Cruz, CA 95062

BULBS
Well known for their **tuberous begonias**, their lath houses are a glorious sight in the summer.
Catalog: $1

Anything Grows Greenhouse
1609 McKean Road
Ambler, PA 19002
(215) 542-9343
Frank J. Niedz

PLANTS
A broad selection of **greenhouse plants**, some quite exotic, including many species and cultivars of sansevieras, rhapis, monstera, jasmines, pandanus and other variegated plants. Catalog has been dropped in favor of specialty lists; the first will be sansevieras. (1977)
Catalog: Free, SS:4-11, $15m, HYB, bn/cn
Nursery: All Year, Sa-Su, By Appointment Only

For Explanations of Abbreviations/Codes Used In Listings See Bookmark or Inside Covers

Appalachian Gardens
P. O. Box 82
Waynesboro, PA 17268
Tom McCloud & Ezra Grubb

PLANTS TOOLS
List of hardy **ornamental trees and shrubs**: azaleas, holly, conifers, crape myrtles, berberis, viburnums, kalmias, rhododendrons: all plants very well described; some hard to find, such as Franklinia alatamaha. Features new items each year; one this year is the Trake (TM), a trowel-rake. (1986)
Catalog: Free, R&W, SS:3-11, $5m
Nursery: All Year, M-F
Garden: All Year, M-F

Appalachian Wildflower Nursery
Route 1, Box 275A
Honey Creek Road
Reedsville, PA 17084
(717) 667-6998
Don Hackenberry

PLANTS
Small nursery specializes in **rock garden plants and garden perennials**, with emphasis on local native plants descended from known wild colonies or from Central Asia, China and Japan. Lists species iris, gentians, phlox, primula, gaultheria, hellebores, dianthus and others. Long SASE for price list.
Catalog: $1, R&W, SS:4-5,9-10, bn
Nursery: All Year, M-Sa (Th-Sa in Shipping Season)

Apple Hill Orchards
P. O. Box 35
Covelo, CA 95428
Russel D. Hill

PLANTS
Specializes only in **scion wood of new and antique apples and pears**: scions of about 300 varieties of apples and over 100 pears available. Plans to add plums, grapes, figs and other fruits and nuts before too long. Current list has no plant descriptions, but the names are delicious! (1984)
Catalog: Long SASE, R&W, MO, CAN/OV, SS:2-3, $3m

Applesource
Route 1
Chapin, IL 62628
(217) 245-7589
Tom Vorbeck

Applesource is NOT a source of plants, but a service which will send you unusual varieties of apples during harvest season so that you can taste before you decide which cultivars to plant. A really nifty idea -- even if you do not have room for a tree! Good holiday gift for yourself or a friend. (1983)
Catalog: Free, MO, SS:10-1, $15m

Applewood Seed Company
P. O. Box 10761, Edgemont Sta.
Golden, CO 80002
(303) 431-6283 TO/CC $10m
Gene & Dee Milstein

SEEDS
Offers **wildflower seeds** from many areas, both as single varieties and in mixtures for all climates in North America and for various growing conditions. Also offers seeds of some ornamental grasses, everlastings and culinary herbs. (1968)
Catalog: Free, R&W, MO, CAN, cn/bn

Arbor & Espalier
201 Buena Vista Avenue East
San Francisco, CA 94117
(415) 626-8880
John C. Hooper & Harry Hull

PLANTS
Offers old-fashioned and unusual **apples** already trained as espaliers. Offered the first year were both apples and pears in several styles of espalier. (1986)
Catalog: Free, R&W, SS:AY
Nursery: By Appointment Only

Armstrong Roses
P. O. Box 1020
Somis, CA 93066
(805) 388-8851
Moet-Hennessey US

PLANTS TOOLS
This old California nursery has passed through several hands and now belongs to the French champagne house. Offers a good selection of hybrid **roses**, some table grapes, pruning tools and, strangely enough, cloned **carnivorous plants**. Color catalog shows and describes everything well.
Catalog: Free, R&W, MO, CAN/OV, SS:W, HYB

Artistic Plants
P. O. Box 1165
Burleson, TX 76028
(817) 295-0802
Estella Flather

PLANTS BOOKS SUPPLIES TOOLS
A **bonsai** nursery, offering plants for bonsai, accent plants and some succulents and tropical plants for display with bonsai: all briefly described. Also sells bonsai tools, pots and books; finished bonsai, some 'in training' for many years, available at the nursery. (1985)
Catalog: $1, R&W, SS:AY, $10m, cn/bn
Nursery: Th-Su, Call Ahead
Garden: Th-Su, Call Ahead

Atkinson's Greenhouse
Route 2, Box 69
Highway 64 East
Morrilton, AR 72110
David Atkinson

PLANTS
Collectors' list of unusual **begonias** (over 200), as well as flowering and other cactus, gesneriads, geraniums, African violets, succulents and other houseplants: all briefly described. Offers introductory collections of begonias which sound tempting. (1975)
Catalog: $1, SS:2-12, $10m, HYB, bn
Nursery: All Year, M-Sa, Su pm
Garden: March-Dec, Daily

Austraflora of Utah
P. O. Box 549
Santa Clara, UT 84765
(801) 537-1448
Dale Rose & Gary Backham

PLANTS SEEDS
Offers seeds and plants of Australian, Mediterranean, Mexican, South American and South Pacific native plants: "rare and experimental items with cultural consultation". Plant list not seen.
Catalog: Long SASE, R&W, MO, CAN, $15m

Avonbank Iris Gardens
708 Noblin Street
Radford, VA 24141
(703) 639-1333
Lloyd Zurbrigg

PLANTS
A selection of **reblooming iris**, bred for the mid-Eastern U.S. Most are quite hardy and succeed in other climate zones: each plant well described; many are their own introductions.
Catalog: 2 FCS, $18m, HYB
Garden: By Appointment Only

Aztekakti/Desertland Nursery
P. O. Box 26126
11306 Gateway East
El Paso, TX 79927
(915) 858-1130 TO/CC
David & Lupina Guerra

PLANTS SEEDS
Specializes in rare and hard to find **Mexican and South American cactus** – plants and seeds, some habitat collected. It's a collectors' list, just names, but seems to be a broad selection, available in large and small quantities. Also sells pottery and Indian crafts at the nursery. (1976)
Catalog: 3 FCS, R&W, SS:AY, bn
Nursery: All Year, Daily, Call Ahead
Garden: Spring-Summer, Daily, Call Ahead

B & B Laboratories
1600 D Dunbar Rd.
Mt. Vernon, WA 98273
(206) 424-5647
Bonnie N. Brown

PLANTS
Propagates **ornamental trees and shrubs and species lilies** by tissue culture. Plants are seedling size, delivered in sterile rooting medium; they will also do custom propagation. Plants and bulbs sold only in quantities of twenty-five or more.
Catalog: Long SASE, CAN/OV, SS:AY

B & D Lilies
330 P Street
Port Townsend, WA 98368
(206) 385-1738 TO/CC $20m
Bob & Dianna Gibson

BULBS
Offers **hybrid and species lilies** and several collections of lilies: each is well described, some shown in color. Working with rare and endangered species through seed production and tissue culture. Also sells alstroemerias. (1978)
Catalog: $1d, R&W, CAN/OV, SS:10-12, HYB, bn
Nursery: July-Aug, Daily, Call Ahead
Garden: July-Aug, Daily, Call Ahead

B & T Associates
Whitnell House, Fiddington
Bridgewater,Somerset, England TA5 1JE
David Sleigh

SEEDS
Seed for thousands of species of **tropical and sub-tropical plants**: fruit, cactus, palms, proteas, bromeliads, carnivorous plants, flowering trees and shrubs: they publish seed lists in 28 categories. Many seeds are collected to order and sent when viable; tell them what you're looking for. (1985)
Catalog: 2 IRC, R&W, MO, OV, $5m, bn

BDK Nursery
P. O. Box 628
2091 Haas Rd.
Apopka, FL 32712
(305) 889-3053
Bill & Dee Downham

PLANTS
Offers a good selection of **miniature roses**, many of them prize winners: all are well described. They also will custom propagate from their huge personal collection and have a few perpetual old garden roses in limited quantities.
Catalog: Free, R&W, SS:AY, $5m
Nursery: All Year, By Appointment Only
Garden: Spring-Summer, By Appointment Only

Fred Bach Epiphyllums
414 South Street
Elmhurst, IL 60126
Frederick O. Bach

PLANTS
Sells only unrooted cuttings of **epiphyllums** ("orchid cactus").
Catalog: Long SASE, MO, SS:4-10

Bailey's
P. O. Box 654
Edmonds, WA 98020
(206) 774-7528
Larry A. Bailey

PLANTS
Small nursery specializes in **exhibition auriculas and Juliana hybrid primulas**: plants very briefly described. You can also make special requests for other hybrid and species primulas.
Catalog: Free, MO, SS:4-5,9-10, bn

Baker & Chantry Orchids
P. O. Box 554
Woodinville, WA 98072
(206) 483-0345
Gary Baker & Will Chantry

PLANTS
Does not publish a catalog; offers **masdevallia, paphiopedilum, miltonia** and **species orchids**. Send your "want-list".
Catalog: See notes, SS:W

Bakker of Holland
U.S. Reservation Center
Louisiana, MO 63353-0050
(314) 754-5511 TO/CC
Clay Logan

PLANTS BULBS
A Dutch bulb company affiliated with Stark Bros. offers a good selection of tulips, daffodils, crocus, lilies, iris and other **spring and summer blooming bulbs** in a color catalog: somewhat florid plant descriptions, some cultural information.
Catalog: Free, MO, SS:Fall,Spring, cn/bn

Baldwin's Iris Gardens

See French Iris Gardens

A Bamboo Shoot
1462 Darby Street
Sebastopol, CA 95472
(707) 823-0131
Richard Waters

PLANTS
Good selection of **bamboo**, both clumping and running, from timber to pigmy, hardy and tropical: listed only by botanical name. (1985)
Catalog: Long SASE, R&W, CAN/OV, SS:11-5, bn
Nursery: All Year, Daily, By Appointment Only
Garden: All Year, Daily, By Appointment Only

Bamboo Sourcery
666 Wagnon Rd.
Sebastopol, CA 95472
(707) 823-5866
Gerald Bol

PLANTS
Collectors' list of **bamboos**: 76 forms, listed only by botanical and cultivar name, some available in 4-inch pots, one or five-gallon containers. Some are rare or newly imported varieties; some are non-invasive and make handsome garden ornamentals; some are very hardy (to -20F). (1985)
Catalog: Long SASE, R&W, CAN/OV, SS:AY, $20m, bn
Nursery: By Appointment Only
Garden: By Appointment Only

The Banana Tree
715 Northampton St.
Easton, PA 18042
Fred Saleet

PLANTS SEEDS
Seed for a wide selection of **tropical plants**, including many types of banana and other tropical fruits, ferns and bromeliads, palms, gingers, proteas, phormiums, cashews, carambola -- all plants well described. Also rhizomes of heliconia and "tuber-like bulbs" of **bananas.**
Catalog: $.75, R&W, CAN/OV, SS:2-12, $7m, bn
Nursery: All Year, Daily, Call Ahead
Garden: All Year, Daily, Call Ahead

Barbara's World of Flowers
3774 Vineyard Ave.
Oxnard, CA 93030
(805) 659-4193
Barbara Schneider

PLANTS
A huge selection of **fuchsias**, hundreds of cultivars, twenty-seven pages of plants: all briefly described. Collectors will know them. Sells rooted cuttings only.
Catalog: $4d, R&W, CAN/OV, SS:W, $20m, HYB
Nursery: All Year, Daily
Garden: All Year, Greenhouses, Daily

Barnee's Garden
Route 10, Box 2010
Nacogdoches, TX 75961
(409) 564-2920
Jean Barnhart

PLANTS
Offers a very broad selection of **daylilies**; grows 2,500 registered cultivars.
Catalog: 1 FCS, R&W, SS:9-10, HYB
Nursery: May-June, Call Ahead

Vernon Barnes & Son Nursery
P. O. Box 250
McMinnville, TN 37110
(615) 668-8576 or 2165 TO/CC $20m

PLANTS
A very broad selection of **fruit and nut trees, berries** of all kinds, and **ornamental trees and shrubs**; many available in small sizes in quantities for hedges or windbreaks. Some plants can't be shipped to CA or AZ. (1950)
Catalog: Free, R&W, MO, SS:10-5, $50m, cn

Bay View Gardens
1201 Bay Street
Santa Cruz, CA 95060
(408) 423-3656
Joseph Ghio

PLANTS SEEDS
A broad selection of **iris**: tall bearded, Louisiana, spuria and Pacific Coast natives -- their famous hybrid 'Pacificas' have good Northern California names (offers seeds of these, too): plants are well described. Also sells collections and even 'surprise packages' at season's end. (1965)
Catalog: $1, MO, CAN/OV, SS:7-10, $10m, HYB

Beahm Epiphyllum Gardens
2686 Paloma Street
Pasadena, CA 91107
(818) 792-6533
Ed & Frances Jagielski

PLANTS
Long list of **epiphyllums, hoyas and rhipsalis**: each well described. List gives detailed information on epiphyllum culture, even how to raise them from seed. (1924)
Catalog: $.50, SS:AY, HYB, bn
Nursery: All Year, F-Tu
Garden: All Year, F-Tu

The Beall Orchid Company
3400 Academy Dr. S.E.
Auburn, WA 98002
(206) 735-1140
Daniel S. Harvey

PLANTS
Big selection of **orchids** -- cattleyas, miltonias, phalaenopsis and odontoglossum-odontioda complex, Colombian miltonias and other species and hybrid orchids: all plants well described. Offers 'experienced' cattleyas which have bloomed; stress service to hobbyists and serious collectors. (1906)
Catalog: Free, R&W, CAN/OV, SS:AY, HYB
Nursery: All Year, Su-F
Garden: Nov-March, Su-F

Bear Creek Nursery
P. O. Box 411
Bear Creek Road
Northport, WA 99157-0411
Larry Geno

PLANTS TOOLS
"**Hardy fruits, nuts, shrubs and rootstocks** for the home gardener and orchardist." Large selection of antique apples and hardy nut trees; specializes in cold-hardy and drought-resistant stocks -- trees and shrubs for windbreaks, wildlife and hardwood; also pruning tools.
Catalog: 2 FCS, R&W, SS:3-5,11, cn/bn
Nursery: By Appointment Only

Beaver Creek Nursery
7526 Pelleaux Road
Knoxville, TN 37938
(615) 922-3961
Mike Stansberry

PLANTS
Specializes in collectors' **trees and shrubs**: species maples, stewartias, viburnums, magnolias, kalmias, crape myrtles and other ornamental plants, most of them Southern natives. A nice selection: each plant well described. Some of the plants are quite recent introductions.
Catalog: $1d, SS:W, $20m, bn/cn
Nursery: All Year, By Appointment Only

Beaverlodge Nursery
P. O. Box 127
Beaverlodge, AB, Canada T0H 0C0
(403) 354-2195
Mrs. I. M. Wallace

PLANTS
Specializes in **fruit trees, berries, flowering trees and shrubs, perennials and gladiolus** for very cold-winter/short-dry-summer areas: all plants well described with cultural suggestions. Catalog lists plants susceptible to rabbit and mouse damage. Canadian orders only.
Catalog: Free, MO, SS:4-5,9-10

Beckers Seed Potatoes
R. R. #1
Trout Creek, ON, Canada P0H 2L0
J. Murray Becker

PLANTS
Offers 35 varieties of **seed potatoes**: listed by maturity date and well described. Also offers 'garden packs' -- ten eyes each of four varieties which will mature over a long period. (1983)
Catalog: $1d, MO, USA, SS:4-5, $6m

Bee Rock Herb Farm
5807 Sawyer Rd.
Signal Mountain, TN 37377
Dan & Georgiana Kotarski

PLANTS BOOKS SUPPLIES
Small new nursery, specializing in **herbs and other perennials**, books on herbs, plant markers for herb gardens and ingredients for potpourri. Nice selection of plants, particularly herbs: each briefly described. (1984)
Catalog: Long SASE, SS:3-6,9-12, $5m, cn/bn
Nursery: March-Dec, Sa-Su, Call Ahead
Garden: Aug-Sept, Sa-Su, Call Ahead

Beersheba Wildflower Garden
P. O. Box 551
Stone Door Road
Beersheba Springs, TN 37305
(615) 692-3575

PLANTS
Color catalog offers a nice selection of **Southeastern wildflowers**, many shown in photographs and described only by botanical and common name. Included are species orchids and lilies, trilliums, ferns and more.
Catalog: Free

Belche Herb Company
P. O. Box 1305
Schenectady, NY 12301
Robert Belche

SEEDS
New company offers brief list of **herbs, tomatoes and other vegetables**: each described for use and flavor. (1986)
Catalog: Free, MO, CAN/OV

For Explanations of Abbreviations/Codes Used In Listings See Bookmark or Inside Covers

Belle Fontaine Nursery
Route 3, Box 546
Theodore, AL 36582
(205) 973-2000
Bea Rogers

PLANTS
Offers **camellias**.

Bentley's Botanical Gardens
P. O. Box 12442
La Crescenta, CA 91214
(818) 249-2182
Terry & Jane Bentley

PLANTS BOOKS SUPPLIES
Color catalog of **succulents and cactus**, as well as several phalaenopsis orchids; a nice selection: plants briefly described. Also offers some growing supplies and books on cactus and succulents. (1985)
Catalog: $2d, R&W, CAN/OV, SS:4-11, $10m, bn/cn
Nursery: By Appointment Only

Bernardo Beach Native Plant Farm
Star Route 7, Box 145
Veguita, NM 87062
Judith Phillips

PLANTS SEEDS BOOKS
Small nursery specializes in **Southwestern native plants** which are tolerant of drought, wind and cold -- trees, shrubs, perennials, wildflowers, vines, grasses and cactus: each well described. Also offers seeds of native plants and a book, "Southwestern Landscaping with Native Plants." (1980)
Catalog: 4 FCS, R&W, SS:10-3, $20m, cn/bn
Nursery: April-Oct, Tu,Th,Sa: 520 Montano NW, Albuquerque
Garden: Growing Area, Veguita, By Appointment Only

Bio-Quest International
P. O. Box 5752
Santa Barbara, CA 93150-5752
(805) 969-4072 TO $10m
Dr. Richard Doutt

SEEDS BULBS
Specializes in **South African bulbs** -- collectors' list offers a broad selection of bulbs, mostly from Cape Province. Small but choice selections -- babiana, lachenalia, ixia, moraea, gladiolus, watsonia, many more. Seed is collected on special order; archival collection is listed. (1980)
Catalog: $1, CAN/OV, SS:5-10, $10m, bn
Nursery: All Year, Daily, By Appointment Only

Bird Rock Tropicals
6523 El Camino Real
Carlsbad, CA 92009-4843
(619) 483-9393 TO $25m (After 1/88)
Pamela Koide

PLANTS
A collectors' list of **tillandsias**; a broad selection, adding more all the time: no plant descriptions. Plants available individually or mounted in a variety of ways.
Catalog: Long SASE, R&W, CAN/OV, SS:AY, $25m, bn
Nursery: All Year, M-Sa, Call Ahead
Garden: April-Aug, M-Sa, Call Ahead

Bisnaga Cactus Nursery
P. O. Box 787-108
1132 E. River Road
Belen, NM 87002
(505) 864-4027
Horst Kuenzler

PLANTS
Specializes in **winter hardy cacti**. Also sells seeds worldwide through New Mexico Cactus Research. (1985)
Catalog: $1d, R&W, SS:3-10, $10m
Nursery: All Year, M-F, Call Ahead
Garden: All Year, By Appointment Only

Bittersweet Farm
6294 Seville Rd.
Seville, OH 44273
(216) 887-5293 TO/CC
Mary Lou Crowe

PLANTS
Offers **herb plants** and herb and wildflower wreaths.
Catalog: $1, R&W, SS:AY
Nursery: March-Dec, T-Sa, Su aft
Garden: March-Dec, T-Sa, Su aft

Black Copper Kits
111 Ringwood Avenue
Pompton Lakes, NJ 07442
(201) 342-2708
Harold Welsh

PLANTS SUPPLIES
Offers a small selection of **carnivorous plants**, terrariums, leaflets and growing supplies: plants not described. Venus fly trap bulbs and plants sold wholesale as well as retail.
Catalog: $.25, R&W, MO, SS:2-11, $5m, cn/bn

Blackmore & Langdon
Pensford
Bristol, England BS18 4JL
(0272) 33-2300
B. J. & J. S. Langdon

SEEDS
Offers seed of their well known **tuberous begonias and delphiniums**, plus polyanthus primroses, gloxinias and aquilegias. Catalogs and seed orders MUST be paid in U.S. bills or money orders for pounds, due to cost of changing foreign checks. Delphiniums and begonias are world-famous. (1900)
Catalog: $3(US notes), R&W, OV, $10m, HYB
Nursery: All Year, M-F, Call Ahead

Blue Dahlia Gardens
P. O. Box 316
San Jose, IL 62682
(309) 247-3210
G. Kenneth Furrer

PLANTS
Dahlia collectors' list: names of cultivars, types and flower color given; only new introductions are described briefly -- fanatics will know them! Offers about 600 cultivars.

Blue Star Lab
P. O. Box 173
Route 13
Williamstown, NY 13493
(315) 964-2295 TO
David & Joan De Graff

PLANTS
Specializes in **hardy blueberries, raspberries and asparagus crowns**. These are grown by special methods to reduce transplant shock and lengthen transplant season. Seven varieties of blueberry, four varieties of raspberry, Jersey Giant asparagus transplants. (1981)
Catalog: Free, CAN/OV, SS 4-11
Nursery: All Year, M-F, Call Ahead
Garden: All Year, Growing Fields, Call Ahead

Blueberry Hill
R. R. 1
Maynooth, ON, Canada K0L 2S0
Roger & Valerie Kelly

PLANTS
Sells **native lowbush blueberry** plants for home gardeners; also to commercial growers under the name Kelly's Farm. Lowbush blueberries are about a foot high and spread by rhizomes; they are very hardy and need cold winters.
Catalog: Free, MO, USA, SS:4-5, $10m

Kurt Bluemel, Inc.
2740 Greene Lane
Baldwin, MD 21013
(301) 557-7229
Kurt Bluemel

PLANTS
A very extensive list of **ornamental grasses, sedges and rushes**, as well as **perennials, bamboos, ferns and aquatic plants**: all very briefly described, with uses and hardiness zones. There are also useful tables listing grasses by desireable traits and for specific purposes. (1964)
Catalog: $2, R&W, CAN/OV, SS:3-5, $25m, HYB, bn/cn
Nursery: All Year, By Appointment Only
Garden: All Year, By Appointment Only

Bluestone Perennials
7211 Middle Ridge Rd.
Madison, OH 44057
(216) 428-7535 TO/CC
R. N. Boonstra

PLANTS
A broad selection of **hardy perennials**. They seem to specialize in chrysanthemums, sedums and groundcovers, but offer a choice of many, many other plants for a perennial border: well described with cultural information and many color photos. Small plants at moderate prices. (1972)
Catalog: Free, R&W, SS:3-6, HYB, bn/cn
Nursery: Spring-Summer, Call Ahead

Arthur Boe Distributor
P. O. Box 6655
New Orleans, LA 70114

PLANTS
Specializes in **bromeliads and tillandsias** from Guatemala.
Catalog: Long SASE, R&W, MO

Boehlke's Woodland Gardens
W 140 N 10829 Country Aire Rd.
Germantown, WI 53022
Daniel Boehlke

PLANTS
"**Native plants and hardy perennials** for northern gardens." Offers plants that naturalize in woodlands, some marsh plants, prairie plants and native Midwestern wildflowers and ferns: nice selection, plants well described with cultural suggestions.
Catalog: $.50d, R&W, MO, SS:5-6,9-10, cn/bn

Bonavista

See Dan's Garden Shop

Bonsai Farm
P. O. Box 130
Lavernia, TX 78121
(512) 649-2109 TO/CC $10m
Edith Sorge

PLANTS BOOKS SUPPLIES TOOLS
List offers a number of **plants to use for bonsai**, as well as a large selection of bonsai supplies -- pots, tools, planting supplies, soil amendments, bonsai display stands and books: plants very well described. (1971)
Catalog: $1, R&W, SS:AY, $10m, cn/bn
Nursery: All Year, Sa-Su
Garden: Spring-Fall, Sa-Su

Boojum Unlimited
P. O. Box 1175
Cortaro, AZ 85652
(602) 682-5441
Bob Perrill

PLANTS SEEDS
Seed grown **boojum** (Fouquieria columnaris) and habitat-collected **seed** of selected **cacti and succulents** of the Southwestern U.S. and N.W. Mexico, including Baja California -- most hardy to 20F.
Catalog: $1d, R&W, SS:5-9, $25m
Nursery: All Year, Daily, By Appointment Only

Boordy Nursery
P. O. Box 38
Riderwood, MD 21139
(301) 823-4624
J. & P. Wagner

PLANTS BOOKS
Proof that "Wine Country" is rapidly spreading all over the country; here's a nursery in Maryland offering **hardy wine grapes** for colder areas, a good selection for both red and white wines; all well described in an informative catalog. Sells two books on winemaking by Philip M. Wagner. (1942)
Catalog: Free, MO, SS:3-5, $16m

Borbeleta Gardens
15974 Canby Ave., Route 5
Faribault, MN 55021
(507) 334-2807 TO
Julius Wadekamper

PLANTS BULBS
"Introduce **daylilies, Siberian and bearded iris, daffodils and lilies** developed by amateur gardeners who in the past have had no commercial outlet. We also develop and introduce our own originations." Catalog has many color illustrations: plants are briefly described. (1972)
Catalog: $3(4 IRC), R&W, CAN/OV, SS:4-10, HYB
Nursery: All Year, M-F, Call Ahead
Garden: April-Sept, Growing Area, Call Ahead

For Explanations of Abbreviations/Codes Used in Listings See Bookmark or Inside Covers

Bosky Dell Nursery
See Northwest Biological Enterprises

Boston Mountain Nurseries
Route 2, Box 405-A
Mountainburg, AR 72946
Pense Family

PLANTS
A good selection of **cane berries (brambles), strawberries and some grapes** and ornamental shade trees, in quantities for home gardeners and for large commercial growers: all plants well described, and hardy to Zones 4 or 5.
Catalog: Long SASE, R&W, MO, SS:Fall,Spring

Botanic Garden Seed Co.
9 Wyckoff Street
Brooklyn, NY 11201
(718) 624-8839
Michael Donnally & Jon Peterson

SEEDS SUPPLIES TOOLS
Wildflower seeds from all regions of the U.S., sold by individual packets or in six-packs or in mixes. They also sell some tools, supplies and gifts for gardeners, greeting cards, handsome posters and tee shirts. Not a large selection, but lovely presentation packs for gifts. (1984)
Catalog: $1, R&W, MO, CAN/OV, $5m

Boulder Valley Orchids
P. O. Box 45
240 2nd Avenue
Niwot, CO 80544
(303) 444-2117
Patricia Trumble

PLANTS
Specializes in **paphiopedilum species and hybrids, cattleya alliance** hybrids and other **species orchids**: plants well decribed. Sells plants, flasks and orchid potting mix. You can sign up for a "parade" of orchids, one-a-month.
Catalog: $2d, R&W, CAN/OV, SS:4-11, HYB, bn/cn
Nursery: All Year, Daily
Garden: All Year, Greenhouse

Bountiful Gardens
5798 Ridgewood Rd.
Willits, CA 95490
(707) 459-3390 TO/CC $5m
Bill & Betsy Bruneau, Mgrs.

SEEDS BOOKS SUPPLIES TOOLS
Catalog offers a broad selection of **open-pollinated vegetable seeds** from Chase Seeds in England, as well as herbs, flowers and green manure crops and grain seeds: all well described in informative catalog. Also sells a wide selection of gardening books, tools and organic supplies. (1983)
Catalog: Free(4 IRC), R&W, CAN/OV, cn/bn
Nursery: Ecology Action of the Midpeninsula, Palo Alto, CA
Garden: Tours: write for information.

The Bovees Nursery
1737 S.W. Coronado
Portland, OR 97219
(503) 244-9341 or 9381 TO/CC $15m
Lucille Sorensen, Mgr.

PLANTS SUPPLIES
A collector's catalog of **species and hybrid rhododendrons**, as well as Japanese maples, camellias, lilacs, clematis, dwarf conifers, alpine and rock garden plants, groundcovers and woodland plants: all well described. They have a separate list offering 250 Vireya rhododendrons. (1953)
Catalog: $2d, CAN/OV, SS:9-11,2-4, $15m, HYB, bn/cn
Nursery: Sept-Dec, Feb-July, Tu, Sa & Su
Garden: Feb-June, Tu, Sa & Su

S & N Brackley
117 Winslow Rd., Wingrave
Aylesbury, Bucks., England HP22 4QB
(0296) 681384
S.& N. Brackley

SEEDS
Specializes in **sweet peas**: offers many cultivars, including many old-fashioned sweet-smelling varieties. Sold by individual cultivar, each briefly described, or in several special mixes. (1890)
Catalog: IRC, R&W, OV
Nursery: All Year, Daily
Garden: June-Aug, Daily

Brand Peony Farm
P. O. Box 842
St. Cloud, MN 56302
Gerald Lund

PLANTS
A good selection of herbaceous **peonies**, many developed by Ben Gilbertson. All plants well described, including Tenuifolia flora plena, the fern leaf peony. Also sells some **tall-bearded iris and daylilies.** (1868)
Catalog: $1d, MO, SS:9-10

Breck's
P. O. Box 1757
Peoria, IL 61656
Spring Hill Nurseries Co., Inc.

PLANTS BULBS
Color catalog offers a large selection of hybrid **Dutch bulbs** -- tulips, daffodils, alliums, and more: each plant glowingly described. Also have a catalog of summer blooming bulbs -- lilies, daylilies, gladiolus, dahlias and tuberous begonias. (1818)
Catalog: Free, MO, SS:4-5,8-11

Breckinridge Orchids
6201 Summit Ave.
Brown Summit, NC 27214-9744
(919) 656-7991 TO/CC $35m
Mark Rose

PLANTS SUPPLIES
Formerly Tamany Tropicals, they relocated from Louisiana in 1986. Offers a good selection of blooming orchids all year, specializes in **phalaenopsis.** Also sells orchids supplies, fertilizers and chemicals. (1957)
Catalog: $2d, R&W, CAN/OV, SS:3-10, $35m, HYB
Nursery: Sept-June, M-F
Garden: Feb-April, M-F

Briarwood Gardens
14 Gully Lane, RFD #1
East Sandwich, MA 02537
(617) 888-2146 TO $15m
Jonathan Leonard

PLANTS
Small nursery specializing in choice selections of **Dexter hybrid rhododendrons** which were originally bred in Sandwich, a few miles away. They have also a few other hybrids, as well as pieris, kalmia and holly at the nursery. Plants are very well described. (1984)
Catalog: $1, R&W, SS:5-6, HYB
Nursery: May-June, By Appointment Only
Garden: May-June, By Appointment Only

Lee Bristol Nursery
P. O. Box 5
Route 55
Gaylordsville, CT 06755-0005
(203) 354-6951 TO/CC $15m
Lee Bristol

PLANTS
Daylilies listed by color with index of cultivar names: plants very well described, with season of bloom and cultural hints. Offers a broad selection and several collections for long seasons of bloom. (1969)
Catalog: Free, R&W, CAN/OV, SS:4-11, HYB
Nursery: April-Nov, Tu-Su
Garden: July-Aug, Tu-Su

Brittingham Plant Farms
P. O. Box 2538
Salisbury, MD 21801
(301) 749-5153 TO/CC
Wayne Robertson & James Brittingham

PLANTS
Specializes in virus-free **strawberry plants**, as well as Mary Washington **asparagus roots, raspberries, blackberries, blueberries and grapes**: all very well described with cultural and hardiness information. (1945)
Catalog: Free, R&W, CAN/OV, SS:AY
Nursery: All Year, M-F

Brookfield Nursery & Tree Plantation
P. O. Box 2490
Christiansburg, VA 24073
(703) 382-9099 or (800) 443-TREE TO/CC
David G. Larson

PLANTS
Sells **living or fresh-cut Christmas trees**, delivered direct by UPS, plus tree stands, wreaths and wooden toys; can't ship to HI or AK. They also run a Bed & Breakfast nearby. (1969)
Catalog: Free, R&W, MO, SS:11-12

Brown's Omaha Plant Farms, Inc.
P. O. Box 787
Omaha, TX 75571
Brown Family

PLANTS
Offers **onion plants** in bunches of about 75 -- several varieties including "Texas Sweeties" in quantities from 2 bunches to 60. They have added other vegetable plants: cabbages, cauliflower, brussels sprouts and broccoli. Also known as W. G. Farrier Plant Co. or Jim Brown Plants. (1935)
Catalog: Free, R&W, MO

Joseph Brown, Native Seeds
Star Route, Box 226
Gloucester Point, VA 23062
(804) 642-4602 TO $12m
Joseph Brown

SEEDS
A wide selection of **seeds of native plants**, some of them habitat-collected. Selection includes: asclepias, asters, echinaceas, eupatorium, liatris, oaks, rudbeckias, species iris, violas and a number of native orchids. Included are seeds of trees and shrubs of the Southeaast. (1984)
Catalog: $1, MO, CAN/OV, $12m, bn

John Brudy Exotics
3411 Westfield Dr.
Brandon, FL 33511
(813) 684-4302
John Brudy

SEEDS BOOKS BULBS
Offers a selection of seeds for **tropical trees, shrubs and fruits**: each plant well described and germination instructions given for each. Many are suitable for greenhouses or as houseplants. Also sells some bulbs and corms, a miniature elephant ear and his own book on growing. (1965)
Catalog: $1d, MO, CAN/OV, cn/bn

Brussel's Bonsai Nursery
8365 Center Hill Rd.
Olive Branch, MS 38654
(601) 895-7457 TO/CC $20m
Brussel & Maury Martin, Susan Straus

PLANTS BOOKS SUPPLIES TOOLS
Grower and importer offers **specimen finished bonsai and plants for bonsai**, as well as plastic and clay bonsai pots, pruners and a soft spray nozzle for bonsai culture: plants briefly described, some specimen plants illustrated. Cannot ship to AK or HI. Ask for book list. (1975)
Catalog: $1d, R&W, SS:9-5, $20m, cn/bn
Nursery: All Year, Tu-F, By Appointment Only
Garden: By Appointment Only

Elizabeth Buck African Violets
9255 Lake Pleasant Rd.
Clifford, MI 48727
(517) 761-7382
Elizabeth Buck

PLANTS
Does not publish a catalog; sells only **African violet leaves** of newest varieties by well-known hybridizers. The leaves come labeled, but the choice is hers. Come in quantities of 12, 25, 50 and 100; a good way to start a collection. Write for further information. (1968)
Catalog: See notes, SS:5-10, $5m
Nursery: All Year, M-F

Buckley Nursery
646 N. River Rd.
Buckley, WA 98321
(206) 829-1811
Don & Penny Marlow

PLANTS
A broad selection of **fruit for the Pacific Northwest**: apples, apricots, cherries, peaches, plums and prunes, pears, nuts and many berries, as well as eating and wine grapes. All plants briefly but well described; will be adding roses to next year's list.
Catalog: Free, R&W, SS:1-4
Nursery: All Year, Daily
Garden: All Year, Daily

Buell's Greenhouse, Inc.
P. O. Box 218
Weeks Road
Eastford, CT 06242
(203) 974-0623
Albert & Diantha Buell

PLANTS SEEDS BOOKS SUPPLIES
A collector's list of **African violets and exotic gesneriads** -- plants, tubers, rhizomes and seeds plus some supplies and books: plants briefly described in concise tables of information. Noted for their 'Buell's Hybrid Gloxinias'. Catalog $.25 plus Long SASE with $.39 postage. (1940)
Catalog: See notes, SS:2-6,9-10, $10m, HYB, bn
Nursery: All Year, M-Sa
Garden: All Year, Greenhouse, M-Sa

Bui, Huan Orchids

See Huan Bui Orchids

Bull Valley Rhododendron Nursery
214 Bull Valley Rd.
Aspers, PA 17304
(717) 677-6313
Faye & Ray Carter

PLANTS
Specializes in Dexter and Wister-Swarthmore **hybrid rhododendrons**, "plants for the serious collector" described only by color of bloom. Have added Gable hybrids and unnamed hybrids of Jack Cowles, and will be adding Leach, Pride, Fuller and Consolini hybrids soon. (1979)
Catalog: Long SASE, SS:5-6,9
Nursery: All Year, By Appointment Only
Garden: May, Rhododendrons, By Appointment Only

Bunch's Seeds

See Miller-Bowie County Farmers Assn.

Bundles of Bulbs
112 Green Springs Valley Rd.
Owings Mills, MD 21117
(301) 363-1371
Kitty Washburne

BULBS
A broad selection of **Dutch bulbs**: tulips, daffodils, crocus, lilies and various small bulbs. All are well described and illustrated with nice block prints; also offer 'span' collections for long seasons of bloom. (1984)
Catalog: $2d, R&W, MO, SS:10-11, $10m
Nursery: By Appointment Only
Garden: March-June, Th, Sa-Su

Burgess Seed & Plant Co.
905 Four Seasons Rd.
Bloomington, IL 61701
Adtron, Inc.

PLANTS SEEDS SUPPLIES
Color tabloid catalog offers seeds and plants, young trees and shrubs for windbreaks and landscaping, fruit trees, houseplants and some supplies.
Catalog: Free

Burkey Gardens

See Hickory Hill Gardens

Burnt Ridge Nursery
432 Burnt Ridge
Onalaska, WA 98570
(206) 985-2873
George Michael Dolan

PLANTS
Small nursery specializes in **perennial crops** -- hardy and regular kiwis, as well as Actinidia kolomitka and A. polygama, fig trees and Akebia quinata, hybrid chestnuts, walnuts and filberts: all plants well described. (1980)
Catalog: Free, R&W, SS:AY, $20m, cn/bn
Nursery: All Year, By Appointment Only
Garden: All Year, By Appointment Only

W. Atlee Burpee Company
300 Park Avenue
Warminster, PA 18974
(215) 674-4900 TO/CC $25m
Jon Burpee, Cust. Svs.

PLANTS SEEDS BOOKS SUPPLIES TOOLS BULBS
A gardening fixture for many years, Burpee offers flowers, vegetables, perennial plants, berries and fruit trees in a fat color catalog: each plant well described. Offers Dutch bulbs in a separate summer catalog. They also carry many tools, supplies, canning equipment and beekeeping supplies. (1876)
Catalog: Free, HYB, cn/bn
Nursery: All Year, Daily
Garden: Summer, Daily, By Appointment Only

D.V. Burrell Seed Growers Co.
P. O. Box 150
405 N. Main Street
Rocky Ford, CO 81067-0150
(303) 254-3318
William E. Burrell

SEEDS BOOKS SUPPLIES TOOLS
A good selection of **vegetable seed**, especially watermelons, canteloupes, hot peppers, tomatoes and onions, as well as annual flowers. Also offers growing supplies and a good deal of growing information. (1899)
Catalog: Free, R&W, CAN/OV
Nursery: All Year, M-F

Bushland Flora (Australian Seed Specialists)
P. O. Box 189
Hillarys, Australia 6025
(09) 401-0187
Brian Hargett

SEEDS BOOKS
Collectors' list with seeds of hundreds of **Australian plants**, each briefly described: also offers some color-illustrated books on these plants. Many acacias, banksias, eucalyptus, melaleucas, callistemons, helicrysums and helipterums (everlastings) and others. Planting guides with orders. (1972)
Catalog: 3 IRC, OV, bn/cn
Nursery: By Appointment Only

Busse Gardens
Route 2, Box 238
Cokato, MN 55321
(612) 286-2654
Ainie H. Busse

PLANTS
A very extensive catalog of **hardy perennials** of all types; offers an especially large selection of hostas, Siberian iris, peonies, daylilies, astilbe, heuchera, phlox, ferns and wildflowers for rock gardens and woodland: well to briefly described. Sells herbaceous, tree and dwarf peonies. (1973)
Catalog: $2d, R&W, OV, SS:4-10, bn/cn
Nursery: April-Oct, Daily
Garden: May-Aug, Daily

The Butchart Gardens
Box 4010, Sta. A
Victoria, BC, Canada V8X 3X4
(604) 652-4422
R. I. Ross

SEEDS
Butchart Gardens in Victoria sells seed of many of the **annual and perennial flowers** grown in their famous gardens: plants well described and prices are very reasonable. They also sell a number of collections: cottage garden, window box, rock garden, children's and hanging baskets. (1904)
Catalog: $1d, USA/OV, $2m
Nursery: All Year, Daily
Garden: April-Sept, world-famous gardens, Admission Charge

Butterbrooke Farm
78 Barry Rd.
Oxford, CT 06483-1598
(203) 888-2000
Tom & Judy Butterworth

SEEDS
Offers seed of **open-pollinated, short-season vegetables** for northern climates, not treated chemically. Regular packets $.35 each, also sold four-times regular size. Sells booklets on organic vegetable growing; customers may join their seed co-op.
Catalog: Long SASE, CAN
Nursery: Daily, Call Ahead
Garden: May-Sept, Call Ahead

C & H Greenhouses

See Carter & Holmes

C 'n C Protea
387 Carmen Plaza
Camarillo, CA 93010-6041
(805) 482-8905
Clifford Severn

SEEDS BOOKS
Seeds of **proteaceae** by individual species or in mixtures. Also offers books on South African proteaceae and does consulting and lecturing. They are distributors of the seed from Akkerdraai Seeds in South Africa, formerly listed under that name. (1949)
Catalog: Free, CAN/OV, bn
Nursery: All Year, M-Sa, Call Ahead

Cactus by Dodie
934 E. Mettler Rd.
Lodi, CA 95242
(209) 368-3692
Dick & Dodie Suess

PLANTS BOOKS SUPPLIES
A broad selection of **cacti** in a collectors' list: no descriptions, some illustrated in b&w photos. Also offers pots, labels, supplies and a few books on cacti. (1981)
Catalog: Free ($2 OV), R&W, CAN/OV, SS:W, $15m, HYB, bn
Nursery: All Year, Th-Sa, Call Ahead
Garden: All Year, Sales Area, Th-Sa

Cactus by Mueller
10411 Rosedale Hwy.
Bakersfield, CA 93312
(805) 589-2674
Gus & Maria Piazza

PLANTS SUPPLIES
A collectors' list of **cacti and succulents**: cereus, echinocereus, echinopsis, gymnocalycium, lobivia, mammillaria, notocactus, opuntia, rebutia, aloe, caralluma, crassula, echeveria, haworthia, huernia, senecio and many more. Sells some **mesembs**: no plant descriptions. Also offers pots. (1966)
Catalog: $1d, R&W, SS:AY, HYB, bn
Nursery: All Year, Th-Tu
Garden: Spring-Fall, Th-Tu

Cactus Gem Nursery
10092 Mann Dr.
Cupertino, CA 95014-1138
(408) 257-1047 TO/CC $15m
James & Elizabeth Daniel

PLANTS BOOKS SUPPLIES
Specializes in **cactus and succulents, echeverias, lithops and epiphyllums**: catalog is a quarterly newsletter offering plants, books and growing supplies. "A wide variety of all succulent plants." (1966)
Catalog: $1, R&W, CAN/OV, SS:AY, $15m, HYB
Nursery: All Year, Th-M, Call Ahead
Garden: May-June, Th-M, Call Ahead

The Cactus Patch
P. O. Box 71
Radium, KS 67571
(316) 982-4670
John Cipra, Jr.

PLANTS BOOKS
Small nursery offers **winter hardy cactus**: opuntias, echinocereus, coryphanthas, as well as yuccas -- a very broad selection of opuntias: all plants well described. Also recommends and sells "Cacti of the Southwest, Revised with Color" by W. Hubert Earle. (1975)
Catalog: $.25, MO, CAN, SS:4-10, $5m, HYB, bn
Nursery: Call Ahead
Garden: Call Ahead

For Explanations of Abbreviations/Codes Used In Listings See Bookmark or Inside Covers

Cal Dixie Iris Gardens
14115 Pear Street
Riverside, CA 92504
Herb & Sara Holk

PLANTS
Large selection of old and new varieties of **bearded iris.**
Catalog: Free, MO

Caladium World
P. O. Drawer 629
Sebring, FL 33871
(813) 385-7661
L. E. & Daniel Selph

BULBS
Specializing in **caladium bulbs**, those brilliantly colored fancy-leaved plants which survive so well through the Southern summers. Several illustrated in their color leaflet. (1979)
Catalog: Free, R&W, CAN, SS:1-5, $10m
Nursery: Jan-Aug, M-F, Call Ahead
Garden: July-Sept, Growing Area, Call Ahead

California Epi Center
P. O. Box 1431
1444 E. Taylor St.
Vista, CA 92083
(619) 758-4290 TO/CC $15m
Lois & Bob Burks

PLANTS
Color catalog offers a broad selection of **flowering cacti** -- epiphyllums, Christmas and Easter cacti, rattail cacti, rhipsalis, night blooming cacti, rare **epiphytic cacti, haworthias, succulents and hoyas**: all plants are well described with general cultural hints by genera. (1975)
Catalog: $2d(8 IRC), R&W, CAN/OV, SS:4-11, HYB, bn
Nursery: April-June, Sa, By Appointment Only
Garden: April-June, Sa, By Appointment Only

California Nursery Co.
P. O. Box 2278
Fremont, CA 94536
(415) 797-3311
George Roeding, Jr.

PLANTS
List offers a broad selection of **fruit and nut trees** for home gardeners and commercial orchardists, including kiwis, persimmons, pistachios, grapes, citrus, avocados, nut trees, bamboo: no plant descriptions. (1865)
Catalog: Free, CAN/OV, $30m

Callahan Seeds
6045 Foley Lane
Central Point, OR 97502
(503) 855-1164
Frank T. Callahan II

SEEDS
An extensive list of seeds of **native Northwestern American trees and shrubs** listed by botanical and common names only. They will also custom collect seeds from "want-lists" -- seeds available in both small packets and in bulk. Small supplier, good list. (1977)
Catalog: Long SASE, R&W, CAN/OV, bn/cn
Nursery: All Year, Daily, By Appointment Only

Camellia Forest Nursery
P. O. Box 291
125 Caroline Forest
Chapel Hill, NC 27514
(919) 967-5529
Kai-Mei Parks

PLANTS
Camellias selected for hardiness and disease resistance, both plants and scions; also species and Japanese maples, ornamental trees and shrubs, dwarf conifers, holly and evergreen azaleas. Wide selection of collectors' plants; some are recent collections from China and Japan, briefly described. (1978)
Catalog: 2FCS, R&W, CAN/OV, SS:11-5, $15m, HYB
Nursery: All Year, By Appointment Only
Garden: Spring, Fall, By Appointment Only

Camelot North
RR 2, Box 398
Pequot Lakes, MN 56472
(218) 568-8922 or 8789
Ruth Peltier

PLANTS BOOKS
List offers a nice selection of very hardy **perennials and perennial herbs** (hardy to Zone 3): very brief plant descriptions. Also listed are a few books on growing annuals, perennials and herbs and a list of plants suitable for drying. (1981)
Catalog: $1d, SS:5-9, $3, bn
Nursery: May-Sept, M-Sa
Garden: Growing Area, M-Sa

Mark S. Cannon

See Ma-Dot-Cha

Canyon Creek Nursery
3527 Dry Creek Rd.
Oroville, CA 95965
(916) 533-2166
John & Susan Whittlesey

PLANTS
A good selection of **perennials**, including many violas and violets, species geraniums, the 'chocolate' cosmos, euphorbias, salvias, campanulas and many more: all very well described. Surely the chief attraction of the Oroville area! (1985)
Catalog: $1, SS:2-5,9-11, bn
Nursery: All Year, M-Sa

Cape Cod Violetry
28 Minot Street
Falmouth, MA 02540
(617) 548-2798
John & Barbara Cook

PLANTS SUPPLIES
A collectors' list of **African violets**, many from well-known hybridizers, and **episcias, sinningias and miniature streptocarpus**: all very briefly described and available as plants or by leaves and stolons. Also sells growing supplies and African violet gift items.
Catalog: $1d($2 OV), R&W, CAN/OV, SS:5-10, HYB
Nursery: By Appointment Only

Cape Seed & Bulb
P. O. Box 4063, Idasvalley
Stellenbosch, Cape, South Africa 7609
(02231) 78367
J. L. Holmes

SEEDS
Color catalog shows a number of the plants offered: a very broad selection of **South African plants -- seed of many bulbous plants.** Descriptions include only height and color, but these plants are worth looking up elsewhere for more complete descriptions. Cannot ship to Australia. (1981)
Catalog: $4, R&W, MO, OV, SS:12-3, $20m, bn

Caprice Farm
15425 S.W. Pleasant Hill Rd.
Sherwood, OR 97140
(503) 625-7241 TO/CC $10m
Allan & Dorothy Rogers

PLANTS
A good selection of **hostas, Japanese iris, daylilies and peonies**, both herbaceous and tree cultivars, some quite rare. All plants are very well described and some are illustrated in color. They are adding Siberian iris in 1988. (1978)
Catalog: $1d, R&W, CAN/OV, SS:AY, $10m, HYB
Nursery: All Year, Daily, Call Ahead
Garden: May-Sept, Call Ahead

Cardinal Nursery
Route 1, Box 316
State Road, NC 28676
(919) 874-2027 TO/CC
Bill & Barbara Storms

PLANTS
List offers over 200 **rhododendron hybrids**, with several sizes available for most plants: all well described with notes on hardiness and bloom time. List is arranged by hybridizer with an index by plant name, reads like a Who's Who of Rhodoland! Cannot ship to CA, OR, WA.
Catalog: Free, SS:AY
Nursery: All Year, Sa; Daily, By Appointment Only

Carino Nurseries
P. O. Box 538
Indiana, PA 15701
(412) 463-3350 or 7480

PLANTS
Specializes in **seedling trees** for windbreaks, wildlife food and Christmas trees and ornamental trees for general garden use.
Catalog: Free

Carlson's Gardens
P. O. Box 305
South Salem, NY 10590
(914) 763-5958
Bob Carlson

PLANTS
A broad selection of **azaleas and rhododendrons** for collectors: native and hybrid azaleas such as Knaphill-Exbury, Robin Hill, Gable, North Tisbury, Glenn Dale and their own 'Face 'em down' evergreens. Also large and small leafed hybrid rhododendrons (Dexter, Leach, Gable) and **kalmia.** (1970)
Catalog: $2d, SS:4-6,9-11, bn/cn
Nursery: Daily, By Appointment Only

Carol's Violets & Gifts
5109 Summit St.
Toledo, OH 43611
(419) 726-9580 TO/CC $10m
Carol Sotkiewicz

PLANTS SUPPLIES
A small **African violet** nursery, specializing in trailers, miniatures and violets with multi-colored blossoms. A nice selection; brief plant descriptions. Also offers pots, fertilizers and other growing supplies. (1980)
Catalog: $1d, CAN/OV, SS:5-10, $10m, HYB
Nursery: All Year, M-Sa, Call Ahead

For Explanations of Abbreviations/Codes Used In Listings See Bookmark or Inside Covers

Carroll Gardens
P. O. Box 310
444 East Main Street
Westminster, MD 21157
(301) 848-5422
Alan L. Summers

PLANTS BOOKS TOOLS
Informative catalog lists a huge selection of **perennials, herbs, roses, vines, conifers, trees, shrubs and summer bulbs**: all very well described with cultural information. Many hollies, lilies, yews, viburnums, box, clematis, species geraniums, dianthus, campanulas and much more.
Catalog: $2d, CAN, SS:W, bn/cn
Nursery: All Year, Daily

Carter & Holmes, Inc.
P. O. Box 668
1 Old Mendenhall Rd.
Newberry, SC 29108
(803) 276-0579 TO $15m
Owen Holmes & Bill Carter

PLANTS SUPPLIES
A broad selection of **orchids**: they are especially well known for their cattleya and phalaenopsis hybrids (I dare you to resist 'Phal. Shanghai Breeze Mendenhall'). Plants are listed by color, with good descriptions. Also sells orchid and greenhouse growing supplies. (1948)
Catalog: $1, R&W, CAN/OV, SS:W, $15m
Nursery: All Year, M-F: Sa am
Garden: Fall & Spring, Greenhouses, M-Sa

Carter Seeds
475 Mar Vista Dr.
Vista, CA 92083
(619) 724-5931
Mrs. M. K. Frick

SEEDS
Essentially a wholesale seed company, their smallest quantity is one ounce of seed, but they offer a broad selection of seeds of **ornamental trees** and **shrubs**: palms, eucalyptus, acacias, conifers, as well as ornamental and lawn grasses, perennials and annuals and wildflowers.
Catalog: Free, R&W, CAN/OV, $15m($25 Flowers), cn/bn
Nursery: All Year, M-F, Call Ahead

Casa Yerba Gardens
3459 Days Creek Rd.
Days Creek, OR 97429
(503) 825-3534
Jim & Carol Hilderbrand

PLANTS SEEDS
Price list, send Long SASE; catalog $1d. Offers a nice selection of **herb** seeds, and some shallots, Egyptian onions, goldenseal roots and **elephant** garlic: no plant descriptions.
Catalog: See Notes: MO, CAN/OV, SS:4-6,9-10, cn/bn

Cascade Forestry Service
Route 1
Cascade, IA 52033
(319) 852-3042

PLANTS
Offers **hardy nut trees, conifers and other trees and shrubs** primarily for reforestation, woodlots and windbreaks: plants not described, informative leaflet free of charge. Plants offered from seedling size to several feet tall, depending on variety.
Catalog: Free, R&W, MO, CAN/OV, $20m, SS:4-5, cn/bn

Catalog of Unusual Succulents

See Altman Specialty Plants

Catnip Acres Farm
67 Christian St.
Oxford, CT 06483-1224
(203) 888-5649
Dean & Gene Pailler

SEEDS
Sells seeds of **herbs and everlastings** by mail, over 350 varieties: each well described with good germination and cultural information. Also sell books on herbs, as well as herbs and scented leaf geranium plants at the nursery.
Catalog: $2, CAN/OV, $5m, cn/bn
Nursery: April-Dec, Tu-Su

Richard G. M. Cawthorne
Lower Daltons Nursery
Swanley Village
Swanley, Kent, England BR8 7NU
Richard G. M. Cawthorne

SEEDS
Seeds from the world's largest collection of **violets and violas**, with 450 named varieties. Plants are for sale at the nursery only, but he will send mixed viola species seed overseas. Plants are well described, selection is mouth-watering. (1951)
Catalog: GB1(2 IRC), MO, OV, HYB

Cedar Ridge Nurseries
Cedar Ridge Road
Allison Park, PA 15101
(412) 443-9073
Walter L. Greenwood

PLANTS SUPPLIES
Here is a one-plant nursery, but what a choice! They offer **nepenthes**, the Asian pitcher plants, both species and hybrids, easily grown in greenhouse, under lights or in terraria: dozens of varieties, well described. Also sells many color slides. Catalog gives good cultural information.
Catalog: Free, R&W, MO, CAN, SS:5-10, bn

Chadwell Himalayan Seed
81 Parlaunt Rd.
Slough, Berks., England SL3 8BE
(0753) 42823
Christopher Chadwell

SEEDS
"Free lance plant hunter/botanist, specializing in the **flora of the North-West Himalaya**, seed available from expeditions and local collectors." List has section of easy seeds for beginners, good plant descriptions and lovely line drawings of many of the plants. Collectors will crow! (1984)
Catalog: 4 IRC(or $1 bill), MO, OV, bn

John Chambers
15 Westleigh Rd., Barton Seagrave
Kettering, Northants, England NN15 5AJ
(0933) 681 632
John Chambers

SEEDS
Seeds of **British wildflowers, herbs, grasses and wildflower bulbs**, mostly by their British common names -- you'll have to use British reference books. Also offers plants to attract butterflies, bees and birds -- should work just as well this side of the ocean. Also herbs and grasses. (1979)
Catalog: Free, R&W, OV, cn/bn
Nursery: All Year, Daily

Chambers Nursery
26874 Ferguson Rd.
Junction City, OR 97448
(503) 998-2467 TO/CC
Vic Chambers

PLANTS
A collectors' list of **rhododendrons and azaleas**: all plants well described with information on hardiness, season of bloom, size and rating. A very broad selection.
Catalog: Free, MO, SS:AY, $30m

Charles Island Gardens
P. O. Box 91471
West Vancouver, BC, Canada V7V 3P2
(604) 921-7383
Wally Thomas

PLANTS
Small nursery specializes in **odontoglossum and miniature cymbidium orchids**: each plant described by parentage and color or expected bloom appearance. The cymbidiums are meristems from the McBeans collection, all have 'Cooksbridge' names. (1977)
Catalog: Free, R&W, USA/OV, SS:4-10, HYB
Nursery: By Appointment Only

Chehalem Gardens
P. O. Box 693
3701 N. Chehalem Dr.
Newberg, OR 97132
(503) 538-8920
Tom & Ellen Abrego

PLANTS
A list for lovers of **Siberian and spuria iris** -- they have 'regular' and tetraploid Siberian iris -- the latter are sturdier and richer in color with larger blooms: each plant briefly but well described. Can't ship to FL or HI. (1982)
Catalog: Free, SS:9-10, HYB
Nursery: May-June, Weekends, Call Ahead
Garden: May-June, Weekends, Call Ahead

Chehalis Rare Plant Nursery
2568 Jackson Highway
Chehalis, WA 98532
(206) 748-7627
Herbert Dickson

SEEDS
Offers only **primula** seed by mail, single, double, show and & alpine auricula, florindae, some petite hybrids and mixed candelabra. Ask for SEED list. At the nursery they sell many miniature and unusual alpine and rock garden plants, dwarf conifers and trees and shrubs. (1968)
Catalog: Long SASE, CAN/OV, $5m
Nursery: All Year, Call Ahead
Garden: Mar-Sept, Call Ahead

Cherry Lane Gardens of Glenn Corlew
2988 Cherry Lane
Walnut Creek, CA 94596
(415) 932-1998
Glenn & Nell Corlew

PLANTS
Mr.Corlew sells his own **tall bearded iris** hybrids, available in small quantities, and a selection of **spuria iris**, his own and others': new introductions well described, others only briefly. (1964)
Catalog: $.50, MO, CAN/OV, SS:7-10, HYB
Garden: April-May, By Appointment Only

Chestnut Hill Nursery, Inc.
Route 1, Box 341
Alachua, FL 32615
(904) 462-2820
R. D. Wallace & Deborah Gaw

PLANTS BOOKS
Specializes in blight-resistant hybrid **chestnuts**: Dunstan hybrids and the Revival (TM) and Heritage (TM) chestnuts: well described and illustrated in a color pamphlet. They also offer 17 varieties of **Oriental persimmons**, five described in order form, and a book on chestnut culture in NZ. (1980)
Catalog: Free, R&W, CAN/OV, SS:1-4, HYB
Nursery: All Year, M-F, Call Ahead
Garden: Nov-March, Orchard, Call Ahead

Chestnuts a Reality
R.D.#1, Box 38
Westbury Cutoff
Red Creek, NY 13143
(315) 754-6621
Earl Douglass

PLANTS SEEDS
Leaflet offers **American-Manchurian chestnut hybrids**, which he claims are resistant to chestnut blight. Offers both seed nuts and seedling trees; will ship seeds to Canada, cannot ship trees to CA, nuts or trees to WA. He's 80; wants to bring back the lovely trees of his youth. (1955)
Catalog: $.25, CAN , SS:Spring, Fall, $4m, HYB
Nursery: All Year, M-Sa, Call Ahead
Garden: All Year, Orchard, Call Ahead

Chiltern Seeds
Bortree Stile
Ulverston, Cumbria, England LA12 7PB
G.D. and B.S. Bowden

SEEDS
Catalog is a sure delight; offers a very extensive selection of plants for every purpose: each very well described; the catalog is a useful reference book containing plants from all over the world. Also sells seed of Oriental, unusual and common vegetables and herbs and British wildflowers. (1976)
Catalog: $2d(US notes), MO, OV, bn/cn

For Explanations of Abbreviations/Codes Used In Listings See Bookmark or Inside Covers

Choice Edibles
584 Riverside Park Rd.
Carlotta, CA 95528
(707) 768-3135
Dan Harkins

SEEDS
A small company specializing in **spawn of morel mushrooms**, a real gourmet's delight. They offer spawn, cultures for spawn productions, a booklet of ten favorite mushroom recipes and detailed indoor and outdoor growing instructions. Cannot ship to South Africa. (1985)
Catalog: Long SASE, R&W, MO, CAN/OV, $4m, HYB

Christa's Cactus
529 W. Pima
Coolidge, AZ 85228
(602) 723-4185
Christa Roberts

SEEDS
Specializes in seed of **cacti and succulents, desert trees and shrubs** -- listed by botanical name, some very briefly described. Broad selection, geographical sources of habitat collected seed mentioned where known. One of those tightly packed collectors' lists. (1979)
Catalog: 1 FCS(3 IRC), R&W, CAN/OV, bn
Nursery: All Year, Call Ahead
Garden: April-June, Call Ahead

Circle 'N' Ranch
18650 Birch St.
Perris, CA 92370
(714) 780-7325
Beverly & Oly Neiiendam

PLANTS
Sells over 3,500 new and old varieties of **bearded iris** in the continental U.S.: bearded iris in all sections and sizes, including arils and arilmeades. Collectors' list: brief descriptions. (1976)
Catalog: 2 FCS, R&W, SS:7-9, $5m
Nursery: April-May, F-Su
Garden: April-May, F-Su

Clargreen Gardens Ltd.
814 Southdown Rd.
Mississauga, ON, Canada L5J 2Y4
(416) 822-0992 TO/CC $45m
Mike Dytnerski, Mgr.

PLANTS BOOKS SUPPLIES TOOLS
Offers phalaenopsis, cattleyas and miniature cattleyas, vandas, paphiopedilums and species **orchids**: each very briefly described. Another catalog lists **tropical plants, roses, perennials, bonsai, general nursery stock**, books, tools, supplies and pots.
Catalog: Free, R&W, USA/OV, SS:5-11, $45m, HYB, bn/cn
Nursery: All Year, Daily
Garden: All Year, Greenhouses, Daily

Clifford's Perennial & Vine
Route 2, Box 320
East Troy, WI 53120
(414) 642-7156 after 5pm EST
Ken & Connie Clifford

PLANTS
"Suppliers of the Cottage Garden", offers a nice selection of **perennials -- iris, peonies, Oriental poppies, rhododendrons, azaleas, clematis**, daylilies and other flowering vines: each plant very well described with cultural notes. (1982)
Catalog: $1d, CAN, $15m, SS:4-5,9-10, bn/cn

Cloud Forest Orchids
P. O. Box 370
Honokaa, HI 96727
(808) 775-9850
Erik & Hillery Gunther

PLANTS
Small nursery specializes in **species and hybrid orchids** for the collector; offered in flasks or as seedlings and mericlones in individual pots: all well described. Ship around the world.
Catalog: Free, R&W, CAN/OV, SS:AY, HYB, bn
Nursery: By Appointment Only
Garden: By Appointment Only

Coastal Gardens & Nursery
Route 3, Box 40
4611 Socastee Blvd. (Route 10)
Myrtle Beach, SC 29577
(803) 293-2000 TO/CC $50m
Rudy & Ursula Herz

PLANTS
A large selection of **hostas**, as well as Japanese and Siberian iris, ornamental grasses, groundcovers, daylilies, perennials, bog and aquatic plants and some flowering shrubs: all briefly but well described. (1974)
Catalog: Free, R&W, CAN/OV, SS:11-3, $50m, HYB, bn
Nursery: All Year, Daily, Call Ahead
Garden: April-Aug, Daily, Call Ahead

Coenosium Gardens
6642 S. Lone Elder Rd.
Aurora, OR 97002
(503) 266-5714
Robert & Diane Fincham

PLANTS BOOKS
A collector of conifers who has recently moved from Pennsylvania to Oregon and bought a nursery. He offers a very broad selection of **conifers, dwarf conifers and plants for bonsai**, some rarer items propagated to order: each plant well described, some b&w photographs. Also specialty books. (1978)
Catalog: $3d, CAN/OV, SS:4-6, 9-11, bn
Nursery: All Year, M-Sa, Call Ahead
Garden: May-Sept., M-Sa, Call Ahead

Cold Stream Farm
2030 Free Soil Rd.
Free Soil, MI 49411-9752
(616) 464-5809 TO $5m
Mike & Kay Hradel

PLANTS
Specializes in hybrid **poplars** for woodlots, wildlife habitat and erosion control. Also offers other trees and shrubs useful for woodland planting in seedling-size and collections for wildlife cover plantings: no descriptions. Nice selection of **native trees and shrubs**, including Am. Chestnut. (1978)
Catalog: Free, R&W, SS:10-7, $5m, cn
Nursery: Oct-July, Daily, Call Ahead

Color Farm Growers
2710 Thornhill Rd.
Auburndale, FL 33823
(813) 967-9895
Vern Ogren

PLANTS
Specializes in **old-fashioned heirloom types of coleus**, which they consider superior garden plants -- some are sun tolerant. They have also hybridized from these plants and offer a large selection: each plant well described in all its glowing colors. New introductions yearly. (1985)
Catalog: $.50, MO, SS:AY, $10m, HYB

Colorado Alpines, Inc.
P. O. Box 2708
Avon, CO 81620
(303) 949-6464 or 6672
Marty & Sandy Jones

PLANTS SEEDS
Specializes in **alpine and rock garden plants** grown at 7,500 feet in the Rocky Mountains: plants well but briefly described and available in several sizes. Seed list not seen.
Catalog: $2, CAN/OV, SS:4-6,9-10, $10m, bn
Nursery: All Year, Daily

Colvos Creek Nursery & Landscaping
1931 2nd Ave., #215
Seattle, WA 98101
(206) 441-1509
Mike Lee & Hector Gaxiola

PLANTS
A broad selection of unusual **trees and shrubs**: acacias, species maples, eucalyptus, conifers, flowering shrubs, oaks, palms and yuccas, among others. They are adding plants all the time and send out catalog supplements as new items are ready for sale; newest list has hardy bamboos.
Catalog: $1d, MO, SS:W, $10m, bn

Comanche Acres Iris Gardens
Route 1, Box 258
Gower, MO 64454
(816) 424-6436 TO
Jim & Vivian Hedgecock

PLANTS BULBS
Specializes in **tall-bearded iris** and offers a selection which includes a number of award winners: all well described. Also offers a few standard dwarf bearded and border bearded iris, 'horned' and Louisiana iris and mixed daffodils. They've purchased the iris division of Gilbert H. Wild. (1981)
Catalog: $1d, R&W, CAN/OV, SS:7-10, $10m, HYB
Nursery: April-Oct, Daily
Garden: April-May, Daily

Companion Plants
7247 N. Coolville Ridge Rd.
Athens, OH 45701
(614) 592-4643 TO/CC $20
Peter & Susan Borchard

PLANTS SEEDS BOOKS
Over 400 **herb** plants for sale and about 120 varieties of seed: all well described in an informative catalog. Selection includes scented geraniums, everlastings, woodland plants and a few books on herbs and herb growing. Will ship only seeds to Canada and Overseas. (1982)
Catalog: $2, R&W, SS:W, $15m, cn/bn
Nursery: March-Nov, Th-Su
Garden: April-June, Th-Su

Comstock, Ferre & Co.
P. O. Box 125
263 Main Street
Wethersfield, CT 06109
Richard G. Willard, Jr.

SEEDS
Offering older varieties of **vegetables** and new varieties proven to be more disease-resistant and productive: plants are well described with some cultural information for each. Also offer seeds of annuals and perennials, a good selection including everlastings. (1820)
Catalog: Free, R&W, CAN/OV, $10m, cn/bn
Nursery: All Year, Daily
Garden: Aug, Call Ahead

Conley's Garden Center
Boothbay Harbor, ME 04538
(207) 633-5020
Conley Family

PLANTS SEEDS
Plants well described in catalog -- a larger selection is offered in the price list, including **native bulbs and orchids, ferns, wildflowers, vines and groundcovers**. Also offers some wildflower seed and seed mixtures.
Catalog: $1.50, SS:3-6,9-11, $25m, bn/cn
Nursery: Daily; Jan-March, Closed Su
Garden: Spring-Fall, "Idea" garden

Connell's Dahlias
10216 40th Ave. East
Tacoma, WA 98446
(206) 531-0292 TO/CC $20
Les Connell

PLANTS
Offers a broad selection of **dahlias**, grouped by type: each briefly but well described, some illustrated in color. Also several collections for those who want to start with only a few! Also offering **gladiolus and pixie-olas**^ and the wonderful annual publication, "Dahlias of Today". (1973)
Catalog: $1d, R&W, CAN/OV, SS:1-4, $10m, HYB
Nursery: All Year, Daily, Call Ahead
Garden: Aug-Sept, Daily

The Cook's Garden
P. O. Box 65
Moffits Bridge
Londonderry, VT 05148
(802) 824-3400 TO/CC $20m
Shepherd & Ellen Ogden

SEEDS BOOKS SUPPLIES
Specializes in **vegetables and salad greens**, edible flowers and ornamental vegetables for home gardeners/cooks and specialty market gardeners. Catalog offers good plant descriptions and growing hints. They have a new book due in Spring 1988 on specialty vegetables. Maple sugar, too! (1977)
Catalog: $1, R&W, CAN/OV
Nursery: May-Oct, Daily, Call Ahead
Garden: June-Aug, Call Ahead

For Explanations of Abbreviations/Codes Used In Listings See Bookmark or Inside Covers

Cook's Geranium Nursery
712 North Grand
Highway 14 North
Lyons, KS 67554
(316) 257-5033 TO/CC
Waldo L. Cook

PLANTS
Offers a huge selection of **geraniums and pelargoniums**: dwarf, fancy leaved (zonal), stellar, scented, ivy leaf, regal -- 850 varieties by their count. There are no species geraniums but some species pelargoniums: all plants are well described. They also offer a number of collections.
Catalog: $1d, CAN/OV, SS:AY
Nursery: All Year, Daily (Call Ahead on Sundays)

Cooley's Gardens
P. O. Box 126
11553 Silverton Rd. N.E.
Silverton, OR 97381

PLANTS
Color catalog offers a large variety of **tall bearded iris**. (1929)
Catalog: $2d

Cooper's Garden
212 West County Rd. C
Roseville, MN 55113
(612) 484-7878
Joan Cooper

PLANTS BULBS
Small nursery specializes in species, spuria, Siberian and Louisiana **iris**, daylilies, perennials and wildflowers and, in a separate list, daffodils; a nice selection, particularly species iris: plants briefly described. Send long SASE for daffodil list. (1975)
Catalog: 1 FCS(2 IRC), CAN/OV, SS:8-9, bn
Nursery: Spring-Fall, Call Ahead
Garden: May-July, Call Ahead

Cordon Bleu Farms
P. O. Box 2033
San Marcos, CA 92069
Bob Brooks & Ray Chesnik

PLANTS
Broad selection of **daylilies** of all types -- tetraploids, diploids, miniatures and doubles -- plus **spuria and Louisiana iris**: plants well but briefly described, some illustrated in color. Can't ship to South Africa.
Catalog: $1, MO, CAN/OV, SS:2-11, $12m

Cornelison Bromeliads
225 San Bernardino St.
North Ft. Myers, FL 33903
(813) 995-4206
Frank Cornelison

PLANTS
A collectors' list of **bromeliads**: aechmeas, billbergias, cryptanthus, neoregelias, nidulariums, tillandsias, vrieseas. Listed only by botanical name and sold bare-root. Some plants are their own hybrids, a few are habitat collected: over 150 varieties in all. (1962)
Catalog: 1 FCS(1 IRC), R&W, CAN/OV, SS:AY, HYB
Nursery: All Year, Daily, Call Ahead

Corns
Rt. 1, Box 32
Turpin, OK 73950
(405) 778-3615
Carl L. Barnes

SEEDS
Corns is a membership organization, devoted to growing and preserving **open-pollinated varieties of corn** of all kinds: 'dent', flour, flint, popcorns, pod corns: they have available several hundred varieties and about 1,000 varieties being maintained in living seed banks. Write for information.
Catalog: $1d, R&W, CAN, $50m
Nursery: All Year, Daily, Call Ahead

Cottage Gardens
11294 Randolph Rd.
Wilton, CA 95693
(916) 687-6134
James McWhirter & Larry Lauer

PLANTS
A small nursery with a broad selection of recent and new **tall bearded iris**, as well as some median, border and dwarf varieties. Quite a few are their own introductions: all are well to briefly described. (1974)
Catalog: $.50, R&W, CAN/OV, SS:7-9, $15m, HYB
Nursery: April-May, Call Ahead
Garden: April-May, Call Ahead

The Cottage Herb Farm Shop
311 State Street
Albany, NY 12210
(518) 465-1130 TO/CC $10m
Betty Jane King

SEEDS
Sells only seeds of **herbs**: plants for cooking, fragrance and medicinal purposes.
Catalog: $.50, CAN, $5m
Nursery: All Year, M-Sa

Country Bloomers Nursery
20091 E. Chapman Avenue
Orange, CA 92669
(714) 633-7222
Mike Morton

PLANTS
A good selection of **old garden roses and miniature roses**, listed by name, color, year of introduction and hybridizer (and old roses by type of rose). The old garden roses are available as liners or as year-old bare root plants and should be reserved in advance of bare root season. (1982)
Catalog: Free, R&W, CAN/OV, SS:AY, HYB, bn
Nursery: All Year, Tu-Su
Garden: April-May, Oct-Nov, Tu-Su

Country Cottage
Route 2, Box 130
Sedgwick, KS 67135
Micki Crozier

PLANTS
"Catering to the enthusiastic gardener", collectors' list of **sempervivums, sedums and jovibarbas**: well to briefly described, with some cultural notes. It makes you think that you must have room for a few of these plants, with their "flushes" of various colors -- sounds irresistible. (1983)
Catalog: 1 FCS(1 IRC), SS:4-9, bn
Nursery: April-Oct, By Appointment Only
Garden: By Appointment Only

The Country Garden
Route 2, Box 455A
Crivitz, WI 54114
(715) 757-2045 TO/CC $20m
Joseph Seals & Susan Sherlag

PLANTS SEEDS BULBS
Specializes in **flowers for cutting gardens** -- a broad selection of seeds and bulbs. Annuals and perennials are available in separate colors for creating special effects; beginning to offer some perennial plants. Offers many old-fashioned varieties and new introductions from abroad -- delightful!
Catalog: Free, R&W, SS:9-10, bn/cn
Nursery: April-Oct, Tu-Sa, Call Ahead

Country Girl Greenhouses
P. O. Box 83
Route 14
Sterling, CT 06377
(203) 564-8227

PLANTS
Specializes in **African violets**: semi-miniatures, trailing and chimeras as plants, leaves and rooted cuttings -- also streptocarpus and other gesneriads and growing supplies.
Catalog: $1, R&W
Nursery: All Year, M-F: Sa morning

Country View Gardens
13253 McKeighan Road
Chesaning, MI 48616
(517) 845-7556
Barb Gibson

PLANTS
Small nursery growing 1,600 different types of **bearded iris**; specializes in dwarfs, medians and some Siberian and spurias. Will soon be offering daylilies, chrysanthemums, dianthus, species geraniums and potentilla. The iris list is extensive, with brief plant descriptions. (1985)
Catalog: Long SASE, SS:7-9, $10m
Nursery: May-Sept, Daily, Call Ahead
Garden: May-June, Call Ahead

Creole Orchids
P. O. Box 24458
New Orleans, LA 70184-4458
(504) 282-5191 TO/CC $30m
Harry A. Freiberg, Jr.

PLANTS
Hybrid orchids of all kinds: cattleya alliance, oncidium alliance, paphiopedilum alliance, dendrobium alliance and cymbidium alliance, both divisions and seedlings. Broad selection, with brief plant descriptions. (1981)
Catalog: Free, R&W, CAN/OV, SS:AY, $30m, HYB
Nursery: All Year, By Appointment Only
Garden: All Year, By Appointment Only

Cricket Hill Herb Farm Ltd.
Glen Street
Rowley, MA 01969
(617) 948-2818
Judy Kehs

PLANTS SEEDS BOOKS
Offers a nice selection of **herbs**, both plants and seeds, and scented geraniums: no plant descriptions. Also sells various herb blends for cooking and books on herbs. Good selection of basils, mints, thymes and sages. (1976)
Catalog: $1, R&W, SS:5-6,9-10, $10m, cn/bn
Nursery: April-Dec, Daily

Cricklewood Nursery
11907 Nevers Road
Snohomish, WA 98290
(206) 568-2829
Evie Douglas

PLANTS TOOLS
Small nursery specializes in old-fashioned "English border **perennials**": a nice selection listed only by botanical name. Offers species geraniums, hebes, species primulas, helianthemums, epimediums, species bulbs and many others. Also offers a selection of quality tools. (1982)
Catalog: Long SASE, R&W, SS:3-4,9, bn
Nursery: All Year, Call Ahead
Garden: May-Sept, Call Ahead

C. Criscola Iris Garden
Route 2, Box 183
Walla Walla, WA 99362

PLANTS
Offers 600 varieties of **iris**.
Catalog: 1 FCS

Crosman Seed Corp.
P. O. Box 110
East Rochester, NY 14445
(716) 586-1928

SEEDS
Offers a good selection of **vegetable, herb and annual flower** seeds: no descriptions of plants, prices very reasonable.
Catalog: Free, R&W
Nursery: All Year, M-F, Call Ahead

Cross Seed Company
HC-69, Box 2
Bunker Hill, KS 67626-9701
(913) 483-6163 or 6240
Dale K. Cross

SEEDS
A small supplier of **grain, bean, sprouting seed and sunflower** seeds, some available organically grown. Offered are: lentils, adzuki, popcorn, mung beans, barley, rye, oats, wheat, buckwheat, millet, triticale, black and striped sunflower seeds and various seeds for sprouting. (1943)
Catalog: Free(1 IRC), R&W, CAN/OV
Nursery: All Year, M-F, Sa am
Garden: Summer, M-F, Sa am

Crownsville Nursery
P. O. Box 797
1241 Generals Highway
Crownsville, MD 21032
(301) 923-2212
Charles Wasitis

PLANTS
Catalog offers a large selection of **perennials**, ornamental grasses, herbs, wildflowers and ferns and some azaleas: each very well described with cultural information. Many aquilegias, dianthus, campanulas, species geraniums, geums, hostas, Japanese and Siberian iris and penstemons.
Catalog: $2d, MO, SS:3-5,9-11, $20m, bn/cn
Nursery: April-Oct, Daily, Call Ahead

For Explanations of Abbreviations/Codes Used In Listings See Bookmark or Inside Covers

C. A. Cruickshank, Ltd.
1015 Mount Pleasant Rd.
Toronto, ON, Canada M4P 2M1
(416) 488-8292 TO/CC $20m
J. S. Williams

PLANTS SEEDS SUPPLIES TOOLS BULBS
Spring catalog offers a large selection of **summer blooming bulbs**: begonias, gladiolus, dahlias, amaryllis, cannas, caladiums, lilies. Also offers perennials such as peonies, daylilies, miniature roses and many more. Canadian distributors of Thompson & Morgan seeds and Van Tubergen bulbs. (1927)
Catalog: $2, USA/OV, SS:W
Nursery: All Year, M-Sa

Cumberland Valley Nurseries, Inc.
P. O. Box 471
McMinnville, TN 37110-0471
W. W. Bragg, Pres.

PLANTS
Specializes in **peaches, plums and nectarines** for larger plantings. Also offers apples (hardy and low-chill), cherries, pears and apricots and pecans. Informative leaflet: a very large selection of peaches listed by ripening sequence. Can't ship to CA, OR or WA. (1902)
Catalog: Free, R&W, MO, SS:12-3, $25m

The Cummins Garden
22 Robertsville Rd.
Marlboro, NJ 07746
(201) 536-2591 TO/CC $20m
Elizabeth K. Cummins

PLANTS
Specializes in **rhododendrons, azaleas and dwarf conifers** for the rock garden and bonsai -- also kalmias, heathers, pieris, box and other acid-loving plants: well described. They are adding new varieties all the time and have an annual plant propagation workshop -- call for details. (1972)
Catalog: $1d(2 IRC), CAN/OV, SS:3-6,9-11, $15m, bn/cn
Nursery: March-Nov, M-F,Su, By Appointment Only
Garden: April-May, Call Ahead

Cycad Gardens
4524 Toland Way
Los Angeles, CA 90041
(213) 255-6651
Loran M. Whitelock

PLANTS
Specializes in **cycad seedlings**: bowenia, ceratozamia, cycas, dioon, encephalartos, lepidozamia, macrozamia, stangeria and zamia -- with notes on origins. Some plants also available in gallon sizes; you can send a "want list" for other rare items which may be available from time to time.
Catalog: Free, R&W, SS:AY, $25m, bn
Nursery: By Appointment Only

Dabney Herbs
P. O. Box 22061
Louisville, KY 40222
(502) 893-5198
Davy Dabney

PLANTS BOOKS SUPPLIES
Recently bought the mail order business of Rutland of Kentucky; offers a big selection of **herbs, scented geraniums, ginseng, perennials and wildflowers**, as well as books, gardening supplies and natural pest controls for pets in an informative catalog. (1986)
Catalog: $3, R&W, MO, CAN/OV, SS:9-6, cn/bn

Dacha Barinka
25232 Strathcona Rd.
Chilliwack, BC, Canada V2P 3T2
(604) 792-0957

SEEDS
Offers **herbs, Oriental vegetables, garlic and everlasting flowers**.
Catalog: Long SASE, MO, USA/OV, SS:3-5

The Daffodil Mart
Route 3, Box 794
Gloucester, VA 23061
(804) 693-3966 TO/CC $20m
Brent & Becky Heath

BOOKS TOOLS BULBS
A very extensive catalog of novelty **daffodils** -- hundreds of varieties, as well as miniature and species daffodils. Plants are arranged by divisions: well described. Also offers growing supplies, tools, books and other spring flowering bulbs. Will also give illustrated lectures. (1935)
Catalog: $1d, R&W, CAN/OV, SS:9-11, $15m, HYB, bn
Nursery: March-April, Sept-Oct, By Appointment Only
Garden: March-April, By Appointment Only

Dahlias by Phil Traff
1316 132nd Avenue East
Sumner, WA 98390
(206) 863-0542
C. Phillip Traff

PLANTS
A collector's list of **dahlias**; many are medal winners: all well described. I especially like a catalog which thanks the nursery cats! Also sells the annual "Dahlias of Today", a publication of the Puget Sound Dahlia Association, very informative and full of the latest dahlia news. (1978)
Catalog: Free, CAN/OV, SS:1-5
Nursery: Aug-Sept, Call Ahead
Garden: Aug-Sept, Call Ahead

The Nursery at the Dallas Nature Center
7575 Wheatland Rd.
Dallas, TX 75249
(214) 296-1955
John H. Weller, Mgr.

PLANTS SEEDS
A source of plants and seeds of **native plants of Texas**: a nice selection listed only by common and botanical name. At the nursery they also sell nature books, bird houses and feeders and other gifts for nature lovers.
Catalog: Free, R&W, CAN/OV, SS:AY, $10m, cn/bn
Nursery: All Year, Th-Su, Call Ahead
Garden: Spring-Fall, Daily

William Dam Seeds
P. O. Box 8400
278 Hwy. 8 (West Flamboro)
Dundas, ON, Canada L9H 6M1
(416) 628-6641
William Dam

SEEDS SUPPLIES
Color catalog of **short-season vegetables, herbs, annuals and perennials**: varieties of European and Oriental vegetables and seeds for houseplants. Plants are well described, some growing and propagation supplies. (1949)
Catalog: $1, USA/OV, SS:W
Nursery: All Year, M-Sa

Dan's Garden Shop
5821 Woodwinds Circle
Frederick, MD 21701
(301) 695-5966 TO/CC $10m
Dan Youngberg

SEEDS SUPPLIES
Seeds for **annuals, perennials and vegetables**: all very well described. Also carries a good selection of growing and propagation supplies and gives general seed starting instructions. Woodwinds Circle sounds the perfect place to do business – Mozart, Haydn, Schumann! (1975)
Catalog: Free, MO

Dane Company
4626 Lamont
Corpus Christi, TX 78411
(512) 852-3806
Rosa Meilleur

PLANTS
A collectors' list of **bromeliads** – aechmea, billbergia, cryptanthus, many neoregelias (including their own 'neo' hybrids), tillandsia species and hybrids: no plant descriptions. All plants shipped bare root by Priority Mail.
Catalog: Long SASE, SS:W, $20m, bn
Nursery: All Year, Daily, Call Ahead

Davidson-Wilson Greenhouses
Ladoga Road
Route 2
Crawfordsville, IN 47933
(317) 364-0556
Barbara Wilson, Marilyn Davidson

PLANTS SUPPLIES
Specializes in **geraniums, begonias, African violets and other gesneriads, ferns, cactus, ivy, hoyas, herbs, succulents, hibiscus** and much more: color catalog illustrates many, briefly describes all. Also sells indoor growing supplies. (1980)
Catalog: Free, R&W, SS:W
Nursery: All Year, M-Sa: April-June, Su
Garden: May-Sept

Corwin Davis Nursery
RFD 1, 20865 Junction Rd.
Bellevue, MI 49021
(616) 781-7402
Corwin Davis

PLANTS SEEDS
Sells plants and seeds of **pawpaw**. Plants are either seedlings or grafts; grafts will be available in Spring 1989. "The forgotten fruit: edible and beautiful trees for landscaping, nothing bothers them, insects or pests or diseases." Sound terrific! Send SASE for free price list.
Catalog: $3.25, SS:4
Nursery: All Year, Call Ahead

Daylily World
P. O. Box 1612
254 N. Old Monroe Rd.
Sanford, FL 32771
(305) 322-4034
D. Kirchhoff

PLANTS
A very broad selection of **daylilies** in a b&w catalog: new introductions well described, older varieties briefly described. They have many diploids and tetraploids, and many blooms seem to be double. They are the exclusive agents for Bertrand Faar, a Silver Medal winner for hybridizing.
Catalog: Free, CAN/OV, $25m
Nursery: By Appointment Only
Garden: May-June, Call Ahead

Daystar
Route 2, Box 250
Litchfield-Hallowell Rd. (West Gardiner)
Litchfield, ME 04350
(207) 724-3369
Marjorie & George Walsh

PLANTS
An extensive list of **alpine, rock garden and dwarf plants**; many are choice, including dwarf conifers and shrubs, daphnes, hardy ferns, ornamental grasses, heathers, dianthus, phlox, holly, azaleas, rhododendrons: plants very briefly described. (1969)
Catalog: $1d, R&W, CAN, SS:4-6, 9-11, $15m, bn
Nursery: March-Nov, Call Ahead
Garden: By Appointment Only

Peter De Jager Bulb Co.
P. O. Box 2010
188 Asbury Street
South Hamilton, MA 01982
(617) 468-4707 TO/CC $10m
Peter De Jager

BULBS
A very broad selection of **Dutch bulbs** – tulips, daffodils, crocuses, lilies, hyacinths and other spring and fall bulbs. Well illustrated and described briefly in a color catalog. (1954)
Catalog: Free, R&W, SS:9-12, $10m
Nursery: M-Sa, Call Ahead

DeGiorgi Company, Inc.
1409 Third Street
P. O. Box 413
Council Bluffs, IA 51502
(712) 323-2372
Vivian Stumpf & Mildred Quick

SEEDS
A good old-fashioned catalog, offering a broad selection of garden **annuals, perennials and vegetables**. All varieties are well described, with cultural suggestions. Packets of many sizes. (1909)
Catalog: $1.25, CAN/OV, bn/cn
Nursery: All Year, By Appointment Only

For Explanations of Abbreviations/Codes Used In Listings See Bookmark or Inside Covers

Del's Japanese Maples
4691 River Road
Eugene, OR 97404
(503) 688-5587 or 688-2174 (evenings)
Del & Pat Loucks

PLANTS
Small nursery sells grafted **Japanese maples** as liners -- offers a broad selection with Japanese cultivar names: no descriptions. Collectors and bonsai folks will be delighted; they grow more than 200 varieties. (1979)
Catalog: Free, R&W, CAN/OV, SS:10-4, $25m
Nursery: All Year, M-Sa, Call Ahead
Garden: Spring-Fall, Call Ahead

Desert Nursery
1301 S. Copper
Deming, NM 88030
(505) 546-6264
Shirley J. Nyerges

PLANTS
Small nursery offers a good selection of winter-hardy **cacti and succulents** for the collector: descriptions are sketchy. Plants include: echinocereus, opuntias, mammillarias, parodias, rebutias, euphorbias and haworthias. Hours vary; be sure to call ahead. (1977)
Catalog: 1 FCS, SS:3-12, $10m, bn
Nursery: March-Sept, Daily, Call Ahead
Garden: Spring, Greenhouse, Call Ahead

Desert Theater
17 Behler Road
Watsonville, CA 95076
(408) 728-5513
Kate & Jay Jackson

PLANTS
A broad selection of **cactus and succulents** including aloes, lithops, notocactus, haworthias, echeverias, euphorbias, gymnocalcyciums, mammillarias, rebutias and sulcorebutias, listed by botanical name: very brief plant descriptions. (1980)
Catalog: 2 FCS(1 IRC), R&W, CAN/OV, SS:AY, $10m, bn
Nursery: All Year, By Appointment Only
Garden: All Year, By Appointment Only

Howard N. Dill
400 College Road, R.R.1
Windsor, NS, Canada B0N 2T0
(902) 798-2728
Howard N. Dill

SEEDS
Sells only seed of **Dill's Atlantic Giant** pumpkin, which has obtained World Class weight of over 400 lbs.
Catalog: 1 FCS(Canada), SAE(USA/OV), R&W, MO

Dionysos' Barn
P. O. Box 31
Bodines, PA 17722
(717) 995-9327
Sandy Klotz

PLANTS
A nice selection of **herbs and scented geraniums**: listed by common name, with very brief plant descriptions. (1977)
Catalog: $.50, R&W, SS:W, $5m, cn/bn
Nursery: Sa-Su, Call Ahead

Bill Dodd's Rare Plants
P. O. Drawer 377
Semmes, AL 36575
William R. Dodd

PLANTS
Price list offers **native azalea and rhododendron species and hybrids**, other ericaceous plant seedlings and native Southern tree seedlings: no plant descriptions, but a nice selection. Among the plants are the Bigleaf Magnolia, Gordonia, several hollies, Michelia figo, osmanthus and others.
Catalog: Long SASE, MO, SS:9-5, $20m, bn

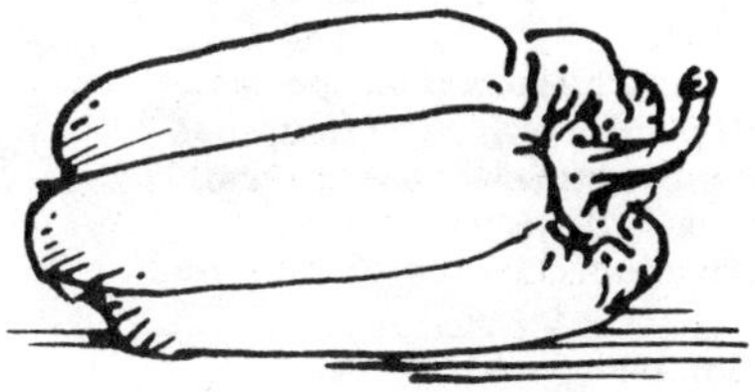

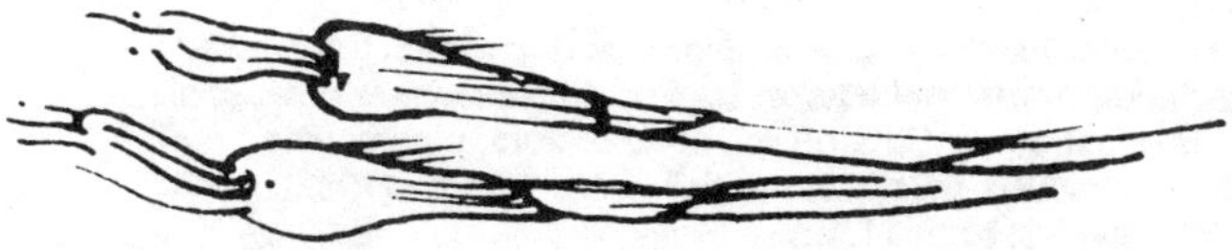

Dominion Seed House
115 Guelph St.
Georgetown, ON, Canada L7G 4A2

SEEDS BOOKS SUPPLIES TOOLS
A Canadian garden emporium, selling seeds of **annuals, perennials and vegetables**, as well as summer blooming bulbs, berries and seed potatoes: many illustrated in color and all well described. In addition, they sell tools, gardening supplies, canning equipment and books. (1927)
Catalog: Free, SS:W, cn/bn

Donnelly's Nursery
Route 7, Box 420
Fairview, NC 28730
(704) 298-0851
Russell Donnelly

PLANTS
A nice selection of **hosta**: all briefly but well described; and about 30 cultivars of **ivy**: briefly described. (1975)
Catalog: Long SASE, SS:4-10, $15m
Nursery: April-Oct, M-Sa, Call Ahead
Garden: April-June, M-Sa, Call Ahead

Dooley Gardens
Route 1
Hutchinson, MN 55350

PLANTS
Offers a broad selection of **chrysanthemums**.
Catalog: Free, R&W

Dos Pueblos Orchid Co.
P. O. Box 158
Dos Pueblos Canyon Rd.
Goleta, CA 93116
(805) 968-3535
Margaret C. Mosher

PLANTS
Specializes in **cymbidium, phalaenopsis, paphiopedilum and dendrobium** orchids.
Catalog: Free, R&W, CAN/OV, SS:AY, HYB
Nursery: All Year, M-F, Call Ahead
Garden: March, Call Ahead

Earl Douglass

See Chestnuts a Reality

Dunford Farms
P. O. Box 238
Sumner, WA 98390
Donald Duncan & Warren Gifford

PLANTS
Sells only **Agapanthus** 'Headbourne Hybrids', Alstoemeria aurantiaca or A. 'Ligtu Hybrids' -- request price list.
Catalog: Free, MO, SS:9-10

Dutch Gardens, Inc.
P. O. Box 200
Adelphia, NJ 07710
(201) 780-2713
Park Marsh, Cust. Svs. Mgr.

PLANTS BULBS
Color catalog of **Dutch bulbs** offers all of the most popular hybrids, with some cultural information. They have bulk order plans for groups and a catalog of **summer bulbs** -- lilies, gladiolus, dahlias, cannas and amaryllis. A wide selection in both catalogs. (1960)
Catalog: $1, MO, SS:9-10,3-4, $20m, cn/bn

Dutch Mountain Nursery
7984 N. 48th Street
Augusta, MI 49012
(616) 731-5232 TO $10m
Walters Family

PLANTS
"Berries for the Birds" and other ornamental fruiting plants to feed wildlife. Included is a sheet on "birdscaping essentials." Also offers a number of flowering trees and shrubs, nuts and rarities such as franklinia and kalopanax. (1952)
Catalog: $.25, MO, SS:3-5,10-12

E & H Products
78260 Darby Road
Bermuda Dunes, CA 92201
(619) 345-0147
Ruben M. Villegas

SEEDS
Offers a good selection of **wildflower** seeds, both by individual species and in mixes for all regions of the U.S. Each plant is well described, seed available from 1/4 oz. to 1/4 lb. Also sell some **herb** seeds and potpourris for various uses. (1985)
Catalog: Free, R&W, MO, CAN, cn/bn

Early's Farm & Garden Centre, Inc.
P. O. Box 3024
2615 Lorne Ave. South
Saskatoon, SK, Canada S7K 3S9
(306) 931-1982 TO/CC $10m
J. C. Bloski, Mgr.

SEEDS SUPPLIES TOOLS BULBS
This old firm re-entered the mail order business in l985 with a color catalog offering **garden flower and vegetable seeds, gladiolus bulbs**, supplies and tools, everything for northern gardening. (1907)
Catalog: $2d, R&W, USA, $10m
Nursery: All Year, M-Sa

Earthstar Herb Gardens
438 W. Perkinsville Rd.
Chino Valley, AZ 86323
(602) 636-2565 TO/CC
Kevin & Mary Smith

PLANTS SEEDS
Catalog offers a broad selection of **herb plants**, including several types of garlic, as well as some herb seeds; plants are grown at 5,000 feet and are very hardy. Common and botanical names only; no plant descriptions.
Catalog: $1d, CAN/OV, SS:W, cn/bn
Nursery: May-Sept, M-Sa, Call Ahead

Eastern Plant Specialties
P. O. Box 40
Colonia, NJ 07067
(201) 388-3101
Mark Stavish

PLANTS SUPPLIES
Offers a broad selection of hardy **rhododendrons and azaleas**, unusual and **dwarf conifers, kalmias, pieris, dwarf shrubs and groundcover plants**: all well described, many illustrated. Catalog full of collectors' plants; lists of plants for special uses. Also sells "Rainmatic" water timers. (1982)
Catalog: $2d, R&W, CAN, SS:4-5,9-11, bn
Nursery: By Appointment Only
Garden: By Appointment Only

For Explanations of Abbreviations/Codes Used In Listings See Bookmark or Inside Covers

Echinational Plant Products
602 Jefferson St.
Vermillion, SD 57069
(605) 624-6848
Darwin Vermaat

PLANTS SEEDS
Small nursery specializing in **echinaceas** grown from habitat-collected seed: in May and June they will ship "sproutlettes", pre-sprouted seeds. They offer seed of six different species and literature on the medicinal uses of echinacea, which is also a handsome perennial. (1982)
Catalog: Long SASE, MO, bn
Garden: June-Aug, Call Ahead

Eco-Gardens
P. O. Box 1227
1346 S. Indian Creek Dr. (Stone Mountain)
Decatur, GA 30031
(404) 294-6468
Don L. Jacobs, Ph.D.

PLANTS BOOKS
Eco-Gardens is a collection of native and exotic plants hardy in the Piedmont region; they sell surplus plants, some of their own breeding, to raise operating funds. Nice selection of **perennials, bog plants, ferns and shrubs**: brief descriptions. Also offers books at a discount. (1976)
Catalog: $1, R&W, CAN/OV, SS:9-6, HYB, bn
Nursery: All Year, By Appointment Only
Garden: All Year, By Appointment Only

Edelweiss Gardens
P. O. Box 66
54 Robb-Allentown Rd.
Robbinsville, NJ 08691

PLANTS
List offers a variety of **house and greenhouse plants** -- species orchids, bromeliads, ferns, begonias, platyceriums, billbergias and others: plants are briefly to well described.
Catalog: $1, SS:4-6,9-11, bn/cn
Nursery: Sept-June, M-Sa
Garden: Sept-June, M-Sa, Greenhouses

Edible Landscaping
P. O. Box 77
Route 4, Box 115 (Waynesboro)
Afton, VA 22920
(703) 949-8408 TO $7m
Michael McConkey

PLANTS
A selection of **fruit for mid-Atlantic gardens**, including Actinidia arguta (hardy kiwi), black currants, several gooseberries, Oriental persimmons, mulberries, jujube, pawpaw and grapes: most plants are well described in a charmingly hand-lettered and illustrated catalog. (1980)
Catalog: Free, R&W, CAN/OV, SS:AY, $7m
Nursery: All Year, M-F, Call Ahead

Eggenberger

See The Plumeria People

Emlong Nurseries
2671 W. Marquette Woods Rd.
Stevensville, MI 49127
(616) 429-3431

PLANTS
Offers **fruit trees, roses and general nursery stock.**
Catalog: Free

Endangered Species
P. O. Box 1830
Tustin, CA 92681
(714) 730-6323
Roger & Hermine Stover

PLANTS BOOKS
A very large selection of **tropical plants**, including many large and small bamboo varieties, small palms, cycads, ferns, grasses, tropical foliage plants, sansevierias, succulents, phormiums and a variety of trees -- plus books. (1978)
Catalog: Free, MO, CAN/OV, SS:AY, $25m, bn
Nursery: All Year, By Appointment Only

Englerth Gardens
2461 22nd St.
Hopkins, MI 49328
(616) 793-7196
Ken & Mary Englerth Herrema

PLANTS
Specializes in **daylilies and hosta** and offers a broad selection of both, as well as tetraploid daylilies and **Siberian iris**: each plant is briefly described. (1931)
Catalog: $.50, R&W, SS:4-6,8-10, $10m, HYB
Nursery: April-June, Aug-Oct, F-Sa
Garden: July, F-Sa

Ensata Gardens
9823 E. Michigan Avenue
Galesburg, MI 49053
(616) 665-7500 TO $15m
Bob Bauer & John Coble

PLANTS
Small nursery specializing in **Japanese and Siberian iris** only. They have a broad selection of Japanese iris, smaller selection of Siberian iris: all plants are well described. They have a Japanese garden display area, for those lucky enough to be close. (1985)
Catalog: 1 FCS, R&W, CAN/OV, SS:5-10, $15m, HYB
Nursery: May-Sept, Daily, Call Ahead
Garden: June-July, Daily, Call Ahead

Ericaceae
P. O. Box 293
6 Kelsey Hill Rd.
Deep River, CT 06417
(203) 525-5100 (after 5 pm EST)
Mathias C. Zack

PLANTS
Offers only the **rhododendron** hybrids of David Leach -- hybridized for superior color and hardiness for the Northeastern climate. Offers a nice selection and will be offering quite a few more in 1988.
Catalog: Free, SS:W
Nursery: By Appointment Only

Ernst Crownvetch Farms
R.D. 5, Box 806
Meadville, PA 16335
(814) 425-7276 or 7897
Calvin & Ted Ernst

PLANTS SEEDS
Mail order farm seed house can supply many grains; also sells several fast growing **trees, crownvetch and grasses** for erosion control, reclamation and groundcover.
Catalog: Free, CAN/OV, SS:4-12, $2m
Nursery: Mar-Nov, M-F

Essie's Violets
115 W. Ida
Lansing, KS 66043
(913) 727-1008

PLANTS
Specializes in **African violets** from well-known hybridizers; sells leaves only.
Catalog: $1d
Nursery: By Appointment Only

Evergreen Y. H. Enterprises
P. O. Box 17538
Anaheim, CA 92817-7538
W. S. Hwang

SEEDS SUPPLIES
Offers a good selection of **Oriental vegetables**: listed in English and Chinese and well described. Also offers Oriental cookbooks; ask for list, as they don't appear in seed catalog. (1978)
Catalog: $1d, R&W, MO

Evon Orchids
P. O. Box 17396
San Diego, CA 92117
(619) 270-1827

PLANTS
Orchids -- seedlings and mature plants.
Catalog: Free

John Ewing Orchids, Inc.
P. O. Box 1318
487 White Road (Watsonville)
Soquel, CA 95076
(408) 684-1111
John & Loraine Ewing

PLANTS
Collectors' list of seedling phalaenopsis **orchids**, available in several sizes, in pink, white, yellow, tan and red stripes or spots on colored backgrounds; available in flasks, as stem propagations or seedlings: informative catalog. Also cymbidiums, miltonias and cattleyas in season. (1969)
Catalog: Free, R&W, CAN/OV, SS:3-11, HYB
Nursery: All Year, M-Sa, Call Ahead
Garden: March-June, Greenhouse

Exotic Blossoms (TM) Topiary Sculptures
P. O. Box 2436
Philadelphia, PA 19147-0436
(215) 925-2440 TO/CC
Lee-John Sobering

PLANTS SUPPLIES
Offers **topiary frames**, which can be plain, stuffed for planting or planted ready for your patio or garden. They also sell "Haddonstone" planters and garden ornaments; 48-page color Haddonstone catalog costs $3.50. They will make custom frames if you have something special in mind. (1982)
Catalog: Long SASE, R&W, CAN/OV, SS:4-12
Nursery: All Year, By Appointment Only

Exotica Seed Co. & Rare Fruit Nursery
P. O. Box 160
Vista, CA 92083
(619) 724-9093
Steve Spangler & Steve Facciola

PLANTS SEEDS
Offers seeds and plants of **tropical fruits and flowering trees and nuts**, Hawaiian ornamentals, palms and Mexican and South American vegetables and fruit -- all for southern climates. They also have a fruit stand at the nursery. (1975)
Catalog: Free, R&W, CAN/OV, bn/cn
Nursery: All Year, Call Ahead
Garden: All Year, Call Ahead

Exotics Hawaii, Inc.
P. O. Box 10416
1344 Hoakoa Place
Honolulu, HI 96816
(808) 732-2105
Kalfred K. Yee

PLANTS
A grower of mericloned **orchids**, but also offers a nice variety of other **tropical foliage plants**, such as dracaenas, polyscias, aroids, ficus, anthuriums and bromeliads. Specify which sort of plants you're interested in. (1958)
Catalog: Long SASE, R&W, SS:AY, $25m, HYB
Nursery: All Year, M-Sa, Call Ahead

F W H Seed Exchange
P. O. Box 651
Pauma Valley, CA 92061

SEEDS BULBS
Not a seed company, but dedicated gardeners who collect seed of garden flowers and heirloom vegetables and exchange among themselves. Their newsletter has a bit of the flavor of Eliz. Lawrence's "Gardening for Love", lists what people have and what they want: you must be willing to contribute, too.
Catalog: $2 + Long SASE, MO, CAN/OV

Fairway Enterprises
114 The Fairway
Albert Lea, MN 56007
(507) 373-5290
Eldred & Nancy Minks

PLANTS
A nice selection of **hostas**, listed by color or leaf type with brief descriptions. Many are their own introductions. (1986)
Catalog: Free, SS:8-9, $30m, HYB
Nursery: Aug-Sept, By Appointment Only

For Explanations of Abbreviations/Codes Used In Listings See Bookmark or Inside Covers

Fairyland Begonia & Lily Garden
1100 Griffith Rd.
McKinleyville, CA 95521
(707) 839-3034
Winkey & Leslie Woodriff

PLANTS SEEDS BULBS
Hybridizes **lilies and begonias, also streptocarpus, hybrid calla lilies** and **lily seed**. Offers a nice selection, including mixed collections of lilies and 'yearling' lilies which will bloom in two years: all plants very well described.
Catalog: $.50(10 IRC), R&W, CAN/OV, SS:W, $10m, HYB
Nursery: All Year, Daily

Fancy Fronds
1911 4th Avenue West
Seattle, WA 98119
(206) 284-5332
Judith I. Jones

PLANTS
A good selection of **hardy ferns**, including ferns from England, China, Japan and New Zealand and other temperate areas: all very well described and some illustrated with line drawings – special requests invited. (1976)
Catalog: $1d, R&W, SS:3-6, 9-10, $10m, bn/cn
Nursery: All Year, By Appointment Only
Garden: May-Oct, By Appointment Only

Far North Gardens
16785 Harrison
Livonia, MI 48154
(313) 422-0747
Karen J. Krusinski

PLANTS SEEDS BOOKS
A very extensive list of seeds, offered in a jumble of categories rather than alphabetically, but rewarding to the collector. Specialties include seed and plants of **Barnhaven primroses**, and they are adding more perennials, seeds and plants all the time: brief to no plant descriptions. (1962)
Catalog: $2d, MO, CAN/OV, bn/cn

Farmer Seed & Nursery
P. O. Box 129
818 N.W. 4th St.
Faribault, MN 55021
(507) 334-1623 TO/CC $20m

PLANTS SEEDS SUPPLIES TOOLS
A **garden emporium** in your mailbox: vegetable seeds, trees and shrubs, fruit and berries, roses, summer blooming bulbs, tools, supplies, canning equipment. Color catalog offers broad selection of northern grown hardy stock, giant and midget vegetables and the gooseneck hoe that I bought and love!
Catalog: Free, R&W, SS:3-5
Nursery: All Year

Farnsworth Orchids
606 N. Lanikai Place
Haiku, Maui, HI 96708
(808) 572-7528 TO $25m
Larry & Kathy Farnsworth

PLANTS
"Our **orchids** are bred and grown for the home environment, for ease of culture and frequent blooming...bright, colorful, and fragrant." Good selection, especially mini-cattleyas, also cattleyas, phalaenopsis, vandaceous and others: plants briefly described. (1978)
Catalog: Free, CAN/OV, SS:AY, $25m, HYB
Nursery: All Year, By Appointment Only
Garden: All Year, Greenhouse, By Appointment Only

Fedco Seeds
52 Mayflower Hill Dr.
Waterville, ME 04901
C. R. Lawn & Gene Frey, Mgrs.

SEEDS BOOKS SUPPLIES
Seeds of short-season **vegetables, herbs and annual and perennial flowers**: plant list in form of order sheet with very brief plant descriptions -- seeds available in small to large quantities. They also offer books on gardening, some supplies and special tee shirts. (1978)
Catalog: Free, MO, SS:4,9, $25m

Fennell's Orchid Jungle
26715 S.W. 157 Ave.
Homestead, FL 33031
(305) 247-4824 or (800) 327-2832 TO/CC
The Fennell Family

PLANTS BOOKS SUPPLIES
Catalog offers a huge selection of **hybrid orchids** -- dendrobiums, epidendrums, miltonias, miltassias, oncidiums, phalaenopsis, vandas, cattleyas: plants well described. Sells other tropical plants as well. Also sells orchid supplies and books and offers orchid tours and tissue culture. (1888)
Catalog: Free, R&W, CAN/OV, SS:W, HYB
Nursery: All Year, Daily
Garden: All Year, Daily

Fern Hill Farm
P. O. Box 185
Clarksboro, NJ 08020
John F. Gyer

SEEDS
Sells only **Dr. Martin Pole Lima Bean seed**: there's no description of this particular variety, but it must be something special.
Catalog: Long SASE, MO, CAN/OV, $5m

Fernald's Hickory Hill Nursery
R R 2
Monmouth, IL 61462
(309) 934-6994
Gary Fernald

PLANTS
Informative leaflet offers lots of growing advice and a good selection of **pecans, hicans, shagback and shellbark hickory, butternuts, black walnuts** and **hazelnuts**. He will do custom grafting to preserve favorite old nut trees for you. (1980)
Catalog: 1 FCS, CAN, SS:AY, HYB
Nursery: All Year, Daily, Call Ahead
Garden: Orchard, Call Ahead

Fiddyment Farms
5000 Fiddyment Rd.
Roseville, CA 95678
(916) 771-0800 TO $4m
David Fiddyment

PLANTS SEEDS
Small nursery specializes in **pistachios**, both seeds and trees, as well as nuts for eating. He also sells hardy and low-chill nut trees, but I haven't see the list. (1978)
Catalog: Free, R&W, CAN/OV, SS:12-1, $4m
Nursery: All Year, M-F, Call Ahead
Garden: All Year, M-F, Call Ahead

Field and Forest Products, Inc.
N3296 Kuzuzek Rd.
Peshtigo, WI 54157
(715) 582-4997 TO:CC $10m
Joseph H. Krawczyk & Mary Ellen Kozak

SEEDS BOOKS SUPPLIES TOOLS
Small company selling **shiitake mushroom spawn** (eleven strains for growing under various temperatures and conditions), and complete growing supplies, books and tools. Shiitake strains well described for commercial and home growers. (1983)
Catalog: Free, R&W, CAN/OV, SS:5-11, $5m
Nursery: All Year, By Appointment Only
Garden: April-May, By Appointment Only

Henry Field Seed & Nursery Co.
407 Sycamore St.
Shenandoah, IA 51602
(712) 246-2011 or (605) 665-9391 TO/CC $10m
Don Kruml, Mgr.

PLANTS SEEDS SUPPLIES TOOLS
A true **garden emporium**: vegetable and flower seeds, fruit and nut trees, grapes, berries, roses, ornamental flowering trees, shrubs and vines and growing supplies and tools. Color catalog shows most of the plants offered and gives good plant descriptions and some growing hints. (1892)
Catalog: Free, R&W, MO, SS:2-6,10-11

The Fig Tree Nursery
P. O. Box 124
Gulf Hammock, FL 32639
(904) 486-2930
Gertrude Watson

PLANTS BOOKS
Offers a variety of **fig trees**, as well as pears, Japanese persimmons, muscadine grapes, mulberries, pomegranates and some flowering trees: each well but briefly described. Also sells her own book on "Growing Fruit Trees and Vines", $3.25 ppd. Can't ship plants to CA or AZ.
Catalog: $1, CAN, SS:10-3
Nursery: M-Sa, Call Ahead

Fischer Greenhouses
Oak Avenue
Linwood, NJ 08221-1398
(609) 927-3399
Charles W. Fischer, Jr.

PLANTS SUPPLIES
Color catalog offers a wide selection of **African violets** and other gesneriads: most plants shown in photographs, all briefly described. They are moving to expanded facilities in Fall 1987; better call ahead before planning a visit. (1888)
Catalog: $.50, CAN/OV, SS:4-11, $15m
Nursery: All Year, Daily
Garden: All Year, Daily

Flad's Glads
2109 Cliff Court
Madison, WI 53713
(608) 255-5274
Stan & Nancy Skolaski

PLANTS
A good selection of **gladiolus**: each plant well described, some shown in color. They offer new varieties and recent prize winners and add new varieties each year. (1963)
Catalog: $1d, R&W, CAN/OV, SS:2-6, $15m, HYB
Nursery: Feb-June, M-Sa, Call Ahead

Fleming's Flower Fields
P. O. Box 4617
3100 Leighton Ave.
Lincoln, NE 68504
Fleming Family

PLANTS
Specializes in **chrysanthemums** of all types; they also offer perennials, including hardy hibiscus, dianthus and 'Filigree' hybrid crape myrtles, which grow three feet high and are heavily branched. All plants well described.
Catalog: Free

Flickingers' Nursery
P. O. Box 245
Sagamore, PA 16250
(412) 783-6528 or 397-4953 TO/CC $30m
Richard Flickinger

PLANTS
A wholesaler of **seedling trees** -- same price to everyone, but a minimum of fifty trees of one variety. A nice variety of spruces, pines and firs and Canadian and Carolina hemlocks, as well as Vinca minor and birch, mountain ash and dogwood. Cannot ship to CA. (1947)
Catalog: Free, SS:4-10, $30m
Nursery: All Year, M-Sa, Call Ahead

Flora Favours
R.R. 4, Box 370
Elkhorn, WI 53121
(414) 742-3342
Thomas Oleshowski

PLANTS
A good selection of hardy **perennials** suitable for the hard winters of the Midwest: very brief plant descriptions. Among plants offered are anemones, aquilegias, asters, astilbes, campanulas, coreopsis, dianthus, species geraniums, monardas, phlox, sedums and veronicas. (1981)
Catalog: $1, SS:3-5,9, $15m, HYB, bn
Nursery: April-June, Daily: July-Oct, Tu-Su, Call Ahead
Garden: April-June, Daily

For Explanations of Abbreviations/Codes Used In Listings See Bookmark or Inside Covers

Flora Lan Nursery
Route 1, Box 357
Forest Grove, OR 97116
(503) 357-3500
Larry Landauer

PLANTS
An extensive list of **rhododendron and azalea hybrids** and magnolias, camellias, Japanese maples, pieris japonica, daphnes, heathers, brooms and other **ornamental plants**. There are no plants descriptions; they're just starting mail order, have been wholesaling since 1945.
Catalog: Free, R&W, CAN, SS:10-4, HYB, bn/cn
Nursery: April-June, Daily
Garden: April-May, Daily

Floridel Gardens
330 George Street
P. O. Box 514
Port Stanley, ON, Canada N0L 2A0
(519) 782-4015 TO $20m
Tom & Rosita Morgan

PLANTS SUPPLIES
Offers **phalaenopsis orchids**, and others, and orchid growing supplies; they send growing instructions with every purchase and will give personalized instructions and repotting demonstrations at the nursery.
Catalog: $2d, CAN, SS:5-9, $20m
Nursery: All Year, M-Sa, Call Ahead

Flowerland
P. O. Box 26
Wynot, NE 68792
Hans Anderson

PLANTS
A good selection of home grown garden **perennials** at reasonable prices: plants are briefly described. Also offers a number of **hardy ferns** and mixed 'get acquainted' collections. (1977)
Catalog: Long SASE, SS:4-6,9-10
Nursery: May-Oct
Garden: May-Oct, Growing Area

Floyd Cove Nursery
11 Shipyard Lane
Setauket, NY 11733-3038
(516) 751-1806
Patrick M. Stamile

PLANTS
A very broad selection of **daylilies**, many of them new cultivars, many tetraploids, as well as many recent introductions and classics. Plants very briefly described.
Catalog: $1d, CAN/OV, SS:4-11
Nursery: July-Aug, Daily, Call Ahead

Foliage Gardens
2003 128th Ave. S.E.
Bellevue, WA 98005
(206) 747-2998
Sue Olson

PLANTS
A very good selection of **ferns, both hardy and for greenhouses**, listed by botanical name with good plant descriptions. All plants grown from spore; new varieties being added all the time. They have also produced a video cassette, "Short Course on Ferns". (1976)
Catalog: $1, R&W, SS:4-6,9-10, $15m, bn
Nursery: All Year, By Appointment Only
Garden: Spring-Summer, By Appointment Only

Fordyce Orchids
1330 Isabel Avenue
Livermore, CA 94550
(415) 447-7171 or 828-3211 TO/CC $25m
Frank & Madge Fordyce

PLANTS
Specialists in **miniature cattleya orchid hybrids**, splashed-petal cattleyas and yellow and red cattleyas -- rooted seedlings in flasks or pots. Offers a broad selection: all briefly described.
Catalog: Free, R&W, CAN/OV, SS:3-11, $10m, HYB
Nursery: All Year, M-Sa, By Appointment Only
Garden: All Year, Greenhouse, By Appointment Only

Forestfarm
990 Tetherow Rd.
Williams, OR 97544
(503) 846-6963
Ray & Peg Prag

PLANTS
A collector's list of interesting **Western natives, garden perennials** and **trees and shrubs**. Offers small plants at reasonable prices, some quite unusual: each plant well described. Also sells hardy eucalyptus, bee plants, conifers, woodland plants and much more: a curl-up-with list. (1973)
Catalog: $2, R&W, SS:2-6,9-11, $20m, bn/cn
Nursery: All Year, Daily, Call Ahead
Garden: All Year, Growing Area, Call Ahead

Fort Caroline Orchids
13147 Fort Caroline Rd.
Jacksonville, FL 32225
(904) 641-9788 TO/CC $20m
W. C. Guthrie

PLANTS
Do not publish a catalog, but will send a free specialty list on request: specify **bromeliads, epiphyllums, ferns or orchids**. The orchid list offers a huge selection of hybrid and species orchids of many kinds.
Catalog: Free, R&W, CAN/OV, SS:AY, $20m
Nursery: All Year, M-Sa
Garden: All Year, Greenhouses, M-Sa

Dean Foster Nurseries
P. O. Box 127
511 S. Center St.
Hartford, MI 49057
(616) 621-2419 TO/CC $20m

PLANTS SUPPLIES
Color catalog offers a large selection of **hardy fruit and nut trees**, all kinds of berries, grapes and vegetable plants: all well described. Also offers growing supplies.
Catalog: Free, R&W, CAN/OV, SS:AY
Nursery: All Year, Call Ahead (Open Daily in Spring)

Four Seasons Nursery
2207 East Oakland Ave.
Bloomington, IL 61701
Adtron, Inc.

PLANTS
Offers **general nursery stock, fruit trees, berries.**
Catalog: Free

Four Winds Growers
P. O. Box 3538
42186 Palm Avenue
Fremont, CA 94539
(415) 656-2591
Donald F. Dillon

PLANTS
Specializes in **dwarf citrus**: oranges, tangerines, mandarin oranges, limes, grapefruit, lemons, tangelos and kumquats, 30 varieties in all. These are true dwarf trees, growing to eight feet; informative leaftlet tells how to grow them. Cannot ship to FL, TX or AZ. (1954)
Catalog: Long SASE, R&W, CAN, SS:4-11, $17m
Nursery: All Year, M-F

Fowler Nurseries, Inc.
525 Fowler Rd.
Newcastle, CA 95658
(916) 645-8191 TO/CC $20m
Robert & Richard Fowler, Nancy F. Johnson

PLANTS
Offers a broad selection of **fruit for the home garden**, including red and Asian "crunch" pears (first planted in California in the 1850's), European, Chinese and hybrid chestnuts, berries, table and wine grapes, pecans and walnuts. Price list is $.25, informative descriptive catalog is $7. (1912)
Catalog: See notes, R&W, SS:1-2, $20m, HYB
Nursery: All Year, Daily
Garden: All Year, Daily

Fox Hill Farm
P. O. Box 9
440 W. Michigan Ave.
Parma, MI 49269
(517) 531-3179
M. J. Hampstead

PLANTS
Broad selection of **herbs and scented geraniums, bee and dye plants**: 350 varieties by their count.
Catalog: $1, Plant/Price List free

Fox Orchids, Inc.
6615 West Markham
Little Rock, AR 72205
(501) 663-4246
John M. Fox

PLANTS BOOKS SUPPLIES
A very extensive list of **cattleya hybrids** and many other hybrid orchids, bromeliads, ferns and other tropical plants: all plants briefly described. Also sells books and orchid growing supplies which they ship at any time of the year. (1945)
Catalog: Free, CAN, SS:W, HYB, bn
Nursery: All Year, M-F, Call Ahead
Garden: All Year, Greenhouse, Call Ahead

Foxborough Nursery
3611 Miller Rd.
Street, MD 21154
(301) 836-7023
David Thompson

PLANTS
A collectors' list of **dwarf and unusual conifers, shrubs and trees**. The selection is broad -- plants for bonsai, heathers, kalmias, holly, rhododendrons, pieris, hamamelis, **Camperdown elm** and other treasures: plants not described, many are very special. (1976)
Catalog: $1d, R&W, CAN/OV, SS:AY, bn/cn
Nursery: By Appointment Only
Garden: May-Nov, By Appointment Only

The Fragrant Path
P. O. Box 328
Ft. Calhoun, NE 68023
E. R. Rasmussen

SEEDS
Catalog is devoted to seeds of **fragrant, rare and old-fashioned plants** of all kinds, with irresistible descriptions, literary quotations and charming sketches. A wide selection: can you live without trying "Kiss-me-over-the-garden-gate"? Cottage gardeners beware! (1982)
Catalog: $1, MO, CAN, $5m, bn/cn

Fred's Plant Farm
P. O. Box 707
Route 1, Dresden Road
Dresden, TN 38225
(901) 364-3754
Fred Stoker

PLANTS SEEDS
Sells only **sweet potato plants**, but fifteen kinds, all described by color of 'meat'. Also sells tobacco seed, not mentioned on sweet potato sheet; write for information. Sadly, no "Fred's" hats this year. (1947)
Catalog: Free, R&W, SS:4-6
Nursery: April-June, M-Sa
Garden: April-June, M-Sa

French Iris Gardens
621 South 3rd Ave.
Walla Walla, WA 99362
(509) 529-4092 TO $25m
Charles A. French

PLANTS
Collectors' list offers a broad selection of **bearded iris** of all classes and sizes; over 400 listed, with very brief plant descriptions. Uses french intensive growing methods; also offers to do research on almost any garden topic for a small fee starting at $3.50 -- write for information. (1987)
Catalog: $2d, R&W, CAN/OV, SS:W
Nursery: April-Sept, By Appointment Only
Garden: May-June, By Appointment Only

For Explanations of Abbreviations/Codes Used In Listings See Bookmark or Inside Covers

Lorine Friedrich
9130 Glenbury
Houston, TX 77034
(713) 448-8976
Lorine H. Friedrich

PLANTS
Offers a wide selection of **sinningias, episcias, columneas and African violets** from leading growers in many sizes: plants not described.
Catalog: $.50

Frosty Hollow Nursery
P. O. Box 53
Langley, WA 98260
(206) 221-2332
Marianne Edain & Steve Erickson

SEEDS
Small company does habitat collection of pre-ordered seeds: they offer a wide variety of **Northwestern native plants** for which they will collect seed -- ornamental trees and shrubs, nut trees, conifers, and wildflowers. Also consult on edible landscaping, restoration and permaculture. (1982)
Catalog: Long SASE, MO, R&W, CAN/OV, $10m, bn/cn

Fruitwood Nursery
P. O. Box 303
Eppinger Bridge Rd.
Molena, GA 30258
Paul Vignos, Mgr.

PLANTS
Small nursery sells **apples** for growers in the South. They've tested 104 varieties and sell those they consider the best for growing in the Piedmont region: plants are well described. They currently offer Yates, Fuji, Granny Smith, Ozark Gold, Mollie and Crispin. (1978)
Catalog: Long SASE, R&W, SS:12-3, $8m
Nursery: Nov-March, By Appointment Only

Fundraising Canada

See McConnell Nurseries, Inc.

Fungi Perfecti
P. O. Box 7634
Olympia, WA 98507
(206) 426-9292 TO/CC $10m
Paul & Cruz Stamets

SEEDS BOOKS SUPPLIES
Catalog offers **mushroom spawn**, growing kits, supplies and books for the amateur and commercial grower. Varieties include shiitake, oyster, button, enoke, Coprinus comatus, and Stropharia rugoso-annulata. They also offer a free brochure. (1980)
Catalog: $3, R&W, MO, CAN/OV, SS:9-6, $10m, HYB, bn/cn

G & B Orchid Laboratory
2426 Cherimoya Dr.
Vista, CA 92084
(619) 727-2611
Barry L. Cohen

PLANTS SUPPLIES
Specializes in **phaleneopsis, cymbidium, cattleya and dendrobium orchids** in great variety: each briefly described. Also sells several types of flasking media, laboratory glassware and a variety of fertilizers and chemicals. Will loan slides of flowering plants. (1970)
Catalog: Free, R&W, CAN/OV, SS:4-12, HYB
Nursery: All Year, M-Sa
Garden: All Year, Glasshouse, M-Sa

G & G Gardens and Growers
6711 Tustin Rd.
Salinas, CA 93907
(408) 663-6252 TO/CC $15m
Sharon & Kermit Gayman

PLANTS
A collectors' list of **fuchsias**, over 125 cultivars and a few species: each plant well described. They also offer a variety of **tuberous begonias** in collections and by individual color: multiflora, carnation, camellia, rose-form, picotee and crispa marginata and hanging basket varieties. (1980)
Catalog: MO, SS:W

Garden of Delights
2018 Mayo Street
Hollywood, FL 33020
(305) 923-2087 TO $50m
Murray & Debby Corman

PLANTS SEEDS
Here's a list of **tropical fruits and nuts** so unusual that I've never heard of many of them -- collectors will swoon! A source of seeds and plants of cherimoyas, cashews, maya breadnut, jelly palm, star apple, governor's plum, lovi-lovi, ice cream bean, yam bean. Intrigued? Super stuff! (1975)
Catalog: $2d, R&W, CAN/OV, SS:AY, $50m, HYB, bn/cn
Nursery: All Year, Daily, Call Ahead
Garden: All Year, Daily, Call Ahead

Garden of the Enchanted Rainbow
Route 4, Box 439-B
Killeen, AL 35645
(205) 757-1518
Jordan & Bernice Miller

PLANTS
Specializes in **tall bearded, median and reblooming iris**, "the best of the old, and the best of the new", some their own introductions. Offers a wide selection: plants very briefly described.
Catalog: 1 FCS, CAN/OV, SS:7-9, $10m
Nursery: July-Sept, Call Ahead

Garden Perennials
Route 1
Wayne, NE 68787
(402) 375-3615
Gail Korn

PLANTS
Sells a broad selection of **perennials**, including many daylilies: all plants are well described with cultural symbols, some illustrated in line drawings. Plants are field-grown clumps.
Catalog: $1d, SS:4-10, bn
Nursery: March-Oct, Daily

Garden Place
P. O. Box 388
6780 Heisley Rd.
Mentor, OH 44061-0388
(216) 255-3705 TO $10m
Jack, John, Jim & Dave Schultz

PLANTS
A very large selection of **perennials**: each well but briefly described. Catalog gives growing tips and has informative tables of plants by color, height, use, exposure, etc. Plants sold by 1, 3 or 12; shipped bareroot. Selection too broad to describe! (1972)
Catalog: $1, MO, CAN, SS:9-5, $10m, bn/cn

The Garden Source, Ltd.
4096 Clairmont Rd.
Atlanta, GA 30341
(404) 451-5356 TO/CC
David E. Cook

PLANTS SUPPLIES
Publishes no catalog at present; you'll have to send a "want-list" to see if they have the **bonsai plants or supplies** you are looking for. Also sells **waterlilies, lotus and bamboo**. Ships overnight anywhere in the U.S. For locals they offer bonsai classes, maintenance and boarding of bonsai. (1975)
Catalog: See notes, SS:AY
Nursery: All Year, T-Sa
Garden: All Year, T-Sa

Garden Valley Dahlias
406 Lower Garden Valley Rd.
Roseburg, OR 97470
(503) 673-8521
Leon V. Olson

PLANTS
A collectors' list of **dahlias**, only briefly described as to color and form.
Catalog: 1 FCS, SS:3-5
Nursery: Aug-Oct, Daily

Garden World
2503 Garfield St.
Laredo, TX 78043
(512) 724-3951
Tony Ramirez

PLANTS SUPPLIES
Bananas -- over 40 varieties, and citrus, bougainvilleas, bromeliads, cactus, bamboo, papayas and other tropical fruit, briefly to well described. Also offers some gowing supplies, and plant collecting expeditions to Mexico -- not for the faint of heart: non-endangered species only! (1976)
Catalog: $1, R&W, CAN/OV, SS:W, $2m, HYB, cn/bn
Nursery: All Year, Daily, Call Ahead
Garden: All Year, Daily, Call Ahead

Gardenimport, Inc.
P. O. Box 760
Thornhill, ON, Canada L3T 4A5
(416) 731-1950
Robert & Dugald Cameron

SEEDS SUPPLIES TOOLS BULBS
Distributor of Sutton's Seeds in Canada. Color catalog offers a broad selection of **garden annuals and perennials, vegetables** and imported garden tools. A separate catalog offers spring bulbs. All plants are well described, many illustrated. (1982)
Catalog: $2, R&W, USA/OV, SS:W, $15m, bn/cn
Nursery: All Year, M-F, Call Ahead

Gardens of the Blue Ridge
P. O. Box 10
U.S. 221 N.
Pineola, NC 28662
(704) 733-2417
Edw. P. Robbins

PLANTS
Catalog lists a good selection of **wildflowers, ferns, native orchids** and native trees and shrubs: all well described and some illustrated in color photos. Many are hard-to-find Southeastern native plants at reasonable prices. (1892)
Catalog: $2, R&W, CAN/OV, SS:3-4,9-11, $10m, bn/cn
Nursery: March-Dec, M-Sa, Call Ahead
Garden: April-Sept, M-Sa, Call Ahead

Gary's Perennials
1122 Welsh Road
Ambler, PA 19002
(215) 628-4070 TO/CC $10m
Gary & Andrea Steinberg

BULBS
Small nursery sells **Dutch bulbs**: tulips, daffodils, crocus, alliums and others. Nice selection, all briefly described and most illustrated in a color pamphlet. (1979)
Catalog: Free, R&W, MO, SS:Fall

Georgetown Greenhouse & Nursery
RD 1, Box 108 B
Georgetown, PA 15043
Joseph Iannetti

PLANTS SUPPLIES
This nursery specializes in **episcias** (called 'Flame Violets', new to me), greenhouse tools and supplies and the Ortho Computerized Gardening and the Plantin' Pal computer programs. The plant selection is good; some not available at all times. They sell several other computer programs, too.
Catalog: Free, R&W, MO, SS:4-10

Gerald's Garden

See Bamboo Sourcery

Louis Gerardi Nursery
R.R. 1, Box 428
Geneva, OH 44041

PLANTS
Offers **rhododendrons, azaleas, flowering shrubs and shade trees**.
Catalog: Free

Gilson Gardens
P. O. Box 277
U.S. Route 20
Perry, OH 44081
Gilson Family

PLANTS
Specializes in plants for **groundcover** and offers a broad selection: 100 varieties of ivy, pachysandra, sedums, plumbago, primroses, vincas and lamiums. Each plant well described, with cultural information. (1947)
Catalog: Free, SS:W, $10m, bn/cn
Nursery: Call Ahead

For Explanations of Abbreviations/Codes Used In Listings See Bookmark or Inside Covers

Girard Nurseries *P. O. Box 428* *6801 North Ridge (US 20)* *Geneva, OH 44041* *(216) 969-1636 or 466-2881 TO/CC $15m* *Pete Girard, Jr.*	PLANTS Offers a broad selection of flowering shrubs, dwarf conifers, garden perennials, rhododendrons and azaleas, holly, ornamental grasses, fruit and nut trees and plants for bonsai. (1942) Catalog: Free, R&W, SS:3-6,9-11, HYB Nursery: March-Nov, Daily
Gladside Gardens *61 Main Street* *Northfield, MA 01360* *(413) 498-2657 $10m* *Corys M. Heselton*	PLANTS BULBS Specializes in **summer blooming and tender bulbs**, particularly gladiolus, cannas, crinums, oxalis, dahlias and many others: each well described. Also offers a number of perennials, greenhouse plants, even Indian corn and decorative popcorn. (1940) Catalog: $1d(4 IRC), R&W, CAN/OV, SS:3-7, $10m, HYB, cn/bn Nursery: Daily, Call Ahead (Closed late Fall-early Winter) Garden: July-Oct, Call Ahead
Glasshouse Works *P. O. Box 97* *10 Church Street* *Stewart, OH 45778-0097* *(614) 622-2142 TO/CC $20m* *Tom Winn & Ken Frieling*	PLANTS A very, very extensive list of **exotic and tropical plants** -- a list to thrill the collector with a greenhouse or tropical climate. Among the many, ferns, gingers, bromeliads, succulents, aroids, acanthus, cactus, euphorbias: briefly described. Specialty is variegated plants of all kinds. (1973) Catalog: $1.50d, R&W, CAN/OV, $15m, HYB, bn/cn Nursery: All Year, Th-Su: Groups By Appt. Only other days. Garden: All Year, Th-Su
Glendale Enterprises *Route 3, Box 77 P* *DeFuniak Springs, FL 32433* *(904) 859-2141 or 2341* *John Alex Wilkerson*	SEEDS Sells seeds of **chufa (Cyperus esculentus)** to feed wild turkeys and other wildlife (cannot be shipped to Canada); advice on how to manage wild turkey habitat and seed of other wildlife food plants – velvet bean, partridge pea, beggarweed and cowpeas. (1979) Catalog: Long SASE, R&W, OV, $5m, cn/bn Nursery: All Year, Daily, Call Ahead Garden: July-Aug, Call Ahead
Gloria Dei *36 East Road* *High Falls Park* *High Falls, NY 12440* *(914) 687-9981* *Marty & Norma Kelly*	PLANTS Specializes in new and recently introduced **miniature roses** from well known hybridizers, plus some old favorites: a good selection, each well described. Catalog: Free, R&W, SS:W, $14m Nursery: By Appointment Only
Glorious Gladiolus	See Flad's Glads
Draig Goch Seed Co. *P. O. Box 113* *Newfield, NY 14867* *Robert Riker*	SEEDS **Northeastern wildflowers and woodland plants** "for those with the patience to watch your plants grow from seed to flower: all seed collected by hand", some habitat-collected. You may also send a want-list for less common Northeastern varieties. Informative catalog, nice selection. (1981) Catalog: $.50, SS:6-10, $2m, bn/cn

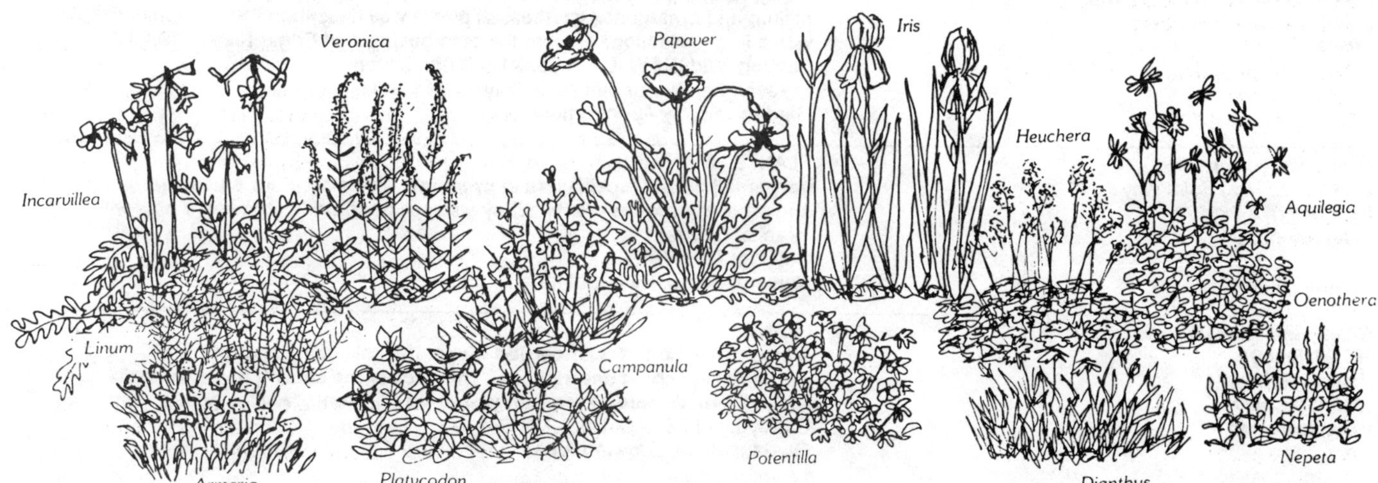

Golden Bough Tree Farm
Marlbank, ON, Canada K0K 2L0
Josef Reeve

PLANTS
A good selection of **hardy fruit trees and grapes for northern climates**, as well as ornamental trees and conifers, English oak, larch, birch and maples and plants for bonsai: all well described with cultural suggestions. (1973)
Catalog: $1, R&W, MO, USA/OV, SS:W, $25m, bn/cn

Good Seed Co.
P. O. Box 702
Tonasket, WA 98855
Will & Lorna Ross (& kids!)

SEEDS BOOKS SUPPLIES
Catalog, full of information, offers advice, opinion, pix of the kids and such items as **amaranth, quinoa, native flour corn, heirloom tomatoes** and **vegetables** suited to the intermountain areas of the Northwest: also sells books. Will boasts of "awesome garlic." (1980)
Catalog: $1, R&W, CAN/OV, bn/cn
Nursery: Random Hours, By Appointment Only
Garden: Aug-Sept, By Appointment Only

Goodwin Creek Gardens
P. O. Box 83
Williams, OR 97544
(503) 846-7357
Jim & Dotti Becker

PLANTS SEEDS BOOKS
Sells plants and seeds of **everlasting annual and perennial flowers, herbs** and **wildflowers**: good selection, plants are well but briefly described. They also sell their book, "A Concise Guide to Growing Everlastings", with illustrations and instructions on growing and drying many plants. (1978)
Catalog: $1, SS:4-6, 9-11, HYB, cn/bn
Nursery: All Year, By Appointment Only
Garden: By Appointment Only

John H. Gordon, Jr., Grower
1385 Campbell Blvd.
N. Tonawanda, NY 14120
(716) 691-9371 (early or eves.)
John H. Gordon, Jr.

PLANTS SEEDS
Small nursery sells **hardy nut trees and seeds, persimmons and pawpaws**: a nice selection, each briefly described. Also sell sample nuts by variety to taste before buying. Offer almonds, filberts, hazels, sweet chestnuts, hickory, pecans and walnuts. Can't ship to West Coast. (1980)
Catalog: Free, SS:3-4,10, $3m, HYB
Nursery: Spring to Fall, Call Ahead
Garden: Sept-Oct, Call Ahead

Gossler Farms Nursery
1200 Weaver Road
Springfield, OR 97478-9663
(503) 746-3922 or 747-0749
Marjory & Roger Gossler

PLANTS
A very large selection of **magnolias**: each well described. Also a number of daphnes, stewartia, franklinia, hamamelis, kalmias, and other unusual trees and shrubs, all well described with cultural suggestions. Collectors of very special trees and shrubs will be delighted!
Catalog: $1, R&W, SS:10-12,2-3, bn/cn
Nursery: All Year, By Appointment Only
Garden: March-June, By Appointment Only

Grace's Gardens
10 Bay Street
Westport, CT 06880
(203) 454-1919 TO/CC $15m
Jess F. Clarke, III

SEEDS
A small seed supplier, specializing in "amazing" and **giant vegetables,** Mexican and Oriental vegetables, chili peppers, gourds and tomatoes: each well described, many illustrated in color. Also sells seeds as "Ripley-Believe-It-or-Not" collections.
Catalog: $1, MO, CAN/OV

Russell Graham, Purveyor of Plants
4030 Eagle Crest Rd. N.W.
Salem, OR 97304
(503) 362-1135
Russell & Yvonne Graham

PLANTS BULBS
A collectors' catalog, full of unusual plants such as **species bulbs** and lilies, iris, fritillaria, hardy cyclamen, novelty daffodils, hardy ferns, trillium and ornamental grasses: all plants well described. Small nursery with a large selection. Bought the bulb business of Edgar Kline. (1980)
Catalog: $2d, R&W, CAN, SS:9-12, $20m, bn/cn
Nursery: Sa, By Appointment Only
Garden: Sa, By Appointment Only

Grand Ridge Nursery
27801 S. E. High Point Way
Issaquah, WA 98027
(206) 392-1896

PLANTS SUPPLIES
Very small nursery specializes in **primulas, dwarf conifers and erigerons** and other ericaceous plants. They also sell handmade stoneware pots with 'granite' glazing.
Catalog: Long SASE
Nursery: Sa-Su, By Appointment Only

Grandview Iris Gardens
HC 86, Box 91
Bayard, NE 69334
(308) 586-1471
Viola Schreiner

PLANTS
A broad selection of **tall bearded iris** for the collector, listed by cultivar name: very brief descriptions. The back of the catalog has a "bargain special" list; it's hard to see how you could go wrong. Aril iris, too.
Catalog: 1 FCS, MO, SS:7-9, $10m
Garden: June, Growing Area

Great Lakes Orchids
28805 Pennsylvania Rd.
Romulus, MI 48174
(313) 941-4696 TO/CC
Alexis Linder

PLANTS
A broad selection of **species and hybrid orchids**: each briefly described with some cultural information. Too many genera to list, including angraecum, ascocentrum, brassavola, doritis, laelia, neobathea, orinthocaphalus, sigmastylis and many more. Type those fast! (1974)
Catalog: Free, R&W, CAN/OV, SS:4-10, HYB
Nursery: All Year, M-Sa

Green Gold Ginseng Co.

See Pick's Ginseng

Green Horizons
218 Quinlan, #571
145 Scenic Hill Rd.
Kerrville, TX 78028
(512) 257-5141
Sherry Miller

SEEDS BOOKS
Devoted to preserving and protecting **Texas wildflowers**, company offers a number of them in small packets to bulk supplies. Also offers scarified bluebonnet seeds for better germination, wildflower books, posters and notecards and books on gardening in Texas and the South.
Catalog: Free, cn/bn
Nursery: Jan-Nov, M-Sa

Green Mountain African Violets
P. O. Box 43-A
Neal Road, RFD 1
White River Junction, VT 05001
(802) 295-6057
Ms. Wilma Boar

PLANTS
Offers a variety of **African violets**, standards and variegated standards, miniatures and chimeras -- and a few episcias -- many from prominent hybridizers: plants are well described. (1982)
Catalog: $.50, SS:W, $10m
Nursery: All Year, Daily, By Appointment Only
Garden: All Year, Daily, By Appointment Only

Green Plant Research
P. O. Box 735
Kaaawa, HI 96730
(808) 237-8672
Ted Green

PLANTS
A good selection of **tropical plants**, listed by families: hoyas, dischidias, plumerias, bougainvilleas, euphorbias, ferns and hibiscus -- and much more: no plant descriptions.
Catalog: $1, CAN/OV, SS:AY, $25m, HYB, bn/cn
Nursery: By Appointment Only
Garden: By Appointment Only

Green Valley Orchids
Route 1, Box 233 S
Folsom, LA 70437
(504) 796-5785 TO $28m
Don Saucier

PLANTS
Specializes in **phalaenopsis and cattleya alliance orchids**, most of their own hybridizing; they also sell ascocendas, vandas and dendrobiums. List is written in that secret code known to orchidists which always sounds like gossip, but has to do with pedigree. (1979)
Catalog: $1d, R&W, CAN/OV, SS:3-11, HYB
Nursery: All Year, Th-Sa, Call Ahead
Garden: March-June, Call Ahead

Greener 'N' Ever Tree Farm & Nursery
P. O. Box 222435
2 Scarlet Rd. (Carmel Valley)
Carmel, CA 93922
(408) 659-3196 or (800) 345-4344 TO $20m
Robert C. Zobel

PLANTS SUPPLIES TOOLS
Seedling conifers for Christmas tree growers, as well as other western native trees for windbreaks and conservation planning: no plant descriptions. Also offers a full line of supplies and equipment for foresters and Christmas tree growers. (1974)
Catalog: Free, R&W, CAN/OV, SS:AY, $20m
Nursery: All Year, M-F, Call Ahead

The Greenery
14450 N.E. 16th Place
Bellevue, WA 98007
(206) 641-1458
Lynn & Marilyn Watts

PLANTS
A broad selection of **species rhododendrons and azaleas**, as well as a selection of hybrids -- collectors will crow! Each plant is briefly to well described; also sells dwarf hybrid rhododendrons and **trilliums** not listed in in the catalog; ask if you are looking for a particular species.
Catalog: $2, R&W, OV, SS:3-6,9-10, bn
Nursery: March-Nov, By Appointment Only

Greenleaf Orchids
158 So. Winterset Ave.
Crystal River, FL 32629
(904) 795-3785
Ralph & Rochelle Flowers

PLANTS
A broad selection of **orchids** -- cattleyas, angraecum, phalaenopsis, vandas and various miniatures and dwarfs: each briefly described, listed by color.
Catalog: Free, R&W, CAN/OV, SS:W, $25m
Nursery: All Year, M-Sa

Greenleaf Seeds
P. O. Box 98
Conway, MA 01341
(413) 369-4615
Robert Wagner

SEEDS
Offers a good selection of unusual **vegetables** from Europe and the Orient: each is very well described. Among the offerings are: amaranth, Japanese and other radishes, green manure crops, annual and everlasting flowers.
Catalog: Free, MO, CAN/OV, SS:2-10, cn/bn

Greenlife Gardens Greenhouses
101 County Line Rd.
Griffin, GA 30223
(404) 228-3669 TO/CC $15m
Ira & Linda Slade

PLANTS
Flowering epiphytic cacti, dwarf crape myrtles, succulents, begonias and gesneriads, ferns and other exotics: most plants are briefly described. In 1988 the catalog will be in color; at present it contains many b&w photographs and a color insert on "holiday cacti". (1967)
Catalog: $2, MO, SS:AY, HYB, cn/bn

Greenmantle Nursery
3010 Ettersburg Rd.
Garberville, CA 95440
(707) 986-7504
Ram & Marissa Fishman

PLANTS
Catalog packed with cultural information, offers **antique apples**, many collected from old homesteads in Humboldt County. Also about 165 **old garden roses**, many rare varieties and species imported from England. Still more: pears, cherries, plums, quinces and disease-resistant chestnuts. (1983)
Catalog: $3, (Rose List, Long SASE), SS:1-4, cn
Nursery: All Year, By Appointment Only
Garden: May-June, By Appointment Only

Greenwood Nursery
P. O. Box 1610
Goleta, CA 93116
(805) 964-2420 TO/CC $25m
Jane & Ken Taylor

PLANTS
Color catalog offers nearly 600 varieties of **daylilies**: each plant well described, and the glimpses of their massed plantings are mouthwatering; unfortunately, they sell mail order only. (1981)
Catalog: $3d, MO, CAN/OV, SS:AY, $25m

Greer Gardens
1280 Goodpasture Island Rd.
Eugene, OR 97401-1794
(503) 686-8266 TO/CC
Harold E. Greer

PLANTS BOOKS SUPPLIES TOOLS
Color catalog offers a very large selection of **rhododendrons and azaleas**, vireyas, ornamental trees, maples (many palmatum cultivars), dwarf conifers, acid-loving shrubs and vines and bonsai materials: all well described in a very informative catalog. Also many books on trees and plants. (1955)
Catalog: $2(5 IRC), R&W, CAN/OV, SS:AY, HYB, bn
Nursery: All Year, Daily
Garden: March-June, Daily

Grianan Gardens
P. O. Box 14492
San Francisco, CA 94114
Colleen & Jim Thomas

SEEDS
Small company offering a nice selection of seeds for **annuals, perennials and herbs**: all plants well described. Packets available in sample and regular sizes; many of the seeds are imported from Europe and Canada. Since I can't bear to thin seedlings overmuch, I like small packets! (1985)
Catalog: $1d(2 IRC), R&W, MO, CAN/OV, $3m

Griffey's Nursery
1680 Highway 25-70
Marshall, NC 28753
(704) 656-2334 or 2681 TO $20m

PLANTS BULBS
A broad selection of **Southeastern native plants**: native orchids, ferns, vines and creepers, violets, aquatic plants, lilies, ornamental trees and shrubs, rhododendrons and azaleas, perennials and berries. Descriptions are very brief; these are choice plants for collectors. (1968)
Catalog: Free, R&W, CAN/OV, SS:8-5, $20m, bn
Nursery: All Year, Daily
Garden: All Year, Daily

Grigsby Cactus Gardens
2354 Bella Vista Dr.
Vista, CA 92084
(619) 727-1323 TO/CC $10m
David B. Grigsby

PLANTS
Catalog profusely illustrated with b&w photos, a real collectors' list of unusual **cacti & succulents**: all well described. They specialize in euphorbias, sansevierias, specimen plants and rare succulents, also send "wish letters" to regular customers offering new and unusual plants. (1965)
Catalog: $2d, R&W, CAN/OV, SS:W, $10m, bn
Nursery: All Year, Tu-Sa
Garden: All Year, Tu-Sa

Grimo Nut Nursery
R.R.3, Lakeshore Rd.
Niagara on the Lake, ON, Canada L0S 1J0
(416) 935-9773 TO $10m
Ernest & Marion Grimo

PLANTS
A selection of **hardy nuts** for northern climates, seedlings and grafted trees: persian walnuts, black walnuts, heartnuts, butternuts, Chinese chestnuts, apricots (sweet kernels), filberts, hickory and more. All well described in an informative list; sells seed nuts, does custom grafts. (1974)
Catalog: $1d, R&W, USA/OV, SS:4, $10m, HYB
Nursery: All Year, Sa-Su, By Appointment Only
Garden: July-Aug, Sa-Su, By Appointment Only

Grootendorst Nurseries
15310 Red Arrow Highway
Lakeside, MI 49116
(616) 469-2865 TO $20m
Theo Grootendorst

PLANTS
Offers **rootstocks** in small quantities for home gardeners, as well as in quantity: East Malling and Malling-Merton varieties for apples, also rootstocks for plums, peaches and cherries. Will do custom grafting and propagates old fruit varieties for Southmeadow Fruit Gardens. (1957)
Catalog: Free, R&W, OV, SS:10-5, $20m
Nursery: All Year, M-F, Call Ahead
Garden: All Year, M-F, Call Ahead

For Explanations of Abbreviations/Codes Used In Listings See Bookmark or Inside Covers

Growin'house
5 Ferndale Drive
Barrie, ON, Canada L4M 4S4
(705) 726-7363
John & Mary Lou Beaulieu

PLANTS SEEDS SUPPLIES
Collectors' list of **African violet leaves**, listed by type -- standards, miniatures, trailers, each briefly described. They also sell episcias and other gesneriads and Nadeau African violet seed and seed of sinningias. A full line of growing supplies and "Floralight" plant carts, too.
Catalog: $1d ($1 bill from US), USA, SS:5-10
Nursery: All Year, M-Sa, Call Ahead

Gurney Seed & Nursery Co.
2nd & Capital
Yankton, SD 57078
(605) 665-4451 or 1930 TO/CC $10m
Don Kruml, Pres.

PLANTS SEEDS SUPPLIES
Color tabloid catalog offers a very broad selection of plants and seeds for the home gardener -- fruit trees, roses, flowering trees and shrubs, nuts, berries, grapes and vegetable and flower seeds: all well described. Also gardening and canning supplies and advice -- even a magazine! (1866)
Catalog: Free, R&W, SS:W, cn/bn
Nursery: All Year, M-Sa (Daily in Spring)

Hager Nurseries, Inc.
RFD 5, Box 2000
Spotsylvania, VA 22553
(703) 582-5031 TO/CC $25m
Don Hager

PLANTS
Azaleas! 1,500 cultivars and species from many well known hybridizers, including their own. List gives only cultivar name and hybridizer: Gable, Glenn Dale, Back Acres, Linwood, Loblolly, Girard, North Tisbury, Beltsville and many more. Descriptive handbook is $4, gives more information. (1955)
Catalog: 2 FCS, R&W, CAN/OV, SS:AY, $25m, HYB
Nursery: March-Nov, M-Sa

Hahn's Rainbow Iris Garden
200 N. School St.
Desloge, MO 63601
(314) 431-3342
Clyde & Anna Hahn

PLANTS
A real collectors' list, tightly packed, offers a broad selection of **iris**, but gives only name, hybridizer, year and price -- hundreds of cultivars. Broad selection of tall bearded, intermediate and dwarf bearded and a nice selection of **daylilies**. (1981)
Catalog: $1d, CAN/OV, SS:4-7,8-9, HYB
Nursery: May-Sept, Call Ahead
Garden: May-July, Call Ahead

Halcyon Gardens
P. O. Box 124
Gibsonia, PA 15044
(412) 443-5544 TO/CC $15m
Peter Shefler

SEEDS
Offers a nice selection of **herb seeds**: each plant very well described with germination and cultural information. They also sell a number of seed collections for various uses and a kit for growing culinary herbs at home.
Catalog: $1d, R&W, MO, CAN, cn/bn

Dr. Joseph C. Halinar
2334 Crooked Finger Rd.
Scotts Mills, OR 97375
Dr. Joseph C. Halinar

SEEDS
Small grower specializing in seed of **species and hybrid lilies, daylilies** and **alliums** for hybridizers and collectors: brief plant notes include information on hybridizing qualities. Supplies limited; you'll have to choose substitutes, but they all sound desireable. (1980)
Catalog: Long SASE(1 IRC), R&W, MO, CAN/OV, SS:10-4, HYB
Garden: By Appointment Only

Hall Rhododendrons
1280 Quince Dr.
Junction City, OR 97448
(503) 998-2060 TO/CC
Stan Hall

PLANTS SUPPLIES
Collectors' list -- a broad selection of **species and hybrid rhododendrons and azaleas**: all well described, with general cultural information. Also sells two styles of aluminum plant labels on which pencil writing "weathers in" and lasts; SASE for free samples. Plants to UPS areas only. (1977)
Catalog: $1, R&W, SS:AY, HYB, bn
Nursery: All Year, Call Ahead
Garden: April-May, Call Ahead

Robert B. Hamm
P. O. Box 160903
Sacramento, CA 95816
Robert B. Hamm

PLANTS
Specializing in **begonias, peperomias, cacti and succulents** and increasing variety all the time: "odd and rare items for indoors and out". Plants are briefly described; price of catalog includes 4 newsletters a year. Formerly called Plants Etcetera. (1981)
Catalog: $3, R&W, CAN, SS:W
Nursery: By Appointment Only

Hanchar Nursery
P. O. Box 407
Carrolltown, PA 15722

PLANTS
Offers seedling **hybrid poplars and red oak, conifers** and other conservation plants.
Catalog: Free

Harmony Farm Supply
P. O. Box 451
4050 Ross Rd.
Graton, CA 95444
(707) 823-9125
Kate Burroughs & David Henry

PLANTS BOOKS SUPPLIES TOOLS
Informative catalog offers a good selection of **fruit and nut trees, dwarf fruit trees and mixed berries**: all well described. Also sells drip irrigation supplies, organic fertilzers and pest controls and tools andV supplies. Specify nursery catalog or growers supply catalog, $2d each. (1980)
Catalog: See notes, R&W, CAN/OV, SS:1-3
Nursery: All Year, M-Sa

Harris Seeds
3670 Buffalo Rd.
Rochester, NY 14624
(716) 594-9411
Joseph Harris

PLANTS SEEDS SUPPLIES TOOLS
Color catalog offers a broad selection of **flower and vegetable seeds**: many developed by their own research staff, and all well described. They list "special merit" vegetables which they feel perform best -- and have those cute 'baby' pumpkins. They also sell some plants, tools and supplies. (1879)
Catalog: Free, R&W, MO

Harstine Island Nursery
E 3021 Harstine Island North Rd.
Shelton, WA 98584
(206) 426-2013
Paul Holden

PLANTS
Does not have a catalog, but will supply plants from "want-lists". Offers a wide variety of **rhododendrons, deciduous and evergreen azaleas, Japanese maples and dwarf conifers, flowering shrubs, dogwood and more**. Send them your want-list by cultivar name; include a long SASE for reply. (1955)
Catalog: See notes, SS:9-6, HYB, bn
Nursery: All Year, Daily, Call Ahead
Garden: April-June, Call Ahead

Hartman's Herb Farm
Old Dana Road
Barre, MA 01005
(617) 355-2015 TO/CC
Lynn & Peter Hartman

PLANTS SUPPLIES
Offers a selection of **herb and scented geranium plants**, as well as essential oils, herb teas, potpourris, dried flower arrangements and wreaths, note papers and an herbal calendar. (1980)
Catalog: $1, SS:AY, $10m
Nursery: March-Dec, Th-Su
Garden: May-Nov, Th-Su

Hartmann's Plantation, Inc.
P. O. Box E
310 60th Street
Grand Junction, MI 49056
(616) 253-4281 TO/CC $10m
Patrick & Daniel Hartmann

PLANTS BOOKS SUPPLIES
Selection of **northern and southern blueberries**, as well as "Artic" kiwis, pineapple guava, pawpaw and wintergreen (Galtheria procumbens). They also carry a line of supplies for fruit growers, including bird repellent devices, and the book "Blueberry Culture" by Dr. Paul Eck. (1942)
Catalog: Free, CAN/OV, SS:AY
Nursery: All Year, M-F, Sa am, Call Ahead

Hass Nursery
24105 Ervin Rd.
Philomath, OR 97370
(503) 929-3739
Henrietta Hass

PLANTS
A collectors' list of **rhododendrons and azaleas** and several cultivars of Pieris japonica: all well described. The many azalea hybrids include those of Back Acres, Gable, Glenn Dale, Harris, Greenwood, Linwood, North Tisbury and others. Also offers a large selection of Satsuki azaleas.
Catalog: $2, SS:9-6, $15m
Nursery: By Appointment Only

Hastings
P. O. Box 4274
Atlanta, GA 30302-4274
(404) 524-8861 or (800) 334-1771 TO/CC

PLANTS SEEDS SUPPLIES
A regional garden emporium: **fruit and nut trees, berries, grapes, kiwis** and seed for **vegetables and garden annuals**. Color catalog has good plant descriptions, also offers tools and supplies. Sells a broad selection of plants for Southern gardens. (1889)
Catalog: Free, R&W
Nursery: All Year, Daily, 2350 Cheshire Bridge Rd.

Hatten's Nursery
6401 Overlook Rd.
Mobile, AL 36608
(205) 342-0505 TO $35m
William Hatten

PLANTS
List offers a broad selection of **bougainvilleas**, including two variegated and four double-flowered varieties: well described with cultural hints. Also Hibiscus rosa-chinensis and Jasminum sambac 'Grand Duke of Tuscany' and other tropical plants; ask for non-bougainvillea list. (1975)
Catalog: Free, R&W, CAN, SS:AY, $35m
Nursery: All Year, M-Sa

Hauser's Superior View Farm
Route 1, Box 199
County Highway J
Bayfield, WI 54814
(715) 779-5404 TO $10m
Jim Hauser

PLANTS
Offers a good selection of hardy field-grown **perennials** -- sold only by the dozen or hundred: only name and flower color given. Good choice of chrysanthemums, lupines, sedums, delphiniums, also asparagus and rhubarb. (1910)
Catalog: Free, R&W, CAN, SS:4-7,9-11, $10m
Nursery: April-Nov, M-Sa, Call Ahead
Garden: May-June, Sept-Oct, M-Sa, Call Ahead

Heard Gardens, Ltd.
5355 Merle Hay Rd.
Johnston, IA 50131
(515) 276-4533 TO/CC $15m
W. R. Heard

PLANTS
Specializes in **lilacs** propagated on their own roots, about 35 varieties: each briefly described, but there are some letters and symbols without explanation which I guess lilac collectors will know. They have the lovely variety "Primrose", which is a soft pale yellow and very hard to find.
Catalog: $2d, MO, SS:3-4,10-11

Heather or Heather Growers

See Heaths & Heathers

Heaths and Heathers
P. O. Box 850
62 Elma-Monte Rd.
Elma, WA 98541
(206) 482-3258 TO/CC $10m
Bob, Alice & Cindy Knight

PLANTS
A collectors' list of many species and cultivars of **erica, calluna** and **daboecia**: each described by color, season of bloom, size and color of foliage. Offers about 280 varieties; if you don't see what you want, write and ask if they have it. (1982)
Catalog: Long SASE, CAN, SS:2-6,9-11, $10m
Nursery: All Year, M-F, Call Ahead
Garden: June-Oct, Call Ahead

Heliconia Haus
12691 S.W. 104 Street
Miami, FL 33186
Charles D. Ullman

PLANTS
Small nursery specializing in **heliconias and gingers**, with a few musaceae and species cannas: a collectors' list with only brief descriptions of these America. (1984)
Catalog: Free, R&W, CAN/OV, SS:AY, bn
Nursery: Feb-Nov, Daily, By Appointment Only
Garden: Feb-Nov, Daily, By Appointment Only

Marc Henny Nursery
10415 72nd Ave. N.E.
Brooks, OR 97305
(503) 792-3448

PLANTS
Offers **hardy evergreen azaleas and daphnes** as liners or one gallon plants: very brief plant descriptions.
Catalog: Free, SS:3-5,9-11, $10m

Herb Gathering Inc.
5742 Kenwood Ave.
Kansas City, MO 64110
(816) 523-2653 TO/CC $20m
Paula Winchester

SEEDS BOOKS
A fresh-herbs business which purchased J.A. Demonchaux, importer of European **gourmet vegetable and herb** seeds. Offers many seeds wanted by cooks. Also sells herb and cookbooks and will ship fresh herbs by overnight Express Mail. Plants and seed germination well described. (1978)
Catalog: $2d, R&W, CAN/OV
Nursery: All Year, W-Sa, (5504 Troost, Kansas City)
Garden: By Appointment Only

The Herbfarm
32804 Issaquah-Fall City Rd.
Fall City, WA 98024
(206) 784-2222
Zimmerman Family

PLANTS BOOKS SUPPLIES
Their regular catalog lists many **herb plants** and a large selection of herb products, gifts and courses offered. They also print a plant list of 425 **herbs, sedums and sempervivums** which they sell ($1.75, ask for #0100). Catalog also lists books and herbal flea collars for cats and dogs. (1974)
Catalog: Free, CAN/OV, SS:AY, cn/bn
Nursery: All Year, Hours Vary, Call Ahead
Garden: April-Sept, Call Ahead

Heritage Rosarium
211 Haviland Mill Rd.
Brookville, MD 20833
(301) 774-2806
Nicholas & Rosanne Weber

PLANTS
Offers a large selection of **old garden, modern shrub and species roses**, available on a custom root basis. About 400 varieties are listed only by by cultivar or species name, with symbols for type, color and date of introduction; get out your 'old' rose books. 50-75 varieties usually in stock.
Catalog: $1d, SS:11, $20m
Nursery: April-Oct, Sa-Su, By Appointment Only

Heritage Rose Gardens
16831 Mitchell Creek Dr.
Ft. Bragg, CA 95437
(707) 984-6959 or 964-3748
Virginia Hopper & Joyce Demits

PLANTS
A broad selection of **species and old garden roses**, including unidentified roses found at old north-coast homesteads and named for location found. Specializes in teas/Chinas, ramblers/climbers and many more and will do custom rooting of additional rare varieties. Garden visits June-July. (1981)
Catalog: $1d, MO, CAN, SS:1-2, HYB, bn
Garden: 40350 Wilderness Rd., Branscomb, By Appt. Only

Hickory Hill Gardens
R. D. 1, Box 11
Loretto, PA 15940
Clayton Burkey

PLANTS
A very broad selection of **daylilies**, also Siberian iris, hosta, bearded iris, herbaceous peonies and other perennials. Each plant briefly but well described. Also advertises as Burkey Gardens. (1981)
Catalog: $1, CAN, SS:5-6,8-10, $10m
Nursery: June-Oct, By Appointment Only
Garden: July-Aug, By Appointment Only

Hidden Springs Nursery - Edible Landscaping
Route 14, Box 159
Cookeville, TN 38501
(615) 268-9889
Hector Black & Jomo MacDermott

PLANTS
Fuchsias for warm climates, including varieties which bloom well in hot weather, with cultural hints. Another list offers "edible" landscaping, **herbs, fruit and nut trees, scented geraniums, berrying shrubs**: all well described. Specify which list you want. (1968)
Catalog: $.40, R&W, OV, SS:9-6, $10m, bn/cn
Nursery: All Year, M-Sa, Call Ahead
Garden: Spring, Fall, M-Sa, Call Ahead

High Altitude Gardens
P. O. Box 4238
620 Sun Valley Rd.
Ketchum, ID 83340
(208) 726-3221 TO/CC
Bill McDorman

SEEDS BOOKS SUPPLIES TOOLS
Seed of open-pollinated **gourmet and heirloom vegetables, herbs, wildflowers** and **native grasses**, adapted to short, cold-season, high altitude climate of the mountain West. Informative catalog with cultural suggestions; also sells tools, growing supplies and books.
Catalog: $2, R&W, CAN/OV, SS:5-8, cn/bn
Nursery: All Year, M-F, Call Ahead
Garden: July-Sept, By Appointment Only

High Country Rosarium
1717 Downing St.
Denver, CO 80218
(303) 832-4026
William & Melinda Campbell

PLANTS SEEDS
Very hardy **old garden roses** grown in the Rockies -- a nice selection of **species, old garden varieties and shrub roses**: all well described. Also offers several collections -- for hedges, bird lovers and dry climates -- and seeds of several species roses. (1971)
Catalog: $1, SS:11-3, HYB, bn/cn
Nursery: May-June, W & Sa, By Appointment Only
Garden: May-June, W & Sa, By Appointment Only

Highland Succulents
Eureka Star Route, Box 133
Gallipolis, OH 45631
(614) 256-1428

PLANTS
"We specialize in hard-to-find **succulents** -- no common varieties." A collectors' list, with periodic specialty lists of new and unusual items, very large selection: plants briefly described.
Catalog: $2, R&W, CAN/OV, SS:AY, $15m, HYB, bn
Nursery: M-F, By Appointment Only

Highlander Nursery
General Delivery
Pettigrew, AR 72752
(501) 677-2300
Lee & Louise McCoy

PLANTS
Formerly Shanti Gardens; specializes in hardy and low-chill **blueberries,** with one dwarf variety, "Tophat", which grows only 9 to 15 inches high and makes a nice container or border plant. (1986)
Catalog: Free, R&W, CAN, SS:W
Nursery: All Year, Daily, Call Ahead
Garden: Spring-Fall, Daily, Call Ahead

Hildenbrandt's Iris Gardens
HC 84, Box 4
Lexington, NE 68850-9304
(308) 324-4334
Les & Tony Hildenbrandt

PLANTS BULBS
Very extensive list of **tall bearded and dwarf iris**: each briefly described. Also offers a good selection of herbaceous peonies, Oriental poppies, hostas and a few hybrid lilies. The color selection of Oriental poppies seems wonderful: apricot, black raspberry, purple! (1956)
Catalog: 2 FCS(2 IRC), R&W, CAN/OV, SS:7-9, $10m
Nursery: All Year, Call Ahead
Garden: May-Sept, Call Ahead

Hill 'n dale
6427 N. Fruit Ave.
Fresno, CA 93711
(209) 439-8249
Dale Kloppenburg

PLANTS
A very extensive list of **hoyas**, both species and named cultivars, with a number of **dischidias** -- cousins of the hoya. Added about 100 new varieties from Australia to their collection in 1987, also went collecting in Guadalcanal and the Solomon Islands, so there are more to come. Cuttings only.
Catalog: Long SASE W/2 FCS, R&W, SS:AY, $25m, bn
Nursery: All Year, By Appointment Only
Garden: June-August, By Appointment Only

Hillhouse Nursery
R. D. 1, Kresson-Gibbsboro Rd.
Voorhees, NJ 08043
(609) 784-6203 TO/CC
Theodore S. Stecki

PLANTS
Specializes in the **Linwood hardy azaleas**, hybridized by the late G. Albert Reid -- all either double, semi-double or hose-in-hose varieties which come in a range of sizes from prostrate and compact to tall, and all very hardy. Very brief descriptions. (1968)
Catalog: Free, SS:4-10, HYB
Nursery: April-Oct, Weekday Evenings and Sa-Su, Call Ahead
Garden: April-Oct, Weekday Evenings and Sa-Su, Call Ahead

For Explanations of Abbreviations/Codes Used in Listings See Bookmark or Inside Covers

Historical Roses
1657 W. Jackson St.
Painesville, OH 44077
(216) 357-7270
Ernest J. Vash

PLANTS
Small nursery offers a wide selection of **old garden roses** of all kinds, a number of fragrant hybrid teas and the very hardy shrub roses of Griffith Buck. All plants very briefly described; over 100 in all. (1982)
Catalog: Long SASE, SS:10-12, $6m
Nursery: All Year, Call Ahead
Garden: June-Aug, By Appointment Only

Holbrook Farm & Nursery
Route 2, Box 223 B
Fletcher, NC 28732
(704) 891-7790 TO/CC $25m
Allen W. Bush

PLANTS BULBS
Offers a broad selection of **garden perennials**, hardy bulbs, native wildflowers, hardy geraniums, hostas and trees and shrubs, including heaths and heathers: all very well described with cultural information. They have recently added daffodils and other Dutch bulbs. (1980)
Catalog: $2d, SS:3-5,9-11, $15m, bn/cn
Nursery: April-Oct, M-Sa
Garden: May-Aug, M-Sa

Holiday Seeds
4276 Durham Circle
Stone Mountain, GA 30083
(404) 294-6594
Jere & Sara Housworth

PLANTS SEEDS
Company originally offered only seeds of **hostas and daylilies** but now sells plants and only a few seeds. They offer a nice selection of hostas, as well as their own seedling hosta, lily and daylily crosses in flats, and a few hardy ferns. (1984)
Catalog: $1, MO, SS:4-5,10, HYB

Holly Hills, Inc.
1216 Hillsdale Rd.
Evansville, IN 47711
(812) 867-3367
Stephen & David Schroeder

PLANTS
Offers their own very hardy H. R. Schroeder **evergreen azaleas**, thirty-eight named cultivars bred for Midwestern winters: plants well described. They also sell species azaleas, hybrid rhododendrons, holly and dwarf conifers -- request a list of these plants or the azalea catalog. (1974)
Catalog: Long SASE(2 FCS), R&W, SS:3-5, $25m, HYB
Nursery: March-Oct, M-Sa
Garden: April-May, M-Sa

Homestead Division of Sunnybrook Farms
9448 Mayfield Rd.
Chesterland, OH 44026
(216) 729-9838
Peter & Jean Ruh

PLANTS SEEDS TOOLS
A retirement business of the founders of Sunnybrook Farms offers a huge selection of **hostas** (and hosta seeds), as well a number of ivies, epimediums, daylilies and two Japanese ferns -- some "retirement"! Plants briefly to well described. They also offer a few of their favorite hand tools. (1980)
Catalog: $1, CAN/OV, SS:5-10, $25m
Nursery: Feb-Sept, Sa-Su, By Appointment Only
Garden: June-Sept, Sa-Su, By Appointment Only

Honeywood Lilies
P. O. Box 63
Parkside, SK, Canada S0J 2A0
(306) 747-3296 or 3776
Dr. A. J. Porter & Allan B. Daku

PLANTS BULBS
Specializes in **lilies**, but also offers a variety of hardy fruit, ornamental trees and shrubs, conifers, perennials, roses and peonies: all plants well described, with planting hints.
Catalog: $1d, R&W, USA/OV, SS:4-5,9-11, HYB, cn/bn
Nursery: April-Oct, M-Sa, Su By Appointment Only
Garden: July-Sept, M-Sa

Hookland's Dahlias
1096 Horn Lane
Eugene, OR 97404
(503) 688-7792
Robert B. Hookland

PLANTS
Offers a good selection of **dahlias**, listed by type with very brief descriptions. Grow more varieties than they list, so you can send a "want-list" to ask for desired cultivars.
Catalog: Free, CAN, SS:12-5
Nursery: Hours Vary, Call Ahead

Horizon Seeds
P. O. Box 886
Hereford, TX 79045
(806) 258-7288 or 7280

SEEDS
Specializes in **native grasses and wildflowers**; also sells hybrid corn and sorghum, legumes and cool season grasses.
Catalog: Free, R&W, MO

Jerry Horne - Rare Plants
10195 S.W. 70th St.
Miami, FL 33173
(305) 270-1235
Jerry Horne

PLANTS
A collectors' list of rare and exotic **tropical plants**. A good selection of of bromeliads, platyceriums, ferns, palms, cycads, aroids and others: all briefly described with cultural suggestions. (1975)
Catalog: Long SASE, CAN/OV, SS:AY, $10m, HYB, bn
Nursery: All Year, M-Sa, Call Ahead
Garden: All Year, M-Sa, Call Ahead

Horsley Rhododendron Nursery
7441 Tracyton Blvd. N.W.
Bremerton, WA 98310
(206) 692-9588
Donald A. Horsley

PLANTS
They ship only two **rhododendrons**: 'One Thousand Butterflies' and 'Arthur Horsley', but will ship others from their rhododendron and Exbury azalea list along with them if you order one of the "shippers". A good selection, but no descriptions except for the special two.
Catalog: Free, SS:3-5,9-10, $25m
Nursery: Sept-Dec, March-June, Daily, Call Ahead

Hortense's African Violets
12406 Alexandria St.
San Antonio, TX 78233
(512) 656-0128
Hortense Pittman

PLANTS
Offers a selection of standard, compact standard, miniature and semi-miniature **African violets**, including their own hybrids, "Hortense's Honeys", both plants and leaves and several collections: all plants briefly described.
Catalog: $.25, SS:W, $10m, HYB

Hortica Gardens
P. O. Box 308
Placerville, CA 95667
(916) 622-7089 TO $15m
Don & Pauline Croxton

PLANTS SEEDS
A good selection of **dwarf conifers, bonsai materials, box, Japanese maples, dwarf lilacs, ornamental grasses, evergreen azaleas**. A choice list from a small nursery -- you MUST call ahead! Also sells seed from many of their trees and shrubs. Collectors' list, brief descriptions. (1969)
Catalog: $.50, CAN, SS:10-4, $15m, bn/cn
Nursery: By Appointment Only
Garden: By Appointment Only

Hortico, Inc.
723 Robson Rd., R.R. 1
Waterdown, ON, Canada L0R 2H0
(416) 689-6984

PLANTS
A very broad selection of garden **perennials**, hardy ornamental trees and shrubs, roses, lilacs, ferns, wildflowers and conifers: briefly described. Essentially a wholesale nursery, they will sell in small quantities to home gardeners at retail prices. Ask for rose or perennial list.
Catalog: See notes, R&W, USA/OV, bn

Horticultural Enterprises
P. O. Box 810082
Dallas, TX 75381-0082

SEEDS
"Chilies are our business." **Chilies and sweet peppers** from around the world: each briefly described and illustrated as to size and shape. Also some **Mexican herbs and vegetables**. Included is a bibliography of cookbooks with publishers' addresses -- uses galore for your harvest! (1973)
Catalog: Free, MO, CAN

C. W. Hosking - Exotic Seed Importer
P. O. Box 500
Hayle, Cornwall, United Kingdom TR27 4BE
(0736) 75-2475
Colin W. Hosking

SEEDS
A collectors' list of **tropic and sub-tropic plants**, about 600 species: listed by botanical name and briefly but well described; includes many tropical fruits, passion flowers, cassias and other greenhouse plants. Will back order seeds until they become available. (1981)
Catalog: $4(6 IRC), R&W, MO, OV, bn/cn

Houston Daylily Gardens

See American Daylily & Perennials

Spencer M. Howard Orchid Imports
11802 Huston Street
North Hollywood, CA 91607
(818) 762-8275
Spencer & Marjorie Howard

PLANTS
Only **species orchids**, collected from all over the world. A collectors' list offers dendrobium, epidendrum, angraceum, oncidium, laelia, rhyncostylis, paphiopedilum, phalaenopsis and many others: very brief descriptions -- get out your reference books and dream. (1957)
Catalog: Long SASE (2 FCS), R&W, CAN/OV, $25m, SS:W, bn
Nursery: All Year, By Appointment Only
Garden: Spring, By Appointment Only

Huan Bui Orchids, Inc.
6900 S.W. 102nd Ave.
Miami, FL 33173
(305) 595-7919
Limrick, Inc.

PLANTS
Offers **hybrid orchids**.
Catalog: $2
Nursery: All Year, M-Sa

J. L. Hudson, Seedsman
P. O. Box 1058
Redwood City, CA 94064
J. L. Hudson

SEEDS BOOKS
"Specialize in **rare seeds** from all over the world -- except Antarctica." Catalog is informative, with broad selection, historic, cultural and literary references and current scientific information, illustrated with old prints. More than a catalog, it's an education; also offers some books. (1911)
Catalog: $1(9 IRC), R&W, MO, CAN/OV, bn/cn

Huff's Garden Mums
P. O. Box 187
618 Juniatta
Burlington, KS 66839-0187
(316) 364-2933 or 2765
Charles & Harry Huff

PLANTS
A huge selection of **chrysanthemums** -- a collectors' list: each very briefly described and organized by type. Also offers a number of collections by type or use for those who are bewildered by the choice. Still carries some old favorites. (1955)
Catalog: Free, R&W, CAN/OV, SS:3-6, $5m
Nursery: Sept-June, M-F
Garden: Sept-Oct, M-F

Huggins Farm Irises
Route 1, Box 348
Hico, TX 76457
(817) 796-4041
Pete & Mary Huggins

PLANTS
A broad selection of **bearded iris**: tall bearded, reblooming, intermediate, border, dwarf, horned, "space age" and "antique" (before 1950 -- by which measure, I'm an antique, too). The "antiques" are used for landscaping restored older homes.
Catalog: $1d, CAN/OV, SS:7-10, $10m
Nursery: Weekends & Eves, Call Ahead
Garden: March-May, Sept-Nov, Weekends & Eves, Call Ahead

Hughes Nursery
1305 Wynooche West
Montesano, WA 98563
Howard Hughes

PLANTS
A collectors' list of **Japanese maples**, mostly listed by their Japanese cultivar names, and a few other species maples: all are well described with cultural suggestions. A broad selection of hard-to-find trees, listed by shape and leaf color/character. Adding rare **beech** cultivars. (1964)
Catalog: $1.50d, CAN, SS:10-3
Nursery: All Year, By Appointment Only
Garden: All Year, By Appointment Only

Ed Hume Seeds, Inc.
P. O. Box 1450
Kent, WA 98035
Jeff Hume

SEEDS BOOKS
Sells a wide variety of untreated **vegetables** for short-season and cool climates, also **perennials, annuals, dahlias and gladiolus**. Also sells Ortho gardening books and video cassettes on vegetable gardening and indoor plants narrated by Ed Hume. (1978)
Catalog: Free, R&W, MO, CAN

Hungry Plants
1216 Cooper Dr.
Raleigh, NC 27607
(919) 851-8699
Ron Gagliardo

PLANTS
Carnivorous plants produced by tissue culture -- sold in tubes: no descriptions. Also does custom tissue culturing for collectors of rare plants. Minimum order of $30 for Overseas shipment. (1982)
Catalog: $1, R&W, CAN/OV, SS:AY, HYB, bn
Nursery: All Year, By Appointment Only

Huronview Nurseries & Garden Centre
1811 Brigden Side Rd.
Bright's Grove, ON, Canada N0N 1C0
(519) 869-4689 or 2837 TO $25m
Dick & Mary Kock

PLANTS
Wide selection of **orchids**: cattleyas, oncidiums, vandas, cymbidiums, paphiopedilums, phalaenopsis and some species orchids: each briefly described. Other catalogs offer a wide selection of nursery stock: roses, ornamental and fruit trees or perennials, wildflowers and ferns. (1950)
Catalog: Free, R&W, USA/OV, SS:4-10, $20m, HYB
Nursery: All Year, M-Sa
Garden: All Year, M-Sa

Brenda Hyatt
1 Toddington Crescent, Bluebell Hill
Chatham, Kent, England ME5 9QT
Medway 63251 (0634)
Brenda Hyatt

SEEDS
Specializes in **Auricula primroses**, both Alpine and Show varieties; sells seeds of both types in packets of mixed colors. Also offers seed of "Diana" primroses (I don't think they are named for you know who), cowslips, candelabras, double Jack in the Green and double single gold laced.
Catalog: 1 IRC (20p), OV, $5m
Nursery: By Appointment Only

Idle Hours Orchids
905 S. W. Coconut Dr.
Ft. Lauderdale, FL 33315
(305) 462-2984

PLANTS
Specializes in orchids: **cattleyas, dendrobiums and phalaenopsis.**
Catalog: R&W

Illini Iris
Route 3, Box 5
North State Street Rd.
Monticello, IL 61856
(217) 762-3446
D. Steve Varner

PLANTS
Breeder of **bearded iris, Siberian iris, daylilies and herbaceous peonies.**
Catalog: $1

Illinois Foundation Seeds, Inc.
P. O. Box 722
Route 45
Champaign, IL 61820
(217) 495-6260
Dale E. Cochran, Gen. Mgr.

SEEDS
Sells only new hybrid "**sweetcorn**": 'Ivory 'n Gold', 'Illini Gold', 'Illini Xtra-Sweet', 'Xtra-Sweet 82', 'Northern Xtra-Sweet' and 'Florida Staysweet'. All are well described, some shown in color in their leaflet.
Catalog: Free, R&W, CAN/OV, HYB
Nursery: All Year, M-F

Innis Violets
8a Maddison Ln.
Lynnfield, MA 01940
(617) 334-6679
Reuben & Kathy Innis

PLANTS SUPPLIES
A selection of **African violets** from prominent breeders in Canada and the U.S., both plants and leaves: good plant descriptions. Also lots of growing supplies and a return address stamp for African violet lovers. (1976)
Catalog: $.50d, CAN/OV, SS:5-10
Nursery: All Year, By Appointment Only
Garden: All Year, By Appointment Only

Intermountain Cactus
2344 South Redwood Road
Salt Lake City, UT 84119
(801) 972-5149
Robert A. Johnson

PLANTS
Offers a selection of **very hardy cactus** (some to -20 to -50F), most of which are profuse bloomers, including opuntia, pediocactus, corypantha and neobesseya. Each plant well described; opuntias sold by pad or by clump.
Catalog: Long SASE, SS:4-11, $15m, bn/cn
Nursery: Spring-Fall, M-Sa, By Appointment Only
Garden: May-Sept, M-Sa, By Appointment Only

International Growers Exchange
P. O. Box 52248
Livonia, MI 48152-0248
(313) 422-0747
Karen J. Krusinski

PLANTS BULBS
The catalog is a collector's dream -- many unusual **alpine plants, species bulbs, orchids, bromeliads, perennials, lilies, Dutch bulbs**, a huge selection of plants very briefly described or only listed by botanical name; some only available in larger quantities. Almost too good to be true!
Catalog: $5d, R&W, MO, CAN/OV, SS:W, bn

International Seed Supplies
P.O. Box 538
Nowra, NSW, Australia 2541
(044) 48 7563
Neville & Pamela Burnett

SEEDS
A very broad selection of seeds, including **Australian native plants**, regular garden flowers, shrubs and trees from all over: each plant is briefly described and there are color photographs of many. They sell seed '6 packs' of Australian native plants -- a dozen assortments. (1983)
Catalog: $3(5 IRC), R&W, OV, $15m, bn/cn
Nursery: All Year, M-Sa

Inter-State Nurseries
P. O. Box 208
Hamburg, IA 51640-0208
(800) 325-4180 TO/CC

PLANTS BULBS
Color catalog offers a selection of **general nursery stock**: roses, fruit trees, flowering shrubs and a selection of Dutch bulbs, iris, daylilies, Oriental poppies and other perennials.
Catalog: Free, SS:9-11,2-5, cn

Iris Acres
R.R. 4, Box 189
Winamac, IN 46996
(219) 946-4197
Thurlow & Jean Sanders

PLANTS
A very extensive list of **bearded iris in all sizes**, including reblooming and 'space age' types: all plants briefly described. List offers some general information on planting and care of iris. (1959)
Catalog: $.50, CAN, SS:7-8
Nursery: May-Sept, Call Ahead
Garden: May-June, Call Ahead

Iris Country
118 So. Lincoln St.
Wayne, NE 68787
(402) 375-3795 or 4436 TO $15m
Roger R. Nelson

PLANTS
A broad selection of **tall bearded iris**, mostly recent selections -- but including a number of "old friends" as well; emphasis on hardy varieties for cold climates: all briefly described. Also **herbaceous and tree peonies** and **dwarf conifers** on another list; specify which list you want. (1969)
Catalog: $.50d, R&W, CAN, SS:7-8, $10m, HYB
Nursery: April-Sept, Daily, Call Ahead
Garden: May-Aug, Daily, Call Ahead

For Explanations of Abbreviations/Codes Used In Listings See Bookmark or Inside Covers

Iris Gardens
109 Sourdough Ridge Rd.
Bozeman, MT 59715
Maureen K. Blackwell

PLANTS
Offers older, often hard-to-find varieties of **tall bearded, intermediate** and **dwarf iris**: list not seen. Sells perennials at the nursery in spring and daffodil bulbs at the nursery in season.
Catalog: Long SASE + $.10, SS: 7-8, $6m
Nursery: June-Sept, By Appointment Only
Garden: June, By Appointment Only

The Iris Pond
7311 Churchill Rd.
McLean, VA 22101
(703) 893-8526
Clarence Mahan

PLANTS
Offers **tall bearded, Japanese, Siberian, reblooming and species iris** and a large selection of miniature tall bearded iris: good selection, plants very briefly described. (1985)
Catalog: $1, MO, CAN/OV, SS:7-9, $12m, HYB
Garden: May-June, By Appointment Only

Iris Test Gardens
1010 Highland Park Dr.
College Place, WA 99324
(509) 525-8804
Austin & Ione Morgan

PLANTS
Very extensive list of **tall bearded iris and some dwarfs**: brief descriptions. Many offerings are their own hybrids. Shipments to Canada and Overseas must be over $400 and include permit costs. (1977)
Catalog: $.50, R&W, CAN/OV, SS:7-9, $5m, HYB
Nursery: July-Sept, Call Ahead
Garden: May, daylight hours

Island Seed Mail Order
P. O. Box 4278, Sta. A
Victoria, BC, Canada V8X 3X8
Muriel R. Coleman

SEEDS
A broad selection of **annual and perennial flowers and vegetables** listed in an informative catalog with good cultural instructions and plant descriptions. Carries some seed for rock garden plants imported from Switzerland and wildflower seed. (1960)
Catalog: $2, MO, USA/OV

Ison's Nursery
Route 1, Box 191
Brooks, GA 30205
(404) 599-6970
William G. Ison

PLANTS
Specializes in **muscadine-scuppernong grapes**, offers many varieties and has a seedless muscadine on the way. They also sell many other fruits -- blackberries, blueberries, raspberries, apricots, low-chill apples, figs, plums, pomegranates, nut trees: well described with cultural hints. (1936)
Catalog: $1, R&W, CAN/OV, SS:11-4, HYB
Nursery: Sept-June, M-F
Garden: Orchard, M-F

Ivies of the World
P. O. Box 408
Highway 42 (3-1/2 mi. East)
Weirsdale, FL 32695
(904) 821-2201 or 2322 TO/CC $20m
J. T. & Judy Rankin

PLANTS
Offers more than 200 cultivars of **ivy**, mainly rooted cuttings: plants are grouped by type and well described. This nursery was formerly Tropexotic Growers, and before that The Alestake of Elkwood, Va. (for those of you who haven't been keeping track). Adding new varieties all the time. (1986)
Catalog: $1.50, CAN/OV, SS:AY, $20m, HYB
Nursery: All Year, M-F, Call Ahead

Izard Ozark Natives
P. O. Box 454
Mountain View, AR 72560
(501) 368-7439
Steven Foster

SEEDS BOOKS
Habitat collected seeds of **native plants of the Ozarks**, most hardy to -15F. Plants include wildflowers and "worthy weeds", shrubs, trees and vines: each plant well described with some germination and cultivation hints. They also sell books on growing wildflowers and medicinal plants.
Catalog: $1d, MO, CAN/OV, $5m, bn/cn

J & L Orchids
20 Sherwood Rd.
Easton, CT 06612
(203) 261-3772 TO/CC
C. Head, M. Webb & L. Winn

PLANTS
A broad selection of **species orchids** from all over the world, as well as hybrids: all well described with lovely illustrations. Specializes in rare and unusual species and miniatures which can be grown in the home under lights or on the windowsill -- also offers 'beginners specials'. (1960)
Catalog: $1, CAN/OV, SS:AY, HYB, bn
Nursery: All Year, Tu-Su
Garden: All Year, Greenhouse, Tu-Su

J & M Tropicals, Inc.
Route 1, Box 619-B
C-97 Hwy. near Pensacola
Cantonment, FL 32533
(904) 477-4935 TO/CC
James & Mary Roberts

PLANTS SUPPLIES
Offers **species orchids** -- phalaenopsis, vandas and vandaceous orchids: very brief descriptions. Also offers growing supplies and Florida cypress and teak orchid baskets. (1975)
Catalog: Free, R&W, SS:W
Nursery: All Year, M-F, Call Ahead
Garden: Fall & Spring, M-F, Call Ahead

J-Lot Gardens
1156 N. Main St.
Joshua, TX 76058
(817) 295-4074
Lottie Ogles

PLANTS
Specializes in **reblooming iris**: 125 varieties.
Catalog: 2 FCS

Jackson & Perkins Co.
P. O. Box 1028
Medford, OR 97501

PLANTS BULBS
Color catalogs (which sometimes come smelling of roses in mid-winter) offer a wide selection of modern **hybrid tea, floribunda, grandiflora and climbing roses**, as well as rhubarb, asparagus, dwarf fruit trees, flowering trees and summer blooming bulbs. Descriptions are effusive. (1872)
Catalog: Free, R&W, MO, CAN
Garden: May-Aug, Roses

Jasperson's Hersey Nursery
R.R. 1, Box 147
Wilson, WI 54027
Lu M. Jasperson

PLANTS
Small nursery specializes in **tall bearded iris and dahlias**: listed by cultivar name. Fresh cut flowers, fresh vegetables available at the nursery, where you can choose and dig other perennials on the spot. (1987)
Catalog: Long SASE, R&W, SS:4-9, $10m
Nursery: April-Oct, Tu-Sa
Garden: April-Oct, Tu-Sa

Jeannette's Jesneriads
2173 Leslie St.
Terrytown/Gretna, LA 70056
(504) 393-6977
Jeannette Domiano

PLANTS SUPPLIES
Offers only her own hybrid **African violets**, standard to large-sized, a number of which have been prize winners. She also offers a few other gesneriad cuttings and growing supplies for pick-up at the nursery. (1982)
Catalog: Long SASE, SS:4-10, $19m, HYB
Nursery: All Year, Daily, Call Ahead
Garden: All Year, Daily, Call Ahead

Klaus R. Jelitto
P. O. Box 560 127
D 2000 Hamburg 56, West Germany
(0 41 03) 89752

SEEDS
A broad selection of **rock garden and alpine plants** listed by botanical name. Catalog is in German, with cultural instructions for germinating seeds in English and French and some color photographs. Particularly good selections of alpines and rock garden plants and perennials. (1957)
Catalog: Free, R&W, OV, $20m, HYB, bn
Nursery: Sept-July, M-F

Jernigan Gardens
Route 6, Box 593
Dunn, NC 28334
(919) 567-2135 (8-9 pm)
Bettie Jernigan

PLANTS
Long collectors' list of **daylilies**: very briefly described with concise tables of information. Also offers a good selection of **hostas and iris** by mail, as well as perennials, which are sold only at the nursery.
Catalog: Long SASE, R&W, SS:4-11, $15m
Nursery: April-July, Daily (Closed 12 to 3), Call Ahead
Garden: April-July, Daylilies (Closed 12-3)

Johnny's Selected Seeds
P. O. Box 2580
Albion, ME 04910
(207) 437-9294 or 4301 TO/CC $15m
Robert L. Johnston, Jr.

SEEDS BOOKS SUPPLIES
Catalog lists **vegetables, herbs and garden annuals**, as well as specialty grains and seed for commercial crops; also a good selection of growing supplies and books. All plants are very well described, with cultural suggestions and germination guides; particularly suited to Northern growing.
Catalog: Free, MO, CAN/OV

Johnson Nursery
Route 5, Box 29 J
Ellijay, GA 30540
(404) 276-3187 TO $20m
Johnson Family

PLANTS SUPPLIES TOOLS
Color catalog offers a good selection of **fruit trees**: apples, old peach varieties, pears, plums, cherries, nuts, many kinds of berries and some grapes: all well described. Also sells supplies and tools.
Catalog: Free, R&W, SS:12-4, $13m
Nursery: All Year, M-Sa
Garden: May-Dec, M-F, By Appointment Only

Johnson Seed Company
227 Ludwig Ave.
Dousman, WI 53118
(715) 965-3745
Jim Johnson

SEEDS
Specializes in open-pollinated vegetables, including many pre-1900 varieties. Catalog offers about 50 varieties of potatoes, including early varieties: these are be sold in small quantities to spread the seed as far as possible.
Catalog: 2 FCS, R&W, CAN/OV

Johnson Seeds
P. O. Box 543
Woodacre, CA 94973
Cathy Johnson

SEEDS
A small company specializing in **seed of California native grasses**: seven varieties, mostly habitat collected. She will try to collect wanted seed if she can locate habitat; send "want list".
Catalog: $.50, R&W, MO, CAN/OV, bn/cn

Jones & Scully
18955 SW 168th Street
Miami, FL 33187-1112
(305) 238-7000 or (800) 672-4437
Robert M. Scully, Jr.

PLANTS
Color catalog offers a broad selection of **orchids**, especially cattleyas, phalaenopsis, vanda and many species. They will assist customers over the phone with cultural challenges -- most plants are shipped Federal Express. Plants are well described, photos mouthwatering! (1945)
Catalog: $5d, R&W, CAN/OV, SS:AY, $25m, HYB, bn
Nursery: All Year, Daily
Garden: All Year, Greenhouses, Daily (Tours 10 and 2)

JoS Violets
402 Dundee St.
Victoria, TX 77904
(512) 575-1344 TO
Joanne Schrimsher

PLANTS SUPPLIES
List of **standard, miniature, semi-miniature and trailing African violets** for sale as plants or leaves: each briefly described. Also sells growing supplies and ceramic, Swift "Moist-rite" and Oyama "Texas style" pots. (1983)
Catalog: Long SASE, R&W, SS:4-11, $5m
Nursery: All Year, Evenings & Weekends, By Appointment Only
Garden: All Year, By Appointment Only

Judy's Violets
9952 Edmil Lane
Overland, MO 63114
(314) 428-4296
Judy Williams

PLANTS
"A long list of **African violets**, leaves and plants, many the best and newest varieties from well-known hybridizers: I am especially interested in variegated foliage and bi-colored blooms and any plants which are abundant bloomers."
Catalog: 2 FCS, SS:W
Nursery: By Appointment Only

J. W. Jung Seed Co.
335 S. High Street
Randolph, WI 53957
(414) 326-3121 TO/CC
Jung Family

PLANTS SEEDS SUPPLIES BULBS
Color catalog offers a broad selection of seeds for the flower and vegetable garden, as well as nursery stock -- fruit trees, roses, perennials, ornamental trees, shrubs and vines. Also issues a Dutch bulb catalog in the summer. Carries tools, supplies; founder is 100 years old this year! (1907)
Catalog: Free, R&W, SS:4-11
Nursery: All Year, M-Sa

Jungle-Gems, Inc.
300 Edgewood Rd.
Edgewood, MD 21040
(301) 676-0672 TO/CC
Charles Williamson

PLANTS
Sells **phalaenopsis from blooming size to seedlings**, as well as miltonopsis, cattleyas, tillandsias and mericlones in mini-flasks. All plants are very briefly described. Their clones include hybrids of the special Phalaenopsis violacea 'Harfords Orange' in orange and red. (1975)
Catalog: Free, R&W, CAN/OV, SS:AY, HYB
Nursery: All Year, M-Sa
Garden: All Year, Glasshouse, M-Sa

Justice Gardens
107 Hight Drive
Watkinsville, GA 30677
(404) 769-8379
Louis Justice

PLANTS
Sells a wide selection of **hybrid azaleas and some rhododendrons** (and some rhododendron species) from a number of well known hybridizers. Plants listed only by species or cultivar name and name of hybridizer. Also sells dwarf crape myrtles, dwarf nandina and Franklinia in 4-inch pots.
Catalog: Long SASE, R&W, SS:3-6,9-12

Justice Miniature Roses
5947 S. W. Kahle Rd.
Wilsonville, OR 97070
(503) 682-2370
Jerry, June & Tara Justice

PLANTS
A broad selection of **miniature roses**, all well described, with some growing advice. In 1987 they started introducing varieties hybridized in Ireland by Sean McCann.
Catalog: Free, R&W, SS:AY
Nursery: All Year, Daily

K & L Cactus Nursery
12712 Stockton Blvd.
Galt, CA 95632
(209) 745-4756 TO/CC $20m
Keith & Lorraine Thomas

PLANTS SEEDS BOOKS SUPPLIES
Color/b&w catalog offers extensive list of **flowering desert and jungle cacti, succulents**, and some seed: each well but briefly described. Also sells some cactus books and a few supplies, including handsome pots. (1971)
Catalog: $2d, CAN/OV, SS:W, $20m, bn
Nursery: All Year, F-Su

KSA Jojoba
19025 Parthenia St.
Northridge, CA 91324
(818) 701-1534
Kathie Aamodt

PLANTS SEEDS SUPPLIES
Sells only **jojoba: seeds, seedlings, rooted cuttings**, and a variety of jojoba products such as soap, shampoos, lotions and automotive products. Cuttings, seedlings may be purchased in bulk: no plant descriptions. (1979)
Catalog: Long SASE w/2 FCS, R&W, CAN/OV
Nursery: All Year, M-F, Call Ahead

Kalmia Farm
P. O. Box 3881
Charlottesville, VA 22903
Ken Klotz

PLANTS BOOKS
Sells only **garlic, shallots and onions** -- but some interesting onions: potato onions, bird's nest onions, Egyptian top onions. The potato onions are an old variety which they say are perennial. Also sells onion and garlic cookbooks.
Catalog: Free, MO, SS:9-12

Karleens Achimenes
1407 W. Magnolia
Valdosta, GA 31601-4235
(912) 242-1368
Karleen Lane

PLANTS
A small hobby business, but offers a wide selection of **achimenes and other gesneriads** -- sinningias, gloxinias, smithiantha, eucodonias and kohlerias: most plants briefly but well described. Get out your glasses; one of those tightly packed lists for the collector! (1978)
Catalog: $1.50, SS:3-6, $12m, bn
Nursery: April-Oct, M-Sa, By Appointment Only
Garden: April-Oct, M-Sa, By Appointment Only

Kartuz Greenhouses
1408 Sunset Drive
Vista, CA 92083
(619) 941-3613 TO/CC $15m
Michael Kartuz

PLANTS
The catalog, a collectors' dream, offers flowering plants for the home, greenhouse and outside in warm areas -- **begonias, gesneriads and African Violets** and many other rare flowering plants and vines: very well described. (1960)
Catalog: $2, R&W, CAN/OV, SS:W, $15m, HYB, bn
Nursery: All Year, W-Sa
Garden: All Year, W-Sa, Greenhouses

Kawamoto Orchid Nursery
2630 Waiomao Road
Honolulu, HI 96816
(808) 732-5808 TO/CC $25m
Leslie Kawamoto

PLANTS
Color catalog, **hybrid and species orchids** -- cattleyas, oncidiums, vandas, dendrobiums: many illustrated and all briefly described. A number of mericlones are listed. They also offer three 'orchid-of-the-month clubs' with various offerings. A wide selection, available in various sizes. (1947)
Catalog: $2d, R&W, CAN, SS:AY, $25m, HYB, bn
Nursery: All Year, M-Sa, Call Ahead
Garden: All Year, M-Sa, Call Ahead

Kelly Nurseries of Dansville, Inc.
19 Maple Street
Dansville, NY 14437
(716) 335-2211 or (800) 828-6977 TO/CC $10m
Thomas Kelly, Gen. Mgr.

PLANTS
Formerly Kelly Bros., offers a broad selection of **general nursery stock**: hardy fruit trees, ornamental trees and shrubs, berries, grapes, groundcovers and conifers. Many plants illustrated in color catalog, each well described. Cannot ship to CA, OR, or WA. (1986)
Catalog: Free, R&W, SS:3-6,9-11, $2m, cn/bn
Nursery: Feb-June, Daily
Garden: May-June, M-Sa

Kensington Orchids
3301 Plyers Mill Rd.
Kensington, MD 20895
(301) 933-0036
Merritt W. Huntington

PLANTS BOOKS SUPPLIES
List offers **phalaenopsis, doritaenopsis and oncidium hybrids, cattleyas, "Cambria types", miltonias and paphiopedilums** in seedling and flowering sizes: briefly described. Also offers books and orchid growing supplies.
Catalog: Free, R&W, CAN/OV, SS:W, $25m
Nursery: All Year, Daily
Garden: All Year, Greenhouses, Daily

Kent's Flowers
320 W. Eagle
Arlington, NE 68002-0398
(402) 478-4011 TO/CC $20m
Kent & Joyce Stork

PLANTS
New and recent **African violets** from various leading hybridizers such as Boone, Harris, Elkin and various others -- including their own prizewinners: plants well described. Sells both plants and leaves. (1977)
Catalog: $.50, SS:9-10, $15m, HYB, bn
Nursery: All Year, M-Sa, Call Ahead
Garden: All Year, M-Sa, Call Ahead

Keith Keppel
P. O. Box 8173
Stockton, CA 95208
(209) 463-0227
Keith Keppel

PLANTS
An extensive list of **tall bearded iris**, many his own introductions: plants very well described with good information on parentage. A small nursery, stock is sometimes limited -- a hobby gone mad! What's really amazing is that there are any names left for iris cultivars! (1955)
Catalog: $.50, SS:7-8, $10m, HYB
Nursery: April-May, By Appointment Only
Garden: April-May, By Appointment Only

Kester's Wild Game Food Nurseries
P. O. Box 516
4582 Highway 116-East
Omro, WI 54963
(414) 685-2929, TO/CC $10m
David & Patricia Kester

PLANTS SEEDS
A wide selection of **plants to feed wildlife**: plants for ponds, various grains and wild rice (including an edible variety). The catalog offers a lot of cultural and wildlife food management information: they offer seed and plants, including aquatic plants, and seed for feeding pet birds. (1899)
Catalog: $2, CAN, SS:2-10, $10m
Nursery: All Year, M-Sa, Call Ahead

For Explanations of Abbreviations/Codes Used In Listings See Bookmark or Inside Covers

Kilgore Seed Company
1400 West First St.
Sanford, FL 32771
(305) 323-6630
J. H. Hunziker

SEEDS SUPPLIES TOOLS
A regional seed company, offering **vegetables and flowers** for the Gulf Coast area of the U.S., but suited to any sub-tropical or tropical climate. A wide selection, each well described; they also sell gardening supplies and tools. (1918)
Catalog: $1d, CAN/OV
Nursery: All Year, M-Sa

Kilworth Flowers
R. R. 3
County Road 14
Komoka, ON, Canada N0L 1R0
(519) 471-9787
Jim & Jo-Anne Eadie

PLANTS BOOKS SUPPLIES
Seedling to blooming size **orchids**: cattleya, phalaenopsis, dendrobium, ascocendas, cymbidium and paphiopedilum hybrids and sophronitis and paphiopedilum species: all briefly described. Also orchid books and growing supplies. (1983)
Catalog: Free, R&W, SS:3-10
Nursery: All Year, Tu-Su, Call Ahead
Garden: May-June, Tu-Su, Call Ahead

Kinder Canna Farm
P. O. Box 7706
Lawton, OK 73506
(405) 353-5118 TO/CC $10m
Johnny & Connie Kinder, Bo Baker

PLANTS
Small nursery specializing in **cannas**: color pamphlets illustrates plants and describes them briefly. Selection is limited, prices very reasonable.
Catalog: Free, R&W, CAN/OV, SS:12-6
Nursery: Dec-June, M-Sa, Call Ahead
Garden: Summer, Call Ahead

King's Mums
P. O. Box 368
20303 E. Liberty Rd.
Clements, CA 95227
(209) 759-3571
Ted & Lanna King

PLANTS
Color catalog offers wide choice of **chrysanthemums** – a real collectors' list: all plants well described, with cultural information. Also sells collections and the handbooks of the National Chrysanthemum Society. (1964)
Catalog: $1d, CAN, SS:2-6, $10m, HYB
Nursery: All Year, Daily
Garden: Oct-Nov, Daily

Kirkland Iris Garden
725 - 20 Avenue West
Kirkland, WA 98033
(206) 828-4907
Carol & George Lankow

PLANTS
Specializes in **dwarf and median bearded irises**, but offers a good selection of all types: all plants are well described, and some cultural information is included in the catalog. (1981)
Catalog: Free, SS:7-8, $10m, HYB
Nursery: Call Ahead
Garden: April-May, Call Ahead

Kitazawa Seed Co.
1748 Laine St.
Santa Clara, CA 95051-3012
Ernest Kitazawa

SEEDS
A good selection of seeds for **Oriental vegetables**: plants briefly described. Nine varieties of daikon, the Japanese radish, and seven kinds of mustard. Cannot ship to Mexico. (1917)
Catalog: Free, R&W, MO, CAN/OV

Arnold J. Klehm Grower, Inc.
44 W 637, Route 72
Hampshire, IL 60193
(312) 683-4761 TO/CC
Arnold J. Klehm

PLANTS
A nice selection of **orchids**, mostly hybrid seedlings of phalaenopsis, but also vandaceous, cattleya alliance, paphiopedilums, ascocenda and species orchids: some are their own "Meriklehms" (an orchid witticism, theirs). All briefly described, some illustrated in color. Special offers, too. (1980)
Catalog: $1d, R&W, CAN/OV, SS:W, HYB, bn
Nursery: All Year, M-F, Call Ahead

Klehm Nursery
Route 5, Box 197
South Barrington, IL 60010
(312) 551-3715 TO/CC
Klehm Family

PLANTS
Color catalog offers many cultivars of **hosta, daylilies, iris and herbaceous and tree peonies**: all plants well described, and many illustrated with some cultural information. (1852)
Catalog: $2d, R&W, CAN/OV, SS:W, HYB, bn
Nursery: Call Ahead
Garden: May-June, Call Ahead

Edgar L. Kline

See Russell Graham, Purveyor of Plants

Gerhard Koehres Cactus & Succulent Nursery
Wingertstrasse 33
Erzhausen/Darmstadt, Germany D-6106
(0 61 50) 72 41
Gerhard Koehres

SEEDS
A very extensive list of **cactus and succulent seeds**, as well as some tillandsias and palms, listed by botanical name: no plant descriptions but sure to please collectors. Offered are: aylostera, copiapoa, frailea, gymnocalciums, parodia, agaves, aloes, euphorbias, mesembs and much more!
Catalog: 1 IRC, R&W, MO, OV, bn

P. Kohli & Co.
Park Road, nr. Neelam Theater
Srinagar, Kashmir, India 190009
73061
Urvashi Suri

SEEDS
Seeds of a broad selection of **Himalayan** plants -- trees, shrubs, vines, perennials, alpines and bulbs from Kashmir and the Western Himalayas. Can also arrange the purchase of sub-tropical seeds and bulbs of India -- write for information. Plants listed by botanical name only. (1928)
Catalog: 5 IRC, R&W, MO, OV, $5m, bn

Kordonowy's Dahlias
P. O. Box 568
401 Quick Rd. (Castle Rock)
Kalama, WA 98625
(206) 673-2426
Sam & Katherine Kordonowy

PLANTS
A collectors' catalog of **dahlias** of all kinds, in a very broad selection: over 800 varieties, each very briefly described as to color and type, with general information. Offers a few collections. (1953)
Catalog: Free, R&W, CAN, SS:3-5, HYB
Nursery: March-Sept, Call Ahead
Garden: July-Sept, Call Ahead

V. Kraus Nurseries, Ltd.
Centre Road
Carlisle, ON, Canada L0R 1H0
(416) 689-4022 or 5704
Victor & Eva Kraus

PLANTS
A broad selection of **flowering and ornamental trees and shrubs**, including many hybrid tea roses, grandifloras, floribundas, climbers, modern shrub and miniature roses. Also sells fruit trees, grapes, berries, rhubarb and asparagus, including many apples and plums. No descriptions. (1951)
Catalog: Free, R&W, USA/OV, SS:10-11,4-5, $6m, bn/cn
Nursery: All Year, M-Sa
Garden: June-Aug, M-Sa

L. Kreeger
91 Newton Wood Rd.(SF)
Ashtead, Surrey, England KT21 1NN
L. Kreeger

SEEDS
A good selection of seeds of **alpine and rock garden** plants: all plants briefly described, with country of origin and type of growing conditions which suit them best. New introductions and re-introductions, including wild-collected seed. (1985)
Catalog: 3 IRC, OV, bn

Krider Nurseries
P. O. Box 29
Middlebury, IN 46540
(219) 825-5714 TO/CC
Roger Krider

PLANTS
A broad selection of **fruit trees, berries, ornamental trees and shrubs and roses**: many illustrated in color and all well described. I may have the wrong impression of Indiana; they offer a hardy rose called "Hoosier Hysteria", pretty enough to warm the blood anywhere. (1896)
Catalog: Free, R&W, SS:2-6,9-11
Nursery: All Year, M-F
Garden: April-Nov, M-F

Michael & Janet Kristick
155 Mockingbird Rd.
Wellsville, PA 17365
(717) 292-2962
Michael & Janet Kristick

PLANTS
The sort of catalog that makes a collector's heart sing! Hundreds of cultivars: **conifers, including many dwarfs, and Japanese and species maples.** No descriptions, just pages and pages of names. Japanese maples listed by Japanese cultivar names. (1970)
Catalog: Free, CAN/OV, SS:4-12, bn
Nursery: All Year, Daily, By Appointment Only
Garden: May-Oct, Daily, By Appointment Only

Krohne Plant Farms
Route 6, Box 586
Dowagiac, MI 49047
(616) 424-3450 or 5423
William & Shiela Krohne

PLANTS
Fifteen varieties of **strawberries** which will produce in northern climates; informative leaflet. Will sell in quantities as low as 25 per customer; quantity discounts for commercial growers. Also offers two kinds of asparagus crowns and horseradish. (1974)
Catalog: Free, R&W, SS:3-6, $6m
Nursery: All Year, Daily, Call Ahead
Garden: Spring-Summer, Daily, Call Ahead

Kusa Research Foundation
P. O. Box 761
Ojai, CA 93023
Non-Profit Foundation

SEEDS
Group devoted to **seedcrops of folk origin, especially cereal grains**. Sells seed of crop which can be grown by home gardeners and small-scale farmers: special strains of millet, hulless barley, Swiss gourmet baking wheat, and grain sorghum and others. (1980)
Catalog: $1d, MO

LaFayette Home Nursery, Inc.
R.R. 1, Box 1A
Lafayette, IL 61449
(309) 495-3311
Corliss Jock Ingels

SEEDS
Broad selection of **prairie grasses, forbs, trees, shrubs and wildflowers** for prairie restoration and development: all plants listed by botanical and common name. They also offer a number of grass and wildflower mixes for various conditions and do consulting and installation. (1887)
Catalog: Free, R&W, MO, bn/cn

For Explanations of Abbreviations/Codes Used In Listings See Bookmark or Inside Covers

Lagomarsino Seeds
5675 Power-Inn Rd.
Sacramento, CA 95824
(916) 381-1024 TO/CC $20m
Thomas & Janna Reimers

PLANTS SEEDS
A broad selection of **vegetable and herb** seeds: no plant descriptions. They ship **onion plants** from February to May; then in May start shipping **sweet potato and yam** plants. Seeds available in sizes from garden packets to one pound.
Catalog: Free, $1m
Nursery: All Year, M-Sa

Lake Odessa Greenhouse
1123 Jordan Lake St.
Lake Odessa, MI 48849
(616) 374-8848
Mark Potter

PLANTS
Offers a large selection of **geraniums**: scented, brocade, rosebud, zonal, 'tulip' and ivy. All plants well but briefly described.
Catalog: Free, R&W, SS:5-10
Nursery: All Year, M-Sa
Garden: All Year, Greenhouse, M-Sa

Lakeland Nursery Sales
340 Poplar St.
Hanover, PA 17331
(717) 637-6000 or 5555 TO/CC
James O. Blasius

PLANTS SUPPLIES TOOLS
Part of a large mail order company, offers an assortment of plants with emphasis on new and novelty items, along with some tools and supplies. Color catalog: glowing plant descriptions. (1934)
Catalog: Free, MO, SS:2-6, cn/bn

Lakeshore Tree Farms, Ltd.
R. R. #3
Saskatoon, SK, Canada S7K 3J6
(306) 382-2077
Rob Krahn

PLANTS
Hardy fruit trees, berries and a good selection of ornamental trees, shrubs and perennials. Color catalog gives good plant descriptions, lists plants by common names. Fruit, including saskatoons, are hardy to 50 below zero. They have a landscaping service for local customers. (1936)
Catalog: $1, R&W, USA/OV, SS:4-5,9
Nursery: All Year, M-Sa
Garden: May-July, M-Sa

Lamb Nurseries
E. 101 Sharp Ave.
Spokane, WA 99202
(509) 328-7956
Nicola Luttropp

PLANTS
Catalog packed with **rock garden and perennial plants, vines, groundcovers, succulents, clematis, violets and flowering shrubs**: each plant very well described with cultural notes. A wide selection of collectors' plants, they are suppliers to many botanical gardens as well as people like us. (1938)
Catalog: Free, R&W, CAN/OV, SS:W, bn/cn
Nursery: Feb-Oct, F-Sa

Lamtree Farm
Route 1, Box 162
Warrensville, NC 28693
(919) 385-6144
Lee A. Morrison

PLANTS
My heart leaps at the word 'Franklinia', and here it is! Small nursery sells a limited but choice selection of **trees and shrubs**: franklinia, leucothoe, native rhododendrons and azaleas, kalmia, seedling maples and conifers and 'Lu shan' (Rhododendron fortunei). No plant descriptions. (1979)
Catalog: Free, R&W, SS:9-4, $25m, bn
Nursery: All Year, Daily, By Appointment Only
Garden: All Year, Daily, By Appointment Only

D. Landreth Seed Company
P. O. Box 6426
180-188 W. Ostend St.
Baltimore, MD 21230
(301) 727-3922

SEEDS
"America's oldest seed house" -- they had George Washington as an early customer! Offers a broad selection of **new and old varieties of vegetables**: all well described with cultural information; also a smaller selection of **herbs and garden annuals.** (1784)
Catalog: $2d, R&W, CAN/OV
Nursery: All Year, M-F

K Lane

See Karleen Achimenes

Larner Seeds
P. O. Box 407
Bolinas, CA 94924-0407
(415) 868-9407
Judith Lowry

SEEDS
"Wildflower seed for the Western landscape": native wildflowers, annual and perennial, and trees, shrubs, vines and grasses. Catalog emphasizes use in natural landscaping and offers several mixes for various habitats. Also offers a series of pamphlets on growing native plants. (1978)
Catalog: $1, R&W, CAN/OV, bn/cn
Nursery: All Year, By Appointment Only
Garden: Spring, By Appointment Only

Las Pilitas Nursery
Star Route, Box 23 X
Las Pilitas Road
Santa Margarita, CA 93453
(805) 438-5992
Bert & Celeste Wilson

PLANTS SEEDS BULBS
A very extensive list of **California native plants** of all kinds, including a few seeds and bulbs. Specifies the number of plants available -- a good indication of what's rare or hard to propagate. Listed by botanical and common name only. Excellent for landscaping and revegetation projects. (1975)
Catalog: $4 (price list free), R&W, SS:AY, $2m, bn/cn
Nursery: All Year, Sa or By Appointment Only
Garden: All Year, Sa or By Appointment Only

Lauray of Salisbury
Undermountain Rd. (Route 41)
Salisbury, CT 06068
(203) 435-2263
Laura & Judy Becker

PLANTS
A very extensive collectors' list of **begonias, gesneriads, cacti, succulents, epiphyllums and hybrid and species orchids**: all briefly described, with some cultural notes by genera.
Catalog: $2(3 IRC), SS:4-10, $10m, bn
Nursery: All Year, Daily, Call Ahead
Garden: All Year, Glasshouse, Call Ahead

Laurel Orchids
18205 S. W. 157th Ave.
Miami, FL 33187
(305) 251-8747 TO/CC $15m
Nancy Priess

PLANTS
Sells orchid plants in flasks, community pots, seedlings and mature specimens, both **hybrids and some jungle collected species**: cattleyas, vandas, ascocendas, oncidiums – and Vanilla planifolia. (1974)
Catalog: $1d, R&W, CAN/OV, SS:3-12, $15m, HYB, bn/cn
Nursery: All Year, Daily, Call Ahead
Garden: All Year, Greenhouse, Call Ahead

Laurie's Garden
41886 McKenzie Highway
Springfield, OR 97478
(503) 896-3756
Lorena M. Reid

PLANTS SEEDS
Specializes in **beardless iris** – Western natives, Japanese, Siberian, Evansia, water iris and other species iris and crosses between Pacific Coast and Siberian iris: broad selection, all briefly described. Also iris seed and a few other hardy perennials. (1964)
Catalog: Long SASE(3 IRC), CAN/OV, SS:8-11, HYB
Nursery: April-Nov, Call Ahead
Garden: March-June, Call Ahead

Lawson's Nursery
Route 1, Box 473
Yellow Creek Road
Ball Ground, GA 30107
(404) 893-2141 TO/CC $25m
Bernice Lawson

PLANTS BOOKS
A good selection of **antique apple and pear trees**: all well described with historical background – even a 14th century apple called "Rambo"! They have added **blueberries, plums, peaches and apricots, nuts** and many other ornamental trees. Also books on fruit growing and cookbooks. (1968)
Catalog: Free, R&W, CAN/OV, SS:11-3
Nursery: All Year, M-Sa
Garden: Sept, M-Sa

Lawyer Nursery, Inc.
950 Highway 200 West
Plains, MT 59859
(406) 826-3881 TO/CC $100m
John N. Lawyer

PLANTS SEEDS
Supplies many types of **ornamental trees, fruit and nut trees, rootstock** for **fruit trees, conifers and shrubs** in large quantities. Also offers a very good selection of seeds of trees and woody plants, including sub-tropical trees and shrubs. $50m on seed orders. (1959)
Catalog: Free, R&W, CAN/OV, SS:6-12, $100m, bn/cn
Nursery: All Year, M-F, Call Ahead

Le Jardin du Gourmet
P. O. Box 44
West Danville, VT 05873-0044
(802) 684-2201
Raymond Saufroy

SEEDS
A broad selection of **European vegetables and herbs**, items for the gourmet kitchen, recipes with shallots and **seeds** in trial packets for $.22, which will appeal to container gardeners. Saufroy claims to have introduced shallots to the U.S. (1954)
Catalog: $.50(1 IRC), R&W, CAN/OV
Nursery: Spring-Fall, Call Ahead
Garden: May-July, Call Ahead

Le Marche Seeds International
P. O. Box 190
Dixon, CA 95620
(916) 678-9244 or 9246 TO/CC $10m
G. Brennan & C. Glenn

SEEDS
Catalog offers over 300 varieties of **vegetables and herbs**, well described and with cultural notes, cooking suggestions and historical notes. A fine selection of 'gourmet' vegetables such as radicchios. Owners are the authors of "The New American Vegetable Cookbook", Aris Books, 1985. (1982)
Catalog: $2, R&W, MO, CAN, $5m, cn/bn

Orol Ledden & Sons
P. O. Box 7
Center & Atlantic Aves.
Sewell, NJ 08080-0007
(609) 468-1000 or 1002 TO/CC $20m
Don & Dale Ledden

SEEDS SUPPLIES TOOLS
Catalog offers over 600 varieties of **flowe crops**: all well described, plants are both hybrid and open-pollinated, most seed available untreated if desired. Also sells a full line of growing supplies and tools, organic pest controls and fertilizers. (1904)
Catalog: Free, R&W, CAN/OV
Nursery: All Year, Daily
Garden: April-Sept, Daily

Lee's Botanical Gardens
12731 S.W. 14th St.
Miami, FL 33184
(305) 223-0496 TO $10m
Bruce Lee Bednar

PLANTS SEEDS
Collectors' list of **carnivorous plants**: heliamphora, sarracenia, nepenthes, dionaea, drosera, pinquicula, utricularia, catopsis and seed of sarracenia. Plants are listed in a jumble of botanical names, but collectors will know them. Some are rare and limited to one per customer. (1980)
Catalog: Free(1 IRC), R&W, CAN/OV, SS:AY, $10m, HYB, bn
Nursery: March-Oct, Weekends, By Appointment Only

For Explanations of Abbreviations/Codes Used In Listings See Bookmark or Inside Covers

Legg Dahlia Gardens
1069 Hastings Rd.
Geneva, NY 14456
(315) 789-1209
Frederick Legg

PLANTS
Catalog offers a very broad selection of **dahlias**: briefly described and listed by flower size -- only a partial listing of the 500+ varieties they grow. Also offers several special collections.
Catalog: Free, SS:W, $5m
Nursery: May-Oct, Daily
Garden: Aug-Oct, Daily

Lenette Greenhouses
4345 Rogers Lake Rd.
Kannapolis, NC 28081
(704) 938-2042
K. G. Griffith

PLANTS
Catalog offers **cattleya and phalaenopsis hybrid orchids**, in community pots, flasks and blooming sizes, even 'stud plants': plants very briefly described. Also offers miniature cymbidium crosses and a few oncidiums, vandas and paphiopedilums. Most are their own hybrids. (1961)
Catalog: Free, R&W, CAN/OV, SS:W, $20m, HYB
Nursery: All Year, M-Sa
Garden: All Year, Greenhouses, M-Sa

Lenington-Long Gardens
7007 Manchester Ave.
Kansas City, MO 64133
(816) 454-9163
Donald L. Long

PLANTS
A very extensive list of **daylilies**, including hybrids of Lenington and Marsh and a long list of diploids and triploids: all briefly described. A large selection sure to appeal to collectors. (1952)
Catalog: 2 FCS, SS:4-6,8-9, $20m, HYB
Nursery: April-Oct, M,W,F,Sa, Call Ahead
Garden: June-Aug, M,W,F,Sa, Call Ahead

W. O. Lessard Nursery
19201 S. W. 248th St.
Homestead, FL 33031
(305) 247-0397 or 248-2666
William O. Lessard

PLANTS
Catalog lists 31 varieties of **bananas** -- even more sold at the nursery. Some available as corms or plants, some up to large specimens: each plant is very well described. Formerly "Tropical Spices Etc." (1978)
Catalog: $1d, R&W, CAN/OV, SS:3-11, HYB
Nursery: All Year, M-Sa, By Appointment Only
Garden: June-Nov, By Appointment Only

Henry Leuthardt Nurseries, Inc.
P. O. Box 666
Montauk Highway
East Moriches, NY 11940
(516) 878-1387
Henry P. Leuthardt

PLANTS
A selection of **fruit trees, berries and grapes**, including some old varieties: all briefly to well described. This nursery is also a source of espaliered apple and pear trees in several styles. Their "handbook" is $1, gives more information than the free catalog.
Catalog: Free, R&W, SS:10-12,3-5
Nursery: All Year, Daily, Call Ahead

Lewis Strawberry Nursery
P. O. Box 24
Rocky Point, NC 28457
(919) 675-2394 TO $10m
C.E. Lewis

PLANTS
Fifty varieties of **strawberries**, sold in quantities of 100 and up: no descriptions, but suggestions for varieties to plant for various hardiness zones and a table comparing the qualities of each variety. Most of the plants are June-bearers; they also carry six 'everbearing' kinds. (1954)
Catalog: Free, R&W, CAN/OV, SS:AY, $10m
Nursery: All Year, M-Sa

Liberty Seed Company
P. O. Box 806
128 1st Drive S.E.
New Philadelphia, OH 44663
(216) 364-1611 TO/CC $10m
William & Connie Watson

SEEDS SUPPLIES
Color catalog offers a broad selection of garden **annuals and perennials**, **vegetables** (including heirloom and open-pollinated varieties), giant pumpkins and super sweet corn: all well described and adapted to the Midwest. Also offers a broad selection of propagation and growing supplies. (1981)
Catalog: Free, R&W, SS:2-5
Nursery: All Year, M-F: Mar-June, Sa

Lilypons Water Gardens
P. O. Box 10
6885 Lilypons Rd.
Lilypons, MD 21717-0010
(301) 874-5133 TO/CC
Charles B. Thomas

PLANTS BOOKS SUPPLIES
Color catalog offers **water lilies, lotus, bog plants**, garden ponds, statues, fountains, fish and supplies. They also have a nursery in Texas, at 839 FM 1489 (P.O. Box 188), Brookshire, TX, 77423, (713) 934-8525, with a display garden, too. The photographs are literally irresistible! (1917)
Catalog: $3.50(8 IRC), R&W, CAN/OV, SS:3-11, HYB, cn/bn
Nursery: March-Oct, Daily: Nov-Feb, M-F
Garden: All Year, Sales Area, M-F

Little Valley Farm
R. R. 1, Box 287
Richland Center, WI 53581
(608) 538-3180
David Kopitzke

PLANTS SEEDS BOOKS
Specializes in **native plants of the Midwest**: wildflowers, trees, shrubs and vines for woods, wetlands and prairie: all plants well described. Also offers seeds of some, books on prairie and woodland plants and local workshops on prairie planting. (1978)
Catalog: $.25, R&W, MO, SS:4-5,9-10, cn/bn

Living Tree Centre
P. O. Box 797
Bolinas, CA 94914
(415) 868-2224
Dr. Jesse Schwartz, John Kozak

PLANTS
Historic **apples** from England, France, Russia and California's pioneering days, including some "highly aromatic" apples -- over 80 kinds: all well described with cultural information on apple growing. Also offers apple scion wood, apricots, persimmons, pawpaws, quince and pears. (1979)
Catalog: $6d, R&W, CAN/OV, SS:1-4
Nursery: By Appointment Only
Garden: By Appointment Only

Lloyd's African Violets
2568 East Main St.
Cato, NY 13033
(315) 626-2314
JoAnn Lloyd

PLANTS
Sells **African violets** by well-known hybridizers: Fredette, Champion Variegates, Granger, Rienhardt, Lyon, Wasmund, Hightower, Tracey and others: each well but briefly described. Leaves, too. (1975)
Catalog: $.50(2 IRC), CAN/OV, SS:5-11, HYB
Nursery: All Year, Daily, Call Ahead
Garden: All Year, Daily, Call Ahead

Lockhart Seeds
3 North Wilson Way
P. O. Box 1361
Stockton, CA 95201
(209) 466-4401 TO/CC $10m
Lockhart Family

SEEDS SUPPLIES
Color catalog with a broad selection of **vegetables** (both hybrid and open-pollinated) and **Oriental vegetables**, with comparative tables on size, season, disease resistance. Specializes in crops for Central California; also offers some growing supplies. (1948)
Catalog: Free, R&W, CAN, $10m, cn/bn
Nursery: All Year, M-F

Logee's Greenhouses
55 North Street
Danielson, CT 06239
(203) 774-8038
Joy Logee Martin

PLANTS
A very extensive list of **begonias and other greenhouse and exotic plants** -- many are outdoor plants in warmer climates: all well described with some cultural suggestions, many illustrated in color. A collector's dream, a houseplant lover's candy store. Catalog price refundable with $25 purchase. (1892)
Catalog: $3, R&W, CAN/OV, SS:W, $10m, HYB, bn/cn
Nursery: All Year, Daily
Garden: All Year, Daily

Lon's Oregon Grapes
4285 Portland Rd. N.E.
Salem, OR 97303
(503) 393-5165
Lon Rombough

PLANTS
New company trying to list **table and wine grapes** for as many climates as possible; offers plants and cuttings of over 50 varieties, with more to come. If he doesn't have it, he'll try to find a source. All plants very well described with notes on hardiness.
Catalog: Long SASE, R&W, CAN/OV, SS:11-4
Nursery: All Year, Call Ahead

Long Hungry Creek Nursery
Red Boiling Springs, TN 37150
(615) 699-2784
Jeff Poppen

PLANTS
Specializing in antique **apples**, as well as newer, hardy, disease-resistant varieties with great taste -- about 50 varieties including Liberty, Arkansas Black, Twenty Ounce, Chenango Strawberry, Rusty Coat, Limbertwig, Ben Davis: very brief descriptions. Choice of two rootstocks. (1976)
Catalog: Long SASE, R&W, CAN/OV, SS:1-4,11-12, $20m
Nursery: All Year, Call Ahead
Garden: All Year, Call Ahead

Long's Gardens
P. O. Box 19
3240 Broadway
Boulder, CO 80306
(303) 442-2353
Catherine Long Gates

PLANTS
List offers broad selection of **tall bearded iris**, with several collections and progressive savings on larger purchases. During bloom time you can visit the nursery, select your favorites and dig them up on the spot. Sells a few border, intermediate and dwarf bearded as well: brief descriptions. (1905)
Catalog: Free, SS:7-8, HYB
Nursery: Late May-Early June, Daily, Call Ahead
Garden: May-June, Tall Bearded Iris, Call Ahead

Lost Prairie Herb Farm
805 Kienas Rd.
Kalispell, MT 59901
(406) 755-3742
Diane Downs

PLANTS SUPPLIES
Hardy herbs, groundcovers and perennials for northern climates: briefly to well described; a broad selection of very hardy plants for extreme winters. Also offers organic pest controls and flea controls for pets. (1977)
Catalog: $1, SS:5-10, $6m, cn/bn
Nursery: April-Oct, Daily, Call Ahead
Garden: June-Aug, Daily, Call Ahead

Loucks Nursery
P. O. Box 102
14200 Campground Rd.
Cloverdale, OR 97112
(503) 392-3166 TO
Mert & Marjorie Loucks

PLANTS
Specializes in **Japanese maples** for bonsai and container growing. Offers a broad selection of cultivars by their Japanese cultivar names: each plant briefly described. Small nursery offers over 100 cultivars. (1955)
Catalog: $1, R&W, CAN, SS:AY
Nursery: All Year, Daily, Call Ahead
Garden: All Year, Daily, Call Ahead

Louisiana Nursery
Route 7, Box 43 (Hwy. 182)
Opelousas, LA 70570
(318) 948-3696 or 942-6404
Ken & Albert Durio

PLANTS
350 cultivars of **magnolia** and many other unusual trees, shrubs, vines and other collectors' plants in catalog (M): catalog (D) has a huge selection of **daylilies, Louisiana, spuria and Pseudacorus iris, cannas, ginger lilies** liriope and related plants. Endless choices: very well described. (1950)
Catalog: $2(D) & $3.50(M), R&W, CAN/OV, bn/cn
Nursery: All Year, Daily

Paul P. Lowe
5741 Dewberry Way
West Palm Beach, FL 33415
Paul P. Lowe

PLANTS
A collectors' list of **bromeliads, species and hybrid orchids, ferns and begonias**: plants very briefly described. Bromeliads sold as unrooted offsets ("pups"), begonias in quantities of 50 or 100 unrooted cuttings. Wide selection; you might send a 'want-list' for special items. (1948)
Catalog: $1, MO, SS:4-11, $10m, HYB

Lowe's own-root Roses
6 Sheffield Rd.
Nashua, NH 03062
(603) 888-2214
Malcolm (Mike) Lowe

PLANTS
A collectors' list of **old roses**, grown on their own roots: a wide selection of many types, including species roses and some of the modern shrub roses of contemporary hybridizers in Europe and the U.S. Some plants in short supply and must be ordered 18 months ahead for propagation. (1979)
Catalog: $2($3 OV), MO, CAN/OV, SS:10, $8m, bn/cn
Garden: June, By Appointment Only

The Lowrey Nursery
2323 Sleepy Hollow Rd.
Conroe, TX 77385
(713) 367-4076
Katie Ferguson

PLANTS
Offers **Southwestern native plants** for use in the landscape; many are selections or hybrids of their own propagation. Plants are well adapted to home or commercial environments. (1970)
Catalog: Free, R&W, SS:11-2, $25m, HYB
Nursery: All Year, M-Sa
Garden: March-June, M-Sa

John D. Lyon, Inc.
143 Alewife Brook Pkwy.
Cambridge, MA 02140
(617) 876-3705

BULBS
Collectors' list of **species bulbs**, mainly hardy, spring-blooming species bulbs native to Europe and Asia, some quite hard to find: brief descriptions with season of bloom. (1929)
Catalog: Free, CAN, SS:9-11, $15m, bn
Nursery: All Year, M-Sa

Lyndon Lyon Greenhouses, Inc.
14 Mutchler St.
Dolgeville, NY 13329-0249
(315) 429-8291
Paul & Sidney Sorano

PLANTS
This firm is the originator of many favorite **African violets** and also sells **streptocarpus, episcias, columneas** and other houseplants: many are illustrated in color photographs, with good brief plant descriptions. (1954)
Catalog: $1, R&W, CAN/OV, SS:5-10, $14m, HYB
Nursery: All Year, Daily
Garden: All Year, Daily

MB Farm Miniature Roses
Jamison Hill Rd.
Clinton Corners, NY 12514
(914) 266-3138 TO/CC $20
M. & B. Florac, J. & T. Cerchiara

PLANTS
Color brochure offers a selection of **miniature roses** and several collections -- plants in leaf are shipped March-September, dormant plants October-February: good plant descriptions, cultural hints with every order. (1980)
Catalog: Free, R&W, CAN, SS:AY
Nursery: All Year, By Appointment Only

McClure & Zimmerman
1422 W. Thorndale
Chicago, IL 60660
(312) 989-0557 TO/CC $20m
Kenneth McClure & Mark Zimmerman

BOOKS BULBS
A very large selection of **bulbs**, both the common spring "Dutch" bulbs and a wide selection of species bulbs not so easy to find -- species tulips, bulbous iris, hardy cyclamen, summer blooming bulbs: all very well described, many charmingly illustrated. Books on bulbs, too. (1980)
Catalog: Free, MO, SS:8-11, bn

McConnell Nurseries, Inc.
R. R. 1
Port Burwell, ON, Canada N0J 1T0
(519) 874-4405 or 4711 TO/CC
M. van Waveren & Sons, Inc.

PLANTS BULBS
Color catalog offers a large selection of **general nursery stock** -- roses, berries of all kinds, ornamental trees and shrubs, spring bulbs and garden perennials: all plants well described. The name "Sears McConnell" appears on the catalog; they also advertise under other names. (1912)
Catalog: Free, R&W, SS:3-11, cn/bn
Nursery: April-Nov, Daily
Garden: May-Sept, Daily

McDaniel's Miniature Roses
7523 Zemco St.
Lemon Grove, CA 92045
(619) 469-4669
Earl & Agnes McDaniel

PLANTS
List offers about a hundred miniature roses, listed by color: all briefly described, frequently gives petal count -- many of their own hybrids. (1973)
Catalog: Free, CAN/OV, SS:AY, HYB
Nursery: All Year, M-Sa, Call Ahead
Garden: April-May, Call Ahead

McFayden Seeds
P. O. Box 1800
Brandon, MB, Canada R7A 6A6
(204) 727-0766

PLANTS SEEDS BOOKS SUPPLIES TOOLS BULBS
Offers a broad selection of **general nursery stock, flower and vegetable** seeds and **Dutch bulbs and perennials**: color catalog also offers tools and supplies as well as kitchen and canning items.
Catalog: $2, MO, SS:4-5,9

McKinney's Glasshouse
89 Mission Rd.
Wichita, KS 67207
(316) 686-9438
James McKinney & Charles Pickard

PLANTS SUPPLIES
"We are **gesneriad specialists**, with a large supply of African violets, episcias and diminuitive terrarium plants." Also lists growing supplies and terrariums in many styles. (1946)
Catalog: $1.50, CAN/OV
Nursery: By Appointment Only

Rod McLellan Co.
1450 El Camino Real
South San Francisco, CA 94080
(415) 871-5655 or (800) USA-8787 TO/CC $10m
David Balster, Mgr.

PLANTS BOOKS SUPPLIES
Color catalog offers many types of **orchids**. Nursery specializes in hybridizing cattleyas and cymbidiums, but also offers miltonias, oncidiums, brassias, odontoglossums, phalaenopsis and more. Also sells books on orchids, orchid food and potting mixture. (1895)
Catalog: $1(3 IRC), R&W, CAN/OV, SS:4-10, $10m, HYB
Nursery: All Year, Daily
Garden: All Year, Greenhouses, Tours

McMillen's Iris Garden
R. R. 1
Norwich, ON, Canada N0J 1P0
(519) 863-6508

PLANTS
Offers a very large selection of **daylilies and iris**: they grow over 100 daylilies and 1,000 iris in their gardens. Iris are tall bearded, dwarf, border, Siberian and spuria.
Catalog: Free
Garden: June-July, Daily

Ma-Dot-Cha Hobby Nursery
300 Montezuma Ave.
Dothan, AL 36303
(205) 792-6970
Mark S. Cannon

PLANTS
Sells only **camellia scions** from his personal collection; write and ask if he has the cultivars you're looking for, send long SASE for reply.
Catalog: See notes, SS:AY, $10m
Nursery: All Year, Call Ahead

Madcap Orchids
48 Pangola Dr.
Ft. Myers, FL 33905
(813) 694-5900
Pauline & Guy Capin

PLANTS SUPPLIES
A small nursery offers **orchids**: cattleyas, "mini-catts", phalaenopsis, vandaceous, equitants -- hybrids and mericlones: brief descriptions in orchid-talk -- collectors will understand. Also sells supplies. (1981)
Catalog: Free, CAN, SS:AY, $25m, HYB
Nursery: Daily, Call Ahead
Garden: Daily, Call Ahead

For Explanations of Abbreviations/Codes Used in Listings See Bookmark or Inside Covers

Magnolia Nursery & Display Garden
Route 1, Box 87
Chunchula, AL 36521
(205) 675-4696 or 8471 (eves)
David Ellis

PLANTS
Offers a good selection of **Southeastern native plants**: species azaleas, Louisiana iris, native magnolias such as the 'bigleaf', as well as Gresham hybrid magnolias, camellias, evergreen azaleas, holly, Japanese iris and other desireable landscape plants. (1985)
Catalog: Free, R&W, CAN/OV, SS:11-3, $25m, bn
Nursery: All Year, M-F: By Appointment Only on Weedends
Garden: All Year, M-F: By Appointment Only on Weekends

Makielski Berry Farm & Nursery
7130 Platt Road
Ypsilanti, MI 48197
(313) 434-3673 or 572-0060 TO/CC
Edward & Diane Makielski

PLANTS
Specializes in **bramble berries**: raspberries, blackberries, currants, gooseberries, all state inspected. Also sells strawberries, rhubarb, blueberries, asparagus, grapes and fruit trees. All plants well described, with information on bearing season, flavor and use. (1954)
Catalog: Free, R&W, CAN/OV, SS:11-5
Nursery: Nov-June, Daily

Ann Mann's Orchids
9045 Ron-Den Lane
Windemere, FL 32786
(305) 876-2625
Ann & Jim Mann

PLANTS BOOKS SUPPLIES
Very large selection of **orchids, bromeliads, hoyas, anthuriums, alocasias** and other **exotic plants**: all briefly described with cultural notes. Also sells water purifiers, cork, charcoal and other growing supplies, including their own potting fiber, "Husky-Fiber", and New Zealand sphagnum moss.
Catalog: $1, R&W, SS:W, $20m, bn
Nursery: By Appointment Only

Maple Tree Gardens
P. O. Box 278
208 First Street
Ponca, NE 68770
(402) 755-2615
Larry L. Harder

PLANTS
Bearded iris: standard tall, miniature and standard dwarf, intermediate, miniature tall and border, as well as arilbred and Siberian. Also **daylilies**, a real collectors' list: broad selection with brief plant descriptions. (1961)
Catalog: Free, CAN/OV, SS:7-10, $10m, HYB
Nursery: By Appointment Only
Garden: May, July, By Appointment Only

Maplethorpe
11296 Sunnyview N.E.
Salem, OR 97301
Noble Bashor

SEEDS
List offers seed of **species maples, Northwestern native trees, shrubs** and **vines and other ornamentals**, some seeds are habitat collected. Plants are very briefly described: germination instructions sent with the seeds. Some seeds in short supply, some are very desireable plants. (1984)
Catalog: Long SASE, R&W, CAN/OV, bn
Nursery: By Appointment Only
Garden: By Appointment Only

Maplewood Seed Company
6219 SW Dawn Street
Lake Oswego, OR 97035
Barbara Ritchie

SEEDS
Offers seed of many cultivars of **Acer palmatum and many species maples**: all seed is freshly harvested. Maples for specialists, collectors and bonsai: no plant descriptions, Japanese maples listed by Japanese cultivar names. (1980)
Catalog: Long SASE, MO, CAN/OV, SS:11-5, bn

Margrave Plant Co.
P. O. Box 146
Gleason, TN 38229
(901) 648-5174
Frank G. Margrave

PLANTS
Specializes in **sweet potato and yam plants**: 15 varieties available, sold by variety or in mixed collections for large or small gardens: can't ship to CA.
Catalog: Free, MO, SS:4-6, $4m

Marilynn's Garden
13421 Sussex Place
8184 Katella Ave (Stanton)
Santa Ana, CA 92705
(714) 955-4133 or 633-1375
Marilynn Cohen

PLANTS
Offers a wide selection of **tropical plants**: bromeliads, plumerias, tillandsias, anthuriums, epiphyllums, gingers, hoyas, cacti, Mexican species orchids and more. They also offer collections: variegated plants, red plants, black plants, grey plants, tropical plants, etc. (1972)
Catalog: $1, R&W, CAN/OV, SS:W, HYB
Nursery: Feb-Dec, By Appointment Only

Maroushek Gardens
120 E. 11th Street
Hastings, MN 55033
(612) 437-9754
Lillian Maroushek

PLANTS
A very extensive selection of **hostas** -- about 100 varieties -- each briefly described. They also have a fine selection of rock garden and shade perennials and species and hybrid clematis for sale only at the nursery. (1976)
Catalog: $.50d, SS:5,8-9, HYB, bn/cn
Nursery: May-Oct, Call Ahead
Garden: May-Aug, Rock Garden, Call Ahead

Marvelous Minis
30840 Wentworth St.
Livonia, MI 48154
(313) 261-6767
Ron Brenton

PLANTS
Specializes in **miniature African violets**, with a few standards from well-known hybridizers. Also other miniature plants for terraria and dish gardens -- begonias, gesneriads, ferns and other very small plants: all plants briefly described.
Catalog: $1d, R&W, SS:5-10, $15m, HYB, bn
Nursery: By Appointment Only

Marvin's Cactus
4410 W. Easton Pl.
Tulsa, OK 74127
(918) 587-8338
Marvin R. Bartlett

PLANTS
Specializes in **cactus and succulents** for the collector and winter hardy plants for outside plantings. Among the selections are discocactus, echinocereus, gymnocalycium, mammillaria, turbinicarpus, euphorbia, haworthia, hoodia and many more, listed only by botanical name. (1969)
Catalog: Long SASE, R&W, SS:AY, $15m, HYB, bn
Nursery: All Year, Call Ahead
Garden: May-June, Greenhouse, Call Ahead

Mary's African Violets
19788 San Juan
Detroit, MI 48221

PLANTS SUPPLIES
Offers **African violets** and growing supplies.
Catalog: 1 FCS, SS:W

Maryott's Gardens
1073 Bird Avenue
San Jose, CA 95125
(408) 971-0444
William R. Maryott

PLANTS
A broad choice of **tall and standard dwarf bearded iris** for collectors: all well described, many illustrated in color and b&w. Also offers several collections to help you get started with this insidious hobby! (1978)
Catalog: $1d, R&W, OV, SS:7-8, $15m, HYB
Nursery: April-May, F-Su, By Appointment Only
Garden: April, F-Su, Call Ahead.

Matsu-Momiji Nursery
P. O. Box 11414
410 Borbeck St.
Philadelphia, PA 19111
(215) 722-6286 (after 4 pm)
Steve Pilacik

PLANTS SUPPLIES TOOLS
A collectors' list of many cultivars of **Japanese black pine** (Pinus thunbergii), spruces and a few Japanese maples and other plants for bonsai: each fairly briefly described. The pines cannot be shipped to several western states -- inquire. Also finished bonsai, supplies and courses. (1980)
Catalog: $1.25d, CAN/OV, SS:AY, $35m
Nursery: All Year, Daily, By Appointment Only
Garden: April-Sept, Daily, By Appointment Only

Mauna Kea Orchids
206 Ainako Ave.
Hilo, HI 96720
(808) 935-4081 or 961-7316
Wendell J. Cabanas

PLANTS
"Concentrates on offering promising **cattleyas and phalaenopsis** clones for the home grower." (1980)
Catalog: Free, MO, CAN/OV, SS:3-11, $25m, HYB

Maver Rare Perennials
RR 2, Box 265 B, Price Road
Asheville, NC 28850
(704) 298-4751
Majella Larochelle & Vee Sharp

PLANTS SEEDS
Offers seed of more than 6,000 **trees, shrubs, alpines, perennials, bulbous plants, ornamental grasses and much more**: a tightly-packed computer list of botanical names, guaranteed to drive you mad with joy if you're looking for unusual plants! A book is on its way -- sure to become essential. (1980)
Catalog: $2d, R&W, CAN/OV, HYB, bn
Nursery: All Year, M-F
Garden: May-June, M-F

Maxim's Greenwood Gardens
2157 Sonoma Street
Redding, CA 96001
(916) 241-0764 TO $15m
Georgia Maxim

PLANTS BULBS
A huge selection of **iris**: bearded in various sizes, Japanese and Siberian iris, Pacific Coast Hybrids, arilbreds, spuria and Louisiana iris, some tetraploid and diploid daylilies and a broad selection of novelty daffodils (offered every three years): all briefly described. (1955)
Catalog: Free, SS:7-11
Nursery: All Year, By Appointment Only
Garden: March-July, By Appointment Only

Earl May Seed & Nursery Co.
P. O. Box 500
208 N. Elm Street
Shenandoah, IA 51603
(712) 246-1020
Rankin Family

PLANTS SEEDS SUPPLIES TOOLS BULBS
Seasonal color catalogs offer **general nursery stock, seeds, bulbs, perennials and garden supplies** -- a traditional garden emporium: all plants well described, with cultural suggestions. (1919)
Catalog: Free, R&W, SS:2-5, $1m
Nursery: Fifty-six garden centers in the Midwest.

Meadowbrook Herb Garden
Route 138
Wyoming, RI 02898
(401) 539-7603 TO/CC $10m
Marjory & Thomas Fortier

SEEDS
A broad selection of **herb seeds**: each well but briefly described. Plants available at the nursery only, where they also sell herb products, books and gifts. (1967)
Catalog: $1($3 OV), R&W, CAN/OV, $10m, cn/bn
Nursery: All Year, M-Sa, Su pm

Mellinger's Inc.
2310 W. South Range Rd.
North Lima, OH 44452
(216) 549-9861 or (800) 321-7444 TO/CC $10m
Philip & Jean Steiner

PLANTS SEEDS BOOKS SUPPLIES TOOLS BULBS
Catalog is a large general store of home and commercial gardening supplies, books, seeds and plants of all kinds -- impossible to fit into any category. It's hard to believe that they can carry so many items -- 4,000 by their count! It's a delightful jumble and great fun to peruse. (1927)
Catalog: Free, R&W, CAN/OV, SS:AY, $10m, cn/bn
Nursery: All Year, M-Sa
Garden: All Year, M-Sa

Merry Gardens
P. O. Box 595
Mechanic Street
Camden, ME 04843
(207) 236-9064
Mary Ellen Ross

PLANTS
Issues two catalogs: #1 ($1) lists **herbs, scented and miniature geraniums**, many ivy cultivars and fuchsias; and #2 ($2) lists **flowering vines, ferns, cacti and succulents and other foliage plants** for home and conservatory. Collectors' list: plants very briefly described. (1947)
Catalog: See notes, CAN, SS:3-12, $10m, bn/cn
Nursery: All Year, M-Sa
Garden: May-Oct, M-Sa

Mesa Flora Nursery
HC 1, Box 4159
1163 Luna Mesa
Yucca Valley, CA 92284-9404
(619) 364-2232
Jim Fiedler

PLANTS SEEDS
A collectors' catalog, illustrated in b&w, offering a broad selection of **cactus and succulents** and seed of both: each plant very briefly described.
Catalog: $2, CAN/OV, SS:AY, $15m, bn
Nursery: All Year, By Appointment Only
Garden: All Year, By Appointment Only

Mesa Garden
P. O. Box 72
Belen, NM 87002
(505) 864-3131
Steven & Linda Brack

PLANTS SEEDS
A very extensive collectors' list of **cacti and succulents**, both seed and seed-grown plants, with very brief descriptions including habitat data: German and British customers may send orders in local currency to agents in those countries. Guaranteed to thrill collectors. (1976)
Catalog: 2 FCS(2 IRC), R&W, CAN/OV, SS:W, bn
Nursery: By Appointment Only
Garden: By Appointment Only

Messelaar Bulb Co.
P. O. Box 269
County Road, Route 150
Ipswich, MA 01938
(617) 356-3737
Pieter Messelaar

BULBS
Importer of **spring and summer flowering Dutch bulbs** sells in quantities from five to hundreds: plants are briefly decribed and many are illustrated in color. (1946)
Catalog: Free, R&W, SS:9-12,2-5, $10m
Nursery: Sept-Dec, Feb-May, M-Sa: Su pm

Meta Horticultural Labs
Meta, KY 41501
(606) 432-1516 TO:CC
Bonnie L. Lawson

SEEDS
Sells seeds of **deciduous fruit and nut trees**: black mulberry, pawpaws, persimmons, black walnuts and some species maples -- some of these seeds are habitat collected. They also sell 15 "true strains" of **gourd** seeds.
Catalog: $1d, CAN/OV
Nursery: All Year, Call Ahead

Meyer Seed Co.
600 South Caroline St.
Baltimore, MD 21231
(301) 342-4224

SEEDS SUPPLIES TOOLS BULBS
Specializes in **vegetable and flower** seeds which do well in the Baltimore-Washington, DC, area. Catalog is informative to the home or commercial grower and also offers supplies and equipment and summer blooming bulbs. (1910)
Catalog: Free, R&W

Michigan Bulb Co.
1950 Waldorf N. W.
Grand Rapids, MI 49550
(616) 453-5401

PLANTS BULBS
Everyone has seen their ads or gotten fliers: offers bulbs, groundcovers, roses, dahlias and gladiolus. Have not seen their catalog.
Catalog: Free

Mid-America Iris Gardens
P. O. Box 12982
3409 N. Geraldine
Oklahoma City, OK 73157
(405) 946-5743
Paul W. Black

PLANTS
Color catalog offers a very broad selection of **bearded iris** in several sizes and **arilbreds**: each plant very briefly described, but new introductions and his twenty favorites get lots of ink. (1978)
Catalog: $1, CAN/OV, SS:7-8, $10m, HYB
Nursery: May-Aug, Call Ahead
Garden: April-May, Call Ahead

Mid-Atlantic Wildflowers

See J. Brown, Native Seeds

Midwest Cactus
P. O. Box 163
New Melle, MO 63365
(314) 828-5389
Chris M. Smith

PLANTS
Specializes in hardy **opuntia cacti** for year round outdoor gardens: plants are shown in b&w photographs, briefly described with good growing information. (1984)
Catalog: $.50, MO, CAN, SS:4-9, $5m, bn

Midwest Seed Growers, Inc.
505 Walnut Street
Kansas City, MO 64106
(816) 842-1493 TO/CC $25m
Mark Pflumm

SEEDS
Seeds for home gardeners and big growers, both **vetegables and annuals**: some are illustrated in color or b&w. They offer a broad selection, particularly vegetables, including 'mini' pumpkins and Indian corn. (1946)
Catalog: Free, R&W, CAN/OV, SS:11-5, $15m
Nursery: All Year, M-F, Call Ahead

Midwest Wildflowers
P. O. Box 64
Rockton, IL 61072
Leroy & Diane Busker

SEEDS BOOKS
Seeds of **wildflowers of the Midwestern US**, "offered with the thought that gardeners would gladly use native plants in home plantings if seed were available." A wide selection, with a booklet describing some of the plants; some seed habitat-collected. Also books on growing wildflowers. (1969)
Catalog: $.50, MO, CAN, $3m, cn/bn

Mighty Minis
7318 Sahara Court
Sacramento, CA 95828
(916) 421-7284
Jean Stokes

PLANTS SUPPLIES
A small nursery selling only **miniature African violets** (plants and leaves) and **episcias**. A broad selection: each brief description has lots of !!!
They also sell plastic 'egg' terrariums for use with tiny plants. (1982)
Catalog: $1d, CAN/OV, SS:4-10, $13m
Nursery: All Year, By Appointment Only
Garden: All Year, By Appointment Only

Milaeger's Gardens
4838 Douglas Ave.
Racine, WI 53402-2498
(414) 639-2371 or 2040 TO/CC $15m
Kevin D. Milaeger

PLANTS
A broad selection of **perennials**, including a good selection of mostly modern **roses, woodland and shade plants, prairie wildflowers and grasses**: all very well described and many illustrated in color photographs. The catalog is accurately called "The Perennial Wishbook." (1960)
Catalog: $1d, R&W, SS:3-6, $15m, bn/cn
Nursery: All Year, Daily
Garden: Spring-Summer, Daily

J. E. Miller Nurseries, Inc.
5060 West Lake Road
Canandaigua, NY 14424
(716) 396-2647 or (800) 828-9630 TO/CC $10m
John & David Miller

PLANTS SUPPLIES
Color catalog offers a broad selection of **fruit and nut trees**, berries of all kinds, grapes, ornamental trees and supplies: each plant well described and many illustrated. (1936)
Catalog: Free, R&W, SS:2-6, 10-11, $5m, cn
Nursery: All Year, M-Sa
Garden: April-May, Growing Area, M-Sa

Miller's Manor Gardens
3167 E. U.S. 224
Ossian, IN 46777
(219) 597-7403
Roger & Lynda Miller

PLANTS BULBS
Offers **bearded iris of all types**, an extensive list: each plant very briefly described. Also offers a number of Siberian iris cultivars, as well as a nice selection of **daylilies and daffodils**. Small nursery; some plants may be in short supply. (1976)
Catalog: $.50, R&W, CAN/OV, SS:7-9, $10m, HYB
Nursery: Nov-March, M-Tu, Th-Sa
Garden: May, M-Tu, Th-Sa

Miller-Bowie County Farmers Assn.
P. O. Box 1110
1007 W. 3rd St.
Texarkana, TX 75502
(214) 794-3631
Harlon Robinson

SEEDS
Formerly Bunch's Seeds, and more recently Aurora Gardens, this seed company has apparently been taken over by their best customers. They offer, among other regional crops, cowhorn okra, rattlesnake beans, willow leaf lima beans and many varieties of Southern peas: **vegetables for Southern gardens**.
Catalog: Free, CAN/OV, $1m
Nursery: All Year, M-F, Sa am

Mini-Roses
P. O. Box 4255, Sta. A
Dallas, TX 75208
(214) 946-3487
Ernest & Minnie Williams

PLANTS
Offers a good selection of **miniature roses** and a number of collections: each plant well described. Their own hybrids are aimed at brilliant colors and hybrid tea form blooms. (1956)
Catalog: Free, R&W, MO, SS:W, $4m, HYB

Miniature Plant Kingdom
4125 Harrison Grade Rd.
Sebastopol, CA 95472
(707) 874-2233
Don Herzog

PLANTS
Offers a large selection of **miniature roses**, including their own hybrids, as well as **Japanese maples, conifers and plants for bonsai**. The bonsai list has grown to a huge computer print-out of desireable plants, many of which have fruit and/or flowers. (1965)
Catalog: $2.50, R&W, SS:W, $7m, HYB
Nursery: All Year, Th-Su: By Appointment Only, M-Tu
Garden: Spring-Summer, Th-Su: By Appointment Only, M-Tu

Miree's Gesneriads
70 Enfield Avenue
Toronto, ON, Canada M8W 1T9
(416) 251-6369
Mrs. M. Lex

PLANTS SEEDS
A collectors' list of **hybrid and species gesneriads** offers plants, tubers or cuttings and some seeds: plants briefly described. (1976)
Catalog: $1, USA, SS:W, $10m, HYB
Nursery: All Year, By Appointment Only

Mission Bell Gardens
2778 West 5600 So.
Roy, UT 84067
Melba & Jim Hamblen

PLANTS
Offers an extensive list of **bearded iris** in all heights; many are their own hybrids: each plant well described.
Catalog: Free, SS:7-8, $25m, HYB

Grant Mitsch Novelty Daffodils
P. O. Box 218
Hubbard, OR 97032
(503) 651-2742 eves.
Dick & Elsie Havens

BULBS
Specializes in rarer hybrids of **daffodils**, including those of Grant E. Mitsch, as well as many others: each plant is very well described, and many are illustrated in color in an informative catalog. Grant Mitsch is nearing 80 and still introducing new cultivars. (1927)
Catalog: $3d, MO, CAN/OV, SS:9-10, HYB
Garden: Spring, Daffodils, Call Ahead

Mo's Greenhouse
185 Swan River Rd.
Bigfork, MT 59911
(406) 837-5128
Robt. & H. Mauree Rost

PLANTS
A nice selection of **alpines, perennials and groundcovers**: delphiniums, dianthus, daylilies, sedums and other hardy plants. They also carry a selection of **edibles**: asparagus, blackberries, currants, raspberries and gooseberries, horseradish and rhubarb. All plants well described.
Catalog: MO, SS:4-5, bn/cn

Mohns, Inc.
P. O. Box 2301
Atascadero, CA 93423
(805) 466-4362

PLANTS
Offers their own "Minicaps" strain of perennial **Oriental poppies**, bred especially for the warm winter climate of Central and Southern California. They come in a choice of several shades of red, pink and orange and in dwarf, standard and tall heights.
Catalog: 2 FCS, MO, SS:3-5

Montrose Nursery
P. O. Box 957
Hillsborough, NC 27278
(919) 732-7787
Nancy Goodwin

PLANTS
Small nursery specializes in seed-grown hardy **species cyclamen** (large selection) and **primulas** -- but also offers other perennials and rock garden plants -- asters, aquilegias, iris, phlox, salvias and more: all very well described. Many are Southeastern native plants. (1984)
Catalog: $1, SS:2-5, 9-11, bn
Nursery: All Year, By Appointment Only
Garden: All Year, By Appointment Only

Moon Mountain Wildflowers
P. O. Box 34
864 Napa Avenue
Morro Bay, CA 93442-0034
(805) 772-2473 TO/CC $15m
Donna Vaiano

SEEDS BOOKS
Informative catalog lists **annual and perennial wildflowers** of many areas, including mixes suitable for many habitats or uses: sold in packets and in bulk. Plants well described with cultural suggestions. Also sells wildflower posters of Calif. Native Plant Society, will be adding books. (1981)
Catalog: $1(5 IRC), R&W, CAN/OV, bn/cn
Nursery: All Year, M-Sa
Garden: Spring-Summer, Call Ahead

Moonshine Gardens
P. O. Box 1019
Clearlake Oaks, CA 95423
(707) 998-3055 or 743-1570
Monty Byers

PLANTS
A very large selection of **bearded iris** of all types: tall bearded, dwarf, border, median, intermediate, horned, reblooming: all plants very well described. Growing area is at 12570-A Powerhouse Rd., Potter Valley. (1985)
Catalog: Free, SS:7-9, HYB
Nursery: April-May, Oct, Daily (take orders at garden)
Garden: April-May, Oct, Daily (See notes)

Moore Water Gardens
P. O. Box 340, Highway 4
Port Stanley, ON, Canada N0L 2A0
(519) 782-4052
Sue See

PLANTS BOOKS SUPPLIES
A good selection of **water lilies, lotus, aquatic plants**, supplies and ponds for water gardens: all well described in an informative catalog, some illustrated in color. Also a number of books on water gardening. (1930)
Catalog: Free, R&W, SS:4-9, $5m, bn/cn
Nursery: All Year, Call Ahead
Garden: May-Aug, Call Ahead

Moose Tubers
P. O. Box 1010
Dixmont, ME 04932
(207) 257-3943
Tom Roberts

PLANTS BULBS
What a great name! Sells sixteen kinds of **seed potatos**, plus onions, gladiolus, lilies, iris, begonias, dahlias, caladiums, cannas, various cover crops and sunchokes. Plants are very briefly described, with some growing information. (1981)
Catalog: 2 FCS, R&W, SS:4, $25
Nursery: April, M-F, By Appointment Only

Moosebell Flower, Fruit & Tree Co.
Route 1, Box 240
St. Francis, ME 04774
Paul Sprung

PLANTS
Small nursery offering very hardy fruit trees for cold climates: **apples, crabapples, cherry-plums, gooseberries and currants.** All plants are very well described as to taste and habit.
Catalog: Free, MO, SS:4-5

Morden Nurseries, Ltd
P. O. Box 1270
Morden, MB, Canada R0G 1J0
(204) 1-822-3311
Herman Temmerman

PLANTS
A good selection of **hardy fruit trees, ornamental trees and shrubs**, and **perennials.** Color catalog, some plants illustrated. Offers fruiting and ornamental crabapples, apples, plums, apricots and berries -- all very hardy.
Nursery: All Year, M-F: Hours vary, Call Ahead

Mt. Leo Nursery
P. O. Box 135
603 Beersheba St.
McMinnville, TN 37110
(615) 473-7833
Virginia Pearsall

PLANTS
List offers a nice selection of **evergreens, flowering trees and shrubs, groundcovers and fruit and nut trees**: sizes listed but no descriptions. List includes 'thornfree' blackberries, apples, apricots, pears, peaches, plums, berries and grapes, flowering trees and shrubs, shade trees. (1982)
Catalog: Free, R&W, CAN/OV, SS:10-4, cn
Nursery: All Year, Daily

Mountain Mist Nursery
23561 Vaughn Road
Veneta, OR 97487
(503) 935-7701
William Barber

PLANTS
Nice selection of **seedling trees and shrubs**, conifers, maples, oaks, crabapples, species roses: listed by botanical and common name only. Minimum order is ten plants per variety, so you'll need space or like-minded friends. Small plants at reasonable prices. (1983)
Catalog: Free, R&W, CAN/OV, SS:11-4, HYB, bn
Nursery: All Year, Daily, Call Ahead

Mountain Valley Seeds & Nursery
1798 N 1200 E
Logan, UT 84321
(801) 752-0247 TO/CC $5m
D. Agathangelides

SEEDS SUPPLIES
A selection of **vegetable seed, many open-pollinated** and suitable for short-season regions, and **annual garden flowers**: all plants well described with planting suggestions. Also sells "Treesaver" trunk protectors and "Solarcap" plant protectors for starting vegetables in cold climates. (1974)
Catalog: Free, R&W, CAN/OV
Nursery: All Year, M-Sa

Mountain West Seeds
P. O. Box 1471
Cheyenne, WY 82003
Robert Dorn

SEEDS
Habitat collected seeds of **Rocky Mountain native plants**: wildflowers, cactus and shrubs: brief list with very good plant descriptions and index to uses, habitat and flower color. Will do custom seed collecting by special order; write for information. (1985)
Catalog: 1 FCS, CAN/OV
Nursery: By Appointment Only

Mowbray Gardens
3318 Mowbray Lane
Cincinnati, OH 45226
(513) 321-0694 TO $25m
Christopher Trautmann

PLANTS
Sells very hardy **species and hybrid rhododendrons** for cold climates, including hybrids of Leach, Pride and Delp.
Catalog: Free, MO, $25m

Mums by Paschke
11286 East Main Road
North East, PA 16428
(814) 725-9860

PLANTS
A good selection of hybrid **chrysanthemums** available to home gardeners from a large wholesaler. Pamphlet gives good plant descriptions, offers forty varieties to choose from, listed by color.
Catalog: Free, R&W, SS:3-6, $10m
Nursery: April-Nov, Daily

Mushroompeople
P. O. Box 159
11435 State Rt. 1 (Pt. Reyes Station)
Inverness, CA 94937
Jennifer Snyder & Bob Snyder

SEEDS BOOKS SUPPLIES TOOLS
Specializes in **shiitake mushrooms** and advises farmers and home growers on setting up shiitake-growing operations. Also offers complete growing supplies and books on mushroom growing, hunting and cooking. They are setting up an electronic bulletin board for mushroom information. (1977)
Catalog: $2d, R&W, CAN/OV, $5m, cn/bn
Nursery: All Year, M-F, By Appointment Only

Musser Forests Inc.
P. O. Box 340
Route 119 North
Indiana, PA 15710-0340
(412) 465-5686 TO/CC $10m
Fred A. Musser

PLANTS
Supplies many varieties of **trees and shrubs in transplant sizes**: conifers, ornamental trees and shrubs and groundcovers for the gardener and commercial grower: good descriptions, some color photographs. (1928)
Catalog: Free, R&W, CAN/OV, SS:3-5,9-12, $10m, cn/bn
Nursery: March-Nov, Daily
Garden: April-May, Trees & Shrubs, Daily

Nationwide Seed & Supply
4801 Fegenbush Lane
Louisville, KY 40228
(502) 499-0115
Harold Payne

SEEDS SUPPLIES
Small company offers **seeds of short-season vegetables and garden annuals**: plants well described with cultural notes. Seed sold by packet or by the cup (or fraction thereof). They also sell elephant garlic and praying mantis egg cases. (1961)
Catalog: Free, MO, CAN/OV, SS:2-7

Native Gardens
Route 1, Box 494
Greenback, TN 37742
(615) 856-3350
Edward & Meredith Clebsch

PLANTS SEEDS
Nursery-propagated **native plants** (and seeds) for meadow and natural landscaping. Very informative plant list groups plants by growing conditions, season and color of flower, habitat and soil, with concise comments. Send long SASE for plant list, $1 for catalog. (1983)
Catalog: $1, R&W, SS:AY, $10m, cn/bn
Nursery: By Appointment Only
Garden: By Appointment Only

Native Seed Foundation
Star Route
Moyie Springs, ID 83845
(208) 267-7938 TO/CC $10m
David & Suzanne Ronniger

SEEDS TOOLS
Seeds of **interior Pacific Northwest native conifers and shrubs** and several hardy nut species: many are habitat collected. They also sell tree-planting "hoedads", special tools for reforestation planting. Separate list of four kinds of **garlic seed and 35 varieties of seed potatoes**. (1977)
Catalog: Free, R&W, MO, CAN/OV, $5m, SS:Fall, bn

Native Seeds, Inc.
14590 Triadelphia Mill Rd.
Dayton, MD 21036
(301) 596-9818 TO
Dr. James A. Saunders

SEEDS
Color brochure offers a selection of **wildflower** seed, chosen to flourish in many regions of the country. Also offers a seed mix with a broad variety of wildflowers and seeds in bulk. Many plants are illustrated, all well described.
Catalog: Free, R&W, MO, CAN/OV, bn/cn

TRICYRTIS hirta
Toad Lily

Native Seeds/SEARCH
3950 W. New York Dr.
Tucson, AZ 85745
(602) 327-9123 (no telephone orders)
Mahina Drees, Dir.

SEEDS BOOKS SUPPLIES
Non-profit group, offers traditional **Southwestern native crops**, many by Spanish names, as well as wild food plants: all plants briefly described. Offers a few related publications, occasional workshops and Indian seed drying baskets. Wide selection of **corn, beans, amaranth, gourds, squash.**
Catalog: $1, CAN/OV, $2m
Garden: Jan-April, Aug-Oct, Daily, Call Ahead

Natural Gardens
113 Jasper Lane
Oak Ridge, TN 37830
Maureen & Jim Cunningham

PLANTS BOOKS
A good selection of **Southeastern native plants and wildflowers** for wetland, woodland, perennial gardens and wildlife food: all plants very well described with a guide to naturalization and information on butterfly gardens. Also sells books on growing wildflowers and perennials. (1984)
Catalog: $1d, MO, SS:3-11, $8m, cn/bn

Nature's Garden Nursery
Route 1, Box 488
Beaverton, OR 97007
Frederick W. Held

PLANTS SEEDS
Plants for the woodland, shady or sunny garden, including some sedum and sempervivums, meconopsis, species primulas, ferns and other choice **rock garden plants**: each briefly described. Also seed of a number of garden perennials in a separate winter seed list. (1974)
Catalog: $1d, R&W, MO, CAN/OV, SS:9-12,3-5, $15m, bn/cn

E. B. Nauman, Nurseryman
688 St. Davids Ln.
Schenectady, NY 12309
E. B. Nauman

PLANTS
"I specialize in **broadleaf evergreens** which are hardy in the Northeast and and Midwest: rhododendrons, azaleas, mountain laurels, featuring young plants of quality, named varieties." A brief list, but each plant well described, with cultural notes. (1973)
Catalog: Free, MO, SS:4-6,9-11, $10m

New Frontiers
3605 N. Berkeley Lake Rd.
Duluth, GA 30136
Teresa Ackerman

PLANTS SEEDS
Sells seeds and plants of **Hawaiian and other tropical plants**: nice selection, listed by common name only, no plant descriptions. Also offers a few varieties of **palms**; most plants listed seem to be offered as seeds only.
Catalog: $2, R&W, MO, CAN, SS:5-9, cn

New Leaf
2456 Foothill Dr.
Vista, CA 92084
(619) 726-9269
Gerald D. Stewart

PLANTS
Catalog offers hundreds of varieties of **geraniums and pelargoniums** of all types: zonal, miniature, ivy, regals, scented and species pelargoniums. Plants well to very briefly described. (1977)
Catalog: $2.50d, R&W, SS:AY, HYB
Nursery: All Year, By Appointment Only
Garden: April-June, By Appointment Only

New Mexico Cactus Research
P. O. Box 787
1132 E. River Rd.
Belen, NM 87002
(505) 864-4027
Horst Kuenzler

SEEDS
A very extensive collectors' list of **cacti and succulent** seeds and mixtures of seeds by genus, listed by botanical name only, with very brief notes on origin. Many of the seeds are habitat collected: no plant descriptions for most, brief notes on some. (1955)
Catalog: $1, R&W, CAN/OV, $5m, bn
Nursery: By Appointment Only
Garden: By Appointment Only

New Mexico Desert Garden
10231 Belnap NW
Albuquerque, NM 87114
(505) 898-0121
Josef Mikulas

SEEDS
A collectors' list with an very wide selection of **cactus and succulent** seed -- listed by botanical name with no descriptions. (1976)
Catalog: Free, R&W, MO, CAN/OV, bn
Garden: By Appointment Only

The New Peony Farm
P. O. Box 18105
St. Paul, MN 55118
(612) 457-8994
Kent Crossley

PLANTS
Catalog lists only a few of the 350 varieties of herbaceous **peonies** which they grow: each plant well described. They bought a lot of the stock of the Brand Peony Farm when it was sold after 100 years in business and specialize in unusual varieties. (1980)
Catalog: Free, R&W, CAN, SS:9-10
Nursery: By Appointment Only
Garden: June, By Appointment Only

New York State Fruit Testing Coop. Assn.
P. O. Box 462
Geneva, NY 14456
(315) 787-2205
John M. Kasper, Mgr.

PLANTS
For a $5 membership fee, fruit testers may buy a large selection of new and older varieties of **hardy fruit**. They must agree not to distribute the new varieties, as well as to report on how their choices perform: all plants well described; prices seem about average. (1918)
Catalog: Free

For Explanations of Abbreviations/Codes Used In Listings See Bookmark or Inside Covers

Niche Gardens
Route 1, Box 290
Chapel Hill, NC 27514
(919) 967-0078
Kim & Bruce Hawks

PLANTS
Small nursery specializing in **Southeastern wildflowers and native plants, perennials, ornamental grasses and herbs** for rock gardens, bogs and dry areas. Plants are well described and come in 4", quart or gallon sizes. Plant list is free; descriptive list is $3d. (1984)
Catalog: See Notes, CAN/OV, SS:3-11, $10m, bn/cn
Nursery: March-Nov, By Appointment Only
Garden: April-Oct, By Appointment Only

Nicholls Gardens
4724 Angus Drive
Gainesville, VA 22065
(703) 754-9623 TO $10m
Diana & Mike Nicholls

PLANTS
Small nursery sells a good selection of **iris** -- Siberian, Japanese, species and bearded, dwarf to tall, as well as **daylilies and dahlias**: all plants are briefly described -- and would provide something in bloom from early spring to late fall. (1984)
Catalog: $1d, SS:4-5,7-9, $10m, HYB
Nursery: April-Sept, Daily, Call Ahead
Garden: April-Sept, Daily, Call Ahead

Nichols Garden Nursery, Inc.
1190 No. Pacific Highway
Albany, OR 97321
(503) 928-9280 TO/CC $10m
E.R. Nichols & Keane and Rose Marie McGee

SEEDS BOOKS SUPPLIES
An extensive selection of **herbs, vegetables and flowers**; many vegetables selected for the coastal conditions of the Northwest: all plants are very well described with cultural hints -- also garden, herbal and winemaking supplies and books on rural subjects. Specializes in elephant garlic. (1950)
Catalog: Free, R&W, CAN, SS:4-5,9-10
Nursery: All Year, M-Sa
Garden: Spring, Summer, M-Sa

Nindethana Seed Service
RMB 939, Washpool Rd.
Woogenilup, Australia 6324
(098) 541066, Intl. +61-98-541066
Peter & Bev Luscombe

SEEDS
A collectors' list of **Australian native plants**, listed only by botanical name with no descriptions: a very broad selection of trees, shrubs and wildflowers, including eucalyptus, acacias, banksias, stylidiums, hakeas, callistemons, cassias, dryandras, leptospermums and grevilleas. (1956)
Catalog: 2 IRC, R&W, OV, $10m, bn
Nursery: All Year, M-F, Call Ahead

Nolin River Nut Tree Nursery
797 Port Wooden Rd.
Upton, KY 42784
John Brittain

PLANTS
Formerly the Leslie Wilmoth Nursery, specializing in grafted **nut trees** -- pecans, hicans, hickories, heartnuts, butternuts, black and Persian walnuts, chestnuts -- over 100 varieties; also grafted **persimmons and pawpaws**: listed by variety name only, no plant descriptions. (1985)
Catalog: Free, SS:3-4, cn/bn
Nursery: All Year, M-Sa, By Appointment Only
Garden: June-Sept, By Appointment Only

Nooitgedag Disa Nursery
7 Sunnybrae Rd.
Rondebosch,Cape Town, South Africa 7700
(021) 689-1919
Dr. L. Vogelpoel

SEEDS
A hobbyist specializing in seed of **Disa uniflora, D. tripetaloides and D. cardinalis and hybrids**: D. Veitchii, Diores, Kewensis, Watsonii, Kirstenbosch Pride, and Langleyensis. Plants well described: grow to flowering size in three years. Growing information included with seeds. (1980)
Catalog: Free, MO, OV, SS:2-6, $20m

Nor'East Miniature Roses
58 Hammond St.
Rowley, MA 01969
(617) 948-7964
Harmon & John Saville

PLANTS
Color catalog of **miniature roses**, including "mini" tree roses and climbers, both single plants and collections. Also have a branch at P. O. Box 473, Ontario, CA 91762, (714) 988-7222. Nice selection, plants well described. (1972)
Catalog: Free, R&W, SS:AY, $6m, HYB
Nursery: May-Sept, Daily, Call Ahead
Garden: June-Sept, AARS Garden, Call Ahead

North American Wildflowers
38 Hillside Avenue
Atlantic Highlands, NJ 07716
(201) 291-4622
Sandra Henning

PLANTS
Offers a selection of plants for use as **groundcovers**: Mahonia repens, Pachistima Canbyi, Arctostaphylos uva-ursi, Psilstrophe Bakerii and Zinnia grandiflora: well described and chosen for easy care. Will be offering perennial borders in a package -- plants, plans, instructions. (1984)
Catalog: Free, R&W, CAN/OV, SS:Spr, Fall, $20m, bn/cn
Nursery: By Appointment Only
Garden: By Appointment Only

North Coast Rhododendron Nursery
P. O. Box 308
Bodega, CA 94922
Parker Smith & Becky Duckles

PLANTS
Rhododendron nursery specializes in plants for mild climates, even some hot ones, and for greenhouses in cold climates. They offer both hybrids and Maddenii and other species: all plants are very well described.
Catalog: $1, MO, CAN/OV, SS:Fall-Winter

North Pine Iris Gardens
P. O. Box 595
308 North Pine
Norfolk, NE 68701
Chuck & Mary Ferguson

PLANTS
Specializes in **bearded iris of all sizes**, a broad selection: brief plant descriptions. Also sells some hosta, as well as windsocks, wind chimes and note cards with iris motifs.
Catalog: $l, CAN/OV, SS:4-9
Nursery: By Appointment Only

Northplan/Mountain Seed
P. O. Box 9107
Moscow, ID 83843
(208) 882-8040 TO/CC
Loring M. Jones

SEEDS
Seeds for disturbed land restoration, erosion control and highway landscaping, and wildflower mixes for various habitats, range and reclamation grass, deciduous trees and shrubs and short-season vegetables and annuals. Garden catalog $1d: send long SASE for native plant list. (1975)
Catalog: See Notes, R&W, CAN/OV
Nursery: By Appointment Only

Northwest Biological Enterprises
23351 S.W. Bosky Dell Lane
West Linn, OR 97068
(503) 638-6029
Stanley G. Jewett, Jr.

PLANTS
Specializes in **Northwestern native plants**, including ferns and azaleas (R. occidentale), conifers, ornamental trees and shrubs and perennials and rock garden plants. Plants briefly but well described. (1971)
Catalog: $2d, R&W, CAN, SS:10-4, $10m, bn/cn
Nursery: Feb-Nov, M-F, Call Ahead
Garden: March-May, M-F, Call Ahead

Northwest Heathers

See Heaths & Heathers

Northwoods Nursery
28696 S. Cramer Rd.
Molalla, OR 97038
(503) 651-3737 TO/CC $10m
Jim Gilbert & Kathy Fives

PLANTS
Offers **hybrid chestnuts, figs, hardy kiwis, pawpaws and oriental pears**, grown by organic methods "as much as possible." A good variety of kiwis, all sorts of shrubs and trees which do well in the Northwest and which are, in many cases, suited to the urban-sized lot. (1979)
Catalog: Free, R&W, SS:1-5, $10m
Nursery: Jan-May, Tu-Su
Garden: Jan-May, Tu-Su

Nourse Farms, Inc.
RFD, Box 485
River Road (Whately)
South Deerfield, MA 01373
(413) 665-2658
Tim Nourse

PLANTS
Growers of tissue-cultured **strawberries** as a means of producing "virus-free" plants -- 31 varieties. They also sell blackberries, raspberries, rhubarb, horseradish and the new Rutgers Univ. varieties of asparagus -- "Jersey Centennial, Jersey Giant and Greenwich". Informative catalog. (1969)
Catalog: Free, R&W, CAN, SS:3-6
Nursery: April-May, M-Sa
Garden: June-Sept, Growing Area, Call Ahead

Novelty Nurseries
P. O. Box 382
Novelty, OH 44072
(216) 338-4425
Patty & Michael Artino

PLANTS
Offers **hardy ferns** suitable to harsh Midwestern winters (Zone 5): each plant well described, grown from spore.
Catalog: Long SASE, R&W, MO, CAN, SS:AY, $10m, bn

Nuccio's Nurseries
P. O. Box 6160
3555 Chaney Trail
Altadena, CA 91001
(818) 794-3383

PLANTS
A very large selection of **camellias and azaleas**: all plants well to briefly described. Camellias include japonica, Sasanqua, reticulata, higo and rusticana hybrids and a number of species camellias. Azalea hybrids of many types, including their own. Also a few gardenias. (1935)
Catalog: Free, R&W, SS:1-11, HYB
Nursery: All Year, F-Tu: June-Dec, Closed Sunday

Oak Hill Gardens
P. O. Box 25
Binnie Road
Dundee, IL 60118-0025
(312) 428-8500 TO/CC
Hermann & Dorothy Pigors

PLANTS BOOKS SUPPLIES
Informative catalog offers a broad selection of **species and hybrid orchids**, as well as bromeliads and other indoor plants: each plant briefly described in table format. Also offers growing supplies and books. (1973)
Catalog: Free, R&W, CAN/OV, SS:W, HYB, bn
Nursery: All Year, M-Sa
Garden: All Year, M-Sa

For Explanations of Abbreviations/Codes Used In Listings See Bookmark or Inside Covers

Oakes Daylilies
Monday Rd., Route 4
Corryton, TN 37721
(615) 689-3036 or 687-1268
Stewart & William Oakes

PLANTS
Just **daylilies**, a collectors' list of hundreds of varieties from many noted hybridizers and AHS award winners. Grows over 1,500 varieties, with concentration on award winners: plants are described in concise but informative tables -- a mind-boggling choice. (1979)
Catalog: Free, R&W, CAN/OV, SS:3-11, HYB
Nursery: March-Oct, Daily, Call Ahead
Garden: June-July, AHS Display Garden, Daily

Oakwood Daffodils
2330 W. Bertrand Rd.
Niles, MI 49120
(616) 695-6848 TO $15m
John R. Reed

BULBS
A broad selection of novelty **daffodils**, many from hybridizers in New Zealand and Australia, but all American grown and acclimatized: all cultivars are very well described. Will be adding their own hybrids soon. (1984)
Catalog: Free, SS:8-9, $10m
Nursery: By Appointment Only
Garden: April-May, By Appointment Only

Oikos
721 N. Fletcher
Kalamazoo, MI 49007-3077
(616) 342-6504 TO
Ken Asmus

PLANTS
Small nursery offers **seedling nut trees**, pines with edible nuts, oaks with edible acorns and hybrid chestnuts: no plant descriptions. Also **berrying shrubs**: bayberry, cornelian cherry, serviceberry, rugosa roses, persimmons and pawpaws. Can't ship to CA, some restrictions to OR and FL. (1980)
Catalog: Free, R&W, OV, SS:3-5, 10-12, $20m, HYB, cn/bn
Nursery: March-Dec, Daily, By Appointment Only
Garden: Growing Area, By Appointment Only

Orchibec
200 Jean Gauvin
Ste Foy, PQ, Canada G2E 3L9
(418) 871-2155
Laurier Nappert

PLANTS
A nice selection of **orchids**: laeliinae, phalaenopsis, paphiopedilum, cattleyas, doritaenopsis and species: plants very briefly described. Catalogs are available in French and English; specify which you want. (1983)
Catalog: Free, SS:4-10, HYB
Nursery: Daily, By Appointment Only
Garden: Daily, By Appointment Only

The Orchid Center
Highway 17 South
P. O. Box 1116
Arcadia, FL 33821
(813) 494-5896 TO/CC $25m
A. P. Hollingsworth

PLANTS
Offers many types of **hybrid orchids**, as well as jungle collected imported species orchids, and some bromeliads, platyceriums, cryptanthus and tillansias: most briefly described.
Catalog: $1d, R&W, CAN/OV, SS:W, HYB, bn
Nursery: All Year, M-F, Sa am
Garden: Fall & Spring, M-Sa, Greenhouse

Orchid Gardens
6700 Splithand Rd.
Grand Rapids, MN 55744
Norma Phillips

PLANTS BOOKS
Collectors' list of **wildflowers and hardy ferns**: good descriptions and concise cultural notes. Mrs. Phillips also wrote and sells "The Root Book" ($10 ppd), covering the culture of native plants -- soils, mulch, moisture and exposure -- in pictures. Nice selection, informative catalog. (1945)
Catalog: $.50, SS:4-5,8-10, cn/bn
Nursery: By Appointment Only
Garden: By Appointment Only

Orchid Haven
900 Rossland Rd. E.
Whitby, ON, Canada L1N 5R5
(416) 668-8534 TO/CC $35m
Joy & Mal Bain

PLANTS
A good selection of **orchids**, both hybrids and species in seedling and blooming sizes: each briefly but well described. Sells phalaenopsis, paphiopedilums, cattleyas, dendrobiums and epidendrums. (1982)
Catalog: Free, R&W, USA/OV, SS:5-11, $35m, HYB, bn
Nursery: Daily, Call Ahead
Garden: Daily, Call Ahead

The Orchid House
1699 Sage Avenue
Los Osos, CA 93402
(805) 528-1417 or (800) 235-4139 TO
N. H. Powell

PLANTS
Specialist in **hybrid and species orchids** -- paphiopedilums, odontoglossums, phalaenopsis, cymbidiums, cattleyas and oncidiums; request list of variety you're interested in. Plants available as seedlings or in flowering size; orchid lovers and collectors can decipher the orchid-speak. (1943)
Catalog: See notes, R&W, CAN/OV, SS:W, HYB
Nursery: All Year, Call Ahead
Garden: All Year, Call Ahead

Orchid Imports
See Spencer M. Howard Orchid Imports

Orchid Jungle
See Fennell's Orchid Jungle

The Orchid People
See Jones & Scully

Orchid Species Specialists
42314 Road #415
Raymond Road
Coarsegold, CA 93614
(209) 683-3239 TO $50m
Walter J. Rybaczyk

PLANTS
Extensive collectors' lists of **species orchids**, collected by the proprietors or other well-known jungle collectors: no descriptions. Award winning species cattleya and laelia clones a specialty, much wanted by hybridizers. Three lists: general botanical, laelia and species cattleya, $1 each. (1972)
Catalog: See notes, R&W, CAN/OV, SS:W, $50m, bn
Nursery: All Year, Daily, Call Ahead
Garden: All Year, Call Ahead

Orchids Bountiful
826 W. 3800 South
Bountiful, UT 84010
(801) 295-6064
Dave Roskelley

PLANTS BOOKS SUPPLIES
A good selection of **hybrid orchids**: cattleya alliance, brassias, dendrobiums, epidendrums, miltonias, odontoglossums, oncidiums and others, including some **species orchids**: plants are very briefly described. They also offer growing supplies and a few books. (1959)
Catalog: Free, R&W, CAN, SS:W, $25m, HYB, bn
Nursery: All Year, M-Sa
Garden: All Year, M-Sa

Orchids by Hausermann, Inc.
2N 134 Addison Rd.
Villa Park, IL 60181
(312) 543-6855 TO/CC $10m
Edwin Hausermann

PLANTS BOOKS SUPPLIES
Color catalog gives brief descriptions of hundreds of species and hybrid orchids: all described in informational tables. Also offers cultural suggestions, orchid growing supplies and books about orchids. (1920)
Catalog: $1, R&W, CAN/OV, SS:3-12, $10m, HYB, bn
Nursery: All Year, M-Sa
Garden: Jan-May, M-Sa, Greenhouses

Orchids Royale
P. O. Box 1289
5902 Via Real
Carpinteria, CA 93013
(805) 684-8066
James Burkey

PLANTS
A very large selection of standard and miniature cymbidiums, miltonias, odontoglossum alliance **orchids** and paphiopedilum divisons -- some obviously very rare: plants briefly described, some in a sort of "orchid shorthand" known to the fanatic. (1978)
Catalog: Free, CAN/OV, SS:W, HYB
Nursery: All Year, M-F, Call Ahead
Garden: All Year, M-F, Call Ahead

Oregon Bulb Farms
14071 N.E. Arndt Rd.
Aurora, OR 97002
Melridge Corp.

BULBS
Home of the "Jagra" **lilies**, they hybridized many well-known garden lilies (including the popular "Enchantment") in "every color except blue!" Color catalog: brief plant descriptions. They have recently produced a 60-minute video cassette on "Perennial Gardening." (1929)
Catalog: $2d, R&W, MO, CAN/OV, SS:10-4, HYB

Oregon Miniature Roses
8285 SW 185th Ave.
Beaverton, OR 97007
(503) 649-4482
Raymond A. Spooner

PLANTS
Color catalog offers a good selection of **miniature roses**, each well described and many illustrated. Sells a few of their own hybrids, miniature tree roses and roses for hanging baskets.
Catalog: Free, R&W, SS:AY, $5m, HYB
Nursery: All Year, Daily, Call Ahead

Orgel's Orchids
18950 S.W. 136 St., R.R. 2
Miami, FL 33187
(305) 233-7168
Orgel C. Bramblett

PLANTS
Collectors' list of **carnivorous plants** -- an especially large selection of nepenthes, droseras, sarracenias and pinguiculas -- and **species orchids** -- dendrobiums, vandas, aerides, cymbidiums, ascocentrums, phalaenopsis and more. Will export only plants not covered by CITIES convention. (1972)
Catalog: Free, R&W, CAN/OV, SS:AY, HYB, bn
Nursery: All Year, By Appointment Only
Garden: All Year, Growing Area, By Appointment Only

D. Orriell - Seed Exporters
45 Frape Avenue
Mt. Yokine, WA, Australia 6060
(09) 344-2290, (+619 Intl. code)
Patricia B. Orriell

SEEDS
A very extensive list of **Australian native plants** for collectors or botanical gardens: each plant briefly described; includes hardy eucalyptus, wildflowers, ferns, palms, proteas, banksias and cycads, acacias, and many tropical/greenhouse plants. Also has list of native plants for bonsai. (1979)
Catalog: $3, R&W, OV, $15m, bn/cn
Nursery: Daily, By Appointment Only

For Explanations of Abbreviations/Codes Used In Listings See Bookmark or Inside Covers

Owen Farms
Route 3, Curve-Nankipoo Rd.
Ripley, TN 38063
Edric & Lillian Owen

PLANTS
Offers **herbs, perennials, hardy ferns, trees and shrubs**: will be putting out a catalog in 1988.
Catalog: $1, R&W, CAN, SS:W, $10m
Nursery: All Year, M-Sa, Call Ahead
Garden: April-Nov, M-Sa, Call Ahead

Richard Owen Nursery
2209 E. Oakland St.
Bloomington, IL 61701
(309) 663-9551
Adtron, Inc.

PLANTS SUPPLIES
Color catalog offers a variety of **nursery stock** -- trees, shrubs, vines, roses, fruit trees and berries, as well as garden supplies and equipment.
Catalog: Free, SS:W, cn/bn
Nursery: All Year, M-Sa

Owens Orchids
P. O. Box 365
18 Orchidheights Dr.
Pisgah Forest, NC 28768-0365
(704) 877-3313 TO/CC
William & Joyce Owens

PLANTS
A good selection of **orchids** -- phalaenopsis and cattleya hybrids, many meristems and some seedlings: plants briefly described. Also offers an Orchid-a-Month Plan and a starter collections for beginners. Several lists a year.
Catalog: Free, SS:W
Nursery: All Year, M-Sa
Garden: All Year, M-Sa

Owl Ridge Alpines
5421 Whipple Lake Rd.
Clarkston, MI 48016
(313) 370-3017 or 394-0158 TO $10m
Judy Pearson

PLANTS
Hardy alpine plants for sunny or shady rock gardens, including campanulas, penstemons, phlox, primulas, delphiniums, dianthus, hardy geraniums, ornamental grasses, species iris, sedums and sempervivums from the mountain tops of the world: plants briefly described. (1980)
Catalog: $.50, SS:4-5,9-10, bn
Nursery: April-Oct, By Appointment Only
Garden: April-June, By Appointment Only

Ozark National Seed Order
P. O. Box 932
Woodstock, NY 12498
(914) 246-1488
Stuart Leiderman

SEEDS
Offers **open-pollinated, untreated garden seeds**: vegetables, herbs and flowers. Price of list includes a sample packet: all packets are $.25.
Catalog: $.50, R&W, MO, CAN/OV

Pacific Berry Works
P. O. Box 54
963 Thomas Rd.
Bow, WA 98232
(206) 757-4385 TO/CC
Mintz & Sakuma

PLANTS BOOKS
A small nursery specializes in **"day neutral" strawberries**, which bear three months after planting, and cane berries: raspberries, boysenberries, loganberries, and tayberries from Scotland. Plants well described. Also sells a couple of berry cookbooks. (1985)
Catalog: Free, R&W, CAN, SS:2-5, HYB
Nursery: Call Ahead
Garden: Growing Area, Call Ahead

Pacific Coast Hybridizers
P. O. Box 972
1170 Steinway Ave.
Campbell, CA 95009-0972
(408) 370-2955
Ted Gromala & Bryce Williamson

PLANTS
Hobbyist hybridizers turned nurserymen: their color catalog is informative and offers a wide selection of tall bearded and reblooming iris and iris-theme gifts: plants well described. (1970)
Catalog: $1d, R&W, CAN/OV, SS:7-9, HYB
Nursery: April 15-May 15, Daily, Call Ahead
Garden: April 15-May 15, Daily, Call Ahead

Pacific Tree Farms
4301 Lynwood Dr.
Chula Vista, CA 92010
(619) 422-2400 TO/CC
William L. Nelson

PLANTS BOOKS SUPPLIES TOOLS
A broad selection of **fruit, nut and ornamental trees** (including 90 varieties of pine), California native trees and shrubs and tender warm-climate fruits like banana: good selection, no plant descriptions. Adding new trees all the time. Also books, grafting supplies and fertilizers. (1970)
Catalog: $1.50, R&W, CAN/OV, SS:AY, bn/cn
Nursery: All Year, Daily
Garden: All Year, Daily

Painted Meadows Seed Co.
P. O. Box 1865
635 W. Moreland
Kingston, PA 18704-0865
(717) 283-2911
Art Frank, Mgr.

SEEDS
Offers a **wildflower** seed mix suitable for most climates except dry or tropical -- best suited to Eastern Seaboard. (1982)
Catalog: $1, R&W, MO, CAN

Carl Pallek & Son Nursery
P. O. Box 137
Highway 55
Virgil, ON, Canada L0S 1T0
(416) 468-7262
Otto Pallek

PLANTS
An extensive list of hybrid tea **roses**, as well as floribundas, grandifloras, climbers and a selection of old garden roses: each very briefly described. Sells in Canada only, but Americans may pick up orders at the nursery; order early to allow preparation of inspection papers. (1959)
Catalog: Free, SS:11-12,3-4
Nursery: All Year, M-Sa
Garden: July-Sept, M-Sa

Panda Products
P. O. Box 104
3900 Barnes Road
Fulton, CA 95434
(707) 527-6777
Hank Yao, Yat Ying Cheung, Timothy Hansken

PLANTS
Small nursery offers a nice selection of **bamboo**, specializing in "Moso Bamboo" (phyllostachys pubescens) for bamboo shoots and timber; it has very beautifully patterned large culms or stalks. (1983)
Catalog: Free, R&W, CAN/OV, SS:AY, $25m, bn
Nursery: By Appointment Only

The PanTree
1150 Beverly Drive
Vista, CA 92084
John Rubesha

PLANTS
Specializing in euphorbias, aloes, crassulas, aeoniums, echeverias, haworthias, gasterias, kalanchoes, monadeniums and other **succulents**. Collectors' list with no plant descriptions; over one hundred euphorbias -- stocks sometimes limited. (1978)
Catalog: $.50, MO, SS:2-11, $10m, bn

Paradise Water Gardens
62 May Street
Whitman, MA 02382
(716) 447-4711 TO/CC

PLANTS BOOKS SUPPLIES
Specializes in plants and supplies for **water gardens** -- water lilies, aquatic plants, books on water gardening, supplies for pools and ponds.
Catalog: $3

Park Seed Company, Inc.
P. O. Box 46
Highway 254 North
Greenwood, SC 29648-0046
(803) 223-7333 TO/CC $20m
Park Family

PLANTS SEEDS BOOKS SUPPLIES TOOLS
Park offers a huge selection of seeds for the home gardener, many illustrated in color. In addition to the usual **flowers and vegetables**, they also have some harder-to-find seeds and some plants. The catalog seems to arrive on December 26th to fight the post-Christmas blues (it works!). (1868)
Catalog: Free, R&W, CAN, cn/bn
Nursery: All Year, M-F
Garden: May-July, M-F

Parsley's Cape Seeds
1 Woodlands Rd.
Somerset West, Cape, South Africa 7130
(024) 512630
Alan and Renate Parsley

SEEDS
Specializes in **Proteaceae**. Collectors' list of South African plants: leucodendrons, proteas, leucospermums, ericas, species pelargoniums, Australian banksias, carnivorous plants, as well as shrubs and trees. (1953)
Catalog: $1d, R&W, MO, OV, bn
Nursery: Call Ahead

Passiflora
Rt. 1, Box 190-A
Germanton, NC 27019
(919) 591-5816
Denise E. Blume

SEEDS BOOKS
Color catalog offers **wildflowers** for naturalizing or for the garden, as well as some mixtures. Plants are well described, arranged by habitat. Also sells books on wildflower identification. (1982)
Catalog: $1, R&W, CAN, SS:4-10, cn/bn
Nursery: All Year, Th-Su, By Appointment Only
Garden: Spring-Summer, By Appointment Only

Theodore Payne Foundation
10459 Tuxford St.
Sun Valley, CA 91352
(818) 768-1802
Non-Profit Foundation

SEEDS BOOKS
This non-profit foundation honors the work of Theodore Payne, who made **California wildflowers and native plants** admired the world over; they sell seeds by mail and plants at their headquarters: no plant descriptions. They also sell many books on native flora -- ask for book list. (1963)
Catalog: Long SASE W/2 FCS, R&W, CAN/OV, bn/cn
Nursery: All Year, Tu-Sa
Garden: Jan-April, Tu-Sa

Peace Seeds
2385 SE Thompson St.
Corvallis, OR 97333
(503) 752-0421
Dr. Alan Kapuler

SEEDS
"A planetary gene pool and research service": they offer a wide variety of seeds for **vegetables, native plants, herbs, heirloom potatos and tomatoes** and **medicinal plants**. Seed list is $1; their catalog and research journal is $5 and presents "an integrated view of the Plant Kingdom". (1979)
Catalog: $1, R&W, CAN/OV, cn/bn
Nursery: By Appointment Only
Garden: April-Oct, By Appointment Only

For Explanations of Abbreviations/Codes Used In Listings See Bookmark or Inside Covers

Peaceful Valley Farm Supply
11173 Peaceful Valley Rd.
Nevada City, CA 95959
(916) 265-FARM TO/CC $20m
Bob Cantisano

PLANTS SEEDS SUPPLIES TOOLS BULBS
A broad selection of **fruit, berries and nuts** for Western climates -- distributes Dave Wilson nursery stock. Also offers landscape trees and shrubs, citrus, grapes, bulbs, organic fertilizers and pest controls, tools and supplies for gardeners and farmers: a real take-to-bed catalog. (1977)
Catalog: $2d, R&W, CAN/OV, SS:AY (1-4 Bare Root), $20m
Nursery: All Year, M,W,F,Sa

Pearl Harbor Orchids
99-007 Kaalakaha Dr.
Aiea, HI 96701
(808) 488-2262

PLANTS
Offers hybrid **brassia and oncidium orchids**.

Peckerwood Gardens

See Yucca Do

Peekskill Nurseries
Shrub Oak, NY 10588

PLANTS
Offers **pachysandra** for groundcover.
Catalog: Free

Penn Valley Orchids
239 Old Gulph Rd.
Wynnewood, PA 19096
(215) 642-9822
William W. Wilson

PLANTS
A very broad selection of **hybrid orchids**, some one of a kind, with some **species orchids** as well: most well but briefly described. Offers a large list of paphiopedilums, cattleya alliance and others. Also sells antique orchid prints. (1946)
Catalog: $1, R&W, CAN/OV, SS:W, HYB, bn
Nursery: All Year, By Appointment Only

The Pepper Gal
10536 119th Ave. N.
Largo, FL 33543
Dorothy L. Van Vleck

SEEDS
An extensive list of **ornamental, hot and sweet peppers**, 200 varieties by her count: no plant descriptions, but she does list her favorites.
Catalog: Free, MO

Perennial Seed Exchange
P. O. Box 1466
Chelan, WA 98816
Michael Pilarski, Coordinator

SEEDS
An exchange open to all gardeners, offering seeds of all types of perennial plants. Write for information, sending Long SASE for reply.
Catalog: See Notes, MO

Peter Pauls Nurseries
R. D. #2
Canandaigua, NY 14424
(716) 394-7397 TO/CC $15m
James & Patricia Pietropaolo

PLANTS SEEDS BOOKS
A good selection of **carnivorous plants**, and seeds thereof, as well as growing supplies, terrarium kits, plant collections and their two books on how to identify and grow carnivorous plants from seed to maturity. Featured are venus fly trap, sarracenias, droseras, darlingtonia, pinguiculas. (1957)
Catalog: Free(4 IRC), R&W, CAN/OV, SS:4-11, $5m, HYB, bn
Nursery: Aug-June, By Appointment Only
Garden: Sales Area, By Appointment Only

Phipps African Violets
R. R. #1
Paris, ON, Canada N3L 3E1
(519) 442-2870 TO/CC $15m
Marie Phipps

PLANTS SUPPLIES
A huge selection of **African violets**, micro-minis, minis, standards and trailing varieties from leading hybridizers including Pat Tracy, Grangers, Lyons and more; over 10,000 plants to chose from -- plants and leaves available. Also growing supplies and fertilizer. (1973)
Catalog: $2d, R&W, USA/OV, SS:5-10, $15m, HYB
Nursery: All Year, Daily

Piccadilly Farm
1971 Whippoorwill Rd.
Bishop, GA 30621
(404) 769-6516 TO $20m
Sam & Carleen Jones

PLANTS
A small selection of **perennials** for Southern gardens -- hostas, helleborus orientalis (Lenten rose) and Ophiopogon japonicus (mondo grass) can be shipped; other perennials available only at the nursery. Brief plant descriptions. (1979)
Catalog: $1d, SS:4-10, $20m
Nursery: April-June, Sa-Su, Call Ahead
Garden: April-June, Sa-Su, Call Ahead

Pick's Ginseng
Crawford Street
Tomkinsville, KY 42167
(502) 487-6441
Morris Pickerel, Sr.

PLANTS SEEDS BOOKS
Offers **ginseng** roots and seeds, goldenseal and comfrey roots and books on their uses. Also buys ginseng roots.
Catalog: R&W, CAN, SS:9-12, $18m
Nursery: All Year, Daily, Call Ahead
Garden: Spring, Daily, Call Ahead

Pickering Nurseries Inc.
670 Kingston Rd. (Hwy. 2)
Pickering, ON, Canada L1V 1A6
(416) 839-2111
Joseph G. Schraven

PLANTS
An extensive list of **roses** -- hybrid tea, floribunda and old garden roses, with tables of information for size, ARA rating, fragrance and color and a section on how to winterize roses in very cold climates. Many roses shown in color photographs. (1956)
Catalog: $2, R&W, USA/OV, SS:10-4, $12m
Nursery: All Year, Call Ahead

Piedmont Gardens
533-577 Piedmont Street
Waterbury, CT 06706
(203) 754-8534 or 3535 TO/CC
Henry & Philip Payne

PLANTS
A good selection of **hostas**:, grouped by leaf size and briefly but well described. They also have a nice selection of hardy ferns and a few other native woodland plants. (1970)
Catalog: $.50, R&W, CAN, SS:4-9, HYB, bn/cn
Nursery: April-Sept, M-F, Call Ahead
Garden: April-Sept, M-F, Call Ahead

Piedmont Plant Company
P. O. Box 424
807 N. Washington St.
Albany, GA 31703
(912) 435-0766 or 883-7029 TO/CC $10m
DuVernet, Jones & Parker

PLANTS
Offers 56 varieties of **vegetable plants** -- onions, cabbage, lettuce, broccoli, cauliflower, tomatoes, peppers and eggplant: some illustrated in color, all well described. Also sells collections and complete vegetable gardens; can't ship to Western States. (1906)
Catalog: Free, R&W, MO, SS:4-6

Pine Ridge Garden Gallery
P. O. Box 222, Brock Rd. N.
Pickering, ON, Canada L1V 2R4
(416) 683-5952 TO/CC
John Patterson

PLANTS
A broad selection of **geraniums**: novelty bloom types, fancy leaf, miniature and dwarf, ivy, regal, scented, species pelargoniums and geraniums. Each plant is very briefly described. (1970)
Catalog: $1, SS:4-10
Nursery: All Year, Daily (except last week of December)
Garden: All Year, Daily

Pinetree Garden Seeds
Route 100, N
New Gloucester, ME 04260
(207) 926-3400
Dick Meiners

SEEDS BOOKS SUPPLIES TOOLS BULBS
Catalog offers a broad selection of **flower and vegetable** seed in smaller, less expensive packets -- specializes in space-saving vegetable cultivars: well described in informative catalog. Also sells Dutch bulbs, tools and supplies and many books on gardening and self-sufficiency. (1979)
Catalog: Free, CAN/OV, bn
Nursery: Summer, Tu-F: Rest of Year, M-F
Garden: Spring-Summer, Tu-F

Pixie Treasures Miniature Rose Nursery
4121 Prospect Ave.
Yorba Linda, CA 92686
(714) 993-6780 TO/CC $10m
Dorothy Cralle & Laurie Chaffin

PLANTS
A huge selection of **miniature roses** -- over 125 varieties, including their own hybrids. Many are illustrated in the color catalog; all are well described. They also offer several special collections. (1972)
Catalog: $1d, SS:AY, $10m, HYB
Nursery: All Year, M-Sa
Garden: April-Nov, M-Sa

Plant Factory
2414 St. Charles Place
Cinnaminson, NJ 08077
(609) 829-5311
Roger Bower, Jr.

PLANTS SUPPLIES
Small nursery specializes in **African violets, episcias and rex begonias**: the catalog I received listed only violets, so specify which plants you are interested in. Offers a nice selection of violets and all the necessary supplies for growing them. (1985)
Catalog: Long SASE, R&W, SS:5-10, $10m, HYB
Nursery: By Appointment Only
Garden: By Appointment Only

The Plant Kingdom
P. O. Box 7273
Lincoln Acres, CA 92047
(619) 267-1991
Patrick J. Worley

PLANTS
A very broad selection of **tropical and greenhouse plants** -- begonias, gesneriads, sinningias, nematanthus, shrubs and vines, including a huge selection of passionflowers and plants for bonsai: all well described, many are award-winning hybrids.
Catalog: $1, CAN/OV, SS:5-9, $10m, HYB, bn

The Plant Shop's Botanical Gardens
18007 Topham St.
Reseda, CA 91335
(213) 881-4831
Bob Cole & Bill Cook

PLANTS
List offers many kinds of **orchid seedlings, both species and hybrids**: good plant descriptions. Nursery offers many tropical plants not listed in the mail order list; they will ship plants purchased at nursery.
Nursery: All Year, W-M

For Explanations of Abbreviations/Codes Used In Listings See Bookmark or Inside Covers

Plant Villa
16 Fullerton
Belleville, IL 62221
(618) 235-6694
Wayne Guttersohn

PLANTS
A long list of **African violets** offered as starter plants or fresh cut leaves: well described. Also offers other gesneriads such as columneas, aeschynanthus, episcias and compact gloxinias.
Catalog: $.35, R&W, SS:4-10, HYB
Nursery: All Year, By Appointment Only
Garden: All Year, By Appointment Only

Plants 'n' Things
R. R. 2
Pollock Road
Keswick, ON, Canada L4P 3E9
(416) 476-7011
Jackie Patterson

PLANTS SUPPLIES
Offers **African violets, streptocarpus, episcias, miniature sinningias**, aeschynanthus, kohleria and other gesneriads: each plant well described. Also sells miniature begonias and indoor growing supplies.
Catalog: $1, USA/OV, SS:4-10, $20m
Nursery: All Year, Daily, Call Ahead

Plants Etcetera

See Hamm, Robert B.

Plants of the Southwest
1812 Second St.
Santa Fe, NM 87501
(505) 983-1548 TO/CC $20m
Gail Haggard

SEEDS BOOKS
Catalog full of landscaping and cultural information, with the object of suggesting water-saving gardens. Offers seeds of **native trees and shrubs, wildflowers, grasses, cacti and succulents -- also native vegetable seeds** and recipes for New Mexican foods. Very useful in the Southwest! (1977)
Catalog: $l.50, R&W, CAN/OV, HYB, bn/cn
Nursery: All Year, Daily
Garden: May-Sept, Daily

Plants of the Wild
P. O. Box 866
Willard Field
Tekoa, WA 99033
Palouse Seed Co.

PLANTS
Broad selection of seedling **Western native trees and shrubs**: all well described. Minimum order is ten plants of each species; plants are useful for natural landscaping, wildlife cover, erosion control and reclamation.
Catalog: Long SASE, R&W, SS:Spr & Fall, $10m, bn/cn
Nursery: All Year, M-F, By Appointment Only
Garden: Spring, M-F, By Appointment Only

Pleasant Hill African Violets
Route 1, Box 73
Brenham, TX 77833
(409) 836-9736
Ruth Goeke

PLANTS SUPPLIES
"**African violet leaves and plants**, episcia stolons and other gesneriads -- aeschynanthus, nemantanthus and columnea cuttings, also some sinningias -- at the moment have about 200 varieties of episcias." Large selection: brief plant descriptions. Also offers growing supplies.
Catalog: $.75, R&W, MO, SS:W

Pleasure Iris Gardens
425 East Luna
Chaparral, NM 88021
(505) 824-4299
Henry & Luella Danielson

PLANTS
A very extensive list of **iris** for collectors, including a number of their own hybrids -- bearded iris of all types, Japanese iris, Siberian iris, aril and arilbred, Louisiana, Sino-Siberian and spuria, oncocylus and regelia species and hybrids: all briefly described, with cultural notes. (1938)
Catalog: $1d, CAN/OV, SS:7-9, HYB
Garden: April, Call Ahead

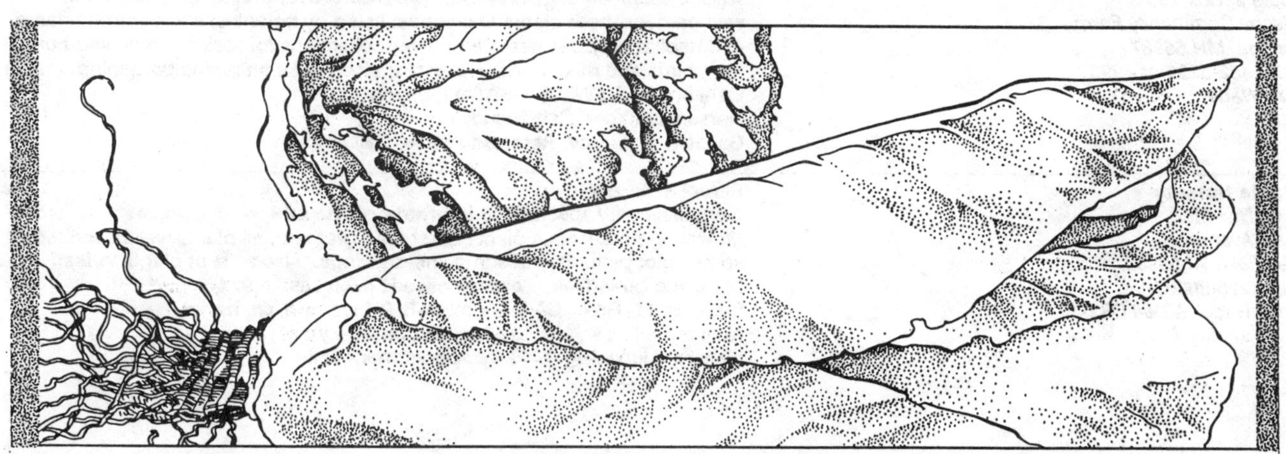

© 1987 Le Marche Seeds Intl. Artist: Amy Pertshuk

The Plumeria People
P. O. Box 820014
Houston, TX 77282-0014
(713) 496-2352
Mary Helen Eggenberger

PLANTS BOOKS SUPPLIES BULBS
Tropical plant specialists: plumerias, bougainvillea, gingers, hibiscus, tender bulbs, daylilies: all very well described. Also a few books on growing tropical plants, including their own "Handbook on Plumeria Culture", and some growing supplies. (1981)
Catalog: $1, R&W, CAN/OV, SS:3-10, $15m, cn/bn
Nursery: By Appointment Only
Garden: By Appointment Only

Pollen Bank
2065 Walnut Blvd.
Walnut Creek, CA 94596
(415) 939-7744
Jack S. Romine

PLANTS
A former President of the California Horticultural Society, Jack is noted as a hybridizer of **daylilies**: he sells unusual tetraploid conversions and seedlings for hybridizers. Pretty special stuff, but hybridizing daylilies seems to be a national mania. Detailed family trees given.
Catalog: Long SASE, SS:W, $20m
Nursery: All Year, M-Sa, By Appointment Only

Pony Creek Nursery
Tilleda, WI 54978
(715) 787-3889 TO/CC
Mildred Maahs

PLANTS SEEDS BOOKS SUPPLIES
Tabloid catalog lists a wide selection of **fruit and nut trees**, ornamental shrubs, berries, flower and vegetable seeds, books, growing supplies and beneficial insects: all well described. Plants best suited to the Midwest; cannot ship to CA. (1950)
Catalog: Free, SS:5-10, $10m, cn/bn
Nursery: April-Sept, Daily
Garden: Growing Area, Daily

Porter & Son
P. O. Box 104
1510 E. Washington St.
Stephensville, TX 76401-0104
Gene Porter

SEEDS BOOKS SUPPLIES
A good selection of **vegetable and flower** seeds for the South, especially **melons, tomatoes and hot peppers**; each variety well described. Also a good selection of gardening supplies, including drip irrigation, and gardening books. (1912)
Catalog: Free, SS:1-4, 10-11, $3m
Nursery: All Year, M-F, Sa am
Garden: Spring-Summer, M-F, Sa am

Possum Trot Tropical Fruit Nursery
14955 SW 214th St.
Miami, FL 33187
(305) 251-5040
Robert Barnum

PLANTS
Tropical fruit for climates which never freeze; a good selection on a price list with no descriptions. Due to problems with shipping, they will not ship in the U.S. except for large shipments for which the buyer is willing to pay air freight. Cannot ship to CA.
Catalog: Long SASE, R&W, CAN/OV, SS:W, $20m
Nursery: All Year, Daily
Garden: All Year, Daily

Powell's Gardens
Route 3, Box 21
Highway 70
Princeton, NC 27569
(919) 936-4421
S. E. Powell

PLANTS
A huge selection of **iris, many daylilies and hosta**, a broad selection of **perennials, dwarf conifers, trees and shrubs**: the pages are tightly packed with only the briefest descriptions -- a true collectors' list. (1953)
Catalog: $1.50, bn/cn
Nursery: All Year, M-Sa: April-June, Su
Garden: May-June, Daily

Prairie Moon Nursery
Route 3, Box 163
Wiscoy Community Farm
Winona, MN 55987
(507) 452-5231 or 4990
Alan Wade

PLANTS SEEDS BOOKS
A good selection of **grasses and wildflowers** for prairie restoration and wild gardens, both plants and seeds: listed by botanical and common name and habitat only. Several forb mixes, collections for rock gardens and hummingbirds and mixed prairie grasses; also books on prairie gardening. (1983)
Catalog: $1, R&W, SS:4-5,10-11, bn/cn
Nursery: All Year, Call Ahead
Garden: April-Nov, Restored Prairie, Call Ahead

Prairie Nursery
P. O. Box 365
Dyke Avenue
Westfield, WI 53964
(608) 296-3679
Brian Bader & Neil Diboll

PLANTS SEEDS
A small nursery specializing in **prairie plants and seed, grasses and forbs** (flowering herbaceous plants other than grasses): all plants well described, some color pictures and some line drawings. Also a list of plants to feed birds and butterflies. Sells only seeds overseas. (1974)
Catalog: $1, R&W, CAN/OV, SS:4-5, 9-11, $15m, cn/bn
Nursery: All Year, M-F, By Appointment Only
Garden: June-Aug, M-F, By Appointment Only

For Explanations of Abbreviations/Codes Used In Listings See Bookmark or Inside Covers

Prairie Ridge Nursery/CRM Ecosystems, Inc.
9738 Overland Road
Mt. Horeb, WI 53572
(608) 437-5245
Joyce Powers, Elizabeth Kanel

PLANTS SEEDS
Specializing in **prairie wildflowers, grasses and forbs**, both plants and seeds: plant information given in concise tables. They also sell plant and seed collections for various growing conditions and do consulting on the establishment of low-maintanence erosion-control plantings. (1974)
Catalog: $.50, R&W, CAN, SS:3-5, 9-11, $20m, bn/cn
Nursery: April-Nov, M-Sa
Garden: June-Aug, M-Sa

Prairie State Commodities
P. O. Box 6
Main Street
Trilla, IL 62469
(217) 235-4322
Charles L. Stodden

SEEDS
Seeds for agriculture, including **open-pollinated corn, alfalfa, clovers, soybeans, buckwheat, sorghum, lawn grasses and cover crops**: also sell seed cleaners, can supply "organically grown" on some items. All items sold in fairly large quantities. (1974)
Catalog: $1, R&W, $5m
Nursery: All Year, M-Sa, Call Ahead

Prentiss Court Ground Covers
P. O. Box 8662
Greenville, SC 29607
(803) 277-4037 TO/CC $15m
Lesesne & Gene Dickson

PLANTS
A small family enterprise offers **groundcover plants**: ajuga, cotoneaster, euonymous, ivy, hypericum, liriope, jasmine, vincas, sedums and more. Plants offered bare root or in pots, in quantities of fifty or more: no plant descriptions. (1978)
Catalog: $.25, R&W, MO, SS:4-10, $15m, bn

The Primrose Path
R. D. 2, Box 110
Scottdale, PA 15683
(412) 887-6756
Charles G. Oliver

PLANTS
A broad selection of **perennials**, including rock garden and woodland plants, all well described and with lists of plants for special uses. They have an active hybridization and selection program in phlox, heuchera, tiarella. They also run a Bed & Breakfast on premises – nice weekend! (1985)
Catalog: $1.50d, R&W, SS:W, HYB, bn/cn
Nursery: All Year, M-Sa, Call Ahead
Garden: April-Oct, M-Sa, Call Ahead

Protea Farms of California
P. O. Box 1806
Fallbrook, CA 92028
(619) 728-4297
Roger Boddaert

PLANTS BULBS
Offers **proteas, leucodendrons, leucospermums, banksias and tender bulbs**, as well as cut protea flowers. Plants are shown in b&w flier; ask for plant and price list, too.
Catalog: $1, R&W, SS:Spring,Fall, $50m, bn

Protea Gardens of Maui
R. R. 2, Box 389
Kula, Maui, HI 96790
(808) 878-6048, 878-6513
Bradish Johnson

PLANTS
Sells **protea** plants, fresh cut blooms and foliage and dried bouquets: color information sheet gives botanical and common names, no plant descriptions. Ask for a price sheet if you want to order plants. (1980)
Catalog: Free, R&W, CAN/OV, SS:AY, $20m, HYB, bn/cn
Nursery: All Year, Th-Su, Call Ahead
Garden: Oct-Feb, Tu-Su, By Appointment Only

Protea Seed & Nursery Suppliers
P. O. Box 98229
Sloanpark, South Africa 2152
011-705-1980
Mrs. I. M. Bruens

SEEDS BOOKS
Offers seeds of proteas, leucodendrons, banksias, ericas and other **South African native plants**: all briefly described. They will also try to supply seed not on their list on request. Also lists several books on growing these plants. (1979)
Catalog: 1 IRC, OV, bn
Nursery: Call Ahead

Putney Nursery, Inc.
Putney, VT 05346
(802) 387-5577

PLANTS SEEDS
Offers **perennials, ferns, herbs and wildflowers**, as well as wildflower and herb seeds.
Catalog: $1d

Qualitree Nursery
11110 Harlan Rd.
Eddyville, OR 97343
(503) 875-4192 TO $50m
Donna Frank

PLANTS
"We grow **conifers and deciduous seedlings** for Christmas tree growers, reforesters and small woodlot owners. We will grow almost any species on contract." Sells only in quantity. (1981)
Catalog: Free, R&W, CAN/OV, SS:11-2, $50m
Nursery: All Year, By Appointment Only
Garden: All Year, By Appointment Only

Quality Cactus
P. O. Box 319
Wisconsin Road (Donna)
Alamo, TX 78516
(512) 464-2357
Roger Brostowicz

PLANTS
Offers **cactus, succulents, epiphyllums, orchids, bromeliads, palms, cycads** and **bananas.**
Catalog: 2 FCS, R&W, SS:AY
Nursery: All Year, Daily, By Appointment Only

Quality Dutch Bulbs
P. O. Box 225
50 Lake Drive
Hillsdale, NJ 07642
(201) 391-6586 TO/CC $20m
Sophie Langeveld

BULBS
Dutch bulbs imported and distributed by the grower: a broad selection of hybrid tulips, daffodils, crocus, hyacinths and amaryllis in a color catalog offering collections and pre-season specials. (1982)
Catalog: Free, R&W, MO, SS:8-11, $5m, cn

Rainbow Gardens Nursery & Bookshop
P. O. Box 721
1574 Dorothea Road
La Habra, CA 90633-0721
(213) 697-1488 TO/CC $10m
C. H. Everson

PLANTS BOOKS
Specializes in **epiphyllums and other rainforest cacti**, hoyas and "holiday" cacti: plants well described and many shown in color photos. Bookshop offers a huge selection of books on cacti, succulents, bromeliads, ferns and greenhouse/propagation in a separate catalog. (1977)
Catalog: $1d(5 IRC), CAN/OV, SS:AY, $10m, bn/cn
Nursery: All Year, By Appointment Only
Garden: All Year, By Appointment Only

Rainforest Flora, Inc.
1927 W. Rosecrans Ave.
Gardena, CA 90249
(213) 515-5200 TO $30m
Jerrold Robinson

PLANTS
Offers **bromeliads, tillandsias, platyceriums, cycads, neoregelia** and other tropical plants. (1976)
Catalog: Long SASE, R&W, CAN/OV, SS:AY, $30m, HYB
Nursery: All Year, Daily
Garden: All Year, Daily

Rainforest Plantes et Fleurs, Inc.
1550 Roycroft St.
Honolulu, HI 96814
(808) 942-1550
Michael Miyashiro

PLANTS SEEDS
Growers and shippers of **hoyas and other tropical plants**; hoya list has good plant descriptions of rare varieties -- they can also provide seeds. Also ship plumeria and bougainvillea and will air ship tropical cut flowers and other flower arranging material. (1985)
Catalog: $1d(2 IRC), R&W, CAN/OV, SS:AY, $30m, HYB, bn
Nursery: All Year, M-Sa
Garden: By Appointment Only

Rainman Succulent Nursery
20101 Hanson Rd.
Ft. Bragg, CA 95437
(707) 964-5148 TO/CC $10m
Marlene P. Rainman

PLANTS
"I carry about 2,000 varieties, for the veriest beginner and the advanced expert -- many extreme rarities." Offers many African and Madagascar **succulents, many cactus and a selection of stapeliads**. No longer issues a list: send your "wish-list" with an SASE for reply. (1975)
Catalog: See notes, SS:5-11, $10m, bn
Nursery: Th-Su, Except Dec 20-Jan 5
Garden: Th-Su, Growing Area

Raintree Nursery
391 Butts Rd.
Morton, WA 98356
(206) 496-5410 TO/CC $10m
Sam Benowitz & Maida Richman

PLANTS BOOKS SUPPLIES
Offers only **edible plants, many fruit and nut varieties** in a very informative catalog full of orchard-lore, edible landscaping and cultural suggestions. They also offer some ornamental trees and shrubs, grafting and pruning supplies and books on fruit growing and edible landscaping. (1976)
Catalog: Free, R&W, SS:1-5, $10m, cn/bn
Nursery: Feb-April, Sa-Su
Garden: Growing Area, Sa-Su

Rainwater Violets
937 B S.E. Third
Lee's Summit, MO 64063
(816) 524-0131 TO/CC $20m
Janet Wickell

PLANTS SUPPLIES
A selection of **African violets** from prominent hybridizers -- available as plants, clumps or leaves: each plant well described. Also offers growing supplies, soil additives and pots. Offers chimeras, minis and semiminis, trailers and will be adding other gesneriads in 1988. (1980)
Catalog: FCS, CAN/OV, SS:5-10, HYB
Nursery: All Year, By Appointment Only

Rakestraw's Perennial Gardens
3094 S. Term Street
Burton, MI 48529

PLANTS
Offers **perennials, sedums, dwarf conifers, alpine plants** and plants for bonsai.
Catalog: $1d

Rancho de la Flor de Lis
P. O. Box 227
Cerrillos, NM 87010
Larry Anaya & Julian Wells

PLANTS
Iris: color catalog offers "the newest of the new, best of the old, growing 4,000 varieties."
Catalog: $1

R. J. Rands Orchids
421 Westlake Blvd.
Malibu, CA 90265
(818) 707-3410

PLANTS
Specializes in **species paphiopedilum** orchids.

Randy's Iris Garden
186 W. 800 N.
Sunset, UT 84015
Randy & Shelly Brown

PLANTS
A real collectors' list of **tall bearded and standard dwarf bearded iris**: wide selection, tiny print, brief descriptions! Many seem to be fairly recent introductions, other obviously old favorites – they also will put together special collections. (1984)
Catalog: 1 FCS, SS:7-8, $10m
Nursery: Call Ahead
Garden: Call Ahead

Rasland Farm
NC 82 at US 13
Godwin, NC 28344
(919) 567-2705
Sylvia Tippett

PLANTS SUPPLIES
A good selection of **herb plants and scented geraniums**: good but brief plant descriptions. Also a broad selection of herbal products: teas, potpourris, cooking herbs and more. No shipments to HI. (1981)
Catalog: $2, R&W, SS:4-6, $10m, cn/bn
Nursery: All Year, M-Sa
Garden: May-Sept, M-Sa

Rawlinson Garden Seed
269 College Rd.
Truro, NS, Canada B2N 2P6
(902) 843-3051
Bill Rawlinson

SEEDS
Catalog offers seeds for a broad selection of **vegetables, some herbs** and **flowers**: all very well described and with cultural information. Included is a heritage baking bean called Jacob's Cattle; it's got to be good! Catalog free in eastern Canada, $.60 other Canada, $1.00 cash U.S. and OV. (1979)
Catalog: See Notes, USA/OV, SS:1-6
Nursery: Feb-June, M-Sa

Ray's African Violets
Route 1, Box 244
College Station, TX 77840
(409) 690-1407 TO/CC $12m
Linda Ray

PLANTS SUPPLIES
Specializes in **miniature, semi-miniature and trailing African violets**, both plants and leaves: plants well described. Also offers growing supplies, self watering pots and fertilizer. (1974)
Catalog: $1d, R&W, CAN/OV, SS:4-11, $12m, HYB
Nursery: All Year, Daily, Call Ahead
Garden: All Year, Daily, Call Ahead

Steve Ray's Bamboo Gardens
909 79th Place So.
Birmingham, AL 35206
(205) 833-3052
Steve Ray

PLANTS
Specializes in **hardy bamboos**, over 25 varieties listed in the catalog: all very well described and many culms shown in b&w photographs. They have other varieties planted on 50 acres, and new varieties will become available as the supply builds up. (1976)
Catalog: $1, SS:9-2, $20m, bn/cn
Nursery: All Year, By Appointment Only
Garden: All Year, By Appointment Only

Rayner Bros.
P. O. Box 1617
Mt. Herman Road
Salisbury, MD 21801
(301) 742-1594 TO/CC
P. Curtis Massey

PLANTS
Offers a wide selection of **strawberries** for many climates: all well described with cultural information. Also offers dwarf fruit trees, blackberries, raspberries, blueberries, nut trees, asparagus roots, grapes and conifers in a color catalog.
Catalog: Free, MO, SS:2-5

Reasoner's
P. O. Box 1881
2501 53rd Avenue East
Oneco, FL 33558
(813) 756-1881
Bud Reasoner

PLANTS BOOKS
Here's a source for **hibiscus**; not the hardy variety but the lovely, tender kind that grows in Florida and Hawaii. They have a very large selection, described only by letter codes; scion wood also available. Also sell a book on growing hibiscus.
Catalog: Free, R&W, CAN/OV, SS:W, $5m
Nursery: All Year, Daily

Reath's Nursery
P. O. Box 521
100 Central Blvd.
Vulcan, MI 49892
(906) 563-9321
David Reath

PLANTS BULBS
Offers only peonies, **herbaceous and tree peonies**, including hybrids of Daphnis, Saunders and his own. Japanese tree peonies listed by Japanese cultivar name – a true collectors' list: catalog has color photographs and good plant descriptions. Has started selling special **daffodils**, too.
Catalog: $1, MO, SS:9-10, HYB

Recor Tree Seed
9164 Huron St.
Denver, CO 80221
(303) 428-2267 or 9883
Anvanette Recor

SEEDS
Offers seeds of **conifers and maples** (not Japanese) by common name: plants well described. Seeds offered in packets and in bulk. They will try to locate seeds of trees not listed and help customers with information if needed. (1981)
Catalog: Long SASE, R&W, MO, CAN, cn

Red Barn Dahlias
2035 East Newton St.
Seattle, WA 98112
(206) 322-0386 TO $10m
Germaine A. Arsove

PLANTS BOOKS
Small nursery offers a good selection of **dahlias**: many varieties and types, described in symbols with brief descriptions. Also sells collections and the informative "Dahlias of Today", published by the Puget Sound Dahlia Society. (1982)
Catalog: Long SASE W/2 FCS, R&W, MO, CAN/OV, SS:3-5, $5m

Red's Rhodies & Alpine Gardens
15920 S. W. Oberst Lane
Sherwood, OR 97140
(503) 625-6331 TO $11m
Dick & Karen Cavender

PLANTS
Offers selected clones of **Rhododendron occidentale** and a very long list of **sempervivums, sedums and jovibarba**: brief descriptions, several illustrated in color. Also sells daphne, vireya rhododendrons and French red and Dutch white shallots. (1977)
Catalog: $.50, R&W, CAN/OV, SS:AY, bn/cn
Nursery: All Year, Daily, Call Ahead
Garden: March-June, Call Ahead

Redfern's Nurseries

See McConnell Nurseries, Inc.

Joseph R. Redlinger Orchids
9236 S. W. 57 St.
Miami, FL 33156
(305) 661-4821

PLANTS
Sells hybrid **phalaenopsis** orchids in community pots.

Redlo Cacti
2315 N.W. Circle Blvd.
Corvallis, OR 97330
(503) 752-2910
Lorne & Lola Hanna

PLANTS SEEDS
Good selection of **cacti, succulents and lithops**: each given a good, brief description and many available in more than one size. Also offers rare "Ant Plants" (**Myrmecodia sp. and Hydnophytum sp.**) and some seeds. There are several pages of detailed cultural information. (1983)
Catalog: $1d(2 IRC), CAN/OV, SS:AY
Nursery: All Year, Daily, Call Ahead

Redwood City Seed Co.
P. O. Box 361
Redwood City, CA 94064
(415) 325-SEED
Craig & Sue Dremann

SEEDS BOOKS
Old fashioned open-pollinated **vegetables and herbs**, mostly developed before 1906; unusual varieties including Oriental types and Native American beans, corn, hot peppers and squash: these and other "useful" plants very well described with growing hints. Books on plants and organic gardening, too.
Catalog: $1(5 IRC), R&W, MO, CAN/OV, cn/bn

Rex Bulb Farms
P. O. Box 774
2568 Washington St.
Port Townsend, WA 98368
(206) 385-4280 TO/CC $20m
Nethalie Shaver

PLANTS BULBS
Color catalog offers a very wide selection of American-grown **lilies**, both species and hybrids, for garden, greenhouse or patio: each plant is well described and many are illustrated. Newest catalog has added dahlias, freesias and tulips. (1946)
Catalog: $1d, CAN/OV, SS:10-11,2-5, $20m, HYB
Nursery: All Year, M-F, Call Ahead

Rhapis Gardens
101 Raphis Rd., Box 287
Gregory, TX 78359
(512) 643-2061 or 5814 TO/CC $20m
Lynn McKamey

PLANTS BOOKS SUPPLIES
Sells **Rhapis excelsa**, grown in the U.S. by division, offering a number of varieties; these subtropical palms have been collectors' plants in Japan for centuries. Also offers cycads, Cissus rhombifolia and 'Ming' aralias: all plants well described. Also designer pottery and a book on Rhapis. (1976)
Catalog: $1, R&W, CAN/OV, SS:2-11, $18m
Nursery: All Year, M-F, Call Ahead
Garden: All Year, Growing Area , Call Ahead

Rhapis Palm Growers
P. O. Box 84
31350 Alta Vista Dr.
Redlands, CA 92373
(714) 794-3823 TO $25m
Leland & Anna Hollenberg

PLANTS
"We offer more than 40 named varieties of **Rhapis excelsa and R. humilis** palms, imported from Japan -- including variegated and all-green varieties." Color catalog is in Japanese, with anglicized Japanese species names given on price list. (1976)
Catalog: $2, R&W, CAN/OV, SS:AY, $25m
Nursery: All Year, By Appointment Only
Garden: All Year, By Appointment Only

For Explanations of Abbreviations/Codes Used In Listings See Bookmark or Inside Covers

The Rhodo Farm
See Horsley Rhododendron Nursery

Rice Creek Gardens
1315 66th Ave. N.E.
Minneapolis, MN 55432
(612) 574-1197
Betty Ann Mech

PLANTS BOOKS
A collectors' list of **alpine and rock garden plants**: dwarf conifers, groundcovers, dwarf flowering shrubs, dwarf ferns and waterside plants. Broad selection of very hardy plants: each briefly described. Also offers some books on gardening and prairie plants. (1972)
Catalog: $1, R&W, SS:5-6,9, $35m, HYB, bn
Nursery: May-Oct, M-Sa, Call Ahead
Garden: May-Oct, Call Ahead

Richters
P. O. Box 26
Highway 47
Goodwood, ON, Canada L0C 1A0
(416) 640-6677 TO/CC
Otto Richter

PLANTS SEEDS BOOKS SUPPLIES TOOLS
Catalog offers seed of many **herbs, wildflowers and everlasting flowers**, as well as dried herbs and spices, herbal gifts and books and posters on herbs; will ship plants in Canada and by UPS to the United States. All plants are well described, with information on culture and traditional uses. (1971)
Catalog: $2.50(6 IRC), R&W, USA/OV, cn/bn
Nursery: All Year, Daily
Garden: Summer, Daily

Rider Nurseries
Route 2, Box 90A
Farmington, IA 52626
(319) 878-3313 TO/CC
Geri & William Rider

PLANTS
Specializes in **strawberries**. Also offers asparagus, horseradish, rhubarb, grapes, raspberries, blackberries and hardy blueberries, some roses, fruit trees, dwarf fruit trees and ornamental shrubs. Very brief plant descriptions. Offers several 'collections' of fruit, berries and roses. (1930)
Catalog: Free, R&W, SS:3-5
Nursery: March-May, M-Sa, Call Ahead

Riverbend Orchids
14220 Lorraine Rd.
Biloxi, MS 39532
(601) 392-2699 TO/CC $15m
Morton Engelberg & James Phillips

PLANTS SUPPLIES
List offers a number of **cattleyas, including mini-cattleyas**, phalaenopsis and dendrobium hybrids, and some species orchids and miscellaneous other hybrids: briefly described. Sold in flasks, community pots and as individuals. Also sells some supplies.
Catalog: Free, R&W, SS:AY, $15m
Nursery: All Year, Daily, Call Ahead
Garden: All Year, Greenhouse, Call Ahead

Riverdale Iris Gardens
7124 Riverdale Rd.
Minneapolis, MN 55430
(612) 561-1748 TO $10m
Zula A. Hanson

PLANTS
Specializes in **dwarf and median iris** and offers a very large selection: each briefly described -- enough for the iris lover. Tough little plants raised in Minnesota, so you know they're hardy! (1968)
Catalog: $1d, R&W, CAN/OV, SS:7-9
Nursery: Summer, Daily, Call Ahead
Garden: May, Daily, Call Ahead

Riverside Gardens
R. R. #5
Saskatoon, SK, Canada S7K 3J8
(306) 374-0494
Art Delahey

BULBS
Small hobby operation raises only **Asiatic lilies** and offers Patterson, Fellner and other hybrids: about 40 cultivars, all well described. (1968)
Catalog: Free, R&W, USA/OV, SS:9-10, $10m
Nursery: Sept, Weekends & Eves., Call Ahead
Garden: July, Growing Area, By Appointment Only

Roberts' Gesneriads
5656 Calyn Road
Baltimore, MD 21228
(301) 788-7723
Barbara Roberts

PLANTS
Formerly offered many types of gesneriads, now specializes in **sinningias** and a few other rhizomatus and fibrous plants. However, their sinningia collection is huge, so collectors will be delighted with the selection. (1977)
Catalog: $1.50, CAN/OV, SS:4-6,9-10, $15m, HYB, bn

Clyde Robin Seed Co.
P. O. Box 2366
Castro Valley, CA 94546
(415) 581-3468
Clyde Robin

SEEDS
Color catalog offers a broad selection of **wildflowers**: plants briefly described. Also available are a number of native seed mixes for habitats all over the U.S. which would suit climates all over the world.
Catalog: $2, CAN/OV, bn/cn

Robinett Bulb Farm
7345 Healdsburg Ave., #9
Sebastopol, CA 95472
James A. Robinett

SEEDS BULBS
Seeds and bulbs of Mediterranean climate plants and California natives: brodaeia, calochortus, species lilies, nerines, fritillaries and others. Seeds and bulbs are nursery grown, and as they are small, may be in short supply. New list every August. (1983)
Catalog: $1d, MO, SS:9-12, $5m, HYB, bn/cn

Rocknoll Nursery
9210 U.S. 50 East
Hillsboro, OH 45133
(513) 393-1278 TO/CC $25m
Eleanor Saur

PLANTS SEEDS
Catalog offers a broad selection of **rock garden plants**, shade plants and native plants, some dwarf evergreens and flowering shrubs and perennials: very brief plant descriptions. Features hostas, dianthus, phlox, penstemons, iris, daylilies, epimediums. Separate seed list available. (1928)
Catalog: 2 FCS, SS:3-11, $20m, bn/cn
Nursery: March-Nov, M-Sa, Call Ahead

Rocky Meadow Orchard & Nursery
Route 1, Box 104
New Salisbury, IN 47161
(812) 347-2213
Ed Fackler

PLANTS SUPPLIES
Specializes in **apples (some antique cultivars), pears and plums** and rootstock for these fruit trees. Also does custom propagation, sells grafting supplies and does consultation on fruit culture. All fruit varieties are chosen with flavor as first priority. Informative catalog. (1975)
Catalog: Long SASE ($.50), R&W, SS:11-4, $25
Nursery: All Year, Tu-Su, Call Ahead
Garden: July-Oct, By Appointment Only

Rocky Waters Farm
4383 Pool Road
Winston, GA 30187
J. Gordon Barrow

PLANTS
A broad selection of **cactus and succulents** for collectors -- echinocereus, echinopsis, gymnocalyciums, lobivias, matucanas, copiapoas, rebutias, echiverias, euphorbias: no plant descriptions. Specializes in South American cacti. (1975)
Catalog: $1d, CAN/OV, SS:4-10, $10m, bn
Nursery: All Year, Th & Sa, Call Ahead
Garden: All Year, Th & Sa, Call Ahead

Rose Acres
6641 Crystal Blvd.
Diamond Springs, CA 95619
(916) 626-1722
Muriel Humenick

PLANTS
Collectors' list offers a selection of hybrid tea, shrub and old garden **roses** and a few species roses: descriptions in letter code with no key; collectors will know them. "Grandmother's Hat" sounds like a good one! Many of the plants are grown on their own roots. (1979)
Catalog: Long SASE, R&W, SS:10-2, $10m, HYB, bn
Nursery: All Year, Call Ahead
Garden: April-June, Call Ahead

The Rose Garden & Mini Rose Nursery
P. O. Box 560
SC Highway 560 (Austin St.)
Cross Hill, SC 29332-0560
(803) 998-4331 TO/CC $20m
Michael & Betty Williams

PLANTS
List offers a selection of award winning **miniature roses** chosen for best performance: each briefly but well described, a few illustrated in color, including their own new introductions. (1983)
Catalog: Free, R&W, SS:AY, HYB
Nursery: All Year, Daily, Call Ahead
Garden: May-Oct, Daily, Call Ahead

Rosehill Farm
Gregg Neck Road
Galena, MD 21635
(301) 648-5538 TO/CC $20m
Nelson Jolly

PLANTS BOOKS
Color catalog offers a good selection of **miniature roses** and several collections: each plant well described. They also sell the book "Miniature Roses" by Sean McCann. (1977)
Catalog: Free, R&W, CAN/OV, SS:AY, HYB
Nursery: All Year, Daily
Garden: March-Sept, Daily

The Rosemary House
120 So. Market Street
Mechanicsburg, PA 17055
(717) 697-5111 or 766-6581
Bertha Reppert

PLANTS SEEDS BOOKS SUPPLIES
Offers a good selection of **herb seeds, some herb plants, scented geraniums** and herbal gifts, supplies, teas, books, cards and kitchenware. Also cookbooks, herb garden plans, bus trips to herb gardens, tea parties and makings for potpourri. Can't ship plants to CA, mints to MT. (1968)
Catalog: $2, R&W, CAN/OV, SS:4-6,9-11, cn
Nursery: All Year, Tu-Sa
Garden: May-Oct, Tu-Sa

Roses by Fred Edmunds
6235 S. W. Kahle Rd.
Wilsonville, OR 97070
(503) 638-4671
Fred Edmunds

PLANTS
An informative color catalog offers a broad selection of modern hybrid tea, floribunda, grandiflora and climbing **roses**: all well described with cultural suggestions.
Catalog: Free, MO, CAN/OV, SS:11-5

Roses of Yesterday & Today
802 Brown's Valley Rd.
Watsonville, CA 95076-0398
(408) 724-3537 or 2755 TO/CC $20m
Patricia Stemler Wiley

PLANTS
Informative catalog lists a broad selection of "old garden" and many other types of **roses** -- modern shrubs, climbers and ramblers, hybrid teas and species: plants very well described, some illustrated in b&w. Included are rare, highly perfumed and some very hardy roses. (1948)
Catalog: $2($3 1st Cl.), CAN/OV, SS:1-5
Nursery: All Year, Daily, Call Ahead
Garden: May-June, Daily

For Explanations of Abbreviations/Codes Used In Listings See Bookmark or Inside Covers

Roslyn Nursery
P. O. Box 69
211 Burrs Lane
Dix Hills, NY 11746
(516) 643-9347 TO/CC $25m
Philip & Harriet Waldman

PLANTS
Collectors' list of hybrid and species rhododendrons, evergreen and deciduous azaleas, dwarf conifers, hollies, pieris, kalmias and other **ornamental shrubs**: each briefly described, some color photographs. A large selection of choice landscape plants. (1980)
Catalog: $2, CAN/OV, SS:4-6,9-12, $25m, bn
Nursery: All Year, Tu-Sa: April-June, Tu-Su
Garden: April-June, Growing Area, Tu-Su

Roswell Seed Co.
P. O. Box 725
115-117 South Main
Roswell, NM 88201
(505) 622-7701 TO/CC $5m
Jim, Ivan & W. L. Gill

SEEDS SUPPLIES
Regional seed company sells **vegetables, grains and grasses** for New Mexico, Arizona, Oklahoma and Utah. Hybrid and open-pollinated crops well described; offers a good variety of grains, cover crops, native grasses, some annual flowers and growing supplies. Can't ship to CA. (1900)
Catalog: Free, R&W, $5m
Nursery: All Year, M-Sa
Garden: All Year, M-Sa

Royal Gardens

See Dutch Gardens

Rupp Seeds, Inc.
5-17919 County Road 13
Wauseon, OH 43567
(419) 337-1841 TO/CC $5m
Roger L. Rupp

SEEDS
A big supplier to commercial farms, they will sell **sweet corn** seeds to home gardeners. They run extensive trials on sweet corn and sell seed from many sources; ask for the corn list for home growers. (1946)
Catalog: Free, R&W, MO, $5m

Jim & Irene Russ Quality Plants
P. O. Box 6450
Buell Road
Igo, CA 96047
(916) 396-2329
Jim & Irene Russ

PLANTS
A very broad selection of **sedums and sempervivums**: well described in a tightly packed collectors' list with good cultural information. Most of the plants are hardy to Zone 1 and come in many colors, leaf textures, even cobweb types. No shipping to Eastern Bloc countries. (1956)
Catalog: $.50(2 IRC), R&W, CAN/OV, SS:3-11, $10m, bn
Nursery: April-Oct, W-M, Call Ahead
Garden: March-May, W-M, Call Ahead

Rust-En-Vrede Nursery
P. O. Box 231
Constantia, South Africa 7848
(021) 74-2574
Hendrik van Zijl

SEEDS
Specializes in the seeds of **South African bulbous plants and disa orchids**: plants listed by botanical name with no descriptions, but collectors will know them. List includes lachenalia, cyrtanthus, moraea, romulea, babiana, species iris and gladiolus, geissorhiza, brunsvigia and many more. (1978)
Catalog: Free, MO, OV, SS:12-5, $15m, HYB, bn

Rutland of Kentucky (Mail Order)

See Dabney Herbs

S & H Organic Acres
P. O. Box 757
12125 Red Hills Rd.
Newberg, OR 97132
(503) 538-6530 TO/CC $56m
Marlene & Jim Courselle

PLANTS BOOKS
A brief list, but offers **"breathtaking" elephant garlic**, other garlics, shallots and Egyptian and potato onions, garlic braids and garlic books -- powerful stuff! (1971)
Catalog: Free, R&W, CAN/OV, SS:8-2
Nursery: Aug-Feb, Daily, Call Ahead

SLO Gardens
4816 Bridgecreek Rd.
San Luis Obispo, CA 93401
(805) 544-3122 TO $20m
Rudy Bachmann

PLANTS
A very extensive list of **hoyas**, many species and cultivars, offered as cuttings or rooted plants: all briefly described, some cultural information is included.
Catalog: 1 FCS($1 OV), CAN/OV, SS:2-11, $20m
Nursery: All Year, Sa-Su, Call Ahead
Garden: All Year, Sa-Su, Call Ahead

SPB Sales
P. O. Box 278
Nash, TN 75569
214 838-5616
Glen McFarlane

SEEDS SUPPLIES TOOLS
Regional seed company specializing in **vegetables for Southern gardens**, particularly tomatoes, melons, onions and onion plants, corn, peas and gourds: all briefly described. Also good selection of growing supplies. (1984)
Catalog: Free, R&W, MO, SS:2-4

Saginaw Valley Nut Nursery
8285 Dixie Hwy, Route 3
Birch Run, MI 48415
Richard D. Goldner

PLANTS SEEDS
A selection of **hardy nut trees** (to -30F) -- black and Persian walnuts, butternuts, buartnuts (butternut X heartnut), hickory, Chinese and Korean chestnuts, mulberries and pawpaws: all very briefly described. Cultivars also listed by state of origin. Trees, seed nuts and scions available. (1980)
Catalog: Long SASE, SS:10-12,4-5

St. Lawrence Nurseries
R. D. 2
Route 345, Potsdam-Madrid Rd.
Potsdam, NY 13676
(315) 265-6739
Diana & Bill MacKentley

PLANTS BOOKS
A broad selection of organically grown **cold-hardy fruit and nut trees**, other edible fruits, berries and scionwood: plants very well described, with comparative tables on hardiness, fruit color and harvest season in an informative catalog. Books on fruit culture available.
Catalog: Free, CAN, SS:4-5, cn/bn
Nursery: M-Sa, Call Ahead
Garden: June-March, Call Ahead

Salter Tree Farm
Route 2, Box 1332
Madison, FL 32340
(904) 973-6312
Charles E. Salter

PLANTS BULBS
A good selection of **Southern native trees and shrubs**, with some lilies, groundcovers and non-natives: there are no plant descriptions, but they are worth looking up elsewhere.
Catalog: Long SASE, R&W, SS:11-3, bn/cn
Nursery: M-Sa, Call Ahead
Garden: M-Sa, Growing Area, Call Ahead

San Luis Gardens

See SLO Gardens

Sanctuary Seeds/Folklore Herb Co.
2388 West 4th Ave.
Vancouver, BC, Canada V6K 1P1
(604) 733-4724
Maha Sarsthi

SEEDS BOOKS
Catalog offers a broad selection of open-pollinated and untreated **veget and herb seeds**, with detailed growing instructions; they do not print instructions on their seed packets. Also offers dried herbs, teas, natural foods and herb and garden books. (1970)
Catalog: $1, R&W, USA, cn/bn
Nursery: All Year, M-Sa

Sand Ridge Greenhouse
Route 2, Box 604
Collinsville, OK 74021
(918) 371-3822
Richard & Betty Govett

PLANTS
A small nursery specializing in **cactus**: a good selection of mammillaria, as well as notocactus, gymnocalyciums, echinocereus and corypanthas. Each plant well but briefly described. (1975)
Catalog: Long SASE, SS:4-10, $10m, bn/cn
Nursery: All Year, Daily, By Appointment Only
Garden: May-Sept, Daily, By Appointment Only

Sandhurst Seeds
R D 1, Box 34
Freedom, NY 14065
(716) 567-8929
Robert Shanks

SEEDS
A small new company with a wide variety of **tomato seeds**, nearly 70: all well described by size or use. Also sells seed of other 'tried and true' vegetables, all seed in small and inexpensive packages. He has the "Siberia" tomato for northern climates, a vine-type paste tomato and shallots. (1986)
Catalog: $.50d, MO

Sandy Mush Herb Nursery
Route 2, Surrett Cove Rd.
Leicester, NC 28748
(704) 683-2014 TO $25m
Fairman & Kate Jayne

PLANTS SEEDS BOOKS
A very broad selection of **herbs**, both seeds and plants: all well described in a nice italic hand. Also offers scented geraniums, iris, hostas, ornamental grasses, primulas, heathers, other perennials, herbal gifts and books. Many salvias, rosemarys, thymes, mints and much more. (1978)
Catalog: $2d, CAN, SS:AY, $10m
Nursery: All Year, Th-Sa, Call Ahead
Garden: May-Sept, Tu-Sa, Call Ahead

Santa Barbara Orchid Estate
1250 Orchid Drive
Santa Barbara, CA 93111
(805) 967-1284 or 3484 TO/CC
Anne P. Gripp

PLANTS SUPPLIES
Offers many **cymbidium orchids** which do well outdoors in coastal California, as well as a huge selection of **species and other orchids**, far too many to list! Each is briefly described; get out your orchid reference books. They also offer growing supplies and plants in flasks. (1957)
Catalog: Free, R&W, CAN/OV, SS:W, HYB
Nursery: All Year, Daily
Garden: All Year, Daily

Santa Barbara Seeds
P. O. Box 6520
Santa Barbara, CA 93160-6520
(805) 967-9679

SEEDS
Seed of a number of **tropical fruits** -- guavas, cherimoyas, carob, papayas, passion fruit, kiwis, sapote and several others: all well described. They are variously suited to tropical, sub-tropical and temperate climates. (1981)
Catalog: Long SASE(2 IRC), MO, CAN/OV, $3m, cn/bn

Santa Barbara Water Gardens
P. O. Box 4353
160 East Mountain Dr.
Santa Barbara, CA 93140
(805) 969-5129 or 5302
Barbara Dobbins & Stephne Sheatsley

PLANTS BOOKS SUPPLIES
A nice selection of **water lilies, lotus, aquatic and bog plants**: each very briefly described. Also sells books and supplies for water gardening and does local water garden design and construction. (1980)
Catalog: $1.50, R&W, CAN/OV, SS:W, cn/bn
Nursery: All Year, W-Sa
Garden: June-Aug, W-Sa

Savage Farms Nursery
P. O. Box 125
Highway 56 South
McMinnville, TN 37110
(615) 668-8902

PLANTS
Color catalog offers **fruit trees, nuts, grapes, berries** and a selection of ornamental trees and shrubs, roses, and conifers: each briefly described. Some of the plants cannot be shipped to CA, OR and WA. (1942)
Catalog: Free, SS:10-4, HYB, cn
Nursery: Oct-May, Daily
Garden: Oct-May, Daily

Savory's Greenhouse
5300 Whiting Ave.
Edina, MN 55435
(612) 941-8755
Arlene, Robert & Dennis Savory

PLANTS
Around two hundred varieties of **hosta**: plants briefly but well described, some illustrated in color. Many are their own introductions. They also sell daylilies and other perennials at the nursery. (1946)
Catalog: $1, R&W, CAN, SS:4-5,9-10, $25m, HYB, bn
Nursery: April-Oct, M-F: May, Daily
Garden: June-Aug, M-F, Call Ahead

Saxton Gardens
1 First Street
Saratoga Springs, NY 12866
Stanley Saxton

PLANTS BULBS
A broad selection of **daylilies and lilies** -- their own "Adirondack" daylily introductions, which are extra hardy, as well as others: plants well described, some illustrated in color. Ask for the lily list; they aren't in the daylily catalog. (1945)
Catalog: $.25, R&W, CAN, SS:5,9-10, $10m, HYB
Nursery: June-Oct, Daily, Call Ahead
Garden: July-Aug, By Appointment Only

John Scheepers, Inc.
63 Wall Street
New York, NY 10005
(212) 422-1177 or 2299

PLANTS BULBS
Issues seasonal catalogs offering **Dutch bulbs and summer blooming bulbs**, many illustrated in color and all well described. The spring catalog also offers many perennials as well as dahlias, begonias, lilies, gladiolus and daylilies.
Catalog: Free, MO

S. Scherer & Sons
104 Waterside Rd.
Northport, NY 11768
(516) 261-7432
Robert W. Scherer

PLANTS SUPPLIES
Offers everything necessary for a garden pool or pond: **waterlilies** and other aquatic plants, fiber glass pools, pool liners, fountain heads, pumps and low-voltage garden lights.
Catalog: Free, SS:4-12, cn/bn
Nursery: All Year, Daily, Call Ahead

Schreiner's Gardens
3625 Quinaby Rd. NE
Salem, OR 97303
(503) 393-3232
David Schreiner

PLANTS
Color catalog describes **tall bearded iris, "lilliputs" and intermediates** and offers a number of collections and cultural advice: all plants very well described, many illustrated. (1925)
Catalog: $2d, R&W, MO, CAN/OV, SS:7-9, $10m, HYB

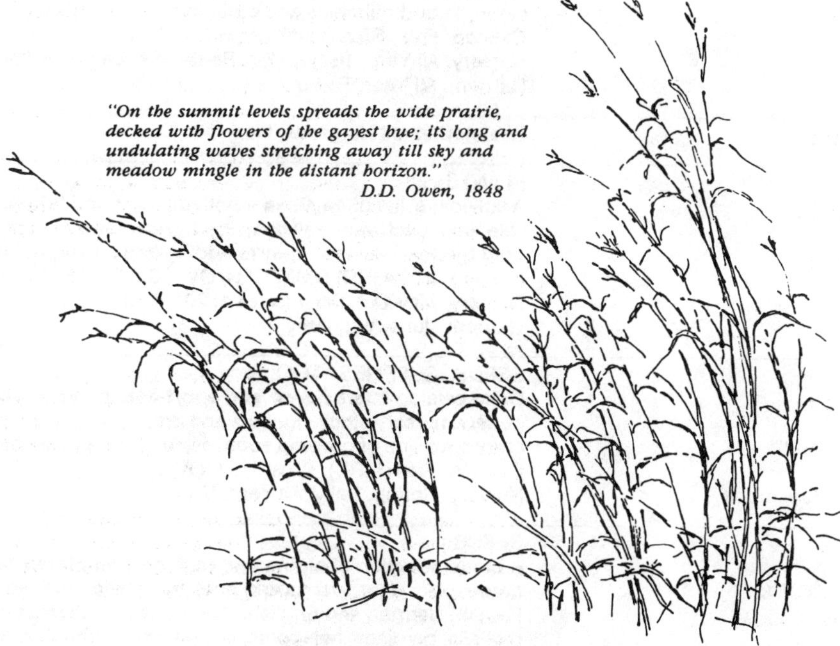

"On the summit levels spreads the wide prairie, decked with flowers of the gayest hue; its long and undulating waves stretching away till sky and meadow mingle in the distant horizon."
D.D. Owen, 1848

Schulz Cactus Gardens
1095 Easy St.
Morgan Hill, CA 95037
(408) 683-4489
Ernst Schulz

PLANTS
A broad selection of **cactus**: coryphanthus, echinocereus, escobaria, ferocactus, matucana, neochilenia, neoporteria, parodia and others, as well as a very large number of mammillaria: listed by botanical name only. (1979)
Catalog: Free, R&W, SS:AY, bn
Nursery: All Year, Daily, Call Ahead
Garden: All Year, Daily, Call Ahead

F. W. Schumacher Co.
36 Spring Hill Rd.
Sandwich, MA 02563-1023
(617) 888-0659
Donald H. Allen

SEEDS BOOKS
A very broad selection of seeds of **trees, shrubs, conifers, rhododendrons** and **azaleas** listed by botanical and common name, and with geographical source where important. Offers species maples, birches, dogwoods, cotoneasters, crabapples, species roses, viburnums and much more. Some books, too.
Catalog: $1, R&W, MO

Sea Breeze Orchids
P. O. Box 1416
Bayville, NY 11709
(516) 496-3513 or 628-2764

PLANTS
Specializes in **species and miniature hybrid orchids.**
Catalog: Free

Sea God Nurseries
P. O. Box 678
Geyserville, CA 95441
Raymond Burr, Robert Benevides

PLANTS
"We specialize in **cattleya seedlings** (3" pots to blooming sizes) but also offer ascocendas, phalaenopsis, vandas, etc." Plants briefly described in orchidese, with information on crosses.
Catalog: R&W, SS 4-10

Sea-Tac Gardens
20020 Des Moines Memorial Dr.
Seattle, WA 98198
(206) 824-3846
Louis & Patti Eckhoff

PLANTS
Collectors' list of **dahlias**, with information given in a compact table -- broad selection. This small nursery also sells **fuchsias** -- "something of interest while waiting for the dahlias to bloom." Their own introductions begin with "Sea" as in "Sea-Miss" a real winner. (1978)
Catalog: Long SASE, R&W, CAN/OV, SS:W, $10m, HYB
Nursery: Feb-Oct, Daily
Garden: Aug-Sept, Daily

Seaborn Del Dios Nursery
Route 3, Box 455
Willow Lane
Escondido, CA 92025
(619) 745-6945
Bill & Estie Seaborn

PLANTS BOOKS
A real collectors' list, just botanical names, but a huge selection of **bromeliads and related plants.** Also offers a color illustrated book on bromeliads and sells palms and cycads at the nursery.
Catalog: R&W, CAN/OV, bn
Nursery: All Year, W-M
Garden: All Year, W-M

Seagulls Landing Orchids
P. O. Box 388
Glen Head, NY 11545
(516) 367-6336 TO/CC $30m
Shell Kanzer

PLANTS
Specializes in hybridizing **"Mini Cats" and "Compact Cats"** -- cattleya hybrids which will bloom two to four times a year; they also sell standard cattleyas and miltonias and other hybrids. Plants well described.
Catalog: Free, R&W, CAN/OV, SS:4-11, HYB
Nursery: All Year, Tu-Su, 1702 Route 25A (Laurel Hollow)
Garden: All Year, Tu-Su

Sears McConnell

See McConnell Nurseries, Inc.

Seawright Gardens
134 Indian Hill
Carlisle, MA 01741
(617) 369-2172 TO/CC $15m
Robert D. Seawright

PLANTS
A collectors' list of **daylilies** -- both diploids and tetraploids -- a wide selection: each very well described. Includes eyed and blotched tetraploids bred by Don Stevens. They're adding hostas and will have a list soon. (1976)
Catalog: $1d(4 IRC) R&W, CAN/OV, SS:5-9, $15m, HYB
Nursery: May-Oct, Daily (sales at 201 Bedford Rd.)
Garden: June-Aug, Daily

Seed Centre Ltd.
Box 3867, Station D
14510 127th Street
Edmonton, AB, Canada T5L 4K1
(403) 456-1052 or 1054
Wigglesworth, Moore & Van Brederode

SEEDS SUPPLIES TOOLS
Color catalog offers **flower and short-season vegetable seeds**, as well as general nursery stock, conifers and ornamental trees and shrubs. They also carry a full line of growing supplies, fertilizers, pest controls and tools.
Catalog: Free(1 IRC), R&W, USA/OV, SS:3-5, $5m
Nursery: Spring, Daily: All Year, M-Sa

Seedalp
P. O. Box 282
Meyrin, Geneve, Switzerland CH 1217
(022) 82 48 78
idem Kroner

SEEDS
A broad selection of **alpine and rock garden plants**, listed by botanical name: color descriptions and brief information in French, key to symbols in French, German and English. Anemones, aquilegias, campanulas, dianthus, digitalis, gentians, helebores, iris, poppies, primulas, pulsatillas. (1981)
Catalog: Free, R&W, OV, $5m, bn
Nursery: All Year, M-F, Call Ahead

For Explanations of Abbreviations/Codes Used In Listings See Bookmark or Inside Covers

Seeds Blum
Idaho City Stage
Boise, ID 83706
(208) 343-2202
Jan Blum

SEEDS BOOKS
Pronounced "Seeds Bloom" -- their catalog is informative, fun and helpful. They offer a number of **vegetables, annuals and perennials** for various conditions, advice on saving seed and opportunities for gardeners to test new "old" seeds and do research. They also sell books -- 'fireside friends'.
Catalog: $2, MO, CAN/OV, cn/bn

Seedway, Inc.
P. O. Box 250
Hall, NY 14463-0250
(315) 526-6391 TO/CC $10m

SEEDS
Color catalog of **vegetable and flower seeds**: each well described and available in quantities for home gardens to large commercial operations. They distribute "Bejo" vegetable seeds in the U.S. and parts of Canada and have their own varieties of sweet corn.
Catalog: Free, R&W, CAN/OV
Nursery: All Year, M-F

Select Seeds
81 Stickney Hill Rd.
Union, CT 06076
(203) 684-5655
Marilyn Barlow

SEEDS
This seed business grew out of an old-garden restoration project: they specialize in **old-fashioned and heirloom perennials** found in cottage and period gardens. Plants are well described -- there's not a 'cultivar' on the list; listed by botanical name with 'old' common names given. (1986)
Catalog: $1, CAN/OV, $2, cn/bn
Nursery: By Appointment Only
Garden: May-July, By Appointment Only

Sequoia Nursery - Moore Miniature Roses
2519 East Noble Ave.
Visalia, CA 93277
(209) 732-0190 or 0309 TO/CC $20m
Ralph S. Moore

PLANTS
Specializes in the hybrids of Ralph Moore, a pioneer in **miniature roses**, patenter of over 150 cultivars and the first to introduce striped flowers to minis. Color leaflets introduce new varieties twice a year and offer popular varieties for sale. (1937)
Catalog: Free, R&W, SS:AY, HYB
Nursery: All Year, M-F
Garden: May-Sept, M-F

Shackleton's Dahlias
30535 Division Dr.
Troutdale, OR 97060
(503) 663-5718
Steve & Linda Shackleton

PLANTS
"Heavy emphasis is placed on quality exhibition **dahlia** varieties -- we carry newer show varieties." A real collectors' list: information given in concise tables, with only color descriptions. (1981)
Catalog: 1 FCS, CAN/OV, SS:12-5, HYB
Nursery: Aug-Oct 10, Daily, Call Ahead
Garden: Sept, Call Ahead

Shady Hill Gardens
821 Walnut Street
Batavia, IL 60510-2999
(312) 879-5665
Chuck & Mary Ellen Heidgen

PLANTS SEEDS
Sells over 900 **geraniums and pelargoniums**, some of their own hybridizing. The selection is huge -- plants of all sizes, indoor and out, scented, variegated, stellar, ivy, dwarf and a nice selection of species geraniums. All plants briefly but well described; also sells seed. (1974)
Catalog: $1d, R&W, SS:3-6,10-11, $5m, HYB, cn
Nursery: All Year, M-Sa: April-June, Thanksgiving-Xmas, Su
Garden: All Year, Glasshouses, M-Sa

Shady Oaks Nursery
700 19th Ave. N.E.
Waseca, MN 56093
(507) 835-5033
Clayton R. Oslund

PLANTS BOOKS
This nursery specializes in **plants which grow well in shade** and offers a good selection of perennials, ferns, wildflowers, groundcovers, hostas and a number of shrubs which tolerate shade: each plant well described. Also offers several books on shade gardening and woodland plants. (1979)
Catalog: $1d, MO, SS:4-5,9-10, bn/cn

Shannon Gardens of Oak Brook Farm
P. O. Box 175
Northfield, MN 55057-0175
(612) 644-0598 Evenings
David E. Shannon

PLANTS
A hobby operation which has grown and grown -- a good selection of **tall bearded iris** for the collector: no plant descriptions. Be sure to call well in advance before trying to visit. Gardens are not at mailing address.
Catalog: SS:8, $10m
Garden: By Appointment Only: Call (612) 257-1153

Shanti Bithi Nursery
3047 High Ridge Road
Stamford, CT 06903
(203) 329-0768

PLANTS BOOKS SUPPLIES TOOLS
Importers of finished **bonsai**, some quite mature; also bonsai tools, pots, supplies and books and two styles of stone lantern.
Catalog: Free
Nursery: Call Ahead

Shanti Gardens

See Highlander Nursery

Shein's Cactus
3360 Drew Street
Marina, CA 93933
(408) 384-7765
Rubin & Anne Shein

PLANTS
A collectors' list of **cactus and succulents** by botanical name: no descriptions, but a large selection of rare and unusual plants. Offered are: copiapoa, coryphanthas, echinocereus, lobivia, gymnocalycium, parodia, rebutia, sulcorebutia, wiengartia, haworthias and many mammillarias.
Catalog: $1d, SS:3-10, $15m, bn
Nursery: Jan-Oct, Sa-Su: Call Ahead other days

Shelldance Nursery
2000 Cabrillo Highway (Hwy 1)
Pacifica, CA 94044
(415) 355-4845 TO/CC $25m
Michael Rothenberg

PLANTS
Offers a broad selection of **bromeliads, primarily tillandsias**, in a collectors' list: no plant descriptions. They suggest sending a "want-list", as sizes and varieties available change so rapidly. Sells aechmea, billbergia, guzmania, neoregelia, nidularium, vriesea and many other tillandsias.
Catalog: $1, R&W, CAN/OV, SS:AY, $25m, bn
Nursery: All Year, M-F, Call Ahead

Shepard Iris Garden
3342 W. Orangewood Ave.
Phoenix, AZ 85051
(602) 841-1231
Don & Bobbie Shepard

PLANTS
A collectors' list offers a very large selection of tall bearded, aril and arilbred, Louisiana, spuria and median **iris**: each plant briefly described with cultural notes. (1970)
Catalog: $1, SS:8-10, HYB
Nursery: April: By Appointment Only other times.
Garden: April, Sa & Su

Shepherd's Garden Seeds
7389 West Zayante Rd.
Felton, CA 95018
(408) 335-5400 TO/CC $15m
Renee Shepherd

SEEDS
Catalog offers European **vegetables** and collections of seeds for various tastes, i.e., Italian, French, Oriental, Mexican, salads and herbs. Each vegetable is carefully described with cultural information and recipes. Also sells everlasting, annual and **edible** flowers. (1983)
Catalog: $1, R&W, CAN,
Nursery: All Year, M-F, Call Ahead
Garden: June-Oct, M-F, Call Ahead

Sherwood's Greenhouses
P. O. Box 6
Sibley, LA 71073
(318) 377-3653
Sherwood Akin

PLANTS
Small nursery sells a selection of **unusual fruits**: mayhaws (hawthorne), jujubes, pawpaw, keriberry, citrange, chinknut. Among the more common fruits are hardy kiwis, pears, grapes and blackberries: all plants very briefly described on single page list. (1975)
Catalog: Long SASE, R&W, SS:1-2
Nursery: All Year, M-Sa, Call Ahead

Shissler Seed Company
R R #3
Elmwood, IL 61529
(309) 742-2211 TO $5m
Jeff Campbell

SEEDS
A big commercial seed supplier, sells seed of three varieties of **sweet** and one variety of **popcorn** to home gardeners. The sweet corns are Great Sweetness, Great Feast and Super Duper -- all their own hybrids. (1934)
Catalog: Long SASE, R&W, CAN/OV, SS:12-5, $5m, HYB
Nursery: By Appointment Only

R. H. Shumway Seedsman
P. O. Box 1
Graniteville, SC 29829
(803) 663-6276 TO/CC $15m
J. Wayne Hilton

SEEDS
An old seed house, they operate in both SC and Illinois (Box 777, Rockford, IL 61105). Catalog offers a good variety of open-pollinated **vegetables, annual and perennial flowers, green manure crops, fruit trees and berries**, illustrated with old-style line art. (1870)
Catalog: $1d(4 IRC), R&W, CAN/OV
Nursery: All Year, M-F: Jan-May, Sa, Call Ahead

Siegers Seed Co.
245 Imlay City Rd.
Imlay City, MI 48444
(313) 724-3155
Linda Timmer, Mgr.

SEEDS
Offers a wide selection of **vegetable** seed, both hybrid and open-pollinated, and some annual flowers as well. All seeds sold in bulk, minimum seems to be based on size of seed. Also offers growing supplies and seeders. (1957)
Catalog: Free, R&W, CAN
Nursery: All Year, M-F

Silvaseed Company, Inc.
P. O. Box 118
17 James Street
Roy, WA 98580
(206) 843-2246
David & Mike Gerdes

PLANTS SEEDS SUPPLIES
Sells only the seed of **Pacific Northwest conifer species**. Minimum order one pound of seed. List includes abies, chamaecyparis, pinus, pseudotsuga, picea, sequoia, thuja and tsuga species. They will do custom collecting and sell seedling trees. Sell "Styroblock" propagating containers. (1968)
Catalog: $1d, R&W, CAN/OV
Nursery: All Year, M-F, Call Ahead

For Explanations of Abbreviations/Codes Used In Listings See Bookmark or Inside Covers

David B. Sindt-Irises
See Adamgrove

Singers' Growing Things
17806 Plummer St.
Northridge, CA 91325
(818) 993-1903 TO/CC $15m
Joseph & Bertha Singer

PLANTS BOOKS SUPPLIES
"We specialize in **caudiciform plants**, plants suitable for bonsai and unusual succulents: sansevierias, monadeniums, pachypodiums, euphorbias and low light plants, as well as other unusual members of the plant kingdom, such as the Baobab tree." Also sells a number of books, some supplies. (1968)
Catalog: $1.50d($3 OV), R&W, CAN/OV, SS:AY, $15m, HYB, bn
Nursery: All Year, Th-Sa
Garden: All Year, Greenhouse, Th-Sa

Siskiyou Rare Plant Nursery
2825 Cummings Rd.
Medford, OR 97501
(503) 772-6846
J. Cobb Colley & Baldassare Mineo

PLANTS BOOKS
A collectors' catalog of **alpine and rock garden plants** offers about 1,500 plants, with rarer items available in small quantities: all very well described with cultural information. Fall supplement with plants for fall planting. Also sells books on alpine and rock garden plants. (1964)
Catalog: $2d, SS:3-5,9-10, bn
Nursery: All Year, By Appointment Only
Garden: April-May, Rock Garden, By Appointment Only

Skagit African Violets
3632 No. Woodland Pl.
Mt. Vernon, WA 98273
(206) 424-1750 TO $15m
Wayne Lindstrom

PLANTS SEEDS
Sells their own hybrid "Skagit African violets" -- plants, leaves and seed: all plants well described.
Catalog: Long SASE, R&W, CAN/OV, SS:5-10, $12m, HYB
Nursery: All Year, M-Sa, By Appointment Only
Garden: All Year, M-Sa, By Appointment Only

Anthony J. Skittone
1415 Eucalyptus
San Francisco, CA 94132
(415) 753-3332
Anthony Skittone

PLANTS SEEDS BOOKS BULBS
Huge selection of **spring and summer bulbs**, many rare species from around the world, including South Africa; also some perennials, iris, lilies and seed of Australian and South African plants. Many shown in color; all well described. Also books on Australian and South African plants. (1980)
Catalog: $1, R&W, CAN/OV, SS:8-4, bn
Nursery: Aug-May, M-F, By Appointment Only

Skyblue Nurseries
P. O. Box 18061
St. Paul, MN 55118-0061
(612) 454-8151
Gary D. Coley

PLANTS
A small nursery specializes in **hardy nuts**: black walnuts, shagbark hickory, heartnuts, butternuts, real American chestnuts and hybrid chestnuts: brief list, all well described. Due to unforeseen circumstances, they can't ship in 1987-88, but will refer inquiries to other sources.
Catalog: Free, MO, CAN, SS:4-5, $6m

Skyline Nursery
464-13 Heath Road
Sequim, WA 98382
(206) 683-2294
Herb Senft

PLANTS
Small nursery offers a good selection of **perennials, alpines and rock garden plants**: anemones, aquilegias, astilbes, campanulas, dianthus, gentians, hellebores, heucheras, penstemons, saxifrages, sisyrinchiums, violets and more. No plant descriptions. Willing to trade plants; write. (1982)
Catalog: $1d, R&W, SS:2-11, $15m, HYB
Nursery: All Year, Tu-Sa

Slocum Water Gardens
1101 Cypress Gardens Blvd.
Winter Haven, FL 33880-6099
(813) 293-7151
Peter D. Slocum

PLANTS BOOKS SUPPLIES
Color catalog offers a wide selection of **water lilies and lotus**, aquatic and bog plants and aquarium plants: all well described. Also offers growing supplies and books for water gardening.
Catalog: $2, R&W, CAN/OV, SS:4-10
Nursery: All Year, M-F: Sa, 1-4
Garden: June-Nov, M-Sa

Smith Nursery Co.
P. O. Box 515
Charles City, IA 50616
(515) 228-3239
Bill Smith

PLANTS
A good selection of **ornamental shrubs and trees** in small sizes: list I received had a jumble of common and botanical names: dogwoods, elderberries, lilacs, euonymus, sumacs, birch, linden, locust, species maples, poplars and willows among others. (1962)
Catalog: Free, R&W, CAN, SS:10-6
Nursery: All Year, M-Sa

Soergel Greenhouses
2573 Brandt School Rd.
Wexford, PA 15090
(412) 935-2090 TO/CC $20m
Randy & Beth Soergel

PLANTS
New nursery sells **perennials**: a nice selection including Shasta daisies, dianthus, sedums, lychnis and others. Plant descriptions in concise tables; and a sheet of color photos comes with the plant list.
Catalog: Free, $20m, bn/cn
Nursery: All Year, Daily

Solar Green, Ltd.
Route 1, Box 115 A
Moore, ID 83255
(208) 554-2821
Patty Slayton

PLANTS
Offers **alpine, rock garden plants and perennials**: each plant very well described. A good selection of very hardy plants -- they also advertise as "Adventure in Cold Climate Gardening".
Catalog: $1.50d, MO, SS:5-6,9-10

Solomon Daylilies
105 Country Club Rd.
Newport News, VA 23606
(804) 595-3850
Sandra Solomon

PLANTS
Tetraploids, miniature and small-flowered, doubles, spiders, **daylilies** for both north and south: all daylilies from tiny to huge, "from oldies-but-goodies to the very newest." Plant descriptions given in concise but informative tables. A very large selection. (1981)
Catalog: Free, SS:4-5, 9-11
Nursery: March-Nov, Call Ahead
Garden: May-June, Call Ahead

Sonoma Antique Apple Nursery
4395 Westside Rd.
Healdsburg, CA 95448
(707) 433-6420 TO/CC $20m
Carolyn & Terry Harrison

PLANTS BOOKS
Offers old English and American cider **apples**, other varieties for cooking or eating and books on fruit growing and cider making. Will select trees suitable for espalier or train them for you. Adding other fruits: antique and Oriental pears, peaches and plums. Sells apples to taste, too.
Catalog: $1d, R&W, CAN, SS:1-4, $8m
Nursery: Feb-May, Sa-Su: By Appointment Only other times
Garden: Small Apple Orchard, By Appointment Only

Sonoma Horticultural Nursery
3970 Azalea Avenue
Sebastopol, CA 95472
(707) 823-6832 TO/CC $30m
Polo DeLorenzo & Warren Smith

PLANTS
Catalog lists a very broad selection of **rhododendrons, azaleas** and other acid-loving trees and shrubs: all plants well described with references to pedigree. Their display garden, which is beautiful, has two flowering **davidia** in the drive; they sometimes have them for sale. (1977)
Catalog: $1.50, R&W, CAN/OV, SS:10-4, HYB, bn
Nursery: All Year, Th-M
Garden: March-May, Th-M

South Florida Seed Supply
16361 Norris Road
Loxahatchee, FL 33470
(305) 790-1422
Carl Bates

SEEDS
Seeds of **tropical and sub-tropical trees and shrubs**: available only in large quantites, usually 1,000. Source of many palms, and poinciana, bauhinia, jacaranda, frangipani and more. Seedlings available at their nursery, called 'Plants for Tomorrow'. (1975)
Catalog: Free, CAN/OV, $25m, bn/cn
Nursery: All Year, M-F, Call Ahead

South Seas Nursery
P. O. Box 4974
1419 Lirio Avenue
Ventura, CA 93004
Rob Brokaw

PLANTS
New nursery sells a wide selection of **tropical fruits**: sapote, carambola, cherimoya, atemoya, feijoa, guava, litchi, loquat, macadamia, papaya, pitanga and others, including a dozen varieties of **avocado**. Plants are greenhouse grown, need a tropical or sub-tropical climate or greenhouse. (1985)
Catalog: Long SASE, R&W, CAN/OV, SS:AY, cn/bn
Nursery: All Year, M-F: Sa am

Southern Exposure
35 Minor Street
Beaumont, TX 77702
(409) 835-0644
Bob Whitman

PLANTS
Offers a huge selection of **cryptanthus**: 300 hybrids from Europe, Australia, the Orient and the U.S., as well as Brazilian species. Also sells aroids, bromeliads and philodendrons.
Catalog: 3 FCS, R&W, CAN/OV, SS:W
Nursery: All Year, Daily, By Appointment Only

Southern Exposure Seed Exchange
P. O. Box 158
North Garden, VA 22959
Jeff McCormack

SEEDS BOOKS SUPPLIES
Specializes in **vegetables for the mid-Atlantic region**, including old "family heirloom" varieties; all seeds are untreated by chemicals and open-pollinated: growing information is given for each, varieties well described. Have rare 'multiplier' onions and shallots, books and supplies. (1982)
Catalog: $2, MO, CAN/OV
Garden: Growing Area, By Appointment Only

Southern Seeds
The Vicarage, Sheffield
Canterbury, New Zealand 8173
(0516) 38 814
The Vestry, Malvern Parish

SEEDS
Specializes in **alpine and rock garden plants of New Zealand**, collected from the scree and tussock-grassland of the Waimakariri Catchment. Plants listed by botanical name only; list of reference books on New Zealand plants is included. Hebes, celmisias, coprosmas, schizeilemas, more. (1982)
Catalog: $2, OV, NZ$10m, bn
Nursery: By Appointment Only
Garden: By Appointment Only

For Explanations of Abbreviations/Codes Used In Listings See Bookmark or Inside Covers

Southmeadow Fruit Gardens
15310 Red Arrow Highway
Lakeside, MI 49116
(616) 469-2865
Theo Grootendorst

PLANTS BOOKS
Free list offers a huge selection of **fruit trees**, many of them antique varieties - apples, pears, peaches, plums, cherries, grapes, gooseberries, even medlars: no descriptions. Sells a detailed reference guide to antique fruit varieties for $8: offers 'conservation fruits' for wildlife. (1961)
Catalog: Free, SS:10-5, $14m
Nursery: All Year, M-F, Call Ahead

Southwest Seeds
200 Spring Road, Kempston
Bedford, England MK42 8ND
(0234) 58970
Doug & Vivi Rowland

SEEDS BOOKS
The ultimate collectors' list, thousands of **cactus, succulents** and other **desert plants**, densely typed in tiny print: no descriptions, enough to make make your heart sing! They specialize in habitat collected desert plant seed of all kinds, also sell books on desert and carnivorous plants. (1971)
Catalog: 2 IRC, MO, OV, bn
Nursery: All Year, Call Ahead
Garden: All Year, Call Ahead

Southwestern Native Seeds
P. O. Box 50503
Tucson, AZ 85703
Tim & Sally Walker

SEEDS
Collectors' list of about 385 species of **Southwestern native plants** "for gardens, nurseries, landscaping, botanical gardens and for many other uses." Information on type, outstanding qualities, size, hardiness and rarity are given in concise tables: many seeds are habitat collected. (1975)
Catalog: $1, MO, CAN/OV, bn

Specialty Seeds
P. O. Box 842
Lompoc, CA 93436
(805) 736-1741
John V. Donlon

SEEDS
Lompoc is a center of the California flower seed industry: this company sells seed of **annuals**: various poppies, marigolds, sweet peas, California wildflowers and others. Very brief plant descriptions, seeds are sold in collections of five packets.
Catalog: Free, R&W, MO, CAN/OV

Spring Garden or Spring Valley Nurseries

See McConnell Nurseries, Inc.

Spring Hill Nurseries Co.
P. O. Box 1758
Peoria, IL 61656
Spring Hill Nurseries Co, Inc.

PLANTS BULBS
Color catalog offers a broad selection of **perennials**, flowering shrubs, groundcovers and some roses, summer blooming bulbs and houseplants: all well described. Alternate address: 110 W. Elm St., Tipp City, OH 45371.
Catalog: Free, MO, SS:2-5,9-11

Square Root Nursery
4764 Deuel Rd.
Canandaigua, NY 14424
(716) 394-3140 TO/CC $15m
James Rose

PLANTS SUPPLIES
Grapes: seedless, wine, desert -- a good selection of cold-hardy varieties. Informative catalog has some color pictures and a lot of cultural information: each plant well described. Also offers some growing supplies. (1984)
Catalog: Free, R&W, CAN/OV, SS:3-5,10-12, HYB
Nursery: March-May, Oct-Dec, M-Sa, Call Ahead
Garden: Summer, Growing Area, M-Sa, Call Ahead

Squaw Mountain Gardens
36212 S.E. Squaw Mtn. Road
Estacada, OR 97023
(503) 630-5458 TO $25m
John & Joyce Hoekstra, Janis Noyes

PLANTS
A broad selection of **sedums, sempervivums** and some arachnoideums, calcareums, ciliosums, jovibarbas, mamoreums and tectorums: all briefly described with general cultural instructions. Sells **lewisias and saxifrage** and other rock garden perennials at the nursery. (1984)
Catalog: Free, R&W, SS:3-9, $10m, bn
Nursery: All Year, Daily, Call Ahead
Garden: All Year, Daily, Call Ahead

Stallings Exotic Nursery
910 Encinitas Blvd.
Encinitas, CA 92024
(619) 753-3079
Steve Brigham, Mail Order Mgr.

PLANTS BULBS
Hold your breath -- hibiscus, jasmines, gingers, ornamental grasses and bamboos, lilies, heliconias, bananas, palms, abutilons, bougainvilleas, cannas; they grow about 1,000 **tropical and sub-tropical plants**: all well described with growing suggestions. A collector's feast! (1945)
Catalog: $2d, CAN/OV, SS:4-11, $25m, bn
Nursery: All Year, Daily
Garden: All Year, Daily

Stanley & Sons Nursery, Inc.
11740 S.E. Orient Dr.
Boring, OR 97009
(503) 663-4391
Larry Stanley

PLANTS
Sixty varieties of **Kiwi plants**, several species and many cultivars; many hardy to Zone 4. Plants are well described by growth habit, flavor and appearance of fruit. (1976)
Catalog: Free, R&W, CAN/OV, SS:AY, HYB
Nursery: All Year, M-Sa, Call Ahead
Garden: Sept-Nov, M-Sa, Call Ahead

Stark Bro's Nurseries & Orchards Co.
Highway 54 West
Louisiana, MO 63353-0010
(314) 754-5511 or (800) 325-4180 TO/CC
Family Corporation

PLANTS SUPPLIES
This firm -- made famous by the "Delicious" apples they developed many years ago -- offers **fruit trees, grapes, ornamental trees and shrubs and roses** in a color catalog, including good plant descriptions and some cultural information. Lots of mouth-watering pictures of pies! (1816)
Catalog: Free, R&W, SS:2-5, 10-12, cn
Nursery: Feb-Dec, M-Sa

Stewart Orchids
P. O. Box 550
3376 Foothill Rd.
Carpinteria, CA 93013
(805) 684-5448 TO/CC $10m
Leo Holguin

PLANTS BOOKS SUPPLIES
Color catalog of **hybrid orchids** and special lists of paphiopedilums, cattleyas and phalaenopsis, a broad selection: all plants well described. Merged with Armacost & Royston in 1986; sixty years of experience. Also sells supplies and orchid books. (1926)
Catalog: $2, R&W, CAN/OV, SS:AY
Nursery: All Year, Daily
Garden: Sales Areas, Daily

Stillpoint Gardens
P. O. Box 24
McKnightstown, PA 17343
(717) 337-3520 TO/CC $20m
Alan and Gretchen Mead

BULBS
Offers **gladiolus and pixiolas**: listed by color and briefly described. Also offers collections and bulblets of individual varieties. They used to be Village Garden of Fairfax, Vt., then moved to Pennsylvania and started a new nursery and a Bed & Breakfast. (1986)
Catalog: Long SASE, R&W, MO, CAN/OV, SS:3-5

Stocking Rose Nursery
785 N. Capitol Ave.
San Jose, CA 95133
(408) 258-3606 TO/CC
George S. Haight

PLANTS SUPPLIES TOOLS
Broad selection of **hybrid tea roses, floribundas, climbers and tree roses**: all well described and some illustrated in color, with good cultural instructions. Also offers some miniature tree roses, supplies and gifts.
Catalog: Free, SS:12-4
Nursery: All Year, F-W
Garden: April-Nov, F-W

Stokes Seed Company
P. O. Box 548
Buffalo, NY 14240
(416) 688-4300 TO/CC

SEEDS SUPPLIES
A very informative catalog, aimed at the commercial farmer and grower, but also sells in smaller packets: each plant well described, with a lot of cultural information. They offer a huge selection of **vegetable and flower** seeds, some available precision sized or pelleted, and some supplies. (1881)
Catalog: Free, R&W, MO, bn/cn
Garden: July-Aug, Trial Gardens, Call Ahead

Stokes Seed Company
39 James Street
St. Catharines, ON, Canada L2R 6R6

SEEDS SUPPLIES
The Canadian division of the Stokes Seed Company of Buffalo, NY. The catalog is the same.
Catalog: Free, R&W, MO, bn/cn

Stonehurst Rare Plants
1 Stonehurst Ct.
Pomona, NY 10970
(914) 354-4049 or 0052
Howard Kellerman

PLANTS
A collector of **rare miniatures of dwarf conifers and Japanese maples**: the choice is staggering -- over 1,200 dwarf conifers and 200 Japanese maples. No plant descriptions, but at this level of specialization it's up to the buyers to have done their homework! This is heady stuff! (1975)
Catalog: $1, SS:4-6,9-11, $20m, bn
Nursery: April-Oct, By Appointment Only
Garden: April-Oct, By Appointment Only

Ed Storms, Inc.
P. O. Box 775
Azle, TX 76020
(817) 444-4121
Ed & Ruth Storms

PLANTS BOOKS SUPPLIES
A wide selection of **lithops, asclepiads, haworthias, euphorbias, mesembryanthemums and other succulents**: well to briefly described, illustrated in color or b&w. Collectors' catalog, with a few books, color photo sets, antique botanical prints, back issues of "Excelsa" and his own book. (1971)
Catalog: $1.50, R&W, MO, CAN/OV, SS:AY, $10m, HYB, bn

Stubbs Shrubs
23225 S.W. Bosky Dell Lane
West Linn, OR 97068
(503) 638-5048
Arthur & Eleanor Stubbs

PLANTS
Small nursery specializes in newer hybrid **evergreen azaleas** -- Kurume, Satsuki, Gable, Glenn Dale, Beltsville Dwarfs, Back Acres, Robin Hill, Linwood Hardy, Harris, North Tisbury and Greenwood: plants well described in an informative catalog. Offers about 600 varieties. (1978)
Catalog: $2d, R&W, SS:3-10
Nursery: All Year, Call Ahead
Garden: Spring, Daily, Call Ahead

For Explanations of Abbreviations/Codes Used In Listings See Bookmark or Inside Covers

Succulenta
P. O. Box 480325
Los Angeles, CA 90048
(213) 933-8676
Deborah Milne & Lykke Coleman

PLANTS
Collectors' lists of **cactus and succulents**, including rare haworthias and euphorbias: plants briefly described in their periodic lists of new and special items. No longer publishes a regular catalog; you can always send a "want-list". All plants are nursery propagated. (1978)
Catalog: $1, MO, SS:4-10, HYB, bn

Suni's Violets
4 Woodlake, South Meadows
Woodbury, CT 06798
(203) 266-0315
Suni Roveto

PLANTS SUPPLIES
African violets graded by ease of culture and offered in several sizes from leaves for rooting to full-grown bloomers: all briefly described. Also sells pots, supplies and custom-made pine plant stands. (1983)
Catalog: $1, MO, SS:4-10, $10m, HYB

Sunlight Gardens
Route 3, Box 286-B
Loudon, TN 37774
(615) 986-6071
Andrea Sessions & Marty Zenni

PLANTS BOOKS
Specializes in **wildflowers of Southeastern and Northeastern North America**: a nice selection, very well described, and with the easy ones pointed out. Also offers collections for special conditions and books on growing wildflowers and perennials. (1984)
Catalog: $1, R&W, SS:9-5, HYB, bn
Nursery: All Year, By Appointment Only
Garden: By Appointment Only

Sunnybrook Farms Nursery
P. O. Box 6
9448 Mayfield Rd.
Chesterland, OH 44026
(216) 729-7232 TO/CC $20m
Timothy Ruh & Martha Sickinger

PLANTS SEEDS BOOKS
Specializing in **herbs, scented geraniums, hoyas, ivies, cactus and houseplants**, they will be adding many perennials in their 1988 catalog. They also offer herb books and gifts and hold herb workshops at the nursery.(1928)
Catalog: $1d, R&W, CAN, SS:3-6,9-10, $10m, cn/bn
Nursery: All Year, Daily
Garden: July-Sept, Daily

Sunnyslope Gardens
8638 Huntington Dr.
San Gabriel, CA 91775
(818) 287-4071

PLANTS
Color catalog offers a good selection of **chrysanthemums** of many types, including spiders, cascades, brush, spoon, anemones, cushion types and even mums for bonsai culture. Also sells a selection of giant everblooming **carnations**; brief descriptions.
Catalog: Free, MO, SS:3-6 Mums:2-9 Carnations, $5m

Sunnyvale Cactus Nursery
679 Pearl Street
Reading, MA 01867
(617) 944-5959
Art Scarpa

PLANTS
Specializes in outdoor **cactus** hardy in New England, needing only protection from moisture during the winter -- most are **opuntias**: briefly but well described. Sells mail order only. (1982)
Catalog: Long SASE(2 IRC), R&W, CAN/OV, SS:5-9, $15m, bn

Sunrise Oriental Seed Co.
P. O. Box 10058
Elmwood, CT 06110-0058
Lucia Fu

PLANTS SEEDS BOOKS
Catalog, in both Chinese and English, offers over a hundred varieties of **Oriental vegetables**: also some flowers, sprouting seeds and gardening and cookbooks in Chinese and English. This year they have added a few hard-to-germinate plants. (1976)
Catalog: $1, R&W, MO, CAN, SS:4,10, cn/bn

Sunset Nursery, Inc.
4007 Elrod Avenue
Tampa, FL 33636-1610
(813) 839-7228 or 837-3003 TO/CC $20m
Robert L. & Vivian V. Perry

PLANTS
Offers 90 varieties of **bamboo**; not all plants available for shipping because of size. Will send fact sheets on growing bamboo with their price list. They are doing genetic research to create new forms and have two to date. (1949)
Catalog: Long SASE, R&W, CAN/OV, SS:W, $18m
Nursery: All Year, M-Sa, Call Ahead
Garden: All Year, M-Sa, Call Ahead

Sunshine Caladium Farms
P. O. Box 905
Sebring, FL 33870
(813) 385-0663 or 655-3530 TO/CC
Eldridge D. Pollard

BULBS
Color brochure offers about thirty varieties of **caladiums**: no plant descriptions, all illustrated. Favorite plants for color in hot summer areas.
Catalog: Free, R&W, MO, CAN, SS:1-5, 100 Bulb Min.

Sunshine Orchids International
Fruitland Road
Barre, MA 01005
(617) 355-2089

PLANTS
Orchid company which sells **African violets, episcias, columneas, fuchsias** and **geraniums** and other houseplants, including some orchids. (1978)
Catalog: $1d, R&W, CAN/OV, SS:W, HYB
Nursery: All Year, W-Su, Call Ahead

Sunswept Laboratories
P. O. Box 1913
Studio City, CA 91604
(818) 506-7271
Robert C. Hull

PLANTS
Broad selection of **hybrid and species orchids**; flask list includes broughtonias, cattleyas, epidendrums, laelias, miltonias, oncidiums, paphiopedilums, phalaenopsis, stanhopeas and other rarities: each briefly described. Also do custom seed-sowing and micropropagation. (1980)
Catalog: Free, CAN/OV, SS:AY, HYB
Nursery: By Appointment Only
Garden: By Appointment Only

Sutton Seeds, Ltd.
Hele Road
Torquay, Devon, England TQ2 7QJ
(0803) 62011
W. Coley, Asst. Mgr.

SEEDS
One of the oldest and largest English seed houses, offering a broad selection of **garden flowers and vegetables**: color catalog. Canadian customers should send their orders to Gardenimport, Inc. (in this section). Visitors to London should visit their shop at 33 Catherine St. near Covent Garden. (1806)
Catalog: Free, R&W, MO, OV, $10m

Swan Island Dahlias
P. O. Box 800
Canby, OR 97013
(503) 266-7711 TO/CC $10m
Nicholas, Ted & Margaret Gitts

PLANTS
Color catalog offers a broad selection of **dahlias**: many shown in photos and all well described. They offer several collections and, for the dahlia fanatic, a powdered drink made from dahlia tubers (caffeine-free). Good cultural and historical information on dahlias. (1930)
Catalog: $2d, CAN, SS:3-6, $10m
Nursery: All Year, M-F
Garden: Aug-Sept, Daylight Hours

The Sweetbriar
P. O. Box 25
13825 132nd N.E. (Kirkland)
Woodinville, WA 98072
(206) 821-2222
Tamara Buchanan

PLANTS BOOKS
A collectors' list of hybrid and species **rhododendrons**, grouped by color with information tables, and a selection of conifers and deciduous trees and shrubs: all well described. Also offers books. (1979)
Catalog: $2d, R&W, MO, CAN, SS:2-7,9-11, $20m, HYB, bn/cn

T & T Seeds, Ltd.
P. O. Box 1710
Winnepeg, MB, Canada R3C 3P6
(204) 943-8483 or 956-2777 TO/CC
P. J. & Kevin Twomey

PLANTS SEEDS SUPPLIES BULBS
Color catalog offers good selection of **vegetables, annuals and perennials**, summer blooming bulbs, perennial plants, trees, shrubs, vines, fruit trees and berries: all well described. They also carry a broad selection of growing supplies. Ship only seeds to the U.S. (1946)
Catalog: $1, MO, USA, SS:W
Nursery: All Year, M-Sa

A.P. & E.V. Tabraham
St. Mary's
Isles of Scilly, England TR21 0JY
(0720) 22759
A. P. Tabraham

SEEDS
The Tabrahams sell seed of their hybrid **fuchsias**, which they claim to be winter hardy in Britain--specify SEED list. They have a good selection, well described, and have added 'rock garden' fuchsias, 4-6 inches high. (1972)
Catalog: Free(3 IRC), OV, $10m, HYB
Nursery: By Appointment Only
Garden: May-June, By Appointment Only

Tansy Farm
R. R. 1, 5888 Else Rd.
Agassiz, BC, Canada V0M 1A0
(604) 796-9316
John Balf & Bonnie Schneider

PLANTS
Catalog offers over 300 **herbs and scented geraniums**: very good descriptions, suggested uses and cultural information. If you want just the free list/order form, send a self-addressed long envelope with a request. They sell at the Granville Island Market on Saturdays and Sundays.
Catalog: $1.50, USA/OV, SS:4-10, $12m, cn/bn
Nursery: April-Oct, By Appointment Only

Taylor's Herb Gardens
1535 Lone Oak Rd.
Vista, CA 92084
(619) 727-3485
Kent Taylor

PLANTS SEEDS
A wide selection of **herb plants and seeds**: each well described in an informative catalog with recipes, some plants illustrated in color. (1947)
Catalog: $1, R&W, SS:AY, $18m, cn/bn
Nursery: All Year, M-F

Ter-El Nursery
P. O. Box 112
Orefield, PA 18069
Cathy Bennett

PLANTS SUPPLIES
Small nursery offers a nice selection of **groundcovers, perennials** and **chrysanthemums**: all plants very well described. They also grow plants not listed and invite "want-lists" for special requests. Offers a few propagating and growing supplies. (1976)
Catalog: $1d, R&W, MO, SS:4-10, bn

For Explanations of Abbreviations/Codes Used In Listings See Bookmark or Inside Covers

Terrapin Springs Farm
P. O. Box 7454
Tifton, GA 31793
(912) 382-1134
John & Sharon Gibson

PLANTS
New nursery offers **rare and native plants for the Southeast**, including introductions from Asia: their first list offers species maples, callicarpas, dogwoods, hollies, crape myrtles, oaks, viburnums, vitex and other desirable plants. (1986)
Catalog: $1, SS:9-3, $10m

Territorial Seed Co.
P. O. Box 27
80030 Territorial Rd.
Lorane, OR 97451
(503) 942-9547 TO/CC $20
Tom Johns

SEEDS BOOKS TOOLS
Informative catalog specializes in **vegetables** for the maritime climate areas of Oregon, Washington, British Columbia and north coastal California. Also offers sprinklers, tools, books and a list of local organic fertilizer suppliers. Also **annuals, herbs and green manure crops**. (1979)
Catalog: Free, CAN, SS:1-9
Nursery: Mar-Aug, M-Sa
Garden: June-Aug, M-Sa

Thomasville Nurseries
P. O. Box 7
1842 Smith Avenue
Thomasville, GA 31799-0007
(912) 226-5568
A. Paul Hjort

PLANTS
Roses, native deciduous and evergreen azaleas, daylilies, liriope and ophiopogon: each well described and illustrated in color or b&w. Also has a large AARS test garden next to the nursery. (1898)
Catalog: Free, R&W, SS:W
Nursery: All Year, M-F: Dec-May, Su pm
Garden: Roses, April-Nov, Daylight Hours

Thompson & Morgan
P. O. Box 1308
Farraday & Gramme Avenues
Jackson, NJ 08527
(201) 363-2225, (800) 367-7333 TO/CC
Bruce J. Sangster

SEEDS
Color catalog with a huge selection of **plants of all types**: good descriptions of plants and good germination and cultural information; catalog creates yearnings on a grand scale. They have recently started a new magazine, "Growing from Seed"; see magazine section. (1855)
Catalog: Free, CAN/OV, bn/cn
Nursery: All Year, M-F

Tiki Nursery
P. O. Box 187
Fairview, NC 28730
(704) 628-2212

PLANTS
African violets, sinningias, achimenes, streptocarpus, begonias and fuchsias. Will send violet list only for long SASE.
Catalog: $1d, CAN
Nursery: By Appointment Only
Garden: By Appointment Only

Tilley's Nursery/The WaterWorks
111 E. Fairmount St.
Coopersburg, PA 18036
(215) 282-4784 TO/CC
Tom Tilley

PLANTS BOOKS SUPPLIES
Good selection of **water lilies, bog and aquatic plants**: all well described. They also sell pools, pond liners, water gardening supplies and books on how to go about it. (1975)
Catalog: $1, R&W, SS:3-10, cn/bn
Nursery: Spring & Summer, Daily, Call Ahead
Garden: June-Oct, Daily, Call Ahead

Tillinghast Seed Co.
P. O. Box 738
623 Morris St.
La Conner, WA 98257
(206) 466-3329
Arberta Lammers & Brian Scheuch

PLANTS SEEDS SUPPLIES BULBS
An old-fashioned garden emporium, offers **general nursery stock and seeds**: flower and vegetable seeds, fruit trees and berries, roses, herbs and bulbs and canning supplies. (1885)
Catalog: Free, CAN/OV, SS:10-4
Nursery: All Year, Daily

Tinari Greenhouses
P. O. Box 190
2325 Valley Road
Huntingdon Valley, PA 19006
(215) 947-0144
Frank & Anne Tinari

PLANTS BOOKS SUPPLIES
A good selection of **African violets** -- many are their own hybrids: all briefly described, many illustrated in color. Also sells books and growing supplies, including plant stands and carts.
Catalog: $.35, SS:5-10, HYB
Nursery: All Year, M-Sa: Oct-May, Su pm
Garden: All Year, M-Sa: Oct-May, Su

Tiny Petals Nursery
489 Minot Ave.
Chula Vista, CA 92010
(619) 422-0385 TO
Dee & Herb Bennett

PLANTS
A broad selection of **miniature roses**, featuring the hybrids of Dee Bennett: minis, micro-minis, trailers and climbers, all well described. Can't ship to AZ and FL, but will refer you to nurseries under contract.
Catalog: Free, SS:1-11, HYB
Nursery: All Year, Daily
Garden: Spring-Summer, Daily

Tolowa Nursery
360 Stephen Way
Williams, OR 97544
(503) 846-7327 TO
Mark Wheeler

PLANTS
A broad variety of **fruit trees**: antique apples, pears and Asian pears, figs and cherries, plums and prunes, apricots, persimmons, kiwis, various berries and grapes. Also offers walnuts, filberts, Chinese chestnuts, almonds, pecans, ornamental trees and rootstock for fruit trees: brief plant notes.
Catalog: Long SASE W/2 FCS, R&W, SS:12-3
Nursery: Dec-April, Daily, Call Ahead

Tomara African Violets
Route 3, Box 116
Fayette, MO 65248
(816) 248-3232
Mrs. R. D. Thompkin

PLANTS
African violets: hybrids by Fredette, Pittmann, Williams, Wrangles and other well known breeders.
Catalog: $.30
Nursery: Call Ahead: Su, By Appointment Only

Tomato Growers Supply Company
P. O. Box 2237
Fort Myers, FL 33902
(813) 332-4157 TO/CC $20m
Linda & Vincent Sapp

SEEDS BOOKS SUPPLIES
Over 150 varieties of **tomato** seed, growing supplies and books: all plants well described, with good general cultural instructions and days to maturity for each variety -- oh, the agony of choices, but they all sound so good it must be hard to go wrong! (1984)
Catalog: Free, MO, $2m

The Tomato Seed Company, Inc.
P. O. Box 323
Metuchen, NJ 08840
Martin Sloan

SEEDS
The ultimate in a world of specialization: **tomato** seed only. Varieties are listed by type and shape and are well described in a hand-lettered catalog; over one hundred varieties, hybrid, heirloom, red, yellow, large and small, round and plum -- I'm suddenly starving! (1983)
Catalog: Free, R&W, MO, CAN/OV

Tradewinds Nursery
P. O. Box 70
Calpella, CA 95418
(707) 485-0835
Gib & Diane Cooper

PLANTS
Offers a selection of **bamboos** -- Phyllostachys pubescens (Moso or Giant Timber Bamboo) and eight other varieties: arundinaria, chimonobambusa, sasa bambusa, pseudosasa and other phyllostachys. Also sells bamboo timber, 1/2 inch to 6 inches in diameter, for special projects. (1986)
Catalog: Free, CAN/OV, SS:AY, $40m, bn
Nursery: All Year, By Appointment Only
Garden: All Year, By Appointment Only

Tranquil Lake Nursery
45 River St.
Rehoboth, MA 02769-1395
(617) 336-6491 or 252-4310
Warren P. Leach & Philip A. Boucher

PLANTS BOOKS
Catalog offers a good selection of **daylilies, Japanese and Siberian iris**; many are recent introductions: plants are well described. Many more are available at the nursery; carries many older varieties and might be able to provide them if you send a "want-list". Also sells a few books. (1958)
Catalog: $.25, CAN/OV, SS:4-6,8-10, $10m, HYB
Nursery: April-Oct, Afternoons & Weekends, Call Ahead
Garden: May-Aug, Call Ahead

For Explanations of Abbreviations/Codes Used In Listings See Bookmark or Inside Covers

Trans Pacific Nursery
29870 Mill Creek Rd.
Sheridan, OR 97378
(503) 843-3588
Jackson Muldoon

PLANTS
A wide selection of **trees, shrubs, vines and perennials** from all over the world, many not easy to find: each plant well described. Among the plants are chorizzma, clianthus, cotula, dryandra, eucalyptus, kennedia, moraea, pleione, pandorea, rhodohypoxis, stylidium and Japanese maples. (1982)
Catalog: Free, R&W, CAN/OV, SS:W, $10m, bn
Nursery: All Year, Daily, Call Ahead

Transplant Nursery
Parkertown Rd.
Lavonia, GA 30553
(404) 356-8947
Mary, Jeff & Lisa Beasley

PLANTS
Collectors' list of Dexter rhododendrons, rare native deciduous azaleas and hybrid azaleas of James Harris, Robin Hill, Ralph Pennington, North Tisbury and several others: brief descriptions and some color photographs. Many are suitable for bonsai -- also offer **kalmia, leucothoe and pieris**. (1975)
Catalog: Free, R&W, CAN/OV, SS:10-4, $25m, HYB, bn
Nursery: April-May, Daily, Call Ahead
Garden: April-May, Daily, Call Ahead

Travis' Violets
P. O. Box 42
Ochlochnee, GA 31773-0042
(912) 574-5167 or 5236 TO/CC $25m
Travis Davis

PLANTS SUPPLIES
African violets, including their own hybrids and many others: Hortense's Honeys, Lyon's, Betty Bryant's and Fredettes included. Sells both leaves and plants: all well described. Also sell pots, fertilizer and a violet potting mix. (1980)
Catalog: $1d, R&W, CAN/OV, SS:W, $15m, HYB
Nursery: All Year, Daily, Call Ahead

Tregunno Seeds
126 Catharine St. North
Hamilton, ON, Canada L8R 1J4
(416) 528-5983
H. Tregunno

SEEDS SUPPLIES BULBS
A very broad selection of **vegetable and flower seeds** for home garden and commercial grower: brief plant descriptions, available in various quantites. Also sells gladiolus, tuberous begonias and lawn grass seed. Offers many garden supplies and fertilizers.
Catalog: Free, R&W, $10m
Nursery: All Year, M-Sa

William Tricker, Inc.
7125 Tanglewood Dr.
Independence, OH 44131
(216) 524-3491
Richard Lee

PLANTS BOOKS SUPPLIES
Color catalog of **water lilies and other aquatic and bog plants**, even a Victoria trickeri with leaves up to 6' across. In addition to a broad selection of plants, they sell books on water gardening, fancy fish, pool supplies and remedies in an informative catalog. (1895)
Catalog: $2d, R&W, CAN/OV, SS:AY, HYB, cn/bn
Nursery: All Year, Daily
Garden: May-Aug, Daily

Trillium Lane Nursery
18855 Trillium Lane
Ft. Bragg, CA 95437
(707) 964-3282
Bruce & Eleanor Philp

PLANTS
Rhododendrons; claims to offer 1,000 cultivars and varieties -- species, dwarf and standard hybrids. Issues no catalog, but you can send a "want-list".
Catalog: See notes

Triple Oaks Nursery
Route 47
Franklinville, NJ 08322
(609) 694-4272 TO/CC $15m
Ted & Lorraine Kiefer

PLANTS SUPPLIES
A list of **herb plants and scented geraniums**: no descriptions. Also offers lectures and classes on herbs and herb crafts at the nursery and a selection of herb products and essential oils.
Catalog: Long SASE, SS:3-11
Nursery: All Year, Daily
Garden: May-July, Daily

Tripple Brook Farm
37 Middle Road
Southampton, MA 01073
(413) 527-4626 (Eves.)
Stephen Breyer

PLANTS
Small nursery with a good selection of **Northeastern native plants**, hardy bamboos, fruiting mulberries and hardy kiwi, iris, flowering shrubs and more -- catalog full of information, as well as pix of plants and the nursery horse, cow, cat and dogs -- a delight!
Catalog: Free, R&W, CAN/OV, SS:4-11, bn
Nursery: By Appointment Only
Garden: Growing Area, By Appointment Only

Tropexotic Growers, Inc.

See Ivies of the World

Tropical Imports
43714 Road 415
Coarsegold, CA 93614
(209) 683-7097

PLANTS
Offers a huge selection of **tillandsias**.
Catalog: Free

Tropicals Unlimited
595 Uluhaku St.
Kailua, HI 96734
(808) 262-6040 TO $25m
Eileen J. Laughlin

PLANTS SEEDS BOOKS
Offers **tropical and greenhouse plants**, some orchids and seeds of tropical fruit. Also offers a few books on Hawaiian plants and gardens. (1980)
Catalog: $1, R&W, MO, SS:4-11, cn/bn

Tsang & Ma
P. O. Box 294
Belmont, CA 94002
(415) 595-2270 TO/CC $10m
Dave Tsang & Bill Sher

SEEDS BOOKS SUPPLIES TOOLS
Offers a selection of **Oriental vegetables**, seasonings, flavored oils and stir-fry sauces, kitchen equipment, utensils and dinnerware -- grow it, cook it, serve it, enjoy it! (1974)
Catalog: Free, R&W, MO, CAN/OV

Tucson Succulents
P. O. Box 5681
50 E. Blacklidge
Tucson, AZ 85705
Gene Joseph

PLANTS
A collectors' list of **succulents and cacti** -- run off on a computer with only botanical names, sizes and prices. Specializes in succulents of the Sonoran Desert, many grown from habitat collected seed. Has added a list of **lithops** to previous offerings. (1983)
Catalog: Long SASE, CAN, SS:4-10, $10m, bn
Nursery: All Year, Th-Sa
Garden: All Year, Th-Sa

Turnipseed Nursery Farms
P. O. Box 792
685 S. Glynn Street
Fayetteville, GA 30214
(404) 461-1654
Steven Stinchcomb

PLANTS
A nice selection of **groundcovers**: ajuga, euonymus, ivy, liriope, mondo grass, vinca minor and daylilies: each plant well described.
Catalog: SS:W, $25m

21st Century Gardens
P. O. Box 1378
Chino Valley, AZ 86323
(602) 636-5313
David R. Spence

PLANTS
Broad selection of **bearded iris** in all sizes, including the "Space-Age" iris of Lloyd Austin and newer hybrids of this type, which are horned, spooned or flounced. Plants well described, many shown in color. (1979)
Catalog: $2d, R&W, CAN/OV, SS:7-9, $5m
Nursery: By Appointment Only
Garden: By Appointment Only

Otis Twilley Seed Co.
P. O. Box 65
Trevose, PA 19047
(800) 622-7333 TO/CC $25m: (800) 232-7333 PA
Corporation (1978)

SEEDS SUPPLIES
Color catalog offers a large selection of **vegetables and garden flowers**: all very well described and with growing suggestions, available in packets or in bulk. Also offers growing supplies and the new seed company status symbol, tee shirts and caps. (1934)
Catalog: Free, R&W, MO, CAN/OV

Twin Peaks Seeds
1814 Dean Street
Eureka, CA 95501
(707) 442-6142
Mark & Susanne Moore

SEEDS
"Hardy, easy to grow, adaptable, **annual and perennial California native wildflowers**": small company, brief list, plants very well described. (1982)
Catalog: Long SASE, R&W, MO, CAN/OV, cn/bn

TyTy Plantation
P. O. Box 159
TyTy, GA 31795
(912) 386-8400 or 382-0404 TO/CC $5m
Patrick A. Malcolm

PLANTS BULBS
Color catalog offers a wide variety of cannas, crinums, lilies, daylilies, hymenocallis, gingers, caladiums, agapanthus, pansies, ferns and other perennials: plants illustrated and well described. There are hardy plants here as well as tender Southerners. (1833)
Catalog: Free, R&W, CAN/OV, SS:AY, $5m, HYB
Nursery: All Year, M-Sa
Garden: July-Nov, M-Sa

Upper Bank Nurseries
P. O. Box 486
Ridley Creek Rd. & Park Ave.
Media, PA 19063
(215) 566-0679 TO $10m
Wirt L. Thompson, Jr.

PLANTS
A nursery selling a nice selection of ornamental trees and shrubs, but they will ship only **bamboo**: eleven varieties of phyllostachys, arundinaria, pseudosasa, shibataea and sasa. No plant descriptions. (1925)
Catalog: Long SASE, R&W, SS:W, bn/cn
Nursery: All Year, M-F
Garden: Spring, M-F

Valente Gardens
RFD 2, Box 234
Dillingham Rd.
East Lebanon, ME 04027
(207) 457-2076
Ron & Cindy Valente

PLANTS
A small new nursery, shipping only **daylilies** at present, a nice selection of newer hybrids and miniatures: briefly described. Visitors to the nursery can buy and dig other perennials, including Siberian and Japanese iris and hostas. Daylilies shipped when it's nice weather in Maine. (1983)
Catalog: $.39 Stamps, SS:W
Nursery: April-Sept, Th-Su
Garden: May-Aug, Th-Su

For Explanations of Abbreviations/Codes Used in Listings See Bookmark or Inside Covers

Valley Creek Nursery
P. O. Box 364
15177 S. Log Cabin Rd.
Three Oaks, MI 49128
(616) 426-3283
Dennis & Mary Schroeder

PLANTS
Offers **herbs, groundcovers, hardy kiwis, miniature roses**. (1980)
Catalog: Free, R&W, SS:4-6,9-11, $10m
Nursery: May-Nov, Su-Th, By Appointment Only

Valley Nursery
P. O. Box 4845
2801 N. Montana Ave.
Helena, MT 59601
(406) 442-8460
Clayton Berg

PLANTS
"Best of old plus newer, hardier plants for cold climates." Ornamental and berrying trees and shrubs are listed by size or use, then by common or or botanical name. Prices not shown on list but will be quoted on available plants as requested. (1961)
Catalog: $.25, R&W, CAN/OV, SS:3-11, $15m, HYB, cn/bn
Nursery: All Year, Daily
Garden: June-Oct, Daily

K. Van Bourgondien & Sons, Inc.
P. O. Box A
245 Farmingdale Rd.
Babylon, NY 11702
(516) 669-3523 or (800) 645-5830 TO/CC
John & Debbie Van Bourgondien

PLANTS BULBS
Color catalogs offer **spring and summer blooming bulbs**, perennials, grapes and berries, ornamental shrubs and houseplants: each plant briefly described, with cultural information given in symbols. Large selection, especially of bulbs, all shown in color; catalogs sent in fall and spring. (1919)
Catalog: Free, R&W, SS:2-6,9-12, cn/bn
Nursery: All Year, M-Sa, Call Ahead

Van Engelen Inc.
307 Maple St.
Litchfield, CT 06759
(203) 567-8734 or 5662 TO/CC $50m
J. S. Ohms

BULBS
Sells **Dutch bulbs** in quantities of 50 and 100 per variety, but anyone who orders a minimum of $50 may take advantage of their bulk prices. Offers a broad selection: brief plant descriptions, cultural suggestions. (1946)
Catalog: Free, MO, SS:8-3, $50m

Van Ness Water Gardens
2460 North Euclid
Upland, CA 91786-1199
(714) 982-2425 TO/CC $15m
William C. Uber

PLANTS BOOKS SUPPLIES
Color catalog offers **everything for water gardens** – water lilies and other aquatic plants, fish, ponds and supplies and books on water gardening, as well as a lot of information on how to do it. (1932)
Catalog: $2($5 OV), OV, SS:W, $15m, HYB, cn/bn
Nursery: All Year, Tu-Sa
Garden: June-Aug, Tu-Sa

Vandenberg
3 Black Meadow Rd.
Chester, NY 10918
(914) 469-2633 TO/CC $15m
John & Connie Vandenberg

PLANTS BULBS
A color catalog of **Dutch and other spring and summer bulbs**: iris, lilies, daylilies, woodland wildflowers and ferns and other perennials: many illustrated and all briefly described. (1860)
Catalog: $2d, R&W, SS:8-10,3-5
Nursery: Aug-May, M-F, Call Ahead

VanWell Nursery, Inc.
P. O. Box 1339
1000 N. Miller St.
Wenatchee, WA 98801
(509) 663-8189
Peter VanWell

PLANTS
A broad selection of **fruit trees**: apples, cherries, pears, peaches, plums and prunes, apricots, berries, nuts, grapes: all well described in an informative catalog. Some apple trees are available on standard to dwarf rootstocks, other dwarf fruit trees are available.
Catalog: Free, R&W, CAN, SS:11-6, $15m, HYB
Nursery: All Year, M-Sa, Call Ahead
Garden: July-Sept, M-Sa, Call Ahead

Varga's Nursery
2631 Pickertown Rd.
Warrington, PA 18976
(215) 343-0646
Barbara L. Varga

PLANTS
A very wide selection of **hardy and greenhouse ferns**, listed only by botanical and common name, with brief notes on size or use. A list of source books is given to help you work your way through the jungle. (1975)
Catalog: $1, R&W, CAN, SS:W, $25m, HYB, bn
Nursery: All Year, Daily, By Appointment Only
Garden: Spring & Fall, Greenhouse, By Appointment Only

Veldheer Tulip Gardens
12755 Quincy Street
Holland, MI 49424
(616) 399-1900 TO/CC
Eric Olson

BULBS
Specializes in **spring and summer blooming Dutch bulbs** – tulips, daffodils, crocus, hyacinths, lilies, alliums and others: all briefly described in a color catalog. (1950)
Catalog: Free, R&W, SS:4-10
Nursery: All Year, M-Sa, Call Ahead
Garden: April-Sept, Daily, Call Ahead

Vermont Bean Seed Co.
Garden Lane
Fair Haven, VT 05743
(802) 265-4212 or 3082 TO/CC $15m
Mary L. Sautter

SEEDS SUPPLIES TOOLS
Specializes in **bean and vegetable seeds**: informative catalog, good descriptions, growing instructions, even a number to call when customers need HELP! Also a selection of growing supplies, some annual, herb and perennial seeds, some color photos and many beautiful drawings. (1975)
Catalog: Free, R&W, CAN/OV
Nursery: All Year, M-Sa
Garden: July-Sept, M-Sa

Vermont Wildflower Farm
Route 7
Charlotte, VT 05445
(802) 425-3500 TO/CC $7m
Chy & Ray Allen

SEEDS
The garden is an tourist attraction in Vermont; they have seeded "thousands" of wildflower species. Offers **wildflower seeds and seed mixes** for sun or shade, regionalized for the entire U.S. (1982)
Catalog: Free, R&W, CAN, $7m, cn/bn
Nursery: May-Oct, Daily
Garden: July-Aug, Wildflowers, Daily

Vesey's Seeds Ltd.
P. O. Box 9000
Charlottetown, PE, Canada C0A 1P0
(902) 892-1048 TO/CC $15m
B. E. & S. F. Simpson

SEEDS BOOKS SUPPLIES
A broad selection of **vegetables and flowers**, all well described with cultural information. Specializes in short-season varieties for Canada and New England (order catalog from Box 6000, Houlton, ME 04730-0814). Also offers growing supplies, gardening books and handmade black-ash baskets. (1939)
Catalog: Free, R&W, USA
Nursery: All Year, M-Sa
Garden: July-Sept, M-Sa

Andre Viette Farm & Nursery
Route 1, Box 16
State Route 608
Fisherville, VA 22939
(703) 943-2315 TO/CC $25m
Andre Viette

PLANTS
A very broad selection of **garden perennials**: brief descriptions. Plants grouped by use or cultural conditions, shade or sun or by type. Many daylilies, iris, hosta, peonies, ornamental grasses, epimediums, astilbes, liriopes, Siberian iris, peonies, Oriental poppies and more.
Catalog: $2, R&W, SS:3-6,9-11, $25m
Nursery: April-Nov, M-Sa, Call Ahead
Garden: April-Oct, M-Sa, Call Ahead

Village Garden (Fairfax, VT)

See Stillpoint Gardens

The Vine and the Branch
11026 Steele Creek Rd.
Charlotte, NC 28217
(704) 588-1788
B. J. & Frances D. Brown

PLANTS
A broad selection of **bearded iris of all types**, Siberian, Louisiana and Japanese iris and daylilies: all plants very well described. They also offer some older iris and daylilies for $1 each, a wonderful way to get a big garden started!
Catalog: $1d, SS:7-9, $10m
Nursery: April-Sept, M-Sa, Call Ahead
Garden: April-July, M-Sa, Call Ahead

Vineland Nurseries
P. O. Box 98
Martin Road
Vineland Station, ON, Canada L0R 2E0
(416) 562-4836
Jim & Barb Lounsbery

PLANTS
A collectors' list of **Japanese maples, dwarf conifers, heathers**, hardy bamboos, rhododendrons, holly, ornamental grasses and ornamental trees and shrubs -- a wide selection: very brief plant descriptions. (1978)
Catalog: $1, USA, SS:Spr,Fall, $15m, bn
Nursery: April-June, Daily: By Appointment Only other times
Garden: April-May, Evenings till dusk: Sa-Su to 5:00.

The Violet Showcase
3147 South Broadway
Englewood, CO 80110
(303) 761-1770
Douglas Crispin

PLANTS SEEDS BOOKS SUPPLIES
A broad selection of **African violets**, each well described. Also some other **gesneriads**. Their supplies catalog offers a wide selection of growing supplies, lights, plant carts, pots, fertilizers (supplies sold in bulk to hobbyists gone mad). Some seed; also books on African Violets. (1969)
Catalog: $1, CAN, SS:5-10, HYB
Nursery: All Year, M,W-Sa

Violets Collectible
1571 Wise Rd.
Lincoln, CA 95648
(916) 645-3487
Jeani Hatfield

PLANTS
A fanatic's list of **African violets**: very large selection with good brief plant descriptions. The list is tightly packed; settle down with your reading glasses -- regular, miniature and semi-miniature and trailers. Big display at greenhouse. Available as plants or leaves. (1981)
Catalog: $1, R&W, CAN/OV, SS:4-10, $10m
Nursery: All Year, Daily, Call Ahead
Garden: Growing Area, Call Ahead

For Explanations of Abbreviations/Codes Used in Listings See Bookmark or Inside Covers

Vireya Specialties Nursery
2701 Malcolm Ave.
Los Angeles, CA 90064
(213) 475-2679
Bette & Bill Moynier

PLANTS
A selection of **hybrid and species Vireya rhododendrons**, suitable for greenhouse/houseplant culture – they grow in warmer climates than other rhododendrons and will bloom anytime during the year, some even year 'round. Color pictures: very good plant descriptions of about 50 varieties. (1980)
Catalog: Long SASE, CAN/OV, SS:AY, HYB, bn

Volkman Bros. Greenhouses
2714 Minert Street
Dallas, TX 75219
(214) 526-3484
Walter & Henry Volkmann

PLANTS SUPPLIES
A selection of **African violets**, many of their own hybridizing: each briefly described and some shown in color. Also offers growing supplies, equipment and plant stands. (1949)
Catalog: Long SASE, R&W, SS:3-11, HYB
Nursery: All Year, M-F, Sa am
Garden: All Year, M-F, Sa am

W. K. Quality Bromeliads
P. O. Box 49621
Los Angeles, CA 90049
(213) 472-6501
Werner Krauspe

PLANTS
Offers a large selection of **bromeliads, tillandsias and species orchids**.
Catalog: Long SASE, R&W

Walden - West
5744 Crooked Finger Rd. N.E.
Scotts Mills, OR 97375
(503) 873-6875
Charles Purtymun & Jay Hyslop

PLANTS SEEDS
Offers **hostas**, both plants and seeds, and other shade plants and groundcovers, including ivy. They hybridize their own introductions.
Catalog: Long SASE, SS:4-9, $10m, HYB
Nursery: April-Sept, Daily, Call Ahead

Mary Walker Bulb Company
P. O. Box 256
Omega, GA 31775
(912) 386-1919

BULBS
A good selection of **summer blooming bulbs**: cannas, crinums, gingers, caladiums, gladiolus, agapanthus, callas, lycoris and others. Mostly listed by common name and color, many shown in color photographs. Also offers a few perennials.
Catalog: MO

Wanda's Hide-a-Way
14812 84th Ave. N.E.
Bothell, WA 98011
(206) 488-2405
Wanda F. Blake

PLANTS
Specializes in **miniature geraniums**, but also offers chrysanthemums and fuchsias: plants briefly described. Offers other geraniums and perennials at the nursery. (1985)
Catalog: $1, R&W, SS:AY, $15m
Nursery: Nov-April, M-F, Call Ahead
Garden: Nov-April, M-F, Call Ahead

Wapumne Native Plant Nursery
3807 Mt. Pleasant Rd.
Lincoln, CA 95648
(916) 383-5154
Everett D. Butts

PLANTS
Specializes in **California native plants**. Has no catalog; write for information.
Catalog: See notes, R&W

Wyrttun Ward
18 Beach Street
Middleboro, MA 02346
(617) 866-4087
Gilbert A. Bliss

PLANTS
Specializes in perennial **herbs, Northeastern wildflowers, woodland plants and dye plants**. (1976)
Catalog: $1, CAN/OV, SS:4-6,9-11
Nursery: April-Nov, Daily, Call Ahead

Washington Evergreen Nursery
P. O. Box 388
Brooks Branch Road
Leicester, NC 28748
(704) 683-4518 TO $15m
Jordan Jack

PLANTS
A collectors' catalog of **dwarf conifers and other dwarf shrubs** such as berberis, box, holly, pieris, and evergreen azaleas: all very well described, with cultural information and estimated size after ten years. (1978)
Catalog: $2d, SS:4-6,9-10, $15m, bn
Nursery: April-Oct, By Appointment Only
Garden: May-Oct, By Appointment Only

Water Lily World
2331 Goodloe
Houston, TX 77093
(713) 694-8801
Glenn Tolman

PLANTS
Offers **water lilies, bog and aquatic plants**.
Catalog: $3d, R&W, CAN/OV, SS:W
Nursery: All Year, M-Sa
Garden: April-Nov, Anahoac, TX, Call Ahead

Water Ways Nursery
Route 2, Box 247
Lovettsville, VA 22080
(703) 822-9052 TO $25m
Sarah R. Kurtz

PLANTS
Small nursery on a historic Virginia farm offers **waterlilies, lotus** and **aquatic plants**. Plants are sold bare-root or potted: brief plant descriptions. (1985)
Catalog: Long SASE, R&W, SS:3-9, $25m, cn/bn
Nursery: March-Oct, By Appointment Only
Garden: June-Aug, By Appointment Only

Waterford Gardens
74 E. Allendale Rd.
Saddle River, NJ 07458
(201) 327-0721 or 0337 TO/CC $10m
James A. Lawrie, Mgr.

PLANTS BOOKS SUPPLIES
Complete selection of **water lilies, lotus and other aquatic and bog plants**, as well as pools, supplies, fish, pumps, filters, remedies and books on water gardening. Many color photographs and good descriptions. I have one water lily, which every visitor is rushed to see when it's blooming! (1985)
Catalog: $3.50, R&W, CAN, SS:4-8, cn/bn
Nursery: All Year, M-Sa
Garden: May-Sept, M-Sa

The WaterWorks

See Tilley's Nursery, Inc.

The Waushara Gardens
Route 2, Box 570
Plainfield, WI 54966
(715) 335-4462 or 4281
George & Robert Melk

PLANTS BOOKS BULBS
Color brochure offers a wide selection of gladiolus and 'Pixiolas', lilies, cannas, dahlias, callas and other **summer blooming bulbs**: well described. Sold in quantities for the cut flower trade, as well as quantities for the the home gardener. Also a few books on glads and lilies. (1924)
Catalog: $1, R&W, CAN/OV, $12m, SS:1-6, HYB
Nursery: Jan-Sept, M-Sa, Call Ahead
Garden: Aug-Sept, M-Sa, Call Ahead

Wavecrest Nursery & Landscaping Co.
2509 Lakeshore Dr.
Fennville, MI 49408
(616) 543-4175
Carol T. Hop

PLANTS SUPPLIES
Offers a broad selection of **ornamental trees and shrubs**: Japanese maples, hybrid azaleas, berberis, flowering quince, dogwoods, hollies, larches, magnolias, crabapples, rhododendrons, spireas, viburnums, conifers and other collectors' trees -- no plant descriptions. Also supplies for birds. (1955)
Catalog: Free, R&W, CAN/OV, SS:W, bn
Nursery: All Year, Daily, By Appointment Only

Waynesboro Nurseries
P. O. Box 987
Route 664
Waynesboro, VA 22980
(703) 942-4141

PLANTS
Color catalog offers a good selection of **fruit and nut trees**, berries and grapes, ornamental trees and shrubs, conifers and groundcovers: each plant briefly to well described. Among the offerings: dogwood, yews, lilacs, hollys and many shade trees and flowering shrubs. (1922)
Catalog: Free

Wayside Gardens
P. O. Box 1
Hodges, SC 29695-0001
(803) 374-3387 or (800) 845-1124 TO/CC $25m
William J. Park

PLANTS
Color catalog of **ornamental trees and shrubs, perennials and roses**: all well described and illustrated, with good cultural information. A Wayside catalog which chanced my way started my passion for ornamental garden plants and was my first tutor. They introduce many new cultivars.
Catalog: $1d, MO, SS:1-5,9-11, bn/cn

We-Du Nurseries
Route 5, Box 724
Marion, NC 28752
(704) 738-8300
Richard Weaver & Rene Duval

PLANTS
A collectors' catalog of **rock garden and woodland plants**, Southern natives, American, Japanese, Korean and Chinese wildflowers; some are quite unusual. Each plant is lovingly described. They also offer several introductory collections for various growing conditions -- sound terrific. (1981)
Catalog: $1d, CAN/OV, SS:2-5,8-11, $20m, HYB, bn
Nursery: All Year, M-Sa, Call Ahead
Garden: April-May, M-Sa, Call Ahead

Webber Gardens
9180 Main Street
Damascus, MD 20872
(301) 253-5335
Steve Webber

PLANTS BOOKS
Offers a broad selection of **daylilies**: all briefly described in reference catalog, including a number of 'classics' and older cultivars, as well as current introductions. Publishing a "Daylily Encyclopedia"; write for information on how to order. (1974)
Catalog: $1d, SS:5-8, $20m, HYB
Nursery: By Appointment Only
Garden: June-Aug, By Appointment Only

Weddle Native Gardens, Inc.
3589 G Road
Palisade, CO 81526
(303) 464-5549
C. Leonard Weddle & Joan B. Cockrane

PLANTS
Offers "hybrid **columbine and eustoma, penstemons, indian paintbrush**, many wildflowers." (1980)
Catalog: $1, R&W, CAN/OV, SS:10-3, $5m, HYB
Nursery: All Year, M-Sa
Garden: April-May, M-Sa

For Explanations of Abbreviations/Codes Used In Listings See Bookmark or Inside Covers

Well-Sweep Herb Farm
317 Mt. Bethel Rd.
Port Murray, NJ 07865
(201) 852-5390
Louise & Cyrus Hyde

PLANTS SEEDS BOOKS SUPPLIES
A broad selection of **herb plants**, as well as perennials and scented geraniums: no plant descriptions. Also offers some herb seeds, dried flowers and other herb gifts and supplies and books. Lectures and open houses in the Spring and Fall. (1971)
Catalog: $1, SS:4-10, $5m, cn/bn
Nursery: April-Dec, Tu-Sa
Garden: June-July, Tu-Sa

West Kootenay Herb Nursery
R. R. 2
Bedford Road (Blewett)
Nelson, BC, Canada V1L 5P5
(604) 352-9479 TO/CC
Mrs. Barbara Tanner

PLANTS
A broad selection of **herb plants**: each very well described as to appearance and taste and giving some traditional uses. Most of the plants are hardy perennials, and more flowering perennials are added each year. (1981)
Catalog: Free($1 in US), R&W, USA, SS:5-9, cn/bn
Nursery: May-Sept, Th-Su, Call Ahead
Garden: June-Sept, Th-Sa, Call Ahead

Ken West Orchids
P. O. Box 1332
Pahoa, HI 96778
(808) 965-9895 TO/CC
Ken & Jean West

PLANTS
List offers a number of **cattleya hybrids**, listed by color, either in small pots or in community pots: each thoroughly described. Some of their hybrids have won awards from the American Orchid Society. Also offers a few other hybrids. (1979)
Catalog: Free, R&W, CAN/OV, SS:W, HYB
Nursery: All Year, Daily, Call Ahead
Garden: All Year, Daily, Call Ahead

Western Biologicals Ltd.
P. O. Box 46466, Sta. G
Vancouver, BC, Canada V4R 4G7
(604) 228-0986
William Chalmers

SEEDS BOOKS SUPPLIES
Offers live cultures and granular spawn for a very broad selection of **mushrooms**, as well as complete growing supplies and books for commercial or home growers. They will also do tissue culture. (1983)
Catalog: C$2, R&W, USA, $10m, bn
Nursery: Call Ahead

Westgate Garden Nursery
751 Westgate Dr.
Eureka, CA 95501
(707) 442-1239 TO $100m
Catherine Weeks

PLANTS
Catalog offers a large selection of **species and hybrid rhododendrons and azaleas**, with good plant descriptions, and some unusual ornamental shrubs and trees as companion plants -- crinodendron, eucryphia, halesia, kalmia, stewartia, styrax: a real collectors' list. (1965)
Catalog: $1d, SS:10-4
Nursery: All Year, Daily
Garden: March-June, Daily

Westside Exotics Palm Nursery
P. O. Box 156
6030 River Rd.
Westley, CA 95387
(209) 894-3492 or 575-2168 TO $20m
Daniel and Susan Lara

PLANTS SEEDS
A very good selection of **palms**, available as seedlings or small plants: no plant descriptions. A small nursery with a fast turn-over of plants, not all palms available at all times; palm and flowering tree seed available in season only. Also a few tropical palms, some hardy to 28F. (1983)
Catalog: Long SASE, SS:2-11, $20m, bn
Nursery: All Year, By Appointment Only
Garden: May-Oct, Growing Area, By Appointment Only

Whistling Wings Farm, Inc.
427 West Street
Biddeford, ME 04005
(207) 282-1146
Don & Julie Harper

PLANTS
This nursery offers just **raspberries**: eight varieties listed in a very informative list full of growing information. During the summer they sell fresh berries at the nursery, and every month but January they sell raspberry jam and 'gourmet' honey (these by mail, too). (1978)
Catalog: Free, R&W, CAN/OV, SS:11,4-5, HYB
Nursery: Feb-Dec: Summer, Daily, Other times, M-F
Garden: July-Aug, Daily

White Flower Farm
Route 63
Litchfield, CT 06759-0050
(203) 567-0801 or 567-4565 TO/CC
Eliot Wadsworth, II

PLANTS BOOKS SUPPLIES TOOLS BULBS
Color catalog offers a broad selection of **shrubs and perennials**: good plant descriptions and detailed cultural suggestions. Also offers books, supplies and tools and has a staff horticulturist who will consult with customers ers over the phone.
Catalog: $5d, SS:3-5,9-10, bn/cn
Nursery: April 12-Oct, Daily
Garden: April-Oct, Garden & Trial Garden, Daily

Whitman Farms
1420 Beaumont St.
Salem, OR 97304
(503) 363-5020 or 364-3076
Lucile Whitman

PLANTS
Seedling trees and rooted cuttings, including species maples, beeches, dogwood, franklinia, oaks, zelkova, stewartia, and other desirable landscape trees and shrubs. Also rooted cuttings of currants, gooseberries, grapes, kiwis and raspberries. Ask for plant list and a price list.
Catalog: Long SASE, MO, CAN, SS:W, $10m

Whitney Gardens
P. O. Box F
31600 Highway 101
Brinnon, WA 98320
(206) 796-4411
Anne Sather

PLANTS
Offers a large selection of **hybrid and species rhododendrons and azaleas**, and **kalmias**: some illustrated in color, all plants very well described, with cultural information. They have a seven-acre display garden; sounds lovely in spring and fall. (1955)
Catalog: $2($3 OV), CAN/OV, SS:W, HYB
Nursery: All Year, Daily
Garden: April-May, Daily

Wicklein's Aquatic Farm & Nursery, Inc.
1820 Cromwell Bridge Rd.
Baltimore, MD 21234
(301) 823-1335 TO/CC $5m
Mr. & Mrs. Walter Wicklein

PLANTS SUPPLIES
Offers a good selection of **water lilies, lotus and other aquatic and bog plants**: all well to briefly described. Also sells fiber glass ponds, PVC pond liners, pumps and other supplies and fancy gold fish and koi.
Catalog: $1, R&W, CAN, $25m
Nursery: April-Aug, Daily; Other months, call for hours.

Gilbert H. Wild & Son, Inc.
P. O. Box 338
1112 Joplin St.
Sarcoxie, MO 64862-0338
Jim Wild, Pres.

PLANTS
Color catalog offers a large selection of **daylilies and herbaceous peonies**: all plants very well described, many illustrated. Offers a number of collections and several your-choice collections at considerable savings. Many of the plants are their own hybrids. (1885)
Catalog: $2d(12 IRC), R&W, CAN/OV, SS:4-11, $10m, HYB
Nursery: Jan 15-Dec 15, M-F, Call Ahead
Garden: May-Aug, M-Sa, Call Ahead

The Wildflower Company

See Botanic Garden Seed Company

The Wildflower Source
P. O. Box 312
Fox Lake, IL 60020
Phill King

PLANTS
Offers hardy native orchids, asarums and double white forms of trillium and bloodroot, **ferns and other woodland wildflowers**: all plants well described; most are propagated by tissue culture. Nice selection of unusual plants for collectors. (1984)
Catalog: $1d, R&W, MO, SS:4-5, 8-11, bn

Wildginger Woodlands
P. O. Box 1091
Webster, NY 14580
Phyllis Farkas

PLANTS SEEDS BOOKS
A collectors' list of **rock garden and woodland plants**, including Northeastern natives and ferns, offered as plants or seeds, and a small selection of shrubs and trees: no descriptions of plants, but many choice items. Also sells a few recommended books on ferns and wildflowers. (1983)
Catalog: $1d, MO, SS:4,10, $6m, bn/cn

Wildwood Farm
10300 Sonoma Highway
Kenwood, CA 95452
(707) 833-1161
Ricardo & Sara Monte

PLANTS
Perennials, sub-tropicals, California native plants.
Catalog: $1, R&W, SS:AY, $25m
Nursery: All Year, Daily

The Wildwood Flower
Route 3, Box 165
Pittsboro, NC 27312
(919) 542-4344
Thurman Maness

PLANTS
Nursery propagated **wildflowers**, including crosses between Lobelia cardinalis and L. siphilitica which have created several new color forms, as well as selected L. cardinalis in white and pink forms. Also hardy **ferns**: all plants well described. (1975)
Catalog: Long SASE, R&W, SS:Spr. & Fall, HYB, bn
Nursery: All Year, Daily, By Appointment Only

Wildwood Gardens
14488 Rock Creek
Chardon, OH 44024
(216) 286-3714 TO $25m
Mrs. Anthony J. Mihalic, Sr.

PLANTS
A collectors' list of **dwarf conifers and other dwarf shrubs**, primarily for bonsai, as well as some **ferns, groundcovers and rock garden plants**: each very briefly described. Also imports bonsai specimens from Japan and the Far East.
Catalog: $.50, CAN/OV, SS:4-5,9-11, $25m, HYB, bn
Nursery: All Year, Daily
Garden: All Year, Daily

For Explanations of Abbreviations/Codes Used In Listings See Bookmark or Inside Covers

Wiley's Nut Grove *2002 Lexington Ave.* *Mansfield, OH 44907-3024* *(419) 589-5239 or 7290* *Dr. Robert F. Wiley*	PLANTS Specializes in **hardy northern nut trees**: chestnuts and Chinese chestnuts, filberts, walnuts, butternuts, hickory nuts, pecans, hicans, as well as persimmons and paw paws. Varieties listed but not described. (1955) Catalog: Long SASE, R&W, CAN/OV, SS:10-5, $10m, HYB Nursery: March-Nov, M-Sa Garden: Aug-Oct, M-Sa
Wilk Orchid Specialties *P. O. Box 1177* *45-212 Nohonani Pl.* *Kaneohe, HI 96744* *(808) 247-6733* *Alice & Chet Wilk*	PLANTS Offers hybrids of many types of orchid: **cattleyas, dendrobiums, ascocendas, phalaenopsis, vanda, oncidiums** and others: each very briefly described. Also offers a number of mericlones. They will try to locate any orchid, not just those listed. (1978) Catalog: Free, R&W, CAN/OV, SS:AY, HYB, bn Nursery: All Year, By Appointment Only Garden: April-Nov, By Appointment Only
Willhite Seed Co. *P. O. Box 23* *Poolville, TX 76076* *(817) 599-8656* *Don Dobles*	SEEDS Color catalog features **watermelons, melons, pumpkins huge and small**, and a broad line of garden vegetables--all very well described. Big selections of corn, tomatoes, cowpeas, peppers, cucumbers, gourds and squash. (1920) Catalog: Free, R&W, MO
Leslie Wilmoth Nursery	See Nolin River Nut Tree Nursery
Nancy Wilson Species & Miniature Narcissus *571 Woodmont Ave.* *Berkeley, CA 94708* *Nancy Wilson*	BULBS A very small nursery specializing in **species and miniature narcissus**: each well described, but stock is limited; these are real collectors' items. She is looking for collectors willing to trade unusual items and wants to create a gene bank and recover old varieties. These are delightful plants. (1980) Catalog: Free, R&W, MO, SS:8-11, $10m, HYB, bn
Wilson's Greenhouse *Route 5, Box 328* *Ozark, MO 65721* *Mrs. Wilbur Wilson*	PLANTS A collectors' list of **begonias and episcias** -- the selection is very large: most are briefly described. You may order plants or cuttings. Catalog: $.50, SS:W, bn/cn Nursery: Call Ahead, M-F, Call Ahead
Wilson's Violet Haven *3900 Carter Creek Parkway* *Bryan, TX 77802* *(409) 846-8970 TO/CC $12m* *Dottie & Bud Wilson*	PLANTS SUPPLIES Offers **African violets** by a number of prominent hybridizers, both plants and leaves: listed by hybridizer and each briefly described. Also offers growing supplies, including their own "Show Plant Soil". (1982) Catalog: $1, R&W, SS:W, $16m, HYB Nursery: All Year, Call Ahead Garden: Spring-Fall, Call Ahead

Wilton's Organic Seed Potatoes
P. O. Box 28
McLain Flats
Aspen, CO 81612
(303) 925-3433 TO $10m
Wilton Jaffee

PLANTS
Sells only Norlands (red) and Norgolds (russet) **seed potatoes**, the "only organic, high altitude certified seed potato in the U.S." -- grown at 8,000 feet. Planting instructions sent with the potatoes: he says they're crisper, firmer, more prolific and flavorful and pass these qualities on. (1975)
Catalog: Free, MO, CAN, SS:12-5, $10m

Wimberlyway Gardens
7024 N.W. 18th Avenue
Gainesville, FL 32605-3237
(904) 372-4922
R. W. Munson, Jr.

PLANTS
A very broad selection of **daylilies**: most plants very well described, many shown in b&w photos. Many are their introductions and those of Betty Hudson.
Catalog: $2, CAN/OV, SS:AY
Nursery: May-Sept, M,Th,Sa

Windrift Prairie Shop
R.D. 2, North Daysville Rd.
Oregon, IL 61061
(815) 732-6890
Dorothy & Douglas Wade

PLANTS SEEDS
Seeds and plants of **prairie forbs** (there's that word again! -- flowering plants other than grasses). Many of the seeds are wild-collected in the "Rock River corridor" of northern Illinois; listed by botanical and common name only. Also sells seed mixtures and **prairie grass seeds**.
Catalog: 2 FCS, SS:4,10, bn/cn
Nursery: All Year, Call Ahead

Windy Ridge Nursery
P. O. Box 301
Hythe, AB, Canada T0H 2C0
(403) 356-2167
John & Carol Jones

PLANTS
Hardy and native fruit -- berries, cherries, apples and a few ornamental trees: all briefly to well described. Offers apples, saskatoons, raspberries and strawberries, Nanking cherries, currants and gooseberries. Will ship only their "smokey saskatoons" to the U.S.
Catalog: $2d, R&W, SS:4-5,9-10, $10m
Nursery: April-Oct, M-Sa, By Appointment Only
Garden: June-Aug, Growing Area, By Appointment Only

Winter Country Cacti
5405 Mohawk Rd.
Littleton, CO 80123
(303) 795-1083
Rod Haenni

PLANTS
Specializes in winter hardy **cactus, yucca and succulents**.
Catalog: $.50

Womack Nursery Co.
Route 1, Box 80
DeLeon, TX 76444
(817) 893-6497 TO $15m
Larry J. Womack

PLANTS BOOKS TOOLS
A very broad selection of **edibles**: pecans, peaches, apples, apricots, figs, persimmons, pears, plums, berries, grapes, as well as some shade and ornamental trees and roses: all well described. They also sell pruning tools, budding and grafting knives and a few books on fruit growing. (1936)
Catalog: Free, SS:12-3, $15m
Nursery: Dec-March, M-Sa

Woodland Nurseries
2151 Camilla Rd.
Mississauga, ON, Canada L5A 2K1
(416) 277-2961
Marjorie & Fraser Hancock

PLANTS
Offers **rhododendrons, azaleas and ornamental trees, shrubs and conifers** for severe winter climates, as well as some hardy perennials: each plant well described. (1930)
Catalog: $1d, R&W, USA/OV, SS:4-5, $50m, HYB, bn/cn
Nursery: April-Dec, M-F, Call Ahead
Garden: May, M-F, Call Ahead

Woodlanders, Inc.
1128 Colleton Ave.
Aiken, SC 29801
(803) 648-7522 TO $15m
Robt. & Julia Mackintosh, Robt. McCartney

PLANTS BOOKS
A collectors' list of **Southeastern native trees, shrubs, groundcovers** and **perennials** and new or hard-to-find exotics: briefly described, with source of further information. Looking up the plants is worth the trouble; list contains many treasures. Also sells books on plants and field guides. (1980)
Catalog: Long SASE W/2 FCS, CAN/OV, SS:10-3, $15m, HYB, bn
Nursery: All Year, By Appointment Only
Garden: March-April, Call Ahead

World Insectivorous Plants
P. O. Box 70513
Marietta, GA 30007-0513
(404) 973-1554
Bob Hanrahan

PLANTS BOOKS SUPPLIES
Illustrated catalog of **insectivorous and carnivorous plants**: good selection with information on each plant family and good cultural information. Also offers books and growing supplies. (1976)
Catalog: $1(3 IRC), R&W, CAN/OV, SS:3-10, $2, HYB, bn/cn
Nursery: March-Oct, M-Sa, By Appointment Only
Garden: May-Aug, M-Sa, By Appointment Only

For Explanations of Abbreviations/Codes Used In Listings See Bookmark or Inside Covers

Wrenwood of Berkeley Springs
Route 4, Box 361
Berkeley Springs, WV 25411
(304) 258-3071
Flora & John Hackimer

PLANTS
Large selection of **herbs, perennials, scented geraniums**, sedums and rock garden plants, listed in an informative catalog. Many thymes, dianthus, salvias, oreganos, mints and basils and other temptations – so many herbs also make wonderful garden perennials. (1981)
Catalog: $1.50, R&W, SS:4-10, $30m, HYB, bn/cn
Nursery: All Year, W-Su
Garden: May-Sept, W-Su

Wright Iris Nursery
6583 Pacheco Pass Hwy.
Gilroy, CA 95020
(408) 848-5991 TO/CC $20m
Ean St. Claire

PLANTS
Offers several lists – tall bearded and standard dwarf bearded iris; Siberian iris; dahlias; cannas; and gladiolus: each plant described briefly. Specify which list(s) you want. (1984)
Catalog: Free, R&W, SS:7-8, $15m, HYB
Nursery: All Year, Tu-Su, Call Ahead
Garden: May-June, Tu-Su, Call Ahead

Guy Wrinkle Exotic Plants
11610 Addison St.
North Hollywood, CA 91601
(818) 766-4820
Guy Wrinkle

PLANTS BULBS
Specializes in collectors' plants – haworthia, succulents, species pelargoniums, species bulbs from South Africa and Portugal, euphorbias, species orchids and a large selection of cycads; some are rare and in short supply: no plant descriptions. (1980)
Catalog: $1d, R&W, CAN/OV, SS:3-12, $15m, bn
Nursery: All Year, By Appointment Only
Garden: All Year, By Appointment Only

Wyatt-Quarles Seed Co.
331 S. Wilmington St. (Raleigh)
P. O. Box 739
Garner, NC 27529
(919) 832-0551 TO/CC $10m
Corporation

SEEDS SUPPLIES BULBS
Color catalog offers seeds of **flowers and vegetables** especially adapted to the Southern states: each briefly described. Also offers some growing supplies and a spring bulb catalog. (1881)
Catalog: Free, R&W, CAN, $5m
Nursery: All Year, M-F, Sa am

Y. O. Ranch Cactus Co.
P. O. Box 1443
Ingram, TX 78025
(512) 367-5110 or 5679
Betty Walton, Mgr.

PLANTS
Collectors' list of **cacti and succulents**: specialties are rare African and native Texas plants, all well described in the list. Also sells Mexican and South American cactus, euphorbias, caudex plants, opuntias and other cacti for hardy landscape use. Most plants nursery propagated. (1981)
Catalog: $1, R&W, CAN/OV, SS:W, $15m, bn
Nursery: All Year, By Appointment Only

Roy Young, Seedsman
23, Westland Chase, West Winch
King's Lynn, Norfolk, England PE33 0QH
(0553) 840 867
Roy Young

SEEDS
"List of approximately 2,000 different **cactus and succulent** seeds obtained from either my own hand-pollinated plants or direct from habitat. Includes a guaranteed accurately named selection of every known lithops."
Catalog: 3 IRC, R&W, OV, $6m
Nursery: All Year, M-Sa, By Appointment Only

Young's Mesa Nursery
2755 Fowler Lane
Arroyo Grande, CA 93420
(805) 489-0548
Kay & Bill Young

PLANTS
A very large selection of **geraniums (pelargoniums)** of all types: brief descriptions with good cultural information. They also offer a few species geraniums and pelargoniums in addition to a huge selection of miniature, scented, ivy and Regale "geraniums". Be sure to call ahead. (1977)
Catalog: $2d, SS:W, $15m
Nursery: Feb-Nov, W-Sa: Su pm, Call Ahead
Garden: April-Nov, Call Ahead

Yucca Do Nursery
P. O. Box 655
FM 359 & Brumlow Rd. (Hempstead)
Waller, TX 77484
(409) 826-6363
John Fairley & Carl Schoenfeld

PLANTS
A nice selection of unusual **trees, shrubs and perennials** for zones 8 and 9: azaleas, cryptomeria, magnolias, maples, itea, cliftonia, cephalotaxus and styrax: listed only by botanical name. Also listed are garden perennials which grow well in that tough summer climate; garden looks lovely. (1986)
Catalog: Long SASE W/2 FCS, SS:10-12,1-3, $15m, bn
Nursery: Jan 15-Dec 15, Su-W, By Appointment Only
Garden: May-June, Oct, Nov, Su-W, By Appointment Only

Zaca Vista Nursery
1190 Alamo Pintado Rd.
Solvang, CA 93463
(805) 688-2585
Steve & Addie Stephens

PLANTS SEEDS BOOKS SUPPLIES
Offers a very broad selection of **African violets**, many from well-known hybridizers – plants, leaves and some seed – and some other Saintpaulia species. Standards, miniatures, semi-miniatures, trailers: all very briefly described. Also African violet supplies and books. (1980)
Catalog: $1d, R&W, CAN/OV, SS:W, HYB
Nursery: All Year, W-Su
Garden: All Year, W-Su

Zuma Canyon Orchids
5949 Bonsall Dr.
Malibu, CA 90265
(213) 457-9771
Amado Vazquez

PLANTS
Specializes in **phalaenopsis orchids**, and the color catalog shows a number of their very beautiful hybrids, many of which have been award winners. Most of the plants for sale are seedlings or in community pots.
Catalog: $3, R&W, CAN/OV, SS:W, $15m
Nursery: All Year, Daily

Buffaloberry

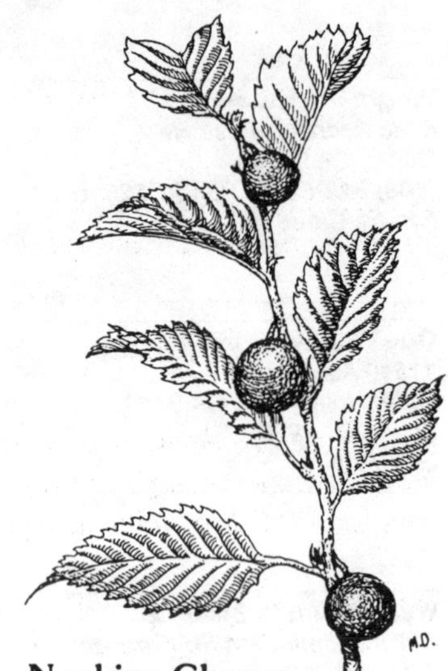

Nanking Cherry

Edible Honeysuckle

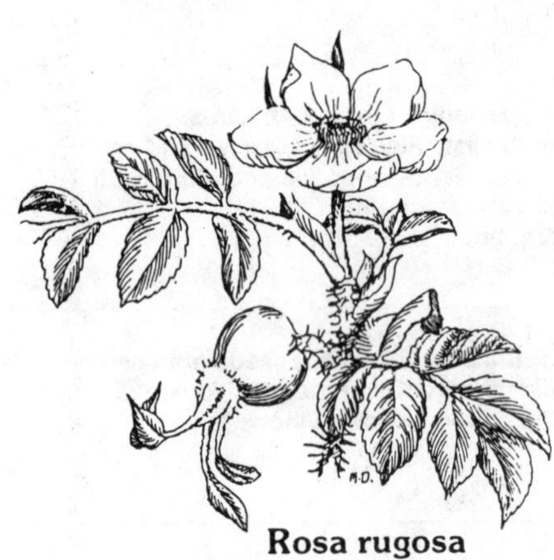

Rosa rugosa

Bog Cranberry

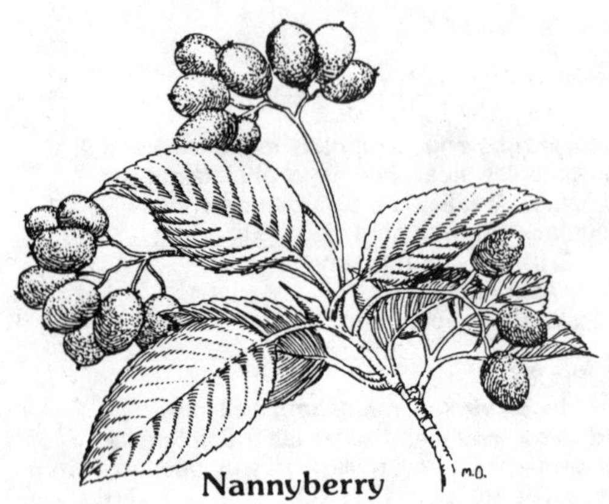

Nannyberry

Pixwell Gooseberry

Garden Suppliers and Services

Sources of garden supplies and services are listed alphabetically. Their specialties (Supplies, Tools, Books, Furniture, Ornaments and Services) are indicated at the top of the notes on catalogs.

See index section for:

K. Product Sources Index: An index of suppliers and services listed by specialties. This index also includes plant and seed sources which offer products or services. Within categories, sources are listed by location, and a symbol indicates if they have a shop to visit.

Be sure to check the Changes and Corrections List at the end of the book (see Practical Matters). This list is updated with each printing.

Sources of supplies and services found too late to include in this edition, as well as changes and deletions to current listings, will be listed in our quarterly updates (see Practical Matters).

Other Sources of Garden Supplies and Services

For tools and garden ornaments, keep your eye on garage sales, salvage yards and dumps – and be ever alert for old buildings and gardens being demolished for "progress". These are good sources of old bricks and paving stones, gates, fences, trellises, benches and more. Sometimes you can strike a deal with the wreckers and haul it away yourself, as I did with a thousand bricks on the hottest day of the year!

For books, many sources of new and used books are listed in this section. If you live near book stores, you should routinely check your local used book stores and the "remainder" tables of new book stores. Many of the societies listed in Section D sell books to their members, some of them highly specialized and hard to find elsewhere.

For garden tours, check the tour programs of horticultural and plant societies. Many have excellent offerings. You might consider joining a tour of an overseas society to make new gardening friends. Several horticultural magazines, such as *Pacific Horticulture* and *Horticulture*, offer tours to their readers, and so do several specialist nurseries.

Table of the Symbols and Abbreviations Used in this Book
Appears Inside the Front and Back Covers and On the Bookmark

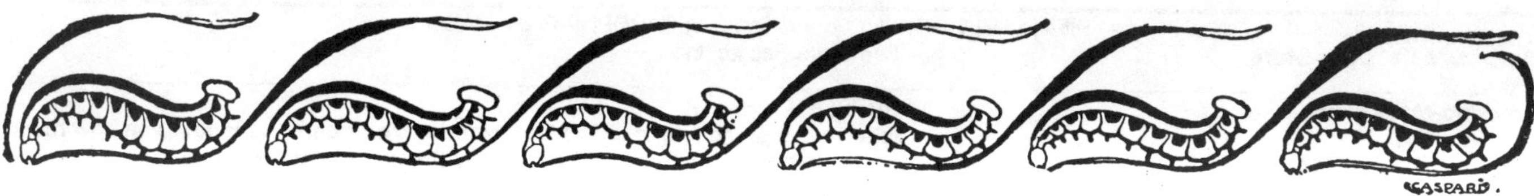

For Explanations of Abbreviations/Codes Used In Listings See Bookmark or Inside Covers

Actagro
4111 N. Motel Dr., Suite 101
Fresno, CA 93722
(209) 275-3600
Gerald Nordstrom

SUPPLIES
Offers 8-inch **plant food discs** made of "Hortopaper" which fertilize as you water and suppress weeds around your vegetables and ornamentals; they have an analysis of 5-5-5. Also sells "Hortopaper", a **ground cover/paper mulch**, which they bought in 1986.
Catalog: Free, R&W, CAN, $3m
Shop: All Year, M-F

Adirondack Designs

See Cypress Street Center

---

agAccess
Box 2008
Davis, CA 95616
(916) 756-7177 TO/CC
David & Karen Katz

BOOKS
A source for **new books in all areas of agriculture**, from water and irrigation to computer uses. While leaning toward agriculture, they also carry books on gardening; all are reviewed in some detail. Also carry computer software for applications in farming. (1979)
Catalog: Free, R&W, CAN/OV
Shop: All Year, M-F, 603 4th St.

Agrilite
P. O. Box 12
93853 River Road
Junction City, OR 97448
(503) 998-3218 TO $20m
Sonny Bekker

SUPPLIES
Sells **growing lights**: halide, sodium and full spectrum high intensity discharge lights, fertilizers and indoor growing supplies. (1979)
Catalog: $2d, R&W, CAN, $20m
Shop: Daily

Alsto's Handy Helpers
P. O. Box 1267
Route 150 East
Galesburg, IL 61401
(309) 343-6181 or (800) 447-8192 TO/CC
A Dick Blick Company

SUPPLIES TOOLS FURNITURE ORNAMENTS
Offers a broad selection of **gadgets for garden and home**: garden carts, tools, supplies, watering equipment, bird houses, animal traps, lawn furniture, items for home and kitchen.
Catalog: Free, MO

Alternative Garden Supply, Inc.
3439 E. 86th St., Suite 259
Indianapolis, IN 46240
(800) 423-0876 or (312) 877-1616 TO/CC $10m
David & Sondi Ittel

SUPPLIES TOOLS
Offers "Felco" pruning tools, the "No Blist'r Trowel", other **garden tools**, sprayers, weather instruments, beneficial insects, insect traps, deer and rabbit repellents, fertilizers and propagation supplies. Many of the tools recommended by Jim Crockett. Can't ship insects out of U.S. (1985)
Catalog: $.22 stamp, R&W, CAN/OV, $5m
Shop: All Year, M-Sa, 599 Williams St., Thornton, IL

Amdega Conservatories
160 Friendship Road
Cranbury, NJ 08512
(201) 329-0999

ORNAMENTS
Offers English **garden rooms and conservatories** which can be built to fit a number of situations, even large enough to use as a pool pavillion. An elegant way to sit outside in cool or windy weather.
Catalog: $3
Shop: Y3

The American Botanist
P. O. Box 143
9526 Lexington Ave.
Brookfield, IL 60513
(312) 485-7805 TO/CC $25m
D. Keith Crotz

BOOKS SERVICES
Specializes in **used and out-of-print books** in all areas of gardening, landscaping and botany. Also offers collection development, book search service and appraisals and will buy book collections in their field. (1983)
Catalog: $1, CAN/OV
Shop: All Year, By Appointment Only

American Standard Co.
P. O. Box 325
Plantsville, CT 06479
(203) 628-9643 TO/CC $17m
Florian Family

TOOLS
Florian "Rachet-Cut" **pruning tools with rachet action** have increased leverage -- need less hand-power; offers hand pruners, loppers and pole pruners.
Catalog: Free, R&W, CAN/OV, $17m
Shop: All Year, M-F, 157 Water St., Southington

American Sundials, Inc.
P. O. Box 677
300 Main St.
Pt. Arena, CA 95468
(707) 884-3082 TO/CC $35m
Wendy Moss

ORNAMENTS
A nice selection of solid **bronze sundials**, with a variety of styles and mottos, some of which are also **birdbaths**.
Catalog: Long SASE, $35m

America's Pet Door Store
See Patio Pacific, Inc.

Amerind-MacKissic
P. O. Box 111
Parker Ford, PA 19457
(215) 495-7181

SUPPLIES
Offers several models of **shredders/grinders/chippers**, depending on how much shredding you want to do and how heavy the material to be shredded is. Also sells portable sprayers and hydraulic log splitters.
Catalog: Free

Anchor & Dolphin Books
P. O. Box 823
30 Franklin Street
Newport, RI 02840
(401) 846-6890
James Hinck

BOOKS
Specializes in **rare, old and out-of-print books** on horticulture and gardening, landscape architecture and garden history. (1977)
Catalog: $1d, CAN/OV
Shop: Call ahead

ANZA Architectural Wood Products
P. O. Box 453
Fairfax, CA 94930
(415) 456-5966
Ruth B. Stein

FURNITURE
Sells **modular planters and benches**, which fit together and can be arranged in several ways. Very nice for decks and small patios where both plants and and seating are wanted. (1983)
Catalog: Free, R&W, CAN/OV
Shop: By Appointment Only

Applied Hydroponics
3135 Kerner Blvd.
San Rafael, CA 94901
(800) 634-9999 or 992-4404 (CA) TO/CC
Peter Wardenburg

SUPPLIES
Offering "Hydrofarm" **hydroponic systems**, as well as supplies and other equipment, and metal halide and high pressure sodium light systems. Also carbon dioxide enrichment systems for home gardeners.
Catalog: Free, R&W, CAN/OV
Shop: All Year, M-Sa

Applied Hydroponics of Canada
2215 Walkley
Montreal, PQ, Canada H4B 2J9
(514) 489-3803 TO/CC $25m
Richard Cohen, Don Stewart

SUPPLIES
Offers a broad selection of "Hydroponix" **equipment and supplies**, including complete hydroponic starter kits. They also sell lighted plant stands and halide lights for indoor gardeners. Catalog in English and French.
Catalog: Free, R&W, USA/OV, $10m
Shop: All Year, M-F, Call Ahead

Aquamonitor
P. O. Box 327
Huntington, NY 11743
(516) 427-5664
Robert and Velma Whitener

SUPPLIES
Complete **mist irrigation systems** and/or automatic controls to monitor soil moisture for propagation in greenhouses; useful for any greenhouse plants, seedlings or cuttings which need constant moisture. Because it monitors the soil, it waters when needed, not on an automatic timer.
Catalog: Free, MO, CAN/OV

Arctic Glass & Window Outlet
Route 1, Box 254
I-94 at County Rd. T
Hammond, WI 54715
(715) 796-2292 TO/CC
Joseph Bacon

SUPPLIES
Ships **insulated (double) glass** nationwide at 25 to 60% below retail; used for greenhouses, sunrooms and windows, doors and roof windows. Panels are unframed; informative leaflet tells you how to install them. (1979)
Catalog: Free, R&W
Shop: All year, M-Sa

Ascot Designs
286 Congress Street
Boston, MA 02210
(617) 451-9173
Hubert S. Moloney

FURNITURE ORNAMENTS SERVICES
Offers "Minsterstone" **garden ornaments and paving** imported from England; specializes in custom design work. The ornaments, made of cast limestone, come in classic designs and are ideal for 'upscale' garden design and historical restoration work. Also sells some one-of-a-kind ornaments. (1983)
Catalog: Free, R&W, CAN/OV

Autumn Forge
1104 N. Buena Vista Ave.
Orlando, FL 32818
(305) 293-3302 TO/CC $10m
Charter & Patricia Murray

ORNAMENTS
A blacksmith who makes several styles of **plant hangers in forged iron**, as well as other handsome hardware -- he also does custom work, making sundials, weathervanes or almost anything else. Offers fire tools, garden dinner bells, racks and sconces, mouse-tail coat hooks and other nice touches.
Catalog: $1, R&W
Shop: All Year, M-F, Call Ahead

Autumn Innovations
P. O. Box 18426
1 East Wendy Ct.
Greensboro, NC 27419
(919) 852-0753 TO/CC
Arne L. Andersson

FURNITURE ORNAMENTS
Offers a number of charming **thatched bird houses and bird feeders** from Devon, Swedish sundials, Sussex trugs and cast aluminum furniture in classic 19th century designs. (1984)
Catalog: Free, R&W

For Explanations of Abbreviations/Codes Used In Listings See Bookmark or Inside Covers

BCS Mosa, Inc.
P. O. Box 1739
13601 Providence Rd.
Matthews, NC 28106
(704) 846-1040 TO/CC $15m
BCS S.p.A., Milan, Italy

SUPPLIES
A very broad selection of **tillers, chipper/shredders, garden carts, sickle-bar mowers, sprayers and power lawn mowers**. They will sell direct if you are not near one of their dealers. (1982)
Catalog: Free, R&W, MO, CAN/OV, $15m

Carol Barnett - Books
3128 S.E. Alder Ct.
Portland, OR 97214
(503) 239-5745
Carol Barnett

BOOKS SERVICES
Issues several catalogs a year, specializes in **used and out-of-print books** on gardens and horticulture, with brief descriptions of contents as well as notes on condition. She will also do book searches if you send her a "want-list." (1983)
Catalog: Free, MO, CAN/OV

Beatrice Farms
Dawson, GA 31742

Offers **earthworms and worm castings**.

Leona Bee Tours & Travel
18305 Biscayne Blvd., #211
Miami, FL 33160-2172
(305) 935-3101

SERVICES
Travel agency specializing in **horticultural tours**, including special tours for orchid-lovers to various habitats of species orchids.
Catalog: Free

Bell's Book Store
536 Emerson St.
Palo Alto, CA 94301
(415) 323-7822 TO/CC $15m
Mr. & Mrs. Herbert Bell

BOOKS
Offers a good selection of **new, used and out-of-print books** on gardening, as well as prints, botanic postcards and greeting cards. They have a good annotated book list on Old Garden Roses ($2.04), but no catalog. Send a "want-list" to see if they have what you want.
Catalog: See notes, CAN/OV
Shop: All Year, M-Sa

Berry-Hill Limited
75 Burwell Road
St. Thomas, ON, Canada N5P 3R5
(519) 631-0480 TO/CC $5m
R. C. Foster & D. L. Roberts

SUPPLIES TOOLS BOOKS
Here's a wonderful old-time **farm equipment and country kitchen catalog**: full of canning supplies, equipment for dairy and poultry yards, garden bells, weather vanes, cider press and tools and equipment for the garden. They also sell a few practical "how-to" books. (1948)
Catalog: Free (2 IRC), R&W, USA/OV, $5m
Shop: All Year, M-F

Beth L. Bibby Books
1225 Sardine Creek Rd.
Gold Hill, OR 97525
(503) 855-1621
George A. Bibby & Nikki A. Wright

BOOKS
Offers **used and out-of-print books** on plants and gardening.
Catalog: $2 and Long SASE, MO, CAN/OV

Dorothy Biddle Service
U.S. Route 6
Greeley, PA 18425-9799
(717) 226-3239
Lynne Dodson

SUPPLIES TOOLS BOOKS
A broad selection of **supplies for flower arrangers** which would be useful to all who cut and bring flowers indoors. Books on arranging and drying flowers, tools and some houseplant supplies. (1936)
Catalog: $.25, R&W, CAN/OV
Shop: All Year, M-F

Bio-Control Co.
P. O. Box 337
57A Zink Road
Berry Creek, CA 95916
(916) 589-5227
Dorothy M. Neva

SUPPLIES
Ladybugs, green lacewings, trichogramma, praying mantis egg cases, fly parasites and "Bio-Control Honeydew" to attract **beneficial insects**. An informative leaflet explains the use of these biological insect controls. (1959)
Catalog: Free, R&W, CAN
Shop: All Year, M,W,F, Call Ahead

Bio-Resources
P. O. Box 902
1210 Birch Street
Santa Paula, CA 93060
(805) 525-0526
Jeri Brandt Mead

SUPPLIES
Predatory mites, green lacewings, ladybugs, fly parasites, trichogramma wasps, mealybug predators and whitefly parasites: uses of **beneficial insects** well described in an informative leaflet.
Catalog: Free, R&W, CAN/OV

BioLogic
418 Briar Lane
Chambersburg, PA 17201
(717) 263-2789
Dr. Albert Pye

SUPPLIES
Sells "Scanmask": a strain of **beneficial, insect-eating nematodes** to control a variety of soil and boring pest insects such as black vine weevils, white grubs, cutworms, caterpillars and fly maggots. (1985)
Catalog: Long SASE, R&W, CAN/OV, $10m
Shop: By Appointment Only

Bird 'n Hand
40 Pearl St.
Framingham, MA 01701
(617) 879-1552
Len Short

SUPPLIES
An informative catalog for serious bird feeders -- offering several mixes of **bird food, feeders and other bird-oriented items**. They also offer an automatic resupply service so that you won't run out of bird food.
Catalog: Free

Geo. C. Birlant & Co.

See Charleston Battery Bench, Inc.

Mary Bland
Augop, Evenjobb
Nr. Presteign, Wales, UK
Whitton 218 or (054-76) 218

BOOKS
Rare, used and out-of-print books for gardeners.

Bloomin' Greenhouse, Inc.
10909-9 Atlantic Blvd.
Jacksonville, FL 32225
(904) 642-8469 TO/CC
Emily D. Boyette

SUPPLIES
Modular aluminum and fiber glass greenhouses can be built in several sizes and expanded with add-on sections. They also sell evaporative cooling systems, heating systems, hydroponic systems, sunscreens and shades.
Catalog: $3d, CAN/OV
Shop: All Year, M-Sa

Bonide Chemical Co., Inc.
2 Wurz Avenue
Yorkville, NY 13495
(315) 736-8231
Jim Wurz

SUPPLIES
Offers a complete line of **home, garden and lawn pesticides**, including the organic products Rotenone, Dipel, Bacillus Thuringiensis, dormant oil, oil and lime surphur spray and many more. (1926)
Catalog: Long SASE, R&W, CAN/OV
Shop: All Year, M-F, Call Ahead

Bonsai Associates, Inc.
3000 Chestnut Ave., #106
Baltimore, MD 21217
(301) 235-5336
Arschel Morell & Barbara Bogash

SUPPLIES TOOLS BOOKS SERVICES
A wide selection of **books, tools and supplies for bonsai**; they also sell some starter plants for bonsai: each well described. They re-pot, refine and board bonsai for local enthusiasts. (1979)
Catalog: $2d, R&W, CAN
Shop: All Year, W-Sa, Call Ahead

Bonsai Creations
2700 N. 29th Ave., #204
Hollywood, FL 33020
(305) 962-6960 TO/CC $25m
Edna Horowitz

SUPPLIES TOOLS BOOKS
Sells **bonsai tools, pots, books and supplies** -- a very broad selection shown in b&w photographs. They also sell finished and pre-bonsai trees, which cannot be shipped to CA or TX. (1982)
Catalog: $2.50d, R&W, MO, CAN/OV

The Book Tree
12 Pine Hill Rd.
Englishtown, NJ 07726
(201) 446-3853
Anne & John Haines

BOOKS SERVICES
Offers **new and recent books** on horticulture, plants and gardening; they will try to locate current books for you.
Catalog: Free, CAN/OV
Shop: By Appointment Only

Bow House, Inc.
92 Randall Road
Bolton, MA 01740
(617) 779-6464
John J. Rogers

ORNAMENTS
Offers **gazebos and other garden structures** of classic design; the "Belvedeary" can be finished in several styles, even cut in half for a bay window. Also sells a domed temple, arbors, pergola, changing structures, Japanese tea house, bridge, even a dog house. All very elegant. (1971)
Catalog: $2, CAN/OV
Shop: All Year, Daily, Call Ahead

Brady-Brooke Farms
3924 N.E. Croco Rd.
Topeka, KS 66617-3903
(913) 286-1126 TO
Scott F. Allen

SUPPLIES
Sells "Kyton Plus" **organic growth stimulant**: soil culture for use on house and garden plants, trees and shrubs, new lawns, even as a seed treatment.
Catalog: Free, R&W, CAN/OV, $12m

Bramen Company, Inc.
P. O. Box 70
Salem, MA 01970-0070
(617) 745-7765 TO/CC $20m
Robert Strom

SUPPLIES TOOLS
Automatic "Thermafor" **ventilation controllers** open and close hinged windows as heavy as 30 lbs -- adjustable for temperatures from 55 to 105F -- and work without electricity. They also offer "Rolcut" pruners and other hand tools, tool hooks, seaweed extract, seed starting cubes and mulch mats.
Catalog: Free, MO, CAN/OV

Brighton By-Products Co., Inc.
P. O. Box 23
New Brighton, PA 15066
(800) 245-3502 or (800) 642-2668 TO/CC $30m
Nathan Ortinberg, Pres.

SUPPLIES
A very broad selection of **growing and landscaping supplies**, sold to anyone by mail; especially good on greenhouse and propagation supplies, irrigation and horticultural chemicals -- including "DuPont Landscape Fabric", a non-chemical mulch/weed barrier.
Catalog: $5, MO, CAN/OV, $30m

Warren F. Broderick - Books
P. O. Box 124
695 4th Avenue
Lansingburgh, NY 12182
(518) 235-4041
Warren F. Broderick

BOOKS
Catalog lists **books** 'usually' in stock, and 'occasionally available'. A broad selection of used, out-of-print and rare books on garden history and design, landscape architecture, botanical illustration and garden art and well written garden classics. (1977)
Catalog: $1.50, R&W, CAN/OV
Shop: All Year, By Appointment Only

Bronwood Worm Gardens
P. O. Box 28
Bronwood, GA 31726-0028
(912) 995-5994
J. F. Seymour

SUPPLIES
Specializes in **bed-run redworms** in mixed sizes for composting and gardening; they also have Gray Nightcrawlers (Georgia wigglers). All shipments are air mail or UPS. Includes instructions for doing your own worm farming.
Catalog: Free, R&W, MO, $11m

Brooks Books
P. O. Box 21473
Concord, CA 94521-0473
(415) 672-4566
Philip & Martha Nesty

BOOKS SERVICES
Sells horticultural and botanical **books, new and used and out-of-print**. Specializes in cacti, succulents, ornamental horticulture, floras and botanicals, plant monographs, native plants, Australian and South African plants and tree and shrubs. Offers a search service; buys book collections. (1986)
Catalog: $1 (2 IRC), CAN/OV
Shop: By Appointment Only

Brookstone Co.
127 Vose Farm Rd.
Peterborough, NH 03458
(603) 924-7181 or 9511 TO/CC

SUPPLIES TOOLS
Offers a variety of **tools and garden equipment and supplies** -- imported and domestic. They are well known for a huge selection of unusual tools for every use and publish several catalogs a year; specify the GARDEN catalog.
Catalog: Free
Shop: Several Stores; list in catalog

Brushy Mountain Bee Farm, Inc.
Rt. 1, Box 135
Moravian Falls, NC 28654
(919) 921-3640 or (800) BEESWAX TO/CC
Steve & Sandy Forrest

SUPPLIES TOOLS BOOKS
Everything for the beekeeper: books, bees, hives, supplies and equipment, including supplies for selling honey -- an informative catalog. Recent additions are videotapes on beekeeping, rockers and porch swings (nobody said beekeepers were as busy as bees), bird houses and feeders.
Catalog: Free, R&W, CAN/OV
Shop: April-Aug, M-Sa; Sept-March, M-F

Builders Booksource
1801 Fourth Street
Berkeley, CA 94710
(415) 845-6874 or (800) 843-2028 TO/CC
George & Sally Kiskaddon

BOOKS
A very broad selection of **books** on architecture and design, construction, interior design, landscaping and gardening, everything from start to finish; the store is a delight! They no longer produce a catalog, but send a monthly newsletter on what's new. Call to see if they have your "wants".
Catalog: Free, CAN/OV
Shop: All Year, Daily

C & C Products
Route 3, Box 438
Hereford, TX 79045
(806) 276-5338 TO/CC
John & Nadine Chance

SUPPLIES
Offers "Big Drop", a **sprinkler which deep waters** up to one inch an hour in a 40' circle or one-half inch an hour over a 60' circle. The base is stable, and the head can be raised to 4' for broad coverage. Good for deep soaking and watering where wind usually blows spray out of the garden.
Catalog: Free, R&W
Shop: All Year, M-F, Call Ahead

Capability's Books & Videos
P. O. Box 144, Highway 46
Deer Park, WI 54007
(800) 247-8154 or (715) 269-5346 TO/CC
Pauline Rickard & Kris Gilbertson

BOOKS
A very broad selection of **horticultural and gardening books and videos**, new or recently published in the United States or Britain. They have nearly 800 books in 69 categories -- something for any special interest. They have added computer programs and will rent videos, too. (1978)
Catalog: Free, R&W, CAN/OV
Shop: All Year, M-F

Cape Cod Worm Farm
30 Center Ave.
Buzzards Bay, MA 02532
(617) 759-5664

SUPPLIES
Sells **earthworms and worm castings**.

Carruth Studio
7035 N. River Rd.
Waterville, OH 43566
(419) 878-8643
George & Deborah Carruth

ORNAMENTS
Handcarved sandstone, limestone and alabaster **garden sculpture, birdbaths and stone benches**, all originals of George Carruth. Also cast concrete and terra cotta birdfeeders, birdbaths and garden accessories. They have a charming, whimsical feeling; some are slyly medieval! Great gifts. (1975)
Catalog: $1d, R&W, CAN/OV
Shop: All Year, Daily

Carter Fishworm Farm
Plains, GA 31780

Offers **earthworms and worm castings**.
Catalog: Free

Carts Warehouse

See Peter Reimuller's Cart Warehouse

Charleston Battery Bench, Inc.
191 King Street
Charleston, SC 29401
(803) 722-3842 TO/CC
Andrew B. Slotin, M/M Phil H. Slotin

FURNITURE
Sells only the "**Charleston Battery Bench**", made using the mold patterns of the original maker; the bench has been in use in Charleston since the 1880's. It has cast-iron sides and cypress wood slats.
Catalog: Free, R&W, CAN
Shop: All Year, M-Sa

Charley's Greenhouse Supply
1569 Memorial Hwy.
Mt. Vernon, WA 98273
(206) 428-2626 TO/CC
Charles & Carol Yaw

SUPPLIES TOOLS BOOKS
A broad selection of **growing supplies, tools, plant lights, irrigation supplies, books** and other items. They also sell greenhouses and greenhouse materials and accessories. (1975)
Catalog: $2, CAN/OV
Shop: All Year, M-F

Chesnutt Corp.
622 Airport Road
Menasha, WI 54952
(800) 433-4475 US or 564-2440 WI TO/CC

SUPPLIES
Manufactures and sells the "Gopher", a special drill bit which fits a regular power drill and makes planting holes pronto! It comes in two models: one for a 3/8-inch drill and a heavy duty model with a longer shaft for a 1/2-inch drill.
Catalog: Free

Chicago Indoor Garden Supply

See Alternative Garden Supply, Inc.

Chippendale Home & Garden Furnishings

See Southern Statuary and Stone

Cindy's Bows
P. O. Box 50718
7 West State St.
Pasadena, CA 91105-0718
(818) 441-6564 or 799-3663
Cindy & Doreen Hambleton

ORNAMENTS
Sells **lead bows and other animal and basket ornaments** for terrace, deck or patio -- many double as small planters; all are charming.
Catalog: Free, R&W

The Clapper Co.
1121 Washington St.
West Newton, MA 02165
(617) 244-7900 TO/CC
Bob & Anette Scaguetti

TOOLS BOOKS FURNITURE ORNAMENTS
A good selection of **tools, garden furniture and ornaments, garden supplies and books**. They sell Barlow Tyrie teak benches and furniture from England and classic American-made hardwood garden furniture, swings and planters.
Catalog: Free

Clarel Laboratories, Inc.
513 Grove St.
Deerfield, IL 60015
(312) 945-4013
Al Toral

SUPPLIES
Sells "Cactus Juice" and "Granny's Bloomers" and other greenhouse and houseplant **fertilizers** especially formulated for African violets, orchids, foliage plants, cacti, ferns and tomatoes. Also sells "Moonshine" biodegradable leaf shine and "Keep 'em Bloomin'" **cut flower extender**.
Catalog: Free, R&W, MO, CAN/OV

J Collard
P. O. Box 40098
Long Beach, CA 90804-6098
Charles E. Tressler & Jane F. Collard

TOOLS FURNITURE ORNAMENTS
New company offers **tools, garden ornaments, bird houses**, even a snow shovel with a crook in its handle which will save your back. They are adding items which are attractive, durable and useful. (1987)
Catalog: Free, MO, CAN/OV

Composting Fast & Easy
709 W. Stonecrest Circle
St. Joseph, MO 64506
(816) 233-0332
Larry Kallauner

SUPPLIES
Offers a **revolving drum for composting**; they claim that it makes finished compost in twelve to sixteen days. Also sells "Load Hog" **garden carts**.
Catalog: Free, R&W
Shop: All Year, M-Sa

Robert Compton, Ltd.
Star Route, Box 6
Bristol, VT 05443
(802) 453-3778 TO/CC
Robert Compton

ORNAMENTS
Sells **stoneware fountains** in a variety of configurations and will make custom orders. Fountains come with submersible pump, ready to plug in and fill; they are completely self-contained and can be used indoors or out.
Catalog: $2, CAN/OV
Shop: All Year, By Appointment Only

CompuGarden, Inc.
1006 Highland Dr.
Silver Spring, MD 20910
(301) 587-7995
Daniel Klein & Rosanne Skirble

SERVICES
Offers **computer software** for the IBM/PC -- a planning system for vegetable gardens -- and a service for an individually prepared garden plan for those without a computer which is Zipcode specific in all regions of the U.S., Canada and Mexico.
Catalog: Free, R&W, CAN/OV
Shop: All Year, By Appointment Only

Computer/Management Services
1426 Medinah Ct.
Arnold, MD 21012
Charles W. Barbour

SERVICES
Custom **computer programs** for orchid lovers and the nursery trade; both run on IBM or compatible computers. "Orchidata" is software for keeping track of an inventory of orchids; "Collector" makes an inventory of any type of collectible, including plants. Here's a chance to organize books or photos!
Catalog: Free, MO, CAN/OV, $40m

Country Casual
17317 Germantown Road
Germantown, MD 20874-2999
(301) 540-0040 TO/CC
Mrs. Bobbie Lopatin

FURNITURE
Offers "Lister" and "Verey" British **teak benches and tables** in a variety of styles and sizes, as well as their own "Chippendale II" designs. Also several styles of garden swing, wooden planting tubs and American-made furniture of their own design in cherry. They pay the freight on purchases.
Catalog: $2, R&W, CAN/OV
Shop: All Year, Call Ahead

Country Home Products, Inc.
P. O. Box 89
Cedar Beach Road
Charlotte, VT 05445
(802) 425-2196 TO/CC $200m
Bill Lockwood

SUPPLIES
Offers the "Dick Raymond" **trimmer/mower and yard and garden wagon** -- two well-thought-out pieces of equipment. The trimmer/mower is a 'string-type' weed cutter on big wheels, which makes it possible to cut high weeds and grass easily; the cart has four wheels and a flat bed for stability. (1985)
Catalog: Free, MO, CAN/OV

Country House Floral Supply
P. O. Box 86, BVL Sta.
Andover, MA 01810
(617) 475-8463 TO/CC $20m
Helga J. Frazzette

SUPPLIES TOOLS BOOKS ORNAMENTS
Offers **flower arranging supplies**, a broad selection, including many styles of vases, bonsai stands, pruning tools and books on flower arranging.
Catalog: Free, MO, CAN/OV

Cox & Kings Travel
21 Dorset Square
London, England NW1 6Q9
(01) 724-6624
Attn: Anne Crawshay-Williams

SERVICES
Offers a number of **horticultural and botanical tours** in Europe and worldwide; flower-painting and birdwatching tours, too, all led by experts. (1758)
Catalog: Free

Creative Playgrounds, Ltd.
P. O. Box 431
Sun Prairie, WI 53590
(608) 837-7363 TO/CC
Jim Lee, V.P., Sales

FURNITURE
Sells "TimberGym" **play structures**, which can be put together in several configurations of various complexity depending on space and size of family. Even comes with a tented clubhouse for secret meetings. (1974)
Catalog: Free, R&W, CAN/OV

Critter Creek Laboratory & Orchids
400 Critter Creek Rd.
Lincoln, CA 95648
(916) 645-8520
Arthur & Beverly Allison

SERVICES
Offers **orchid testing** for cymbidium mosaic virus and tobacco mosaic virus using the accurate ELISA technique, and the capability of testing other plants for viruses. They also offer a self-testing kit and virus testing anti-serums.
Catalog: Free, R&W
Shop: By Appointment Only, Allison Ranch

Cropking Greenhouses
P. O. Box 310
6142 Wooster Pike
Medina, OH 44258
(216) 725-5656 TO $25m
Dan J. Brentlinger

SUPPLIES
Specializes in **greenhouses and supplies** and equipment for the larger scale hydroponic grower; they offer a hydroponic growers' newsletter and an annual growers' seminar in March. Much of their equipment is suitable for any greenhouse. They sell rockwool, the last word in growing media. (1981)
Catalog: $2d, R&W, CAN/OV
Shop: All Year, M-F, Call ahead

Cumberland Woodcraft
P. O. Box 609
Carlisle, PA 17013
(717) 243-0063
John Lopp, Mgr.

ORNAMENTS
Offers a broad line of Victorian "gingerbread" for remodeling, but also two charming **gazebos**, garden benches and other historical reproductions.
Catalog: $3.75, R&W, CAN/OV, $75m
Shop: All Year, M-F

Custom Orchid Propagation
221 Delayen Place
Saskatoon, SK, CANADA S7N 2T9
(306) 249-1073
Marvin Swartz

SERVICES
Offers **custom propagation of orchids**; will germinate seeds and return seedlings, do tissue culture and meristem cloning. Helpful to amateur and professional growers alike; write for information. (1987)
Catalog: See notes, R&W, USA/OV
Shop: All Year, Call Ahead

Cypress Street Center
350 Cypress St.
Fort Bragg, CA 95437
(707) 964-4940 TO/CC
George Griffith, Mgr.

FURNITURE
Sells the "Adirondack" **garden chair**, a garden classic, as well as a similar loveseat, side table and a tea/drinks trolly -- all made from California redwood for durability. Canadian readers: they will ship to BC, ON and the city of Montreal.
Catalog: Free
Shop: All Year, M-F

Dalen Products, Inc.
11110 Gilbert Dr.
Knoxville, TN 37932
(615) 966-3256 TO/CC
E. Neal Caldwell

SUPPLIES
Offers a number of **products for gardeners** -- "Solarvent" automatic greenhouse vent openers, bird and trellis netting, inflatable snake and owl scarecrows, "Miracle Mulch" porous film, the "Automator" tomato watering device, coldframes and 'floating' row covers. (1973)
Catalog: Long SASE, R&W, CAN
Shop: All Year, M-F

Jim Dalton Garden House Co.
7260-68 Oakley Street
Philadelphia, PA 19111
(215) 342-9804

ORNAMENTS
Offers **red cedar gazebos** in various sizes and styles.

Day-Dex Co.
4725 N.W. 36th Ave.
Miami, FL 33142
(305) 635-5241 or 5259
Ernie & Kim Motsinger

SUPPLIES
Offers **galvanized steel tiered benches** for orchids and other indoor and patio plants; also sells shade canopies with 55 to 73% shade. In addition, they manufacture and sell "Kinsman" carts, dollies and flat barrows for moving heavy nursery loads.
Catalog: Free, R&W, CAN/OV
Shop: All Year, M-F, Call Ahead

John Deere Catalog
1400 Third Avenue
Moline, IL 61265
(800) 544-2122
John Deere Company

SUPPLIES TOOLS BOOKS ORNAMENTS
A new venture of an old company -- a home and garden catalog offering **tools and supplies, garden ornaments and games, fireplace equipment** and more -- even John Deere maple syrup! Color catalog; nice selection. (1838)
Catalog: Free, MO, CAN/OV

Direct Book Service
P. O. Box 230
Rose Bay, NSW, Australia 2029

BOOKS
A source of all **new and current books published in Australia**; send your "want-list". Payment is by bank draft in Australian currency.
Catalog: See notes, MO

DoDe's Gardens, Inc.
1490 Saturn Street
Merritt Island, FL 32953
(305) 452-5670 TO/CC
Dorothy & James Whitaker

SUPPLIES BOOKS
Growing supplies and equipment for African violets and other indoor plants, including some books and the "Floracart" for indoor light gardening.
Catalog: 2 FCS, R&W, CAN/OV, $7.50m
Shop: By Appointment Only

Down to Earth Distributors
850 W. 2nd St.
Eugene, OR 97402
(503) 485-5932 or (800) 547-7556 TO $50m
Jack Bates & Zeph Van Allen

SUPPLIES TOOLS
Specializing in **organic fertilizers, soil amendments, pest controls and pet supplies**, as well as goods for home and kitchen. Products include bat guano, Maxicrop, greensand, bone meal, rock phosphate, Safers and Attack pest controls, worm castings and canning equipment and supplies. (1977)
Catalog: Free, R&W, CAN/OV, $50m
Shop: All Year, M-F, Call Ahead

For Explanations of Abbreviations/Codes Used In Listings See Bookmark or Inside Covers

The Dramm Company
P. O. Box 528
Manitowoc, WI 54220
(414) 684-0227 TO/CC $10m
Kurt Dramm

SUPPLIES TOOLS
Known for the "Dramm Water Breaker" **nozzles** which break the water flow into a gentle shower, offers a whole line of **watering equipment**, including watering cans and sprayers. Also sells hand-forged plant hangers, grafting and budding knives and bat guano.
Catalog: Free, R&W, MO, CAN/OV, $10m

Dressler & Co.
P. O. Box 67
Silver City, NV 89428
(702) 847-0519
Chad Dressler

ORNAMENTS
Offers a Victorian-style **cast-iron boot scraper**.
Catalog: Free, R&W, CAN/OV, $20m
Shop: Spring-Fall, Daily (Chollar Mine, Virginia City)

Drip Irrigation Garden
16216 Raymer Street
Van Nuys, CA 91406
(818) 989-5999
Joyce Schiffer & David Levy

SUPPLIES
Drip and mist irrigation supplies for the do-it-yourselfer -- including micro-sprinklers for indoors and out. Informative brochure gives basics and how to get started and what you'll need. Also "Liquick" sprayers.
Catalog: Free, R&W, CAN/OV
Shop: All Year, M-F, Call Ahead

Duncraft, Inc.
33 Fisherville Rd.
Penacook, NH 03303
(603) 224-0200 TO/CC $15m
Mike Dunn

SUPPLIES BOOKS ORNAMENTS
Broad selection of **bird feeders, bird houses and other bird related items**, including birdbaths and books. They also sell sundials with bird decorations.
Catalog: Free, R&W
Shop: All Year, M-Sa

Earlee, Inc.
2002 Highway 62
Jeffersonville, IN 47130
(812) 282-9134 TO/CC $5m
Earl Stewart, Mary Stewart, Brent Stewart

SUPPLIES
A broad selection of **organic products** for farmer and gardener; they manufacture "Nature's Way" African violet supplies and sell soil amendments, fertilizers, pest controls, bird repellents and tillers.
Catalog: Free, R&W, MO, CAN/OV, $3m

Economy Label Sales Co., Inc.
P. O. Box 350
Daytona Beach, FL 32015
(904) 253-4741 or (800) 874-4465 TO/CC
Barbara Powell-Cameron

SUPPLIES
Various styles of **plastic, paper and metal plant and garden labels**, label printers and custom labels to customer design, computer labels and software. Minimum order for most items is 1,000 of any one style, but you can get your friends or club to share an order.
Catalog: Free, R&W, CAN/OV

EcoSafe Laboratories, Inc.
P. O. Box 8702
Oakland, CA 94662
(415) 530-6586
Scott Fickes

SUPPLIES
This one's in here for Alice, Kelpie and Trout, my faithful companions: this company offers **natural flea controls** for pets, as well as vitamins and supplements. Also sells mosquito repellent, cedar spray and non-toxic plant soap.
Catalog: Free, R&W, CAN, $15m

Editions
Boiceville, NY 12412
(914) 657-7000 TO/CC $25m
Joan & Norman Levine

BOOKS
A dealer in **used and out-of-print books** in many fields; each catalog has a nice selection of books on gardening and horticulture.
Catalog: $1, CAN/OV

Laura D. Eisener, Landscape Design
59 Maple Street
Waltham, MA 02154
(617) 891-3902
Laura Eisener

BOOKS SERVICES
Sells **garden bulletins** on various aspects of planting design and plant choices, garden plans by mail and plant and garden photos from your "want-list."
Catalog: Long SASE, R&W
Shop: By Appointment Only

Electric Mobility Corp
1 Mobility Plaza
Sewell, NJ 08080
(800) 662-4548

SUPPLIES
Electric **chair-cart** to allow non-walkers to move around a garden and work from a seated position.
Catalog: Free

EnP Inc.
2001 Main St., Box 218
603 14th St.
Mendota, IL 61342
(815) 539-7471 or (800) 255-4906 TO/CC $20m
Tom Smith

SUPPLIES
Offers various **seed treatments, soil amendments, wetting agents, seaweed concentrate and humic acid products**. Informative leaflet explains purpose and use of each product. Offers "Enliven" and "Fertile Grower" products; demonstrates the effectiveness of the products in their own greenhouses.
Catalog: Free
Shop: All Year, M-Sa

Environmental Concepts
710 N. W. 57th St.
Ft. Lauderdale, FL 33309
(305) 491-4490 TO/CC $20m
Joe Lindell

SUPPLIES
Meters to measure pH, soil salts, temperature, moisture, light intensity or soil fertility. Each comes with a comprehensive book on use. Recently introduced is a light meter which measures all types of light: sun, fluorescent, grow lights and high intensity discharge lights. (1975)
Catalog: Free, CAN/OV, $20m
Shop: All Year, M-Sa

Eon Industries
P. O. Box 853
Holland, OH 43537
John H. Noe

SUPPLIES
Offers all-metal **plant and flower markers** -- zinc name plates will last for many years; galvanized wire standards are rust-resistant. Can be written on with pencils and markers which they also sell. The plates are sold separately, so you can reuse the standards. Originally the "Everlasting Label Co."
Catalog: Free, R&W, MO, CAN/OV

Erkins Studios, Inc.
604 Thames St.
Newport, RI 02840
(401) 849-2660 or 2665 TO/CC
Ann Gerrish, Mgr.

FURNITURE ORNAMENTS
Importers of **statues, fountains and other garden ornaments** in lead, iron and terra cotta: also stone, wood and metal garden benches. Styles are classic; they have some very handsome terra cotta jars and planters, as nice on city decks as in estate gardens. (1910)
Catalog: $4, R&W, CAN/OV
Shop: March-Dec, M-F, Call Ahead

Evans BioControl, Inc.
895 Interlocken Parkway, Unit A
Broomfield, CO 80020
(303) 460-1780 TO/CC
Steve Heising, Marketing Dir.

SUPPLIES
Sells "Nolo Bait", a **biological control for grasshoppers**. They say it works on fifty-eight species of grasshopper and some crickets.
Catalog: Free, R&W, MO, OV, $15m

Evergreen Garden Plant Labels
P.O. Box 922
Cloverdale, CA 95425
(707) 894-3225
Philip Edinger & Gary Patterson

SUPPLIES
Sells **metal plant label holders with metal name plates** for many types of plants, including irises, roses, daylilies, daffodils and peonies, and can make custom printed labels for favorite plants. They also sell 30-inch "Bloomstalk Supports" for tall growing flowers. (1983)
Catalog: 1 FCS, MO, CAN, $10m

Everlight Greenhouses, Inc.
9305 Gerwig Lane
Columbia, MD 21046
(301) 381-3880
William Bender & William Tisano

SUPPLIES
Offers "Everlite" **greenhouses and solariums** in many configurations for home and commercial uses, both single or double glazed. They have added a line of conservatories and garden rooms which are very "English" in style.
Catalog: $5, R&W, CAN/OV, $25m
Shop: All Year, M-F

FXG Corporation
3 Sullivan Street
Woburn, MA 01801
(617) 933-8428 or 935-1544
Frank Graney

SUPPLIES
Offers two sizes of **garden cart**: the "Log'n'Lawn" cart converts to carry wood or beehives in a rack; the "Log'n'Lawn Jr." will haul wood in a rack or barrels or trash containers. Also sells mechanical log-splitters.
Catalog: Free, R&W, CAN/OV, $25m
Shop: All Year, M-F, Call Ahead

Fireside & Green Conserver Products

See Green Hand Tools

Floracolour
21 Oakleigh Rd., Hillingdon
Uxbridge, Middlesex, England UB10 9EL
(0895) 51831
H.C.W. Shaw

SERVICES
Here's the answer to my perennial problem of loading the film incorrectly: Mr. Shaw offers sets of slides of famous gardens, the Chelsea Flower Shows, interesting plants and flowers in England and abroad, the 'stately homes' and even a steam train and vintage car rally -- and he can wait for the sun!
Catalog: Free, OV
Shop: All Year, Daily, Call Ahead

Floral Accents
Route I, Box 69
Rustburg, VA 24588
Elizabeth Blanks

SUPPLIES
Sells **flower arranging supplies** in bulk for garden clubs and classes; all supplies seem to be sold by the case. (1984)
Catalog: Long SASE, MO

Floralight Gardens Canada, Inc.
P. O. Box 247, Sta. A
Willowdale, ON, Canada M2N 5S9
(416) 920-4769 or 665-4000 TO/CC
Alan Patte

SUPPLIES
Manufactures and sells "Floralight" **plant stands** -- multi-tiered systems for propagation or for indoor growing of African violets, orchids and other houseplants; can even be used for hydroponics.
Catalog: Free, R&W, MO, USA

Florapersonnel
P. O. Box 1732
Deland, FL 32721
(904) 738-5151
Robert F. Zahra, Mgr.

SERVICES
A **horticultural employment agency** which lists many types of job: managers of commercial operations, florists, landscape architects, estate managers, nursery supply and management, import and export -- you name it! A good way to find a job or a qualified worker. (1982)
Catalog: Free

Florentine Craftsmen, Inc.
46-24 28th Street
Long Island City, NY 11101
(212) 532-3926 or (718) 937-7632
Graham Brown

FURNITURE ORNAMENTS
A wide selection of fine **lead statuary, fountains, cast aluminum and cast iron furniture** in classic styles. Also sundials, birdbaths, weathervanes, planters and cherubs and animals of the most appealing sort. (1928)
Catalog: $3, R&W, CAN/OV
Shop: All Year, M-F

Florist Products, Inc.
2242 North Palmer Dr.
Schaumburg, IL 60173
(312) 885-2242
Paul Lange

SUPPLIES TOOLS
A broad selection of **gardening supplies, tools and equipment, pots, fertilizers and mist systems**; also sells the "Wonder Garden", a lighted plant stand for indoor light gardening. They have another catalog for commercial growers with a complete line of supplies; request on letterhead.
Catalog: Free, R&W, CAN
Shop: All Year, M-F (Closed first two weeks of July)

Foothill Agricultural Research, Inc.
510 W. Chase Drive
Corona, CA 91720
(805) 371-0120 TO $10m
Reed Finfrock & Jim Davis

SUPPLIES
Offers a wide selection of **beneficial insects**: parasitic wasps, fly parasites, ladybugs, predatory mites, green lacewings, preying mantids and decollate snails. Also Chilocorus nigritus, a voracious predatory beetle which attacks scale insects, including red scale. (1978)
Catalog: Free, R&W, CAN/OV, $10m
Shop: All Year, Daily, Call Ahead

Fountain Sierra Bug Company
P. O. Box 114
Rough & Ready, CA 95975
(916) 273-0513
H. H. Fountain

SUPPLIES
Sells **ladybugs**, those little charmers who really earn their keep; offered from one-half pint to one gallon, sent by Air Mail.
Catalog: Free, SS:1-9

Four Seasons Greenhouses
425 Smith Street
Farmingdale, NY 11735
(516) 694-4400 or (800) 645-9527

SUPPLIES
Sells **greenhouses and lean-to solariums**.
Catalog: Free

Freedom Soil Lab
P. O. Box 1144
1234 Highway 1 (Watsonville)
Freedom, CA 95019-1144
Frank Shields

BOOKS SERVICES
Offers **soil testing** by mail; issues a report showing your results in primary and secondary nutrients, toxic salts, pH value and organic matter; and compares them to typical fertile soil. Also sells books on soil management and crop production. Quantity discounts to clubs and garden shops. (1987)
Catalog: Free, CAN/OV, $10m
Shop: All Year, M-F

Full Circle Garden Products
P. O. Box 6
77 Ave. of the Giants (Phillipsville)
Redway, CA 95560
(800) 426-5511 TO/CC
Michael & Rhona Martin

SUPPLIES BOOKS
Offers a broad selection of **growing supplies**: fertilizers, irrigation supplies, sprayers, tools, pruning tools, plant lights and pest controls. Also sells rockwool for hydroponic growing; it's becoming 'the thing' for orchids, too. Sells bat guano in 10-3-1 and 2-8-.05 formulas. (1983)
Catalog: $2d, R&W, CAN/OV, $10m
Shop: All Year, M-F

The Garden Book Club
250 W. 57th St.
New York, NY 10107
(212) 582-6912
New York Review of Books

BOOKS
Just like that big **book club**, monthly selections and other new garden books offered at a discount. Has had a series of terrific introductory offers in the past and has had the ineffable good taste to offer this book to its members since it first came out.
Catalog: Write for information

The Garden Concepts Collection
4646 Poplar Avenue
Memphis, TN 38117
(901) 682-1109 or 1156 TO/CC $100m
John B. Painter

FURNITURE ORNAMENTS
A broad selection of **ornaments and furnishings** for the garden: pavilions, arbors, pergolas, bridges, gates, lighting systems, planters, plant stands, garden furniture -- in a variety of historical styles.
Catalog: $2, R&W
Shop: All Year, M-F

Garden Way Manufacturing Co.
102nd St. and 9th Ave.
Troy, NY 12180
(800) 828-5500 TO/CC

SUPPLIES
Manufactures and sells "Troy-Bilt" tillers, "Garden Way" carts and "Tomahawk" chipper/shredders. The **tillers** come in several sizes to suit various uses and power requirements, as do the **chipper/shredders**. They also have a **sickle-bar mower** for rough stuff.
Catalog: Free, MO, CAN/OV

Gardener's Eden
Box 7307
San Francisco, CA 94120-7307
(415) 428-9292 TO/CC
Williams-Sonoma

SUPPLIES FURNITURE ORNAMENTS
Offers a broad selection of **tools, equipment and gadgets** for gardening, including ornaments and many unusual and appropriate gifts for gardeners.
Catalog: Free

Gardener's Supply Company
128 Intervale Rd.
Burlington, VT 05401
(802) 863-1700 TO/CC
Will Raap

SUPPLIES TOOLS ORNAMENTS
A broad selection of **tools and equipment, organic fertilizers and pesticides, tillers and food preservation supplies** -- most illustrated in color catalog. They also sell greenhouses, composters, garden swings and chairs, shredder/chippers, carts, sprayers, knee pads, a wind-driven mole-repeller.
Catalog: Free
Shop: All Year, M-Sa

Gardenworks
P. O. Box 112
Coloma, CA 95613
(916) 622-3895 TO $100m
Jeffrey Brees

ORNAMENTS
A good selection of **topiary frames**, all painted with green enamel and fitted with watering tubes where appropriate. They will do custom orders and have garden club specials for group orders.
Catalog: Free, R&W, CAN/OV, $100m
Shop: May-Nov, By Appointment Only

V. L. T. Gardner
30026 Avenida Celestial
Rancho Palos Verdes, CA 90274
(213) 541-1372
Virginia Gardner

BOOKS SERVICES
Offers **new and used books** on horticulture, gardening, botany, landscape architecture and plants and gardens appropriate to Southern California and other dry areas; and will search for out-of-print books on those subjects. No catalog at present; call or send "want list". (1982)
Catalog: See notes, R&W, CAN/OV
Shop: By Appointment Only

Genie House
P. O. Box 2478
Vincentown, NJ 08088
(609) 654-8303

SUPPLIES
Hand-crafted brass and copper light fixtures in classic styles; they will also do custom work.
Catalog: Free

Gladstone & Campbell
North Park Studio
Hawarden, Clwyd, Wales, U.K. CH5 3NY
(244) 535306
Francis Gladstone & Josephine Gladstone

BOOKS
Catalog of **British, American and European garden books**, both rare and used and out-of-print, is $2. Invoices are payable in U.S. dollars. They also carry a large stock of old botanical prints; a catalog of hand-colored prints is $5, deductible from first order.
Catalog: See notes, OV
Shop: By Appointment Only

Goodly Publishing
Route 3, Box 252
Stanfield, NC 28163
Michael & Loni Woodward

SUPPLIES
Sells a "Garden Log", a **diary for planning and keeping garden records**; it has a month-by-month reminder section, planning grids and blank pages for keeping notes. They have no catalog; the diary is $7 ppd.
Catalog: See notes, R&W, MO, CAN/OV

Gothic Arch Greenhouses
P. O. Box 1564
1059 Sutton Ave.
Mobile, AL 36633-1564
(205) 432-7529 TO/CC
W. H. Sierke, Jr.

SUPPLIES
Redwood or red cedar **greenhouses** with fiber glass glazing in a pointed-arch style, either attached or free-standing. Also sells heating/cooling systems, shade cloth, benches and supplies. (1945)
Catalog: Free
Shop: All Year, M-F, Call Ahead

Great Lakes IPM
10220 Church Rd. N.E.
Vestaburg, MI 48891
(517) 268-5693
James Hansel

SUPPLIES
A good selection of **supplies and equipment for integrated pest management**, insect traps of all kinds and controlled-release pheromone dispensers; an informative catalog.
Catalog: Free, R&W, CAN
Shop: All Year, M-F

For Explanations of Abbreviations/Codes Used in Listings See Bookmark or Inside Covers

Green Earth Organics
9422 144th St. East
Puyallup, WA 98373
(206) 845-2321
Joel & MariLou Holland

SUPPLIES TOOLS
Offers a number of **organic products** for soil improvement, fertilizing and insect control; they manufacture their own "Multi-Crop Liquid Seaweed". Also sells seeds for green manure crops, watering equipment and general growing supplies.
Catalog: Free, R&W, CAN/OV
Shop: Feb-May, M-Sa: June-Jan, By Appointment Only

Green Hand Tools
2301 Avenue C North
Saskatoon, SK, Canada S7L 5Z5
(306) 665-6707 TO/CC
David Van Vliet

TOOLS BOOKS FURNITURE
A broad selection of **garden tools and equipment**, mostly imported from England and Japan, as well as some gardening books, furniture and watering equipment. Also known as Fireside & Green Conserver Products. (1982)
Catalog: $2d, R&W, USA

The Green House
1432 W. Kerrick St.
Lancaster, CA 93534
(805) 948-1959 TO $50m
John Mankc

SUPPLIES
Sells only the "Gro-Cart" and accessories: a **lighted plant stand** for indoor gardening. Shipped only to UPS areas.
Catalog: Free
Shop: Sept-June, By Appointment Only

Green River Tools

See The Plow & Hearth

Green Thumb Hygro-Gardens
P. O. Box 1314
Sheboygan, WI 53081-1314
(414) 459-8989
Robert Van Derslice

SUPPLIES
"We offer several **hydroponic systems** for the home hydroponic enthusiast: can be used inside or outside, and can be expanded."
Catalog: $1, R&W, CAN/OV
Shop: By Appointment Only

The Greener Thumb
P. O. Box 704
Littlefield, TX 79339
Richard A. Ferrill

SUPPLIES TOOLS
New company offers "Spear & Jackson" and "True Friends" tools, organic pest controls, "Gloria" sprayers, the "Earthtumbler" compost maker and "Nature's Raindrops" sprinkler, which puts out large drops, so there's less drift in the wind. (1987)
Catalog: Free

Greenhouse Builders Supply
Rt. 3, Box 80
Epping, NH 03042
(603) 679-1208
Robert Daley

SUPPLIES
Sells **greenhouses and greenhouse building materials** for the hobbyist or the large commercial installation; also lean-to greenhouses and wooden solariums. Also offers greenhouse accessories and ventilation systems and controls, in a well illustrated catalog -- lots of construction detail drawings.
Catalog: $2, R&W, CAN, $10m
Shop: By Appointment Only

Greenhouse Specialties Co.
P. O. Box 4920
Princeton, FL 33092
Frank G. Finck, Jr.

SUPPLIES
Building materials for people who want to build their own greenhouses; there's a small plan for building a 14 x 14 greenhouse included, with all the details a builder or knowledgable do-it-yourselfer would need.
Catalog: $1d, R&W, MO

Greenleaf Technologies
P. O. Box 12726
746 Galloway Ave.
Memphis, TN 38182
(901) 521-1758 TO/CC
Bill Smart

SUPPLIES
Offers **portable, battery operated sprayers** in 2-1/2, 5 and 15 gallon capacity. The batteries are rechargable; sprayers deliver from .4 to .85 gallons per minute, and will spray up to 40 feet. They are mounted on two-wheeled carts with big wheels.
Catalog: Free, CAN
Shop: All Year, M-F

Gro-n-Energy
P. O. Box 1114
Matthews, NC 28106-1114
Sandy Enes

SUPPLIES
Offers a good selection of **greenhouse and propagation supplies** for the home gardener, including pots, flats, watering nozzles, fertilizers and insecticides.
Catalog: 1 FCS

Gro-Tek
RFD 1, Box 518A
South Berwick, ME 03908
(207) 676-2209 TO/CC $25m
Tin Smith

A good selection of **indoor and greenhouse growing supplies**, including irrigation, propagation, glazing and shade cloth, ventilation and organic soil amendments and insect controls.
Catalog: $1, CAN
Shop: All Year, Daily, By Appointment Only

The Growing Company
P. O. Box 1276
Los Angeles, CA 90069
(213) 659-GROW
Stephen Morey

SUPPLIES
Here's an **organizer for the gardener**, like the ones the Yuppies use, only not for aerobics and power lunchs, but for really important stuff -- organizing your garden. Has a diary, maintenance schedule, room for plans and shopping lists and more. It's loose leaf, so you can add your own pages.
Catalog: Free, R&W, MO, $30m

H. P. Supplies, Inc.
P. O. Box 2053
Livonia, MI 48150
(313) 422-2420 TO/CC
John Walter

SUPPLIES
Sells **lighted plant carts** and accessories for indoor growing.
Catalog: Free, R&W

Hanover Lantern
470 High Street
Hanover, PA 17331
(717) 632-6464
Michael Hoffman

SUPPLIES
Sells the "Hanover Lantern", a **12-volt lighting system** for gardens; the fixtures come in a variety of styles both traditional and modern.
Catalog: R&W

Happy Valley Ranch
Route 2, Box 83-4
Paola, KS 66071
(913) 849-3103 TO/CC
Ray & Wanda Stagg

SUPPLIES
Offers **cider and wine presses** for the home orchardist or winemaker: single and double presses, presses in kit form; separate apple grinders and picking bags, loppers, pole saws and pruners. They also have a cider cookbook.
Catalog: $1, CAN/OV
Shop: Call Ahead

Harlane Company, Inc.
266 Orangeburgh Rd.
Old Tappan, NJ 07675
(201) 768-0158
Frank & June Benardella

SUPPLIES TOOLS
Sells **garden markers** with removable name plates, marking pens, "Felco" **pruning shears**, a rose pruning saw and pH testing meters. They will custom print rose nameplates.
Catalog: Free

Harper Horticultural Slide Library
219 Robanna Shores
Seaford, VA 23696
(804) 898-6453
Pamela Harper

SERVICES
Huge selection of **photographic slides of plants, gardens, landscaping and natural scenery**, available for purchase or rent (some sets with lecture notes); catalog well arranged by subject. Ms. Harper is a well-known photographer and garden writer. (1973)
Catalog: $2, MO, CAN/OV

Harvest Glow Systems
32 E. Fillmore Ave.
St. Paul, MN 55107
(612) 291-7383 TO/CC
Matt Storm

SUPPLIES TOOLS
Offers **hydroponic systems and planters, supplies, tools, plant lights and nutrients**, even seeds specially chosen for hydroponic growing. (1983)
Catalog: Free, R&W, CAN/OV, $4m
Shop: All Year, M-F

Hatchard's
187 Piccadilly
London, England W1V 9DA
01-439-9921

BOOKS
Long-established bookseller which issues a periodic catalog offering a broad selection of **gardening and horticultural books** -- they will accept credit card orders from overseas. The Royal Horticultural Society was founded in the back room. Write for information.

Philip Hawk & Company
159 E. College Ave.
Pleasant Gap, PA 16823
(814) 355-7177
Philip Hawk

ORNAMENTS
Handcarved **stone lanterns** for outdoor lighting, in traditional Japanese and and original designs; they are naturally not cheap, but beautiful, and would make a lovely commemorative gift. (1978)
Catalog: $3, R&W, CAN/OV
Shop: By Appointment Only

Hayes Equipment Co.
150 New Britain Ave.
Unionville, CT 06085
(203) 673-2556 TO/CC

SUPPLIES
Offers two models of **garden cart**, to carry 350 or 500 lbs., and several small trailers for hauling small equipment, wood, hay, furniture and similar light loads behind a car.
Catalog: Free, R&W, CAN

Heritage Arts
16651 S.E. 235th St.
Kent, WA 98042
(206) 631-1318
Sharon Muth

SUPPLIES TOOLS BOOKS SERVICES
A broad selection of **bonsai pots, tools, supplies** and some books; they offer "Kaneshin" bonsai tools and "Tokoname" bonsai pots. They also offer classes on bonsai and repotting and styling services at the shop.
Catalog: $2, R&W, CAN
Shop: All Year, Th-Sa

Heritage Lanterns
70A Main Street
Yarmouth, ME 04096
(207) 846-3911 or (800) 544-6070 TO/CC
H. William Geoffrion

Beautiful hand-crafted **lanterns and light fixtures in copper, pewter and brass**, available in a variety of classic styles for outdoors and indoors. They will also do custom work.
Catalog: $3, R&W, CAN/OV
Shop: All Year, M-F

Heritage Sundial
7340 East 131st St.
Bixby, OK 74008
(918) 747-1390 or (800) 537-5412 TO/CC $20m
Connie Hollingsworth

ORNAMENTS
Sells a nice selection of **sundials** in handsome designs with brass and bronze finishes and in terra cotta. There are styles to suit many gardens, from cottages to palaces, including a nice lily-pad with a frog or a duck sitting on it.
Catalog: Free, R&W, MO, $20m

Hermitage Gardens
P. O. Box 361
Canastota, NY 13032
(315) 697-9093
Russell Rielle

ORNAMENTS
Sells a number of fiber glass **fountains, pools, waterfalls**, redwood water-wheels and equipment for water gardening such as pumps and lights; many of their illustrations show indoor installations. They also sell ornamental **bridges** in several styles.
Catalog: Free, R&W, CAN, $100m
Shop: All Year, Daily, Call Ahead

Historical Landscapes
RD 2, Box 242A
Bernville, PA 19506
Amy White Gernsheimer

SERVICES
Historical garden designs for period homes, based on your information and the style of your house. Will also do planting designs based on plants used during various historical eras and does research and consultation.
Catalog: Free, R&W, CAN/OV
Shop: By Appointment Only

Homestead Carts
6098 Topaz Street N.E.
Salem, OR 97305
(503) 390-5586
Marvin Botts

SUPPLIES
Offers a 26" **garden cart** with a 400 lb. carrying capacity -- also available as a kit -- and a 20" cart for smaller gardens. They will sell wheels and axles separately.
Catalog: Free

Honigklip Nurseries & Book Sales
13 Lady Anne Avenue
Newlands, Cape Town, South Africa 7700
(021) 644410
Mrs. E. R. Middelmann

BOOKS SERVICES
Price list offers a broad selection of **books on South African plants and gardens**; they also will search for used and out-of-print books. Payment is in U.S. dollars.
Catalog: Free, R&W, OV
Shop: All Year, M-F

House of Violets
936-940 Garland St. S.W.
Camden, AR 71701
(501) 836-3016
Charlyne & Ralph Reed

SUPPLIES
Sells only the Swift "Moist-Rite" **self-**
and other small plants, singly or by the case.
Catalog: Free, R&W

Hubbard Folding Box Co. *15980 Rush Creek Rd.* *Osseo, MN 55369* *(612) 420-2875* *Floyd Nelson*	SUPPLIES **Folding wooden fruit harvesting boxes**; can have names or logos printed on the side; can be used over and over again. They come in several sizes and styles. Great for moving all sorts of belongings; nice gift. (1898) Catalog: Free, R&W, CAN/OV
H. D. Hudson Mfg. Co. *500 N. Michigan Ave.* *Chicago, IL 60611* *(312) 644-2830* *R. C. Hudson, Jr.*	SUPPLIES Offers many styles of **garden sprayers**, from hand pumping sprayers and dusters to back packs and a power sprayer on wheels; offer economy to top-of-the-line models. Catalog: R&W
Hurley Books *R.R. 1, Box 160* *Route 12* *Westmoreland, NH 03467* *(603) 399-4342* *Henry & Janet Hurley*	BOOKS **Historical or textual books** on agriculture, horticulture, animal husbandry, cottage industry and rural miscellany. They also have older seed catalogs, 19th century horticultural periodicals: a selection of over 2,000 titles. Catalog: $1, CAN, $10m Shop: All Year, Call Ahead
Hyde Bird Feeder Co. *P. O. Box 168* *Waltham, MA 02254* *(617) 893-6780* *Donald B. Hyde, Jr., & Jim Flewelling*	SUPPLIES ORNAMENTS Sells **bird feeders, houses, bird seed and gifts for the bird lover**: Canadian customers contact Yule-Hyde Assoc., 329 Rayette, Unit 7 & 8, Concord, ON L4K 2G1. (1942) Catalog: Free, R&W, MO
Hydro-Gardens of Denver *P. O. Box 9707* *Colorado Springs, CO 80932* *(303) 495-2266 or (800) 634-6362 TO/CC $10m* *Mike Morton or Stan Benson*	SUPPLIES **Greenhouse and hydroponic growing supplies** of all kinds for the home grower or large commercial operator, including their "Chem-Gro Nutrient". A very broad selection; ask for either home catalog or commercial catalog. (1972) Catalog: Free, R&W, CAN/OV, $10m Shop: All Year, M-F
I. F. M. *333-B Ohme Garden Road* *Wenatchee, WA 98801* *(509) 662-3179 or 662-1922 TO/CC* *Phillip Unterschuetz*	SUPPLIES SERVICES **Organic garden products and pest controls**: a good selection, with products and their uses well described. They are specialists in organic fruit production and toxic residue testing. Offer soil amendments, natural pest controls, beneficial insects, traps and baits, soaps and green manure seed. Catalog: Free, R&W, CAN/OV Shop: All Year, M-Sa
ISBS, Inc.	See International Specialized Book Services, Inc.
Idaho Wood Industries, Inc. *P. O. Box 488* *3425 Meadow Creek Dr.* *Sandpoint, ID 83864-0488* *(800) 635-1100 or (208) 263-9521 TO/CC* *Leon Lewis & Linda Mitchell*	ORNAMENTS **Natural wood garden lights**, mostly lights on standards for paths and gardens; also sell handsome indoor and outdoor wall and ceiling fixtures in natural wood and wooden bathroom accessories. (1975) Catalog: Free, R&W, CAN/OV Shop: All Year, M-F, Call Ahead
Indoor Gardening Supplies *P. O. Box 40567* *Detroit, MI 48240* *(313) 427-6160 TO/CC* *Nancy Allen*	SUPPLIES Offers a good selection of **growing supplies** for indoor and light gardening and plant propagation: lighted plant stands, plant lights, capillary matting, meters, timers, pots, trays and more. Catalog: Free
Integrated Fertility Management	See I.F.M.
International Bonsai Containers *412 Pinnacle Road* *Rochester, NY 14623* *(716) 344-2595*	SUPPLIES TOOLS Offers a broad selection of **bonsai pots, tools, books and supplies**; pots are sold by the case for groups and clubs. They also offer a series of **video cassettes** teaching master bonsai techniques. Catalog: Free, CAN/OV, $25m
International Irrigation Systems *P. O. Box 1133* *St. Catharines, ON, Canada L2R 7A3* *(416) 688-4090 or 2242* *Robert L. Neff*	SUPPLIES "Irrigro" **drip irrigation systems** based on micro-porous tubing, for continuous watering from gravity flow tank or house faucet; also offer "Fertil--Matic" system for continuous fertilizing. U.S. buyers see Irrigro of Niagara Falls, NY. Catalog: Free, R&W, OV Shop: All Year, M-F, By Appointment Only

For Explanations of Abbreviations/Codes Used In Listings See Bookmark or Inside Covers

International Nursery Labels
7000 Soquel Dr., #333
Aptos, CA 95003
(408) 684-1007
Nick & Patty Russo

Sells a broad selection of **plant labels** (attached to plant or put in pot) and **garden markers** (to stick in ground near plant). These can be pre-printed with plant names or custom designed for your needs.
Catalog: Long SASE, R&W, CAN/OV, $1.50m

International Specialized Book Services, Inc.
5602 N.E. Hassalo St.
Portland, OR 97213
(503) 287-3093 or (800) 547-7734 TO/CC
John F. Knapp

BOOKS
A good selection of **gardening books** from all over the world, as well as the beautiful books published by Timber Press, with which they are affiliated.
Catalog: Free, R&W, CAN/OV, $10m
Shop: All Year, M-F

InterNet, Inc.
2730 Nevada Ave. N.
Minneapolis, MN 55427
(800) 328-8456 or (612) 541-9690
William B. Richardson

SUPPLIES
Offers two weights of black polypropylene **bird netting** with an ultraviolet inhibitor, used by home gardeners and to keep birds from nesting on buildings, etc. Also sells clips to attach the panels to buildings or cables.
Catalog: Free, R&W, CAN/OV
Shop: All Year, M-F, By Appointment Only

Irrigro
P. O. Box 160
Niagara Falls, NY 14304
(416) 688-4090 TO/CC
Robert L. Neff

SUPPLIES
The "Irrigro" system is based on a **porous plastic tubing**; they offer kits and supplies for building your own system, as well as a gravity feed system which can also apply fertilizers. Canadian buyers see International Irrigation Systems in St. Catharines, ON.
Catalog: Free

Ivelet Books
18 Fairlawn Dr.
Redhill, Surrey, England RH1 6JP
(0737) 64520 or (+44) 737-64520 TO/CC $10m
S. A. Ahern

BOOKS
Used, out-of-print and rare books on horticulture, gardening, garden design and history, plant collecting and related subjects.
Catalog: Free, R&W, OV
Shop: By Appointment Only

Ian Jackson
P. O. Box 9075
Berkeley, CA 94709
(415) 548-1431
Ian Jackson

BOOKS
Offers **used and out-of-print books** on plants, gardens and horticulture; a good selection. Issues three or four catalogs a year.
Catalog: Free, R&W, MO, CAN/OV

Jaffrey Mfg. Co.
P. O.Box 421
Jaffrey, NH 03452
(603) 673-8466 TO/CC
Bruce Holt

SUPPLIES
Sells a **cider and wine press** with frame parts made of solid maple for strength; you can buy it assembled, as a kit or the hardware parts only. They also sell an old-fashioned wooden wheelbarrow made from oak.
Catalog: Free, R&W, CAN, $100m

Janco Greenhouses
9390 Davis Avenue
Laurel, MD 20707
(301) 498-5700
J.A. Nearing Co.

SUPPLIES
Offers **greenhouses and greenhouse additions** in a variety of configurations for home and commercial uses. Also sells accessories, controls and ventilators for greenhouses.
Catalog: $2, R&W

Jersey Village Gardener
P. O. Box 40526
Houston, TX 77240-0526
(713) 466-3123 TO/CC
Dan Agan

Ah! The wonders of the computer. I learned four days before going to the printer that this company has gone out of business. Just in time to put in a note, but not in time to take it out of the index. Now you see why we make such a point of offering updates!

David Kay Garden & Gift Catalogue, Inc.
4509 Taylor Lane
Cleveland, OH 44128
(216) 464-5125 or (800) 872-5588 TO/CC
David A. Kay

SUPPLIES TOOLS FURNITURE ORNAMENTS
A good selection of **tools, supplies and gifts for gardeners** and nature lovers, garden ornaments and furniture, decorations for the lunch table -- all shown in a color catalog. They also offer wildflower seeds and plants and some exotic plants for indoors. (1982)
Catalog: Free, CAN/OV
Shop: All Year, M-F, Call Ahead

Kemp Company
160 Koser Rd.
Lititz, PA 17543
(717) 627-7979 TO/CC
Mike Peck & Howard Livingston

SUPPLIES
Offers **shredder/chippers** in various models, depending on the volume of material to be handled.
Catalog: Free, CAN/OV, $10m
Shop: All Year, M-F

The Ken-L-Questor
32255 N. Highway 99 W
Newburg, OR 97132
(503) 538-2051
Kenneth M. Lewis

BOOKS
Specializes in **used, rare and out-of-print books** on cacti and succulents, lilies, mushrooms and fungi. Each is on a separate list; please specify which list you want. Dog books, too!
Catalog: $1d(2 IRC), CAN/OV
Shop: All Year, Daily, Call Ahead

The Keth Company
P. O. Box 645
Corona del Mar, CA 92625
Mary Keth

SUPPLIES
A good selection of **supplies for flower arrangers**, including the "Keth Candlestick Cup" for putting flowers on candle holders, and sets of tiny lights which run off small batteries and would make flower arrangements really sparkle.
Catalog: $1d, MO, CAN/OV

Myron Kimnach
1600 Orlando Rd.
San Marino, CA 91108
(818) 792-4881
Myron Kimnach

BOOKS
Specializes in **books on ferns, bromeliads and cactus and succulents.**
Catalog: Free, MO, CAN/OV

Kinco Manufacturing
170 N. Pascal St.
St. Paul, MN 55104
(612) 644-4666 TO
John Kinkead & Tom Fiske

SUPPLIES
Sells a gas-powered heavy duty **sickle-bar mower** for cutting heavy weeds and brush, even saplings; can be used over rough terrain. (1972)
Catalog: Free, R&W, CAN/OV
Shop: All Year, M-F

Sue Fisher King
3075 Sacramento St.
San Francisco, CA 94115
(415) 922-7276
Sue Fisher King

ORNAMENTS
Classic Italian **terra cotta planters** in several styles, which they will pack very carefully and ship. Also **seats and gazebos** of elaborate wire design, very lacy and Victorian, and false-lead planters in molded fiber glass in classic English designs.
Catalog: $1, R&W
Shop: All Year, M-Sa

Kinsman Company, Inc.
River Road
Point Pleasant, PA 18950
(215) 297-5613 TO/CC
Graham & Michele Kinsman

SUPPLIES TOOLS
Importers of English **garden tools and equipment**: electric and hand-powered shredders, compost bins, sieves, strawberry tubs and modular arbors. These items sold in Canada by Dominion Seed House, Georgetown, ON, L7G 4A2.
Catalog: Free, R&W
Shop: All Year, M-F, Call (Doylestown) (215) 348-0840

Kinsmen Corp.
214 Permalune Pl. N.W.
Atlanta, CA 30318
(404) 355-9550
James P. Walsh, Sr.

SUPPLIES
Offers horticultural-grade **pumice** for growing cactus; it comes in Grades 5 and -1/4+1/8 (smaller than 1/4-inch, larger than 1/8-inch) and is shipped in 50 pound bags.
Catalog: Free, R&W, MO

Kohan-Matlick Productions
1016 N. Sycamore
Hollywood, CA 90038
(213) 876-4055 TO/CC $30m
John & Felisa Kohan-Matlick

SUPPLIES
Offers a **video cassette** on "How to Care for Cymbidium Orchids", which do particularly well outdoors in frost-free areas.
Catalog: Free, R&W, $30m
Shop: All Year, M-F, Call Ahead

Ladybug Sales

See West Coast Lady Bug Sales

Landscape Books
P. O. Box 483
Exeter, NH 03833
(603) 964-9333
Jane W. Robie

BOOKS
Broad selection of **books on garden history, landscape architecture** and **city planning**: books are new, used and out-of-print and rare; all are well described as to contents and condition. (1972)
Catalog: $3, MO, CAN/OV

LaRamie Soils Service
P. O. Box 255
Laramie, WY 82070
(307) 742-4185
Michael McFaul

SERVICES
Soil testing for organic and non-organic gardeners, with suggestions for amendments, crop suitability and rotation -- designed to build organically rich soils as quickly as possible. They do not send a catalog, but mail you a bag for a soil sample, with collection instructions.
Catalog: See notes, MO

C. M. Leonard, Inc.
P. O. Box 816
Piqua, OH 45356
(800) 543-8955 TO/CC $25m
P. E. Dunlavy

SUPPLIES TOOLS
A very broad selection of **tools, supplies and equipment** for home and commercial gardeners -- almost everything for gardening and growing. As they specialize in supplies for commercial operators, some of the supplies come in large quantities. (1885)
Catalog: Free, R&W, MO, CAN/OV

For Explanations of Abbreviations/Codes Used In Listings See Bookmark or Inside Covers

Lexigrow
P. O. Box 1491
Indianapolis, IN 46206-1491
(317) 844-5691
Jack Miles Langston

SUPPLIES
Offers "Leximulch", a **fabric mulch** which can be used in many ways to cut down on weeding and tilling; even discourages moles. It can be used to keep weeds from growing between paving materials, for erosion control and as a frost cover for plants. They also sell clamps to anchor it in place.
Catalog: Free

Limewalk Tours
102 Lake Street
Burlington, VT 05401
(802) 863-5790
Cecelia M. Lindberg

SERVICES
Offers **garden tours** to Britain, Ireland and Europe -- different tours each year; gardens always visited with the owner and/or head gardener, and tours include significant historical and cultural sites.
Catalog: Free

The Live Oak Railroad Co.
111 East Howard St.
Live Oak, FL 32060
(904) 362-4419 TO/CC

FURNITURE
Offers turn-of-the-century **cast iron benches and street lamp posts**.
Catalog: Free

Living Green, Inc.
4091 E. LaPalma Ave., Ste. E
Anaheim, CA 92807
(714) 630-3914 or (800) LG-HYDRO TO/CC
Frank Bramante

SUPPLIES
Sells a self-contained **hydroponic planter/garden** for the home; it takes up about 3 square feet and can provide tomatoes all winter, herbs or whatever you want. (1985)
Catalog: Free, R&W, CAN/OV
Shop: All Year, M-F, Call Ahead

Living Wall Gardening Co.
2044 Chili Avenue
Tobey Street (Naples)
Rochester, NY 14624
(716) 247-0080 or 374-2340 TO/CC

SUPPLIES
Sells polyethylene modules which fit together and form **vertical planters** with many planting pockets -- good for small spaces such as decks or patios, can be joined together to make a screen or hedge for privacy and beauty -- planted with vegetables or ornamentals. Great for the handicapped.
Catalog: Free, R&W, CAN/OV
Shop: All Year, M-Sa

Lloyds' of Kew
9, Mortlake Terrace
Kew, Surrey, England TW9 3DT
(01) 940-2512 TO/CC
Daniel Lloyd

BOOKS SERVICES
A very broad selection of **used and out-of-print books** in gardening and horticulture, with many new and recent books; they will search for wanted items not on their list. Shop is very near to Kew Gardens and fun to include on a visit there -- or to the Maids of Honour tea shop down the road.
Catalog: $1d(2 IRC), OV
Shop: All Year, M-Tu, Th-Sa

Lord & Burnham
CSB 3181
Melville, NY 11747
Burnham Corp.

SUPPLIES
Offers "Evenspan" **greenhouses and lean-to additions**.
Catalog: $2

Kenneth Lynch & Sons, Inc.
78 Danbury Rd.
Wilton, CT 06897
(203) 762-8363
Lynch Family

FURNITURE ORNAMENTS
Offers a huge selection of **garden ornaments**: furniture, statues, planters and urns, gates, topiary frames, weather vanes, fountains and pools. Over 10,000 different items. Heaven must look like the Lynch catalog!
Catalog: $8, CAN/OV

MAC Industries
8125 S I-35
Oklahoma City, OK 73149

SUPPLIES
Offers **purple martin houses**.
Catalog: $.50

McDermott Garden Products
P. O. Box 129
1300 South Grand Ave.
Charles City, IA 50616
(515) 228-5086 or 228-6334 TO/CC $20m
Leon McDermott

SUPPLIES
Sells **raised planters made of coated steel**; they come 14 or 28 inches high, are open at the bottom for good drainage. The 28-inch model is ideal for gardeners who cannot bend or stoop. They also sell a revolving drum compost maker for quick conversion of garden clippings to compost.
Catalog: Free, R&W, CAN/OV, $20m
Shop: All Year, M-F, Call Ahead

Mrs. McGregor's Garden Shop
4801 - 1st Street North
Arlington, VA 22203
(703) 528-8773 TO/CC
Nancy Schuhmann

TOOLS ORNAMENTS
Offers several styles of **natural wood planters**: some carved with rabbits and cabbages, others in simple classic styles. Also sells other garden ornaments, hand tools, window boxes and gifts for your gardening friends.
Catalog: Free, R&W, CAN/OV
Shop: All Year, Daily

McQuerry Orchid Books
5700 W. Salerno Rd.
Jacksonville, FL 32244
(904) 387-5044 (8-8 EST)
Mary & Jack McQuerry

BOOKS
Specializes in **new, used, out-of-print and rare books on orchids** and also offers back issues of orchid magazines, old plant catalogs (orchids only) and antique orchid prints. They also publish and sell the "You Can Grow Orchids" series by Mary Noble.
Catalog: Free, R&W, MO, CAN/OV

Machin Designs (USA) Inc.
557 Danbury Rd. (Route 7)
Wilton, CT 06987
(203) 348-5319
Francis Machin & Miranda Ketrewell

SUPPLIES FURNITURE
Offers period design English **conservatories**, summerhouses and other garden buildings, as well as garden furniture and pots.
Catalog: $5, CAN

Mainline of North America
P. O. Box 526
Junction of U.S. 40 & State Route 38
London, OH 43140
(614) 852-9733
Paul A. Sullivan

SUPPLIES
Offers **tillers, sickle-bar mowers, log splitters, snow throwers, rotary** and **power lawnmowers**. All are gear driven -- no belts or chains -- they say, "entirely automotive in design"; thirty models to chose from.
Catalog: Free, R&W, CAN/OV
Shop: All Year, M-Sa

Mantis Manufacturing Co.
1458 County Line Rd.
Huntingdon Valley, PA 19006
(215) 355-9700, (800) 344-4030 TO/CC
HJS Enterprises, Inc.

SUPPLIES
Offers a small, lightweight garden **tiller**, with attachments which convert it to a lawn de-thatcher or aerator, edge cutter or hedge trimmer. They also sell a **portable power sprayer**.
Catalog: Free, CAN/OV
Shop: All Year, M-F, By Appointment Only

Marion Designs
594 Front Street
Marion, MA 02738
(617) 748-2540 TO/CC $35
William S. Harrison III, Partner

FURNITURE
Sells **potting benches, plant stands and display tables for plants**, all made of redwood for strength and durability. Potting benches come with wooden or plastic pans and with coated or stainless steel hardware for high humidity.
Catalog: $1d, R&W, CAN
Shop: All Year, M-F, Call Ahead

The Matrix Group
P. O. Box 1176
Southport, CT 06490

SUPPLIES
Sells **video cassettes** of "The Home Gardener", John Lenaton's popular series of 30 gardening programs organized by subject. Also offers a **videodisc**, "Gardening at Home", a complete A-to-Z of gardening basics, coordinated with Lenaton's book, "The Home Gardener". He's lively and fun.
Catalog: Free, MO, CAN/OV

Don Mattern
267 Filbert St.
San Francisco, CA 94133
(415) 781-6066
Don Mattern

SUPPLIES
Offers the "HERRmidifier", a **humidifier with humidistat** for greenhouse and orchid growers, available in 110 or 220 volts.
Catalog: Free, R&W, MO, CAN/OV

Timothy Mawson
Main Street
New Preston, CT 06777
(212) 874-6839
Timothy Mawson

BOOKS
Offers **used and out-of-print books** on gardening and other country pursuits.
Catalog: $1

Emi Meade, Importer
16000 Fern Way
Guerneville, CA 95446
(707) 869-3218
Emi & Eugene Meade

SUPPLIES
Offers two styles of "Jollys", **waterproof garden clogs** from Europe in six colors; soft and comfortable, easy to rinse clean -- one of my good friends lives in them! They also sell a skin buffer called "Atomocoll" to smooth rough skin and calluses; take it from a rhinoceros, it really works! (1981)
Catalog: Free, R&W, CAN/OV
Shop: By Appointment Only

Memory Metals, Inc.
84 West Park Place
Stamford, CT 06901
(203) 357-9777 TO/CC

SUPPLIES
Offers "Memrytec", an **automatic greenhouse vent opener** with a 14-pound lifting capacity which operates by sun power and will open partially to fully depending on the temperature.
Catalog: Free, R&W, CAN/OV

Meridian Equipment Corporation
2055 Bee's Ferry Road
Charleston, SC 29407
(803) 763-6616
Loretta Nickel

TOOLS
Importers of English hand and pruning **tools, spades, forks and rakes**, they also sell **shredders, weathervanes and hand weeders**; their "Elite" line is made from hand-forged stainless steel.
Catalog: R&W
Shop: All Year, M-F

For Explanations of Abbreviations/Codes Used In Listings See Bookmark or Inside Covers

Meyer Manufacturing

See Safe-N-Sound Live Traps

Micro Essential Laboratory, Inc.
4224 Avenue H
Brooklyn, NY 11210
(718) 338-3618 TO $25m
Joel, Mark, & Walter Florin

SUPPLIES
Offers "Hydrion" **test papers for pH soil testing** and a kit for testing hydroponic solutions. They sell mostly to big operators; if you want small quantities, please tell them so when you request the catalog. (1935)
Catalog: Free, R&W, MO, CAN/OV, $25m

Modern Farm
P. O. Box 1420
1825 Big Horn Avenue
Cody, WY 82414
(307) 587-5515 or (800) 443-4934 TO/CC
Paul C. Clymer

SUPPLIES TOOLS ORNAMENTS
General catalog for country living, offering much of interest to the gardener: **carts, sundials, weather instruments, weathervanes, tools, hammocks, canning supplies**. (1967)
Catalog: Free, MO

Modern Homesteader

See Modern Farm

Moss Products, Inc.
P. O. Box 72
Palmetto, FL 34220
(813) 729-5433
Graham Wilson

SUPPLIES
Watering systems: drip, sprinkler and mist sprayers -- very flexible and adaptable to many garden situations and types of plants.
Catalog: Free, R&W, MO, CAN

Raoul Moxley Travel
76 Elmbourne Rd.
London, England SW17 8JJ
01-672-2437

SERVICES
Offers **horticultural tours and treks** and archeology, history and culture tours all over the world. Write for information.

Mr. Birdhouse
2307 B Highway 2 West
Grand Rapids, MN 55744
(218) 326-3044
Larry Lessin

SUPPLIES
Martin houses, made of riveted aluminum alloy for strength and care-free maintainance. Available in various sizes, well ventilated and easy to clean.
Catalog: Free, R&W, CAN/OV
Shop: All Year, M-Sa

Nampara Gardens
2004 Golfcourse Rd.
Bayside, CA 95524
(707) 822-5744 TO/CC
Stefan & Rebecca Hall

FURNITURE ORNAMENTS
Redwood garden ornaments: **bridges, gates, benches and lanterns** in Japanese style. They will also do custom designs or build from yours. Products are elegant and made from almost indestructible redwood heartwood.
Catalog: Free, R&W, CAN/OV
Shop: All Year, By Appointment Only

The Natural Gardening Company
27 Rutherford Avenue
San Anselmo, CA 94960
(415) 456-5060 TO/CC
David Baldwin & Karin Kramer

SUPPLIES TOOLS BOOKS
New company offers a nice selection of **imported garden tools**, some books and supplies and a copper snail barrier which gives the little devils a mild shock -- they won't cross it. Also sells some birdhouses which mimic tree cavities for small garden birds.
Catalog: $1, R&W, MO, CAN

Natural Gardening Research Center
P. O. Box 149
Sunman, IN 47041
(812) 623-3800 TO/CC
Niles Kinerk

SUPPLIES
Natural insect and disease controls, supplies and equipment for organic gardening; all explained in an informative catalog. Offers organic insect controls, beneficial insects, fertilizers, worm castings and drip irrigation systems. There's a color guide to insects in the catalog.
Catalog: Free, MO

Nature's Control
P. O. Box 35
Medford, OR 97501
(503) 899-8318 TO/CC
Don Jackson

SUPPLIES
Predator mites, ladybugs, whitefly traps and parasites, mealy bug predators and insecticidal soap for **natural pest control**; all especially useful for indoor or greenhouse growing. Stress helpful advice and fast service. (1980)
Catalog: Free, R&W
Shop: All Year, By Appointment Only

Necessary Trading Co.
P. O. Box 305
626 Main Street
New Castle, VA 24127
(703) 864-5103 TO/CC
Bill Wolf

SUPPLIES TOOLS BOOKS
Large selection of **organic insect controls, tools, books and soil amendments** for 'biological agriculture'. The catalog is informative; they also offer organic pest controls for pets and live traps for critters. (1979)
Catalog: $2d, R&W, CAN/OV
Shop: All Year, M-F; March-June, Sa

Walter Nicke Company
P. O. Box 433
Topsfield, MA 01983
(617) 887-3388 or 9693 TO/CC $50m
Katrina Nicke Neefus

SUPPLIES TOOLS BOOKS
Garden tools, gadgets and supplies, many imported: a broad selection. One of my favorite tools is a heavy duty steel trowel with a long handle which I bought from them years ago. There's much in the catalog which is useful, decorative or just desireable.
Catalog: $.50, CAN
Shop: All Year, M-F, Call Ahead

Nitron Industries, Inc.
P. O. Box 400
100 W. Rock Street
Fayetteville, AR 72702
(501) 521-0055 or (800) 835-0123 TO/CC $15m
Frank & Gay E. Finger

SUPPLIES TOOLS
Offers a good selection of **organic growing supplies**, fertilizers, their own "Nitron" soil amendment, "Wet Flex" porous hose and mulch film. Informative catalog also offers greenhouses, hand tools, cover crop seed. (1977)
Catalog: Free, R&W, CAN/OV
Shop: All Year, M-F

North American Kelp
R.R. 1, Box 279A
Cross Street
Waldoboro, ME 04572
(207) 832-7506
Robert C. Morse

SUPPLIES
Offers "Sea Crop" and "Sea Life Soil Conditioner" and other **soil conditioners** made from kelp; catalog has detailed information on use, even as a supplement to livestock feed.
Catalog: Free, R&W, CAN/OV

North Country Organics
P. O. Box 107
Route 5
Newbury, VT 05051
(802) 866-5562 or 866-3325 TO $20m
Paul Sachs

SUPPLIES BOOKS
Sells **organic fertilizers and soil amendments** for commercial growers and home gardeners; carries "Harvest King", "Crop Booster", "Farm Tech Service", "Erth-Rite" brands, as well as greensand, bone meal, soft rock phosphate, diatomaceous earth, seaweed extract and some books on building soil. (1983)
Catalog: $1d, R&W, CAN
Shop: All Year, By Appointment Only

North Star Evergreens
P. O. Box 253
Eastwood Plaza Bldg.
Park Rapids, MN 56470
(800) 732-5819 or 336-3361 TO/CC
Thom & Cathy Peterson

SUPPLIES TOOLS
Tools, supplies and equipment for foresters and Christmas tree growers, but many items of use to serious gardeners and nurseries, too: sprayers, hand tools and saws, safety equipment and animal repellents. A broad selection, including "True Friends" & "Wilkinson" tools.
Catalog: Free, R&W, CAN/OV
Shop: All Year, M-Sa

North Star Seed & Plant Search
RR 1, Box 2310
Troy, ME 04987
(207) 948-2401
Sandy Olson

SERVICES
Offers a custom **plant and seed search service** for gardeners and landscapers looking for a particular plant. Closed June-September.
Catalog: Long SASE

Northern Greenhouse Sales
P. O. Box 42
Neche, ND 58265
(204) 327-5540
Bob Davis & Margaret Smith

SUPPLIES
Offers **woven polyethylene** and other supplies for making your own greenhouse plus advice from the Far North on how to make them. The plastic poly is 9.5 mils thick and very strong, with an average life of 3 years; they will sell small amounts. Canadian address: Box 1450, Altona, MB, R0G 0B0. (1979)
Catalog: 3 FCS, R&W, CAN/OV
Shop: All Year, Daily, Call Ahead

Northern Hydraulics, Inc.
P. O. Box 1499
Burnsville, MN 55337-0499
(612) 894-8310 or (800) 533-5545

SUPPLIES TOOLS
A **tool and equipment** catalog, containing useful items for gardening, from boots to portable generators, from small trailers to ladders; not for the small garden, but useful if you have a larger garden or live in the country.
Catalog: Free
Shop: Three retail stores in MN.

Norwood Engineering, Inc.
529 E. Main St.
Stoughton, WI 53589
(608) 873-8664 TO/CC
Eric Lysne

SUPPLIES
Sells two models of **garden cart** -- the "Carryall", 42 inches wide, and the "Carryette", 32 inches wide for going through doorways; sold complete or as kits for you to put together with your own wood.
Catalog: Free, R&W, CAN/OV
Shop: All Year, M-F, Call Ahead

OFE International, Inc.
Box 161302
Miami, FL 33116
(305) 253-7080 or 255-2175 TO/CC $20m
Jose Hortensi

SUPPLIES TOOLS
Offers **growing supplies for orchids and bromeliads**: clay orchid pots, wood and wire plant baskets, fertilizers, sprayers, watering accessories, growing media, plant labels and plant stands. (1980)
Catalog: $2d, R&W, MO, CAN, $20m

For Explanations of Abbreviations/Codes Used In Listings See Bookmark or Inside Covers

Ohio Earth Food, Inc.
13737 Duquette Ave., N.E.
Hartville, OH 44632
(216) 877-9356
Larry Ringer & Glenn Graber

SUPPLIES SERVICES
Offers a broad selection of **natural soil conditioners and amendments**, including "Erth-Rite" and "Maxicrop", insect controls, flea controls for pets. They also will do soil testing with suggestions for using natural products. Farmers may request their quantity prices. (1972)
Catalog: Free, R&W, CAN/OV
Shop: All Year, M-Sa

One Up Productions
P. O. Box 410777
San Francisco, CA 94141
(415) 558-8688 or (800) 331-6304 TO/CC $16m
Hamilton V. Bryan

SUPPLIES
Company specializing in **videos** for the gardener; they cover a number of subjects, from "how to" to landscaping and arm-chair tours of famous gardens. Adding new subjects all the time, such as vegetables, lawns, pests and diseases and pruning. (1982)
Catalog: Free, R&W, MO, CAN, $16m

Orchis Laboratories
86 F Mason Street
Burdett, NY 14818

SERVICES
Will do **virus testing and tissue culture on orchids**; also sells a home virus-testing kit and a home seed-sowing kit for orchid hobbyists.
Catalog: Free, R&W, CAN/OV

Organic Farm & Garden Supply
131 Organic Lane
West Columbia, SC 29169
(803) 794-5504 TO/CC
Margaret Locklear

SUPPLIES
Offers a broad selection of **organic fertilizers, beneficial insects, pet supplies, and growing supplies** in an informative catalog. Also offers open-pollinated vegetable and cover crop seeds. Two other businesses as well: natural cosmetics and herb products and supplies. (1983)
Catalog: $2d, R&W, CAN/OV
Shop: All Year, M-Sa, Call Ahead

Organic Gardening Book Club
33 East Minor Street
Emmaus, PA 18049
(215) 967-5171
Rodale Press

BOOKS
The focus of this book club is generally food growing and organic gardening, but it offers books on other aspects of gardening, too. While run by a big publisher of gardening books, it sells books from many publishers, even Tusker Press.

Organic Pest Management
P. O. Box 55267
Seattle, WA 98155
(206) 367-0707
David & Audrey Mirgon

SUPPLIES
Sells **beneficial insects, bird repellents, earthworms and organic garden products** including rodent and insect traps, humane live traps and pest controls for dogs and cats. Formerly called Organic Pest Control Naturally.
Catalog: Free, R&W, CAN/OV, $14m
Shop: All Year, Tu-Sa, Call Ahead

Organic Research Laboratories
P. O. Box 289
St. Marys, OH 45885
(419) 394-5944 or 753-2642 TO/CC $100m
Dr. Richard D. Pifer, Owner

SUPPLIES
Offers several **soil amendments** containing bacteria, which make soil into 'virgin-like' fertility; special mixtures for African violets, roses, greenhouse plants and "Vita-Loam II" for soil rejuvenation and improvement. Informative catalog describes products and their uses and history.
Catalog: $1d, R&W, CAN
Shop: By Appointment Only

Original Home Gardener's Video Catalog

See One Up Productions

ORLabs Products, Inc.

See Organic Research Laboratories

Ortho Information Services
575 Market St.
San Francisco, CA 94105
(415) 894-0277 TO/CC
Chevron Chemical Co.

BOOKS SERVICES
"Ortho's Computerized Gardening" program for IBM, Apple, Macintosh and Commodore 64: some 800 plants by zipcode -- you can specify type of plant, flower color and season, shade tolerance, height. It includes a plant encyclopedia, garden diary and calendar. Also many gardening books and videos. (1973)
Catalog: Free, R&W, MO, CAN/OV

Ozark Handle & Hardware
P. O. Box 390
91 S. Main Street
Eureka Springs, AR 72632
(501) 423-6888 TO/CC
Eddie Silver

SUPPLIES TOOLS
Offers a very broad selection of **hardwood replacement handles** for tools of all sorts -- who else has wooden plow handles? Also carries fiber glass handles for hammers and axes and has a space-age divining rod for finding cables and pipes. Also sells woven poly tarps. (1977)
Catalog: $2d, R&W, CAN/OV
Shop: All Year, Daily

Pacific Coast Greenhouse Mfg. Co.
8360 Industrial Ave.
Cotati, CA 94928
(707) 795-2164 or 8812 TO/CC
Bill Snow

SUPPLIES
Sells **greenhouses, greenhouse supplies and controls** and "residential sunspaces" (solariums). They also manufacture and sell "Frisco Fog" humidifiers. (1928)
Catalog: $1, CAN/OV
Shop: All Year, M-Sa, Call Ahead

John Palmer Bonsai
P. O. Box 29
Sudbury, MA 01776
(617) 443-5084
W. John Palmer

SUPPLIES TOOLS BOOKS
Specializes in **bonsai books, tools, pots and supplies** -- with many books on Japanese gardens and bonsai techniques. He also carries some books on camellias.
Catalog: Free, CAN/OV
Shop: By Appointment Only

Park Place
2251 Wisconsin Ave. N.W.
Washington, DC 20007
(202) 342-6294 TO/CC
C. Philip Mitchell & Charles H. Betts

FURNITURE ORNAMENTS
Offers many types of **garden furniture, light fixtures, street lamps, urns, rockers, swings and gliders**; styles are elegant and the very thing for your stately home.
Catalog: $2, R&W, CAN/OV
Shop: All Year

Patio Pacific, Inc.
24433 Hawthorne Blvd.
Torrance, CA 90505-6506
(213) 378-9286 or (800) 826-2871 TO/CC
Alan Lethers

SUPPLIES
Readers who pay close attention realize that Tusker was a favorite cat and that I'm partial to cats and dogs. This company carries nearly every brand of **pet doors**, both traditional flap models and panel pet doors which fit sliding glass doors; 79 models to fit gardeners' helpers of all sizes. (1972)
Catalog: Free, R&W, CAN/OV
Shop: All Year, M-Sa

Paw Paw Everlast Label Co.
P. O. Box 93
Paw Paw, MI 49079-0093
Arthur & Dorothy Arens

SUPPLIES
Manufactures and sells **metal plant and garden labels** with zinc nameplates. They offer styles to put in the ground and to hang on the plant; also sell special marking pencils and crayons to write on the labels. (1962)
Catalog: Free, R&W, MO, CAN/OV

PeCo Inc.
P. O. Box 1197
100 Airport Road
Arden, NC 28704
(704) 684-1234 OR (800) 438-5823 TO/CC $10m

SUPPLIES
Sells a completely self-contained **12-volt electric sprayer** which runs up to five hours on its rechargeable battery. It features a cart with big wheels to make it easy to move around and has a plug-in charger, an 8-foot hose and an opaque tank to keep track of fluid level.
Catalog: Free, R&W, MO, CAN/OV

Phologistics
P. O. Box 1411
Ventura, CA 93002
(805) 658-0111 or (800) 541-5471 in CA TO/CC
Florence Naylor

SUPPLIES
Sells "Nifty Scoops" for transplanting African violets; also offers several brands of **water distillers** and other equipment for making and storing pure water, pH test papers -- and a cleaner to get label-gum off of glass, metal, etc. Hallelujah!!
Catalog: 2 FCS, R&W, CAN/OV
Shop: All Year, M-F, 1860 Eastman Ave., Suite 101

Plant Collectibles
103 Kenview Ave.
Buffalo, NY 14217
(716) 875-1221
Marseille Luxenberg

SUPPLIES BOOKS
Growing and propagating supplies for indoors and out: pots in many sizes, fertilizers, potting soil, hanging baskets, peat pots and pellets, nozzles, Ortho and Sunset books and more.
Catalog: 2 FCS, MO, CAN/OV, $8m

Plant Magic Products, Inc.
3003 N. 85th Ave. W.
Duluth, MN 55810-1410
(218) 628-3234

SUPPLIES
Sells "Plant Magic", a **fertilizer made from earthworm castings**.
Catalog: Free, R&W, MO, CAN/OV

Plastic Plumbing Products, Inc.
P. O. Box 186
17005 Manchester Rd.
Grover, MO 63040
(314) 458-2226
Bob Pisarkiewicz

SUPPLIES
Sells "Biwall" and "Rain Run" kits for **drip and mist irrigation**, as well as doing custom-designed systems in Missouri. They also carry a large selection of parts and fittings for drip and mist irrigation.
Catalog: $1d, R&W, CAN
Shop: All Year, M-Sa, Call Ahead

The Plow & Hearth
560 Main Street
Madison, VA 22727
(703) 948-6821 TO/CC
Peter G. Rice

TOOLS FURNITURE ORNAMENTS
Color catalog offers **goods for home and garden**; they bought Green River Tools in 1986 and sell many products from that source. Also garden furniture, ornaments, birdhouses, fireplace accessories, pet supplies and other useful home goods.
Catalog: Free, CAN
Shop: All Year, Daily (Route 250 West, Charlottesville)

For Explanations of Abbreviations/Codes Used In Listings See Bookmark or Inside Covers

Pomona Book Exchange
Highway 52
Rockton P.O.
Rockton, ON, Canada L0R 1X0
(519) 621-8897
Frederic & Walda Janson

BOOKS SERVICES
Offers **books on plants, botany, gardening and horticulture, landscape design, fruit growing and related fields** and will search for hard-to-find books. They also have a museum orchard and can supply propagating material of several hundred varieties of apples to local collectors!
Catalog: $1, USA/OV
Shop: South of Wentworth Heritage Village, Call Ahead

Pompeian Studios
90 Rockledge Road
Bronxville, NY 10708
(914) 337-5595
Pamela Humbert

ORNAMENTS
Marble, bronze, limestone, mosaic and wrought-iron **garden ornaments**, made to order in Italy and hand-carved or hand-finished; the styles are classic and charming. Prices are very upscale and vary with the exchange rate with the lira. Statues and fountains, mostly -- all very elegant and lovely.
Catalog: $10d, R&W, CAN/OV

Popovitch & Associates, Inc.
346 Ashland Avenue
Pittsburgh, PA 15228
(412) 344-6097
Don & Rose Popovitch

ORNAMENTS
Sells three styles of **light fixtures** for gardens in natural styles; they are handcrafted in copper and ceramic. Two styles are flower-shaped, one is shaped like a mushroom; all are elegant ornaments as well as functional.
Catalog: Free, R&W, MO

Pot Lock
1032-21 Street
Rock Island, IL 61201
(309) 786-5949
Charles J. White

SUPPLIES
Offers a unique **device to lock bonsai and other pots** to your shelf -- good insurance on tempting or valuable specimens! (1984)
Catalog: Free, R&W, MO, CAN, $8m

Public Service Lamp Corp.
410 W. 16th St.
New York, NY 10011
(212) 989-5557 or (800) 221-4392 TO/CC $30m
Jack Howard, Sales Mgr.

SUPPLIES
Sells "Wonderlites", a self-ballasted **mercury vapor flood lamp** for any screw-socket -- excellent for growing plants indoors, even those with higher light requirements.
Catalog: Free, R&W, CAN/OV, $10m

Putnam's
Main Street
Wilton, NH 03086
(603) 654-6564 TO/CC
Richard & Victoria Putnam

SUPPLIES
Offers goatskin gardening **gloves**, a bug hat (veiled) for working outside under attack, overalls and other clothing in 100% cotton or wool.
Catalog: Free, R&W, CAN
Shop: All Year, M-Sa

Putterin Press
P. O. Box 72
Burlingame, CA 94011-0072
(415) 343-8426 TO/CC $13m
Nancy Fisher

SUPPLIES
Offers a **practical five-year garden diary**, with room for weather notes and other information -- a useful garden gift, even to non-gardeners. Well made, well designed and easy to write in because it lies flat!
Catalog: Free, R&W, MO, CAN/OV, $12m

RAM Log Splitters
1240 Harrison Ave.
Rockford, IL 61108-7292
(815) 963-0953 TO $25m
Thomas D. Skibba and Michael L. Rohrbacher

SUPPLIES TOOLS
Makes "RAM Heavy Haulers" -- **garden carts** with 20 or 26-inch wheels, and a model with a trailer hitch for pulling behind a garden tractor. They also sell "RAM Log Splitters" in various sizes;: you can cut your wood and wheel it to the woodpile.
Catalog: Free, R&W, MO, CAN/OV, $25m

Raindrip, Inc.
P. O. Box 2173
21305 Itasca St.
Chatsworth, CA 91313-2173
(800) 222-3747 or 367-3747 (CA) TO/CC $10m
Barry Hanish

SUPPLIES
Sells "Raindrip" **drip irrigation systems and supplies**; informative booklet tells you how to get started and what you'll need. They have a multiplex dripper which will fit the sprinkler fittings of existing underground systems. They also sell a video on how-to-do-it. (1975)
Catalog: Free, R&W, MO, CAN/OV, $10m

The Ram Company
R.R. 723
Lowesville, VA 22951
(804) 277-8511
R. H. Fleming

SUPPLIES
Sells the Fleming Hydro-Ram **pump**, which operates by the pressure of flowing water rather than by electricity or gas. It can pump water uphill as much as ten times the downhill "fall or drop" of the water supply.
Catalog: $3, R&W, CAN/OV

Reed Bros.
Turner Station
Sebastopol, CA 95472
(707) 795-6261
Duncan Reed

FURNITURE ORNAMENTS
Makers of one-of-a-kind hand carved **outdoor and indoor redwood furniture** and accessories, definitely up-market and very charming in a country-rustic style. They also do custom carving.
Catalog: $7, R&W, CAN/OV
Shop: All Year, M-F, By Appointment Only

Joe Reed, Woodsmith
Georgetown, ME 04548

SUPPLIES
'Versailles' boxes -- the classic **planter** -- wood finished with white polyurethane and equipped with plastic inserts; several sizes, several designs.
Catalog: $1d

Peter Reimuller's Cart Warehouse
200 Center St.
Point Arena, CA 95468
(707) 882-2422
Peter Reimuller

SUPPLIES
Sells major brands of **garden carts** at a discount; brands include "Garden Way", "Stanley Forge" and "Sotz", as well as their own "Muller" brand. They also sell wheels, axles and plans for making your own cart and replacement wheels, pneumatic tires, bearings and iron wheels for carts. (1984)
Catalog: Free, R&W, MO, CAN/OV

Replogle Globes, Inc.
2801 S. 25th Ave.
Chicago, IL 60153
(312) 343-0900 TO/CC
William Nichols

ORNAMENTS
Company specializes in regular earth and sky globes, but also sells two styles of **sundials**, a flat and an 'equatorial' style made of solid bronze.
Catalog: $1d, R&W, MO, CAN/OV

Ringer Research
9959 Valley View Rd.
Eden Prairie, MN 55344-3585
(612) 941-4180 OR 829-5430 TO/CC
Mike Colehour, V.P. Mktg.

SUPPLIES TOOLS SERVICES
A wide selection of **organic garden products**: soil amendments, potting soil boosters, insect controls, compost makers, lawn care products and various tools and equipment in an informative catalog. (1962)
Catalog: Free, R&W
Shop: All Year, M-F, Call Ahead

Rocky Mountain Insectary
P. O. Box 152
Palisade, CO 81526
Linda Mowrer

SUPPLIES
Sells **"Pedio" wasps** for control of the Mexican Bean Beetle; informative leaflet explains how to get them established. (1983)
Catalog: Free, R&W, MO, CAN, SS:4-10, $8m

Rodco Products Co., Inc.
P. O. Box 944
Columbus, NE 68601
(402) 563-3596 or (800) 443-0100 x 109 TO/CC
Rodney F. Bahlen

SUPPLIES
"Computemp" **temperature monitor and alarm**: takes Fahrenheit or Celcius readings, both indoors and out; records high and low of the day; will monitor air, soil or water; will sound an alarm at a pre-set temperature -- it won't get up to fix things! Can monitor up to nine locations. (1977)
Catalog: Free, R&W, MO, CAN/OV
Shop: All Year, M-F

A. I. Root Company
P. O. Box 706
Medina, OH 44258-0706
(216) 725-6677 TO/CC $15m
Kim Flottum & Dick Kehl

SUPPLIES BOOKS
Everything for the home or commercial beekeeper and honey producer, even bee toys -- they've been in business since 1869 and have branches in three states. Also publish "Gleanings in Bee Culture", the monthly magazine of the beekeeping industry. (1869)
Catalog: Free, R&W, CAN/OV
Shop: All Year, M-Sa; branches listed in catalog

Rose Tender
1049 Mockingbird Lane
Van Wert, OH 45891
(419) 238-4851 TO $12m
Jon Rhoades

SUPPLIES
Offers a low-level **sprinkler to water roses below the leaves** to reduce water spots and mildew; also a rose soaker and adapter heads which convert sprinklers for long narrow rose beds or regular lawn and garden use. (1962)
Catalog: Free, R&W, MO, CAN/OV

For Explanations of Abbreviations/Codes Used In Listings See Bookmark or Inside Covers

Royal Tidewater Collection, Inc.
P. O. Box 26
Main Street
Hillsboro, VA 22132-0026
(703) 668-6066 TO/CC
Tom Horvath

ORNAMENTS
Pier and garden sculpture: original and limited editions by international artists, priced from $200 to $150,000. Works are generally realistic and dramatic in style, usually cast bronze. They will also do custom work and design consultation. (1978)
Catalog: $4 (3 IRC), R&W, CAN/OV
Shop: All Year, M-Sa, By Appointment Only

Safe-N-Sound Live Traps
Box 153
Garrison, IA 52229
(319) 477-5041 or (800) 255-2255 TO/CC $20m
Steve Meyer

SUPPLIES
Offers a humane solution to the problem of critters in the garden: **animal traps** which do not harm the animals -- but leave you with the problem of where to release them! They also make larger cages for transporting and kenneling dogs.
Catalog: Free, R&W, MO, CAN/OV, $20m

San Luis Plastic Products
P. O. Box 12559
San Luis Obispo, CA 93406
(805) 549-0700 or (800) 538-0423 TO/CC

SUPPLIES
Offers **stacking plastic pocket planters** in which you can grow flowers, vegetables, strawberries, bulbs or anything else you like. They come in seven colors and have a base which catches surplus water. Great for patios and small space gardens.
Catalog: Free

Santa Barbara Greenhouses
1115J Ave. Acaso
Camarillo, CA 93010
(805) 482-3765 TO/CC $50m
Robert Solakian

SUPPLIES
Offers redwood and fiber glass pre-fabricated **greenhouses** in various sizes, as well as all of the accessories to fit them out, such as benches, mist systems, heaters and fans. They also have a line of "Deluxe" redwood and glass greenhouses, which are shipped in preglazed sections.
Catalog: Free, R&W, CAN/OV
Shop: All Year, M-F, Call Ahead

Santa Barbara Orchid Garden & Library
1350 More Ranch Road
Santa Barbara, CA 93111
(805) 967-9798
Paul Gripp

SERVICES
A retired orchid nurseryman who offers five-day **orchid study vacations** in Santa Barbara, with tours of nurseries, etc. Santa Barbara is a great orchid center, with many other attractions. He also provides an **orchid advice service**; write for details.

Savoy Books
P. O. Box 271
Lanesboro, MA 01237
(413) 499-9968
Robert Fraker

BOOKS
Specializes in American, English and French **books** on agriculture and horticulture, mostly fairly old and rare for collectors. Also old prints, nursery catalogs and other empemera related to the history of gardening and agriculture. Material generally covers the 16th to 19th centuries. (1971)
Catalog: Free, CAN/OV
Shop: By Appointment Only

Scanmask

See BioLogic

Jack Schmidling Productions
4501 N. Moody Ave.
Chicago, IL 60630
(312) 685-1878
Jack Schmidling

SUPPLIES
Sells two horticultural **video cassettes**: one on tropical rainforest flora and the danger of destroying such habitats, the other on mushrooms and other fungi. (1983)
Catalog: Free, R&W, MO, CAN/OV

Science Associates
P. O. Box 230
Princeton, NJ 08542
(609) 924-4470 TO $25m
Thomas Tesauro

SUPPLIES
Offers a large selection of **weather instruments**; those of special interest to gardeners are a temperature-time indicator, growing degree-day totalizers, humidity indicators and recorders for greenhouses, wind speed indicators, soil thermometers and rain gauges. Even sells complete weather stations.
Catalog: $1d, CAN/OV, $25m
Shop: All Year, By Appointment Only

The Scotchmen
R.D. 1
Pottstown, PA 19464
(215) 495-6282 TO/CC
Inductotherm Corp.

SUPPLIES
Offers "The Scotchmen", a **shredder/grinder/chipper** with a 3 HP Briggs & Stratton engine -- they say it will handle branches up to 1-3/4". They also sell a **sprayer** which can be towed by a mower or garden tractor;: it has a 22-gallon tank and will spray up to 25' high.
Catalog: Free, MO, CAN/OV

Sculpture Cast Editions
P. O. Box 426
15 Tamara Dr.
Roosevelt, NJ 08555
(609) 426-0942
James Mills

ORNAMENTS
Cast stone or bronze statues for special gardens. Selection is small; most are charming young girls by well known sculptors -- definitely upscale.
Catalog: Free, R&W, CAN/OV
Shop: By Appointment Only

Seabright Enterprises
4026 Harlan St.
Emeryville, CA 94608
(415) 655-3126 or 3127 TO/CC $5m
John W. Cutter

SUPPLIES
"Stickem Special" is a **non-poisonous compound which traps flying and crawling pests and discourages cats.** They also sell a 'smart' and humane mouse trap, whitefly traps, a yellow jacket trap and "Bird Begone", a colorless repellent. (1979)
Catalog: Free, R&W, CAN/OV, $5m
Shop: All Year, M-F

Serendipity Garden Tours
3 Channing Circle
Cambridge, MA 02138
(617) 354-1879

SERVICES
Garden tours in the U.S., Britain and Europe; specializes in small groups and hotels, a tranquil pace and good cooking.
Catalog: Free

Robert Shuhi - Books
P. O. Box 268
Morris, CT 06763
(203) 567-5231 or 9384

BOOKS
Offers an extensive list of **used and out-of-print books** covering a broad field of travel, archeology, nature, science and, of course, plants and gardening.
Catalog: Free, MO

Skagit Gardens
1695 Johnson Road
Mt. Vernon, WA 98273
(206) 424-6760 TO/CC
Gary Lorenz

SUPPLIES
A broad selection of **growing and greenhouse supplies, tools, propagation supplies** and much more; professional supplies for home gardeners. (1967)
Catalog: $2d, CAN/OV
Shop: All Year, Daily

Edward F. Smiley, Bookseller
43 Liberty Hill Rd.
Bedford, NH 03102
(603) 472-5800

BOOKS SERVICES
Offers **antiquarian and out-of-print books** and book search services.
Catalog: $1

Smith & Hawken
25 Corte Madera
Mill Valley, CA 94941
(415) 381-0359 TO/CC
Paul Hawken & Dave Smith

TOOLS BOOKS FURNITURE ORNAMENTS
Offers a very broad selection of **garden tools**, many imported from England or Japan, irrigation supplies, composting equipment and gardening clothing, books and gifts and garden furniture. They've opened a store at the Stanford Shopping Center, have a nursery at the store in Mill Valley.
Catalog: Free
Shop: All Year, Daily

South Pacific Books, Ltd.
P. O. Box 3533
Auckland, New Zealand
541-224
Valery & Alan McEldowney

BOOKS
Offers a selection of **books** on New Zealand, Australian and South Pacific horticulture and plants; invoices are in U.S. dollars. Books are new or recently published. They will also search for books published Down Under; provide them with all the details.
Catalog: Free, R&W, OV

Southern Statuary and Stone
3401 Fifth Avenue So.
Birmingham, AL 35222
(205) 322-0379

FURNITURE ORNAMENTS
Offers **statues, garden ornaments and light fixtures** of cast-stone and cast-lead, and also "Chippendale" **garden furniture** made of cypress for durability.
Catalog: $1(Furniture), $5 (Furniture & Gdn. Ornaments)

Spalding Laboratories
760 Printz Rd.
Arroyo Grande, CA 93420
(805) 489-5946 TO/CC $10m
Pat Spalding

SUPPLIES
Sells "Fly Predators", **beneficial insects** for fly control, and non-toxic "Good-Bye-Fly" traps, useful wherever flies are a problem -- around indoor plants, animals, farm buildings, greenhouses -- who doesn't have flies?
Catalog: Free, R&W, MO, CAN/OV, $10m

Spiral Filtration
747 N. Twin Oaks Valley Rd., #13
San Marcos, CA 92069
(619) 744-3012

SUPPLIES
Makers of **reverse osmosis water purifiers** for hobbyists and others who need very pure water. Two models: will purify 100 or 150 gallons a day -- enough for a vacation cabin. They also make small portable models for up to 25 gallons a day.
Catalog: $5

Spot Systems Div., Wisdom Ind.
5812 Machine Drive
Huntington Beach, CA 92649
(714) 891-1115 or (800) 854-7649 TO $20m
W. R. Graziani

SUPPLIES
"Spot System" **supplies for drip and mist irrigation**, filters, separators, even spot heaters; systems in kits for home gardeners. In addition to drip 'vortex' emitters, they have spot spray and spot mist sprinklers. (1975)
Catalog: Free, R&W, CAN/OV, $20m
Shop: All Year, M-F

Spray-N-Grow
P. O. Box 722038
Houston, TX 77272
Bill J. Muskopf

SUPPLIES
Offers "Spray-N-Grow", a **growth stimulant** which they say will make all plants grow better and have better fruit or flowers. Also sell "Triple Action 20", a **fungicide** which also controls bacteria and mildew.
Catalog: Free, MO

Standard Humidifier
100 Ashton Street
Pawtucket, RI 02860
(401) 722-0238 TO/CC
Thomas A. Barber

SUPPLIES
Sells **humidifiers** in several sizes, both free standing and overhead, available for 110V or 220V, with various controls.
Catalog: Free, R&W, CAN/OV
Shop: All Year, M-F

The Stanley Forge Co., Inc.
P. O. Box 23156
Stanley, KS 66223
(816) 421-4265 TO/CC

SUPPLIES
Sells two models of the "Big Wheeler" **garden cart**, one with 7-cubic-foot capacity, the other with 13 1/2-cubic-foot capacity; sold either as kits or assembled.

Strassacker Bronze, Inc.
P. O. Box 931, 23A Metro Dr.
Spartanburg, SC 29304
(803) 573-7438 TO/CC
Guenther F. Nebel

ORNAMENTS
Representatives of a German manufacturer of bronze garden **sculptures, ornaments, fountains, lighting fixtures and plaques**. Scale is generally large and best suited to larger gardens and public spaces. (1977)
Catalog: $10d, R&W, CAN/OV
Shop: All Year, M-F

Stuppy Greenhouse Manufacturing, Inc.
P. O. Box 12456
North Kansas City, MO 64116
(800) 821-2132 or (800) 892-5044 TO/CC $25m

SUPPLIES
Everything for the commercial greenhouse grower, including the greenhouses: **shade cloth, drip irrigation supplies, greenhouse controls and equipment**. They will also sell to the home gardener; there is a $3.50 handling charge on orders less than $25.
Catalog: Free, CAN/OV, $25m

Sturdi-Built Mfg. Co.
11304 S.W. Boones Ferry Rd.
Portland, OR 97219
(503) 244-4100
Bill Warner

SUPPLIES
Offers redwood **greenhouses** in a number of styles, both free-standing and lean-to; also sells accessories and equipment. One model is round. They can be single or double glazed and customized to fit your exact space. (1952)
Catalog: $2, OV, $10m
Shop: All Year, M-F, Call Ahead

Submatic Irrigation Systems
P. O. Box 246
Lubbock, TX 79408
(806) 747-9000 or (800) 858-4016 TO/CC

SUPPLIES
A broad selection of supplies for **drip and mist irrigation systems**, subsurface lawn irrigation and mini-sprinklers for a variety of uses -- both for home gardeners and commercial use.
Catalog: $1, R&W, CAN/OV
Shop: All Year, M-Sa

Sun Designs
P. O. Box 206
173 E. Wisconsin Ave. (Oconomowoc)
Delafield, WI 53018-0206
(414) 567-4255 TO/CC
Richard & Janet Strombeck

ORNAMENTS
Publishes several books of **garden structure designs**: gazebos, bridges, privies, storage sheds, arbors; and sells detailed plans for their designs. They have charming styles to fit almost any garden. Gazebo book $9.45 ppd, Garden Structures book $10.45 ppd. (1978)
Catalog: See notes, R&W, CAN/OV
Shop: All Year, M-Sa

Sun System Greenhouses
60-D Vanderbilt Motor Pkwy.
Commack, NY 11725
(516) 543-7766

SUPPLIES
Metal framed **greenhouses, solar additions and sun rooms** in many sizes and configurations for home or commercial use; also greenhouse windows and greenhouse accessories.
Catalog: Free

Sunbird Products, Inc.
P. O. Box 144
Millersburg, OH 44654
(216) 674-2966 TO/CC
Daniel Breckenridge

SUPPLIES
Offers the "Sunbird" **tiller/cultivator**, a lightweight machine which comes with a variety of labor-saving attachments: lawn dethatcher, snow thrower, brushcutter, string trimmer, water pump. The engine even comes off to make a hedge trimmer -- but you still have to get out of the hammock! (1985)
Catalog: Free, CAN/OV
Shop: All Year, Call Ahead

Suncraft, Inc.
414 South Street
Elmhurst, IL 60126
(312) 530-1552
Frederick Bach & Arthur Pudark

SUPPLIES
"Superior Greenhouses" -- several models of **aluminum greenhouses and lean-tos** with all necessary accessories -- exhaust fans, heaters and bench frame fittings. Greenhouses have curved eaves, anodized aluminum frames and full-length roof vents. Also sells material kits for do-it-yourselfers. (1982)
Catalog: $1d, R&W, MO

Sunglo Solar Greenhouses *4441 26th Ave. West* *Seattle, WA 98199* *(206) 284-8900 or (800) 647-0606 TO/CC* *Robert and Ron Goldsberry*	SUPPLIES Manufactures and sells **greenhouses in kit form**, with double or triple wall construction; also offers greenhouse accessories. Catalog: Free, CAN/OV Shop: All Year, M-F
Sunstream Bee Supply *P. O. Box 225* *Eighty Four, PA 15330* *(412) 222-3330* *Francis Yost*	SUPPLIES BOOKS Offers a complete line of **beekeeping supplies and equipment**: bees, books, hives, honey extracting equipment, clothing and gloves, even seeds of plants attractive to bees. You can buy a complete's beginner's outfit with or without bees. Catalog: Free, CAN/OV, $5m Shop: April-Oct, M,W,F,Su, By Appointment Only
Superior Autovents *17422 LaMesa Lane* *Huntington Beach, CA 92647* *(714) 848-0412*	SUPPLIES Sells the "Bayliss Solarvent", an **automatic vent opener** for greenhouses and coldframes; it comes in several models and can be set to open at temperatures between 55 and 75F. Catalog: Free, R&W, CAN, $40m Shop: By Appointment Only, Call Ahead
Superior Greenhouse	See Suncraft, Inc.
Jane Sutley Horticultural Books *1105 W. Cherry Street* *Centralia, WA 98531* *(206) 736-5251* *Jane & Bruce Sutley*	BOOKS Offers **new, used and out-of-print books** on gardening, horticulture, farming and forestry -- emphasizing useful books for the gardener and researcher. Good selection, indexed by subject. Catalog: $1, CAN/OV
Swallowtail Corporation *1705 14th St., Ste. 331* *Boulder, CO 80302* *(303) 499-5914 or 355-0266* *T. Williams, R. Kraemer, L. Williams*	SUPPLIES Sells "Vita-Gro Liquid Plantfood", a 'high-tech' **fertilizer** for houseplants. (1984) Catalog: R&W, MO, CAN/OV, $4m
Sylvandale Gardens	See Full Circle Garden Products
Talisman Cove Productions *1120 Cove Road* *Mamaroneck, NY 10543* *(914) 698-6439 or 698-6631* *Charles Marden Fitch*	SERVICES A photographer-author with an extensive file of **horticultural photographs**, which may be purchased for publication. He will also accept photographic assignments for specific projects. (1965) Catalog: Free, CAN/OV, $35m
Tecnu Enterprises, Inc. *828 E. 1st Avenue* *Albany, OR 97321* *(503) 926-4577 or (800) ITCHING TO/CC $5m*	SUPPLIES Tecnu really works! I only have to look at poison oak or poison ivy to start scratching -- but if you wash at once you can avoid the rash, and if you're too late, it lessens the itch; it sits on my kitchen sink. They also sell a venom remover for insect bites and stings and a 10-hour insect repellent. Catalog: Free, R&W, MO, $5m
Texas Greenhouse Co. *2773 St. Louis Ave.* *Ft. Worth, TX 76110* *(817) 926-5447 or (800) 227-5447 TO/CC* *T. F. Lange*	SUPPLIES Sells **greenhouses and lean-tos** with curved glass eaves, automatic venting and aluminum or redwood frames; also greenhouse accessories. (1948) Catalog: Free ($1 First Class) Shop: All Year, M-F
There's Always the Garden *32 W. Anapamu, #267* *Santa Barbara, CA 93101* *(805) 687-6478 TO/CC* *Linda Cole*	SUPPLIES Charming **tee shirts, sweatshirts and totes** silk-screened "There's always the garden" and in styles for flower or vegetable gardeners and bird lovers, new designs for herb and rose growers. Also adding note cards and rubber stamps with the same designs -- gardeners love to broadcast their passion. Catalog: Free, R&W, MO, CAN/OV
Thurston Distributing, Inc. *914 Lee Street* *Boise, ID 83702* *(208) 342-1212* *Bob Thurston*	SUPPLIES Sells **diatomaceous earth** in a product called "Got-cha", which kills many insects but is harmless to pets and humans -- they claim you can even brush your teeth with it. A completely natural and non-toxic pest control. Catalog: Free, R&W, CAN/OV

For Explanations of Abbreviations/Codes Used In Listings See Bookmark or Inside Covers

Topiary, Inc.
41 Bering
Tampa, FL 33606
(813) 254-3229

ORNAMENTS
Painted galvanized wire **topiary frames** in many animal and other shapes, some available already planted.
Catalog: Free, R&W

Trade-Wind Instruments
1076 Loraine St.
Enumclaw, WA 98022
(206) 825-2294 TO/CC
Ronald Tyler

SUPPLIES
Weather instruments: wind anemometers, wind odometers, rain gauge and tide clock. Useful to sailors, seaside dwellers, birdwatchers -- and gardeners, too. (1970)
Catalog: Free, R&W, CAN/OV
Shop: All Year, M-F, Call Ahead

Trans-Sphere Corp.

See Gothic Arch Greenhouses

Trickle Soak Systems
P. O. Box 38
8733 Magnolia, Ste. 100
Santee, CA 92071
(619) 449-6408 TO/CC $20m
Tom Strong

SUPPLIES
A broad selection of **supplies for drip irrigation systems** and free design advice for the customer; they sell a "Drip Irrigation Design Manual" for $3.95 ppd, 37 pages of practical advice. Newest product is the "Add-It" fertilizer injector for drip systems or any hose bibb in the garden. (1977)
Catalog: Free, R&W, CAN/OV
Shop: All Year, M-Sa

Tropexotic Growers, Inc.
708 - 60th St., N.W.
Bradenton, FL 34209
(813) 792-3574 TO $5m
Darwin Ralston

SUPPLIES
Offers "Superthrive", a **plant vitamin/hormone food** useful in transplanting and starting cuttings. One of life's mysteries is how customers are supposed to pour "one drop" out of a 1/2 inch wide bottle mouth; put eye dropper tops on it, Superthrive!
Catalog: SASE, R&W, OV
Shop: All Year, M-Sa, By Appointment Only

Tropical Plant Products, Inc.
P. O. Box 547754
1715 Silver Star Rd.
Orlando, FL 32804
(305) 293-2451 or 2453
Kenneth & Janet Lewis

SUPPLIES
Sells **orchid growing supplies**: fertilizers, wire hanging baskets, coconut fiber, fir bark, moss, tree fern baskets, sphagnum moss and osmunda fiber, totems and plaques for mounting bromeliads and more. (1974)
Catalog: Long SASE, R&W, CAN/OV
Shop: All Year, M-F

Turner Greenhouses
Highway 117 South
Goldsboro, NC 27530
(919) 734-8345 TO/CC $10m
Sumpter Turner, Gary Smithwick

SUPPLIES
Galvanized steel framed **greenhouses** in various sizes and configurations, available with fiber glass or polyethylene coverings, as well as a full line of equipment and accessories. (1958)
Catalog: Free, CAN/OV, $10m
Shop: All Year, M-F, Call Ahead

Twin Oaks Books
4343 Causeway Dr.
Lowell, MI 49331
(616) 897-7479 TO/CC
George E. Woolfson

BOOKS
Specializes in **books about orchids** -- only orchids, but they have a broad selection, and each book is described in great detail; they will pay the 'book rate' postage on purchases anywhere in the world. (1977)
Catalog: Free, SASE, MO, CAN/OV

Unique Insect Control
5504 Sperry Drive
Sacramento, CA 95621
(916) 961-7945 or 967-7082
Foley Family

SUPPLIES
Offers several types of **beneficial insects**: ladybugs, green lacewings, trichogramma wasps, praying mantis, fly parasites, white-fly parasites, predatory mites, mealybug predators and earthworms. Informative flier.
Catalog: Free, R&W, SS:AY

F. R. Unruh
37 Oaknoll Rd.
Wilmington, DE 19808
(302) 994-2328
F. R. Unruh

SUPPLIES
Wire and aluminum garden markers, either 4-1/2 or 11-1/2 inches high -- can be written on with wax pencil or stenciling tape; come in white, light green or beige. (Garden markers are stuck in the ground next to the plant; plant labels are attached to the plant.)
Catalog: Free, R&W, $20m

The Urban Farmer Store
2833 Vicente Street
San Francisco, CA 94116
(415) 661-2204 TO/CC
Tom Bressan & John Stokes

SUPPLIES
Specializes in **drip and automatic irrigation systems**; publishes a good all around introduction to the subject and sells all the necessary equipment. Carries products by Eintal, Toro, Rainbird, Maxijet, Irritrol and Hardie.
Catalog: $1, R&W, CAN/OV
Shop: All Year, M-Sa

VT Productions
P. O. Box 339
Soquel, CA 95073
Monica Meyer

SUPPLIES
Sells a **videodisc of exotic plants**, including a visual encyclopedia of plant habitats, family groupings, time-lapse of flowering plants and a computer-generated index to each frame. Produced for use at all levels of teaching botany, horticulture and landscaping. (1980)
Catalog: Long SASE, MO, CAN

Vegetable Factory, Inc.
P. O. Box 2235
71 Vanderbilt Avenue
New York, NY 10163
(212) 867-0113 TO/CC
Dean Schwartz, Cust. Svs. Mgr.

SUPPLIES
Sells a complete line of double-walled **greenhouses** in various sizes and configurations. Their "Sun-Porch" lean-to model converts to a screen porch for summer use. Also offers insulated glazing panels for do-it-yourself construction. (1972)
Catalog: $2, R&W, MO, CAN

Verilux, Inc.
P. O. Box 1512
Greenwich, CT 06836
(203) 869-3750 TO $55m
H. Jackson Scott

SUPPLIES
Verilux "Tru Bloom" **fluorescent plant lights** balanced to promote normal, compact growth -- long lasting and available in various sizes for home or commercial use. (1956)
Catalog: Free, R&W, MO, CAN/OV, $55m

Vermont Castings
Prince Street
Randolph, VT 05060
(802) 728-3181
Duncan Syme

FURNITURE
Famous for their cast iron stoves, they also make a **garden bench of cast iron and teak** which could be used indoors or out, in a simple and elegant eighteenth century style.
Catalog: Free, R&W, CAN/OV
Shop: All Year, M-Sa

Victory Garden Supply Co.
1428 East High Street
Charlottesville, VA 22901
(804) 293-2298 TO/CC
Robert W. Sandow

SUPPLIES
New company offers several models of aluminum **greenhouse**, benches, vent openers, shades and ventilated shelving. (1987)
Catalog: Free, CAN/OV, $5m
Shop: All Year, M-F

Videodiscovery, Inc.
P. O. Box 85878
1515 Dexter Ave. N.
Seattle, WA 98145
(206) 285-5400
Joe Clark

SUPPLIES
Offers an "Encyclopedia of Landscape Horticulture" on **videodisc** -- over 7,000 still images of 1,000 woody landscape plants. Photos show full plant, winter foliage, leaf, usage and identification characteristics; associated database helps landscapers and students with plant selection. (1983)
Catalog: Free, R&W, MO, CAN

Vine Arts
P. O. Box 03014
Portland, OR 97203
(503) 289-7505
Janet Schuster

ORNAMENTS
Topiary frames in various animal shapes; will also do custom frames. Frames are made of galvanized steel and treated with rust-proof paint; their life-size deer and foxes are popular.
Catalog: $2d

Vintage Wood Works
P. O. Box 980
513 S. Adams
Fredericksburg, TX 78624
(512) 997-9513 TO/CC
Gregory Tatsch

ORNAMENTS
Offers a charming Victorian **gazebo**, but also a broad selection of Victorian and period trim for houses, posts and balustrades for porches, entrances and fences -- a terrific way to perk up a lackluster house or outbuilding.
Catalog: $2, CAN/OV
Shop: All Year, M-F

The Violet House
P. O. Box 1274
Gainesville, FL 32601
(904) 377-8465 TO $8m
Dick & Anne Maduro

SUPPLIES
Offers **indoor growing supplies**: plastic pots, wick watering reservoirs, fertilizers, pesticides and potting materials for growing African violets and other houseplants. Also sells Nadeau sinningia and African violet seed.
Catalog: Free, R&W, CAN/OV, $8m
Shop: All Year, M-F, Call Ahead

Vixen Hill Gazebos
Main Street
Elverson, PA 19520
(215) 286-0909 or 827-7972
Douglas Jefferys & Christopher Peeples

ORNAMENTS
Makes easy-to-assemble **prefabricated gazebos**, available in four sizes, Victorian or Colonial, made of cedar and assembled with brass acorn nuts. They also make benches and tables to fit.
Catalog: $5d, CAN/OV

Walpole Woodworkers
767 East Street
Walpole, MA 02081
(617) 668-2800 or (800) 343-6948 TO/CC
Arthur W. Clapp, Chmn.

SUPPLIES FURNITURE
Offers **rustic cedar outdoor furniture** -- chairs, picnic tables, swings, chaises, benches and more; also sells a number of prefabricated garden buildings for storage, studios, stables and poolhouses. They even have croquet and horseshoe sets!
Catalog: $1, CAN/OV

For Explanations of Abbreviations/Codes Used In Listings See Bookmark or Inside Covers

Warnico/USA, Inc.
59 Rutter St.
Rochester, NY 14610
NY (800) 537-0047 or US (800) 451-1118 TO/CC
Edward E. Warnick

TOOLS
Sells the "Easy Weeder", a long-handled device for cutting and lifting long-rooted weeds without stooping -- great for gardeners with bad backs. They've just come out with an extra-lightweight model. (1986)
Catalog: Free, R&W, CAN/OV
Shop: All Year, M-F, Call Ahead

Gary Wayner - Bookseller
Rt. 3, Box 18
Ft. Payne, AL 35967-9501
(205) 845-5866 TO/CC $20m
Gary Wayner

BOOKS
Specializes in scholarly **out-of-print books** on botany, gardening and natural history. (1976)
Catalog: $1, MO, CAN/OV

Wendelighting
2445 N. Naomi St.
Burbank, CA 91504
(818) 955-8066
Peter Jens Jacksen

SUPPLIES
Offers a variety of **indoor and outdoor lighting systems**, aimed at the professional, but available to anyone; they can also provide design services and consultation. Systems are low-voltage and inconspicuous, can be used in numerous configurations.
Catalog: Free, R&W, CAN/OV
Shop: All Year, M-F, By Appointment Only

West Coast Ladybug Sales
P. O. Box 903
Gridley, CA 95948
(916) 534-0840 or 846-2738
Russell E. Smith

SUPPLIES SERVICES
Offers a selection of **beneficial insects** -- ladybugs, fly parasites, trichogramma parasitic wasps, cryptolaemus mealybug destroyers, green lacewings and praying mantis egg cases; informative leaflets on their benefits and how to release and establish them. (1968)
Catalog: Free, R&W, CAN/OV, $3m
Shop: All Year, Call Ahead

Westwind Mfg. Co.
P. O. Box 948
Kemp, TX 75143-0948
(214) 498-6753
Glenn Thorpe

SUPPLIES
Offers **redwood gazebos** in four sizes; also sells garden furniture and swings.

Wikco Industries, Inc.
Route 2, Box 154
Broken Bow, NE 68822
(308) 872-5327 or (800) 247-6167 x 734
Jackson M. Ideen

TOOLS FURNITURE
Offers the "Clear Creek" **garden bench** in turn-of-the-century wrought-iron style, with green, black or white enamel finish. Also sells the "Super Spear Log Splitter" for splitting firewood without an ax -- I've got a new wood stove, and suddenly such items look very appealing!
Catalog: Free, R&W, MO, CAN

Wilkerson Books
31 Old Winter St.
Lincoln, MA 01773
(617) 259-1110
Robin Wilkerson

BOOKS SERVICES
A good selection of **used and out-of-print books** on gardening and horticulture, herbs, plant exploration, garden history and design. Some are fairly recent; will search for out-of-print titles.
Catalog: $1d, R&W, CAN/OV
Shop: By Appointment Only

Willsboro Wood Products
P. O. Box 336
Willsboro, NY 12996
(800) 342-3373

FURNITURE
Adirondack-style **cedar furniture** -- chairs, chaises, settees, tables, picnic tables and benches.
Catalog: Free, R&W, CAN/OV

Winterthur Museum & Gardens
Catalogue Division
115 Brand Road
Salem, VA 24156
(800) 848-2929

ORNAMENTS
Catalog from the Winterthur Museum & Gardens offers beautiful reproductions of items on display both in the gardens and in the house, as well as special plants from the gardens. A good selection of gifts and garden ornaments for any garden or gardener -- many tempting items.
Catalog: Free
Shop: Shop at Museum & Gardens

Wisconsin Wagon Co.
507 Laurel Ave.
Janesville, WI 53545
(608) 754-0026 TO/CC
Albert & Lois Hough

SUPPLIES
Makes wooden children's toys, including **wheelbarrows** and great "Janesville" wagons. They also make an awning-covered **patio cart** useful as a bar or buffet and have added an adult-size wheelbarrow, probably because the little one is so cute that grown-ups had to have their own. (1979)
Catalog:]ree
Shop: Feb-Xmas, M-Sa, Call Ahead

Womanswork
RD 539K
Berwick, ME 03908
(207) 676-3332
Karen Smiley

SUPPLIES
Specializes in **gardening and work gloves~ made to fit women's hands; come in** either supple suede pigskin or pigskin back and split-cowhide palms for heavy duty. They also make a practical work-apron with 15 pockets. (1985)
Catalog: Free, R&W, MO, CAN/OV, $8m

Wood Classics, Inc.
RD 1, P. O. Box 455E
High Falls, NY 12440
(914) 687-7288 TO/CC
Eric & Barbara Goodwin

FURNITURE
Nicely crafted **wooden outdoor furniture** in rustic and classic styles – tables, chairs, lounges, porch swings and rockers, made of mahogany or teak. All available finished or in kit form.
Catalog: $3, R&W, CAN/OV
Shop: All Year, By Appointment Only

Wood Violet Books
291 North Main St.
Oregon, WI 53575
(608) 835-7954
Debra S. Cravens

BOOKS SERVICES
New and used books, specializing in books on herbs and other garden subjects; will search for hard-to-find books. (1983)
Catalog: Free, CAN/OV
Shop: All Year, Various Hours, Call Ahead

Elisabeth Woodburn
P. O. Box 398
Booknoll Farm
Hopewell, NJ 08525
(609) 466-0522
Elisabeth Woodburn

BOOKS
A specialist in **horticultural books**, including new, used, out-of-print and very rare for libraries and serious gardeners; separate catalogs for various categories are $2 each.
Catalog: See notes, CAN/OV, $10m
Shop: By Appointment Only

Woodventure, Inc.
15 Island Drive
Savannah, GA 31406
(912) 354-8857 or 236-8689
George G. Quaile

FURNITURE
Offers **garden furniture** made of pine and teak -- chairs and porch swings, chairs for children, a patio cart, table, rocker, planters and more. Styles are solid and rustic. Write for information.

Gary W. Woolson, Bookseller
RFD 1, Box 1576
Rt. 9 (Newburgh)
Hampden, ME 04444
(207) 234-4931 TO
Gary W. Woolson

BOOKS
Specializes in **used and out-of-print books** on plants and gardening. (1967)
Catalog: Free, R&W
Shop: All Year, M-Th, Call Ahead

Yonah Manufacturing Co.
P. O. Box 280
Airport Road
Cornelia, GA 30531
(404) 778-2126 TO/CC
James Bruce, Jr.

SUPPLIES
Sells **shade cloth** providing from 30 to 92% actual shade -- used for greenhouses and shade structures, patio covers, etc. Sold with bindings and grommets to your specifications.
Catalog: Free, R&W, CAN/OV
Shop: All Year, M-F, Call Ahead

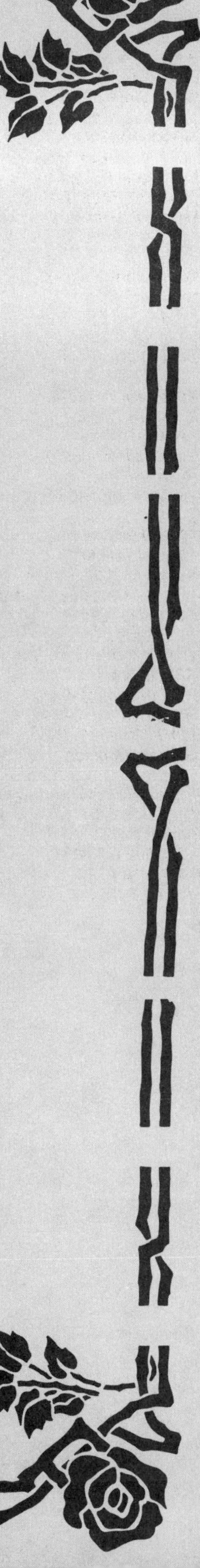

Professional Societies and Trade Associations

Professional societies, trade associations and umbrella groups are listed alphabetically.

See index section for:

M. Magazine Index: An index to the magazines offered by societies — as well as other horticultural and gardening magazines and newsletters.

Be sure to check the Changes and Corrections List at the end of the book (see Practical Matters). This list is updated with each printing.

Professional Societies and Trade Associations found too late to include in this edition, as well as changes and deletions to current listings, will be listed in our quarterly updates (see Practical Matters).

Associations

While usually limited in membership, these associations are excellent sources of special information. The umbrella groups, while not open to general membership, will put you in touch with local affiliates who do accept members — if you can't find a local group, contact them and inquire.

A Table of the Symbols and Abbreviations Used in this Book
Appears Inside the Front and Back Covers and On the Bookmark

For Explanations of Abbreviations/Codes Used In Listings See Bookmark or Inside Covers

All-America Selections
Nona Wolfram-Koivula
1311 Butterfield Rd., Suite 310
Downers Grove, IL 60515
(312) 963-6999

Trade association to evaluate and promote new cultivars of flowers and vegetables from seed: send out annual information to gardening press. Will send list of their 230 test gardens in the U.S. and Canada on request.

American Assn. of Botanical Gardens & Arboreta
Susan Lathrop, Exec. Dir.
P. O. Box 206
Swarthmore, PA 19081
(215) 328-9145
Bulletin (4)
Newsletter (12)

Professional association of botanical gardens: have regional meetings in various locations. News letter lists positions available in botanical gardens, they also have a job hotline with recorded announcements (215) 328-9146.
Annual Dues: US$40. (IMO)

American Association of Nurserymen
Terri Gore
1250 I Street, No. 500
Washington, DC 20005
(202) 789-2900

Trade association: provides services and information to nurserymen. Publish a directory of the nursery industry with a classified directory of goods and services; it includes many wholesale nurseries.

American Community Gardening Association
Box 500, c/o Chicago Botanical Garden
Glencoe, IL 60022-0400
ACGA Journal (4)

Umbrella association for the community gardening movement: write for information.
Annual Dues: US$15 Individuals: US$30 Organizations

American Forestry Association
Kathy Amberger
P. O. Box 2000
Washington, DC 20013
(202) 467-5810
American Forests (12)

Society is dedicated to balanced forest use; founded in 1875.
Annual Dues: US$24: C$27.50: US$27.50 OV

American Horticultural Therapy Association
Steve Gallison
9220 Wightman Road, Suite 300
Gaithersburg, MD 20879
(301) 948-3010
Journal of Therapeutic Horticulture

Professional association devoted to using horticulture to enhance the lives of special populations through therapy and vocational rehabilitation.
Annual Dues: US$35

American Seed Trade Association
1030 15th St.N.W., Suite 964
Washington, DC 20005
(202) 223-4080
ASTA Newsletter (12)

Trade association of seed companies: write for information.

American Society of Consulting Arborists
700 Canterbury Rd.
Clearwater, FL 33546
Arboriculture Consultant (7)

Trade association of qualified arborists; purpose is to educate the public on the value of trees and to refer them to members for consultation.
Annual Dues: US$125

American Society of Landscape Architects
Edward H. Able, Jr. Exec. Dir.
1733 Connecticut Ave. N.W.
Washington, DC 20009
(202) 466-7730
Landscape Architecture (6)

Professional association: write for information.

Associated Landscape Contractors of America
Terry Peters
405 N. Washington Street
Falls Church, VA 22046
(703) 241-4004

Trade assocation to provide exchange of business and technical information among its members; they have many educational programs and conferences.
Annual Dues: Based on annual volume.

The Association for Women in Aboriculture
Kimberly Dunn
277-285 Martinel Dr., Suite 100
Kent, OH 44240

"New organization for women in arboriculture, forestry, landscaping, nursery work, gardening and lawncare, with special emphasis on enhancing career opportunities." Mentioned in Hortideas: write for information.

Center for Plant Conservation
125 The Arborway
Jamaica Plain, MA 02130
(617) 524-6988

Formed in 1984 to create a systematic, comprehensive national program of conservation of endangered American plants, coordinates programs of botanical gardens.

The Council on Botanical & Horticultural Libraries
John F. Reed
The New York Botanical Garden
Bronx, NY 10458

Association of libraries in the field of botany and horticulture.

The Fertilizer Institute
H. Wm. Hale
1015 18th Street. N.W.
Washington, DC 20036
(202) 861-4934

Trade association: write for information.

Future Farmers of America
Ted Amick
P. O. Box 15160
Alexandria, VA 22309-0160
(703) 360-3600
The National Future Farmer (4)
Newsletter (6)

Umbrella organization for 8,350 local chapters: purpose is to prepare students for careers in agriculture.
Annual Dues: $2.50

Garden Centers of America
Patrick Redding
1250 I Street N.W., Suite 500
Washington, DC 20005
(202) 789-2900
G.G.A. Newsletter (10)

Trade association of the nursery/landscape industry with over 3,500 member firms.
Annual Dues: Based on volume of business.

The Garden Club of America
Mrs. E. Murphy
598 Madison Avenue
New York, NY 10022
(212) 753-8287
GCA Bulletin (2)
Newsletter (6)

Umbrella organization for 185 local garden clubs: they have a program of awards and scholarships, civic improvement and education to promote the love of gardening.

Garden Writers Association of America
W. J. Jung
1218 Overlook Road
Eustis, FL 32726
(904) 589-8888
Bulletin (6)

Association of professional garden writers, dedicated to improving the standards of horticultural journalism in print and broadcast media.
Annual Dues: US$40

Horticultural Research Institute
1250 I Street N.W., Suite 500
Washington, DC 20005
(202) 789-2900

Trade association: the research arm of the American Association of Nurserymen.
Annual Dues: US$100

International Plant Propagator's Society
Dr. John A. Wott, Sec.-Tres.
Ctr. for Urban Hort., GF-15, Univ. of Wash.
Seattle, WA 98195
(206) 543-8602
Proceedings, Intl. Plant Propagators Society

Professional group: devoted to art and science of plant propagation.
Annual Dues: US$30

International Society of Arboriculture
Box 71-5 Lincoln Square
Urbana, IL 61801
(217) 328-2032
Journal of Arboriculture (12)

Write for information.

For Explanations of Abbreviations/Codes Used In Listings See Bookmark or Inside Covers

The Irrigation Association
Joseph Venable
1911 N. Fort Myer Dr., Suite 1009
Arlington, VA 22209
(703) 524-1200
Irrigation News (12)

Trade association to promote use of modern irrigation equipment, and water and soil conservation.
Annual Dues: Vary according to category.

The Lawn Institute
Beverly Roberts
P. O. Box 108, County Line Road
Pleasant Hill, TN 38578-0108
(615) 277-3722
Harvests Newsletter (4)

Non-profit trade association to enhance lawn grass research and education. Periodical "Harvests" available on separate subscription.
Annual Dues: US$75 US & CAN: US$100 OV

Mailorder Association of Nurserymen, Inc.
Ann Reilly
210 Cartwright Blvd.
Massapequa Park, NY 11762
(516) 541-6902

Trade association of larger mail-order businesses: write for information.

Master Gardeners of the Cooperative Extension Service
Diane Relf or Judy Schwab
Dept. of Horticulture, Virginia Tech. Univ.
Blacksburg, VA 24061
(703) 961-6254

This group is in organization as this book goes to press. Its aim is to serve as a clearinghouse of information on programs and training for Master Gardeners. There are 45 state chapters.

Men's Garden Clubs of America, Inc.
Nancy D. Gorden, Exec. Sec.
5560 Merle Hay Rd.
Johnston, IA 50131
(515) 278-0295
The Gardener (6)
MGCA Newsletter (6)

Umbrella organization for local men's garden clubs.
Annual Dues: US$10: C$12: US$15 OV

National Association of Women in Horticulture
Betty Hensinger, Pres.
P. O. Box 1485
Mt. Dora, FL 32757
(904) 383-8811

Group founded early in l987: write for information.

National Council of State Garden Clubs, Inc.
401 Magnolia Avenue
St. Louis, MO 63110
The National Gardener (6)

Umbrella group for state garden clubs, which in themselves are umbrella organizations for 11,000 local garden clubs.
Annual Dues: Membership through local garden clubs.
Chapters: 11,000

National Garden Bureau
Nona Wolfram-Koivula
1311 Butterfield Rd., Suite 310
Downers Grove, IL 60515
(312) 963-6999

Trade association: purpose is to encourage home gardening from seed, annual convention held in conjunction with American Seed Trade Association.
Annual Dues: Based on Gross Sales.

National Junior Horticulture Association
Jan Hoffman
441 E. Pine St.
Fremont, MI 49412
Going & Growing (3)

Umbrella organization for state and local chapters: students join chapters in their schools or through other local clubs.
Annual Dues: Through local chapters.

National Wildflower Research Center
Mae Daniller
2600 FM 973 North
Austin, TX 78725
(512) 929-3600

National group to promote conservation and use of native plants in public and private landscapes.

National Xeriscape Council, Inc.
Pat Miller, Exec. Dir.
940 East 51st Street
Austin, TX 78751
(512) 454-8626

Non-profit association devoted to "xeriscaping": landscaping to make gardens and plantings more water efficient. Write for information.

Ontario Horticultural Association
Ruth Friendship
P. O. Box 1030, Guelph Horticultural Centre
Guelph, ON, Canada N1H 6N1
(519) 823-5700
Horticultural Societies Newsletter

Umbrella organization for horticultural societies in Ontario; publishes a schedule of Agricultural Fairs and Exihibitions, and helps local groups with suggestions for programs and useful resources.

Outdoor Power Equipment Institute
Dennis Dix
1901 L Street N.W., Suite 700
Washington, DC 20036
(202) 296-3484

Trade association: write for information.

Perennial Plant Association
Steven M. Still
217 Howlett Hall
Columbus, OH 43210
(614) 292-6027
Perennial Plant Symposium Proceedings (1)
Newsletter (4)

Trade association: promotes the development of the perennial plant industry, holds symposia and conferences.
Annual Dues: Based on Gross Income.
Privileges: CONVENTIONS BOOKS

Plant Sciences Data Center
American Horticultural Society
7931 East Boulevard Dr.
Alexandria, VA 22308
(703) 768-5700
Master Inventory of Botanical Taxa

Provides services to horticultural societies and botanical gardens, maintains a master list of holdings of cooperating botanical gardens worldwide, registers new plant varieties.

Regenerative Agriculture Association
Jim Morgan
222 Main Street
Emmaus, PA 18049
(215) 967-5171
The New Farm (7)

An association of commercial farmers using organic methods: has educational conferences.
Annual Dues: US$15: C$19: US$21 OV

Seedpeople Network
Michael Pilarski
P. O. Box 1466
Chelan, WA 98816
Newsletter (4)

Coalition of small seed companies, growers and collectors in the Northwest: all welcome. Goal is diverse and sustainable agriculture, sharing information and preserving old varieties.
Annual Dues: US$12

Soil & Water Conservation Society
Ann Thornton
7515 N.E. Ankeny Rd.
Ankeny, IA 50021
(515) 289-2331
Journal of Soil & Water Conservation (6)
Conservogram (6)

Purpose is to advance the science and art of good land use. Periodical available on separate subscription: US$25 or US$28 overseas.
Annual Dues: US$32 US&CAN: US$37 OV (IMO)

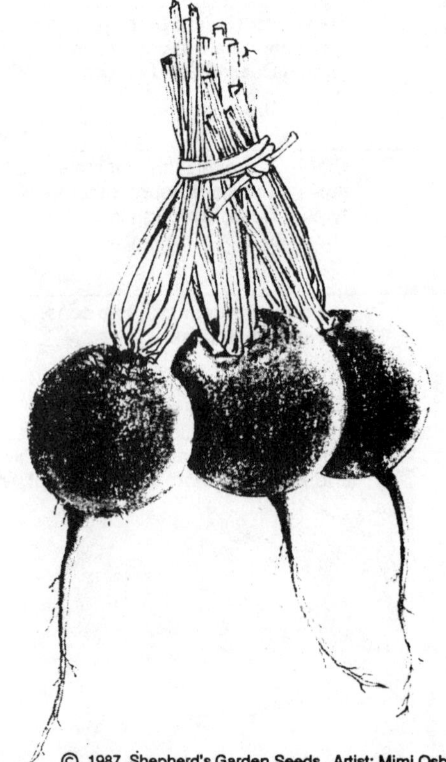

Horticultural Societies

Horticultural Societies are listed alphabetically.

See index section for:

L. Society Index: An index of horticultural societies listed by plants and/or other special interests.

M. Magazine Index: An index to the magazines offered by societies as well as other horticultural and gardening magazines and newsletters.

Be sure to check the Changes and Corrections List at the end of the book (see Practical Matters). This list is updated with each printing.

Horticultural Societies found too late to include in this edition, as well as changes and deletions to current listings, will be listed in our quarterly updates (see Practical Matters).

Societies

I have listed only societies which are of international, national or regional interest and membership. There are also local garden clubs, regional chapters of national and state organizations and the "friends" groups at botanical gardens – any of which would have activities and programs. Ask your garden center, recreation department, chamber of commerce or the ornamental horticulture department of your local college to find out about local groups.

To my distress, fewer than half of the societies listed answered my requests for updated addresses and other information. In my quest for more information, I was told that **Gardening by Mail** has the most current listing in the U.S. – apparently everyone has the same problem keeping current. Mailing addresses are frequently the addresses of the current society officers and change when they do. I suggest that you write to the address given, and your request for information should be forwarded. Readers who can supply more current information are begged to do so!

If you travel, consider the advantages of joining an international or foreign group a year or so before you go in order to find out about events and places you'd like to include in your plans.

I have to laugh now when I think how shy I was about daring to join the "experts". My experience has been pure pleasure. I've learned a lot, volunteered time to useful projects and made many new friends – and I usually come home from meetings with a new plant. The gardener's greatest resource is other gardeners. The more you get into the network, the greater your pleasure will be!

A Table of the Symbols and Abbreviations Used in this Book
Appears Inside the Front and Back Covers and On the Bookmark

Society Abbreviations and Conventions

Society publications are listed after the address with the number of issues per year indicated in parentheses – e.g. (6).

Available membership privileges are indicated as follows:

Conventions – conferences or annual meetings

Library – library for use of members

Books – book sales to members

Seeds – seed exchanges or sales to members

Plants – plant sales at meetings

Exhibits – plant shows or exhibits sponsored by society

Trips – local field trips for members

Tours – tours or travel program for members

For Explanations of Abbreviations/Codes Used In Listings See Bookmark or Inside Covers

African Violet Society of America, Inc.
P. O. Box 3609
Beaumont, TX 77704
(409) 839-4725
African Violet Magazine (6)

Annual Dues: US$13.50: US$15.50 CAN & OV
Privileges: CONVENTIONS LIBRARY EXHIBITS

African Violet Society of Canada
1573 Arbordale Ave.
Victoria, BC, Canada V8N 5J1
Chatter (4)

Annual Dues: C$10

Alabama Wildflower Society
George Wood
Route 2, Box 115
Northport, AL 35478

Write for information.
Chapters: 5

Alaska Native Plant Society
Verna Pratt
P. O. Box 141613
Anchorage, AK 99514
(907) 333-8212
Newsletter (8)

Annual Dues: US$10: US$12.50 (IMO) OV
Privileges: SEEDS EXHIBITS TRIPS

Aloe, Cactus & Succulent Society of Zimbabwe
Rosemary Kimberley
P. O. Box 8514, Causeway
Harare, Zimbabwe
(263) (0) 39175
Bulletin (2)
Excelsa (1)

Periodically hold major international conventions; next one in 1988. Also offer quarterly newsletter to members.
Annual Dues: US$10 (PC)
Privileges: CONVENTIONS BOOKS SEEDS PLANTS TRIPS TOURS

Alpine Garden Club of British Columbia
Erika Hobeck
13751, 56A Avenue
Surrey, BC, Canada V3W 1J4
Monthly Bulletin

One of the best and most extensive seed exchanges in the world!
Annual Dues: C$13, C$15 family
Privileges: CONVENTIONS LIBRARY BOOKS SEEDS PLANTS EXHIBITS TRIPS

Alpine Garden Society
E. Michael Upward
Lye End Link, St. John's
Woking, Surrey, England GU21 1SW
(04862) Woking 69327
Alpine Gardening (4)

Publish a very interesting Bulletin; have an excellent seed exchange.
Annual Dues: US$15 (IMO) OV
Privileges: CONVENTIONS LIBRARY BOOKS SEEDS PLANTS EXHIBITS TOURS

American Bamboo Society
Richard Haubrich
1101 San Leon Ct.
Solana Beach, CA 92075
(619) 481-9869
Journal (2)
Newsletter (6)

Annual Dues: US$15 (IMO from Overseas)
Garden: Quail Botanical Gardens, Encinitas, CA
Privileges: CONVENTIONS LIBRARY BOOKS SEEDS PLANTS EXHIBITS TRIPS

American Begonia Society
John Ingles, Jr.
8922 Conway Drive
Riverside, CA 92503
(714) 687-3728
The Begonian (6)

There are sixty-four special interest round robin letter "flights" -- members meet at Conventions. Have a seed exchange and seed sales.
Annual Dues: US$15 US & CAN: US$19 OV
Chapters: 50
Privileges: CONVENTIONS BOOKS SEEDS PLANTS EXHIBITS TOURS

American Bonsai Society
Anne Moyle
P. O. Box 358
Keene, NH 03431
(603) 352-9034
Bonsai Journal (4)
ABStracts (3)

Annual Dues: US$18: C$22: US$22 OV (IMO or PC)
Privileges: CONVENTIONS LIBRARY BOOKS

American Boxwood Society
Katherine D. Ward
P. O. Box 85
Boyce, VA 22620
(703) 837-1758
The Boxwood Bulletin (4)

Another plant collection: Orlando White Arboretum, Blandy Experimental Farm, Boyce, VA 22620. Have Boxwood Workshops twice a year, annual tour in Mid-Atlantic states. Their "Buyers Guide", $3, is listed in the book section.
Annual Dues: US$10 (PC or IMO from OV)
Garden: National Arboretum, Washington, DC
Privileges: CONVENTIONS

American Camellia Society
Ann Blair Brown
P. O. Box 1217
Fort Valley, GA 31030-1217
(912) 967-2358
The Camellia Journal (4)
American Camellia Yearbook

Annual Dues: US$15: US$19 OV
Chapters: 70
Garden: Historic Massee Lane Gardens, Ft. Valley, GA
Privileges: CONVENTIONS LIBRARY BOOKS

American Conifer Society
Mrs. Maxine Schwarz
P.O. Box 242
Severna Park, MD 21146
Bulletin (4)

Annual Dues: US$20
Privileges: CONVENTIONS

American Daffodil Society, Inc.
Miss Leslie E. Anderson
Route 3, 2302 Byhalia Road
Hernando, MS 38632
(601) 368-6337
The Daffodil Journal (4)

Annual Dues: US$10: US$7.50 OV (IMO)
Privileges: CONVENTIONS LIBRARY BOOKS

American Dahlia Society
Michael Martinolich
159 Pine St.
New Hyde Park, NY 11040
Bulletin (4)

Annual Dues: US$8: US$9 OV
Chapters: 6
Privileges: EXHIBITS TOURS

American Fern Society
James D. Caponetti, Treas.
Dept. of Botany, The Univ. of Tennessee
Knoxville, TN 37996-1100
American Fern Journal (4)
Fiddlehead Forum (6)

Membership without the more scholarly American Fern Journal is US$6, $8 OV. The spore exchange has fresh spore free or at nominal cost. Membership is by calendar year only. Also publish Pteridologia (irregular).
Annual Dues: US$10: US$14 OV
Chapters: 5
Privileges: SEEDS

American Fuchsia Society
Hall of Flowers
Golden Gate Park
San Francisco, CA 94122
Monthly Bulletin

A number of chapters on the Pacific Coast.
Annual Dues: US$9: US$11 OV (PC or IMO)
Privileges: CONVENTIONS LIBRARY BOOKS PLANTS EXHIBITS TRIPS

American Ginger Society
Tom Wood
P. O. Box 600
Archer, FL 32618
(904) 495-9168
Zingiber (2)

Society founded in l985. Display garden open by appointment only from July to September.
Annual Dues: US$15 US & CAN: US$20 OV (IMO)
Garden: Tom Wood Herb Farm, Archer, FL, By Appointment Only
Privileges: CONVENTIONS LIBRARY SEEDS PLANTS EXHIBITS TRIPS

American Gloxinia & Gesneriad Society, Inc.
Ellen Todd, Membership Secy.
P. O. Box 493
Beverly Farms, MA 01915
The Gloxinian (6)

Seeds are sold at a nominal cost to members.
Annual Dues: US$10: US$13 OV
Chapters: 42
Privileges: CONVENTIONS LIBRARY SEEDS EXHIBITS

American Gourd Society
John Stevens
P. O. Box 274
Mount Gilead, OH 43338-0274
(419) 946-3302
The Gourd (3)

Annual meeting at Mt. Gilead Fairgrounds in July; annual show first full weekend in October, same location. Promote the use of gourds for decorative and useful purposes; magazines show beautifully decorated gourds.
Annual Dues: US$3
Chapters: 2 State chapters.
Privileges: CONVENTIONS BOOKS SEEDS

American Hemerocallis Society
Elly Launius, Secretary
1454 Rebel Drive
Jackson, MS 39211
Daylily Journal (4)

They have a slide library for members; publish an extensive source list; have many round robins on topics of special interest.
Annual Dues: US$12.50 (IMO)
Garden: Many; see publications
Privileges: CONVENTIONS PLANTS EXHIBITS TRIPS

For Explanations of Abbreviations/Codes Used In Listings See Bookmark or Inside Covers

American Hibiscus Society
P. O. Drawer 1540
Cocoa Beach, FL 32931
The Seed Pod (4)

Local chapters have shows and sales, exchange wood for grafting.
Annual Dues: US$10: US$20 OV
Chapters: 21
Privileges: PLANTS EXHIBITS

American Horticultural Society
Sallie S. Hutcheson
P. O. Box 0105
Mount Vernon, VA 22121
(703) 768-5700
American Horticulturist (6)
American Horticulturist News (6)

They have an extensive tour program, a gardener's information service for your problems and plant labels and books for members at special prices.
Annual Dues: US$20: C$35: US$35 OV (IMO)
Garden: River Farm, Mount Vernon, VA
Privileges: CONVENTIONS LIBRARY BOOKS SEEDS PLANTS EXHIBITS TOURS

American Hosta Society
Jack A. Freedman
3103 Heatherhill
Huntsville, AL 35802
(205) 883-6109
American Hosta Society Bulletin (2)
Newsletter (1)

If you love Hostas, their 15th Anniversary Issue (l984) is packed with information -- ask about buying a copy when you join. Maybe they'll put out another one in 1989.
Annual Dues: US$12.50: C$15: US$15 OV (IMO)
Garden: Planning a display garden
Privileges: CONVENTIONS EXHIBITS

American Iris Society
Carol Ramsey
6518 Beachy Ave.
Wichita, KS 67206
Bulletin (4)

Have sections by types of iris; 24 regional affiliates and 127 chapters.
Annual Dues: US$9.50
Garden: Many test gardens; see literature
Privileges: CONVENTIONS PLANTS EXHIBITS

American Ivy Society
Elizabeth Carrick
P. O. Box 520
West Carrollton, OH 45449-0520
(513) 434-7069
The Ivy Journal (3)

Regional display garden at Mendocino Coast Botanical Garden, Fort Bragg, CA. Ivy Research Center may be contacted at the Society's address in West Carrollton, OH.
Annual Dues: US$15: C$19: US$19 OV (IMO or IBD)
Chapters: 2
Garden: Amer. Hort. Soc. Garden, River Farm, Mt. Vernon, VA
Privileges: CONVENTIONS LIBRARY BOOKS

American Magnolia Society
Phelan A. Bright
907 S. Chestnut St.
Hammond, LA 70403-5102
Magnolia, Jnl. of the AMS (2)

Seeds offered to members for a nominal fee.
Annual Dues: US$12: US$15 OV
Privileges: CONVENTIONS SEEDS

American Orchid Society
Membership Department
6000 S. Olive Ave.
West Palm Beach, FL 33405
(305) 585-8666
American Orchid Society Bulletin (12)
A.O.S. Awards Quarterly (4)

Have two meetings a year in different locations; publish handbooks on various orchid subjects.
Annual Dues: US$28, US$34 OV
Privileges: CONVENTIONS LIBRARY BOOKS

American Penstemon Society
Orville Steward
P. O. Box 33
Plymouth, VT 05056
(412) 238-4208
Bulletin of the Amer. Penstemon Society (2)

Publish a very good "Manual for Beginners". They have a second display collection at the Denver Botanical Garden.
Annual Dues: US$7.50: C$7.50: US$8 OV (PC or IMO)
Garden: Cox Arboretum, Dayton, OH
Privileges: CONVENTIONS LIBRARY SEEDS PLANTS TRIPS

American Peony Society
250 Interlachen Rd.
Hopkins, MN 55343
(612) 938-4706
Bulletin (4)

Write for information and list of publications.
Annual Dues: $7.50

American Plant Life Society
R. Mitchel Beauchamp, Editor
P. O. Box 985
National City, CA 92050
(619) 477-5333
Herbertia (2)
Newsletter (4)

Devoted to the culture and preservation of bulbous plants and species bulbs, especially Amaryllidaceae.
Annual Dues: US$20
Privileges: CONVENTIONS SEEDS

American Poinsettia Society
P. O. Box 706
Mission, TX 78572-1256
(512) 585-1256

Write for information.

American Pomological Society
Dr. L. D. Tukey, Bus. Mgr.
103 Tyson Building
University Park, PA 16802
(814) 863-2198
Fruit Varieties Journal (4)

Promotes fruit variety and rootstock improvement through breeding and testing. Open to all; founded in 1848.
Annual Dues: US$12 (IMO or PC)
Privileges: CONVENTIONS BOOKS

American Primrose Society
Brian Skidmore, Treas.
6730 West Mercer Way
Mercer Iland, WA 98040
(206) 242-3846
Primroses (4)

Have slide programs and round robins.
Annual Dues: US$10
Chapters: 7
Privileges: CONVENTIONS SEEDS PLANTS EXHIBITS

American Rhododendron Society
Paula L. Cash, Exec. Secy.
4885 S.W. Sunrise Lane
Tigard, OR 97224
(503) 620-4038
Journal (4)

Slide programs to rent, pollen bank, in addition to seed exchange. Local chapters have active programs and tours; some have libraries.
Annual Dues: US$20
Chapters: 54
Garden: Local chapters maintain gardens
Privileges: CONVENTIONS BOOKS SEEDS PLANTS EXHIBITS

American Rock Garden Society
Buffy Parker
15 Fairmead Road
Darien, CT 06820
Bulletin (4)

A very active society, many local chapters. Winter study weekends: one on East coast, one on West Coast; annual Spring meeting. Have an excellent bookstore for members.
Annual Dues: US$15 (US Funds or IMO)
Chapters: 27
Privileges: CONVENTIONS LIBRARY BOOKS SEEDS PLANTS EXHIBITS TRIPS

American Rose Society
Harold Goldstein
P. O. Box 30,000
Shreveport, LA 71130
(318) 938-5402
The American Rose Magazine (12)

Annual Dues: US$25: US$40 OV (IMO)
Garden: Shreveport, LA. Call for directions.

Aril Society International
Donna Downey
5500 Constitution N.E.
Albuquerque, NM 87110
(505) 255-8207
Yearbook

A society of aril iris lovers; write for information.

Arizona Native Plant Society
David Ingram
P. O. Box 41206
Tucson, AZ 85717
Plant Press (4)

Have informal seed exchanges among members.
Annual Dues: US$15
Chapters: 5
Privileges: CONVENTIONS SEEDS EXHIBITS TRIPS TOURS

Arkansas Native Plant Society
Don Peach
Route 1, Box 282
Mena, AR 71953

Write for information.

Australian Fuchsia Society
Patricia Morris
P. O. Box 97
Norwood, SA, Australia 5062

Information incomplete; they have very few overseas members.

Australian Garden History Society
Membership Secy.
P. O. Box 588
Bowral, NSW, Australia 2576
Australian Garden Journal (6)

Found too late to contact; write for information.
Annual Dues: A$20: A$25 OV
Chapters: 7
Privileges: CONVENTIONS TRIPS TOURS

Australian Geranium Society
27 Chichester St.
Maroubra, NSW, Australia 2035
Journal (4)

Write for information.
Annual Dues: A$6

Australian Hibiscus Society
Miss J. Taylor, Memb. Secy.
8 Girraman Street
West Chermside, Qld., Australia 4032
The Hibiscus (6)

Annual Dues: A$10 (Surface), A$12 (Airmail) OV

Australian Rhododendron Society
Miss. M. Rickards
28 Dequetteville Terrace
Kent Town, SA, Australia 5067
The Rhododendron (4)

Annual Dues: A$15
Chapters: 6
Garden: Some local chapters have display gardens
Privileges: CONVENTIONS SEEDS

Azalea Society of America
Marjorie Taylor
P. O. Box 6244
Silver Spring, MD 20901
(301) 593-2415
The Azalean (4)

Local societies have plant shows and sales.
Annual Dues: US$15
Chapters: 12
Privileges: CONVENTIONS

Bio-Dynamic Farming & Gardening Assn.
Roderick Shouldice
P. O. Box 550
Kimberton, PA 19442
(215) 327-2420
Bio-Dynamics (4)

Promotes bio-dynamic method of farming and gardening.
Annual Dues: US$20: US$25 CAN: US$26 OV (IMO)
Chapters: 9
Privileges: CONVENTIONS BOOKS

Bio-Integral Resource Center (BIRC)
P. O. Box 7414
Berkeley, CA 94707
(415) 524-2567
The IPM Practitioner (Technical) (11)
Common Sense Pest Control (Non-technical) (4)

Society devoted to least-toxic methods of pest management; issue periodicals for both home gardeners and pest control professionals.
Annual Dues: US$25 Prof: US$30 Public
Privileges: CONVENTIONS BOOKS

Bonsai Canada
Norman Haddrick
12 Beardmore Crescent
Willowdale, ON, Canada M2K 2P5
Yearbook

Membership limited to Canadians with advanced bonsai skills; they provide support to seven bonsai groups across Canada.
Annual Dues: Donation
Privileges: EXHIBITS TRIPS

Bonsai Clubs International
Virginia Ellerman
2636 West Mission Road #277
Tallahassee, FL 32304
(904) 575-1442
Bonsai Clubs International (6)

A large society, with many local chapters and activities.
Annual Dues: US$15: US$18 CAN & OV (IMO)
Chapters: 150
Privileges: CONVENTIONS LIBRARY BOOKS EXHIBITS TOURS

Botanical Club of Wisconsin
Rudy G. Koch, Biology Dept.
Univ. of Wisconsin, La Crosse
LaCrosse, WI 54601

Write for information.

Botanical Society of South Africa
Mrs. Diana Peters
Kirstenbosch
Claremont, Cape, South Africa 7735
(021) 771725
Veld & Flora (4)

Personal check for equivalent in dollars may be sent. In addition to Kirstenbosch, they have seven other botanical gardens.
Annual Dues: SA Rand 18 (IMO or US$ Notes; see notes)
Chapters: 8
Garden: Kirstenbosch Botanical Garden
Privileges: LIBRARY BOOKS SEEDS PLANTS EXHIBITS TRIPS TOURS

British & European Geranium Society
Ray Plowright
1 Roslyn Rd., Hathersage
Sheffield, England S30 1BY
Gazette (3)
Year Book

Annual Dues: US$ 5: UK2 (IMO)
Chapters: 8
Privileges: CONVENTIONS BOOKS PLANTS EXHIBITS TRIPS TOURS

The British Cactus & Succulent Society
c/o Miss W. E. Dunn
43 Dewer Drive
Sheffield, England S7 2GR
British Cactus and Succulents Journal (4)
Bradleya (1)

Members can send personal checks for dues; no seed exchange, but seeds are sold to members. "Bradleya" available on separate subscription.
Annual Dues: US$15 (PC)
Chapters: 100
Privileges: CONVENTIONS LIBRARY BOOKS SEEDS PLANTS EXHIBITS

British Columbia Fuchsia & Begonia Society
Mrs. E. I. Hood
2175 W. 16th Avenue
Vancouver, BC, Canada V6K 3B1

Write for information.

British Fuchsia Society
Ron Ewart
29 Princes Crescent
Dollar, Northampton, England FK14 7BW

Write for information.

British Iris Society
Mrs. E. M. Wise
197 The Parkway, Iver Heath
Iver, Bucks., England SL0 0RQ
The Iris Year Book

Three shows a year at the RHS Hall in London; conventions every five years or so.
Annual Dues: UK7 OV (IMO or PC)
Privileges: CONVENTIONS LIBRARY BOOKS SEEDS PLANTS EXHIBITS

The British Ivy Society
Mr. W. F. Kennedy, Mem. Secy.
66 Corwall Rd.
Ruislip, Middlesex, England HA4 6AN
Journal (2)
Occasional Papers

Found too late to contact; please write for information.

British Pelargonium & Geranium Society
Mrs. J. Taylor
23 Beech Crescent, Kidlington
Oxford, England OX5 1DW
KID 5063
Pelargonium News (3)
Yearbook

Have a Geraniaceae group for those interested in species geraniums.
Annual Dues: UK4 or US$10 (US Notes or IMO)
Privileges: CONVENTIONS BOOKS EXHIBITS

Bromeliad Society, Inc.
2355 B Rusk Street
Beaumont, TX 77702
Journal of the Bromeliad Society (6)

Local affiliates have exhibits and plant sales, libraries and field trips.
Annual Dues: US$15
Chapters: 50
Privileges: CONVENTIONS BOOKS SEEDS PLANTS EXHIBITS TRIPS

Bromeliad Study Group of Northern California
Daniel Arcos
1334 S. Van Ness
San Francisco, CA 94110
The Bromeliad Hobbyist (12)

A very enthusiastic and friendly group; periodical is a joint effort of four Bromeliad Study Groups in California, from San Diego to the Bay Area.
Annual Dues: US$10: US$12 OV (IMO)
Privileges: SEEDS PLANTS EXHIBITS TRIPS

Cactus & Succulent Society of America
Louise Lippold
P. O. Box 3010
Santa Barbara, CA 93130
Cactus & Succulent Journal (6)
C.S.S.A. Newsletter (6)

Subscription to journal is separate from membership; see Cactus & Succulent Journal in the magazine section.
Annual Dues: US$20 US & CAN: US$21 OV
Chapters: 50
Privileges: CONVENTIONS LIBRARY EXHIBITS

For Explanations of Abbreviations/Codes Used In Listings See Bookmark or Inside Covers

California Horticultural Society
Mrs. Elsie Mueller
1847 34th Street
San Francisco, CA 94122
(415) 566-5222
Pacific Horticulture (4)
Newsletter (11)

Society active in the San Francisco Bay Area; see also Southern California Horticultural Institute and the Western Horticultural Society.
Annual Dues: US$17.50
Privileges: LIBRARY BOOKS SEEDS PLANTS EXHIBITS TRIPS TOURS

California Native Plant Society
Kristina Schierenbeck
909 12th Street, #116
Sacramento, CA 95814
(916) 447-2677
Fremontia (4)
Bulletin (4)

Some local chapters have seed exchanges.
Annual Dues: US$18 (IMO)
Chapters: 26
Privileges: CONVENTIONS BOOKS SEEDS PLANTS EXHIBITS TRIPS

California Rare Fruit Growers, Inc.
Dianne M. Hand
California State Univ. Arboretum
Fullerton, CA 92634
The Fruit Gardener (4)
Journal (1)

For better understanding on growing sub-tropical fruits. Additional display gardens at the San Diego Zoo and at California Polytechnic Univ. in Pomona.
Annual Dues: US$10: C$15: US$15 OV (IMO)
Chapters: 12
Garden: Fullerton Arboretum, Fullerton, CA
Privileges: CONVENTIONS BOOKS SEEDS PLANTS TRIPS TOURS

Canadian Chrysanthemum & Dahlia Society
G. H. Lawrence
83 Aramaman Dr.
Agincourt, ON, Canada M1T 2PM
(416) 293-6372

Write for information.
Privileges: CONVENTIONS EXHIBITS

Canadian Geranium & Pelargonium Society

Our last mailing to this society was returned. Can any reader send us current information to put into our updates?

Canadian Gladiolus Society
P. Q. Drysdale
3770 Hardy Road, R.R. #1
Agassiz, BC, Canada V0M 1A0
(604) 796-2548
Canadian Gladiolus Annual
Fall Bulletin (1)

Annual Dues: C$8
Chapters: 15
Privileges: CONVENTIONS

Canadian Iris Society
Miss Verna Laurin, Secy.
199 Florence Ave.
Willowdale, ON, Canada M2N 1G5
(416) 225-1088
Newsletter (4)

Canadian members only. Iris shows and auctions, annual educational and awards program, regional activities.
Annual Dues: C$3
Garden: Laking Garden, Royal Botanical Gardens, Hamilton, ON
Privileges: CONVENTIONS LIBRARY PLANTS EXHIBITS

Canadian Orchid Society
President
128 Adelaide St.
Winnipeg, Manitoba, Canada R3A 0W5
(204) 943-6870
The Canadian Orchid Journal (4)

Enthusiastic greenhouse growers, held together over long distances by an interesting magazine.
Annual Dues: US$25: C$25: US$28 OV (PC or IMO)
Privileges: SEEDS PLANTS

Canadian Organic Growers
Lida Martin
146 Elveston Dr.
Toronto, ON, Canada M4A 1N6
(416) 848-9345
COGnition (4)

Hope to develop a Heritage Garden.
Annual Dues: C$10 US: C$5 CAN: C$10 OV (IMO)
Privileges: CONVENTIONS LIBRARY SEEDS TRIPS

Canadian Prairie Lily Society
A. E. Delahay
R. R. 5
Saskatoon, SK, Canada S7K 3J8
Newsletter (3-4)

Concerned with growing the native prairie lilies of Canada.
Annual Dues: $3 US or CAN
Privileges: BOOKS PLANTS EXHIBITS TOURS

Canadian Rose Society
Dianne D. Lask
686 Pharmacy Avenue
Scarborough, ON, Canada M1L 3H8
The Rosarian (3)
Canadian Rose Annual

Promotes knowledge of rose-growing in northern climates; has a slide library and an annual garden tour.
Annual Dues: C$15
Chapters: 32
Privileges: LIBRARY PLANTS EXHIBITS

The Canadian Wildflower Society
James A. French
35 Bauer Crescent
Unionville, ON, Canada L3R 4H3
(416) 477-3992 eves.
Wildflower (4)

New society with a handsome magazine, the only one devoted exclusively to the wild flora of North America.
Annual Dues: C&US$15: $25 Libraries & OV
Privileges: CONVENTIONS BOOKS SEEDS EXHIBITS TRIPS

Alan Chadwick Society
50 Oak Mountain Dr.
San Rafael, CA 94903

Write for information; devoted to bio-dynamic organic gardening.

Colorado Native Plant Society
Myrna P. Steinkamp
P. O. Box 200
Fort Collins, CO 80522
Newsletter (4-6)

Planning to have seed exchanges for members.
Annual Dues: US$8
Chapters: 4
Privileges: CONVENTIONS PLANTS TRIPS

Cottage Garden Society
Mrs. Phililla Carr
15 Faenol Ave.
Abergele, Clwyd, Britain LL22 7HT
(0745) 822059
Newsletter (4)

Members may pay dues in personal checks on U.S. banks. Arrange garden visits in the summer.
Annual Dues: UK3, US$10
Chapters: 5
Privileges: CONVENTIONS SEEDS PLANTS TRIPS

The Cryptanthus Society
2355-E Rusk
Beaumont, TX 77702
Journal (4)

Send a first class stamp for information or $2.50 for sample copy of the journal.
Annual Dues: See Notes

The Cycad Society
David Mayo
1161 Phyllis Court
Mountain View, CA 94040
The Cycad Newsletter (4)

Seed and pollen bank.
Annual Dues: US$10
Privileges: SEEDS

Cyclamen Society
c/o Dr. David V. Bent
9 Tudor Dr.
Otford, Kent, England TN14 SQP
(09592) 2322
Cyclamen Journal (2)

Good exchange of viable seed in late summer; advice from experts.
Annual Dues: UK5.50 OV (IMO or US Bills)
Privileges: CONVENTIONS LIBRARY SEEDS EXHIBITS

Cymbidium Society of America
Mrs. Richard L. Johnston
6881 Wheeler Avenue
Westminster, CA 92683
(714) 894-5421
The Orchid Advocate (6)

Annual Dues: US$12.50
Chapters: 4
Privileges: EXHIBITS

The Daffodil Society (UK)
Ivor Fox
44 Wargrave Rd., Twyford
Reading, Berks, England
Bulletin (2)

Write for information.
Annual Dues: UK3 (IMO)

The Delphinium Society
Mrs. Shirley E. Bassett
"Takakkaw," Ice House Wood
Oxted, Surrey, England RH8 9DW
Delphinium Year Book

Annual Dues: US$6 US & CAN (IMO)
Garden: Delphinium Trial Ground, RHS, Wisley, Surrey
Privileges: CONVENTIONS BOOKS SEEDS EXHIBITS

Desert Plant Society of Vancouver
2941 Parker Street
Vancouver, BC, Canada V5K 2T9
(604) 255-0606

Write for information.

Epiphyllum Society of America
Betty Berg
P. O. Box 1395
Monrovia, CA 91016
Epiphyllum Society Bulletin (6)

Annual Dues: US$6 US & CAN: US$12 OV (IMO)
Chapters: 3
Privileges: PLANTS EXHIBITS TRIPS

For Explanations of Abbreviations/Codes Used in Listings See Bookmark or Inside Covers

Federation of International Rose Exhibitors
Francine Cowley
3109 Triunfo Canyon Rd.
Agoura, CA 91301
(818) 991-0943
ARS Rosaceae (4)

A chapter of the American Rose Society. Promotes the skill and art of growing and exhibiting roses; exchanges information.
Annual Dues: US$15 (IMO)

Friends of the Farm
Hopewell Farms
Route 1, Box 32
Dalton City, IL 61925
(217) 864-2679

Write for information.

Friends of the Fig
Fred W. Born
5715 W. Paul Bryant Dr.
Crystal River, FL 32629
(904) 795-0489 eves.
The Fig Leaflet (4)

All are welcome; newsletter "The Fig Leaflet" is delightfully jolly. They exchange plants and cuttings; once a year publish their membership list, with information on collections.
Annual Dues: US$5: C$5: US$5 OV (PC)
Privileges: CONVENTIONS LIBRARY BOOKS PLANTS EXHIBITS TRIPS

Friends of the Trees
Michael Pilarski
P. O. Box 1466
Chelan, WA 98816
Friends of the Trees Yearbook
Actinidia Enthusiasts Newsletter (1)

Promotes reforestation and Earth-healing worldwide; distributes seeds and plants and information on horticulture, forestry and permaculture.
Annual Dues: US$3 US & CAN: US$4 (IMO) OV
Privileges: SEEDS PLANTS TRIPS

Garden History Society
Mrs. Anne Richards
5 The Knoll
Hereford, England HR1 1RU
0432-354479
Garden History (2)
Newsletter (3)

They have excellent tours in Europe and elsewhere.
Annual Dues: $US30: UK13.50 (PC or IMO)
Privileges: CONVENTIONS TRIPS TOURS

Gardenia Society of America
Lyman Duncan
P. O. Box 879
Atwater, CA 95301
(209) 385-4251
Gardenia Quarterly

Annual Dues: US$5

Georgia Botanical Society
Dr. Frank McCamey, Treas.
4676 Andover Court
Doraville, GA 30360

Write for information.

Gesneriad Hybridizers Association
Meg Stephenson
4115 Pillar Dr., Route 1
Whitmore Lake, MI 48189
Crosswords (3)

Annual Dues: $5

Gesneriad Society International
P. O. Box 102
Greenwood, IN 46142
Gesneriad Saintpaulia News (6)

Membership dues include membership in Saintpaulia International. They have a slide library.
Annual Dues: US$12.75: US$15.75 CAN & OV (IMO)
Privileges: CONVENTIONS BOOKS SEEDS PLANTS EXHIBITS

Hardy Plant Society (UK)
10 St. Barnabas Rd.
Emmer Green, Cabersham
Reading, England RG4 8RA
Bulletin of the Hardy Plant Society (2)
News Letter (2)

See also Hardy Plant Society of Oregon.
Annual Dues: UK4 (IMO)
Chapters: 10
Privileges: CONVENTIONS SEEDS PLANTS EXHIBITS TRIPS

Hardy Plant Society of Oregon
Connie Hanni
33530 S.E. Bluff Road
Boring, OR 97009
Newsletter

They have a much admired annual study weekend in the Northwest.
Annual Dues: $12
Chapters: 2
Privileges: CONVENTIONS SEEDS PLANTS EXHIBITS TOURS

Hawaiian Botanical Society
Univ. of Hawaii, Botany Dept.
3190 Maile Way
Honolulu, HI 96822

Write for information.

The Heather Society
Mrs. A. Small
Denbeigh, All Saints Road, Creeting St. Mary
Ipswich, Suffolk, England 1P6 8PJ
(0449) 711220
Bulletin (3)
Year Book

Have a slide library and a cultivar location service.
Annual Dues: US$10: C$14: UK6 (IMO or PC)
Garden: RHS Garden, Wisley; NHS Garden, Harlow Car, Harrogate
Privileges: CONVENTIONS

Heliconia Society International
David Bar-Zvi, Vice Pres.
Flamingo Gardens, 3750 Flamingo Road
Ft. Lauderdale, FL 33330
(305) 473-4988
HSI Bulletin (4)

New society in l985. Plant collection centers: Flamingo Gardens, Fort Lauderdale, FL; Harold L. Lyon Arboretum, Honolulu, HI; Andromeda Gardens, Barbados, West Indies; Pacific Tropical Botanical Garden, Kauai, HI.
Annual Dues: US$20
Garden: See notes
Privileges: CONVENTIONS PLANTS EXHIBITS TOURS

Herb Research Foundation
Bobbi Close
HRF, P. O. Box 2602
Longmont, CO 80501
(303) 449-2265
Herbalgram (4)

Formed to initiate, disseminate and publish research into common/uncommon herbs, primarily medicinal herbs.
Annual Dues: US$25 (IMO)
Privileges: CONVENTIONS

Herb Society of America
2 Independence Court
Concord, MA 01742
(617) 371-1486
The Herbarist (1)

Write for information; periodical contains no information on membership. They publish a "Traveler's Guide to Herb Gardens", listing 480 gardens in the U.S. and Canada, for $3.75 postpaid.
Chapters: 26
Privileges: CONVENTIONS

Heritage Roses Group
Miriam Wilkins
925 Galvin Dr.
El Cerrito, CA 94530
(415) 526-6960
Heritage Rose Letter (4)

Local chapters have meetings.
Annual Dues: US$4: US$ 4.25 CAN: US$7.50 OV

Hobby Greenhouse Association
Fran L. Melzer
432 Templeton Hills Rd.
Templeton, CA 93465
(617) 275-0377
Hobby Greenhouse (4)

Annual Dues: US$10: C$12: US$14 OV (IMO)
Chapters: 7

Holly Society of America
c/o Kit Richardson
304 North Wind Rd.
Baltimore, MD 21204
(301) 825-8133
Holly Society Journal (4)

They have holly auctions and cutting exchanges, informative pamphlets, local chapters and annual meetings in various locations near notable holly collections.
Annual Dues: US$15
Chapters: 8

Home Orchard Society
P. O. Box 776
Clackamas, OR 97015
(503) 655-1939
Pome News (4)
Handbook

Have scion and rootstock exchanges, fruit exhibits. For members in the Northwest there are various events, including an annual cider-squeeze.
Annual Dues: US$10 (PC or MO)
Privileges: CONVENTIONS PLANTS EXHIBITS

Horticultural Society of New York
128 W. 58th Street
New York, NY 10019
(212) 757-0915
Garden (6)
HSNY Newsletter (6)

Sponsor of the New York Flower Show, held on the Hudson River Pier every March.
Annual Dues: US$25
Privileges: LIBRARY BOOKS PLANTS EXHIBITS TRIPS TOURS

The Hoya Society International
Christine M. Burton
P. O. Box 54271
Atlanta, GA 30308
The Hoyan (4)

Write for information.

For Explanations of Abbreviations/Codes Used In Listings See Bookmark or Inside Covers

Hydroponic Society of America
Gene Brisbon
P. O. Box 6067
Concord, CA 94524
(415) 682-4193
Newsletter (6-8)
Annual Conference Proceedings

Non-members may buy a copy of the Annual Conference Proceedings -- write for information.
Annual Dues: US$25 US & CAN: US$35 OV (IMO)
Privileges: CONVENTIONS BOOKS TRIPS TOURS

Hydroponic Society of Victoria
Miss Eva Best
6/38 Maroo St.
Hughesdale, Victoria, Australia 3166
Newsletter (10)

To encourage hobbist and commercial growers.
Annual Dues: AUS$15 (IMO)
Privileges: CONVENTIONS LIBRARY EXHIBITS TRIPS

Idaho Native Plant Society - Pahvoe Chapter
Box 9451
Boise, ID 83707
Sage Notes (6)

Annual Dues: US$6

Indigenous Bulb Growers Assn. of South Africa
Mr. P. von Stein
P. O. Box 141, Woodstock
Capetown, South Africa 7915
IBSA Bulletin (1)

Society devoted to the conservation of South African bulbous plants by means of cultivation and propagation.
Annual Dues: R5
Privileges: PLANTS EXHIBITS TRIPS

Indoor Citrus & Rare Fruit Society
176 Coronado Ave.
Los Altos, CA 94022
Quarterly Newsletter

One of the best newsletters, full of information and interest and letters from around the world. Will help members find information, seeds and plants of citrus and rare fruit.
Annual Dues: US$15: US$18 OV (IMO)
Privileges: BOOKS SEEDS

Indoor Gardening Society of America
Robert D. Morrison
5305 S.W. Hamilton St.
Portland, OR 97221
(503) 292-9785
Indoor Garden (6)

Formerly the Indoor Light Gardening Society of America. Chapters have plant sales and exhibits; members grow plants under lights, on windowsills and in greenhouses.
Annual Dues: US$10: US$12 OV (IMO)
Chapters: 18
Privileges: BOOKS SEEDS

The Indoor Gardening Society of Canada
Anne Marie Van Nest
16 Edgar Woods Rd.
Willowdale, ON, Canada M2H 2Y7
Inside Green (10)

Members may attend 10 meetings a year; have access to indoor gardening supplies as well as other benefits.
Annual Dues: C$10
Privileges: BOOKS PLANTS EXHIBITS TRIPS

International Aroid Society
Bruce McManus
P. O. Box 43-1853
South Miami, FL 33143
(305) 271-3767
Aroideana (4)

Society devoted to members of the arum family (Aroidaceae); write for information.

International Asclepiad Society
Mrs. M. Thompson
10 Moorside Terrace, Driglington
Bradford, England BD11 1HX

Annual Dues: UK8

International Cactus & Succulent Society

Lost contact; can any reader give us current information?

International Camellia Society
Thomas H. Perkins, III
P. O. Box 750
Brookhaven, MS 39601-0750
(601) 833-7351
International Camellia Journal (1)
Mid-Year Newsletter (1)

Meet every other year in different host countries; dues may be paid in local currency through regional membership representatives.
Annual Dues: US$9
Privileges: CONVENTIONS EXHIBITS

International Carnivorous Plant Society
Leo Song, Co-Editor
c/o Fullerton Arboretum, Calif. State Univ.
Fullerton, CA 92634
Carnivorous Plant Newsletter (4)

Have a very interesting magazine with color photographs and articles on plant hunting.
Annual Dues: US$10 US & CAN: US$15 OV (IMO)
Privileges: SEEDS

The International Clematis Society
Mrs. Hildegard Widman-Evison
Clematis Nursery, Domarie Vin., Les Sauvages
St. Sampson's, Guern, Channel Islands
Newsletter (2)

Have meetings in various countries. St. Sampson's is in Guernsey -- didn't have room to fit it in.
Annual Dues: UK5 + UK2 entrance fee.
Privileges: CONVENTIONS SEEDS EXHIBITS

International Dwarf Fruit Tree Association
303 Department of Horticulture
Michigan State University
East Lansing, MI 48824
(517) 355-5200

Write for information.

International Geranium Society
Mrs. Robin Schultz
5861 Walnut Dr.
Eureka, CA 95501
Geraniums Around the World (4)

Annual Dues: US$12.50
Chapters: 8
Privileges: CONVENTIONS BOOKS SEEDS

International Lilac Society
Walter W. Oakes
P. O. Box 315
Rumford, ME 04276
(207) 562-7453
Newsletter (11)
Proceedings

Publish a book on lilac culture.
Annual Dues: US$10
Privileges: CONVENTIONS SEEDS

International Oleander Society
Elizabeth S. Head, Cor. Secy.
P. O. Box 3431
Galveston, TX 77552-0431
(713) 762-9334
Nerium News (4)

Annual Dues: US$5
Garden: One is being planned
Privileges: SEEDS TRIPS

International Ornamental Crabapple Society
Thomas L. Green
Morton Arboretum
Lisle, IL 60532
(312) 968-0074
Crab Gab (4)

Annual Dues: US$15
Privileges: CONVENTIONS

The International Palm Society
P. O. Box 368
Lawrence, KS 66044
Principes (4)

Published Genera Palmarum in l987, 600 pages. Seeds sold to members at a nominal fee.
Annual Dues: US$15: US$25 OV (IMO)
Privileges: CONVENTIONS BOOKS SEEDS PLANTS EXHIBITS TRIPS TOURS

International Tropical Fern Society
Elaine Spear
8720 S.W. 34th Street
Miami, FL 33165
(305)221-0502
Chapter Bulletins

Annual Dues: US$6-10; varies by chapter
Chapters: 21
Garden: Emerald Forest, 8720 SW 34th St., Miami FL
Privileges: CONVENTIONS LIBRARY BOOKS SEEDS PLANTS EXHIBITS TRIPS TOURS

Kansas Wildflower Society
Virginia Hocker
Mulvane Arts Center, Washburn University
Topeka, KS 66621
Kansas Wildflower Society Newsletter (4)

Annual Dues: US$10
Privileges: LIBRARY BOOKS SEEDS TRIPS

Light Gardening Society of America
Robert Morrison
5305 S.W. Hamilton Street
Portland, OR 97221

Annual Dues: US$8

Los Angeles International Fern Society
P. O. Box 90943
Pasadena, CA 91109-0943
LAIFS Journal
Monthly Fern Lesson

They have a spore store and round robins on various subjects. Also hold educational programs.
Annual Dues: US$15
Privileges: BOOKS

For Explanations of Abbreviations/Codes Used In Listings See Bookmark or Inside Covers

Louisiana Native Plant Society
Richard Johnson, Pres.
Route 1, Box 151
Saline, LA 71070

Write for information.
Chapters: 2

Marigold Society of America, Inc.
Gordon Marten
P. O. Box 112
New Britain, PA 18901
Amerigold Newsletter (4)

Annual Dues: US$10 US & CAN: US$12 OV (IMO)
Garden: AHS Gardens, River Farm, Mt. Vernon, VA
Privileges: CONVENTIONS SEEDS

Massachusetts Horticultural Association
300 Massachusetts Ave.
Boston, MA 02115
(617) 536-9280

Write for information.

Michigan Botanical Club
Mathaei Botanical Gardens
1800 Dixboro Road
Ann Arbor, MI 48105

Write for information.

Minnesota Native Plant Society
University of Minnesota
1445 Gortner Ave., 220 BioSci Center
St. Paul, MN 55108

Write for information.

Minnesota State Horticultural Society
161 Alderman Hall
University of Minnesota
St. Paul, MN 55108
(612) 373-1031
Minnesota Horticulturist (9)

Of interest to all Northern gardeners.
Annual Dues: US$12: C$18: US$18 OV (IMO)
Privileges: CONVENTIONS LIBRARY BOOKS EXHIBITS TRIPS TOURS

Mississippi Native Plant Society
Travis Salley, Sec/Treas.
202 N. Andrews Ave.
Cleveland, MS 38732
(601) 843-2330
Mississippi N. P. S. Newsletter (4)

Annual Dues: US$5
Privileges: TRIPS

Missouri Native Plant Society
John Darel, Treas.
P. O. Box 176, Dept. of Nat. Resources
Jefferson City, MO 65102

Write for information.

National Auricula & Primula Society
Mr. B. Goalby
99 Somerfield Road, Bloxwich
Walsall, W. Midlands, England
Yearbook

Found too late to contact; write for information.
Chapters: 3

National Chrysanthemum Society (UK)
H. B. Locke
2 Lucas House, Craven Rd.
Rugby, Warwicks., England CV21 3JQ
Rugby 0788 69039
Bulletin/Panorama (2)
Year Book

They have a second display garden at Brackenhill Park, Bradford (near Leeds).
Annual Dues: UK9 to all (IMO)
Garden: RHS Gardens, Wisley, Surrey
Privileges: CONVENTIONS BOOKS EXHIBITS

National Chrysanthemum Society, Inc. (USA)
Galen L. Goss
5012 Kingston Dr.
Annandale, VA 22003
(703) 941-1791 eves.
The Chrysanthemum (5)

Annual Dues: US$8.50 (IMO)
Chapters: 54
Privileges: CONVENTIONS BOOKS

National Fuchsia Society
P. O. Box 4687
Downey, CA 92041
Fuchsia Fan (12)

Write for information; dues in Canada and Overseas are higher.
Annual Dues: US$12

National Gardening Association
Vicki Gaylord
180 Flynn Ave.
Burlington, VT 05401
(802) 863-1308
National Gardening (12)

Dedicated to teaching people to garden; have a seed search service, answer service, group rate insurance, new books at a discount and a very nice magazine for home food gardeners.
Annual Dues: US$15: US$24 CAN & OV (IMO)
Privileges: CONVENTIONS LIBRARY BOOKS SEEDS

National Sweet Pea Society
L. H. O. Williams
Acacia Cottage, Down Ampney
Cirencester, Glos., England GL7 5QW
0793-750385
Bulletin (2)
Annual

By paying a little more, you can elect yourself a Vice President. All societies should consider this!!
Annual Dues: UK10 US & CAN: UK12 for Vice Presidents
Garden: Trial Grounds, RHS Garden, Wisley, Surrey
Privileges: BOOKS SEEDS PLANTS EXHIBITS TRIPS

Native Plant Society of New Mexico
Judith Phillips
P. O. Box 5917
Santa Fe, NM 87502
Newsletter (6)

Seed exchange to be established soon.
Annual Dues: US$8: $US14 OV (IMO)
Chapters: 5
Privileges: CONVENTIONS LIBRARY BOOKS PLANTS TRIPS

Native Plant Society of Oregon
Mary Falconer, Memb. Chm.
1920 Engel Ave. N.W.
Salem, OR 97304
Bulletin (12)

Annual Dues: US$10
Chapters: 10
Privileges: TRIPS

Native Plant Society of Texas
Bettye Jane Dodds
1204 S. Trinity St.
Decatur, TX 76234
(817) 627-2862
Texas Native Plant Society News (6)

Annual Dues: $US15 (IMO)
Chapters: 7
Privileges: CONVENTIONS SEEDS PLANTS EXHIBITS TRIPS

Nerine Society
Brookend House
Welland, Worcs., England

Write for information.

New England Botanical Club
Botanical Museum
Oxford Street
Cambridge, MA 02138

Write for information.

New England Wild Flower Society
Bee Entwisle
Hemenway Road
Framingham, MA 01701
Newsletter (4)
Wild Flower Notes (1-2)

Chapters in each Northeastern state; seed exchanges with botanical gardens.
Annual Dues: $US15
Garden: Garden in the Woods, Framingham, MA
Privileges: CONVENTIONS LIBRARY BOOKS PLANTS EXHIBITS TRIPS TOURS

New Jersey Native Plant Society
Frelinghuysen Arboretum
P. O. Box 1295 R
Morristown, NJ 07960

Write for information.

New Zealand Camellia Society
New Zealand Camellia Bulletin (4)

You can join through the Southern California Camellia Society, U.S. agent, c/o M. Schmidt, 1523 Highland Oaks Dr., Arcadia, CA 91006. Our last mailing to New Zealand was returned.
Annual Dues: NZ$10
Chapters: 19
Privileges: CONVENTIONS EXHIBITS

New Zealand Fuchsia Society
Miss Joan Byres
P. O. Box 11-082
Ellerslie, Auckland, New Zealand
Auckland 872-118
News Letter (11)

Annual Dues: NZ$3 (IMO)
Privileges: CONVENTIONS LIBRARY PLANTS EXHIBITS TRIPS

For Explanations of Abbreviations/Codes Used In Listings See Bookmark or Inside Covers

North American Fruit Explorers
Jill Vorbeck, Memb. Chm.
Rte. 1, Box 94
Chapin, IL 62628
Pomona (4)

Dedicated fruit growers who locate, test and preserve special fruit and nut varieties. New members get their "Handbook for Fruit Explorers". Scion and budstock exchanges, computer programs for test groups.
Annual Dues: US$8
Privileges: CONVENTIONS BOOKS SEEDS EXHIBITS TRIPS

North American Gladiolus Council
R. A. Vogt
9338 Manzanita Dr.
Sun City, AZ 85373
(602) 972-4177
Bulletin (4)

Annual Dues: US$7.50 US & CAN: US$10 OV (IMO)
Chapters: 57
Privileges: CONVENTIONS LIBRARY BOOKS

North American Heather Society
Alice E. Knight
62 Elma-Monte Rd.
Elma, WA 98541
(206) 482-3258
Heather News (4)

Annual Dues: US$10 (IMO)
Chapters: 2
Privileges: CONVENTIONS LIBRARY BOOKS PLANTS

North American Lily Society, Inc.
Mrs. Dorothy B. Schaefer
P. O. Box 476
Waukee, IA 50263
(515) 987-1371
Quarterly Bulletin
Yearbook

Annual Dues: US$12.50 (IMO)
Garden: Some affiliated local societies have display gardens
Privileges: CONVENTIONS LIBRARY BOOKS SEEDS EXHIBITS

North Carolina Wild Flower Preservation Soc.
Mrs. S. M. Cozart
900 West Nash St.
Wilson, NC 27893
Newsletter (2)

Offer a "North Carolina native plant propagation handbook" for $3, including postage. Send check to N.C. Botanical Garden, Totten Center 457-A, UNC-CH, Chapel Hill, NC 27514.
Annual Dues: US$5.
Garden: N.C. Botanical Garden, Chapel Hill, NC
Privileges: SEEDS EXHIBITS TRIPS

Northern Nevada Native Plant Society
Loring Williams
P. O. Box 8965
Reno, NV 89507
(702) 358-7759
Newsletter (9)
Menzelia (irregular)

Annual Dues: US$7.50 (IMO)
Privileges: LIBRARY BOOKS SEEDS PLANTS EXHIBITS TRIPS

Northern Nut Growers Association
Kenneth Bauman
9870 S. Palmer Rd.
New Carlisle, OH 45344
(513) 878-2610
Nutshell (4)
Annual Report

Publish "Nut Tree Culture in North America", for $17.50 in U.S. and Canada, $18.50 overseas, including postage.
Annual Dues: US$15 US & CAN: US$17 OV (IMO)
Privileges: CONVENTIONS BOOKS

Northwest Fuchsia Society
P. O. Box 33071, Bitter Lake Station
Seattle, WA 98133-0071
Bulletin (12)

Found too late to contact; write for information.
Annual Dues: US$8: US$10 CAN & OV
Chapters: 11
Privileges: CONVENTIONS BOOKS EXHIBITS

Northwest Horticultural Society
Center for Urban Horticulture
University of Washington, GF-15
Seattle, WA 98195
Pacific Horticulture (4)

Annual Dues: US$25
Privileges: SEEDS PLANTS EXHIBITS TRIPS TOURS

Ohio Native Plant Society
6 Louise Dr.
Chagrin Falls, OH 44022
(216) 338-6622
On the Fringe (6)

Annual Dues: US$7.50
Chapters: 7
Garden: Garden Center of Greater Cleveland, OH
Privileges: CONVENTIONS LIBRARY BOOKS SEEDS PLANTS EXHIBITS TRIPS TOURS

Ontario Regional Lily Society
Mrs. Gordon Brown
R. R. 1
Harley, ON, Canada N0E 1E0
Newsletter (3)

Have an annual garden picnic at the Royal Botanical Gardens, Hamilton, ON.
Annual Dues: C$3
Privileges: CONVENTIONS LIBRARY PLANTS EXHIBITS

Orchid Correspondence Club
Doreen Vander Tuin, Editor
1230 Plum Ave.
Simi Valley, CA 93065
The Orchid Information Exchange (12)

Publish a monthly newsletter that covers all aspects of growing orchids in the home and in greenhouses.
Annual Dues: US$10 US & CAN: US$14 OV

Pacific Northwest Lily Society
Mary Hoffman
19766 S. Impala Lane
Oregon City, OR 97045
Bulletin (3 or 4)

Annual Dues: US$5
Privileges: CONVENTIONS LIBRARY BOOKS PLANTS EXHIBITS TRIPS

Pacific Orchid Society
Barbara Schafer
P. O. Box 1091
Honolulu, HI 96808
Na Okika O Hawaii/Hawaiian Orchid Journal (4)

Annual Dues: US$10: US$15 CAN/OV (PC or IMO)
Privileges: LIBRARY PLANTS EXHIBITS TRIPS

The Pennsylvania Horticultural Society
Betsy Gullan
325 Walnut Street
Philadelphia, PA 19106
(215) 625-8250
The Green Scene (6)
PHS News (11)

The Green Scene is available on subscription for $8 a year.
Annual Dues: US$25 (IMO)
Garden: 325 Walnut Street, Philadelphia, PA
Privileges: LIBRARY EXHIBITS TRIPS TOURS

Pennsylvania Native Plant Society
1806 Commonwealth Bldg.
316 Fourth Avenue
Pittsburgh, PA 15222

Write for information.

Peperomia Society International
5240 W. 20th St.
Vero Beach, FL 32960
The Gazette (4)

Annual Dues: US$5 US & CAN: $US8 OV
Garden: Glasshouse Works, Stewart, OH
Privileges: LIBRARY SEEDS

The Plumeria Society of America, Inc.
37 Stillforest
Houston, TX 77024
(713) 468-6275
Newsletter (4)

Write for information.

Puget Sound Dahlia Association
Roger L. Walker
544 129th Ave. S.E.
Bellevue, WA 98005
Bulletin (12)

Their annual "Dahlias of Today" is terrific; available from Mrs. Dorothy Rasmussen, 14021 Sunnyside Ave. N., Seattle, WA 98133, for $3 postpaid, $1 more overseas, $3 more airmail. Also sold by dahlia nurseries.
Annual Dues: US$10 (Members in WA & OR only)
Garden: Volunteer Park in Seattle, WA
Privileges: CONVENTIONS PLANTS EXHIBITS

For Explanations of Abbreviations/Codes Used In Listings See Bookmark or Inside Covers

Rare Fruit Council International, Inc.
13609 Old Cutler Rd.
Miami, FL 33158
(305) 238-1360
Newsletter (12)
Yearbook

Have plant exchanges; publish a cookbook for $10.95.
Annual Dues: US$20
Chapters: 3
Privileges: LIBRARY SEEDS PLANTS EXHIBITS

Rhododendron Society of Canada
R. Dickhout
5200 Timothy Cr.
Niagara Falls, ON, Canada L2E 5G3
Bulletin (2)

Annual Dues: C$15.
Chapters: 3
Privileges: CONVENTIONS LIBRARY BOOKS SEEDS PLANTS EXHIBITS TOURS

Rhododendron Species Foundation
Pam Elms
P. O. Box 3798
Federal Way, WA 98063-3798
(206) 927-6960
RSF Newsletter (4)
Vireya Vine (4)

Offer classes, lectures and an independent study course by mail; and have a rhododendron library. Also have pollen distribution for hybridizers.
Annual Dues: US$25 (IMO)
Garden: Rhododendron Species Foundation, Federal Way, WA
Privileges: CONVENTIONS LIBRARY BOOKS SEEDS PLANTS EXHIBITS TOURS

Rose Hybridizers Association
Larry D. Peterson
3245 Wheaton Road
Horseheads, NY 14845
(607) 562-8592
Rose Hybridizers Association Newsletter (4)

Annual Dues: US$5 US & CAN: US$7 OV (IMO)
Garden: Test Garden, American Rose Center, Shreveport, LA
Privileges: CONVENTIONS LIBRARY SEEDS

The Royal Horticultural Society
Membership Secretary
80 Vincent Square
London, England SW1P 2PE
The Garden (12)

Many plant and flower shows in London, including the grand-daddy of them all, the Chelsea Flower Show. They also have wonderful library at Vincent Square.
Annual Dues: UK19 (accept pmt. in $)
Garden: RHS Garden, Wisley, Surrey
Privileges: LIBRARY BOOKS SEEDS PLANTS EXHIBITS TRIPS TOURS

Royal National Rose Society
The Secretary
Chiswell Green
St. Albans, Herts., England AL2 3NR
(0727) 50461
The Rose (4)

Claim to be one of the oldest, largest and FRIENDLIEST plant societies in the world.
Annual Dues: UK8.50 (IMO)
Garden: The Gardens of the Rose, St. Albans
Privileges: CONVENTIONS LIBRARY BOOKS EXHIBITS TOURS

Saintpaulia International
Rt. 1, Box 143
Greenwood, IN 46142
Gesneriad Saintpaulia News (6)

Dues include membership in the Gesneriad Society International.
Annual Dues: US$9.25
Privileges: CONVENTIONS SEEDS PLANTS EXHIBITS

Saskatchewan Orchid Society
Marvin Swartz
221 Delayen Place
Saskatoon, SK, Canada S7N 2T9
(306) 249-1073
Newsletter (6)

Annual Dues: C$10
Privileges: LIBRARY PLANTS

Scottish Rock Garden Club
Miss K. M. Gibb
21 Merchiston Park
Edinburgh, Scotland EH10 4PW
0786-822295
The Rock Garden (2)
Year Book

Have a very extensive seed exchange.
Annual Dues: US$12 US & CAN: UK5
Privileges: CONVENTIONS LIBRARY BOOKS SEEDS PLANTS EXHIBITS TRIPS

Seattle Tilth Association
L. Elder-LaCroix or J. Gordon
4548 Sunnyside Avenue No.
Seattle, WA 98103
(206) 633-0451
Sea-Tilth (12)

Part of a regional association in Pacific Northwest, promoting sustainable regional agriculture. They may be able to put you in touch with groups in your part of the Northwest.
Annual Dues: US$12
Garden: Urban Agr. Ctr., 4649 Sunnyside Ave. No., Seattle
Privileges: CONVENTIONS LIBRARY BOOKS SEEDS PLANTS EXHIBITS TRIPS

Seed Savers Exchange
c/o Kent Whealy
203 Rural Avenue
Decorah, IA 52101
Winter Yearbook

Sell the "Garden Seed Inventory", a huge and wonderful inventory of open-pollinated and heirloom vegetable seeds and where to get them, $12 postpaid. Hooray for Kent Whealy!!
Annual Dues: US$10: US$14 CAN & MEX: US$20 OV (IMO)

Sempervivum Fanciers Association
Dr. C. William Nixon
37 Oxbow Lane
Randolph, MA 02368
(617) 963-6737
Sempervivum Fanciers Assn. Newsletter (4)

Largely the effort of Dr. Nixon; not a formal "association".
Annual Dues: US$12

The Sempervivum Society
Peter J. Mitchell
11 Wingle Tye Rd.
Burgess Hill, W. Sus, England RH15 9HR
044 46 6848
Houseleeks (3)
Newsletter (3)

Annual Dues: UK5.50 (IMO)
Garden: Burgess Hill, W. Sussex, England
Privileges: CONVENTIONS LIBRARY BOOKS PLANTS EXHIBITS

The Society for Growing Australian Plants
Glen Harvey
5 Ellesmere Rd.
Crymea Bay, NSW, Australia 2227
Australian Plants (4)

Magazine available on separate subscription for $9 a year; send an International Money Order.
Annual Dues: US$15 OV (IMO)
Privileges: CONVENTIONS LIBRARY BOOKS SEEDS PLANTS EXHIBITS TRIPS TOURS

The Society for Japanese Irises
Mrs. Andrew C. Warner
16815 Falls Rd.
Upperco, MD 21155
(301) 374-4788
The Review (2)

A section of the American Iris Society.
Annual Dues: US$3.50
Privileges: CONVENTIONS BOOKS SEEDS PLANTS EXHIBITS

Society for Louisiana Irises
P. O. Box 40175, USL
Lafayette, LA 70504
(318) 264-6203
Newsletter (4)

Write for information.

Society for Pacific Coast Native Iris
c/o Mrs. Dorothy Foster
977 Meredith Ct.
Somoma, CA 95476
SPCNI Almanac (2)

A section of the American Iris Society.
Annual Dues: US$4
Privileges: SEEDS

Solanaceae Enthusiasts
John M. Riley
3370 Princeton Ct.
Santa Clara, CA 95051
(408) 241-9440
Solanaceae Quarterly

Devoted to edible members of the Solanaceae family, growers of rare fruit.
Annual Dues: US$5 US & CAN: US$10 OV (IMO)

South African Fuchsia Society
P. O. Box 193
Hilton, South Africa 3245
(011) 869-7697 RSA
The South African Fuchsia Fanfare (3)

Annual Dues: R10 (IMO)
Chapters: 5
Privileges: LIBRARY PLANTS EXHIBITS TRIPS

Southern California Botanists
Alan Romspert
Dept. of Biology, Fullerton State
Fullerton, CA 92634
(714) 773-3614
Crossosoma (6)

Study, preservation and conservation of native plants of California. Have an annual symposium and pot luck.
Annual Dues: US$8
Privileges: CONVENTIONS BOOKS PLANTS TRIPS

Southern California Horticultural Institute
Joan DeFato
P. O. Box 49798, Barrington Station
Los Angeles, CA 90045-0798
Pacific Horticulture (4)
Monthly Bulletin

Annual Dues: US$15
Privileges: BOOKS PLANTS EXHIBITS TRIPS TOURS

Southern Garden History Association
Mrs. Zachary T. Bynum
Old Salem, Inc., Drawer F, Salem Station
Winston-Salem, NC 27101
(919) 724-3125
Newsletter (4)

Encourages research and preservation of materials on the history of gardens in the "Old South", with conferences on garden restoration.
Annual Dues: US$15
Privileges: CONVENTIONS

For Explanations of Abbreviations/Codes Used In Listings See Bookmark or Inside Covers

Southern Illinois Native Plant Society
Dr. Robert Mohlenbrock
Botany Dept., Southern Illinois Univ.
Carbondale, IL 52901

Write for information.

Species Iris Group of North America
Florence Stout
150 N. Main St.
Lombard, IL 60148
(703) 745-2603
SIGNA (2)

They have an excellent seed exchange.
Annual Dues: US$3.50
Privileges: CONVENTIONS SEEDS

Tallgrass Prairie Alliance
Tallgrass Prairie News (4)
Tallgrass Prairie Alliance (1)

Formerly Save the Tallgrass Prairie, Inc. Reader alert! Last mailing returned -- please let us know if you have current information!
Annual Dues: US$10 US & CAN: US$15 OV (IMO)
Garden: Access to several private prairie preserves
Privileges: CONVENTIONS LIBRARY BOOKS SEEDS TRIPS

Tennessee Native Plant Society
Dept. of Botany
University of Tennessee
Knoxville, TN 37996
(615) 974-2256
Newsletter TNPS (6)

Annual Dues: US$5
Privileges: CONVENTIONS SEEDS TRIPS TOURS

The Terrarium Association
Robert C. Baur
57 Wolfpit Ave.
Norwalk, CT 06851
(203) 847-7019

Not a real society, but a source of information and literature on terrarium growing.

Texas Horticultural Society
P. O. Box 10025
College Station, TX 77840
(713) 693-7308
The Texas Gardener (4)
Yearbook

Annual Dues: US$10

The Toronto Bonsai Society
495 Deloraine Ave.
Toronto, ON, Canada M5M 2C1
(416) 782-2403

Write for information.

The Toronto Cactus & Succulent Club
P. O. Box 334
Brampton, ON, Canada L6V 2L3

Write for information.

Toronto Gesneriad Society
70 Enfield Rd.
Etabicoke, ON, Canada M8W 1T9

Write for information.

Tubers
Steve Neal
Route 1, Box 151-A
Norwood, MO 65717
Tater Talk (2)

Group dedicated to lovers of the potato -- and who isn't!
Annual Dues: US$10

Utah Native Plant Society
Pam Poulsen, Treas.
3631 So. Carolyn St.
Salt Lake City, UT 84106
Sego Lily (12)

They have an annual mushroom hunt.
Annual Dues: US$10
Privileges: SEEDS PLANTS TRIPS

Vancouver Island Rock & Alpine Garden Society
c/o Secretary
P. O. Box 6507, Station C
Victoria, BC, Canada V8P 5M4
(604) 479-3230
Newsletter (9)
Occasional Papers

Local members only.
Annual Dues: C$6 (Local members only)
Garden: Rock Garden, Beacon Hill Park, Victoria, BC
Privileges: CONVENTIONS LIBRARY PLANTS EXHIBITS TRIPS

Victoria Orchid Society
P. O. Box 337
Victoria, BC, Canada V8W 2N2

Write for information.

Vinifera Wine Growers Association
Mrs. Juanita Swedenburg
P. O. Box P
The Plains, VA 22171
Vinifera Wine Growers Journal (4)

Have an annual seminar at Middleburg, VA, at the Virginia Wine Festival, the last Saturday in August. Open to anyone interested in home or commercial viticulture and enology.
Annual Dues: US$17
Privileges: CONVENTIONS LIBRARY TOURS

Virginia Wildflower Preservation Society
Membership Chairman
P. O. Box 844
Annandale, VA 22003
Bulletin (4)

Have a good book and gift sales list for members.
Annual Dues: US$10
Chapters: 6
Privileges: CONVENTIONS LIBRARY BOOKS PLANTS TRIPS TOURS

Washington Native Plant Society
Department of Botany, KB-15
University of Washington
Seattle, WA 98195
(206) 543-1942
Douglasia (4)
Occasional Papers

They have annual backpack trips and study weekends.
Annual Dues: US$10 to all.
Chapters: 7
Privileges: CONVENTIONS BOOKS TRIPS TOURS

Water Lily Society
Charles B. Thomas
P. O. Box 104
Buckeystown, MD 21717
(301) 622-2230
Water Lily Journal (4)

Have an annual symposium in various locations.
Annual Dues: US$12.50 (IMO)
Privileges: CONVENTIONS LIBRARY TOURS

Western Horticultural Society
Jean Fowkes
P. O. Box 60507
Palo Alto, CA 94306
(415) 941-1332
Pacific Horticulture (4)

Have plant raffles at every meeting.
Annual Dues: US$15
Privileges: PLANTS TRIPS

World Pumpkin Confederation
14050 Gowanda State Rd.
Collins, NY 14034
Newsletter

Found too late to contact; I suspect that it is connected with a pumpkin seed company, but it unites people with a common interest in giant pumpkins.

Wyoming Native Plant Society
Secretary-Treasurer
P. O. Box 1471
Cheyenne, WY 82003
WNPS Newsletter (3)

Annual meeting is usually a field trip.
Annual Dues: US$7 to join, US$3 annual dues.
Privileges: CONVENTIONS TRIPS

Magazines

Horticultural magazines and newsletters, published in English and available on subscription from all over the world, are listed alphabetically by title.

See index section for:

M. Magazine Index: An index to horticultural and gardening magazines and newsletters as well as the magazines offered by societies.

Be sure to check the Changes and Corrections List at the end of the book (see Practical Matters). This list is updated with each printing.

Magazines found too late to include in this edition, as well as changes and deletions to current listings, will be listed in our quarterly updates (see Practical Matters).

Magazines

The true gardener pulls the gardening magazines out of the mail and plops right down to look at them first. They have an alarming way of multiplying — must be by invasive root systems. At any rate, they are very difficult to weed!

Be sure to notice the new annual *Gardener's Index*, listed in this section — it indexes the five most popular gardening magazines for 1986 and will be adding more for 1987. A very welcome new publication!

A Table of the Symbols and Abbreviations Used in this Book
Appears Inside the Front and Back Covers and On the Bookmark

For Explanations of Abbreviations/Codes Used In Listings See Bookmark or Inside Covers

Actinidia Enthusiasts Newsletter *Friends of the Trees* *P. O. Box 1466* *Chelan, WA 98816*	Issued by Friends of the Trees, sold by the issue.Information on available species, growing suggestions, sources, propagation, and more. Price: $1.50 per issue, US$3 OV Issues/Year: 1
Amaranth Today *Rodale Press, Inc.* *33 E. Minor St.* *Emmaus, PA 18049*	Write for information. I think the focus is on developing Amaranth as a commercial crop, but it would be of interest to serious home food gardeners. Price: $15 Issues/Year: 4
Bulletin of American Garden History *Ellen Richards Samuels* *P. O. Box 397A, Planetarium Sta.* *New York, NY 10024*	Newsletter on garden history, restoration, and exibitions and events, covering the whole country. Useful to historically-minded travelers, interesting. Price: US$7 Issues/Year: 4
Arnoldia *Harvard Univ., The Arnold Arboretum* *The Arborway* *Jamaica Plain, MA 02130*	Devoted to all aspects of plants. Price: US$12 Issues/Year: 4
Australian Orchid Review *14 McGill Street* *Lewisham, NSW, Australia 2049*	Back issues available for US7.50 each: send self-addressed envelope for list. Price: US$22 OV: US$33 OV Airmail Issues/Year: 4
The Avant Gardener *Horticultural Data Processors* *P. O. Box 489* *New York, NY 10028*	Sumarizes new information on all phases of gardening. Lists new sources of garden materials, sometimes has special interest issues. Price: US$15: US$16.50 OV (IMO) Issues/Year: 12
Baer's Garden Newsletter *John Baer's Sons* *Box 328* *Lancaster, PA 17603*	Write for information: they say it's for the lively, intelligent gardener, but aren't we all? Price: US$3.50 Issues/Year: 4
Bev Dobson's Rose Letter *Beverly R. Dobson* *215 Harriman Rd.* *Irvington, NY 10533*	Newsletter for the enthusiastic rose lover, up-dates her annual Combined Rose List: full of rose news. See Combined Rose List on book list. Price: US$9: US$16 OV (Airmail) Issues/Year: 6
Blair & Ketchum's Country Journal *Historical Times, Inc.* *P. O. Box 392* *Mt. Morris, IL 61054-9956*	Generally a magazine on country living, but it has many articles on gardening and fruit growing. The focus is generally Northeastern. Price: US$16.95: US$21.95 CAN & OV Issues/Year: 12 Region: Northeast
John E. Bryan Gardening Newsletter *John E. Bryan Inc.* *1505 Bridgeway, Suite 107* *Sausalito, CA 94965-1967*	A gardening newsletter which focuses on Northern California growing conditions, but it contains a lot of general information and musings as well. Price: US$30 Issues/Year: 12 Region: Northern California
The Bu$iness of Herbs *Portia Meares* *P. O. Box 559* *Madison, VA 22727*	Newsletter for the small herb grower & seller, expanding into more general articles about herbs of "more lasting significance". Price: US$21: US$25 CAN: US$30 OV Issues/Year: 6
Cactus & Succulent Journal *Abbey Garden Press* *P. O. Box 3010* *Santa Barbara, CA 93130-3010*	Magazine for the cactus and succulent enthusiast -- from beginner to professional botanist. Price: US$20 US & CAN: US$21 OV (IMO) Issues/Year: 6

Canadian Horticultural History
Royal Botanical Gardens (CCHHS)
Box 399
Hamilton, ON, Canada L8N 3H8

New journal which will feature Canadian gardens, historical restorations, plant collectors, early nurseries, etc. Subscriptions is for 4 issues.
Price: US$16: C$14 CAN: US$20 OV
Issues/Year: Irreg.
Region: Canada

Chestnutworks
Chestnut Growers Exchange
Rt. 1, Box 341
Alachua, FL 32615

A new periodical devoted wholly to the Chestnut: culture, propagation, resea rch, history and recipes and sources of these magnificent trees.
Price: US$10
Issues/Year: irreg

The Cultivar
UCSC Agroecology Program
Agroecology Program, College Eight
Santa Cruz, CA 95064

Newsletter for researchers, farmers and gardeners interested in agro-ecological approaches to farming and gardening.
Issues/Year: 2

Desert Plants
Boyce Thompson Southwestern Arboretum
P. O. Box AB
Superior, AZ 85273

Devoted to cultivated and wild desert plants: fairly scholarly.
Price: US$12 US & CAN:US$15 OV
Issues/Year: 4

Dwarf Conifer Notes
Theophrastus
P. O. Box 458
Little Compton, RI 02837-0458

Theophrastus publishes books on conifers and other subjects, and reprints of garden classics: will send Dwarf Confer Notes to book buyers if they ask.
Price: Sent free to buyers of books.
Issues/Year: Irregular

Euphorbia Journal
Strawberry Press
227 Strawberry Dr.
Mill Valley, CA 94941

A beautiful annual publication with many color photographs of euphorbias and related genera: will be a 10 vol. set. Book on Caudiciforms is $60.
Price: US$35 + CA Tax & Postage
Issues/Year: 1 (Bound)

Fine Gardening
The Taunton Press
63 South Main Street, Box 355
Newtown, CT 06470

I received an advertisement for this new magazine one week before going to press! Write for information: publisher also issues Fine Woodworking.
Price: US$19
Issues/Year: 6

Flower & Garden
Modern Handcraft, Inc.
4251 Pennsylvania Ave.
Kansas City, MO 64111

A general interest gardening magazine, with arti- cles on all phases of home gardening, regional re-ports, and reports on new cultivars and products.
Price: US$6: C$9: US$9 OV (IMO)
Issues/Year: 6

The Four Seasons
East Bay Regional Park District
Tilden Regional Park, Botanic Garden
Berkeley, CA 94708

Magazine covering all aspects of California nativeplants: both technical and semi-popular articles. For the experienced enthusiast and botanists.
Price: US$10 for 4 issues.
Issues/Year: 4
Region: California (Native Plants)

Garden
Subscription Department
New York Botanical Garden
Bronx, NY 10458

Published by a consortium of horticultural societies. Covers the plant world: gardening, botany, plant sciences, art, agriculture, and history.
Price: US$12: US$14.50 CAN & OV (IMO)
Issues/Year: 6

The Garden
New Perspectives Publishing, Ltd.
19 Garrick St.
London, England WC2E 9AX

The Journal of the Royal Horticultural Society, available by subscription to those who want it without becoming a "Fellow" of the Society.
Price: UK16.50 surface mail
Issues/Year: 12

Garden Design
American Society of Landscape Architects
1733 Connecticut Ave. NW
Washington, DC 20009

The only periodical that I'm aware of that concentrates on residential garden design: domestic, international and historical.
Price: US$20 US & CAN: US$25 OV
Issues/Year: 4

Gardener's Index
Compudex Press
P. O. Box 27041
Kansas City, MO 64110

A terrific combined annual index to Amer. Horticulturist, Flower & Garden, Horticulture, Natl. Gardening & Rodale's Organic Gardening: very thorough!
Price: US$10
Issues/Year: 1 Yr.

Gardening Newsletter by Bob Flagg
Morningside Associates
P.O. Box 2306
Houston, TX 77001

A general gardening newsletter oriented to the SunBelt and Gulf Coast south.
Price: US$12.95
Issues/Year: 12
Region: Gulf Coast & Sun Belt South

Greener Gardening, Easier *E. Dexter Davis, Horticulturist* *26 Norfolk St.* *Holliston, MA 01746*	A gardening newsletter oriented to New England: good information on gardening events in the area, book reviews, seasonal gardening advice. Price: US$12 Issues/Year: 12
Growing from Seed *Thompson & Morgan* *P. O. Box 1308* *Jackson, NJ 08527*	Started in 1987, a new magazine on growing from seed: nice feature is an A to Z Seed Raiser's Directory, giving details on germination on many seeds. Price: US$9.95 Issues/Year: 4
Gurney's Gardening News *Gurney Seed & Nursery Company* *2nd & Capitol* *Yankton, SD 57079*	Tabloid paper: full of information oriented to the home flower and fruit and vegetable gardener. Price: US$5.95 Issues/Year: 6
Harrowsmith *Camden House Publishing* *The Creamery* *Charlotte, VT 05445*	Magazine on all phases of country living, quite a lot of articles on gardening, particularly growing vegetables and fruit. Price: US$18: US$22 CAN: US$26 OV Issues/Year: 6
Helping Each Other *Judy Huber* *HCR, Box 78* *Bowdle, SD 67428*	Published by a farm-wife to share gardening tips and recipes: each issue features a vegetable group, with many delicious uses for the product. Price: US$12: US$18 OV Issues/Year: 12 Region: Northern Mid-West
The Herb Quarterly *Uphill Press, Inc.* *P. O. Box 275* *Newfane, VT 05345*	Publication devoted to herbs: their culture, history, use and recipes. A regular feature is information on herb gardens to visit. Price: US$20: US$24 CAN & OV (IMO) Issues/Year: 4
The Herb, Spice and Medicinal Plant Digest *University of Massachusetts* *Dept. of Plant & Soil Sci., Stockbridge Hall* *Amherst, MA 01003*	Quarterly for herb growers and those interested in uses of herbs: issues have surveys of recent literature, some technical material--not for beginners. Price: US$6 Issues/Year: 4 yr.
The Herbal Kitchen *Diane Lea Mathews* *Box 134* *Salisbury Center, NY 13454*	Gardening and culinary information on herbs, herb sources and herbal lore. Price: US$15: US$18 OV (IMO) Issues/Year: 5
Himalayan Plant Journal *Primulaceae Books* *Abhijit Villa, BPO Ecchey* *Kalimpong/Darjeeling, WB, India 734301*	Dealing with conservation, culture, history, hybridization and identification Himalayan flora. Send subscription money by Registered Airmail. Price: US$25 Airmail: UK 20 Airmail Issues/Year: 2 or 4 Region: Himalayas
Horticulture *Subscription Department* *P. O. Box 2595* *Boulder, CO 80323*	A general interest magazine devoted to all aspects of gardening and horticulture. Price: US$18: US$25 CAN & OV Issues/Year: 12
HortIdeas *Greg & Pat Williams* *Route 1, Box 302* *Gravel Switch, KY 40328*	A gardeners' "digest": the latest research, new sources of plants & supplies, a tour of the home gardening world. Emphasis is serious food gardening. Price: US$10: US$12 CAN: US$15 OV Issues/Year: 12
Hortline *Tom's World Horticulture Consulting* *P. O. Box 5238* *Charleston, WV 25361*	Focuses on the how-to and when-to of ornamental gardening in Zones 4 - 7: subscription lets you call the editor for consultation (no collect calls). Price: US$15: $20 CAN: US$28 OV (IMO) Issues/Year: 12 yr. Region: USDA Zones 4 - 7
Hortus *P. O. Box 90* *Farnham, Surrey, England GU9 8SX*	New quarterly devoted of writings of distinquished British gardeners, with a sprinking of American writers: enough reading for several evenings. Price: UK 28 US & CAN: UK 22 Europe Issues/Year: 4
Houseplant Forum **A Fleur de Pot (French edition)** *HortiCom Inc.* *1449 Avenue William* *Sillery, PQ, Canada G1S 4G5*	A new newsletter, well illustrated by drawings, with in-depth information on indoor plants: helpful to beginner and those looking for new challenges. Price: $7.50: US7.50 OV Issues/Year: 6 yr.

Indian Orchid Journal
Ganesh Mani Pradhan & Udai C. Pradhan
Ganesh Villa
Kalimpong 734-301, WB, India

Price: US$15 (US20 Airmail)
Issues/Year: 4

International Bonsai
Intl. Bonsai Arboretum
412 Pinnacle Rd.
Rochester, NY 14623

Quarterly for the serious bonsai enthusiast.
Price: US$20: US$25 OV
Issues/Year: 4

The IPM Practitioner
Bio Integral Resource Center
1307 Acton Street
Berkeley, CA 94706

Journal covers the field of integrated pest management: research, new developments, products and publications: oriented to professionals.
Price: US$25 Individuals: US$50 Inst.
Issues/Year: 11

Journal of Garden History
Taylor & Francis, Inc.
242 Cherry Street
Philadelphia, PA 19106-1906

Write for information.
Price: US$48 US & CAN
Issues/Year: 4

The Kew Magazine
c/o Timber Press
9999 S. W. Wilshire
Portland, OR 97225

Devoted to plants, with beautiful illustrations. Articles are scientific but understandable, deal with plant habitats and taxonomy.
Price: US$50 or UK37.50 OV
Issues/Year: 4

Lindleyana
American Orchid Society
6000 S. Olive Ave.
West Palm Beach, FL 33405

The scientific journal of the American Orchid Society.
Price: US$20: US$22 OV
Issues/Year: 4

Living off the Land, Subtropic Newsletter
Geraventure
P. O. Box 2131
Melbourne, FL 32902-2131

A newsletter oriented to growing edibles, particularly tropical fruits and crops: list seeds wanted and available in each issue.
Price: US$12 US & CAN: US$15 OV (IMO)
Issues/Year: 6

The New England Gardener
New England Horticultural Services, Inc.
P. O. Box 2699
Nantucket, MA 02584

Newsletter on gardening in New England, how-to and when-to, with longer articles on plants and special projects. Also covers gardening events.
Price: US$14.95: C$17.95: US17.95 OV
Issues/Year: 12
Region: New England

The Orchid Digest
Mrs. N. H. Atkinson, Memb. Secy.
P. O. Box 916
Carmichael, CA 95609-0916

A quarterly magazine for orchid growers, many color photographs.
Price: US$18
Issues/Year: 4

The Orchid Review
The Orchid Review, Ltd.
5 Orchid Ave., Kingsteignton
Newton Abbot, Devon, UK TQ12 3HG

International in scope: many color photographs. Subscriptions run from January to December.
Price: US$31 or UK17 OV
Issues/Year: 12

Pacific Horticulture
Pacific Horticultural Foundation
P.O. Box 485
Berkeley, CA 94701

Magazine published by a consortium of Pacific Coast horticultural societies: a very interesting and beautiful magazine with worldwide readership.
Price: US$12: US$14 CAN: US$16 OV
Issues/Year: 4

Permaculture with Native Plants
Curtin Mitchell
Box 38
Lorane, OR 97451

Newsletter devoted to growing and using edible and useful native plants of Pacific Northwest. Informative, carries seed exchange offers and sources.
Price: Free: Donation Appreciated.
Issues/Year: 3 to 4
Region: Pacific Northwest

Plant Lore
16 Oak Street
Genesse, NY 14454

No reply received: write for information.
Price: US$6
Issues/Year: 2

Plants & Gardens
Plants & Gardens News
Brooklyn Botanical Garden
1000 Washington Ave.
Brooklyn, NY 11225

Each very informative issue covers one subject in depth: herbs, rock gardens, propagation, shade gardening or other garden subjects. Very good value!
Price: US$20: US$35 OV
Issues/Year: 4

For Explanations of Abbreviations/Codes Used In Listings See Bookmark or Inside Covers

The Plantsman
N. P. Publishing
19 Garrick Street
London, England WC2E 9AX

Fairly scholarly coverage of all types of plants in garden use, several well illustrated articles in each issue, scope is international.
Price: UK11.50 OV
Issues/Year: 4

Rodale's Organic Gardening
Rodale Press, Inc.
33 East Minor St.
Emmaus, PA 18098

Primarily devoted to vegetable and fruit growing, recently they have added garden ornamentals; full of practical organic gardening ideas and sources.
Price: US$13: US$18 CAN: US$19 OV
Issues/Year: 12

Rosy Outlook Magazine
'Rosy' McKenney
1014 Enslen St.
Modesto, CA 95350

New independent quarterly magazine all about roses.
Price: US$10: C$15 CAN
Issues/Year: 4

Solanaceae Quarterly
3370 Princeton Ct.
Santa Clara, CA 95051

Devoted to edible members of the Solanaceae family.
Price: $3
Issues/Year: 4

Southern Herbs
Eve Elliott
400 S. Hawthorne Circle, Box 3722
Winter Springs, FL 32708

Newsletter for the Southern herb grower, cook and herb crafter.
Price: US$9
Issues/Year: 4
Region: South

Southern Living
820 Shades Creek Parkway
Birmingham, AL 35209

Magazine has frequent articles on gardening in the South.
Price: $19.95 in South: $24 Elsewhere
Issues/Year: 12
Region: Southeast

Sunset Magazine
Lane Publishing Co.
80 Willow Road
Menlo Park, CA 94025-3691

Familiar to all in the 13 western states: there are 4 regional editions, and each issue carries gardening features customized by region.
Price: US$14, 13 Western States.
Issues/Year: 12
Region: Western States

The Weekend Garden Journal
Jim Bennett
P. O. Drawer 1607
Aiken, SC 29802

General interest magazine, with articles stressing practical gardening.
Price: US$11.95: US$15.95 CAN
Issues/Year: 7

Westscape
Rick Hassett
369 E. 900 S.
Salt Lake City, UT 84111

General gardening newsletter oriented to the inter-mountain West.
Price: US$10
Issues/Year: 4

 Artist: Claudette Stewart

The Advantages of Fall Planting

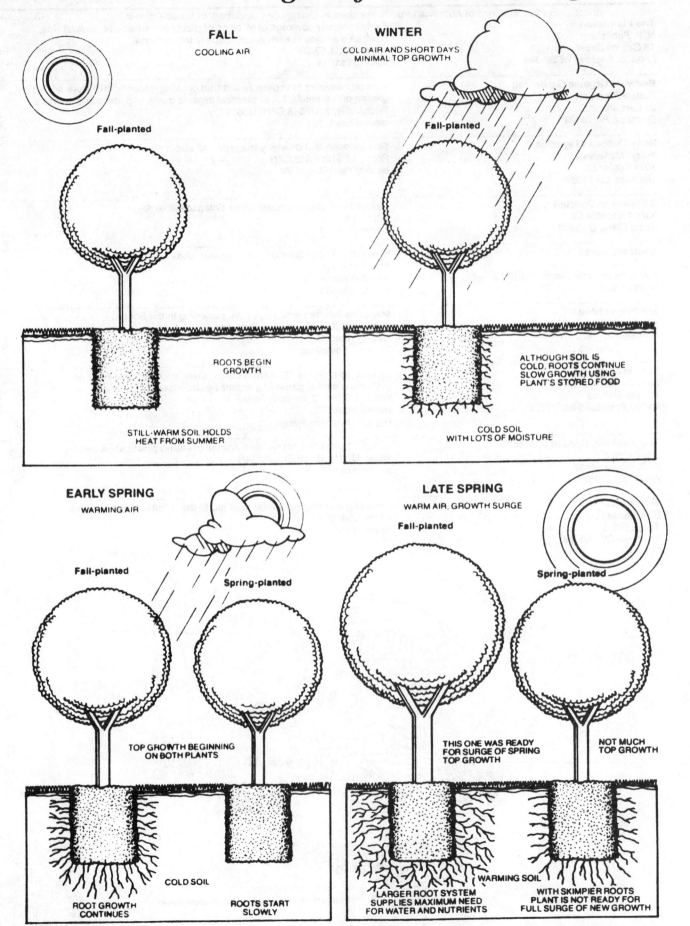

Courtesy of Hartmann's Plantation, Inc., artist unknown.

F

Libraries

Libraries with special horticultural collections are listed by state or province and city.

Be sure to check the Changes and Corrections List at the end of the book (see Practical Matters). This list is updated with each printing.

Libraries found too late to include in this edition, as well as changes and deletions to current listings, will be listed in our quarterly updates (see Practical Matters).

Libraries

Many public libraries have excellent collections of books on plants and gardening and will try to borrow books they don't have through inter-library loan for you. Some cities such as Philadelphia (The Library Company of Philadelphia) and San Francisco (The Mechanics Institute) have membership libraries which also have good gardening collections. Some colleges and universities will allow alumni and local residents to use their libraries for an annual fee, or you could sign up for a horticultural course and get library privileges for a semester.

Many of the libraries listed are supported by membership groups, frequently horticultural societies or "friends" of botanical gardens. It is well worth joining such a group to have the use of a good library, to say nothing of all the other activities they offer.

A Table of the Symbols and Abbreviations Used in this Book
Appears Inside the Front and Back Covers and On the Bookmark

Library Abbreviations and Conventions

Available library services are indicated as follows:

Members Only — only members may borrow books

Reference Only — books do not circulate

Inter-library loans — other libraries may borrow books

Loans to Public — public may borrow books, subject to library rules.

For Explanations of Abbreviations/Codes Used In Listings See Bookmark or Inside Covers

ALABAMA

Horace Hammond Memorial Library
Birmingham Botanical Gardens
2612 Lane Park Road
Birmingham, AL 35223
(205) 879-1227
Ida Burns

Open: M-F 7-5
Number of Books: 3,000
Periodical Titles: 125
Services: REFERENCE ONLY LOANS TO PUBLIC

ALASKA

Library
University of Alaska Museum Herbarium
907 Yukon Drive
Fairbanks, AL 99701
(907) 479-7108

Call or write for information.

ALBERTA, CANADA

Library
Faculty of Environmental Design
University of Calgary
Calgary, AB, Canada T2N 1N4

Call or write for information.

ARIZONA

Richter Memorial Library
Desert Botanical Garden
1202 N. Galvin Parkway, Papago Park
Phoenix, AZ 85008
(602) 941-1217, Ext. 110
Jane B. Cole

Particularly strong collection on desert plants. They have a collection of garden catalogs.
Open: M,W,F 9-1: Tu,Th 1-5
Number of Books: 10,000
Periodical Titles: 126
Services: REFERENCE ONLY

Boyce Thompson Southwestern Arboretum Library
Box AB
Superior, AZ 85273
(602) 689-2811
Carole Crosswhite

No reply received: call or write for information.

BRITISH COLUMBIA, CANADA

Library
University of British Columbia Botanical Gdn.
6501 N.W. Marine Dr.
Vancouver, BC, Canada V5T 1W5
(604) 228-3928
Dr. Gerald B. Straley

Open: M-F 8:30-4:30
Number of Books: 1,500
Periodical Titles: 200
Services: REFERENCE ONLY

VanDusen Gardens Library
Vancouver Botanical Garden Assn.
5251 Oak Street
Vancouver, BC, Canada V6M 4H1
(604) 266-7194
Charlaine Corbett

Open: Tu-F 10-3: W 7-9 p.m.
Number of Books: 2,700
Periodical Titles: 50
Services: REFERENCE ONLY

CALIFORNIA

Plant Science Library
Los Angeles State & County Arboretum
301 North Baldwin Avenue
Arcadia, CA 91006-2697
(213) 446-8251, Ext. 32
Joan DeFato

Open: M-F 9-5
Number of Books: 12,000
Periodical Titles: 200
Services: REFERENCE ONLY

Rancho Santa Ana Botanic Garden Library
1500 North College Avenue
Claremont, CA 91711
(714) 626-3922
Beatrice M. Beck

Call or write for information.

Fullerton Arboretum Library
California State University
Fullerton, CA 92634
(714) 773-3579
Celia Kutcher

Call for information on location.
Number of Books: 1,000
Periodical Titles: 15
Services: REFERENCE ONLY

The Traub Plant Life Library
The American Plant Life Society
P. O. Box 150
La Jolla, CA 92038

Collection specialized in Amaryllidaceae.

R. Mitchel Beauchamp Botanical Library
1843 E. 16th Street
National City, CA 92050
(714) 477-0295

Call or write for information.

South Coast Plant Science Library
South Coast Botanic Garden
26300 Crenshaw Boulevard
Palos Verdes Penin., CA 90274
(213) 377-0468
Virginia Gardner

Open: W, 12:30-3:30, Su 1-4
Number of Books: 500
Periodical Titles: 10
Services: MEMBERS ONLY REFERENCE ONLY

Helen Crocker Russell Library
Strybing Arboretum Society
Ninth Avenue at Lincoln Way
San Francisco, CA 94122
(415) 661-1514
Jane Gates

Open: Daily 10-4
Number of Books: 12,000
Periodical Titles: 250
Services: REFERENCE ONLY

Library
Huntington Botanical Gardens
1151 Oxford Road
San Marino, CA 91108
(818) 405-2100
Daniel Woodward

Call or write for information.

Library
Ganna Walska Lotusland Foundation
695 Ashley Road
Santa Barbara, CA 93108
c/o Dr. Steven Timbrook

Heard about this one too late to contact: library in organization, call or write for information.

Library
Santa Barbara Botanic Garden
1212 Mission Canyon Road
Santa Barbara, CA 93105
(805) 682-4726
Nancy Hawver

Collection strong in California native plants: members may use Library for reference, general public must make appointments in advance. Active society.
Open: M-F 9-5
Number of Books: 6,100
Periodical Titles: 110
Services: REFERENCE ONLY

Wallace Sterling Library of Landscape Arch.
Filoli Center & Friends of Filoli
Canada Road
Woodside, CA 94062
(415) 364-8300
Hadley Osborn

Call or write for information.
Open: By Appointment Only
Number of Books: 2,000
Services: REFERENCE ONLY

For Explanations of Abbreviations/Codes Used In Listings See Bookmark or Inside Covers

COLORADO

Helen Fowler Library
Denver Botanic Gardens
909 York Street
Denver, CO 80206
(303) 575-3751
Solange G. Gignac (Ext. 32 or 33)

Members of the Botanic Garden get in free, may borrow from the Library. Entry fee to the public is $3 to go into the Garden. Active society.
Open: M-Sa 10-4
Number of Books: 15,500
Periodical Titles: 378
Services: MEMBERS ONLY REFERENCE ONLY INTER-LIBRARY LOANS

CONNECTICUT

Library
The Greenwich Garden Center
Bible Street
Cos Cob, CT 06807
(203) 869-9242
Mrs. D. M. McAvity

Call or write for information.

Bartlett Arboretum Library
Univ. of Connecticut, Dept. of Plant Science
151 Brookdale Road
Stamford, CT 06903-4199
(203) 322-6971
Director

Open: M-F 8:30-4
Number of Books: 2,500
Periodical Titles: 35
Services: MEMBERS ONLY LOANS TO PUBLIC

DELEWARE

Wilmington Garden Center Library
503 Market Street Mall
Wilmington, DE 19801
(302) 658-1913 A
Karin Bidus

Open: M-F 10-3
Number of Books: 1,700
Periodical Titles: 50
Services: REFERENCE ONLY

DISTRICT OF COLUMBIA

Library
Society of American Foresters
5400 Grosvenor Lane
Washington, DC 20014
(301) 897-8720
Barry Walsh

Call or write for information.

Library
Dumbarton Oaks Garden
1703 32nd Street N.W.
Washington, DC 20007
(202) 342-3280
Laura Byers

Call or write for information.

Library
Landscape Architecture Foundation
1733 Connecticut Ave., N.W.
Washington, DC 20015
(202) 233-6229

Small collection focused on landscape architectureand design.
Open: M-F 9-5
Services: MEMBERS ONLY REFERENCE ONLY LOANS TO PUBLIC

U.S. National Arboretum Library
USDA, Agricultural Research Service
3501 New York Avenue N.E.
Washington, DC 20002
(202) 475-4828
Susan Whitmore

Open: Tu & Th 8:30-4:30
Number of Books: 5,000
Periodical Titles: 500
Services: REFERENCE ONLY

Office of Horticulture Branch Library
Arts & Industries Bldg., Rm. 2401
Smithsonian Institution
Washington, DC 20560
(202) 357-1544
Susan Gurney

Library has 15,000 nursery and seed catalogs: focus is garden history and design. Also an excellent Botany Library in the Natural History Museum.
Open: M-F 10-5 by appointment
Number of Books: 2,500
Periodical Titles: 200
Services: REFERENCE ONLY INTER-LIBRARY LOANS

FLORIDA

Montgomery Library
Fairchild Tropical Garden
10901 Old Cutler Rd.
Miami, FL 33156
(305) 667-1651

Active membership organization.
Open: Daily 9:30-4:30
Number of Books: 7,000
Services: MEMBERS ONLY REFERENCE ONLY

Library
Rare Fruit & Vegetable Council
408 N.E. 23rd Ave.
Pompano Beach, FL 33062
(305) 942-4493
Jayne H. Morgenstern

Collection on use of food producing plants for permaculture.
Open: 1st Monday, 7:30-10p.m.
Number of Books: 300
Services: MEMBERS ONLY

Research Library
Marie Selby Botanical Gardens
811 South Palm Avenue
Sarasota, FL 33577
(813) 366-5730, Ext. 39
Janet Kuhn

Members may use the Library for reference by appointment.
Open: By appointment only.
Number of Books: 4,500
Periodical Titles: 140
Services: MEMBERS ONLY

GEORGIA

Library
Atlanta Botanical Garden
1345 Piedmont Ave. N.E.
Atlanta, GA 30309

Just getting organized; not contacted. Call or write for information.

Cherokee Garden Library
Atlanta Historical Society
3099 Andrews Dr.
Atlanta, GA 30305
(404) 261-1837
Sally Bruce McClatchey

Open: M-Sa 9-5
Number of Books: 3,000
Periodical Titles: 100
Services: REFERENCE ONLY

Fernbank Science Center Library
156 Heaton Park Dr. N.E.
Atlanta, GA 30307
(404) 378-4311
Mary Larsen or Shirley Brown

Hours are M 8-5: Tu-Th 8am-9pm: F 8-5: Sa 10-5.
Open: See notes.
Number of Books: 18,500
Periodical Titles: 355
Services: REFERENCE ONLY INTER-LIBRARY LOANS

Library
American Camellia Society
P. O. Box 1217
Fort Valley, GA 31030
(912) 967-2358
Joseph H. Pyron

Call or write for information.

HAWAII

Library
Waimea Arboretum & Botanical Garden
59-865 Kamehameha Highway
Haleiwa, HI 96712
(808) 638-8655
K. R. Woolliams

Call or write for information.

Bishop Museum Library
Bernice Pauani Bishop Museum
1525 Bernice Street (P. O. Box 19000-A)
Honolulu, HI 96817
(808) 848-4147
Marguerite K. Ashford

Library includes horticultural collection.
Open: Tu-F 10-3: SA 9-12
Number of Books: 90,000
Periodical Titles: 2500
Services: REFERENCE ONLY INTER-LIBRARY LOANS

Lyon Arboretum Reference Collection
Harold L. Lyon Arboretum
3860 Manoa Road
Honolulu, HI 96822
(808) 988-3177

Materials available to staff only.
Open: M-F 9-3
Services: REFERENCE ONLY

(continued next page)

For Explanations of Abbreviations/Codes Used In Listings See Bookmark or Inside Covers

HAWAII (continued)

Pacific Tropical Botanic Garden Library
Papalina Rd., Kalaheo (Box 340, Lawai)
Kauai, HI 96765
(808) 332-7324 or7325
Lynwood M. Hume

A strong collection on tropical plants: members may use the Library for research, visiting researchers should write ahead to make arrangements.
Open: M-F 7-3:30
Number of Books: 3,000
Periodical Titles: 875
Services: REFERENCE ONLY

ILLINOIS

Library
Field Museum of Natural History
Roosevelt Road & Lake Shore Dr.
Chicago, IL 60605
(312) 922-9410

Public may use botanical and horticultural books for reference in the Readin g Room.
Open: M-F 9-4:30
Number of Books: 40,000
Services: REFERENCE ONLY INTER-LIBRARY LOANS

Chicago Botanic Garden Library
Chicago Horticultural Society
Lake-Cook Road
Glencoe, IL 60022
(312) 835-5440 X200. 27
Sue O'Brien

Open: M-Sa 9-4: Su 1-4 May-Sep
Number of Books: 8,000
Periodical Titles: 200
Services: MEMBERS ONLY REFERENCE ONLY

Sterling Morton Library
Morton Arboretum
Route 53
Lisle, IL 60532
(312) 719-2427, Ext. 30
Rita M. Hassert

Open: M-F 9-5: Sa 10-4
Number of Books: 23,000
Periodical Titles: 400
Services: MEMBERS ONLY REFERENCE ONLY INTER-LIBRARY LOANS

Agricultural Library
University of Illinois
1301 W. Gregory Dr. (226 Mumford)
Urbana, IL 61801
(217) 333-2416
Carol Boast or Maria Porta

Open Sundays from 1-10pm.
Open: M-Th 8-10pm: F,Sa 8-5
Number of Books: 200,000
Periodical Titles: 3,000
Services: REFERENCE ONLY INTER-LIBRARY LOANS

INDIANA

Library
Indianapolis Museum of Art Horticultural Soc.
1200 W. 38th St.
Indianapolis, IN 46208

Call or write for information.

(continued next page)

INDIANA (continued)

The Hayes Regional Arboretum Library
801 Elks Road
Richmond, IN 47374
(317) 962-3745

Please call and make an appointment to use the Libraray.
Open: Tu-Sa 1-5
Number of Books: 1,000
Services: REFERENCE ONLY

IOWA

Library, Bickelhaupt Arboretum
340 So. 14th St.
Clinton, IA 52732
(319) 242-4771
Francie Hill

Open: Daily, 9-6
Number of Books: 900
Periodical Titles: 36
Services: REFERENCE ONLY LOANS TO PUBLIC

LOUISIANA

Library
R.S. Barnwell Memorial Gardens & Art Center
501 Clyde Fant Parkway
Shreveport, LA 71101
(318) 226-6495
Sheila Nuttall

Call or write for information.

MAINE

Thuya Lodge Library
Asticou Terraces
Northeast Harbor, ME 04662
(207) 276-5456

Call or write for information.

MARYLAND

The Cylburn Horticultural Library
Cylburn Park Mansion
4915 Greenspring Avenue
Baltimore, MD 21209
(301) 367-2217
Adelaide C. Rackemann

Call to find out dates of Open House Sundays.
Open: Th 1-3, Some Sundays 2-4
Number of Books: 1,600
Periodical Titles: 4
Services: MEMBERS ONLY REFERENCE ONLY

National Agricultural Library
U.S. Department of Agriculture
10301 Baltimore Blvd.
Beltsville, MD 20705
(301) 344-3755

Probably the largest of all the Libraries--public may use it for reference only. Branch reading room in DC: USDA South, Room 1052, (202) 447-3434.
Open: M-F 8-4:30
Services: REFERENCE ONLY

Brookside Gardens Library
Maryland-National Capital Park & Plan. Comm.
1500 Glenallan Ave.
Wheaton, MD 20902
(301) 949-8231
Rebecca Zastrow

Open: M-F 9-5: Sa & Su 12-5
Number of Books: 2,000
Periodical Titles: 20
Services: REFERENCE ONLY

MASSACHUSETTS

Massachusetts Horticultural Society Library
300 Massachusetts Avenue
Boston, MA 02115
(617) 536-9280
Walter T. Punch

Open M-Tu & Th-F 8:30-4:30: W 8:30-8 pm: Sa l0-2.
Open: See Notes.
Number of Books: 29,500
Periodical Titles: 300
Services: MEMBERS ONLY REFERENCE ONLY INTER-LIBRARY LOANS

Library
Worcester County Horticultural Society
30 Tower Hill Road
Boylston, MA 01505
(617) 869-6111
Julie O'Shea

Open l0-4 Sa & Su, May to October.
Open: M-F 8:20-5
Number of Books: 6,000
Periodical Titles: 25
Services: REFERENCE ONLY

(continued next page)

MASSACHUSETTS (continued)

The Arnold Arboretum Library
Harvard University Herbaria Bldg.
22 Divinity Ave.
Cambridge, MA 02138
(617) 495-2366
Barbara A. Callahan

Call or write for information.

Library
Herb Society of America
2 Independence Court
Concord, MA 01742
(617) 371-1486
Mrs. Michael Ruettgers

Open: M-F 9:30-4:30
Number of Books: 700
Services: MEMBERS ONLY REFERENCE ONLY

Lawrence Necomb Library
New England Wild Flower Society
Hemenway Road
Framingham, MA 01701
(617) 877-7630
Mary M. Walker

Open: Tu-F 9-4
Number of Books: 2,500
Periodical Titles: 10
Services: MEMBERS ONLY REFERENCE ONLY INTER-LIBRARY LOANS

Berkshire Garden Center Library
Stockbridge, MA 01262
(413) 298-3926

Call or write for information.

MICHIGAN

The Detroit Garden Center Library
1460 East Jefferson Avenue
Detroit, MI 48207
(313) 259-6363
Margaret Grazier

Open: Tu,W,Th 9:30-3:30
Number of Books: 5,500
Periodical Titles: 10
Services: MEMBERS ONLY REFERENCE ONLY

Detroit Public Library
5201 Woodward Ave.
Detroit, MI 48202
(313) 833-1400 or 1450

They have a collection on gardening, botany and agriculture.
Open: Call
Number of Books: 5,500
Periodical Titles: 61
Services: REFERENCE ONLY INTER-LIBRARY LOANS LOANS TO PUBLIC

Library
Chippewa Nature Center
400 S. Badour Rd, Rt. 9
Midland, MI 48640
(517) 631-0803
Meg Ulery

Librarian on duty M,W,Th 8-3.
Open: M-F 8-5: Sa 9-5: Su 1-5
Number of Books: 2500
Periodical Titles: 86
Services: MEMBERS ONLY REFERENCE ONLY

The Dow Gardens Library
The Dow Gardens
1018 W. Main Street
Midland, MI 48640
(517) 631-2677
Tina J. Podboy

Library not staffed all the time, please call ahead if your need assistance with your research.
Open: M-F 10-4:30
Number of Books: 1,000
Periodical Titles: 30
Services: REFERENCE ONLY

The Fernwood Botanic Garden Library
13988 Range Line Rd.
Niles, MI 49120
(616) 695-6491
Ramona Hines

They have a collection of garden catalogs.
Open: M-F 9-5
Number of Books: 3,000
Periodical Titles: 45
Services: REFERENCE ONLY

Hidden Lake Gardens Library
Michigan State University
Tipton, MI 49287
(517) 431-2060
Laura Furgason

Open: Call for hours.
Number of Books: 3,000
Periodical Titles: 8
Services: REFERENCE ONLY

(continued next page)

MICHIGAN (continued)

Library, Matthaei Botanical Gardens
The University of Michigan
1800 N. Dixboro Road
Ypsilanti, MI 48105
(313) 763-7060
Mrs. Annie Hannan

Members may use the Library for reference.
Open: M-F 8-5
Number of Books: 1,700
Periodical Titles: 30
Services: MEMBERS ONLY REFERENCE ONLY

MINNESOTA

Anderson Horticultural Library
Minnesota Landscape Arboretum
3675 Arboretum Drive, Box 39
Chanhassen, MN 55317
(612) 443-2460
Nancy Allison

Open: M-F 8-4:30: Sa-Su 11-4:30
Number of Books: 8,000
Periodical Titles: 350
Services: REFERENCE ONLY

MISSOURI

St. Louis Parks Department Library
The Jewel Box Conservatory
5600 Clayton Road
St. Louis, MO 63110
(316) 535-0400
Susan Baker

Call or write for information.

Missouri Botanical Garden Library
P. O. Box 299
St. Louis, MO 63166
(314) 577-5155
Connie Wolfd

Call or write for information.

NEW JERSEY

Elvin McDonald Horticultural Library
Monmouth County Park System
Deep Cut Park, Red Hill Road
Middletown, NJ 07748
(201) 671-6050
Mrs. Mae H. Fisher

Open: Daily, 8-4:30
Number of Books: 1700
Periodical Titles: 18
Services: MEMBERS ONLY REFERENCE ONLY

Elizabeth Donnell Kay Botanical Library
George Griswold Frelinghuysen Arboretum
Box 1295R, 53 East Hanover Ave.
Morristown, NJ 07960
(201) 285-6166
Helen Hesselgrave

Call or write for information.

NEW YORK

Library of the New York Botanical Garden
Bronx, NY 10458
(212) 220-8751
Bernadette G. Callery

Call or write for information.

The Library
Brooklyn Botanic Garden
1000 Washington Avenue
Brooklyn, NY 11225
(718) 622-4433
Marie Giasi

Botanic Garden has an active society: excellent publications.
Open: Tu-F 9:30-4:30
Number of Books: 40,000
Periodical Titles: 500
Services: REFERENCE ONLY

George Landis Arboretum Library
Esperance, NY 12066
(518) 875-6935
Fred Lape

Call or write for information.

(continued next page)

For Explanations of Abbreviations/Codes Used In Listings See Bookmark or Inside Covers

NEW YORK (continued)

Library
Queens Botanical Garden
43-50 Main Street
Flushing, NY 11355

Call or write for information.

Library
Liberty Hyde Bailey Hortorium
467 Mann Library, Cornell University
Ithaca, NY 14853
(607) 256-2131
Dr. John Ingram

Collection in taxonomic botany: open to qualified researchers only, call to m ake arrangements in advance. Similar collection in Mann Library.
Open: M-F 8-5
Number of Books: 10,000
Periodical Titles: 350

Library
The Cary Arboretum
P. O. Box AB
Millbrook, NY 12545
(914) 677-5343
Betsy Calvin

Call or write for information.

Garden Club of America Library
598 Madison Avenue
New York, NY 10022
(212) 753-8287
Anne C. Shomer

Members must pay a fee of $1 to borrow a book.
Open: M-F 9-4:30
Number of Books: 3,000
Services: MEMBERS ONLY REFERENCE ONLY

The Horticultural Society of New York Library
The Horticultural Society of New York
128 W. 58th Street
New York, NY 10019
(212) 757-0915
Vicki Moeser

Big collection of seed & nursery catalogs.
Open: M-F 9-5, W 12-7
Number of Books: 16,000
Periodical Titles: 160
Services: MEMBERS ONLY REFERENCE ONLY

Planting Fields Arboretum Library
Oyster Bay, NY 11732
(516) 922-9024
Elizabeth Reilley

Open: W 11-4, Sa 10-3
Number of Books: 4,800
Periodical Titles: 50
Services: MEMBERS ONLY REFERENCE ONLY

Herbarium Library
Monroe County Parks Arboretum
375 Westfall Rd.
Rochester, NY 14620
(716) 244-4640
James W. Kelly

Open: M-F 9-5
Number of Books: 837
Periodical Titles: 30
Services: REFERENCE ONLY INTER-LIBRARY LOANS

Library
Garden Center of Rochester
5 Castle Park
Rochester, NY 14620

Call or write for information.

NORTH CAROLINA

Totten Library
North Carolina Botanic Garden
Laurel Hill Rd. off 15-501/54 Bypass
Chapel Hill, NC 27514
(919) 967-2246
Elisa Jones

Botanic Garden has an active society with many programs.
Open: M-F 8-5
Number of Books: 2,000
Periodical Titles: 30
Services: REFERENCE ONLY

OHIO

Library
Civic Garden Center of Greater Cincinnati
2715 Reading Road
Cincinnati, OH 45206
(513) 221-0981
Jeanne Bridewell

Call or write for information.

(continued next page)

OHIO (continued)

Lloyd Library and Museum
917 Plum Street
Cincinnati, OH 45202
(513) 721-3707
Rebecca A. Perry

Open: M-F 8:30-4
Number of Books: 65,000
Periodical Titles: 5,000
Services: REFERENCE ONLY

Eleanor Squire Library
The Garden Center of Greater Cleveland
11030 East Boulevard
Cleveland, OH 44106
(216) 721-1600
Richard R. Isaacson

Open: M-F 9-5: Su 2-5
Number of Books: 11,000
Periodical Titles: 200
Services: MEMBERS ONLY REFERENCE ONLY INTER-LIBRARY LOANS

Franklin Park Reference Library
Franklin Park Conservatory & Garden Center
1777 East Broad Street
Columbus, OH 43203
(614) 222-7447
Jack Zimmerman

Open: M-F 10-4
Number of Books: 600
Periodical Titles: 7
Services: MEMBERS ONLY REFERENCE ONLY

Biological Sciences Library
Ohio State University
1735 Neil Avenue
Columbus, OH 43210
(614) 422-1744

Call or write for information.

Cox Arboretum Library
James M. Cox Arboretum
6733 Springboro Pike
Dayton, OH 45449
(513) 434-9005
Ruth McManis

Arboretum has an active support group with many activities.
Open: M-F 10-4
Number of Books: 2,000
Periodical Titles: 10
Services: MEMBERS ONLY REFERENCE ONLY

Kingwood Center Library
900 Park Avenue West
Mansfield, OH 44906
(419) 522-0211
Timothy J. Gardener

Residents of Richland and five surrounding counties may borrow books.
Open: Tu-Sa 9-5
Number of Books: 7,000
Periodical Titles: 100
Services: REFERENCE ONLY INTER-LIBRARY LOANS LOANS TO PUBLIC

Warren H. Corning Library
The Holden Arboretum
9500 Sperry Road
Mentor, OH 44060
(216) 946-4400
Paul C. Spector

Open: Tu-Su 10-5
Number of Books: 6,000
Periodical Titles: 125
Services: REFERENCE ONLY

The Dawes Arboretum Library
7770 Jacksontown Road S.E.
Newark, OH 43055
(614) 323-2355
Alan D. Cook or Linda Milligan

Members may use the Library for reference.
Open: M-F 8-4:30
Number of Books: 3,000
Periodical Titles: 30

Library
Gardenview Horticultural Park
16711 Pearl Road
Strongsville, OH 44136
(216) 238-6653
Henry A. Ross

Library open to members only, who may use it at any time.
Number of Books: 3,000
Services: MEMBERS ONLY

Environmental Library
George P. Crosby Gardens
5403 Elmer Drive
Toledo, OH 43651
(419) 536-8365
Mary Tucker

Call or write for information.

For Explanations of Abbreviations/Codes Used In Listings See Bookmark or Inside Covers

OKLAHOMA

Tulsa Garden Center Library
2453 South Peoria
Tulsa, OK 74114
(918) 749-6401
Mrs. Donald Ross

Call or write for information.

ONTARIO, CANADA

Library
The Civic Garden Centre, Ontario, Canada
777 Lawrence Ave. East
Don Mills, ON, Canada M3C 1P2
(416) 445-1552
Pamela Mackenzie

Open: M-F 9:30-5: Sa-Su 12-5
Number of Books: 6,000
Periodical Titles: 40
Services: REFERENCE ONLY INTER-LIBRARY LOANS

Royal Botanical Gardens Library
Royal Botanical Gardens
P. O. Box 399
Hamilton, ON, Canada L8N 3H8
(416) 527-1158, Ext. 159
Ina Vrugtman

Open: M-F 9-5: Sa 9-12
Number of Books: 7,000
Periodical Titles: 450
Services: MEMBERS ONLY REFERENCE ONLY INTER-LIBRARY LOANS

School of Horticulture Library
Niagara Parks Commission
Niagara Parkway (P.O.Box 150)
Niagara Falls, ON, Canada L2E 6T2
(416) 356-8554
Mrs. Shirley Stoner

The public may use the library for research only by prior arrangement: please call a day or two in advance.
Open: M-F (see Notes)
Number of Books: 2,700
Periodical Titles: 65
Services: INTER-LIBRARY LOANS

Ottawa Research Station Library
Agriculture Canada
Central Experimental Farm, Bldg. 75
Ottawa, ON, Canada K1A OC6
(613) 995-9428, Ext. 30
Gail A. Waters

Open: M-F 8-4
Number of Books: 25,000
Periodical Titles: 250
Services: MEMBERS ONLY REFERENCE ONLY INTER-LIBRARY LOANS

OREGON

Library
Berry Botanic Garden
11505 S. W. Summerville Rd.
Portland, OR 97219
(503) 636-4112
Myrtle R. Snyder

Members may use the library and borrow books.
Open: Weekdays 8-5
Number of Books: 600
Services: MEMBERS ONLY

PENNSYLVANIA

Joseph Krauskopf Library
Delaware Valley College
Doylestown, PA 18901
(215) 345-1500, Ext 2255
Constance Shook

Open M-Th 8:30-11pm: F 8:30-9:30: Sa 12-3: Su 2-11. Building a collection of seed and nursery catalogs; specializes in science and agriculture.
Open: See notes.
Number of Books: 65,000
Periodical Titles: 600
Services: REFERENCE ONLY INTER-LIBRARY LOANS

Longwood Gardens Library
Kennett Square, PA 19348
(215) 388-6741, Ext. 501
Enola J. N. Teeter

There is a small fee to use the Library for reference.
Open: M-F 8-4
Number of Books: 17,000
Periodical Titles: 236
Services: REFERENCE ONLY INTER-LIBRARY LOANS

Pennsylvania Horticultural Society Library
325 Walnut Street
Philadelphia, PA 19106
(215) 625-8261
Janet Evans

Open: M-F 9-5
Number of Books: 14,000
Periodical Titles: 200
Services: REFERENCE ONLY INTER-LIBRARY LOANS

(continued next page)

PENNSYLVANIA (continued)

The Library Company of Philadelphia
1314 Locust Street
Philadelphia, PA 19107
(215) 546-3181
Phil Lapsansky, Reference

Large research collection, some horticulture.
Open: Call
Number of Books: 400,000
Periodical Titles: 1000
Services: REFERENCE ONLY INTER-LIBRARY LOANS

Library
Academy of Natural Sciences
19th & The Parkway
Philadelphia, PA 19103
(215) 299-1040
Janet Evans

Open: M-F 9-5
Number of Books: 190,000
Periodical Titles: 9,999
Services: REFERENCE ONLY INTER-LIBRARY LOANS

Morris Arboretum Library
University of Pennsylvania
9414 Meadowbrook Ave.
Philadelphia, PA 19118
(215) 247-5777
Karen D. Stevens

Call or write for information.

Library
Carnegie Museum of Natural History
4400 Forbes Avenue
Pittsburgh, PA 15213
(412) 622-3264
Gerard McKiernan

Large collection includes books on botany and horticulture.
Open: Daily 8:30-12, 1-5
Number of Books: 100,000
Periodical Titles: 3,200
Services: REFERENCE ONLY INTER-LIBRARY LOANS

Hunt Botanical Library
Hunt Institute for Botanical Documentation
Carnegie Mellon University
Pittsburgh, PA 15213
(412) 268-2436
Anita Karg

Open: M-F 1-5
Number of Books: 22,000
Periodical Titles: 300
Services: REFERENCE ONLY INTER-LIBRARY LOANS

Pittsburgh Civic Garden Center Library
1059 Shady Lane
Pittsburgh, PA 15232
(412) 441-4442
Mrs. Malcolm Farnsworth

Call or write for information.

Barbara Spaulding Cramer Library
Arthur Hoyt Scott Horticultural Foundation
Swarthmore College
Swarthmore, PA l9081
(215) 447-7025
Judith Zuk

Open: M-F 8:30-4:30
Number of Books: 800
Periodical Titles: 45
Services: MEMBERS ONLY REFERENCE ONLY

QUEBEC, CANADA

Montreal Botanical Garden Library
Jardin Botanique de Montreal
4101 rue Sherbrooke est
Montreal, PQ, Canada H1X 2B2
(514) 872-1824
Celine Arseneault

Open: M-F 8:30-12, 1:15-4:30
Number of Books: 12,000
Periodical Titles: 200
Services: REFERENCE ONLY INTER-LIBRARY LOANS

SOUTH CAROLINA

Orangeberg County Library
P. O. Box 1367
Orangeberg, SC 29115
(803) 531-4636

Call or write for information.

For Explanations of Abbreviations/Codes Used In Listings See Bookmark or Inside Covers

TENNESSEE

Library
Dixon Gallery & Gardens
4339 Park Avenue
Memphis, TN 38117
(901) 761-5250
Carol Griffin

Open: Tu-Sa 11-5: Su 1-5
Number of Books: 1,000
Periodical Titles: 40
Services: MEMBERS ONLY REFERENCE ONLY

Sybil G. Malloy Memorial Library
Memphis Botanic Garden
750 Cherry Road
Memphis, TN 38117
(901) 685-1566

Call or write for information.

The Botanical Gardens Library
Cheekwood
Forrest Park Drive
Nashville, TN 37205
(615) 356-3306
Muriel H. Connell

Members may borrow books; the general public may use materials there.
Open: T-Sa 9-5: Su 1-5
Number of Books: 4500
Services: MEMBERS ONLY REFERENCE ONLY

TEXAS

Library
Fort Worth Botanic Garden
3220 Botanic Garden Drive North
Fort Worth, TX 76107
(817) 870-7686
Jana Johnson

General public may borrow books if they have a Fort Worth Public Library card.
Open: M-F 8-5: Sa 10-5: Su 1-5
Number of Books: 3,000
Periodical Titles: 20
Services: MEMBERS ONLY LOANS TO PUBLIC

VIRGINIA

Harold B. Tukey Memorial Library
American Horticultural Society
7931 East Boulevard Dr.
Alexandria, VA 22308
(703) 768-5700
Raymond J. Rogers

Members may use the library for reference.
Open: M-F 8:30-5
Number of Books: 2,500
Periodical Titles: 200

Blandy Farm Library
University of Virginia
Boyce, VA 22620
(703) 837-1758
Tom Ewert

Open: M-F 7:30-4
Number of Books: 2,000
Periodical Titles: 20
Services: MEMBERS ONLY REFERENCE ONLY INTER-LIBRARY LOANS LOANS TO PUBLIC

Library
Norfolk Botanical Gardens
Norfolk, VA 23518
(804) 855-0194
Marion Cole

Members may borrow from the Library.
Open: M-F 8:30-5
Number of Books: 1,935
Periodical Titles: 16
Services: MEMBERS ONLY REFERENCE ONLY

WASHINGTON

Rhododendron Reference Library
Rhododendron Species Foundation
P. O. Box 3798
Federal Way, WA 98003
(206) 927-6960
Mrs. Richard B. Johnson

Call or write for information.

Elisabeth C. Miller Horticultural Library
Center for Urban Horticulture
GF-15, University of Washington
Seattle, WA 98195
(206) 543-8616
Valerie Easton

Open: M-F 9-5
Number of Books: 3,000
Periodical Titles: 200
Services: REFERENCE ONLY

(continued next page)

WASHINGTON (continued)

Library
University of Washington Arboretum
East Madison and Lake Washington Blvd. East
Seattle, WA 98195
(206) 543-8800

Call or write for information.

WEST VIRGINIA

Library
Wheeling Garden Center
Oglebay Park
Wheeling, WV 26003
(304) 242-0665

Call or write for information.

WISCONSIN

Reference Library
Boerner Botanical Gardens
5879 South 92nd St.
Hales Corners, WI 53130
(414) 425-1131

Hours: March-Oct, Daily, 8-Sunset: Nov & Dec, Daily, 8-4: Jan & Feb M-F, 8-4
Open: See notes.
Number of Books: 2,000
Services: REFERENCE ONLY

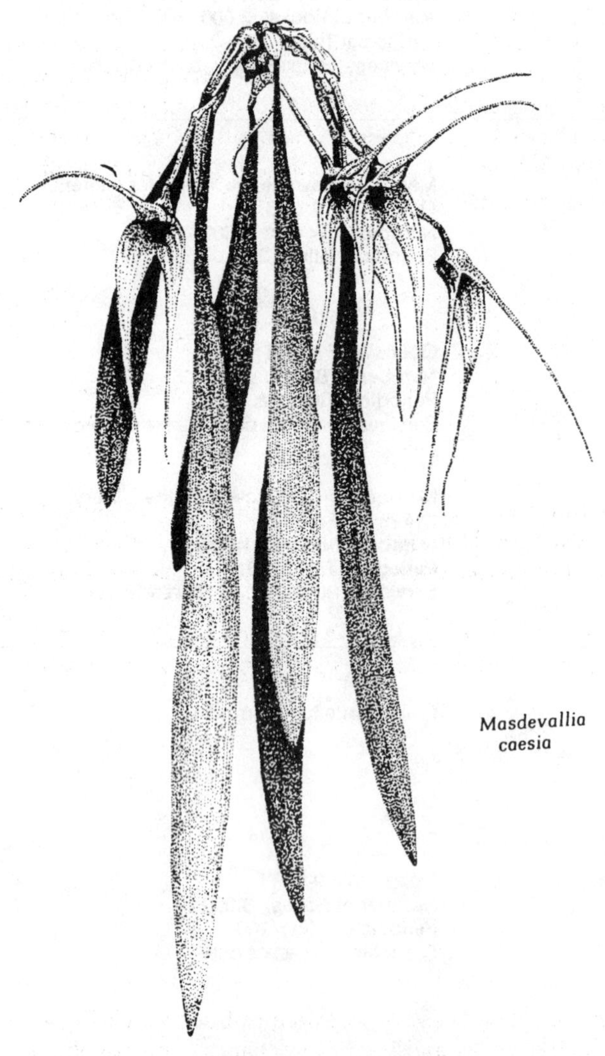

Books

Useful books on plants and gardening, for reference and daily use as well as for pleasure reading, are grouped into general categories by plant groups or plant uses.

Books found too late to include in this edition, as well as changes and deletions to current listings, will be listed in our quarterly updates (see Practical Matters).

Books

The books listed in this section are ones I have myself, have received for review, or which I have found in the Helen Crocker Russell Library at Strybing Arboretum in San Francisco. The notes are my own opinions, based on general garden and plant knowledge, but no great expertise in any one field. Most of them are fairly recent and should be available in public libraries, bookstores — including the many horticultural book suppliers listed in this book — or perhaps in second-hand book shops or on remainder tables. I have not tried to list the most scholarly, but rather those which seem to me to be good introductions to many kinds of plants and have good illustrations.

The frequent appearance of books from Britain reflects the state of garden book publishing. The British produce many beautiful garden books targeted at the American market, but they are frequently inappropriate to our conditions and to the plants available to us. It can be very disappointing and frustrating trying to recreate the perfect English garden in our own backyards. So, don't forget to seek out the wonderful writers in our midst who tell us how to garden in our own regions.

Mail order sources of new and used books are listed in the Product Sources Index. Books on specific plants or areas of horticultural interest are often available from nurseries and seed companies. In addition, many societies make books available to their readers, often at special prices.

The addresses of publishers can be found in *Books in Print* and *Forthcoming Books*, found in most libraries and larger book stores. Society addresses not given are listed in the Horticultural Societies section of this book.

A Table of the Symbols and Abbreviations Used in this Book
Appears Inside the Front and Back Covers and On the Bookmark

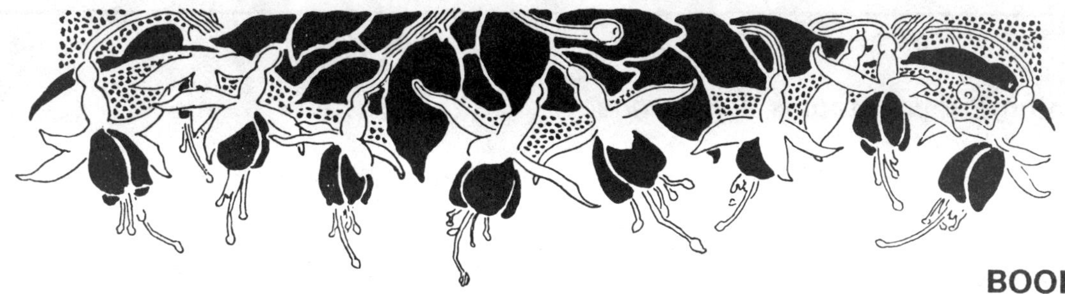

Useful Reference Books

Hortus Third: New York, Macmillan, 1976. A dictionary of plants cultivated in the U.S. and Canada – which means a very great many! It is the standard North American reference and should be in almost any library.

The New York Botanical Garden Illustrated Encyclopedia of Horticulture: Thomas Everett. New York, Garland, 1982. This work, in 10 volumes, is really monumental – descriptions more complete and easier to read than *Hortus Third*. Quite a bit of cultural information; most of the photographs are in black and white.

The Royal Horticultural Society Dictionary of Gardening: Patrick Synge, ed. Oxford, Clarendon Press, 1974. This work, in 4 volumes with a supplement, covers plants cultivated in Great Britain – also a very great many.

The European Garden Flora: Cambridge University Press, 1984. Recommended by a very knowledgeable reader who has the first two volumes; there are four more to come. He says it will become the standard reference for identification of cultivated ornamental plants. Expensive; you might try to get your library interested.

Exotica 4: Alfred B. Graf. East Rutherford, NJ, Roehrs, 1985. 2 v. A pictorial encyclopedia of exotic and tropical plants, including most plants which are grown indoors or in greenhouses.

Tropica: Alfred B. Graf. East Rutherford, NJ, Roehrs, 1986. 3rd ed. A color encyclopedia of tropical and sub–tropical plants of all kinds.

The Ortho Problem Solver: Michael Smith, ed. 2nd ed. San Francisco, Ortho Information Services, 1982. A color encyclopedia of plant diseases and pest problems, with color photographs of the problem, a discussion of the conditions which cause it and suggested solutions. Includes some cultural information and suggestions. Problems are entered by plant, making them fairly easy to locate.

Flowering Plant Index of Illustration and Information: The Garden Center of Greater Cleveland. Boston, G. K. Hall, 1979. 2 v. Supplement, 1982. 2 v. Only available in large horticultural libraries, very useful if you need to locate color illustrations of unusual plants. Each entry indicates if the illustration is of flower, fruit or general plant habit; there are 55,000 entries in the first two volumes. The two–volume supplement, equally thick, covers books published from 1965 – 1977.

The Seedlist Handbook: Mabel G. Harkness. 4th ed. Portland, Timber Press, 1986. Originally a handbook for people requesting unfamiliar seeds from seed exchange lists, it briefly describes the plant, its type, size, flower color, origin and gives references to information and illustrations on the plant in authoritative books.

Directory of Regional Gardening Resources: New York, Garden Club of America, 1987. This is a gem! It covers the country by regions, giving a bibliography of books on regional gardening and plants, nurseries and gardens to visit listed by state and a list of general reference books. $3.50 ppd. from The Garden Club of America. A steal for so much information!

Gardening Encyclopedias

A Gardener's Dictionary of Plant Names: William T. Stearn & Isadore Smith. New York, St. Martin's, 1972. A useful dictionary of plant names.

Gardening Encyclopedias – *continued*

Dictionary of Plant Names: Allen J. Coombes. Portland,Timber Press, 1985. Handy small book with a lot of information in concise entries.

Plant Names Simplified: A. T. Johnson and H. A. Smith. London,Hamlyn, 1972. Pocket–sized; gives derivation of plant names.

Wyman's Gardening Encyclopedia: Donald Wyman. Updated edition. New York, Macmillan, 1977. My favorite of the popular gardening encyclopedias, easy to read and use, but with a Northeastern point of view.

Taylor's Encyclopedia of Gardening: Norman Taylor. 4th ed. Boston, Houghton Mifflin, 1961. Another "Northeastern" gardening guide, which sometimes has things I can't find in Wyman. Good guide to gardening by state. Still in print.

Taylor's Guides: Multi–volume set, each book is written by a committee of experts and illustrated with many color photographs. Books on Roses, Annuals, Perennials, Bulbs, Ground Covers, Shrubs, Vegetables and Houseplants. Why "Taylor's"?

America's Garden Book: James and Louise Bush–Brown. Revised ed. New York, Scribner, 1980. Highly recommended by a reader.

The Complete Book of Gardening: Michael Wright, ed. New York,Warner Books, 1979. Well illustrated and packed with information on all phases of gardening.

Sunset New Western Garden Book: Menlo Park, Sunset Books, 1979. An excellent guide to gardening anywhere in the Western U.S. They have divided the West into 24 climate zones, and their plant encyclopedia indicates in which zones each plant will grow, very useful for choosing plants.

Reader's Digest Illustrated Guide to Gardening: Pleasantville, NY, The Reader's Digest Association, Inc., 1978. One of the very best how–to gardening guides, with lots of illustrations and extensive sections on choosing appropriate plants.

The Royal Horticultural Society's Concise Encyclopedia of Gardening Techniques: Christopher Brickell, ed. London, Mitchell Beazley, 1981. A compilation of an earlier series of books on garden techniques and problems; detailed and profusely illustrated coverage of pruning, propagation, greenhouse growing and fruit and vegetable growing, with a brief section on pests and diseases.

The Encyclopedia of Organic Gardening: New revised edition. Emmaus, PA, Rodale Press, 1978. A comprehensive encyclopedia on organic gardening, methods and crops, easy to read and use.

What Makes the Crops Rejoice: Robert Howard. Boston, Little Brown, 1986. A very interesting and enjoyable introduction to organic gardening, with beautiful illustrations.

Gardening and Beyond: Florence Bellis, Portland, Timber, 1986. Another interesting book on organic gardening and soil fertility. Her method of getting rid of moles is worth the price of the book.

The Encyclopedia of Natural Insect & Disease Control: Roger B. Yepson, Jr. Emmaus, PA, Rodale, 1984. A basic guide to non–toxic pest and disease control, arranged by plant.

Controlling Lawn and Garden Insects: San Francisco, Ortho Books, 1987. Offers good color pictures of the pests, advice on chemical and non–toxic methods of control.

Pruning Simplified: Lewis Hill. Updated edition. Pownal, VT, Storey Communications, 1986. A good, easy–to–understand introduction to the principles.

Sunset Pruning Handbook: Menlo Park, Lane Publishing Company, 1983. A good introduction, with basic principles explained, and an encyclopedia of how to prune many common garden plants.

Illustrated Books Useful for Finding and Identifying Plants

Reader's Digest Encyclopedia of Garden Plants and Flowers: London, The Reader's Digest Association, 1975. My copy of this is nearly worn out. It has small color pictures of a great variety of plants, with good descriptions and some information on growing.

The Color Dictionary of Flowers and Plants for Home and Garden: Roy Hay and Patrick M. Synge. Compact edition. New York, Crown, 1982. A very useful book, with good color photographs and brief descriptions of many common garden plants.

The Complete Handbook of Garden Plants: Michael Wright. New York, Facts on File, 1984. A concise guide to popular garden trees, shrubs and flowers, with color paintings of many.

2850 House & Garden Plants: Rob Herwig. New York, Crescent Books, 1986. Color encyclopedia of popular house and garden plants, all shown in color and briefly described with symbols for cultural requirements.

Right Plant, Right Place: Nicola Ferguson. New York, Summit, 1984. A good illustrated guide to popular garden plants, organized by garden and growing conditions.

The Concise Encyclopedia of Garden Plants: Kenneth A. Beckett. Topsfield, MA, Salem House, 1983. More than 2,000 color photographs of popular garden plants, with brief plant descriptions and growing requirements.

The Gardener's Illustrated Encyclopedia of Trees & Shrubs: Brian Davis. Emmaus, PA, Rodale Press, 1987. Concise information; color photos are mostly close–ups, with black and white silhouettes of plants.

The Illustrated Book of Food Plants: A Guide to the Fruit, Vegetables, Herbs & Spices of the World: S. G. Harrison, G. B. Masefield, & Michael Wallis. London, Peerage Books, 1985. Illustrated by color paintings, it will show you what almost any edible looks like – usually leaves and fruit.

Reader's Digest Guide to Creative Gardening: London, The Reader's Digest Association, 1984. A guide to choosing garden plants which is lavishly and romantically illustrated; more than most of the books of this kind, it shows plants in association and something of the habit of the whole plant. Pretty weak on plant descriptions and growing requirements, more a "looker".

Poisonous Plants: A Color Field Guide: Lucia Woodward. New York, Hippocrene Books, 1985. Color photos, descriptions, symptoms, treatment and tables of season and types of danger.

Weeds of the United States and Their Control: Harri J. Lorenzi and Larry S. Jeffery. New York, Van Nostrand Reinhold, 1987. Color photos, maps, descriptions, habitat and suggested controls.

Books on Plants for Specific Conditions & Effects

Scented Flora of the World: Roy Genders. New York, St. Martin's, 1977. A very interesting and readable book on scented plants – his nose is very lenient, coverage broad. There are newer books, but this one's my favorite.

Trees, Shrubs and Vines for Attracting Birds, A Manual for the Northeast: Richard DeGraff and Gretchen Whitman. Amherst, University of Massachusetts, 1979. Informative book with excellent cultural notes, lovely drawings.

Books on Plants for Specific Conditions & Effects – *continued*

The Complete Shade Gardener: George Schenk. Boston, Houghton Mifflin, 1984. Written by an experienced plantsman whose style and humor put him high on my list of "good reads".

Shade Gardening: A. Cort Sinnes. San Francisco, Ortho Books, 1982. Good illustrations and plant directory, plenty of help with creative and practical aspects.

Ponds and Water Gardens: Bill Heritage. New York, Stirling, 1981. Setting up pools and ponds and choosing appropriate aquatic plants, including water lilies.

The Water Garden: Anthony Paul and Yvonne Rees. New York, Viking Penguin, 1986. Not as practical as the book above, but full of inspirational photos which will spark your ideas.

All About Groundcovers: rev. ed. San Francisco, Ortho Books, 1982. Color guide to choosing groundcovers, good photos.

Hedges, Screens and Espaliers: Susan Chamberlin. Tucson, HP Books, 1982. Well illustrated guide to choosing and caring for hedges, screens, espaliered shrubs and fruit trees.

Flowering Plants in the Landscape: Mildred E. Mathias, ed. Berkeley, University of California Press, 1982. Excellent color photographs of trees, shrubs and vines for sub–tropical climates – hardiness indicated.

Trees and Shrubs for Dry California Landscapes: Bob Perry. San Dimas, CA, Land Design Publications, 1981. This book has fast become a standard in California. Good discussion of planting for erosion and fire control, and an excellent section on appropriate plants.

Plants for Dry Climates: How to Select, Grow and Enjoy: Mary Rose Duffield and Warren D. Jones. Tucson, HP Books, 1981. Plants for very dry conditions, especially the Southwestern deserts.

Southern Gardens, Southern Gardening: William L. Hunt. Durham, Duke University Press, 1982. This book is full of advice on how to grow plants under Southern growing conditions.

A Southern Garden: A Handbook for the Middle South. Elizabeth Lawrence. Revised edition. Chapel Hill, University of North Carolina Press, 1984. I've only recently discovered Lawrence, another "regional" writer who gives great pleasure with her information. I also enjoyed her *Gardening for Love: The Market Bulletins*. Allen Lacy, ed. Durham, Duke University Press, 1987.

The Year in Bloom: Gardening for All Seasons in the Pacific Northwest: Ann Lovejoy. Seattle, Sasquatch Books, 1987. Ann Lovejoy writes so well that if her name was Vita she'd be the rage. Forget the "Pacific Northwest" in the title and read her for the fun of it; after all, Vita was a "local" writer, too.

The Best of the Hardiest: John J. Sabuco. 2nd ed. Flossmoor, IL, Good Earth Publishing, 1987. Essential to the cold climate gardener; covers many types of plants, source lists.

Trees and Shrubs for Northern Gardens and *Flowers for Northern Gardens:* Leon Snyder, University of Minnesota Press, 1981 and 1983. Suggested by a reader in Wisconsin; I haven't seen them.

Propagation

Secrets of Plant Propagation: Lewis Hill. Pownal, VT, Storey Communications, 1985. Good overview of the subject, easy to understand.

The Seed Starter's Handbook: Nancy Bubel. Emmaus, Pa, Rodale Press, 1978. Recommended by a knowledgeable seedsman; his recommendation is enough for me. I haven't used it.

Park's Success With Seeds: Ann Reilly. Greenwood, SC, Park Seed Company, 1978. Brief information on habit, uses, germination and culture; very useful color photos of the seedlings.

Growing Plants From Seed: Richard Gorer. Boston, Faber and Faber, 1978. Concise information; section on special treatments.

Trees & Shrubs

Trees & Shrubs Hardy in the British Isles: W. J. Bean. 8th ed. rev. London, John Murray, 1976 – 1980. "Bean" is the British standard for looking up trees and shrubs – lists almost any woody plant hardy enough to grow in some part of Britain, no matter what the origin. Plant descriptions are exhaustive, all too few illustrations.

Illustrated Encyclopedia of Trees: Hugh Johnson. New York, W. H. Smith, 1987? A good overview of all aspects of trees, well illustrated and interesting to read. Updated version of "The International Book of Trees".

Trees for American Gardens and *Shrubs & Vines for American Gardens:* Donald Wyman. New York, Macmillan, 1965 and 1969. Two excellent books for choosing garden trees, shrubs and vines.

Plants that Merit Attention: V. 1, Trees. Janet Poor, ed. Portland, Timber Press, 1984. Suggests the use of beautiful trees not well known or widely used in the past.

100 Great Garden Plants: William H. Frederick, Jr. Portland, Timber Press, 1986. Like the book above, this one draws attention to all types of garden plants off the beaten path.

Manual of Cultivated Conifers: Gerd Krussmann. Portland, Timber Press, 1985. Maps, good descriptions, black and white photographs and drawings, descriptions of many cultivars. There is also a multi–volume set coming out of Krussmann's *Manual of Cultivated Broad–Leaved Trees & Shrubs.* A challenge to "Bean".

Conifers: D. M. Van Gelderen & J. R. P. van Hoey Smith. Portland, Timber Press, 1986. A good companion to the book above; many color photographs showing trees in gardens and in their natural habitats. Many cultivars illustrated.

Ornamental Conifers: Charles R. Harrison. New York, Hafner Press, 1975. A very good treatment of conifers, both large and dwarf – good color photographs and plant descriptions, with notes on hardiness. Harrison is a New Zealander.

Japanese Maples: J. D. Vertrees. Portland, Timber Press, 1987. Certainly the definitive book on Japanese maples – at least in English. Well illustrated in color, with excellent plant descriptions and information on culture. A beautiful book in itself, updated from the 1978 edition.

Palms: Alec Blombery and Tony Rodd. Topsfield, MA, Salem House, 1983. Good color photographs and plant descriptions of palms from all over the world. There is some cultural and propagation information in a separate section.

The Color Dictionary of Camellias: Stirling Macoboy. Topsfield, MA, Merrimack Pubs. Cir., 1983. Good color photographs of many cultivars, good introductory treatment.

The Book of Bamboo: David Farrelly. San Francisco, Sierra Club Books, 1984. A very lovely book, giving an inspiring introduction to bamboo and it many uses.

Azaleas: Fred Galle. Beaverton, OR, Timber Press, 1985. According to Azalea people, this is the "bible".

Trees & Shrubs – *continued*

Greer's Guidebook to Available Rhododendrons, Species & Hybrids: Harold E. Greer. Eugene, OR, Offshoot Pub., 1987. An overview of rhododendrons available in commerce, with some information on growing and a number of color photographs. Available from Greer Gardens (see Plant Sources) and in book shops.

Azaleas, Rhododendrons, Camellias: Menlo Park, Lane Publishing Company, 1982. Basic introduction to selection and culture, with color photographs.

House & Greenhouse Plants

Reader's Digest Success With Houseplants: New York, Random House, 1979. Very good information on plants and their cultural requirements, with nice color paintings throughout.

Essential Guide to Perfect House Plants: George Seddon. New York, Summit Books, 1985. By the author of my old favorite *The Best Plant Book Ever.*

House Plants for the Purple Thumb: Maggie Baylis. San Francisco, 101 Productions, 1981. The first indoor plant book I bought, it has recently been revised, but has retained its wit and charm. A confidence builder for the beginner, with good plant use suggestions.

Complete Indoor Gardener: Michael Wright. New York, Random House, 1975. Prolific writer of plant and gardening books, well organized and informative.

Orchids for Everyone: Brian Williams et al. New York, Crown, 1980. This book is a nice pictorial introduction to an enormous field – just a dip in what seems to become an obsession.

Orchid Care: Walter Richter. New York, Van Nostrand Reinhold, 1982. A practical little book, well illustrated and giving confidence to neophytes.

The Manual of Cultivated Orchid Species: Helmut Bechtel, Phillip Cribb and Edmund Laurent. Cambridge, MIT Press, 1981. Fairly technical, good color photos, pen and ink drawings, cultural notes.

How to Select and Grow African Violets and Other Gesneriads: Theodore James, Jr. Tucson, HP Books, 1983. A nice introduction to what seem to be the most popular plants in America.

The Miracle House Plants, African Violets and Other Easy-to-bloom Plants in the Gesneriad Family: Virginie & George Elbert. New York, Crown, 1976. A more detailed study of gesneriads and their care.

The Illustrated Encyclopedia of Succulents: A Guide to the Natural History and Cultivation of Cactus and Cactus-like Plants: Gordon Rowley. New York, Crown, 1978. Enter at your peril, you'll fall in love and want every plant you see! Good color photographs.

Books on Miscellaneous Plants

Alpines for Your Garden: Alan Bloom. Chicago, Floraprint, 1981. Many color photographs, brief information on growing.

Rock Gardens: William Schacht. New York, Universe Books, 1983. Written by a German expert, this is a good basic introduction to rock gardening.

Rock Gardening: A Guide to Growing Alpines & Other Wildflowers in the American Garden: H. Lincoln Foster. Portland, Timber Pr., 1982. Remains the standard; it has recently been reissued.

Perennial Garden Plants Or the Modern Florilegium: Graham Stuart Thomas. 2nd ed. London, Dent, 1982. Written by one of the great English plantsmen, this is a good read, with sound advice on plant selection. See also his excellent *The Art of Planting (Godine, 1984)*. Also three admired books on "old" roses.

Perennials: How to Select, Grow & Enjoy: Pamela Harper and Frederick McGourty. Tucson, HP Books, 1985. An excellent joint effort of two experts, with situation and growing well covered, beautiful color photographs.

All About Perennials: A. Cort Sinnes. San Francisco, Ortho Books, 1981. Another well written and illustrated guide to choosing perennials – good color photographs, ideas for planting perennial borders, plant descriptions and cultural requirements.

Landscaping With Perennials: Emily Brown. Portland, Timber Press, 1986. Not well organized, but full of information for the determined digger. It will take some getting used to.

The Perennial Garden: Color Harmonies Through the Season. Jeff and Marilyn Cox. Emmaus, PA, Rodale Press, 1985. Extensive tables of plants, their seasons, qualities and requirements.

Color in Your Garden: Penelope Hobhouse. Boston, Little Brown, 1985. Extending your garden pleasure through the use of plants to provide interest at different seasons of the year. Worth study.

The Well Chosen Garden: Christopher Lloyd. New York, Harper & Row, 1984. Advice on choosing garden plants from a well known British plantsman. Also see his *The Well Tempered Gardener* and *The Adventurous Gardener*, both New York, Random House, 1984.

A Garden of Wildflowers: 101 Native Species and How to Grow Them: Henry W. Art. Pownal, VT, Storey Communications, 1986. National in scope; maps, culture and propagation, list of sources and botanical gardens with native plant collections.

Roses: How to Select, Grow and Enjoy: Richard Ray and Michael McCaskey. Tucson, HP Books, 1981. A good general introduction to roses and rose growing, full of general information and color photographs and descriptions of many popular roses.

My World of Old Roses: Trevor Griffiths. Christchurch, Whitcoulls Publishers, 1983. By a jolly New Zealander, besotted by "old garden roses", this book is both a good read and a feast for the eyes. These roses have slowly been regaining popularity, but Griffiths may make them the rage with his infectious enthusiasm. He has a new book coming soon called *The Book of Classic Old Roses.*

Classic Roses: Peter Beales. New York, Holt, Reinhart & Winston, 1985. Another book on "old" roses, comprehensive coverage with hundreds of color photographs. Author is a British rose grower and expert; one of my bedside winter–dreaming books.

The World of Irises: Wichita, KS, American Iris Society, 1978. A very thorough treatment of a very popular group of plants, it should make all of the confusing categories clear.

All About Bulbs: Revised ed. San Francisco, Ortho Books, 1986. Color guide to growing bulbs, good cultural advice, broad coverage of "Dutch" and species bulbs.

Bulbs: How to Select, Grow and Enjoy: George H. Scott. Tucson, HP Books, 1982. A fine color–illustrated introduction to bulbs of all types and seasons.

The Bulb Book: A Photographic Guide to Over 800 Hardy Bulbs: Martin Rix and Roger Phillips. London, Pan Books, 1981. Good for identification of both plants and bulbs; mostly species bulbs.

Books on Miscellaneous Plants – *continued*

The Little Bulbs: Elizabeth Lawrence. Durham, NC, Duke University Press, 1986. Both a good read and good information on species bulbs, especially narcissus.

The Bromeliads: Victoria Padilla. New York, Crown, 1986. A good, well illustrated introduction.

Ferns to Know and Grow: F. Gordon Foster. 3rd ed. Portland, Timber Press, 1984. A practical guide to choosing and growing ferns in the home garden.

Fern Growers Manual: Barbara Joe Hoshizaki. New York, Knopf, 1975. Another fine book on ferns; practical advice.

Encyclopedia of Ferns: David L. Jones. Portland, Timber Press, 1987. Growing, propagation, disease control, good descriptions and color and black and white photos.

Vegetable, Herb & Fruit Growing

The Self–Sufficient Gardener: John Seymour. Garden City, NY, Doubleday, 1979. This is a book which has started a revolution among home gardeners – people were gardening organically, but he fanned the spark into flame with a popular book.

High–Yield Gardening: How to Get More From Your Garden Space and More From Your Garden Season: Marjorie B. Hunt and Brenda Bortz. Emmaus, PA, Rodale Press, 1986. A very practical guide, with sources and reading lists.

Gardening: The Complete Guide to Growing America's Favorite Fruits and Vegetables: National Gardening Association. Reading, MA, Addison–Wesley, 1986. Good introduction to the food garden.

How to Grow More Vegetables Than You Ever Thought Possible on Less Land Than You Can Imagine: John Jeavons. Rev. ed. Berkeley, Ten Speed Press, 1982. Good book on the bio–dynamic or French intensive method of organic growing, by a disciple of Alan Chadwick.

Register of New Fruit & Nut Varieties: Brooks & Olmo. Berkeley, Univ. of California Press, 1972. Suggested by a reader, varieties are "new" since 1920 – he says it's the best book on hardy fruit and nuts.

Citrus – How to Select, Grow, and Enjoy: Richard Ray and Lance Walheim. Tucson, HP Books, 1980. An informative and well illustrated book on growing all sorts of citrus, including unusual kinds.

All About Citrus & Subtropical Fruits: San Francisco, Ortho Books, 1985. A new book which covers citrus and other fruit for warmer climates.

Herb Gardening At Its Best: Sal Gilbertie & Larry Sheehan. New York, Atheneum/SMI, 1982. A nice introduction, interesting and well illustrated.

Herbs: Gardens, Decorations & Recipes: Emelie Tolley & Chris Mead. N.Y., Clarkson Potter, 1985. A very beautiful new book with many color photographs, showing herb garden design and plant selection, making decorations with herbs and using herbs in cooking. A real feast for the eyes – full of inspiration.

Rodale's Illustrated Encyclopedia of Herbs: C. Kowalchik and William H. Hylton, eds. Emmaus, PA, Rodale Press, 1987. Color photos and drawings; history, uses and cultivation, index of botanical names and medicinal uses, bibliography of books and newsletters.

Landscape History and Design

The Principles of Gardening: Hugh Johnson. New York, Simon & Schuster, 1979. This is one of my very favorite books – an all around discussion of gardening in all aspects, it will open your eyes to the "look" of a garden and everything that goes into making one. I wish he'd write more gardening books.

Visions of Paradise: Themes and Variations on the Garden: Marina Schinz. New York, Stewart, Tabori & Chang, 1985. A terrific companion to Hugh Johnson's book; a feast for the eye and the imagination.

The Education of a Gardener: Russell Page. New York, Random House, 1983. Again, not a how–to book, but a thoughtful discussion of making gardens by a master. It will repay reading many times over; my copy is heavily marked up so that I can find points which struck my fancy.

The Quest for Paradise: The History of the World's Gardens: Ronald King. New York, W.H. Smith Pubs., 1979. It is the best one–volume introduction to garden history that I have found, covering major gardens the world over, with good color illustrations.

The House of Boughs: Elizabeth Wilkinson & Marjorie Henderson. New York, Viking, 1985. A very interesting compendium of garden ornament in many periods and garden styles – well worth studying, especially for creating period gardens – full of ideas to trigger your creativity.

The Well Furnished Garden: Michael Balston. New York, Simon & Schuster, 1986. By a well known English landscape architect, not as exhaustive as the book above.

The Oxford Companion to Gardens: Geoffrey & Susan Jellicoe, Patrick Goode, Michael Lancaster. New York, Oxford University Press, 1986. An encyclopedic reference to garden history, design and ornament; European in emphasis.

The Garden Book: Designing, Creating and Maintaining Your Garden: John Brookes. New York, Crown, 1984. A very practical and interesting guide to achieving the garden effects you want, well illustrated with construction and planting details. See also his *The Small Garden* (New York, Macmillan, 1978), and *A Place in the Country* (London, Thames Hudson, 1984).

Gardens Are for People: Thomas Church. 2nd ed. New York, McGraw–Hill, 1983. A treatise on creating gardens by a celebrated California landscape architect, illustrated primarily with photographs of gardens he designed.

Nature's Design: A Practical Guide to Natural Landscaping: Carol A. Smyser. Emmaus, PA, Rodale Press, 1982. A practical guide to landscaping with native plants for a natural effect – full of how–tos.

Reader's Digest Practical Guide to Home Landscaping: Reader's Digest Association. Pleasantville, NY, 1972. The title tells it all, a practical and well illustrated book.

Herb Garden Design: Faith Swanson & Virginia Rady. Hanover, NH, University Press of New England, 1984. Full of plans and suggestions for planting herb gardens of all kinds and styles.

The Complete Book of Edible Landscaping: Rosaline Creasy. San Francisco, Sierra Club Books, 1982. An inspiring book, which makes you think twice about plant choices for your garden! She gives lots of information on mixing edibles with ornamentals and choosing the right edibles for your garden, with detailed information on the plants.

Designing and Maintaining Your Edible Landscape Naturally: Robert Kourik. Santa Rosa, CA, Metamorphic Press, 1986. Everything there is to know about growing vegetables and fruit to make your food garden attractive as well. More "nuts and bolts" than the book above.

Landscape History and Design – *continued*

Gardens By Design: Step–by–step Plans for 12 Imaginative Gardens: Peter Loewer. Emmaus, PA, Rodale Press, 1986. Practical advice, wonderful illustrations, good source lists.

Theme Gardens: Barbara Damrosch. New York, Workman, 1982. A charming book on creating small theme gardens, sixteen in all. With detailed planting suggestions for color and interest over several seasons.

Good Reads (This is not to say that many of the books above aren't!)

The Essential Earthman: Henry Mitchell on Gardening. Bloomington, Indiana University Press, 1981. My dream is to stroll around Henry Mitchell's garden – this book is so full of plant–love and humor that you'll want to start over again when you finish – he should be forced to publish an annual update. You have a feeling that he would not look down his nose at your efforts or dare to brag about his own!

Onward and Upward in the Garden: Katharine S. White. New York, Farrar, Strauss, Giroux, 1979. A book full of vinegary opinions, a super read, but if you don't live in New England, you'll get no sympathy from her!

Green Thoughts: A Writer in the Garden: Eleanor Perenyi. New York, Random House, 1981. Another New Englander, writing well about gardening – but honestly, it's possible to live and garden in mild climates – you don't have to freeze to be happy.

V. Sackville–West's Garden Book: New York, Atheneum, 1979. Excerpts from Vita Sackville–West's garden books and columns, organized by the months of the year. Her love of plants and ideas for plantings bubble out of the pages. A visit to Sissinghurst Castle proves that she knew her stuff.

The Illustrated Garden Book: A New Anthology. Robin Lane Fox, ed. New York, Atheneum, 1986. Mostly new excerpts from the London Observer garden columns of Vita Sackville–West. Nice illustrations, pictures of Sissinghurst Castle in all seasons.

Home Ground: A Gardener's Miscellany: Allen Lacy. New York, Ballentine, 1985. A collection of essays by one of our very best garden writers. See also his *Further Afield: A Gardener's Excursions* (Farrar, Straus & Giroux, 1986).

The Gardener's Year: Karel Capek. Madison, University of Wisconsin, 1984. Proof that gardening knows no boundaries, this little book written in Prague in the 1930's will make you laugh out loud – his wry observations are timeless.

Gertrude Jekyll on Gardening: Penelope Hobhouse. London, Collins, 1983. Do I have to admit that Jekyll puts me right to sleep? Apparently Hobhouse had the same problem, so she made excerpts of the books for readers like me.

Guides to Gardens

Handbook on American Gardens: A Traveler's Guide: Brooklyn, Brooklyn Botanical Garden, 1986. Newly revised, it gives concise coverage of gardens in the United States. It's #111 in the series Plants and Gardens.

A Traveler's Guide to North American Gardens: Harry Britton Logan. New York, Scribner's, 1974. Well illustrated in black and white, with good descriptions of gardens in the United States, Canada, Hawaii, Puerto Rico and the Virgin Islands. This book is dated, but gardens don't move around very much.

Gardens of North America and Hawaii: A Traveler's Guide: Irene & Walter Jacob. Beaverton, OR, Timber Press, 1986. Very useful, small enough to take with you on a trip; rates the gardens.

Collins Book of British Gardens: A Guide to 200 Gardens in England, Scotland & Wales: George Plumptre. London, Collins, 1985. Organized by region, then by county; black and white photos, regional maps, a page or two on each garden.

Guide to Herb Gardens: Herb Society of America. A guide to 480 herb gardens to visit in the U.S. and Canada. $3.75 ppd.

Plant Finding Source Books

Andersen Horticultural Library's Source List of Plants and Seeds: Completely indexes over 200 retail and wholesale catalogs, lists 20,000 plants by scientific name. Available in October 1987, $29.95 ppd. Minnesota Landscape Arboretum, Box 39, Chanhassen, MN, 55317. They hope to update it every two years.

Nursery Source Manual, A Handbook: Brooklyn, Brooklyn Botanic Garden, 1988. New edition in the works, will be available in mid–1988. Last edition listed 1,300 trees and shrubs with retail and wholesale sources.

Wonder Crops, 1986: Fultonville, NY, Natural Food Institute, 1986. Where to buy 200 fruits, nuts, grains and vegetables (mostly open–pollinated varieties). Send US$5 ($6 outside the U.S.) to Natural Food Institute, P. O. Box 606, Fultonville, NY 12072. I think it's published every year or two.

The Combined Rose List: Irvington NY, Beverly Dobson, annual. This is a tour–de–force: Beverly Dobson compiles a list every year of every species and hybrid rose cultivar listed by dozens of rose nurseries in the U.S., Canada and overseas. They are listed by cultivar name, with brief information on year of introduction, breeder, color of flower and where you can get it. You can't grow roses and not have it! Current issue is $10.00 ppd; write to 215 Harriman Road, Irvington NY 10533.

Longwood Gardens Plant and Seed Sources: Kennett Square, PA, Longwood Gardens, no date. Copyright date not given, but I think it's new in 1985. It lists mail–order sources for many of the plants grown in the Gardens, from trees to vegetables. Plants listed by botanical, common and cultivar names, with nursery sources; many hundreds of plants are listed. US$3.50 ppd; write to Longwood Gardens, Box 501, Kennett Square, PA 19348– 0501.

Selected California Native Plants With Commercial Sources: Saratoga Horticultural Foundation. Sources by plant, from both retail and wholesale nurseries. $4.65 ppd from SHF, 151 Murphy Ave., San Marcos, CA 95046.

Nursery Sources, Native Plants and Wild Flowers: Framingham, MA, New England Wild Flower Society, 1987. A list of wholesale and retail nurseries which specialize in native plants and wild flowers, listed by region, with notes as to plant and seed sources. US$3.50 ppd.

Sources of Native Seeds and Plants: Ankeny, IA, Soil and Water Conservation Society, 1987. A source book for plants to use in conservation and restoration work – native plants, grasses and trees, both seed and plants. Sources listed by state. US$3 ppd.

Graham Center Seed and Nursery Directory: Pittsboro, NC, Rural Advancement Fund, new edition due in 1988. They call it "a gardener's and farmer's guide to sources of traditional, old–timey vegetables, fruit and nut varieties, herbs and native plants." It lists sources by plant type, gives information on saving seed. Send a self–addressed stamped envelope for information: RAF, Box 1029, Pittsboro NC 27312.

Garden Seed Inventory: Kent Whealy. Decorah, IA, Seed Savers Exchange, new edition due in 1988. This is an amazing example of what computers can do in gardening – an inventory of hundreds of open–pollinated vegetables and sources for all of them, including a long list of seed companies and their specialties – it is terrific and must have taken forever. It will be US$15 ppd.

Plant Finding Source Books — *continued*

The Buyers Guide to Boxwood: American Boxwood Society. Boyce, VA, no date. A guide to retail, mail order and wholesale sources of boxwood, approximately 40 species and cultivars: a model for society plant source lists, indexed by cultivar and location of source. $3 ppd.

The Orchid Lover's Sales Directory & Guide to Regional Sources: Dody Ellenberger. A guide to mail order and retail sources of orchids and orchid supplies. Available from Twin Oaks Books, or from Ellenbergers Orchid Eden, 6764 Gillis Road, Victor, NY 14564. ($9.95 ppd)

Orchid Species Source Book III: Jim Spatzek. Haven't seen this one, recommended by Dody Ellenberger. It helps the orchid lover to locate 4,400 species orchids in 400 genera, from sources all over the world, with some information on importing for the collector. Revised edition due in 1988, available from Twin Oaks Books.

Herb Gardener's Resource Guide: Paula Oliver. 2nd ed. Five hundred sources of herbs, herb supplies and products, herb gardens and more. It's available from Northwind Farm, Rt. 2, Box 246, Shevlin, MN 56676. US$7.95 ppd, US$8.95 to Canada, US$10.95 to all other countries.

The Herb Directory: Shops and gardens to visit, plant and seed sources, festivals and workshops to attend. For information, send SASE to Diane Lea Mathews, Box 134, Salisbury Center, New York 13454.

The Reference Guide to Ornamental Plant Cultivars: Laurence Hatch. An inventory of cultivars of ornamental plants, with descriptions of the newer ones and nursery sources. The database will be constantly updated. Send SASE for information. Taxonomic Computer Research, P. O. Box 5747, Raleigh, NC, 27650.

Perennial Seed Exchange Directory: Perennial Seed Exchange. The Perennial Seed Exchange promotes exchange of seeds of trees, shrubs, vines, herbaceous perennials, alpines, wildflowers, seed grains and more. Send SASE for information to PSE, P. O. Box 1466, Chelan, WA 98816.

The American Association of Nurserymen has compiled a list of commercial plant locating services and state commercial nursery source publications; send a long SASE for their *Plant Locators* list.

* *

Well, that's more than 165 books on many facets of gardening, certainly not THE definitive list, but enough to get you started. By the time you're familiar with fifty garden books, no one will need to suggest more — you'll have books stacked everywhere waiting to be read! As space permits, I'll try to mention interesting new books which come my way in the quarterly updates.

One reader wrote to tell me that she was disabled and unable to physically work in a garden, but had become an avid "gardener of the imagination" through reading. I found this very touching but also very satisfying; so much of my pleasure also comes from the fun of reading and learning from books. I've had many letters from gardeners telling me they liked my book for its practical information; I'm very happy that I've found a friend who gardens happily in her mind. Truth to tell, our mind–gardens are always the most beautiful.

Indexes

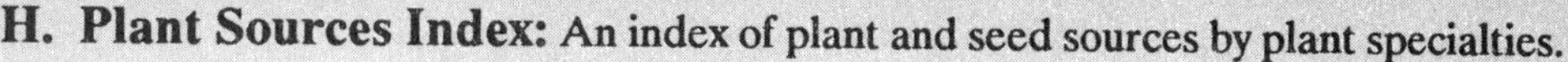

H. Plant Sources Index: An index of plant and seed sources by plant specialties.

J. Geographical Index: An index of plant and seed sources by location. United States and Canadian sources are listed by state or province. Overseas sources are listed by country. Within each primary location, sources are listed alphabetically by city or post office. Symbols indicate which sources have nurseries or shops and which sell by mail order only, if we have been given this information.

K. Product Sources Index: An index of suppliers and services listed by specialty. This index also includes plant and seed sources which offer products or services. Within categories, sources are listed by location, and a symbol indicates if they have a shop to visit.

L. Society Index: An index of horticultural societies listed by plants and/or other special interests.

M. Magazine Index: An index of magazines offered by societies as well as other horticultural and gardening magazines, newsletters and other occasional publications. If the magazine is issued by a society, a symbol indicates whether it is available to members only.

Notes on Indexing

Each plant source or supplier is indexed on up to eight specialties and/or trade names. When they didn't indicate which specialties they preferred, I have chosen for them from a study of their catalog. The companies vary from small to large, and their specialties from narrow to very broad.

For those with few specialties, the indexing is very specific, but as their offerings become greater, the indexing becomes broader. For example, a small nursery that offers only ivy would be listed under "Ivy", but a large nursery that includes ivy as one of its many offerings would be listed under "Groundcovers". Similarly, "Sundials" would be a specific category versus the more general "Garden Ornaments".

You should check both the specific category and the general category to be sure you find all possible sources.

The notes on catalogs in the alphabetical listings include some specialites which we were unable to index because each "listee" was limited to eight categories. To jog your memory, you could jot the company name into the index next to the appropriate category.

Table of the Symbols and Abbreviations Used in this Book
Appears Inside the Front and Back Covers and On the Bookmark

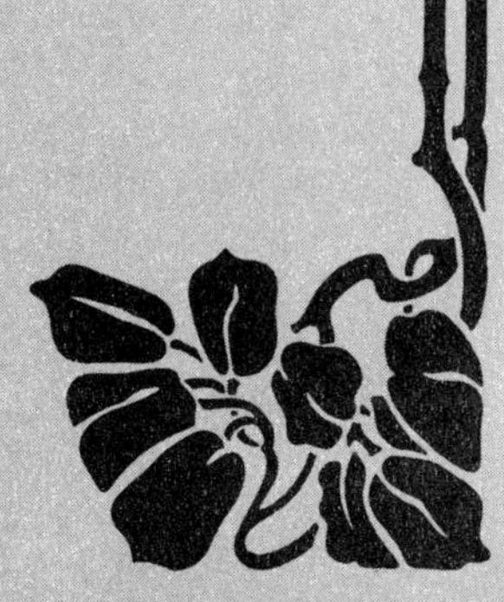

PAGE SOURCE

ACACIAS
A 13 Bushland Flora (Australian Seed Specialists)
A 17 Carter Seeds
A 19 Christa's Cactus
A 46 International Seed Supplies
A 67 Nindethana Seed Service

ACHIMENES
A 13 Buell's Greenhouse, Inc.
A 50 Karleens Achimenes
A 95 Tiki Nursery

AECHMEAS
A 21 Cornelison Bromeliads
A 24 Dane Company
A 88 Shelldance Nursery

AESCHYNANTHUS
A 63 Miree's Gesneriads
A 75 Plant Villa
A 75 Plants 'n' Things
A 75 Pleasant Hill African Violets
A 78 Rainwater Violets

AFRICAN VIOLET LEAVES
A 12 Elizabeth Buck African Violets
A 16 Cape Cod Violetry
A 16 Carol's Violets & Gifts
A 22 Country Girl Greenhouses
A 28 Essie's Violets
A 39 Growin'house
A 44 Hortense's African Violets
A 46 Innis Violets
A 49 JoS Violets
A 49 Judy's Violets
A 50 Kent's Flowers
A 56 Lloyd's African Violets
A 60 Marvelous Minis
A 62 Mighty Minis
A 73 Phipps African Violets
A 75 Plant Villa
A 75 Pleasant Hill African Violets
A 78 Rainwater Violets
A 79 Ray's African Violets
A 89 Skagit African Violets
A 93 Suni's Violets
A 97 Travis' Violets
A 100 The Violet Showcase
A 100 Violets Collectible
A 105 Wilson's Violet Haven
A 107 Zaca Vista Nursery

AFRICAN VIOLETS
A 2 Alice's Violet Room
A 13 Buell's Greenhouse, Inc.
A 16 Cape Cod Violetry
A 16 Carol's Violets & Gifts
A 22 Country Girl Greenhouses
A 24 Davidson-Wilson Greenhouses
A 30 Fischer Greenhouses
A 33 Lorine Friedrich
A 37 Green Mountain African Violets
A 44 Hortense's African Violets
A 46 Innis Violets
A 48 Jeannette's Jesneriads

PAGE SOURCE

AFRICAN VIOLETS
A 49 JoS Violets
A 49 Judy's Violets
A 50 Kartuz Greenhouses
A 50 Kent's Flowers
A 56 Lloyd's African Violets
A 57 Lyndon Lyon Greenhouses, Inc.
A 58 McKinney's Glasshouse
A 60 Marvelous Minis
A 60 Mary's African Violets
A 62 Mighty Minis
A 73 Phipps African Violets
A 74 Plant Factory
A 75 Plant Villa
A 75 Plants 'n' Things
A 78 Rainwater Violets
A 79 Ray's African Violets
A 89 Skagit African Violets
A 93 Suni's Violets
A 93 Sunshine Orchids International
A 95 Tiki Nursery
A 96 Tinari Greenhouses
A 96 Tomara African Violets
A 97 Travis' Violets
A 100 The Violet Showcase
A 100 Violets Collectible
A 101 Volkman Bros. Greenhouses
A 105 Wilson's Violet Haven
A 107 Zaca Vista Nursery

AGAPANTHUS
A 3 Amaryllis, Inc.
A 9 Bio-Quest International
A 26 Dunford Farms
A 98 TyTy Plantation

AGAVES
A 19 Christa's Cactus
A 51 Gerhard Koehres Cactus & Succulent Nursery
A 61 Mesa Garden
A 66 New Mexico Cactus Research
A 93 Sunnyvale Cactus Nursery

AJUGAS
A 77 Prentiss Court Ground Covers
A 94 Ter-El Nursery
A 98 Turnipseed Nursery Farms

ALLIUMS
A 13 Bundles of Bulbs
A 23 The Daffodil Mart
A 24 Peter De Jager Bulb Co.
A 39 Dr. Joseph C. Halinar
A 99 Van Engelen Inc.
A 99 Veldheer Tulip Gardens

ALOES
A 6 Atkinson's Greenhouse
A 14 Cactus by Mueller
A 25 Desert Theater
A 38 Grigsby Cactus Gardens
A 51 Gerhard Koehres Cactus & Succulent Nursery
A 59 Marilynn's Garden
A 61 Mesa Garden
A 72 The PanTree
(continued next page)

PAGE SOURCE

ALOES (continued)
A 98 Tucson Succulents

ALPINE PLANTS
See Also - Specific Plants
A 3 Alpenflora Gardens
A 3 Alpine Gardens & Calico Shop
A 3 Alpine Plants
A 15 Callahan Seeds
A 17 Chadwell Himalayan Seed
A 18 Chehalis Rare Plant Nursery
A 18 Chiltern Seeds
A 20 Colorado Alpines, Inc.
A 42 High Altitude Gardens
A 44 J. L. Hudson, Seedsman
A 48 Klaus R. Jelitto
A 52 P. Kohli & Co.
A 52 L. Kreeger
A 63 Mo's Greenhouse
A 64 Mountain West Seeds
A 71 Owl Ridge Alpines
A 78 Rakestraw's Perennial Gardens
A 80 Red's Rhodies & Alpine Gardens
A 81 Rice Creek Gardens
A 83 Jim & Irene Russ Quality Plants
A 86 Seedalp
A 89 Siskiyou Rare Plant Nursery
A 89 Skyline Nursery
A 90 Solar Green, Ltd.
A 90 Southern Seeds
A 91 Southwestern Native Seeds

ALSTROEMERIAS
A 3 Alpine Valley Gardens
A 6 B & D Lilies
A 26 Dunford Farms
A 38 Grianan Gardens

AMARANTH
A 36 Good Seed Co.
A 66 Native Seeds/SEARCH
A 75 Plants of the Southwest

AMARYLLIS
A 3 Amaryllis, Inc.
A 9 Bio-Quest International
A 23 The Daffodil Mart
A 24 Peter De Jager Bulb Co.
A 26 Dutch Gardens, Inc.
A 61 Messelaar Bulb Co.
A 78 Quality Dutch Bulbs

ANNUALS
A 2 Alberta Nurseries & Seed Company
A 2 Allen, Sterling & Lothrop
A 5 Applewood Seed Company
A 13 W. Atlee Burpee Company
A 13 D.V. Burrell Seed Growers Co.
A 13 Bushland Flora (Australian Seed Specialists)
A 14 The Butchart Gardens
A 17 Carter Seeds
A 18 Chiltern Seeds
A 20 Comstock, Ferre & Co.
A 22 The Country Garden
A 22 Crosman Seed Corp.
A 24 William Dam Seeds
A 24 Dan's Garden Shop
A 24 DeGiorgi Company, Inc.
A 26 Dominion Seed House
A 26 E & H Products
A 26 Early's Farm & Garden Centre, Inc.
A 28 F W H Seed Exchange
A 29 Fedco Seeds

PAGE SOURCE

ANNUALS
A 30 Henry Field Seed & Nursery Co.
A 32 The Fragrant Path
A 34 Gardenimport, Inc.
A 37 Greenleaf Seeds
A 38 Grianan Gardens
A 39 Gurney Seed & Nursery Co.
A 40 Harris Seeds
A 40 Hastings
A 44 J. L. Hudson, Seedsman
A 45 Ed Hume Seeds, Inc.
A 47 Island Seed Mail Order
A 48 Johnny's Selected Seeds
A 49 J. W. Jung Seed Co.
A 51 Kilgore Seed Company
A 53 D. Landreth Seed Company
A 54 Orol Ledden & Sons
A 56 Liberty Seed Company
A 58 McFayden Seeds
A 60 Earl May Seed & Nursery Co.
A 61 Meyer Seed Co.
A 64 Mountain Valley Seeds & Nursery
A 65 Nationwide Seed & Supply
A 65 Native Seeds, Inc.
A 67 Nindethana Seed Service
A 68 Northplan/Mountain Seed
A 71 Ozark National Seed Order
A 72 Park Seed Company, Inc.
A 74 Pinetree Garden Seeds
A 76 Pony Creek Nursery
A 79 Rawlinson Garden Seed
A 86 Seed Centre Ltd.
A 87 Seeds Blum
A 87 Seedway, Inc.
A 88 Shepherd's Garden Seeds
A 88 Siegers Seed Co.
A 91 Specialty Seeds
A 92 Stokes Seed Company
A 94 Sutton Seeds, Ltd.
A 94 T & T Seeds, Ltd.
A 95 Territorial Seed Co.
A 95 Thompson & Morgan
A 96 Tillinghast Seed Co.
A 97 Tregunno Seeds
A 98 Otis Twilley Seed Co.
A 100 Vermont Bean Seed Co.
A 100 Vesey's Seeds Ltd.
A 107 Wyatt-Quarles Seed Co.

ANTHURIUMS
A 28 Exotics Hawaii, Inc.
A 32 Fox Orchids, Inc.
A 59 Marilynn's Garden
A 98 Tropicals Unlimited

APPLES
A 1 Adams County Nursery, Inc.
A 5 Apple Hill Orchards
A 36 Golden Bough Tree Farm
A 48 Johnson Nursery
A 56 Long Hungry Creek Nursery
A 64 Moosebell Flower, Fruit & Tree Co.
A 82 Rocky Meadow Orchard & Nursery
A 84 St. Lawrence Nurseries
A 92 Stark Bro's Nurseries & Orchards Co.
A 99 VanWell Nursery, Inc.
A 106 Windy Ridge Nursery

APPLES, ANTIQUE
A 4 Ames' Orchard and Nursery
A 5 Apple Hill Orchards
A 5 Arbor & Espalier
A 8 Bear Creek Nursery
(continued next page)

SYMBOLS & ABBREVIATIONS USED IN THE LISTINGS

Name & Address		Current to the best of our knowledge. Use first address for letters and orders where two are given.
Telephone	**TO**	Accepts telephone orders: usually ships on payment.
	TO/CC	Telephone orders with credit cards.
	$0m	Minimum amount of telephone order.
Catalog	**$0**	Price of catalog.
	$0d	Price of catalog deductible from first order.
	IRC	International Reply Coupon(s): purchase at Post Office
	FCS	First Class Stamp(s)
	SASE	LONG self-addressed stamped envelope (9 1/2" or 24 cm).
	R &W	Business sells both retail and wholesale to the trade.
	MO	Business sells only by mail order.
	USA	Business ships to the U.S. from Canada.
	CAN	Business ships to Canada from the U.S.
	OV	Business ships Overseas FROM the U.S. or Canada, or TO the U.S. and Canada from Overseas
	SS:	Shipping season: followed by months when live orders are shipped.
	SS:W	Live orders are shipped when weather permits.
	AY	All year.
	$0m	Minimum mail order: shipping extra. Minimum orders for Overseas are usually higher.
	HYB	Nursery sells plants which they hybridize themselves.
	cn	Plants listed by common names.
	bn	Plants listed by botanical names.
	bn/cn	Plants are listed by botanical name, then by common name.
	cn/bn	Plants are listed by common name, with botanical name given.
Supply Index	**(R)**	Registered Trade Mark.
	(TM)	Trade Mark
Currencies	**US$**	United States dollars
	C$	Canadian Dollars
	IMO	International money order
	PC	Personal checks accepted (ask for amount before sending.

(See Introduction for information on other currencies and overseas payments).

Gardening by Mail 2: A Source Book

SYMBOLS & ABBREVIATIONS USED IN THE LISTINGS

Name & Address		Current to the best of our knowledge. Use first address for letters and orders where two are given.
Telephone	**TO**	Accepts telephone orders: usually ships on payment.
	TO/CC	Telephone orders with credit cards.
	$0m	Minimum amount of telephone order.
Catalog	**$0**	Price of catalog.
	$0d	Price of catalog deductible from first order.
	IRC	International Reply Coupon(s): purchase at Post Office
	FCS	First Class Stamp(s)
	SASE	LONG self-addressed stamped envelope (9 1/2" or 24 cm).
	R &W	Business sells both retail and wholesale to the trade.
	MO	Business sells only by mail order.
	USA	Business ships to the U.S. from Canada.
	CAN	Business ships to Canada from the U.S.
	OV	Business ships Overseas FROM the U.S. or Canada, or TO the U.S. and Canada from Overseas
	SS:	Shipping season: followed by months when live orders are shipped.
	SS:W	Live orders are shipped when weather permits.
	AY	All year.
	$0m	Minimum mail order: shipping extra. Minimum orders for Overseas are usually higher.
	HYB	Nursery sells plants which they hybridize themselves.
	cn	Plants listed by common names.
	bn	Plants listed by botanical names.
	bn/cn	Plants are listed by botanical name, then by common name.
	cn/bn	Plants are listed by common name, with botanical name given.
Supply Index	**(R)**	Registered Trade Mark.
	(TM)	Trade Mark
Currencies	**US$**	United States dollars
	C$	Canadian Dollars
	IMO	International money order
	PC	Personal checks accepted (ask for amount before sending.

(See Introduction for information on other currencies and overseas payments).

Gardening by Mail 2: A Source Book

Don't Forget to Send In Your Reader Feedback Form

Don't Forget to Send In Your Reader Feedback Form

PAGE SOURCE

APPLES, ANTIQUE (continued)
A 27 Edible Landscaping
A 33 Fruitwood Nursery
A 38 Greenmantle Nursery
A 54 Lawson's Nursery
A 56 Living Tree Centre
A 56 Long Hungry Creek Nursery
B 25 Pomona Book Exchange
A 90 Sonoma Antique Apple Nursery
A 91 Southmeadow Fruit Gardens
A 96 Tolowa Nursery

APPLES, ANTIQUE (SAMPLES TO TASTE)
A 5 Applesource
A 90 Sonoma Antique Apple Nursery

APPLES, LOW-CHILL
A 23 Cumberland Valley Nurseries, Inc.
A 47 Ison's Nursery
A 90 Sonoma Antique Apple Nursery
A 106 Womack Nursery Co.

APRICOTS
A 1 Adams County Nursery, Inc.
A 12 Buckley Nursery
A 23 Cumberland Valley Nurseries, Inc.
A 38 Grimo Nut Nursery
A 47 Ison's Nursery
A 56 Living Tree Centre

AQUATIC PLANTS
See Also - Bog Plants
See Also - Specific Plants
A 10 Kurt Bluemel, Inc.
A 19 Coastal Gardens & Nursery
A 27 Eco-Gardens
A 38 Griffey's Nursery
A 50 Kester's Wild Game Food Nurseries
A 54 Laurie's Garden
A 56 Lilypons Water Gardens
A 64 Moore Water Gardens
A 72 Paradise Water Gardens
A 84 Santa Barbara Water Gardens
A 85 S. Scherer & Sons
A 89 Slocum Water Gardens
A 95 Tilley's Nursery/The WaterWorks
A 97 William Tricker, Inc.
A 99 Van Ness Water Gardens
A 101 Water Lily World
A 102 Water Ways Nursery
A 102 Waterford Gardens
A 104 Wicklein's Aquatic Farm & Nursery, Inc.

AQUILEGIAS
A 9 Blackmore & Langdon
A 16 Canyon Creek Nursery
A 20 Colorado Alpines, Inc.
A 22 Cricklewood Nursery
A 22 Crownsville Nursery
A 32 The Fragrant Path
A 63 Montrose Nursery
A 86 Seedalp
A 87 Select Seeds
A 102 Weddle Native Gardens, Inc.

AROIDS
A 28 Exotics Hawaii, Inc.
A 32 Fox Orchids, Inc.
A 41 Heliconia Haus
A 59 Ann Mann's Orchids
A 90 Southern Exposure

PAGE SOURCE

ASPARAGUS
A 1 Ahrens Strawberry Nursery
A 2 Allen Company
A 10 Blue Star Lab
A 12 Brittingham Plant Farms
A 48 Jackson & Perkins Co.
A 52 Krohne Plant Farms
A 53 D. Landreth Seed Company
A 63 Mo's Greenhouse
A 68 Nourse Farms, Inc.
A 79 Rayner Bros.
A 81 Rider Nurseries

ASTILBES
A 14 Busse Gardens
A 30 Flora Favours

AVOCADOS
A 15 California Nursery Co.
A 90 South Seas Nursery

AZALEAS, DECIDUOUS
A 16 Carlson's Gardens
A 23 The Cummins Garden
A 31 Flora Lan Nursery
A 39 Hager Nurseries, Inc.
A 40 Harstine Island Nursery
A 44 Horsley Rhododendron Nursery
A 83 Roslyn Nursery
A 95 Thomasville Nurseries
A 97 Transplant Nursery
A 103 Westgate Garden Nursery
A 104 Whitney Gardens

AZALEAS, EVERGREEN
A 15 Camellia Forest Nursery
A 16 Carlson's Gardens
A 23 The Cummins Garden
A 31 Flora Lan Nursery
A 37 The Greenery
A 39 Hager Nurseries, Inc.
A 40 Harstine Island Nursery
A 41 Marc Henny Nursery
A 43 Holly Hills, Inc.
A 44 Hortica Gardens
A 59 Magnolia Nursery & Display Garden
A 66 E. B. Nauman, Nurseryman
A 83 Roslyn Nursery
A 92 Stubbs Shrubs
A 95 Thomasville Nurseries
A 97 Transplant Nursery
A 101 Washington Evergreen Nursery
A 103 Westgate Garden Nursery
A 104 Whitney Gardens
A 107 Yucca Do Nursery

AZALEAS, HYBRIDS
A 5 Appalachian Gardens
A 11 The Bovees Nursery
A 16 Carlson's Gardens
A 18 Chambers Nursery
A 22 Crownsville Nursery
A 34 Louis Gerardi Nursery
A 38 Greer Gardens
A 39 Hager Nurseries, Inc.
A 40 Hass Nursery
A 42 Hillhouse Nursery
A 43 Holly Hills, Inc.
A 44 Horsley Rhododendron Nursery
A 49 Justice Gardens
A 68 Nuccio's Nurseries
A 90 Sonoma Horticultural Nursery
A 95 Thomasville Nurseries
(continued next page)

PAGE SOURCE

AZALEAS, HYBRIDS (continued)
A 97 Transplant Nursery
A 104 Whitney Gardens
B 33 Winterthur Museum & Gardens

AZALEAS, SPECIES
A 11 The Bovees Nursery
A 15 Camellia Forest Nursery
A 16 Carlson's Gardens
A 25 Bill Dodd's Rare Plants
A 39 Hager Nurseries, Inc.
A 39 Hall Rhododendrons
A 43 Holly Hills, Inc.
A 53 Lamtree Farm
A 57 The Lowrey Nursery
A 59 Magnolia Nursery & Display Garden
A 68 Northwest Biological Enterprises
A 86 F. W. Schumacher Co.
A 90 Sonoma Horticultural Nursery
A 97 Transplant Nursery
A 104 Whitney Gardens
A 106 Woodlanders, Inc.
A 107 Yucca Do Nursery

BAMBOOS
A 7 A Bamboo Shoot
A 7 Bamboo Sourcery
A 10 Kurt Bluemel, Inc.
A 15 California Nursery Co.
A 27 Endangered Species
A 34 The Garden Source, Ltd.
A 34 Garden World
A 35 Glasshouse Works
A 57 Louisiana Nursery
A 72 Panda Products
A 93 Sunset Nursery, Inc.
A 96 Tradewinds Nursery
A 98 Upper Bank Nurseries

BAMBOOS, HARDY
A 4 American Bamboo Company
A 7 A Bamboo Shoot
A 7 Bamboo Sourcery
A 10 Kurt Bluemel, Inc.
A 20 Colvos Creek Nursery & Landscaping
A 72 Panda Products
A 79 Steve Ray's Bamboo Gardens
A 93 Sunset Nursery, Inc.
A 96 Tradewinds Nursery
A 97 Tripple Brook Farm
A 98 Upper Bank Nurseries

BANANAS
A 7 The Banana Tree
A 34 Garden World
A 44 C. W. Hosking - Exotic Seed Importer
A 55 W. O. Lessard Nursery
A 78 Quality Cactus

BANKSIAS
A 13 Bushland Flora (Australian Seed Specialists)
A 14 C 'n C Protea
A 44 C. W. Hosking - Exotic Seed Importer
A 46 International Seed Supplies
A 67 Nindethana Seed Service
A 70 D. Orriell - Seed Exporters
A 77 Protea Farms of California
A 77 Protea Seed & Nursery Suppliers

BEANS
A 22 Cross Seed Company
A 29 Fern Hill Farm
A 62 Midwest Seed Growers, Inc.

PAGE SOURCE

BEANS
A 62 Miller-Bowie County Farmers Assn.
A 64 Mountain Valley Seeds & Nursery
A 66 Native Seeds/SEARCH
A 100 Vermont Bean Seed Co.
A 105 Willhite Seed Co.

BEE PLANTS
A 1 Abundant Life Seed Foundation
A 8 Bee Rock Herb Farm
A 18 John Chambers
A 20 Companion Plants
A 32 Fox Hill Farm
A 39 Halcyon Gardens
A 41 The Herbfarm
A 79 Rasland Farm
A 84 Sandy Mush Herb Nursery
A 94 Taylor's Herb Gardens

BEECHES
A 45 Hughes Nursery
A 52 Michael & Janet Kristick
A 104 Whitman Farms

BEGONIAS
A 4 Antonelli Brothers
A 6 Atkinson's Greenhouse
A 9 Blackmore & Langdon
A 11 Breck's
A 23 C. A. Cruickshank, Ltd.
A 26 Dutch Gardens, Inc.
A 27 Edelweiss Gardens
A 29 Fairyland Begonia & Lily Garden
A 33 G & G Gardens and Growers
A 39 Robert B. Hamm
A 46 International Growers Exchange
A 50 Kartuz Greenhouses
A 54 Lauray of Salisbury
A 56 Logee's Greenhouses
A 57 Paul P. Lowe
A 60 Marvelous Minis
A 63 Miree's Gesneriads
A 64 Moose Tubers
A 74 Plant Factory
A 74 The Plant Kingdom
A 75 Plants 'n' Things
A 85 John Scheepers, Inc.
A 95 Tiki Nursery
A 99 K. Van Bourgondien & Sons, Inc.
A 105 Wilson's Greenhouse

BERBERBIS
A 101 Washington Evergreen Nursery

BERBERIS
A 102 Wavecrest Nursery & Landscaping Co.

BERRIES, MIXED
A 4 Ames' Orchard and Nursery
A 7 Vernon Barnes & Son Nursery
A 8 Bear Creek Nursery
A 11 Boston Mountain Nurseries
A 26 Dominion Seed House
A 29 Farmer Seed & Nursery
A 31 Dean Foster Nurseries
A 32 Fowler Nurseries, Inc.
A 40 Harmony Farm Supply
A 40 Hastings
A 48 Johnson Nursery
A 49 J. W. Jung Seed Co.
A 50 Kelly Nurseries of Dansville, Inc.
A 52 Krider Nurseries
A 55 Henry Leuthardt Nurseries, Inc.
(continued next page)

PAGE SOURCE

BERRIES, MIXED (continued)
A 58 McConnell Nurseries, Inc.
A 62 J. E. Miller Nurseries, Inc.
A 63 Mo's Greenhouse
A 64 Morden Nurseries, Ltd
A 65 Native Seed Foundation
A 71 Richard Owen Nursery
A 71 Pacific Berry Works
A 71 Pacific Tree Farms
A 76 Pony Creek Nursery
A 78 Raintree Nursery
A 79 Rayner Bros.
A 85 Savage Farms Nursery
A 92 Stark Bro's Nurseries & Orchards Co.
A 94 T & T Seeds, Ltd.
A 96 Tillinghast Seed Co.

BILLBERGIAS
A 21 Cornelison Bromeliads
A 24 Dane Company
A 27 Edelweiss Gardens
A 88 Shelldance Nursery

BLACKBERRIES
A 1 Ahrens Strawberry Nursery
A 2 Allen Company
A 12 Brittingham Plant Farms
A 12 Buckley Nursery
A 47 Ison's Nursery
A 59 Makielski Berry Farm & Nursery
A 64 Mt. Leo Nursery
A 68 Nourse Farms, Inc.
A 79 Rayner Bros.
A 106 Womack Nursery Co.

BLUEBERRIES, HARDY
A 2 Allen Company
A 10 Blue Star Lab
A 10 Blueberry Hill
A 12 Brittingham Plant Farms
A 27 Edible Landscaping
A 40 Hartmann's Plantation, Inc.
A 42 Highlander Nursery
A 59 Makielski Berry Farm & Nursery
A 79 Rayner Bros.
A 84 St. Lawrence Nurseries

BLUEBERRIES, RABBITEYE (LOW-CHILL)
A 40 Hartmann's Plantation, Inc.
A 42 Highlander Nursery
A 47 Ison's Nursery
A 54 Lawson's Nursery

BOG PLANTS
See Also - Aquatic Plants
A 4 American Daylily & Perennials
A 54 Lee's Botanical Gardens
A 56 Lilypons Water Gardens
A 56 Little Valley Farm
A 64 Moore Water Gardens
A 67 Niche Gardens
A 69 Orchid Gardens
A 73 Peter Pauls Nurseries
A 77 Prairie Ridge Nursery/CRM Ecosystems, Inc.
A 81 Rice Creek Gardens
A 84 Santa Barbara Water Gardens
A 89 Slocum Water Gardens
A 95 Tilley's Nursery/The WaterWorks
A 97 William Tricker, Inc.
A 97 Tripple Brook Farm
A 99 Van Ness Water Gardens
A 101 Water Lily World
A 102 Waterford Gardens

PAGE SOURCE

BOG PLANTS
A 104 Wicklein's Aquatic Farm & Nursery, Inc.

BONSAI, FINISHED
B 4 Bonsai Creations
A 12 Brussel's Bonsai Nursery
A 19 Clargreen Gardens Ltd.
A 34 The Garden Source, Ltd.
A 34 Garden World
A 60 Matsu-Momiji Nursery
A 63 Miniature Plant Kingdom
A 87 Shanti Bithi Nursery

BONSAI, PLANTS FOR
See Also - Specific Plants
A 6 Artistic Plants
B 4 Bonsai Associates, Inc.
B 4 Bonsai Creations
A 10 Bonsai Farm
A 12 Brussel's Bonsai Nursery
A 15 Camellia Forest Nursery
A 19 Coenosium Gardens
A 25 Del's Japanese Maples
A 32 Foxborough Nursery
A 34 The Garden Source, Ltd.
A 35 Girard Nurseries
A 35 Glasshouse Works
A 36 Golden Bough Tree Farm
A 38 Greenlife Gardens Greenhouses
A 44 Hortica Gardens
A 52 Michael & Janet Kristick
A 57 Loucks Nursery
A 59 Maplewood Seed Company
A 60 Matsu-Momiji Nursery
A 63 Miniature Plant Kingdom
A 71 Owen Farms
A 74 The Plant Kingdom
A 78 Rakestraw's Perennial Gardens
A 90 Southern Seeds
A 91 Stallings Exotic Nursery
A 97 Trans Pacific Nursery
A 97 Transplant Nursery
A 104 Wildwood Gardens

BOOJUM
A 10 Boojum Unlimited

BOUGAINVILLEA
A 24 Davidson-Wilson Greenhouses
A 34 Garden World
A 37 Green Plant Research
A 40 Hatten's Nursery
A 76 The Plumeria People
A 78 Rainforest Plantes et Fleurs, Inc.

BOX
A 17 Carroll Gardens
A 23 The Cummins Garden
A 24 Daystar
A 44 Hortica Gardens
A 101 Washington Evergreen Nursery

BROMELIADS
See Also - Specific Plants
A 2 Alberts & Merkel Bros., Inc.
A 10 Arthur Boe Distributor
A 21 Cornelison Bromeliads
A 24 Dane Company
A 27 Edelweiss Gardens
A 31 Fort Caroline Orchids
A 32 Fox Orchids, Inc.
A 43 Jerry Horne - Rare Plants
A 57 Paul P. Lowe
(continued next page)

PAGE SOURCE

BROMELIADS (continued)
A 59 Ann Mann's Orchids
A 59 Marilynn's Garden
A 68 Oak Hill Gardens
A 69 The Orchid Center
A 78 Quality Cactus
A 78 Rainforest Flora, Inc.
A 86 Seaborn Del Dios Nursery
A 88 Shelldance Nursery
A 90 Southern Exposure
A 101 W. K. Quality Bromeliads
A 107 Guy Wrinkle Exotic Plants

BUCKWHEAT
A 22 Cross Seed Company
A 64 Moose Tubers
A 77 Prairie State Commodities

BULBS, DUTCH
See Also - Specific Plants
A 3 Amaryllis, Inc.
A 7 Bakker of Holland
A 11 Breck's
A 13 Bundles of Bulbs
A 23 The Daffodil Mart
A 24 Peter De Jager Bulb Co.
A 26 Dutch Gardens, Inc.
A 34 Gardenimport, Inc.
A 34 Gary's Perennials
A 46 International Growers Exchange
A 46 Inter-State Nurseries
A 49 J. W. Jung Seed Co.
A 50 Kelly Nurseries of Dansville, Inc.
A 58 McClure & Zimmerman
A 58 McConnell Nurseries, Inc.
A 58 McFayden Seeds
A 60 Earl May Seed & Nursery Co.
A 61 Messelaar Bulb Co.
A 61 Michigan Bulb Co.
A 74 Pinetree Garden Seeds
A 78 Quality Dutch Bulbs
A 85 John Scheepers, Inc.
A 96 Tillinghast Seed Co.
A 99 K. Van Bourgondien & Sons, Inc.
A 99 Van Engelen Inc.
A 99 Vandenberg
A 99 Veldheer Tulip Gardens
A 102 Wayside Gardens
A 103 White Flower Farm

BULBS, SPECIES
See Also - Specific Plants
A 9 Bio-Quest International
A 13 Bundles of Bulbs
A 16 Cape Seed & Bulb
A 17 Chadwell Himalayan Seed
A 20 Conley's Garden Center
A 22 The Country Garden
A 22 Cricklewood Nursery
A 23 The Daffodil Mart
A 36 Russell Graham, Purveyor of Plants
A 38 Griffey's Nursery
A 43 Holbrook Farm & Nursery
A 46 International Growers Exchange
A 57 John D. Lyon, Inc.
A 58 McClure & Zimmerman
A 61 Messelaar Bulb Co.
A 81 Robinett Bulb Farm
A 83 Rust-En-Vrede Nursery
A 89 Anthony J. Skittone
A 99 K. Van Bourgondien & Sons, Inc.
A 105 Nancy Wilson Species & Miniature Narcissus
A 107 Guy Wrinkle Exotic Plants

PAGE SOURCE

BULBS, SUMMER BLOOMING
See Also - Specific Plants
A 9 Bio-Quest International
A 11 Breck's
A 17 Carroll Gardens
A 23 C. A. Cruickshank, Ltd.
A 26 Dominion Seed House
A 26 Dutch Gardens, Inc.
A 29 Fairyland Begonia & Lily Garden
A 30 Flad's Glads
A 34 Gardenimport, Inc.
A 35 Gladside Gardens
A 46 International Growers Exchange
A 51 Kinder Canna Farm
A 52 Kordonowy's Dahlias
A 58 McClure & Zimmerman
A 61 Meyer Seed Co.
A 64 Moose Tubers
A 72 Park Seed Company, Inc.
A 85 John Scheepers, Inc.
A 89 Anthony J. Skittone
A 91 Spring Hill Nurseries Co.
A 94 T & T Seeds, Ltd.
A 98 TyTy Plantation
A 99 K. Van Bourgondien & Sons, Inc.
A 101 Mary Walker Bulb Company
A 102 The Waushara Gardens
A 102 Wayside Gardens
A 105 Nancy Wilson Species & Miniature Narcissus

BULBS, TENDER
See Also - Specific Plants
A 9 Bio-Quest International
A 23 The Daffodil Mart
A 35 Gladside Gardens
A 76 The Plumeria People
A 77 Protea Farms of California
A 99 K. Van Bourgondien & Sons, Inc.
A 101 Mary Walker Bulb Company
A 105 Nancy Wilson Species & Miniature Narcissus

BUTTERNUTS
A 29 Fernald's Hickory Hill Nursery
A 38 Grimo Nut Nursery
A 67 Nolin River Nut Tree Nursery
A 83 Saginaw Valley Nut Nursery

CACTUS
See Also - Specific Plants
A 1 Abbey Gardens
A 3 Altman Specialty Plants
A 6 Atkinson's Greenhouse
A 6 Aztekakti/Desertland Nursery
A 6 B & T Associates
A 9 Bentley's Botanical Gardens
A 10 Boojum Unlimited
A 14 Cactus by Dodie
A 14 Cactus by Mueller
A 14 Cactus Gem Nursery
A 25 Desert Theater
A 38 Grigsby Cactus Gardens
A 49 K & L Cactus Nursery
A 51 Gerhard Koehres Cactus & Succulent Nursery
A 54 Lauray of Salisbury
A 60 Marvin's Cactus
A 61 Merry Gardens
A 61 Mesa Flora Nursery
A 61 Mesa Garden
A 66 New Mexico Cactus Research
A 66 New Mexico Desert Garden
A 78 Quality Cactus
A 78 Rainman Succulent Nursery
A 80 Redlo Cacti
(continued next page)

PAGE SOURCE

CACTUS (continued)
A 82 Rocky Waters Farm
A 84 Sand Ridge Greenhouse
A 86 Schulz Cactus Gardens
A 88 Shein's Cactus
A 91 Southwest Seeds
A 95 Thompson & Morgan
A 98 Tucson Succulents
A 107 Roy Young, Seedsman

CACTUS, WINTER HARDY
See Also - Specific Plants
A 6 Aztekakti/Desertland Nursery
A 9 Bernardo Beach Native Plant Farm
A 9 Bisnaga Cactus Nursery
A 14 The Cactus Patch
A 19 Christa's Cactus
A 20 Colvos Creek Nursery & Landscaping
A 25 Desert Nursery
A 46 Intermountain Cactus
A 51 Gerhard Koehres Cactus & Succulent Nursery
A 60 Marvin's Cactus
A 62 Midwest Cactus
A 64 Mountain West Seeds
A 93 Sunnyvale Cactus Nursery
A 106 Winter Country Cacti
A 107 Y. O. Ranch Cactus Co.

CALADIUMS
A 15 Caladium World
A 93 Sunshine Caladium Farms
A 98 TyTy Plantation

CALLA LILIES
A 29 Fairyland Begonia & Lily Garden

CALLICARPAS
A 95 Terrapin Springs Farm

CALLUNAS
A 41 Heaths and Heathers

CAMELLIAS
A 9 Belle Fontaine Nursery
A 11 The Bovees Nursery
A 15 Camellia Forest Nursery
A 31 Flora Lan Nursery
A 58 Ma-Dot-Cha Hobby Nursery
A 59 Magnolia Nursery & Display Garden
A 68 Nuccio's Nurseries

CAMPANULAS
A 3 Alpina Research & Montane Garden
A 16 Canyon Creek Nursery
A 29 Far North Gardens
A 30 Flora Favours
A 38 Grianan Gardens
A 48 Klaus R. Jelitto
A 71 Owl Ridge Alpines
A 81 Rice Creek Gardens
A 86 Seedalp
A 87 Select Seeds
A 89 Skyline Nursery
A 90 Solar Green, Ltd.

CANNAS
A 4 American Daylily & Perennials
A 35 Gladside Gardens
A 51 Kinder Canna Farm
A 101 Mary Walker Bulb Company
A 102 The Waushara Gardens
A 107 Wright Iris Nursery

PAGE SOURCE

CANTALOUPES
A 13 D.V. Burrell Seed Growers Co.

CARNATIONS
A 2 Allwood Bros. (Hassocks) Ltd.
A 22 The Country Garden
A 93 Sunnyslope Gardens

CARNIVOROUS PLANTS
See Also - Specific Plants
A 2 Arthur Eames Allgrove
A 5 Armstrong Roses
A 9 Black Copper Kits
A 17 Cedar Ridge Nurseries
A 35 Glasshouse Works
A 43 Jerry Horne - Rare Plants
A 45 Hungry Plants
A 54 Lee's Botanical Gardens
A 70 Orgel's Orchids
A 73 Peter Pauls Nurseries
A 91 Southwest Seeds
A 106 World Insectivorous Plants

CAUDICIFORMS
A 1 Abbey Gardens
A 4 Anything Grows Greenhouse
A 6 Artistic Plants
A 14 Cactus by Mueller
A 19 Christa's Cactus
A 60 Marvin's Cactus
A 80 Redlo Cacti
A 89 Singers' Growing Things
A 93 Succulenta
A 98 Tucson Succulents
A 107 Guy Wrinkle Exotic Plants
A 107 Y. O. Ranch Cactus Co.

CHERIMOYAS
A 33 Garden of Delights
A 90 South Seas Nursery

CHERRIES
A 1 Adams County Nursery, Inc.
A 12 Buckley Nursery
A 23 Cumberland Valley Nurseries, Inc.

CHESTNUTS, HYBRID
A 8 Bear Creek Nursery
A 13 Burnt Ridge Nursery
A 18 Chestnut Hill Nursery, Inc.
A 18 Chestnuts a Reality
A 32 Fowler Nurseries, Inc.
A 36 John H. Gordon, Jr., Grower
A 38 Greenmantle Nursery
A 38 Grimo Nut Nursery
A 67 Nolin River Nut Tree Nursery
A 69 Oikos
A 83 Saginaw Valley Nut Nursery
A 89 Skyblue Nurseries
A 105 Wiley's Nut Grove

CHRISTMAS TREES, LIVING
A 12 Brookfield Nursery & Tree Plantation

CHRYSANTHEMUMS
A 10 Bluestone Perennials
A 26 Dooley Gardens
A 30 Fleming's Flower Fields
A 40 Hauser's Superior View Farm
A 44 Huff's Garden Mums
A 51 King's Mums
A 64 Mums by Paschke
A 93 Sunnyslope Gardens

(continued next page)

PAGE SOURCE

CHRYSANTHEMUMS (continued)
A 101 Wanda's Hide-a-Way

CITRUS
A 15 California Nursery Co.
A 34 Garden World
A 78 Raintree Nursery

CITRUS, DWARF
A 32 Four Winds Growers
A 40 Harmony Farm Supply

CLEMATIS
A 17 Carroll Gardens
A 19 Clifford's Perennial & Vine
A 32 The Fragrant Path
A 72 Park Seed Company, Inc.
A 90 Southern Seeds

COLCHICUMS
A 57 John D. Lyon, Inc.

COLEUS
A 20 Color Farm Growers

COLUMNEAS
A 33 Lorine Friedrich
A 57 Lyndon Lyon Greenhouses, Inc.
A 63 Miree's Gesneriads
A 75 Plant Villa
A 75 Pleasant Hill African Violets
A 78 Rainwater Violets
A 93 Sunshine Orchids International
A 100 The Violet Showcase

CONIFERS
A 5 Appalachian Gardens
A 15 Callahan Seeds
A 15 Camellia Forest Nursery
A 17 Carter Seeds
A 17 Cascade Forestry Service
A 18 Chiltern Seeds
A 19 Coenosium Gardens
A 31 Forestfarm
A 33 Frosty Hollow Nursery
A 35 Girard Nurseries
A 36 Golden Bough Tree Farm
A 43 Honeywood Lilies
A 44 Hortico, Inc.
A 52 V. Kraus Nurseries, Ltd.
A 52 Michael & Janet Kristick
A 58 McConnell Nurseries, Inc.
A 59 Maplethorpe
A 64 Mt. Leo Nursery
A 65 Musser Forests Inc.
A 65 Native Seed Foundation
A 68 Northwest Biological Enterprises
A 71 Pacific Tree Farms
A 80 Recor Tree Seed
A 86 F. W. Schumacher Co.
A 88 Silvaseed Company, Inc.
A 106 Woodland Nurseries

CONIFERS, DWARF
A 15 Camellia Forest Nursery
A 19 Coenosium Gardens
A 23 The Cummins Garden
A 24 Daystar
A 26 Eastern Plant Specialties
A 32 Foxborough Nursery
A 35 Girard Nurseries
A 36 Grand Ridge Nursery
A 40 Harstine Island Nursery

PAGE SOURCE

CONIFERS, DWARF
A 43 Holly Hills, Inc.
A 44 Hortica Gardens
A 46 Iris Country
A 52 Michael & Janet Kristick
A 60 Matsu-Momiji Nursery
A 63 Miniature Plant Kingdom
A 76 Powell's Gardens
A 78 Rakestraw's Perennial Gardens
A 81 Rice Creek Gardens
A 82 Rocknoll Nursery
A 83 Roslyn Nursery
A 89 Siskiyou Rare Plant Nursery
A 92 Stonehurst Rare Plants
A 94 The Sweetbriar
A 100 Vineland Nurseries
A 101 Washington Evergreen Nursery
A 104 Wildwood Gardens
A 107 Yucca Do Nursery

CONIFERS, SEEDLING
A 16 Carino Nurseries
A 19 Cold Stream Farm
A 30 Flickingers' Nursery
A 37 Greener 'N' Ever Tree Farm & Nursery
A 39 Hanchar Nursery
A 53 Lamtree Farm
A 54 Lawyer Nursery, Inc.
A 64 Mountain Mist Nursery
A 65 Musser Forests Inc.
A 77 Qualitree Nursery
A 79 Rayner Bros.
A 88 Silvaseed Company, Inc.

CORN
A 22 Cross Seed Company
A 43 Horizon Seeds
A 46 Illinois Foundation Seeds, Inc.
A 56 Liberty Seed Company
A 62 Midwest Seed Growers, Inc.
A 64 Mountain Valley Seeds & Nursery
A 77 Prairie State Commodities
A 83 Rupp Seeds, Inc.
A 83 SPB Sales
A 87 Seedway, Inc.
A 88 Shissler Seed Company
A 105 Willhite Seed Co.

CORN, HEIRLOOM
A 3 Alston Seed Growers
A 21 Corns
A 36 Good Seed Co.
A 66 Native Seeds/SEARCH
A 88 R. H. Shumway Seedsman

CORYPHANTHAS
A 14 The Cactus Patch
A 84 Sand Ridge Greenhouse
A 86 Schulz Cactus Gardens
A 88 Shein's Cactus

CRABAPPLES
A 64 Moosebell Flower, Fruit & Tree Co.
A 64 Morden Nurseries, Ltd
A 64 Mountain Mist Nursery
A 86 F. W. Schumacher Co.
A 102 Wavecrest Nursery & Landscaping Co.

CRANBERRIES
A 84 St. Lawrence Nurseries

CRAPE MYRTLES, DWARF
A 5 Appalachian Gardens
(continued next page)

PAGE SOURCE

CRAPE MYRTLES, DWARF (continued)
A 30 Fleming's Flower Fields
A 38 Greenlife Gardens Greenhouses
A 49 Justice Gardens

CRASSULAS
A 38 Greenlife Gardens Greenhouses
A 72 Parsley's Cape Seeds
A 80 Redlo Cacti

CRINUMS
A 35 Gladside Gardens
A 101 Mary Walker Bulb Company

CROCUS
A 7 Bakker of Holland
A 34 Gary's Perennials
A 57 John D. Lyon, Inc.
A 61 Messelaar Bulb Co.
A 99 Van Engelen Inc.

CROWN VETCH
A 28 Ernst Crownvetch Farms
A 53 Lakeland Nursery Sales

CRYPTANTHUS
A 21 Cornelison Bromeliads
A 24 Dane Company
A 69 The Orchid Center
A 90 Southern Exposure

CURRANTS
A 59 Makielski Berry Farm & Nursery
A 64 Moosebell Flower, Fruit & Tree Co.
A 104 Whitman Farms
A 106 Windy Ridge Nursery

CYCADS
See Also - Specific Plants
A 23 Cycad Gardens
A 27 Endangered Species
A 43 Jerry Horne - Rare Plants
A 44 C. W. Hosking - Exotic Seed Importer
A 70 D. Orriell - Seed Exporters
A 78 Quality Cactus
A 78 Rainforest Flora, Inc.
A 80 Rhapis Gardens
A 107 Guy Wrinkle Exotic Plants

CYCLAMEN, HARDY
A 29 Far North Gardens
A 36 Russell Graham, Purveyor of Plants
A 63 Montrose Nursery

DABOECIAS
A 41 Heaths and Heathers

DAFFODILS
A 7 Bakker of Holland
A 10 Borbeleta Gardens
A 11 Breck's
A 13 Bundles of Bulbs
A 20 Comanche Acres Iris Gardens
A 21 Cooper's Garden
A 23 The Daffodil Mart
A 24 Peter De Jager Bulb Co.
A 26 Dutch Gardens, Inc.
A 34 Gary's Perennials
A 36 Russell Graham, Purveyor of Plants
A 57 John D. Lyon, Inc.
A 58 McClure & Zimmerman
A 60 Maxim's Greenwood Gardens
A 61 Messelaar Bulb Co.

PAGE SOURCE

DAFFODILS
A 62 Miller's Manor Gardens
A 63 Grant Mitsch Novelty Daffodils
A 69 Oakwood Daffodils
A 78 Quality Dutch Bulbs
A 79 Reath's Nursery
A 99 K. Van Bourgondien & Sons, Inc.
A 99 Van Engelen Inc.
A 99 Vandenberg
A 99 Veldheer Tulip Gardens
A 105 Nancy Wilson Species & Miniature Narcissus

DAHLIAS
A 3 Alpen Gardens
A 9 Blue Dahlia Gardens
A 11 Breck's
A 20 Connell's Dahlias
A 23 C. A. Cruickshank, Ltd.
A 23 Dahlias by Phil Traff
A 26 Dutch Gardens, Inc.
A 34 Garden Valley Dahlias
A 35 Gladside Gardens
A 43 Hookland's Dahlias
A 45 Ed Hume Seeds, Inc.
A 46 International Growers Exchange
A 48 Jasperson's Hersey Nursery
A 52 Kordonowy's Dahlias
A 55 Legg Dahlia Gardens
A 67 Nicholls Gardens
A 80 Red Barn Dahlias
A 85 John Scheepers, Inc.
A 86 Sea-Tac Gardens
A 87 Shackleton's Dahlias
A 94 Swan Island Dahlias
A 107 Wright Iris Nursery

DAPHNES
A 31 Flora Lan Nursery
A 41 Marc Henny Nursery
A 59 Maplethorpe
A 80 Red's Rhodies & Alpine Gardens

DATURAS
A 44 C. W. Hosking - Exotic Seed Importer

DAYLILIES
A 1 Adamgrove
A 3 Alpine Valley Gardens
A 3 Amaryllis, Inc.
A 4 American Daylily & Perennials
A 7 Barnee's Garden
A 10 Borbeleta Gardens
A 11 Brand Peony Farm
A 12 Lee Bristol Nursery
A 16 Caprice Farm
A 19 Clifford's Perennial & Vine
A 19 Coastal Gardens & Nursery
A 21 Cooper's Garden
A 21 Cordon Bleu Farms
A 23 C. A. Cruickshank, Ltd.
A 24 Daylily World
A 27 Englerth Gardens
A 31 Floyd Cove Nursery
A 33 Garden Perennials
A 38 Greenwood Nursery
A 39 Hahn's Rainbow Iris Garden
A 39 Dr. Joseph C. Halinar
A 41 Hickory Hill Gardens
A 43 Holiday Seeds
A 43 Homestead Division of Sunnybrook Farms
A 46 Illini Iris
A 46 Inter-State Nurseries
A 48 Jernigan Gardens
(continued next page)

PAGE SOURCE

DAYLILIES (continued)
A 51 Klehm Nursery
A 55 Lenington-Long Gardens
A 57 Louisiana Nursery
A 58 McMillen's Iris Garden
A 59 Maple Tree Gardens
A 60 Maxim's Greenwood Gardens
A 62 Miller's Manor Gardens
A 67 Nicholls Gardens
A 69 Oakes Daylilies
A 76 The Plumeria People
A 76 Pollen Bank
A 76 Powell's Gardens
A 77 Prentiss Court Ground Covers
A 85 Saxton Gardens
A 86 Seawright Gardens
A 87 Shady Oaks Nursery
A 90 Solomon Daylilies
A 94 Ter-El Nursery
A 95 Thomasville Nurseries
A 96 Tranquil Lake Nursery
A 98 TyTy Plantation
A 98 Valente Gardens
A 99 Vandenberg
A 100 Andre Viette Farm & Nursery
A 100 The Vine and the Branch
A 102 Webber Gardens
A 103 White Flower Farm
A 104 Gilbert H. Wild & Son, Inc.
A 106 Wimberlyway Gardens

DELPHINIUMS
A 9 Blackmore & Langdon
A 63 Mo's Greenhouse
A 71 Owl Ridge Alpines
A 87 Select Seeds

DESERT PLANTS
See Also - Specific Plants
A 3 Altman Specialty Plants
A 6 Aztekakti/Desertland Nursery
A 9 Bentley's Botanical Gardens
A 9 Bernardo Beach Native Plant Farm
A 23 The Nursery at the Dallas Nature Center
A 25 Desert Nursery
A 46 Intermountain Cactus
A 62 Midwest Cactus
A 66 Native Seeds/SEARCH
A 67 Nindethana Seed Service
A 72 The PanTree
A 84 Sand Ridge Greenhouse
A 86 Schulz Cactus Gardens
A 91 Southwest Seeds
A 92 Ed Storms, Inc.
A 93 Succulenta
A 98 Tucson Succulents

DIANTHUS
A 2 Allwood Bros. (Hassocks) Ltd.
A 5 Appalachian Wildflower Nursery
A 14 Busse Gardens
A 29 Far North Gardens
A 30 Fleming's Flower Fields
A 30 Flora Favours
A 32 The Fragrant Path
A 38 Grianan Gardens
A 48 Klaus R. Jelitto
A 53 Lamb Nurseries
A 71 Owl Ridge Alpines
A 82 Rocknoll Nursery
A 86 Seedalp
A 89 Soergel Greenhouses
A 90 Solar Green, Ltd.

PAGE SOURCE

DIGITALIS
A 40 Hauser's Superior View Farm

DISCHIDIAS
A 37 Green Plant Research
A 42 Hill 'n dale

DOGWOODS
A 40 Harstine Island Nursery
A 89 Smith Nursery Co.

DROUGHT-TOLERANT PLANTS
See Also - Specific Plants
A 1 Abbey Gardens
A 3 Alpine Plants
A 6 Austraflora of Utah
A 6 Aztekakti/Desertland Nursery
A 9 Bernardo Beach Native Plant Farm
A 9 Bird Rock Tropicals
A 12 Joseph Brown, Native Seeds
A 13 Bushland Flora (Australian Seed Specialists)
A 14 C 'n C Protea
A 15 Callahan Seeds
A 19 Christa's Cactus
A 23 The Nursery at the Dallas Nature Center
A 25 Desert Nursery
A 38 Grigsby Cactus Gardens
A 44 J. L. Hudson, Seedsman
A 53 Larner Seeds
A 53 Las Pilitas Nursery
A 60 Marvin's Cactus
A 62 Midwest Cactus
A 63 Moon Mountain Wildflowers
A 64 Mountain West Seeds
A 65 Native Seeds, Inc.
A 66 Native Seeds/SEARCH
A 67 Niche Gardens
A 68 Northplan/Mountain Seed
A 70 D. Orriell - Seed Exporters
A 72 The PanTree
A 72 Theodore Payne Foundation
A 75 Plants of the Southwest
A 76 Prairie Moon Nursery
A 77 Prairie Ridge Nursery/CRM Ecosystems, Inc.
A 80 Redwood City Seed Co.
A 84 Sand Ridge Greenhouse
A 91 Southwest Seeds
A 93 Succulenta

DRYANDRAS
A 67 Nindethana Seed Service
A 97 Trans Pacific Nursery

DYE PLANTS
A 17 Casa Yerba Gardens
A 20 Companion Plants
A 22 Cricket Hill Herb Farm Ltd.
A 32 Fox Hill Farm
A 36 Goodwin Creek Gardens
A 57 Lost Prairie Herb Farm
A 79 Rasland Farm
A 82 The Rosemary House
A 101 Wyrttun Ward

ECHEVERIAS
A 1 Abbey Gardens
A 14 Cactus by Mueller
A 14 Cactus Gem Nursery
A 82 Rocky Waters Farm

ECHINACEAS
A 26 Earthstar Herb Gardens
A 27 Echinational Plant Products
(continued next page)

PAGE SOURCE

ECHINACEAS (continued)
A 47 Izard Ozark Natives

ECHINOCEREUS
A 14 The Cactus Patch
A 25 Desert Nursery
A 46 Intermountain Cactus
A 60 Marvin's Cactus
A 66 New Mexico Cactus Research
A 82 Rocky Waters Farm
A 84 Sand Ridge Greenhouse
A 86 Schulz Cactus Gardens
A 88 Shein's Cactus
A 91 Southwest Seeds
A 93 Sunnyvale Cactus Nursery
A 98 Tucson Succulents

EPAZOTE
A 72 Peace Seeds

EPIMEDIUMS
A 22 Cricklewood Nursery
A 43 Homestead Division of Sunnybrook Farms
A 82 Rocknoll Nursery

EPIPHYLLUMS
A 3 Altman Specialty Plants
A 7 Fred Bach Epiphyllums
A 8 Beahm Epiphyllum Gardens
A 14 Cactus Gem Nursery
A 15 California Epi Center
A 31 Fort Caroline Orchids
A 38 Greenlife Gardens Greenhouses
A 54 Lauray of Salisbury
A 59 Marilynn's Garden
A 78 Quality Cactus
A 78 Rainbow Gardens Nursery & Bookshop

EPISCIAS
A 13 Buell's Greenhouse, Inc.
A 16 Cape Cod Violetry
A 33 Lorine Friedrich
A 34 Georgetown Greenhouse & Nursery
A 37 Green Mountain African Violets
A 39 Growin'house
A 57 Lyndon Lyon Greenhouses, Inc.
A 58 McKinney's Glasshouse
A 63 Miree's Gesneriads
A 74 Plant Factory
A 75 Plant Villa
A 75 Plants 'n' Things
A 75 Pleasant Hill African Violets
A 93 Sunshine Orchids International
A 100 The Violet Showcase
A 105 Wilson's Greenhouse

ERICAS
A 24 Daystar
A 41 Heaths and Heathers
A 72 Parsley's Cape Seeds
A 77 Protea Seed & Nursery Suppliers

ERIGERONS
A 36 Grand Ridge Nursery

ERIOGONUMS
A 53 Las Pilitas Nursery

EUCALYPTUS
A 17 Carter Seeds
A 37 Greener 'N' Ever Tree Farm & Nursery
A 46 International Seed Supplies
A 67 Nindethana Seed Service

PAGE SOURCE

EUCALYPTUS
A 70 D. Orriell - Seed Exporters

EUCALYPTUS, HARDY
A 6 Austraflora of Utah
A 13 Bushland Flora (Australian Seed Specialists)
A 20 Colvos Creek Nursery & Landscaping
A 97 Trans Pacific Nursery

EUCODONIAS
A 50 Karleens Achimenes

EUPHORBIAS
A 1 Abbey Gardens
A 4 Anything Grows Greenhouse
A 14 Cactus by Mueller
A 25 Desert Theater
A 37 Green Plant Research
A 38 Grigsby Cactus Gardens
A 60 Marvin's Cactus
A 66 New Mexico Cactus Research
A 72 The PanTree
A 82 Rocky Waters Farm
A 89 Singers' Growing Things
A 92 Ed Storms, Inc.
A 93 Succulenta
A 107 Y. O. Ranch Cactus Co.

EVERLASTING FLOWERS
A 4 Angel Seed Company
A 5 Applewood Seed Company
A 16 Camelot North
A 17 Catnip Acres Farm
A 20 Companion Plants
A 20 Comstock, Ferre & Co.
A 22 The Country Garden
A 23 Dacha Barinka
A 29 Fedco Seeds
A 36 Goodwin Creek Gardens
A 37 Greenleaf Seeds
A 41 Herb Gathering Inc.
A 67 Nindethana Seed Service
A 79 Rasland Farm

FERNS
A 6 Atkinson's Greenhouse
A 10 Kurt Bluemel, Inc.
A 19 Coastal Gardens & Nursery
A 27 Edelweiss Gardens
A 31 Foliage Gardens
A 31 Fort Caroline Orchids
A 43 Jerry Horne - Rare Plants
A 45 Huronview Nurseries & Garden Centre
A 56 Logee's Greenhouses
A 57 Paul P. Lowe
A 60 Marvelous Minis
A 99 Varga's Nursery

FERNS, HARDY
A 10 Kurt Bluemel, Inc.
A 10 Boehlke's Woodland Gardens
A 14 Busse Gardens
A 20 Conley's Garden Center
A 29 Fancy Fronds
A 31 Flowerland
A 31 Foliage Gardens
A 34 Gardens of the Blue Ridge
A 36 Russell Graham, Purveyor of Plants
A 38 Griffey's Nursery
A 43 Holbrook Farm & Nursery
A 43 Holiday Seeds
A 43 Homestead Division of Sunnybrook Farms
A 44 Hortico, Inc.
(continued next page)

PAGE SOURCE

FERNS, HARDY (continued)
A 53 Lamtree Farm
A 62 Milaeger's Gardens
A 66 Nature's Garden Nursery
A 68 Novelty Nurseries
A 69 Orchid Gardens
A 71 Owen Farms
A 74 Piedmont Gardens
A 77 The Primrose Path
A 77 Putney Nursery, Inc.
A 87 Shady Oaks Nursery
A 99 Varga's Nursery
A 103 White Flower Farm
A 104 The Wildflower Source
A 104 Wildginger Woodlands
A 104 The Wildwood Flower
A 106 Woodlanders, Inc.

FIG TREES
A 13 Burnt Ridge Nursery
A 27 Edible Landscaping
A 30 The Fig Tree Nursery
A 42 Hidden Springs Nursery - Edible Landscaping
A 47 Ison's Nursery
A 68 Northwoods Nursery
A 96 Tolowa Nursery

FILBERTS
A 13 Burnt Ridge Nursery
A 69 Oikos
A 83 Saginaw Valley Nut Nursery
A 105 Wiley's Nut Grove

FRAGRANT PLANTS
A 8 Bee Rock Herb Farm
A 16 Canyon Creek Nursery
A 16 Cape Seed & Bulb
A 20 Companion Plants
A 21 The Cottage Herb Farm Shop
A 22 Cricket Hill Herb Farm Ltd.
A 23 Dabney Herbs
A 32 The Fragrant Path
A 36 Goodwin Creek Gardens
A 38 Grianan Gardens
A 39 Halcyon Gardens
A 40 Hartman's Herb Farm
A 41 The Herbfarm
A 57 Lost Prairie Herb Farm
A 61 Meadowbrook Herb Garden
A 76 The Plumeria People
A 79 Rasland Farm
A 81 Richters
A 82 The Rosemary House
A 84 Sandy Mush Herb Nursery
A 87 Seeds Blum
A 87 Select Seeds
A 87 Shady Hill Gardens
A 89 Skyline Nursery
A 91 Stallings Exotic Nursery
A 94 Sutton Seeds, Ltd.
A 94 Taylor's Herb Gardens
A 97 Triple Oaks Nursery
A 99 Valley Creek Nursery

FRANKLINIA
A 5 Appalachian Gardens
A 26 Dutch Mountain Nursery
A 36 Gossler Farms Nursery
A 49 Justice Gardens
A 53 Lamtree Farm
A 104 Whitman Farms

PAGE SOURCE

FRITILLARIAS
A 36 Russell Graham, Purveyor of Plants
A 57 John D. Lyon, Inc.

FRUIT TREES
See Also - Specific Fruits
A 1 Ahrens Strawberry Nursery
A 4 Ames' Orchard and Nursery
A 7 Vernon Barnes & Son Nursery
A 13 Burgess Seed & Plant Co.
A 13 Burnt Ridge Nursery
A 23 Cumberland Valley Nurseries, Inc.
A 27 Emlong Nurseries
A 32 Fowler Nurseries, Inc.
A 33 Fruitwood Nursery
A 35 Girard Nurseries
A 42 Hidden Springs Nursery - Edible Landscaping
A 46 Inter-State Nurseries
A 52 V. Kraus Nurseries, Ltd.
A 52 Krider Nurseries
A 53 Lakeland Nursery Sales
A 54 Lawson's Nursery
A 64 Mt. Leo Nursery
A 68 Northwoods Nursery
A 71 Richard Owen Nursery
A 76 Pony Creek Nursery
A 78 Raintree Nursery
A 81 Rider Nurseries
A 85 Savage Farms Nursery
A 92 Stark Bro's Nurseries & Orchards Co.
A 96 Tillinghast Seed Co.
A 99 VanWell Nursery, Inc.
A 102 Waynesboro Nurseries
A 106 Womack Nursery Co.

FRUIT TREES, ANTIQUE
A 38 Greenmantle Nursery
A 40 Harmony Farm Supply
A 54 Lawson's Nursery
A 55 Henry Leuthardt Nurseries, Inc.
A 91 Southmeadow Fruit Gardens

FRUIT TREES, DWARF
A 4 Ames' Orchard and Nursery
A 32 Four Winds Growers
A 33 Fruitwood Nursery
A 40 Harmony Farm Supply
A 50 Kelly Nurseries of Dansville, Inc.
A 55 Henry Leuthardt Nurseries, Inc.
A 79 Rayner Bros.
A 82 Rocky Meadow Orchard & Nursery
A 91 Southmeadow Fruit Gardens
A 99 VanWell Nursery, Inc.
A 102 Waynesboro Nurseries

FRUIT TREES, ESPALIERED
A 5 Arbor & Espalier
A 55 Henry Leuthardt Nurseries, Inc.
A 90 Sonoma Antique Apple Nursery

FRUIT TREES, HARDY
See Also - Specific Fruits
A 1 Adams County Nursery, Inc.
A 8 Bear Creek Nursery
A 8 Beaverlodge Nursery
A 29 Farmer Seed & Nursery
A 31 Dean Foster Nurseries
A 36 Golden Bough Tree Farm
A 43 Honeywood Lilies
A 49 J. W. Jung Seed Co.
A 53 Lakeshore Tree Farms, Ltd.
A 54 Lawyer Nursery, Inc.
A 58 McConnell Nurseries, Inc.
(continued next page)

PAGE SOURCE

FRUIT TREES, HARDY (continued)
A 59 Makielski Berry Farm & Nursery
A 62 J. E. Miller Nurseries, Inc.
A 64 Moosebell Flower, Fruit & Tree Co.
A 64 Morden Nurseries, Ltd
A 66 New York State Fruit Testing Coop. Assn.
A 84 St. Lawrence Nurseries
A 94 T & T Seeds, Ltd.

FRUIT TREES, LOW-CHILL
A 33 Fruitwood Nursery
A 57 The Lowrey Nursery
A 90 South Seas Nursery

FRUIT, NEW VARIETIES
See Also - Specific Fruits
A 33 Fruitwood Nursery
A 33 Garden of Delights
A 38 Greenmantle Nursery
A 42 Highlander Nursery
A 66 New York State Fruit Testing Coop. Assn.
A 71 Pacific Tree Farms
A 73 Peaceful Valley Farm Supply
A 78 Raintree Nursery
A 82 Rocky Meadow Orchard & Nursery
A 88 Sherwood's Greenhouses

FRUIT, TROPICAL
See Also - Specific Fruits
A 6 B & T Associates
A 7 The Banana Tree
A 12 John Brudy Exotics
A 28 Exotica Seed Co. & Rare Fruit Nursery
A 33 Garden of Delights
A 34 Garden World
A 44 C. W. Hosking - Exotic Seed Importer
A 71 Pacific Tree Farms
A 76 Possum Trot Tropical Fruit Nursery
A 84 Santa Barbara Seeds
A 90 South Seas Nursery
A 98 Tropicals Unlimited

FUCHSIAS
A 7 Barbara's World of Flowers
A 33 G & G Gardens and Growers
A 42 Hidden Springs Nursery - Edible Landscaping
A 61 Merry Gardens
A 86 Sea-Tac Gardens
A 90 Southern Seeds
A 93 Sunshine Orchids International
A 95 Tiki Nursery
A 101 Wanda's Hide-a-Way

FUCHSIAS, HARDY
A 53 Lamb Nurseries
A 94 A.P. & E.V. Tabraham

GARDENIAS
A 68 Nuccio's Nurseries

GARLIC
A 17 Casa Yerba Gardens
A 23 Dacha Barinka
A 26 Earthstar Herb Gardens
A 36 Good Seed Co.
A 50 Kalmia Farm
A 65 Nationwide Seed & Supply
A 65 Native Seed Foundation
A 67 Nichols Garden Nursery, Inc.
A 83 S & H Organic Acres

GENERAL NURSERY STOCK
See Also - Specific Plants

PAGE SOURCE

GENERAL NURSERY STOCK
A 2 Alberta Nurseries & Seed Company
A 4 Ames' Orchard and Nursery
A 8 Bear Creek Nursery
A 12 Brittingham Plant Farms
A 12 Buckley Nursery
A 13 W. Atlee Burpee Company
A 19 Cold Stream Farm
A 27 Emlong Nurseries
A 29 Farmer Seed & Nursery
A 30 Henry Field Seed & Nursery Co.
A 31 Dean Foster Nurseries
A 32 Four Seasons Nursery
A 32 Fowler Nurseries, Inc.
A 39 Gurney Seed & Nursery Co.
A 40 Harstine Island Nursery
A 40 Hastings
A 45 Huronview Nurseries & Garden Centre
A 46 Inter-State Nurseries
A 48 Jackson & Perkins Co.
A 48 Johnson Nursery
A 49 J. W. Jung Seed Co.
A 50 Kelly Nurseries of Dansville, Inc.
A 52 V. Kraus Nurseries, Ltd.
A 52 Krider Nurseries
A 53 Lakeland Nursery Sales
A 53 Lakeshore Tree Farms, Ltd.
A 54 Lawson's Nursery
A 54 Lawyer Nursery, Inc.
A 58 McFayden Seeds
A 60 Earl May Seed & Nursery Co.
A 61 Mellinger's Inc.
A 62 J. E. Miller Nurseries, Inc.
A 64 Morden Nurseries, Ltd
A 71 Richard Owen Nursery
A 73 Peaceful Valley Farm Supply
A 76 Pony Creek Nursery
A 81 Rider Nurseries
A 86 Seed Centre Ltd.
A 88 R. H. Shumway Seedsman
A 92 Stark Bro's Nurseries & Orchards Co.
A 94 T & T Seeds, Ltd.
A 99 VanWell Nursery, Inc.
A 102 Waynesboro Nurseries

GENTIANS
A 5 Appalachian Wildflower Nursery
A 86 Seedalp

GERANIUMS
A 21 Cook's Geranium Nursery
A 53 Lake Odessa Greenhouse
A 56 Logee's Greenhouses
A 62 Midwest Seed Growers, Inc.
A 66 New Leaf
A 74 Pine Ridge Garden Gallery
A 87 Shady Hill Gardens
A 107 Young's Mesa Nursery

GERANIUMS, MINIATURE
A 21 Cook's Geranium Nursery
A 61 Merry Gardens
A 66 New Leaf
A 74 Pine Ridge Garden Gallery
A 87 Shady Hill Gardens
A 101 Wanda's Hide-a-Way
A 107 Young's Mesa Nursery

GERANIUMS, SCENTED
A 8 Bee Rock Herb Farm
A 16 Cape Seed & Bulb
A 21 Cook's Geranium Nursery
A 22 Cricket Hill Herb Farm Ltd.

(continued next page)

PAGE SOURCE

GERANIUMS, SCENTED (continued)
A 23 Dabney Herbs
A 24 Davidson-Wilson Greenhouses
A 26 Earthstar Herb Gardens
A 32 Fox Hill Farm
A 40 Hartman's Herb Farm
A 53 Lake Odessa Greenhouse
A 57 Lost Prairie Herb Farm
A 61 Merry Gardens
A 66 New Leaf
A 74 Pine Ridge Garden Gallery
A 79 Rasland Farm
A 82 The Rosemary House
A 84 Sandy Mush Herb Nursery
A 87 Shady Hill Gardens
A 93 Sunnybrook Farms Nursery
A 93 Sunshine Orchids International
A 94 Tansy Farm
A 103 Well-Sweep Herb Farm
A 107 Wrenwood of Berkeley Springs
A 107 Young's Mesa Nursery

GERANIUMS, SPECIES
A 16 Canyon Creek Nursery
A 16 Cape Seed & Bulb
A 22 Cricklewood Nursery
A 30 Flora Favours
A 34 Garden Place
A 53 Lamb Nurseries
A 63 Montrose Nursery
A 66 New Leaf
A 74 Pine Ridge Garden Gallery
A 87 Shady Hill Gardens
A 90 Southern Seeds
A 107 Young's Mesa Nursery

GESNERIADS
See Also - Specific Plants
A 6 Atkinson's Greenhouse
A 13 Buell's Greenhouse, Inc.
A 22 Country Girl Greenhouses
A 24 Davidson-Wilson Greenhouses
A 30 Fischer Greenhouses
A 35 Glasshouse Works
A 39 Growin'house
A 48 Jeannette's Jesneriads
A 50 Karleens Achimenes
A 50 Kartuz Greenhouses
A 54 Lauray of Salisbury
A 56 Logee's Greenhouses
A 57 Lyndon Lyon Greenhouses, Inc.
A 60 Marvelous Minis
A 63 Miree's Gesneriads
A 74 The Plant Kingdom
A 75 Plant Villa
A 75 Pleasant Hill African Violets
A 81 Roberts' Gesneriads
A 93 Sunshine Orchids International
A 107 Zaca Vista Nursery

GINGERS
A 35 Glasshouse Works
A 41 Heliconia Haus
A 76 The Plumeria People
A 91 Stallings Exotic Nursery
A 98 TyTy Plantation
A 101 Mary Walker Bulb Company

GINSENG
A 23 Dabney Herbs
A 73 Pick's Ginseng

PAGE SOURCE

GLADIOLUS
A 11 Breck's
A 20 Connell's Dahlias
A 23 C. A. Cruickshank, Ltd.
A 26 Early's Farm & Garden Centre, Inc.
A 30 Flad's Glads
A 35 Gladside Gardens
A 45 Ed Hume Seeds, Inc.
A 61 Michigan Bulb Co.
A 85 John Scheepers, Inc.
A 92 Stillpoint Gardens
A 99 K. Van Bourgondien & Sons, Inc.
A 101 Mary Walker Bulb Company
A 102 The Waushara Gardens
A 107 Wright Iris Nursery

GLADIOLUS, SPECIES
A 9 Bio-Quest International
A 16 Cape Seed & Bulb
A 35 Gladside Gardens
A 72 Parsley's Cape Seeds
A 83 Rust-En-Vrede Nursery
A 89 Anthony J. Skittone

GLOXINIAS
A 9 Blackmore & Langdon
A 13 Buell's Greenhouse, Inc.
A 50 Karleens Achimenes
A 75 Plant Villa

GOOSEBERRIES
A 27 Edible Landscaping
A 59 Makielski Berry Farm & Nursery
A 63 Mo's Greenhouse
A 64 Moosebell Flower, Fruit & Tree Co.
A 104 Whitman Farms

GOURDS
A 3 Alston Seed Growers
A 36 Grace's Gardens
A 51 Kilgore Seed Company
A 61 Meta Horticultural Labs
A 83 SPB Sales
A 93 Sunrise Oriental Seed Co.

GRAINS
A 11 Bountiful Gardens
A 22 Cross Seed Company
A 28 Ernst Crownvetch Farms
A 48 Johnny's Selected Seeds
A 50 Kester's Wild Game Food Nurseries
A 52 Kusa Research Foundation
A 64 Moose Tubers
A 83 Roswell Seed Co.

GRAPE SCIONS
A 56 Lon's Oregon Grapes

GRAPES
A 1 Ahrens Strawberry Nursery
A 5 Armstrong Roses
A 10 Boordy Nursery
A 11 Boston Mountain Nurseries
A 12 Brittingham Plant Farms
A 12 Buckley Nursery
A 15 California Nursery Co.
A 27 Edible Landscaping
A 30 The Fig Tree Nursery
A 31 Dean Foster Nurseries
A 32 Fowler Nurseries, Inc.
A 40 Hastings
A 47 Ison's Nursery
A 48 Johnson Nursery
(continued next page)

PAGE SOURCE

GRAPES (continued)
A 55 Henry Leuthardt Nurseries, Inc.
A 56 Lon's Oregon Grapes
A 59 Makielski Berry Farm & Nursery
A 62 J. E. Miller Nurseries, Inc.
A 81 Rider Nurseries
A 84 St. Lawrence Nurseries
A 85 Savage Farms Nursery
A 91 Square Root Nursery
A 92 Stark Bro's Nurseries & Orchards Co.
A 99 VanWell Nursery, Inc.
A 104 Whitman Farms

GRASSES, LAWN AND TURF
A 53 D. Landreth Seed Company
A 54 Orol Ledden & Sons
A 77 Prairie State Commodities
A 83 Roswell Seed Co.
A 86 Seed Centre Ltd.
A 97 Tregunno Seeds

GRASSES, ORNAMENTAL
A 3 Alpina Research & Montane Garden
A 5 Applewood Seed Company
A 10 Kurt Bluemel, Inc.
A 17 Carroll Gardens
A 17 Carter Seeds
A 22 The Country Garden
A 22 Crownsville Nursery
A 34 Garden Place
A 35 Girard Nurseries
A 42 High Altitude Gardens
A 44 Hortica Gardens
A 48 Johnson Seeds
A 60 Maver Rare Perennials
A 63 Miniature Plant Kingdom
A 67 Niche Gardens
A 89 Skyline Nursery
A 91 Stallings Exotic Nursery
A 97 Trans Pacific Nursery
A 100 Andre Viette Farm & Nursery

GRASSES, PRAIRIE
A 23 The Nursery at the Dallas Nature Center
A 43 Horizon Seeds
A 52 LaFayette Home Nursery, Inc.
A 62 Milaeger's Gardens
A 76 Prairie Moon Nursery
A 76 Prairie Nursery
A 106 Windrift Prairie Shop

GRASSES, RANGE AND RECLAMATION
A 28 Ernst Crownvetch Farms
A 43 Horizon Seeds
A 48 Johnson Seeds
A 53 Larner Seeds
A 75 Plants of the Southwest
A 80 Redwood City Seed Co.
A 83 Roswell Seed Co.

GREEN MANURE CROPS
A 11 Bountiful Gardens
A 36 Good Seed Co.
A 37 Greenleaf Seeds
A 64 Moose Tubers
B 23 Organic Farm & Garden Supply
A 77 Prairie State Commodities
A 88 R. H. Shumway Seedsman
A 95 Territorial Seed Co.

GREENHOUSE/TROPICAL PLANTS
See Also - Specific Plants
A 2 Alberts & Merkel Bros., Inc.

PAGE SOURCE

GREENHOUSE/TROPICAL PLANTS
A 4 Anything Grows Greenhouse
A 6 B & T Associates
A 7 The Banana Tree
A 9 Bird Rock Tropicals
A 10 Arthur Boe Distributor
A 12 John Brudy Exotics
A 15 California Epi Center
A 17 Carter Seeds
A 17 Cedar Ridge Nurseries
A 19 Clargreen Gardens Ltd.
A 24 Dane Company
A 24 Davidson-Wilson Greenhouses
A 24 DeGiorgi Company, Inc.
A 27 Edelweiss Gardens
A 27 Endangered Species
A 28 Exotica Seed Co. & Rare Fruit Nursery
A 28 Exotics Hawaii, Inc.
A 30 Fischer Greenhouses
A 31 Foliage Gardens
A 31 Fort Caroline Orchids
A 32 Fox Orchids, Inc.
A 33 G & B Orchid Laboratory
A 33 Garden of Delights
A 35 Glasshouse Works
A 37 Green Plant Research
A 39 Robert B. Hamm
A 40 Hatten's Nursery
A 41 Heliconia Haus
A 43 Jerry Horne - Rare Plants
A 44 C. W. Hosking - Exotic Seed Importer
A 50 Kartuz Greenhouses
A 55 W. O. Lessard Nursery
A 56 Logee's Greenhouses
A 59 Ann Mann's Orchids
A 59 Marilynn's Garden
A 61 Merry Gardens
A 66 New Frontiers
A 68 Oak Hill Gardens
A 70 Orchids Royale
A 74 The Plant Kingdom
A 74 The Plant Shop's Botanical Gardens
A 76 The Plumeria People
A 78 Rainforest Flora, Inc.
A 78 Rainforest Plantes et Fleurs, Inc.
A 80 Rhapis Gardens
A 83 SLO Gardens
A 84 Santa Barbara Seeds
A 86 Seaborn Del Dios Nursery
A 88 Shelldance Nursery
A 90 South Florida Seed Supply
A 90 South Seas Nursery
A 94 Sutton Seeds, Ltd.
A 95 Thompson & Morgan
A 98 Tropicals Unlimited
A 100 Violets Collectible
A 101 Vireya Specialties Nursery
A 103 Westside Exotics Palm Nursery

GROUNDCOVERS
See Also - Specific Plants
A 2 Allen, Sterling & Lothrop
A 3 Alpenflora Gardens
A 4 American Daylily & Perennials
A 4 Angelwood Nursery
A 10 Kurt Bluemel, Inc.
A 10 Bluestone Perennials
A 16 Camelot North
A 20 Conley's Garden Center
A 28 Ernst Crownvetch Farms
A 30 Henry Field Seed & Nursery Co.
A 34 Garden Place
A 34 Gilson Gardens
(continued next page)

PAGE SOURCE

GROUNDCOVERS (continued)
A 47 Ivies of the World
A 57 Lost Prairie Herb Farm
A 57 Louisiana Nursery
A 57 The Lowrey Nursery
A 61 Michigan Bulb Co.
A 63 Mo's Greenhouse
A 64 Mt. Leo Nursery
A 65 Musser Forests Inc.
A 65 Native Gardens
A 67 North American Wildflowers
A 75 Plants of the Wild
A 76 Powell's Gardens
A 77 Prentiss Court Ground Covers
A 84 Salter Tree Farm
A 91 Spring Hill Nurseries Co.
A 91 Squaw Mountain Gardens
A 94 The Sweetbriar
A 94 Ter-El Nursery
A 98 Turnipseed Nursery Farms
A 99 Valley Creek Nursery
A 101 Walden - West
A 104 Wildwood Gardens
A 107 Wrenwood of Berkeley Springs

GUZMANIAS
A 88 Shelldance Nursery

GYMNOCALYCIUMS
A 25 Desert Theater
A 82 Rocky Waters Farm
A 84 Sand Ridge Greenhouse
A 86 Schulz Cactus Gardens

HAWORTHIAS
A 6 Atkinson's Greenhouse
A 15 California Epi Center
A 25 Desert Nursery
A 38 Grigsby Cactus Gardens
A 60 Marvin's Cactus
A 80 Redlo Cacti
A 88 Shein's Cactus
A 92 Ed Storms, Inc.
A 93 Succulenta
A 107 Guy Wrinkle Exotic Plants

HAZELNUTS
A 8 Bear Creek Nursery
A 29 Fernald's Hickory Hill Nursery
A 38 Grimo Nut Nursery
A 89 Smith Nursery Co.

HEATHERS
See Also - Specific Plants
A 23 The Cummins Garden
A 24 Daystar
A 26 Eastern Plant Specialties
A 32 Foxborough Nursery
A 41 Heaths and Heathers
A 84 Sandy Mush Herb Nursery
A 100 Vineland Nurseries

HELICONIAS
A 7 The Banana Tree
A 41 Heliconia Haus

HELLEBORES
A 5 Appalachian Wildflower Nursery
A 73 Piccadilly Farm
A 86 Seedalp

HERBS
A 1 Abundant Life Seed Foundation

PAGE SOURCE

HERBS
A 4 Angel Seed Company
A 5 Applewood Seed Company
A 8 Bee Rock Herb Farm
A 8 Belche Herb Company
A 9 Bittersweet Farm
A 11 Bountiful Gardens
A 16 Camelot North
A 17 Casa Yerba Gardens
A 17 Catnip Acres Farm
A 18 John Chambers
A 20 Companion Plants
A 20 The Cook's Garden
A 21 The Cottage Herb Farm Shop
A 22 Cricket Hill Herb Farm Ltd.
A 22 Crosman Seed Corp.
A 22 Crownsville Nursery
A 23 Dabney Herbs
A 23 Dacha Barinka
A 25 Dionysos' Barn
A 26 E & H Products
A 26 Earthstar Herb Gardens
A 29 Fedco Seeds
A 32 Fox Hill Farm
A 32 The Fragrant Path
A 33 Garden Perennials
A 34 Garden Place
A 36 Goodwin Creek Gardens
A 39 Halcyon Gardens
A 40 Hartman's Herb Farm
A 41 Herb Gathering Inc.
A 41 The Herbfarm
A 47 Island Seed Mail Order
A 48 Johnny's Selected Seeds
A 51 Kilgore Seed Company
A 53 Lagomarsino Seeds
A 53 D. Landreth Seed Company
A 54 Le Jardin du Gourmet
A 54 Le Marche Seeds International
A 56 Logee's Greenhouses
A 57 Lost Prairie Herb Farm
A 57 The Lowrey Nursery
A 61 Meadowbrook Herb Garden
A 61 Merry Gardens
A 61 Meyer Seed Co.
A 62 Midwest Seed Growers, Inc.
A 64 Mountain Valley Seeds & Nursery
A 67 Niche Gardens
A 67 Nichols Garden Nursery, Inc.
A 71 Owen Farms
A 71 Ozark National Seed Order
A 72 Peace Seeds
A 73 Pick's Ginseng
A 74 Pinetree Garden Seeds
A 77 Putney Nursery, Inc.
A 79 Rasland Farm
A 79 Rawlinson Garden Seed
A 81 Richters
A 82 The Rosemary House
A 84 Sanctuary Seeds/Folklore Herb Co.
A 84 Sandy Mush Herb Nursery
A 87 Seeds Blum
A 88 Shepherd's Garden Seeds
A 93 Sunnybrook Farms Nursery
A 94 Tansy Farm
A 94 Taylor's Herb Gardens
A 95 Territorial Seed Co.
A 96 Tillinghast Seed Co.
A 97 Tregunno Seeds
A 97 Triple Oaks Nursery
A 99 Valley Creek Nursery
A 100 Vermont Bean Seed Co.
A 101 Wyrttun Ward
(continued next page)

PAGE SOURCE

HERBS (continued)
A 103 Well-Sweep Herb Farm
A 103 West Kootenay Herb Nursery
A 107 Wrenwood of Berkeley Springs

HERBS, ORIENTAL
A 9 Bittersweet Farm
A 93 Sunrise Oriental Seed Co.

HEUCHERAS
A 40 Hauser's Superior View Farm
A 77 The Primrose Path

HIBISCUS
A 1 Air Expose
A 37 Green Plant Research
A 40 Hatten's Nursery
A 76 The Plumeria People
A 79 Reasoner's
A 91 Stallings Exotic Nursery

HIBISCUS, HARDY
A 1 Air Expose
A 30 Fleming's Flower Fields
A 59 Magnolia Nursery & Display Garden

HICKORY NUTS
A 38 Grimo Nut Nursery

HOLLY
A 5 Appalachian Gardens
A 25 Bill Dodd's Rare Plants
A 32 Foxborough Nursery
A 35 Girard Nurseries
A 43 Holly Hills, Inc.
A 59 Magnolia Nursery & Display Garden
A 83 Roslyn Nursery
A 95 Terrapin Springs Farm
A 101 Washington Evergreen Nursery
A 102 Wavecrest Nursery & Landscaping Co.
A 102 Waynesboro Nurseries

HOSTAS
A 14 Busse Gardens
A 16 Caprice Farm
A 19 Coastal Gardens & Nursery
A 22 Crownsville Nursery
A 26 Donnelly's Nursery
A 27 Englerth Gardens
A 28 Fairway Enterprises
A 41 Hickory Hill Gardens
A 42 Hildenbrandt's Iris Gardens
A 43 Holbrook Farm & Nursery
A 43 Holiday Seeds
A 43 Homestead Division of Sunnybrook Farms
A 48 Jernigan Gardens
A 51 Klehm Nursery
A 59 Maroushek Gardens
A 73 Piccadilly Farm
A 74 Piedmont Gardens
A 76 Powell's Gardens
A 82 Rocknoll Nursery
A 84 Sandy Mush Herb Nursery
A 85 Savory's Greenhouse
A 86 Seawright Gardens
A 87 Shady Oaks Nursery
A 99 Vandenberg
A 100 Andre Viette Farm & Nursery
A 101 Walden - West

HOUSEPLANTS
See Also - Specific Plants
A 4 Anything Grows Greenhouse

PAGE SOURCE

HOUSEPLANTS
A 6 Atkinson's Greenhouse
A 6 B & T Associates
A 12 John Brudy Exotics
A 13 Burgess Seed & Plant Co.
A 20 Color Farm Growers
A 24 William Dam Seeds
A 24 Davidson-Wilson Greenhouses
A 27 Edelweiss Gardens
A 30 Henry Field Seed & Nursery Co.
A 35 Glasshouse Works
A 38 Greenlife Gardens Greenhouses
A 39 Robert B. Hamm
A 44 C. W. Hosking - Exotic Seed Importer
A 50 Kartuz Greenhouses
A 56 Logee's Greenhouses
A 57 Lyndon Lyon Greenhouses, Inc.
A 61 Merry Gardens
A 68 Oak Hill Gardens
A 73 Peter Pauls Nurseries
A 74 The Plant Kingdom
A 75 Pleasant Hill African Violets
A 80 Rhapis Gardens
A 80 Rhapis Palm Growers
A 81 Roberts' Gesneriads
A 91 Spring Hill Nurseries Co.
A 92 Stokes Seed Company
A 93 Sunnybrook Farms Nursery
A 93 Sunshine Orchids International
A 94 Sutton Seeds, Ltd.

HOYAS
A 1 Abbey Gardens
A 8 Beahm Epiphyllum Gardens
A 15 California Epi Center
A 37 Green Plant Research
A 42 Hill 'n dale
A 50 Kartuz Greenhouses
A 54 Lauray of Salisbury
A 59 Ann Mann's Orchids
A 78 Rainbow Gardens Nursery & Bookshop
A 78 Rainforest Plantes et Fleurs, Inc.
A 83 SLO Gardens
A 93 Sunnybrook Farms Nursery

HYACINTHS
A 23 The Daffodil Mart
A 24 Peter De Jager Bulb Co.
A 58 McClure & Zimmerman
A 78 Quality Dutch Bulbs
A 99 Van Engelen Inc.
A 99 Veldheer Tulip Gardens

IRIS
See Also - Specific Type
A 1 Adamgrove
A 7 Bakker of Holland
A 19 Circle 'N' Ranch
A 20 Comanche Acres Iris Gardens
A 21 Cooley's Gardens
A 22 C. Criscola Iris Garden
A 24 Peter De Jager Bulb Co.
A 36 Grandview Iris Gardens
A 39 Hahn's Rainbow Iris Garden
A 42 Hildenbrandt's Iris Gardens
A 47 Iris Gardens
A 54 Laurie's Garden
A 59 Maple Tree Gardens
A 79 Rancho de la Flor de Lis
A 89 Skyline Nursery

IRIS, ARIL & ARILBRED
A 61 Mid-America Iris Gardens
(continued next page)

PAGE SOURCE

IRIS, ARIL & ARILBRED (continued)
A 75 Pleasure Iris Gardens
A 88 Shepard Iris Garden

IRIS, BEARDED (VARIOUS TYPES)
See Also - Specific Type
A 1 Adamgrove
A 2 Aitken's Salmon Creek Garden
A 10 Borbeleta Gardens
A 15 Cal Dixie Iris Gardens
A 19 Circle 'N' Ranch
A 20 Comanche Acres Iris Gardens
A 21 Cottage Gardens
A 22 Country View Gardens
A 26 Dutch Gardens, Inc.
A 32 French Iris Gardens
A 46 Illini Iris
A 46 Iris Acres
A 47 Iris Gardens
A 51 Kirkland Iris Garden
A 57 Long's Gardens
A 58 McMillen's Iris Garden
A 59 Maple Tree Gardens
A 60 Maryott's Gardens
A 60 Maxim's Greenwood Gardens
A 63 Mission Bell Gardens
A 63 Moonshine Gardens
A 67 Nicholls Gardens
A 68 North Pine Iris Gardens
A 75 Pleasure Iris Gardens
A 76 Powell's Gardens
A 79 Randy's Iris Garden
A 98 21st Century Gardens
A 100 The Vine and the Branch

IRIS, BORDER
A 21 Cottage Gardens
A 22 Country View Gardens
A 32 French Iris Gardens
A 45 Huggins Farm Irises
A 57 Long's Gardens
A 58 McMillen's Iris Garden
A 63 Moonshine Gardens
A 68 North Pine Iris Gardens
A 81 Riverdale Iris Gardens
A 100 The Vine and the Branch

IRIS, DWARF
A 10 Borbeleta Gardens
A 21 Cottage Gardens
A 22 Country View Gardens
A 32 French Iris Gardens
A 39 Hahn's Rainbow Iris Garden
A 42 Hildenbrandt's Iris Gardens
A 45 Huggins Farm Irises
A 46 Iris Acres
A 47 Iris Gardens
A 47 Iris Test Gardens
A 51 Kirkland Iris Garden
A 57 Long's Gardens
A 58 McMillen's Iris Garden
A 60 Maryott's Gardens
A 62 Miller's Manor Gardens
A 63 Moonshine Gardens
A 68 North Pine Iris Gardens
A 81 Riverdale Iris Gardens
A 85 Schreiner's Gardens
A 100 The Vine and the Branch
A 107 Wright Iris Nursery

IRIS, HORNED
A 20 Comanche Acres Iris Gardens
A 45 Huggins Farm Irises

PAGE SOURCE

IRIS, HORNED
A 63 Moonshine Gardens
A 98 21st Century Gardens

IRIS, INTERMEDIATE
A 10 Borbeleta Gardens
A 39 Hahn's Rainbow Iris Garden
A 45 Huggins Farm Irises
A 47 Iris Gardens
A 51 Kirkland Iris Garden
A 57 Long's Gardens
A 62 Miller's Manor Gardens
A 63 Moonshine Gardens
A 81 Riverdale Iris Gardens
A 85 Schreiner's Gardens

IRIS, JAPANESE
A 2 Aitken's Salmon Creek Garden
A 16 Caprice Farm
A 19 Coastal Gardens & Nursery
A 22 Crownsville Nursery
A 27 Ensata Gardens
A 47 The Iris Pond
A 54 Laurie's Garden
A 59 Magnolia Nursery & Display Garden
A 60 Maxim's Greenwood Gardens
A 67 Nicholls Gardens
A 75 Pleasure Iris Gardens
A 96 Tranquil Lake Nursery
A 100 The Vine and the Branch

IRIS, LOUISIANA
A 4 American Daylily & Perennials
A 8 Bay View Gardens
A 20 Comanche Acres Iris Gardens
A 21 Cooper's Garden
A 21 Cordon Bleu Farms
A 57 Louisiana Nursery
A 59 Magnolia Nursery & Display Garden
A 60 Maxim's Greenwood Gardens
A 75 Pleasure Iris Gardens
A 84 Santa Barbara Water Gardens
A 88 Shepard Iris Garden
A 100 The Vine and the Branch

IRIS, MEDIAN
A 20 Comanche Acres Iris Gardens
A 21 Cottage Gardens
A 22 Country View Gardens
A 33 Garden of the Enchanted Rainbow
A 46 Iris Acres
A 51 Kirkland Iris Garden
A 59 Maple Tree Gardens
A 61 Mid-America Iris Gardens
A 62 Miller's Manor Gardens
A 63 Moonshine Gardens
A 81 Riverdale Iris Gardens
A 88 Shepard Iris Garden

IRIS, PACIFIC COAST NATIVES
A 2 Aitken's Salmon Creek Garden
A 8 Bay View Gardens
A 51 Kirkland Iris Garden
A 53 Larner Seeds
A 54 Laurie's Garden
A 60 Maxim's Greenwood Gardens

IRIS, PUMILA
A 1 Adamgrove
A 22 Country View Gardens
A 62 Miller's Manor Gardens
A 81 Riverdale Iris Gardens

PAGE SOURCE

IRIS, REBLOOMING
A 6 Avonbank Iris Gardens
A 33 Garden of the Enchanted Rainbow
A 45 Huggins Farm Irises
A 46 Iris Acres
A 47 The Iris Pond
A 48 J-Lot Gardens
A 63 Moonshine Gardens
A 71 Pacific Coast Hybridizers

IRIS, SIBERIAN
A 2 Aitken's Salmon Creek Garden
A 10 Borbeleta Gardens
A 14 Busse Gardens
A 16 Caprice Farm
A 18 Chehalem Gardens
A 21 Cooper's Garden
A 22 Country View Gardens
A 22 Crownsville Nursery
A 27 Englerth Gardens
A 27 Ensata Gardens
A 41 Hickory Hill Gardens
A 46 Illini Iris
A 47 The Iris Pond
A 54 Laurie's Garden
A 58 McMillen's Iris Garden
A 59 Maple Tree Gardens
A 60 Maxim's Greenwood Gardens
A 62 Miller's Manor Gardens
A 67 Nicholls Gardens
A 75 Pleasure Iris Gardens
A 84 Santa Barbara Water Gardens
A 89 Anthony J. Skittone
A 96 Tranquil Lake Nursery
A 100 Andre Viette Farm & Nursery
A 100 The Vine and the Branch
A 107 Wright Iris Nursery

IRIS, SPECIES
A 1 Adamgrove
A 2 Aitken's Salmon Creek Garden
A 3 Alpenflora Gardens
A 5 Appalachian Wildflower Nursery
A 13 Bundles of Bulbs
A 17 Chadwell Himalayan Seed
A 19 Coastal Gardens & Nursery
A 20 Colorado Alpines, Inc.
A 21 Cooper's Garden
A 47 The Iris Pond
A 48 Klaus R. Jelitto
A 54 Laurie's Garden
A 59 Maplethorpe
A 63 Montrose Nursery
A 67 Nicholls Gardens
A 75 Pleasure Iris Gardens
A 83 Rust-En-Vrede Nursery
A 87 Select Seeds

IRIS, SPURIA
A 8 Bay View Gardens
A 18 Chehalem Gardens
A 18 Cherry Lane Gardens of Glenn Corlew
A 21 Cordon Bleu Farms
A 60 Maxim's Greenwood Gardens
A 75 Pleasure Iris Gardens
A 88 Shepard Iris Garden

IRIS, TALL BEARDED
A 4 Anderson Iris Gardens
A 8 Bay View Gardens
A 11 Brand Peony Farm
A 18 Cherry Lane Gardens of Glenn Corlew
A 20 Comanche Acres Iris Gardens

PAGE SOURCE

IRIS, TALL BEARDED
A 21 Cooley's Gardens
A 21 Cottage Gardens
A 22 Country View Gardens
A 33 Garden of the Enchanted Rainbow
A 36 Grandview Iris Gardens
A 39 Hahn's Rainbow Iris Garden
A 41 Hickory Hill Gardens
A 42 Hildenbrandt's Iris Gardens
A 45 Huggins Farm Irises
A 46 Iris Acres
A 46 Iris Country
A 47 The Iris Pond
A 47 Iris Test Gardens
A 48 Jasperson's Hersey Nursery
A 48 Jernigan Gardens
A 50 Keith Keppel
A 51 Klehm Nursery
A 57 Long's Gardens
A 58 McMillen's Iris Garden
A 59 Maple Tree Gardens
A 60 Maryott's Gardens
A 61 Mid-America Iris Gardens
A 62 Miller's Manor Gardens
A 63 Mission Bell Gardens
A 63 Moonshine Gardens
A 68 North Pine Iris Gardens
A 71 Pacific Coast Hybridizers
A 79 Rancho de la Flor de Lis
A 79 Randy's Iris Garden
A 85 Schreiner's Gardens
A 88 Shepard Iris Garden
A 100 Andre Viette Farm & Nursery
A 100 The Vine and the Branch
A 107 Wright Iris Nursery

IVY
A 4 Angelwood Nursery
A 26 Donnelly's Nursery
A 34 Gilson Gardens
A 43 Homestead Division of Sunnybrook Farms
A 47 Ivies of the World
A 61 Merry Gardens
A 77 Prentiss Court Ground Covers
A 93 Sunnybrook Farms Nursery
A 94 Ter-El Nursery
A 101 Walden - West

JASMINES
A 4 Anything Grows Greenhouse
A 77 Prentiss Court Ground Covers
A 91 Stallings Exotic Nursery

JOJOBA
A 49 KSA Jojoba

JOVIBARBA
A 3 Alpine Gardens & Calico Shop
A 21 Country Cottage
A 83 Jim & Irene Russ Quality Plants

KALMIAS
A 8 Beaver Creek Nursery
A 16 Carlson's Gardens
A 23 The Cummins Garden
A 32 Foxborough Nursery
A 50 Kelly Nurseries of Dansville, Inc.
A 66 E. B. Nauman, Nurseryman
A 83 Roslyn Nursery
A 97 Transplant Nursery
A 100 Vineland Nurseries
A 103 Westgate Garden Nursery
A 104 Whitney Gardens

PAGE SOURCE

KIWIS
A 13 Burnt Ridge Nursery
A 15 California Nursery Co.
A 68 Northwoods Nursery
A 90 South Seas Nursery
A 91 Stanley & Sons Nursery, Inc.

KIWIS, HARDY
A 13 Burnt Ridge Nursery
A 27 Edible Landscaping
A 40 Hartmann's Plantation, Inc.
A 42 Hidden Springs Nursery - Edible Landscaping
A 53 Lakeland Nursery Sales
A 68 Northwoods Nursery
A 88 Sherwood's Greenhouses
A 91 Stanley & Sons Nursery, Inc.
A 97 Tripple Brook Farm
A 99 Valley Creek Nursery

LEPTOSPERMUMS
A 46 International Seed Supplies

LEUCODENDRONS
A 14 C 'n C Protea
A 46 International Seed Supplies
A 72 Parsley's Cape Seeds
A 77 Protea Farms of California
A 77 Protea Seed & Nursery Suppliers

LEUCOSPERMUMS
A 14 C 'n C Protea
A 72 Parsley's Cape Seeds
A 77 Protea Farms of California
A 77 Protea Gardens of Maui

LILACS
A 41 Heard Gardens, Ltd.
A 44 Hortica Gardens
A 44 Hortico, Inc.
A 64 Morden Nurseries, Ltd
A 89 Smith Nursery Co.

LILIES, HYBRID
A 6 B & D Lilies
A 7 Bakker of Holland
A 10 Borbeleta Gardens
A 13 Bundles of Bulbs
A 23 C. A. Cruickshank, Ltd.
A 24 Peter De Jager Bulb Co.
A 29 Fairyland Begonia & Lily Garden
A 39 Dr. Joseph C. Halinar
A 42 Hildenbrandt's Iris Gardens
A 43 Holiday Seeds
A 43 Honeywood Lilies
A 61 Messelaar Bulb Co.
A 64 Moose Tubers
A 70 Oregon Bulb Farms
A 80 Rex Bulb Farms
A 81 Riverside Gardens
A 81 Robinett Bulb Farm
A 85 Saxton Gardens
A 85 John Scheepers, Inc.
A 98 TyTy Plantation
A 99 Vandenberg
A 102 The Waushara Gardens

LILIES, SPECIES
A 6 B & B Laboratories
A 6 B & D Lilies
A 8 Beersheba Wildflower Garden
A 13 Bundles of Bulbs
A 17 Chadwell Himalayan Seed
A 34 Gardens of the Blue Ridge

PAGE SOURCE

LILIES, SPECIES
A 36 Russell Graham, Purveyor of Plants
A 39 Dr. Joseph C. Halinar
A 80 Rex Bulb Farms
A 81 Robinett Bulb Farm
A 85 Saxton Gardens

LIMA BEANS
A 29 Fern Hill Farm

LIRIOPES
A 4 American Daylily & Perennials
A 77 Prentiss Court Ground Covers
A 95 Thomasville Nurseries
A 98 Turnipseed Nursery Farms

LITHOPS
A 1 Abbey Gardens
A 14 Cactus Gem Nursery
A 61 Mesa Garden
A 80 Redlo Cacti
A 91 Southwest Seeds
A 92 Ed Storms, Inc.
A 98 Tucson Succulents
A 107 Roy Young, Seedsman

LOBELIA, PERENNIAL
A 104 The Wildwood Flower

LOBIVIAS
A 82 Rocky Waters Farm
A 88 Shein's Cactus

LOTUS
A 34 The Garden Source, Ltd.
A 56 Lilypons Water Gardens
A 84 Santa Barbara Water Gardens
A 89 Slocum Water Gardens
A 97 William Tricker, Inc.
A 102 Water Ways Nursery
A 102 Waterford Gardens
A 104 Wicklein's Aquatic Farm & Nursery, Inc.

LUPINES
A 40 Hauser's Superior View Farm
A 72 Theodore Payne Foundation

MAGNOLIAS
A 8 Beaver Creek Nursery
A 31 Flora Lan Nursery
A 36 Gossler Farms Nursery
A 38 Greer Gardens
A 57 Louisiana Nursery
A 59 Magnolia Nursery & Display Garden
A 102 Wavecrest Nursery & Landscaping Co.
A 107 Yucca Do Nursery

MAMMILLARIAS
A 14 Cactus by Mueller
A 25 Desert Nursery
A 25 Desert Theater
A 38 Grigsby Cactus Gardens
A 51 Gerhard Koehres Cactus & Succulent Nursery
A 61 Mesa Garden
A 66 New Mexico Cactus Research
A 80 Redlo Cacti
A 84 Sand Ridge Greenhouse
A 86 Schulz Cactus Gardens
A 88 Shein's Cactus
A 91 Southwest Seeds

MAPLES, JAPANESE
A 25 Del's Japanese Maples
(continued next page)

PAGE SOURCE

MAPLES, JAPANESE (continued)
A 31 Flora Lan Nursery
A 32 Foxborough Nursery
A 38 Greer Gardens
A 40 Harstine Island Nursery
A 44 Hortica Gardens
A 45 Hughes Nursery
A 52 Michael & Janet Kristick
A 53 Lamtree Farm
A 57 Loucks Nursery
A 59 Maplewood Seed Company
A 60 Matsu-Momiji Nursery
A 63 Miniature Plant Kingdom
A 90 Sonoma Horticultural Nursery
A 92 Stonehurst Rare Plants
A 97 Trans Pacific Nursery
A 100 Vineland Nurseries
A 102 Wavecrest Nursery & Landscaping Co.

MAPLES, SPECIES
A 8 Beaver Creek Nursery
A 15 Camellia Forest Nursery
A 19 Cold Stream Farm
A 20 Colvos Creek Nursery & Landscaping
A 31 Forestfarm
A 45 Hughes Nursery
A 52 Michael & Janet Kristick
A 59 Maplethorpe
A 59 Maplewood Seed Company
A 61 Meta Horticultural Labs
A 80 Recor Tree Seed
A 89 Smith Nursery Co.
A 95 Terrapin Springs Farm
A 104 Whitman Farms

MEADOW PLANTS
A 104 Wildginger Woodlands

MELONS
A 41 Herb Gathering Inc.
A 62 Midwest Seed Growers, Inc.
A 98 Otis Twilley Seed Co.
A 105 Willhite Seed Co.

MESEMBS
A 66 New Mexico Cactus Research
A 92 Ed Storms, Inc.

MULBERRIES
A 30 The Fig Tree Nursery
A 42 Hidden Springs Nursery - Edible Landscaping
A 61 Meta Horticultural Labs
A 83 Saginaw Valley Nut Nursery
A 88 Sherwood's Greenhouses
A 97 Tripple Brook Farm

MUSHROOM SPAWN
A 19 Choice Edibles
A 30 Field and Forest Products, Inc.
A 33 Fungi Perfecti
A 65 Mushroompeople
A 103 Western Biologicals Ltd.

MUSHROOMS, MOREL
A 19 Choice Edibles

MUSHROOMS, SHIITAKE
A 30 Field and Forest Products, Inc.
A 33 Fungi Perfecti
A 65 Mushroompeople

NATIVE PLANTS
See Also - Specific Plants

PAGE SOURCE

NATIVE PLANTS
See Also - Specific Regions

NATIVE PLANTS, AUSTRALIAN
A 6 Austraflora of Utah
A 6 B & T Associates
A 13 Bushland Flora (Australian Seed Specialists)
A 14 C 'n C Protea
A 23 Cycad Gardens
A 44 J. L. Hudson, Seedsman
A 46 International Seed Supplies
A 67 Nindethana Seed Service
A 70 D. Orriell - Seed Exporters
A 77 Protea Gardens of Maui
A 97 Trans Pacific Nursery

NATIVE PLANTS, CALIFORNIAN
A 3 Alpine Plants
A 15 Callahan Seeds
A 53 Larner Seeds
A 53 Las Pilitas Nursery
A 71 Pacific Tree Farms
A 72 Theodore Payne Foundation
A 73 Peaceful Valley Farm Supply
A 80 Redwood City Seed Co.
A 81 Robinett Bulb Farm
A 101 Wapumne Native Plant Nursery

NATIVE PLANTS, CENTRAL & SOUTH AMERICAN
A 6 Austraflora of Utah
A 6 Aztekakti/Desertland Nursery
A 41 Heliconia Haus
A 81 Robinett Bulb Farm
A 82 Rocky Waters Farm

NATIVE PLANTS, HAWAIIAN
A 7 The Banana Tree
A 28 Exotica Seed Co. & Rare Fruit Nursery
A 66 New Frontiers

NATIVE PLANTS, HIMALAYAN
A 17 Chadwell Himalayan Seed
A 36 Gossler Farms Nursery
A 44 J. L. Hudson, Seedsman
A 52 P. Kohli & Co.
A 94 The Sweetbriar

NATIVE PLANTS, INDIAN
A 7 The Banana Tree
A 52 P. Kohli & Co.

NATIVE PLANTS, MEXICAN & CENTRAL AMERICAN
A 6 Austraflora of Utah
A 9 Bird Rock Tropicals
A 23 Cycad Gardens
A 91 Southwestern Native Seeds
A 107 Y. O. Ranch Cactus Co.

NATIVE PLANTS, MIDWESTERN U.S.
A 3 Alpine Gardens & Calico Shop
A 10 Boehlke's Woodland Gardens
A 27 Echinational Plant Products
A 52 LaFayette Home Nursery, Inc.
A 56 Little Valley Farm
A 62 Milaeger's Gardens
A 69 Oikos
A 69 Orchid Gardens
A 76 Prairie Moon Nursery
A 76 Prairie Nursery
A 77 Prairie Ridge Nursery/CRM Ecosystems, Inc.
A 106 Windrift Prairie Shop

PAGE SOURCE

NATIVE PLANTS, NEW ZEALAND
A 6 B & T Associates
A 7 The Banana Tree
A 90 Southern Seeds
A 97 Trans Pacific Nursery

NATIVE PLANTS, NORTH AMERICAN
A 3 Alpina Research & Montane Garden
A 10 Blueberry Hill
A 12 Joseph Brown, Native Seeds
A 26 Eastern Plant Specialties
A 43 Holbrook Farm & Nursery
A 44 J. L. Hudson, Seedsman
A 53 Lamtree Farm
A 54 Lee's Botanical Gardens
A 60 Maver Rare Perennials
A 64 Mountain Mist Nursery
A 65 Native Gardens
A 67 North American Wildflowers
A 72 Peace Seeds
A 81 Clyde Robin Seed Co.
A 87 Shady Oaks Nursery

NATIVE PLANTS, NORTHEASTERN U.S.
A 20 Companion Plants
A 24 Daystar
A 35 Draig Goch Seed Co.
A 66 Natural Gardens
A 77 The Primrose Path

NATIVE PLANTS, NORTHWESTERN U.S.
A 1 Abundant Life Seed Foundation
A 15 Callahan Seeds
A 20 Colvos Creek Nursery & Landscaping
A 31 Forestfarm
A 33 Frosty Hollow Nursery
A 54 Laurie's Garden
A 59 Maplethorpe
A 64 Mountain Mist Nursery
A 65 Native Seed Foundation
A 68 Northplan/Mountain Seed
A 68 Northwest Biological Enterprises
A 75 Plants of the Wild
A 88 Silvaseed Company, Inc.
A 89 Siskiyou Rare Plant Nursery

NATIVE PLANTS, ROCKY MOUNTAIN
A 54 Lawyer Nursery, Inc.
A 62 Midwest Cactus
A 64 Mountain West Seeds
A 68 Northplan/Mountain Seed
A 80 Recor Tree Seed
A 90 Solar Green, Ltd.
A 102 Weddle Native Gardens, Inc.

NATIVE PLANTS, SOUTH AFRICAN
A 7 The Banana Tree
A 9 Bio-Quest International
A 14 C 'n C Protea
A 16 Cape Seed & Bulb
A 72 Parsley's Cape Seeds
A 77 Protea Farms of California
A 77 Protea Gardens of Maui
A 77 Protea Seed & Nursery Suppliers
A 81 Robinett Bulb Farm
A 83 Rust-En-Vrede Nursery
A 92 Ed Storms, Inc.
A 97 Trans Pacific Nursery
A 107 Guy Wrinkle Exotic Plants
A 107 Y. O. Ranch Cactus Co.

NATIVE PLANTS, SOUTHEASTERN U.S.
A 25 Bill Dodd's Rare Plants

PAGE SOURCE

NATIVE PLANTS, SOUTHEASTERN U.S.
A 27 Eco-Gardens
A 34 Gardens of the Blue Ridge
A 47 Izard Ozark Natives
A 65 Native Gardens
A 66 Natural Gardens
A 67 Niche Gardens
A 73 Piccadilly Farm
A 84 Salter Tree Farm
A 90 South Florida Seed Supply
A 102 We-Du Nurseries
A 106 Woodlanders, Inc.

NATIVE PLANTS, SOUTHWESTERN U.S.
A 6 Artistic Plants
A 6 Aztekakti/Desertland Nursery
A 9 Bernardo Beach Native Plant Farm
A 23 The Nursery at the Dallas Nature Center
A 37 Greener 'N' Ever Tree Farm & Nursery
A 53 Larner Seeds
A 57 The Lowrey Nursery
A 66 Native Seeds/SEARCH
A 75 Plants of the Southwest
A 75 Plants of the Wild
A 91 Southwestern Native Seeds
A 98 Tucson Succulents
A 102 Weddle Native Gardens, Inc.
A 107 Y. O. Ranch Cactus Co.
A 107 Yucca Do Nursery

NEOREGELIAS
A 21 Cornelison Bromeliads
A 24 Dane Company
A 78 Rainforest Flora, Inc.
A 88 Shelldance Nursery

NEPENTHES
A 17 Cedar Ridge Nurseries
A 54 Lee's Botanical Gardens
A 70 Orgel's Orchids

NERINES
A 29 Fairyland Begonia & Lily Garden

NOTOCACTUS
A 14 Cactus by Mueller
A 25 Desert Theater
A 80 Redlo Cacti
A 84 Sand Ridge Greenhouse

NUT TREES, HARDY
See Also - Specific Nuts
A 7 Vernon Barnes & Son Nursery
A 8 Bear Creek Nursery
A 17 Cascade Forestry Service
A 19 Cold Stream Farm
A 26 Dutch Mountain Nursery
A 29 Fernald's Hickory Hill Nursery
A 30 Fiddyment Farms
A 31 Dean Foster Nurseries
A 36 Golden Bough Tree Farm
A 36 John H. Gordon, Jr., Grower
A 38 Grimo Nut Nursery
A 47 Ison's Nursery
A 62 J. E. Miller Nurseries, Inc.
A 64 Mt. Leo Nursery
A 67 Nolin River Nut Tree Nursery
A 69 Oikos
A 78 Raintree Nursery
A 83 Saginaw Valley Nut Nursery
A 84 St. Lawrence Nurseries
A 89 Skyblue Nurseries
A 96 Tolowa Nursery
(continued next page)

PAGE SOURCE

NUT TREES, HARDY (continued)
A 102 Waynesboro Nurseries
A 105 Wiley's Nut Grove

NUT TREES, LOW-CHILL
See Also - Specific Nuts
A 28 Exotica Seed Co. & Rare Fruit Nursery
A 30 Fiddyment Farms
A 33 Garden of Delights
A 85 Savage Farms Nursery

OAKS
A 12 Joseph Brown, Native Seeds
A 15 Callahan Seeds
A 17 Cascade Forestry Service
A 20 Colvos Creek Nursery & Landscaping
A 31 Forestfarm
A 39 Hanchar Nursery
A 53 Larner Seeds
A 53 Las Pilitas Nursery
A 64 Mountain Mist Nursery
A 69 Oikos
A 89 Smith Nursery Co.
A 95 Terrapin Springs Farm

ONION PLANTS
A 12 Brown's Omaha Plant Farms, Inc.
A 53 Lagomarsino Seeds
A 74 Piedmont Plant Company
A 83 SPB Sales

ONIONS
A 13 D.V. Burrell Seed Growers Co.
A 50 Kalmia Farm
A 53 D. Landreth Seed Company
A 64 Moose Tubers
A 83 S & H Organic Acres

OPUNTIAS
A 14 The Cactus Patch
A 25 Desert Nursery
A 46 Intermountain Cactus
A 61 Mesa Garden
A 62 Midwest Cactus
A 66 New Mexico Cactus Research
A 93 Sunnyvale Cactus Nursery
A 107 Y. O. Ranch Cactus Co.

ORCHIDS, ANGRAECUM
A 4 The Angraecum House
A 37 Greenleaf Orchids

ORCHIDS, ASCOCENDAS
A 29 Farnsworth Orchids
A 37 Green Valley Orchids
A 47 J & M Tropicals, Inc.
A 49 Jones & Scully
A 51 Kilworth Flowers
A 51 Arnold J. Klehm Grower, Inc.
A 54 Laurel Orchids
A 70 Orgel's Orchids
A 84 Santa Barbara Orchid Estate
A 86 Sea God Nurseries
A 105 Wilk Orchid Specialties

ORCHIDS, BRASSAVOLAS
A 70 Orchid Species Specialists
A 73 Pearl Harbor Orchids
A 81 Riverbend Orchids
A 84 Santa Barbara Orchid Estate

ORCHIDS, CATTLEYAS
A 8 The Beall Orchid Company

PAGE SOURCE

ORCHIDS, CATTLEYAS
A 11 Boulder Valley Orchids
A 17 Carter & Holmes, Inc.
A 22 Creole Orchids
A 29 Farnsworth Orchids
A 29 Fennell's Orchid Jungle
A 31 Fordyce Orchids
A 32 Fox Orchids, Inc.
A 33 G & B Orchid Laboratory
A 37 Great Lakes Orchids
A 37 Green Valley Orchids
A 37 Greenleaf Orchids
A 44 Spencer M. Howard Orchid Imports
A 46 Idle Hours Orchids
A 47 J & M Tropicals, Inc.
A 49 Jones & Scully
A 49 Jungle-Gems, Inc.
A 50 Kawamoto Orchid Nursery
A 50 Kensington Orchids
A 51 Kilworth Flowers
A 51 Arnold J. Klehm Grower, Inc.
A 54 Laurel Orchids
A 55 Lenette Greenhouses
A 58 Rod McLellan Co.
A 58 Madcap Orchids
A 60 Mauna Kea Orchids
A 68 Oak Hill Gardens
A 69 Orchibec
A 69 Orchid Haven
A 69 The Orchid House
A 70 Orchid Species Specialists
A 70 Orchids Bountiful
A 71 Owens Orchids
A 73 Penn Valley Orchids
A 81 Riverbend Orchids
A 86 Sea God Nurseries
A 86 Seagulls Landing Orchids
A 92 Stewart Orchids
A 94 Sunswept Laboratories
A 103 Ken West Orchids
A 105 Wilk Orchid Specialties

ORCHIDS, CYMBIDIUMS
A 18 Charles Island Gardens
A 22 Creole Orchids
A 26 Dos Pueblos Orchid Co.
A 33 G & B Orchid Laboratory
A 50 Kensington Orchids
A 51 Kilworth Flowers
A 58 Rod McLellan Co.
A 68 Oak Hill Gardens
A 69 The Orchid House
A 70 Orchids Royale
A 84 Santa Barbara Orchid Estate
A 94 Sunswept Laboratories

ORCHIDS, DENDROBIUMS
A 22 Creole Orchids
A 26 Dos Pueblos Orchid Co.
A 28 Exotics Hawaii, Inc.
A 29 Fennell's Orchid Jungle
A 33 G & B Orchid Laboratory
A 37 Green Valley Orchids
A 44 Spencer M. Howard Orchid Imports
A 46 Idle Hours Orchids
A 47 J & L Orchids
A 47 J & M Tropicals, Inc.
A 49 Jones & Scully
A 50 Kawamoto Orchid Nursery
A 69 Orchid Haven
A 70 Orgel's Orchids
A 73 Penn Valley Orchids
A 105 Wilk Orchid Specialties

PAGE SOURCE

ORCHIDS, DISA
A 16 Cape Seed & Bulb
A 67 Nooitgedag Disa Nursery
A 83 Rust-En-Vrede Nursery

ORCHIDS, DORITAENOPSIS
A 28 John Ewing Orchids, Inc.
A 37 Green Valley Orchids
A 47 J & M Tropicals, Inc.
A 69 Orchibec

ORCHIDS, EPIDENDRUMS
A 44 Spencer M. Howard Orchid Imports
A 47 J & L Orchids
A 69 Orchid Haven
A 70 Orchid Species Specialists
A 70 Orgel's Orchids
A 73 Penn Valley Orchids

ORCHIDS, HYBRIDS
See Also - Specific Genera
A 1 A & P Orchids
A 2 Alberts & Merkel Bros., Inc.
A 8 The Beall Orchid Company
A 11 Breckinridge Orchids
A 17 Carter & Holmes, Inc.
A 18 Charles Island Gardens
A 19 Clargreen Gardens Ltd.
A 19 Cloud Forest Orchids
A 28 Evon Orchids
A 28 John Ewing Orchids, Inc.
A 29 Farnsworth Orchids
A 29 Fennell's Orchid Jungle
A 31 Floridel Gardens
A 31 Fordyce Orchids
A 31 Fort Caroline Orchids
A 33 G & B Orchid Laboratory
A 37 Great Lakes Orchids
A 37 Greenleaf Orchids
A 44 Huan Bui Orchids, Inc.
A 45 Huronview Nurseries & Garden Centre
A 47 J & L Orchids
A 49 Jones & Scully
A 49 Jungle-Gems, Inc.
A 50 Kawamoto Orchid Nursery
A 50 Kensington Orchids
A 51 Arnold J. Klehm Grower, Inc.
A 54 Lauray of Salisbury
A 54 Laurel Orchids
A 55 Lenette Greenhouses
A 57 Paul P. Lowe
A 58 Madcap Orchids
A 59 Ann Mann's Orchids
A 60 Mauna Kea Orchids
A 68 Oak Hill Gardens
A 69 Orchibec
A 69 The Orchid Center
A 69 Orchid Haven
A 69 The Orchid House
A 70 Orchids Bountiful
A 70 Orchids by Hausermann, Inc.
A 70 Orchids Royale
A 73 Penn Valley Orchids
A 74 The Plant Shop's Botanical Gardens
A 78 Quality Cactus
A 81 Riverbend Orchids
A 84 Santa Barbara Orchid Estate
A 86 Seagulls Landing Orchids
A 92 Stewart Orchids
A 93 Sunshine Orchids International
A 94 Sunswept Laboratories
A 103 Ken West Orchids
A 108 Zuma Canyon Orchids

PAGE SOURCE

ORCHIDS, LAELIAS
A 29 Farnsworth Orchids
A 44 Spencer M. Howard Orchid Imports
A 47 J & L Orchids
A 70 Orchid Species Specialists
A 86 Seagulls Landing Orchids
A 103 Ken West Orchids

ORCHIDS, MASDEVALLIAS
A 7 Baker & Chantry Orchids
A 8 The Beall Orchid Company
A 37 Great Lakes Orchids
A 47 J & L Orchids

ORCHIDS, MERICLONES
A 17 Carter & Holmes, Inc.
A 19 Cloud Forest Orchids
A 28 John Ewing Orchids, Inc.
A 28 Exotics Hawaii, Inc.
A 29 Farnsworth Orchids
A 37 Green Valley Orchids
A 45 Huronview Nurseries & Garden Centre
A 49 Jones & Scully
A 50 Kawamoto Orchid Nursery
A 51 Arnold J. Klehm Grower, Inc.
A 58 Rod McLellan Co.
A 69 Orchibec
A 69 Orchid Haven
A 70 Orchids Bountiful
A 71 Owens Orchids
A 86 Seagulls Landing Orchids
A 94 Sunswept Laboratories
A 105 Wilk Orchid Specialties

ORCHIDS, MILTONIAS
A 7 Baker & Chantry Orchids
A 28 John Ewing Orchids, Inc.
A 29 Fennell's Orchid Jungle
A 50 Kensington Orchids
A 70 Orchid Species Specialists
A 70 Orchids Royale

ORCHIDS, MILTONOPSIS
A 8 The Beall Orchid Company
A 29 Farnsworth Orchids
A 49 Jungle-Gems, Inc.
A 86 Seagulls Landing Orchids

ORCHIDS, MINIATURE
A 18 Charles Island Gardens
A 29 Farnsworth Orchids
A 31 Fordyce Orchids
A 37 Great Lakes Orchids
A 37 Green Valley Orchids
A 44 Spencer M. Howard Orchid Imports
A 47 J & L Orchids
A 51 Kilworth Flowers
A 58 Madcap Orchids
A 69 Orchibec
A 70 Orchid Species Specialists
A 71 Owens Orchids
A 81 Riverbend Orchids
A 86 Sea Breeze Orchids
A 86 Seagulls Landing Orchids
A 94 Sunswept Laboratories

ORCHIDS, NATIVE SPECIES (U.S.)
A 12 Joseph Brown, Native Seeds
A 20 Conley's Garden Center
A 34 Gardens of the Blue Ridge
A 38 Griffey's Nursery
A 69 Orchid Gardens
A 104 The Wildflower Source

PAGE SOURCE

ORCHIDS, ODONTOGLOSSUMS
A 8 The Beall Orchid Company
A 18 Charles Island Gardens
A 69 The Orchid House
A 70 Orchids Bountiful
A 70 Orchids Royale

ORCHIDS, ONCIDIUMS
A 8 The Beall Orchid Company
A 22 Creole Orchids
A 29 Fennell's Orchid Jungle
A 37 Great Lakes Orchids
A 44 Spencer M. Howard Orchid Imports
A 47 J & L Orchids
A 54 Laurel Orchids
A 69 The Orchid House
A 70 Orchid Species Specialists
A 73 Pearl Harbor Orchids
A 73 Penn Valley Orchids
A 105 Wilk Orchid Specialties

ORCHIDS, PAPHIOPEDILUMS
A 1 A & P Orchids
A 7 Baker & Chantry Orchids
A 8 The Beall Orchid Company
A 11 Boulder Valley Orchids
A 22 Creole Orchids
A 26 Dos Pueblos Orchid Co.
A 32 Fox Orchids, Inc.
A 37 Great Lakes Orchids
A 44 Spencer M. Howard Orchid Imports
A 50 Kensington Orchids
A 51 Arnold J. Klehm Grower, Inc.
A 55 Lenette Greenhouses
A 58 Rod McLellan Co.
A 69 Orchibec
A 69 Orchid Haven
A 69 The Orchid House
A 70 Orchids Royale
A 70 Orgel's Orchids
A 73 Penn Valley Orchids
A 79 R. J. Rands Orchids
A 92 Stewart Orchids
A 94 Sunswept Laboratories

ORCHIDS, PHALAENOPSIS
A 1 A & P Orchids
A 8 The Beall Orchid Company
A 9 Bentley's Botanical Gardens
A 11 Breckinridge Orchids
A 17 Carter & Holmes, Inc.
A 26 Dos Pueblos Orchid Co.
A 28 John Ewing Orchids, Inc.
A 28 Exotics Hawaii, Inc.
A 29 Farnsworth Orchids
A 31 Floridel Gardens
A 32 Fox Orchids, Inc.
A 33 G & B Orchid Laboratory
A 37 Great Lakes Orchids
A 37 Green Valley Orchids
A 37 Greenleaf Orchids
A 46 Idle Hours Orchids
A 47 J & M Tropicals, Inc.
A 49 Jones & Scully
A 49 Jungle-Gems, Inc.
A 50 Kensington Orchids
A 51 Kilworth Flowers
A 51 Arnold J. Klehm Grower, Inc.
A 55 Lenette Greenhouses
A 58 Madcap Orchids
A 60 Mauna Kea Orchids
A 69 Orchibec
A 69 Orchid Haven

PAGE SOURCE

ORCHIDS, PHALAENOPSIS
A 69 The Orchid House
A 71 Owens Orchids
A 80 Joseph R. Redlinger Orchids
A 81 Riverbend Orchids
A 86 Sea God Nurseries
A 86 Seagulls Landing Orchids
A 92 Stewart Orchids
A 94 Sunswept Laboratories
A 105 Wilk Orchid Specialties
A 108 Zuma Canyon Orchids

ORCHIDS, SPECIES
A 4 The Angraecum House
A 7 Baker & Chantry Orchids
A 8 Beersheba Wildflower Garden
A 11 Boulder Valley Orchids
A 19 Cloud Forest Orchids
A 31 Fort Caroline Orchids
A 33 G & B Orchid Laboratory
A 37 Great Lakes Orchids
A 37 Greenleaf Orchids
A 44 Spencer M. Howard Orchid Imports
A 45 Huronview Nurseries & Garden Centre
A 46 International Growers Exchange
A 47 J & L Orchids
A 47 J & M Tropicals, Inc.
A 49 Jones & Scully
A 50 Kawamoto Orchid Nursery
A 51 Kilworth Flowers
A 51 Arnold J. Klehm Grower, Inc.
A 54 Lauray of Salisbury
A 54 Laurel Orchids
A 57 Paul P. Lowe
A 68 Oak Hill Gardens
A 69 Orchibec
A 69 The Orchid Center
A 69 Orchid Haven
A 69 The Orchid House
A 70 Orchid Species Specialists
A 70 Orchids Bountiful
A 70 Orchids by Hausermann, Inc.
A 70 Orgel's Orchids
A 73 Penn Valley Orchids
A 74 The Plant Shop's Botanical Gardens
A 84 Santa Barbara Orchid Estate
A 86 Sea Breeze Orchids
A 94 Sunswept Laboratories
A 101 W. K. Quality Bromeliads

ORCHIDS, VANDAS
A 22 Creole Orchids
A 37 Green Valley Orchids
A 37 Greenleaf Orchids
A 47 J & M Tropicals, Inc.
A 49 Jones & Scully
A 50 Kawamoto Orchid Nursery
A 51 Arnold J. Klehm Grower, Inc.
A 54 Laurel Orchids
A 58 Madcap Orchids
A 70 Orgel's Orchids
A 86 Sea God Nurseries
A 105 Wilk Orchid Specialties

PACHYSANDRA
A 34 Gilson Gardens
A 73 Peekskill Nurseries
A 77 Prentiss Court Ground Covers
A 94 Ter-El Nursery

PALMS
A 20 Colvos Creek Nursery & Landscaping
A 28 Exotica Seed Co. & Rare Fruit Nursery
(continued next page)

PAGE SOURCE

PALMS (continued)
A 33 Garden of Delights
A 46 International Seed Supplies
A 51 Gerhard Koehres Cactus & Succulent Nursery
A 66 New Frontiers
A 70 D. Orriell - Seed Exporters
A 78 Quality Cactus
A 90 South Florida Seed Supply
A 103 Westside Exotics Palm Nursery
A 106 Woodlanders, Inc.

PALMS, RHAPIS
A 4 Anything Grows Greenhouse
A 80 Rhapis Gardens
A 80 Rhapis Palm Growers

PALMS, TROPICAL
A 6 B & T Associates
A 17 Carter Seeds
A 27 Endangered Species
A 43 Jerry Horne - Rare Plants
A 80 Rhapis Palm Growers
A 103 Westside Exotics Palm Nursery

PANSIES
A 98 TyTy Plantation

PAPAYAS
A 34 Garden World
A 90 South Seas Nursery

PARODIAS
A 86 Schulz Cactus Gardens
A 88 Shein's Cactus

PASSIONFLOWERS
A 44 C. W. Hosking - Exotic Seed Importer
A 74 The Plant Kingdom

PAWPAWS
A 24 Corwin Davis Nursery
A 27 Edible Landscaping
A 36 John H. Gordon, Jr., Grower
A 40 Hartmann's Plantation, Inc.
A 56 Living Tree Centre
A 61 Meta Horticultural Labs
A 67 Nolin River Nut Tree Nursery
A 69 Oikos
A 83 Saginaw Valley Nut Nursery
A 88 Sherwood's Greenhouses
A 105 Wiley's Nut Grove

PEACHES
A 1 Adams County Nursery, Inc.
A 4 Ames' Orchard and Nursery
A 23 Cumberland Valley Nurseries, Inc.
A 48 Johnson Nursery
A 91 Southmeadow Fruit Gardens
A 92 Stark Bro's Nurseries & Orchards Co.
A 106 Womack Nursery Co.

PEARS
A 1 Adams County Nursery, Inc.
A 5 Apple Hill Orchards
A 23 Cumberland Valley Nurseries, Inc.
A 30 The Fig Tree Nursery
A 48 Johnson Nursery
A 56 Living Tree Centre
A 82 Rocky Meadow Orchard & Nursery
A 84 St. Lawrence Nurseries
A 88 Sherwood's Greenhouses
A 92 Stark Bro's Nurseries & Orchards Co.
A 99 VanWell Nursery, Inc.

PAGE SOURCE

PEARS, ANTIQUE
A 5 Apple Hill Orchards
A 5 Arbor & Espalier
A 90 Sonoma Antique Apple Nursery
A 91 Southmeadow Fruit Gardens
A 96 Tolowa Nursery

PEARS, ORIENTAL
A 1 Adams County Nursery, Inc.
A 5 Apple Hill Orchards
A 12 Buckley Nursery
A 32 Fowler Nurseries, Inc.
A 90 Sonoma Antique Apple Nursery
A 96 Tolowa Nursery

PECANS
A 23 Cumberland Valley Nurseries, Inc.
A 29 Fernald's Hickory Hill Nursery
A 32 Fowler Nurseries, Inc.
A 38 Grimo Nut Nursery
A 67 Nolin River Nut Tree Nursery
A 69 Oikos
A 105 Wiley's Nut Grove
A 106 Womack Nursery Co.

PELARGONIUMS
A 21 Cook's Geranium Nursery
A 24 Davidson-Wilson Greenhouses
A 66 New Leaf
A 74 Pine Ridge Garden Gallery
A 87 Shady Hill Gardens
A 107 Young's Mesa Nursery

PELARGONIUMS, SPECIES
A 16 Cape Seed & Bulb
A 21 Cook's Geranium Nursery
A 66 New Leaf
A 72 Parsley's Cape Seeds
A 74 Pine Ridge Garden Gallery
A 83 Rust-En-Vrede Nursery
A 87 Shady Hill Gardens
A 107 Young's Mesa Nursery

PENSTEMONS
A 9 Bernardo Beach Native Plant Farm
A 20 Colorado Alpines, Inc.
A 48 Klaus R. Jelitto
A 53 Las Pilitas Nursery
A 64 Mountain West Seeds
A 71 Owl Ridge Alpines
A 72 Theodore Payne Foundation
A 87 Select Seeds
A 90 Solar Green, Ltd.

PEONIES, HERBACEOUS
A 4 Anderson Iris Gardens
A 11 Brand Peony Farm
A 14 Busse Gardens
A 16 Caprice Farm
A 34 Gardenimport, Inc.
A 41 Hickory Hill Gardens
A 42 Hildenbrandt's Iris Gardens
A 46 Illini Iris
A 46 Iris Country
A 51 Klehm Nursery
A 66 The New Peony Farm
A 79 Reath's Nursery
A 100 Andre Viette Farm & Nursery
A 102 Wayside Gardens
A 103 White Flower Farm
A 104 Gilbert H. Wild & Son, Inc.

PAGE SOURCE

PEONIES, TREE
A 14 Busse Gardens
A 16 Caprice Farm
A 46 Iris Country
A 51 Klehm Nursery
A 79 Reath's Nursery

PEPEROMIAS
A 39 Robert B. Hamm
A 60 Marvelous Minis

PEPPERS, HOT
A 2 Alfrey -- Peter Pepper Seeds
A 13 D.V. Burrell Seed Growers Co.
A 36 Grace's Gardens
A 44 Horticultural Enterprises
A 66 Native Seeds/SEARCH
A 73 The Pepper Gal
A 76 Porter & Son
A 80 Redwood City Seed Co.
A 100 Vermont Bean Seed Co.
A 105 Willhite Seed Co.

PERENNIALS
See Also - Specific Plants
A 1 Adamgrove
A 2 Allen, Sterling & Lothrop
A 3 Alpenflora Gardens
A 3 Alpina Research & Montane Garden
A 3 Alpine Plants
A 3 Alpine Valley Gardens
A 4 American Daylily & Perennials
A 4 Angel Seed Company
A 5 Appalachian Wildflower Nursery
A 5 Applewood Seed Company
A 7 Vernon Barnes & Son Nursery
A 8 Beaverlodge Nursery
A 8 Bee Rock Herb Farm
A 10 Kurt Bluemel, Inc.
A 10 Bluestone Perennials
A 10 Borbeleta Gardens
A 12 Joseph Brown, Native Seeds
A 13 W. Atlee Burpee Company
A 14 Busse Gardens
A 14 The Butchart Gardens
A 16 Camelot North
A 16 Canyon Creek Nursery
A 16 Caprice Farm
A 17 Carroll Gardens
A 17 Catnip Acres Farm
A 17 Chadwell Himalayan Seed
A 18 Chiltern Seeds
A 19 Clargreen Gardens Ltd.
A 19 Clifford's Perennial & Vine
A 19 Coastal Gardens & Nursery
A 20 Comstock, Ferre & Co.
A 21 Cooper's Garden
A 22 The Country Garden
A 22 Country View Gardens
A 22 Cricklewood Nursery
A 22 Crosman Seed Corp.
A 22 Crownsville Nursery
A 23 C. A. Cruickshank, Ltd.
A 23 Dabney Herbs
A 23 The Nursery at the Dallas Nature Center
A 24 William Dam Seeds
A 24 Dan's Garden Shop
A 24 Daystar
A 24 DeGiorgi Company, Inc.
A 25 Dionysos' Barn
A 26 Dominion Seed House
A 26 E & H Products
A 26 Early's Farm & Garden Centre, Inc.

PAGE SOURCE

PERENNIALS
A 27 Echinational Plant Products
A 27 Eco-Gardens
A 27 Englerth Gardens
A 28 F W H Seed Exchange
A 29 Far North Gardens
A 29 Fedco Seeds
A 30 Henry Field Seed & Nursery Co.
A 30 Flora Favours
A 31 Flowerland
A 31 Forestfarm
A 32 The Fragrant Path
A 33 Garden Perennials
A 34 Garden Place
A 34 Gardenimport, Inc.
A 35 Girard Nurseries
A 35 Gladside Gardens
A 36 Goodwin Creek Gardens
A 36 Russell Graham, Purveyor of Plants
A 38 Grianan Gardens
A 39 Gurney Seed & Nursery Co.
A 40 Harris Seeds
A 40 Hauser's Superior View Farm
A 41 Hickory Hill Gardens
A 43 Holbrook Farm & Nursery
A 43 Honeywood Lilies
A 44 Hortico, Inc.
A 44 J. L. Hudson, Seedsman
A 45 Ed Hume Seeds, Inc.
A 45 Huronview Nurseries & Garden Centre
A 46 International Growers Exchange
A 46 Inter-State Nurseries
A 47 Island Seed Mail Order
A 48 Klaus R. Jelitto
A 48 Jernigan Gardens
A 49 J. W. Jung Seed Co.
A 50 Kelly Nurseries of Dansville, Inc.
A 51 Klehm Nursery
A 52 P. Kohli & Co.
A 52 Kordonowy's Dahlias
A 53 Lakeland Nursery Sales
A 53 Lakeshore Tree Farms, Ltd.
A 54 Orol Ledden & Sons
A 56 Liberty Seed Company
A 57 Lost Prairie Herb Farm
A 57 Louisiana Nursery
A 58 McConnell Nurseries, Inc.
A 58 McFayden Seeds
A 59 Maple Tree Gardens
A 59 Maplethorpe
A 60 Maver Rare Perennials
A 60 Earl May Seed & Nursery Co.
A 61 Meadowbrook Herb Garden
A 61 Mellinger's Inc.
A 62 Milaeger's Gardens
A 63 Miniature Plant Kingdom
A 63 Mo's Greenhouse
A 63 Montrose Nursery
A 65 Native Gardens
A 65 Native Seeds, Inc.
A 66 Natural Gardens
A 66 Nature's Garden Nursery
A 67 Niche Gardens
A 67 North American Wildflowers
A 68 Northwest Biological Enterprises
A 71 Owen Farms
A 71 Owl Ridge Alpines
A 72 Park Seed Company, Inc.
A 72 Theodore Payne Foundation
A 73 Perennial Seed Exchange
A 73 Piccadilly Farm
A 74 Pinetree Garden Seeds
A 76 Powell's Gardens
(continued next page)

PAGE SOURCE

PERENNIALS (continued)
A 77 The Primrose Path
A 77 Putney Nursery, Inc.
A 78 Rakestraw's Perennial Gardens
A 81 Rice Creek Gardens
A 81 Richters
A 82 Rocknoll Nursery
A 84 Sandy Mush Herb Nursery
A 85 Savory's Greenhouse
A 85 John Scheepers, Inc.
A 86 Seed Centre Ltd.
A 87 Seeds Blum
A 87 Select Seeds
A 87 Shady Oaks Nursery
A 89 Skyline Nursery
A 89 Soergel Greenhouses
A 90 Solar Green, Ltd.
A 91 Spring Hill Nurseries Co.
A 92 Stokes Seed Company
A 93 Sunlight Gardens
A 93 Sunnybrook Farms Nursery
A 94 Sutton Seeds, Ltd.
A 94 T & T Seeds, Ltd.
A 94 Ter-El Nursery
A 95 Thompson & Morgan
A 97 Tregunno Seeds
A 97 Triple Oaks Nursery
A 99 Vandenberg
A 100 Vesey's Seeds Ltd.
A 101 Mary Walker Bulb Company
A 102 The Waushara Gardens
A 102 Wayside Gardens
A 102 We-Du Nurseries
A 103 Well-Sweep Herb Farm
A 103 West Kootenay Herb Nursery
A 103 White Flower Farm
A 104 The Wildwood Flower
A 106 Windrift Prairie Shop
A 106 Woodlanders, Inc.
A 107 Wrenwood of Berkeley Springs
A 107 Wright Iris Nursery
A 107 Wyatt-Quarles Seed Co.
A 107 Yucca Do Nursery

PERSIMMONS
A 15 California Nursery Co.
A 18 Chestnut Hill Nursery, Inc.
A 27 Edible Landscaping
A 30 The Fig Tree Nursery
A 36 John H. Gordon, Jr., Grower
A 56 Living Tree Centre
A 61 Meta Horticultural Labs
A 67 Nolin River Nut Tree Nursery
A 68 Northwoods Nursery
A 88 Sherwood's Greenhouses
A 105 Wiley's Nut Grove

PHILODENDRONS
A 90 Southern Exposure

PHLOX
A 5 Appalachian Wildflower Nursery
A 10 Bluestone Perennials
A 20 Colorado Alpines, Inc.
A 30 Flora Favours
A 100 Andre Viette Farm & Nursery

PIERIS
A 31 Flora Lan Nursery
A 32 Foxborough Nursery
A 40 Hass Nursery
A 83 Roslyn Nursery
A 100 Vineland Nurseries

PAGE SOURCE

PIERIS
A 101 Washington Evergreen Nursery

PISTACHIOS
A 15 California Nursery Co.
A 30 Fiddyment Farms

PLATYCERIUMS
A 27 Edelweiss Gardens
A 41 Heliconia Haus
A 43 Jerry Horne - Rare Plants
A 69 The Orchid Center
A 78 Rainforest Flora, Inc.

PLUMERIAS
A 37 Green Plant Research
A 59 Marilynn's Garden
A 66 New Frontiers
A 76 The Plumeria People
A 78 Rainforest Plantes et Fleurs, Inc.

PLUMS
A 1 Adams County Nursery, Inc.
A 23 Cumberland Valley Nurseries, Inc.
A 48 Johnson Nursery
A 82 Rocky Meadow Orchard & Nursery
A 91 Southmeadow Fruit Gardens
A 106 Womack Nursery Co.

POPCORN
A 21 Corns
A 22 Cross Seed Company
A 29 Farmer Seed & Nursery
A 87 Seedway, Inc.
A 88 Shissler Seed Company

POPLARS, HYBRID
A 19 Cold Stream Farm
A 39 Hanchar Nursery
A 96 Tolowa Nursery

POPPIES, ORIENTAL
A 19 Clifford's Perennial & Vine
A 34 Garden Place
A 42 Hildenbrandt's Iris Gardens
A 53 Lamb Nurseries
A 63 Mohns, Inc.
A 100 Andre Viette Farm & Nursery
A 102 Wayside Gardens
A 103 White Flower Farm

POTATOES, SEED
A 8 Beckers Seed Potatoes
A 26 Dominion Seed House
A 26 Early's Farm & Garden Centre, Inc.
A 48 Johnson Seed Company
A 64 Moose Tubers
A 65 Native Seed Foundation
A 72 Peace Seeds
A 106 Wilton's Organic Seed Potatoes

PRAIRIE PLANTS
See Also - Grasses, Prairie
See Also - Wildflowers, Prairie
A 9 Bernardo Beach Native Plant Farm
A 10 Boehlke's Woodland Gardens
A 12 Joseph Brown, Native Seeds
A 23 The Nursery at the Dallas Nature Center
A 27 Echinational Plant Products
A 52 LaFayette Home Nursery, Inc.
A 56 Little Valley Farm
A 62 Midwest Wildflowers
A 62 Milaeger's Gardens
(continued next page)

PAGE SOURCE

PRAIRIE PLANTS (continued)
A 76 Prairie Moon Nursery
A 76 Prairie Nursery
A 77 Prairie Ridge Nursery/CRM Ecosystems, Inc.
A 106 Windrift Prairie Shop

PRIMULAS
A 5 Appalachian Wildflower Nursery
A 7 Bailey's
A 9 Blackmore & Langdon
A 17 Chadwell Himalayan Seed
A 18 Chehalis Rare Plant Nursery
A 20 Colorado Alpines, Inc.
A 22 Cricklewood Nursery
A 24 Daystar
A 29 Far North Gardens
A 36 Russell Graham, Purveyor of Plants
A 36 Grand Ridge Nursery
A 45 Brenda Hyatt
A 48 Klaus R. Jelitto
A 63 Montrose Nursery
A 66 Nature's Garden Nursery
A 77 The Primrose Path
A 86 Seedalp

PROTEACEAE
A 6 B & T Associates
A 14 C 'n C Protea
A 70 D. Orriell - Seed Exporters
A 77 Protea Seed & Nursery Suppliers
A 89 Anthony J. Skittone

PROTEAS
A 72 Parsley's Cape Seeds
A 77 Protea Farms of California
A 77 Protea Gardens of Maui

PUMPKINS, GIANT
A 25 Howard N. Dill
A 62 Midwest Seed Growers, Inc.
A 64 Mountain Valley Seeds & Nursery
A 88 Shepherd's Garden Seeds
A 100 Vesey's Seeds Ltd.
A 105 Willhite Seed Co.

PYRETHRUMS
A 40 Hauser's Superior View Farm

PYRRHOCACTUS
A 66 New Mexico Cactus Research

QUINCES
A 38 Greenmantle Nursery
A 42 Hidden Springs Nursery - Edible Landscaping
A 56 Living Tree Centre
A 102 Wavecrest Nursery & Landscaping Co.

RASPBERRIES
A 1 Ahrens Strawberry Nursery
A 2 Allen Company
A 10 Blue Star Lab
A 12 Brittingham Plant Farms
A 47 Ison's Nursery
A 59 Makielski Berry Farm & Nursery
A 68 Nourse Farms, Inc.
A 71 Pacific Berry Works
A 81 Rider Nurseries
A 103 Whistling Wings Farm, Inc.
A 106 Windy Ridge Nursery

REDWOOD, DAWN
A 90 Sonoma Horticultural Nursery

PAGE SOURCE

RHIPSALIS
A 8 Beahm Epiphyllum Gardens
A 15 California Epi Center
A 78 Rainbow Gardens Nursery & Bookshop

RHODODENDRONS, HYBRIDS
A 11 The Bovees Nursery
A 12 Briarwood Gardens
A 13 Bull Valley Rhododendron Nursery
A 16 Cardinal Nursery
A 16 Carlson's Gardens
A 18 Chambers Nursery
A 23 The Cummins Garden
A 26 Eastern Plant Specialties
A 27 Ericaceae
A 31 Flora Lan Nursery
A 34 Louis Gerardi Nursery
A 37 The Greenery
A 38 Greer Gardens
A 39 Hall Rhododendrons
A 40 Harstine Island Nursery
A 43 Holly Hills, Inc.
A 44 Horsley Rhododendron Nursery
A 49 Justice Gardens
A 64 Mowbray Gardens
A 66 E. B. Nauman, Nurseryman
A 68 North Coast Rhododendron Nursery
A 83 Roslyn Nursery
A 90 Sonoma Horticultural Nursery
A 94 The Sweetbriar
A 97 Transplant Nursery
A 97 Trillium Lane Nursery
A 100 Vineland Nurseries
A 103 Westgate Garden Nursery
A 104 Whitney Gardens
A 106 Woodland Nurseries

RHODODENDRONS, SPECIES
A 11 The Bovees Nursery
A 23 The Cummins Garden
A 25 Bill Dodd's Rare Plants
A 37 The Greenery
A 38 Greer Gardens
A 39 Hall Rhododendrons
A 49 Justice Gardens
A 53 Lamtree Farm
A 64 Mowbray Gardens
A 68 North Coast Rhododendron Nursery
A 83 Roslyn Nursery
A 86 F. W. Schumacher Co.
A 90 Sonoma Horticultural Nursery
A 94 The Sweetbriar
A 97 Transplant Nursery
A 97 Trillium Lane Nursery
A 103 Westgate Garden Nursery
A 104 Whitney Gardens

RHODODENDRONS, VIREYA
A 11 The Bovees Nursery
A 38 Greer Gardens
A 80 Red's Rhodies & Alpine Gardens
A 90 Sonoma Horticultural Nursery
A 101 Vireya Specialties Nursery

RHUBARB
A 1 Ahrens Strawberry Nursery
A 12 Buckley Nursery
A 48 Jackson & Perkins Co.
A 53 D. Landreth Seed Company
A 63 Mo's Greenhouse
A 68 Nourse Farms, Inc.
A 81 Rider Nurseries

PAGE SOURCE

RIBES
A 53 Las Pilitas Nursery

ROCK GARDEN PLANTS
See Also - Specific Plants
A 1 Adamgrove
A 3 Alpenflora Gardens
A 3 Alpina Research & Montane Garden
A 3 Alpine Plants
A 5 Appalachian Wildflower Nursery
A 10 Bluestone Perennials
A 11 The Bovees Nursery
A 13 Bushland Flora (Australian Seed Specialists)
A 14 The Butchart Gardens
A 17 Chadwell Himalayan Seed
A 18 Chehalis Rare Plant Nursery
A 18 Chiltern Seeds
A 19 Coenosium Gardens
A 20 Colorado Alpines, Inc.
A 22 Cricklewood Nursery
A 23 The Nursery at the Dallas Nature Center
A 27 Eco-Gardens
A 29 Fancy Fronds
A 29 Far North Gardens
A 30 Flora Favours
A 38 Grianan Gardens
A 47 Island Seed Mail Order
A 48 Klaus R. Jelitto
A 52 P. Kohli & Co.
A 52 L. Kreeger
A 52 Michael & Janet Kristick
A 53 Lamb Nurseries
A 57 Lost Prairie Herb Farm
A 58 McClure & Zimmerman
A 60 Maver Rare Perennials
A 63 Montrose Nursery
A 64 Mountain West Seeds
A 65 Native Gardens
A 66 Nature's Garden Nursery
A 67 Niche Gardens
A 68 Northwest Biological Enterprises
A 71 Owl Ridge Alpines
A 75 Plants of the Wild
A 76 Prairie Moon Nursery
A 77 The Primrose Path
A 80 Red's Rhodies & Alpine Gardens
A 81 Rice Creek Gardens
A 82 Rocknoll Nursery
A 83 Jim & Irene Russ Quality Plants
A 83 Rust-En-Vrede Nursery
A 84 Sandy Mush Herb Nursery
A 86 Seedalp
A 89 Siskiyou Rare Plant Nursery
A 89 Skyline Nursery
A 89 Soergel Greenhouses
A 90 Solar Green, Ltd.
A 90 Southern Seeds
A 91 Southwestern Native Seeds
A 91 Squaw Mountain Gardens
A 93 Sunlight Gardens
A 94 Sutton Seeds, Ltd.
A 95 Thompson & Morgan
A 102 We-Du Nurseries
A 104 Wildginger Woodlands
A 104 Wildwood Gardens
A 107 Wrenwood of Berkeley Springs

ROOTSTOCKS, FRUIT TREES
A 38 Grootendorst Nurseries
A 78 Raintree Nursery
A 82 Rocky Meadow Orchard & Nursery

PAGE SOURCE

ROSES
A 5 Armstrong Roses
A 6 BDK Nursery
A 21 Country Bloomers Nursery
A 27 Emlong Nurseries
A 39 Gurney Seed & Nursery Co.
A 40 Hastings
A 41 Heritage Rosarium
A 41 Heritage Rose Gardens
A 43 Historical Roses
A 43 Honeywood Lilies
A 44 Hortico, Inc.
A 46 Inter-State Nurseries
A 48 Jackson & Perkins Co.
A 50 Kelly Nurseries of Dansville, Inc.
A 52 V. Kraus Nurseries, Ltd.
A 52 Krider Nurseries
A 57 Lowe's own-root Roses
A 58 McConnell Nurseries, Inc.
A 62 Milaeger's Gardens
A 64 Morden Nurseries, Ltd
A 71 Richard Owen Nursery
A 72 Carl Pallek & Son Nursery
A 74 Pickering Nurseries Inc.
A 81 Rider Nurseries
A 82 Rose Acres
A 82 Roses by Fred Edmunds
A 85 Savage Farms Nursery
A 88 R. H. Shumway Seedsman
A 91 Spring Hill Nurseries Co.
A 92 Stark Bro's Nurseries & Orchards Co.
A 92 Stocking Rose Nursery
A 94 T & T Seeds, Ltd.
A 95 Thomasville Nurseries
A 96 Tillinghast Seed Co.
A 102 Wayside Gardens

ROSES, MINIATURE
A 3 Alpenflora Gardens
A 5 Armstrong Roses
A 6 BDK Nursery
A 21 Country Bloomers Nursery
A 35 Gloria Dei
A 49 Justice Miniature Roses
A 58 MB Farm Miniature Roses
A 58 McDaniel's Miniature Roses
A 62 Mini-Roses
A 63 Miniature Plant Kingdom
A 67 Nor'East Miniature Roses
A 70 Oregon Miniature Roses
A 74 Pixie Treasures Miniature Rose Nursery
A 82 Rose Acres
A 82 The Rose Garden & Mini Rose Nursery
A 82 Rosehill Farm
A 87 Sequoia Nursery - Moore Miniature Roses
A 92 Stocking Rose Nursery
A 96 Tiny Petals Nursery
A 99 Valley Creek Nursery

ROSES, MODERN SHRUB
A 38 Greenmantle Nursery
A 41 Heritage Rosarium
A 41 Heritage Rose Gardens
A 42 High Country Rosarium
A 43 Historical Roses
A 57 Lowe's own-root Roses
A 74 Pickering Nurseries Inc.
A 82 Rose Acres
A 82 Roses of Yesterday & Today

ROSES, OLD GARDEN
A 4 Antique Rose Emporium
A 6 BDK Nursery

(continued next page)

PAGE SOURCE

ROSES, OLD GARDEN (continued)
A 21 Country Bloomers Nursery
A 38 Greenmantle Nursery
A 41 Heritage Rosarium
A 41 Heritage Rose Gardens
A 42 High Country Rosarium
A 43 Historical Roses
A 57 Lowe's own-root Roses
A 72 Carl Pallek & Son Nursery
A 74 Pickering Nurseries Inc.
A 82 Rose Acres
A 82 Roses of Yesterday & Today

ROSES, SPECIES
A 6 BDK Nursery
A 21 Country Bloomers Nursery
A 38 Greenmantle Nursery
A 41 Heritage Rosarium
A 41 Heritage Rose Gardens
A 42 High Country Rosarium
A 57 Lowe's own-root Roses
A 64 Mountain Mist Nursery
A 74 Pickering Nurseries Inc.
A 82 Roses of Yesterday & Today

RUDBECKIAS
A 40 Hauser's Superior View Farm

SALAD VEGETABLES
A 20 The Cook's Garden
A 41 Herb Gathering Inc.
A 88 Shepherd's Garden Seeds

SALVIAS
A 16 Canyon Creek Nursery
A 53 Las Pilitas Nursery
A 63 Montrose Nursery

SANSEVIERIAS
A 4 Anything Grows Greenhouse
A 35 Glasshouse Works
A 38 Grigsby Cactus Gardens
A 78 Rainbow Gardens Nursery & Bookshop
A 89 Singers' Growing Things

SASKATOONS
A 53 Lakeshore Tree Farms, Ltd.
A 65 Native Seed Foundation
A 106 Windy Ridge Nursery

SEDUMS
A 3 Alpine Gardens & Calico Shop
A 10 Bluestone Perennials
A 21 Country Cottage
A 34 Garden Place
A 34 Gilson Gardens
A 41 The Herbfarm
A 53 Lamb Nurseries
A 66 Nature's Garden Nursery
A 76 Powell's Gardens
A 78 Rakestraw's Perennial Gardens
A 80 Red's Rhodies & Alpine Gardens
A 81 Rice Creek Gardens
A 83 Jim & Irene Russ Quality Plants
A 91 Squaw Mountain Gardens
A 94 Ter-El Nursery
A 107 Wrenwood of Berkeley Springs

SEMPERVIVUMS
A 3 Alpine Gardens & Calico Shop
A 14 Cactus Gem Nursery
A 21 Country Cottage
A 41 The Herbfarm

PAGE SOURCE

SEMPERVIVUMS
A 53 Lamb Nurseries
A 80 Red's Rhodies & Alpine Gardens
A 82 Rocknoll Nursery
A 83 Jim & Irene Russ Quality Plants
A 91 Squaw Mountain Gardens
A 94 Ter-El Nursery
A 107 Wrenwood of Berkeley Springs

SHADE PLANTS
See Also - Specific Plants
See Also - Woodland Plants
A 3 Alpine Plants
A 19 Coastal Gardens & Nursery
A 20 Color Farm Growers
A 21 Cooper's Garden
A 23 Dabney Herbs
A 26 Eastern Plant Specialties
A 27 Eco-Gardens
A 29 Fancy Fronds
A 31 Foliage Gardens
A 52 V. Kraus Nurseries, Ltd.
A 57 The Lowrey Nursery
A 59 Maroushek Gardens
A 65 Native Gardens
A 66 Nature's Garden Nursery
A 80 Rhapis Palm Growers
A 85 Savory's Greenhouse
A 87 Shady Oaks Nursery
A 93 Sunlight Gardens
A 94 Sutton Seeds, Ltd.
A 95 Thompson & Morgan
A 97 Tripple Brook Farm
A 101 Walden - West
A 102 We-Du Nurseries

SHALLOTS
A 17 Casa Yerba Gardens
A 41 Herb Gathering Inc.
A 50 Kalmia Farm
A 54 Le Jardin du Gourmet
A 80 Red's Rhodies & Alpine Gardens
A 83 S & H Organic Acres
A 84 Sandhurst Seeds
A 90 Southern Exposure Seed Exchange

SHASTA DAISIES
A 10 Bluestone Perennials
A 34 Garden Place
A 40 Hauser's Superior View Farm
A 89 Soergel Greenhouses

SHRUBS, DWARF
See Also - Bonsai, Plants for
A 3 Alpenflora Gardens
A 26 Eastern Plant Specialties
A 36 Gossler Farms Nursery
A 43 Holbrook Farm & Nursery
A 44 Hortica Gardens
A 100 Vineland Nurseries
A 101 Washington Evergreen Nursery
A 104 Wildwood Gardens
A 107 Yucca Do Nursery

SHRUBS, FLOWERING
See Also - Specific Plants
A 3 Alpina Research & Montane Garden
A 6 B & B Laboratories
A 8 Beaver Creek Nursery
A 8 Beaverlodge Nursery
A 15 Callahan Seeds
A 17 Carroll Gardens
A 18 Chiltern Seeds
(continued next page)

PAGE SOURCE

SHRUBS, FLOWERING (continued)
A 19 Cold Stream Farm
A 24 Daystar
A 25 Bill Dodd's Rare Plants
A 26 Dutch Mountain Nursery
A 29 Farmer Seed & Nursery
A 31 Forestfarm
A 34 Gardens of the Blue Ridge
A 34 Louis Gerardi Nursery
A 35 Girard Nurseries
A 38 Griffey's Nursery
A 39 Hall Rhododendrons
A 40 Harstine Island Nursery
A 43 Holbrook Farm & Nursery
A 44 Hortico, Inc.
A 52 V. Kraus Nurseries, Ltd.
A 52 Krider Nurseries
A 53 Lakeshore Tree Farms, Ltd.
A 53 Las Pilitas Nursery
A 54 Lawyer Nursery, Inc.
A 57 Louisiana Nursery
A 58 McConnell Nurseries, Inc.
A 60 Maver Rare Perennials
A 61 Mellinger's Inc.
A 64 Morden Nurseries, Ltd
A 64 Mt. Leo Nursery
A 73 Perennial Seed Exchange
A 76 Powell's Gardens
A 86 F. W. Schumacher Co.
A 91 Southwestern Native Seeds
A 91 Spring Hill Nurseries Co.
A 91 Stallings Exotic Nursery
A 97 Tripple Brook Farm
A 99 Valley Nursery
A 102 Waynesboro Nurseries
A 102 Wayside Gardens

SHRUBS, FOLIAGE
See Also - Specific Plants
A 8 Beaver Creek Nursery
A 13 Burgess Seed & Plant Co.
A 15 Camellia Forest Nursery
A 56 Little Valley Farm
A 68 Northwest Biological Enterprises
A 71 Owen Farms
A 86 F. W. Schumacher Co.
A 89 Smith Nursery Co.
A 99 Valley Nursery

SINNINGIAS
A 13 Buell's Greenhouse, Inc.
A 33 Lorine Friedrich
A 39 Growin'house
A 50 Karleens Achimenes
A 63 Miree's Gesneriads
A 74 The Plant Kingdom
A 75 Plants 'n' Things
A 75 Pleasant Hill African Violets
A 81 Roberts' Gesneriads
A 95 Tiki Nursery

STAPELIADS
A 3 Altman Specialty Plants
A 61 Mesa Garden
A 78 Rainman Succulent Nursery

STEWARTIAS
A 8 Beaver Creek Nursery
A 36 Gossler Farms Nursery
A 90 Sonoma Horticultural Nursery
A 103 Westgate Garden Nursery
A 104 Whitman Farms

PAGE SOURCE

STRAWBERRIES
A 1 Ahrens Strawberry Nursery
A 2 Allen Company
A 11 Boston Mountain Nurseries
A 12 Buckley Nursery
A 52 Krohne Plant Farms
A 55 Lewis Strawberry Nursery
A 59 Makielski Berry Farm & Nursery
A 68 Nourse Farms, Inc.
A 71 Pacific Berry Works
A 79 Rayner Bros.
A 81 Rider Nurseries

STRAWBERRIES, HARDY
A 2 Allen Company
A 12 Brittingham Plant Farms
A 52 Krohne Plant Farms
A 55 Lewis Strawberry Nursery
A 79 Rayner Bros.
A 106 Windy Ridge Nursery

STREPTOCARPUS
A 13 Buell's Greenhouse, Inc.
A 16 Cape Cod Violetry
A 22 Country Girl Greenhouses
A 29 Fairyland Begonia & Lily Garden
A 30 Fischer Greenhouses
A 39 Growin'house
A 57 Lyndon Lyon Greenhouses, Inc.
A 63 Miree's Gesneriads
A 95 Tiki Nursery

SUCCULENTS
See Also - Specific Plants
A 3 Altman Specialty Plants
A 6 Artistic Plants
A 6 Atkinson's Greenhouse
A 6 Aztekakti/Desertland Nursery
A 9 Bentley's Botanical Gardens
A 10 Boojum Unlimited
A 14 Cactus by Mueller
A 14 Cactus Gem Nursery
A 15 California Epi Center
A 19 Christa's Cactus
A 25 Desert Nursery
A 25 Desert Theater
A 38 Greenlife Gardens Greenhouses
A 38 Grigsby Cactus Gardens
A 39 Robert B. Hamm
A 42 Highland Succulents
A 49 K & L Cactus Nursery
A 51 Gerhard Koehres Cactus & Succulent Nursery
A 54 Lauray of Salisbury
A 59 Marilynn's Garden
A 60 Marvin's Cactus
A 61 Mesa Flora Nursery
A 61 Mesa Garden
A 66 New Mexico Desert Garden
A 72 The PanTree
A 78 Quality Cactus
A 78 Rainman Succulent Nursery
A 80 Red's Rhodies & Alpine Gardens
A 80 Redlo Cacti
A 82 Rocky Waters Farm
A 88 Shein's Cactus
A 89 Singers' Growing Things
A 91 Southwest Seeds
A 92 Ed Storms, Inc.
A 98 Tucson Succulents
A 106 Winter Country Cacti
A 107 Guy Wrinkle Exotic Plants
A 107 Y. O. Ranch Cactus Co.
A 107 Roy Young, Seedsman

PAGE SOURCE

SUNFLOWERS
A 22 The Country Garden

SWEET PEAS
A 11 S & N Brackley
A 18 Chiltern Seeds
A 22 The Country Garden
A 64 Mountain Valley Seeds & Nursery

SWEET POTATO PLANTS
A 32 Fred's Plant Farm
A 53 Lagomarsino Seeds
A 59 Margrave Plant Co.

TERRARIUM PLANTS
See Also - Specific Plants
A 2 Arthur Eames Allgrove
A 6 Artistic Plants
A 17 Cedar Ridge Nurseries
A 50 Kartuz Greenhouses
A 54 Lee's Botanical Gardens
A 58 McKinney's Glasshouse
A 73 Peter Pauls Nurseries
A 81 Roberts' Gesneriads

TILLANDSIAS
A 9 Bird Rock Tropicals
A 10 Arthur Boe Distributor
A 21 Cornelison Bromeliads
A 24 Dane Company
A 34 Garden World
A 49 Jungle-Gems, Inc.
A 51 Gerhard Koehres Cactus & Succulent Nursery
A 59 Marilynn's Garden
A 69 The Orchid Center
A 78 Rainforest Flora, Inc.
A 88 Shelldance Nursery
A 97 Tropical Imports
A 101 W. K. Quality Bromeliads
A 107 Guy Wrinkle Exotic Plants

TOMATOES
A 2 Alfrey – Peter Pepper Seeds
A 13 D.V. Burrell Seed Growers Co.
A 36 Grace's Gardens
A 41 Herb Gathering Inc.
A 62 Midwest Seed Growers, Inc.
A 76 Porter & Son
A 84 Sandhurst Seeds
A 88 Shepherd's Garden Seeds
A 96 Tomato Growers Supply Company
A 96 The Tomato Seed Company, Inc.
A 100 Vermont Bean Seed Co.
A 105 Willhite Seed Co.

TOMATOES, HEIRLOOM
A 3 Alston Seed Growers
A 36 Good Seed Co.
A 72 Peace Seeds
A 84 Sandhurst Seeds
A 90 Southern Exposure Seed Exchange
A 96 The Tomato Seed Company, Inc.

TOMATOES, HYBRID
A 83 SPB Sales
A 87 Seedway, Inc.
A 96 Tomato Growers Supply Company
A 96 The Tomato Seed Company, Inc.
A 98 Otis Twilley Seed Co.

TOPIARY, PLANTED
A 28 Exotic Blossoms (TM) Topiary Sculptures

PAGE SOURCE

TREES, FLOWERING
See Also - Specific Plants
A 5 Appalachian Gardens
A 6 B & B Laboratories
A 8 Beaver Creek Nursery
A 8 Beaverlodge Nursery
A 17 Carroll Gardens
A 18 Chiltern Seeds
A 25 Bill Dodd's Rare Plants
A 26 Dutch Mountain Nursery
A 28 Exotica Seed Co. & Rare Fruit Nursery
A 30 Henry Field Seed & Nursery Co.
A 30 Flickingers' Nursery
A 31 Forestfarm
A 36 Golden Bough Tree Farm
A 36 Gossler Farms Nursery
A 38 Greer Gardens
A 38 Griffey's Nursery
A 40 Hastings
A 43 Holbrook Farm & Nursery
A 44 Hortico, Inc.
A 48 Jackson & Perkins Co.
A 50 Kelly Nurseries of Dansville, Inc.
A 52 V. Kraus Nurseries, Ltd.
A 52 Krider Nurseries
A 54 Lawson's Nursery
A 54 Lawyer Nursery, Inc.
A 57 Louisiana Nursery
A 61 Mellinger's Inc.
A 64 Mt. Leo Nursery
A 71 Pacific Tree Farms
A 86 F. W. Schumacher Co.
A 90 South Florida Seed Supply
A 91 Southwestern Native Seeds
A 91 Spring Hill Nurseries Co.
A 94 The Sweetbriar
A 96 Tolowa Nursery
A 99 Valley Nursery
A 102 Wayside Gardens
A 103 Westgate Garden Nursery
B 33 Winterthur Museum & Gardens
A 107 Yucca Do Nursery

TREES, FOLIAGE
See Also - Specific Plants
A 7 Vernon Barnes & Son Nursery
A 11 Boston Mountain Nurseries
A 13 Burgess Seed & Plant Co.
A 15 Callahan Seeds
A 17 Cascade Forestry Service
A 29 Farmer Seed & Nursery
A 33 Frosty Hollow Nursery
A 34 Louis Gerardi Nursery
A 36 Golden Bough Tree Farm
A 36 Gossler Farms Nursery
A 52 V. Kraus Nurseries, Ltd.
A 52 Krider Nurseries
A 60 Maver Rare Perennials
A 62 J. E. Miller Nurseries, Inc.
A 64 Morden Nurseries, Ltd
A 64 Mt. Leo Nursery
A 65 Musser Forests Inc.
A 71 Owen Farms
A 73 Perennial Seed Exchange
A 86 F. W. Schumacher Co.
A 90 South Florida Seed Supply
A 96 Tolowa Nursery
A 102 Waynesboro Nurseries
A 106 Woodland Nurseries

TREES, SEEDLING
See Also - Specific Plants
A 16 Carino Nurseries

(continued next page)

PAGE SOURCE

TREES, SEEDLING (continued)
A 19 Cold Stream Farm
A 28 Ernst Crownvetch Farms
A 30 Flickingers' Nursery
A 39 Hanchar Nursery
A 53 Lamtree Farm
A 54 Lawyer Nursery, Inc.
A 64 Mountain Mist Nursery
A 65 Musser Forests Inc.
A 69 Oikos
A 77 Qualitree Nursery
A 88 Silvaseed Company, Inc.
A 104 Whitman Farms

TRICHOCEREUS
A 19 Christa's Cactus

TRILLIUMS
A 8 Beersheba Wildflower Garden
A 34 Gardens of the Blue Ridge
A 37 The Greenery
A 89 Siskiyou Rare Plant Nursery
A 104 The Wildflower Source
A 104 Wildginger Woodlands

TULIPS
A 7 Bakker of Holland
A 11 Breck's
A 13 Bundles of Bulbs
A 23 The Daffodil Mart
A 24 Peter De Jager Bulb Co.
A 26 Dutch Gardens, Inc.
A 34 Gary's Perennials
A 57 John D. Lyon, Inc.
A 58 McClure & Zimmerman
A 61 Messelaar Bulb Co.
A 78 Quality Dutch Bulbs
A 99 Van Engelen Inc.
A 99 Vandenberg
A 99 Veldheer Tulip Gardens

VEGETABLE PLANTS
A 12 Brown's Omaha Plant Farms, Inc.
A 31 Dean Foster Nurseries
A 74 Piedmont Plant Company

VEGETABLES - WIDE ASSORTMENT
See Also - Specific Vegetables
A 1 Abundant Life Seed Foundation
A 2 Allen, Sterling & Lothrop
A 13 W. Atlee Burpee Company
A 14 Butterbrooke Farm
A 20 Comstock, Ferre & Co.
A 22 Crosman Seed Corp.
A 24 Dan's Garden Shop
A 24 DeGiorgi Company, Inc.
A 26 Dominion Seed House
A 26 Early's Farm & Garden Centre, Inc.
A 29 Farmer Seed & Nursery
A 29 Fedco Seeds
A 30 Henry Field Seed & Nursery Co.
A 34 Gardenimport, Inc.
A 36 Good Seed Co.
A 39 Gurney Seed & Nursery Co.
A 40 Harris Seeds
A 40 Hastings
A 45 Ed Hume Seeds, Inc.
A 47 Island Seed Mail Order
A 48 Johnny's Selected Seeds
A 49 J. W. Jung Seed Co.
A 53 Lagomarsino Seeds
A 53 D. Landreth Seed Company
A 54 Le Jardin du Gourmet

PAGE SOURCE

VEGETABLES - WIDE ASSORTMENT
A 54 Le Marche Seeds International
A 54 Orol Ledden & Sons
A 56 Liberty Seed Company
A 56 Lockhart Seeds
A 58 McFayden Seeds
A 60 Earl May Seed & Nursery Co.
A 61 Meyer Seed Co.
A 62 Miller-Bowie County Farmers Assn.
A 64 Mountain Valley Seeds & Nursery
A 65 Nationwide Seed & Supply
A 67 Nichols Garden Nursery, Inc.
A 72 Park Seed Company, Inc.
A 72 Peace Seeds
A 74 Piedmont Plant Company
A 74 Pinetree Garden Seeds
A 76 Pony Creek Nursery
A 76 Porter & Son
A 80 Redwood City Seed Co.
A 83 Roswell Seed Co.
A 83 SPB Sales
A 84 Sanctuary Seeds/Folklore Herb Co.
A 86 Seed Centre Ltd.
A 87 Seeds Blum
A 87 Seedway, Inc.
A 88 Shepherd's Garden Seeds
A 88 R. H. Shumway Seedsman
A 88 Siegers Seed Co.
A 92 Stokes Seed Company
A 94 Sutton Seeds, Ltd.
A 95 Territorial Seed Co.
A 95 Thompson & Morgan
A 96 Tillinghast Seed Co.
A 97 Tregunno Seeds
A 98 Otis Twilley Seed Co.
A 100 Vermont Bean Seed Co.
A 105 Willhite Seed Co.
A 107 Wyatt-Quarles Seed Co.

VEGETABLES, EUROPEAN
See Also - Specific Vegetables
A 4 Angel Seed Company
A 20 The Cook's Garden
A 24 William Dam Seeds
A 36 Grace's Gardens
A 37 Greenleaf Seeds
A 41 Herb Gathering Inc.
A 42 High Altitude Gardens
A 54 Le Jardin du Gourmet
A 54 Le Marche Seeds International
A 67 Nichols Garden Nursery, Inc.
A 80 Redwood City Seed Co.
A 88 Shepherd's Garden Seeds

VEGETABLES, GIANT
A 25 Howard N. Dill
A 29 Farmer Seed & Nursery
A 36 Grace's Gardens

VEGETABLES, HEIRLOOM
See Also - Specific Vegetables
A 1 Abundant Life Seed Foundation
A 11 Bountiful Gardens
A 14 Butterbrooke Farm
A 20 The Cook's Garden
A 28 F W H Seed Exchange
A 42 High Altitude Gardens
A 54 Le Marche Seeds International
A 72 Peace Seeds
A 88 R. H. Shumway Seedsman
A 90 Southern Exposure Seed Exchange

(continued next page)

PAGE SOURCE

VEGETABLES, HYBRID
See Also - Specific Vegetables
A 13 W. Atlee Burpee Company
A 20 The Cook's Garden
A 51 Kilgore Seed Company
A 56 Lockhart Seeds
A 62 Midwest Seed Growers, Inc.
A 76 Porter & Son
A 88 Siegers Seed Co.

VEGETABLES, LATIN AMERICAN
A 28 Exotica Seed Co. & Rare Fruit Nursery
A 36 Grace's Gardens
A 44 Horticultural Enterprises
A 54 Le Marche Seeds International
A 88 Shepherd's Garden Seeds

VEGETABLES, NATIVE AMERICAN
A 66 Native Seeds/SEARCH
A 75 Plants of the Southwest
A 80 Redwood City Seed Co.

VEGETABLES, OPEN-POLLINATED
See Also - Specific Vegetables
A 1 Abundant Life Seed Foundation
A 11 Bountiful Gardens
A 14 Butterbrooke Farm
A 36 Good Seed Co.
A 42 High Altitude Gardens
A 48 Johnson Seed Company
A 51 Kilgore Seed Company
A 53 D. Landreth Seed Company
A 54 Le Marche Seeds International
A 56 Liberty Seed Company
A 56 Lockhart Seeds
B 23 Organic Farm & Garden Supply
A 71 Ozark National Seed Order
A 72 Peace Seeds
A 76 Porter & Son
A 80 Redwood City Seed Co.
A 84 Sanctuary Seeds/Folklore Herb Co.
A 84 Sandhurst Seeds
A 87 Seeds Blum
A 88 R. H. Shumway Seedsman
A 88 Siegers Seed Co.
A 90 Southern Exposure Seed Exchange

VEGETABLES, ORIENTAL
A 23 Dacha Barinka
A 24 William Dam Seeds
A 28 Evergreen Y. H. Enterprises
A 36 Grace's Gardens
A 37 Greenleaf Seeds
A 51 Kitazawa Seed Co.
A 54 Le Marche Seeds International
A 56 Lockhart Seeds
A 67 Nichols Garden Nursery, Inc.
A 93 Sunrise Oriental Seed Co.
A 98 Tsang & Ma

VEGETABLES, ORNAMENTAL
A 2 Alfrey -- Peter Pepper Seeds
A 20 The Cook's Garden
A 100 Vesey's Seeds Ltd.

VEGETABLES, PATIO-SIZED
A 24 William Dam Seeds
A 72 Park Seed Company, Inc.
A 96 The Tomato Seed Company, Inc.

VEGETABLES, SHORT-SEASON
See Also - Specific Vegetables
A 2 Alberta Nurseries & Seed Company

PAGE SOURCE

VEGETABLES, SHORT-SEASON
A 2 Allen, Sterling & Lothrop
A 14 Butterbrooke Farm
A 24 William Dam Seeds
A 45 Ed Hume Seeds, Inc.
A 48 Johnny's Selected Seeds
A 64 Mountain Valley Seeds & Nursery
A 68 Northplan/Mountain Seed
A 79 Rawlinson Garden Seed
A 84 Sandhurst Seeds
A 86 Seed Centre Ltd.
A 87 Seeds Blum
A 94 T & T Seeds, Ltd.
A 100 Vesey's Seeds Ltd.

VENUS FLY TRAP
A 9 Black Copper Kits
A 54 Lee's Botanical Gardens
A 106 World Insectivorous Plants

VERONICAS
A 30 Flora Favours

VIBURNUMS
A 5 Appalachian Gardens
A 8 Beaver Creek Nursery
A 17 Carroll Gardens
A 102 Wavecrest Nursery & Landscaping Co.

VINCAS
A 30 Flickingers' Nursery
A 34 Gilson Gardens
A 77 Prentiss Court Ground Covers
A 98 Turnipseed Nursery Farms

VINES
See Also - Specific Plants
A 19 Clifford's Perennial & Vine
A 20 Conley's Garden Center
A 32 The Fragrant Path
A 38 Griffey's Nursery
A 44 J. L. Hudson, Seedsman
A 50 Kartuz Greenhouses
A 52 P. Kohli & Co.
A 56 Little Valley Farm
A 56 Logee's Greenhouses
A 71 Richard Owen Nursery
A 74 The Plant Kingdom
A 89 Smith Nursery Co.
A 91 Stallings Exotic Nursery
A 106 Woodlanders, Inc.

VIOLAS
A 10 Bluestone Perennials
A 12 Joseph Brown, Native Seeds
A 16 Canyon Creek Nursery
A 17 Richard G. M. Cawthorne
A 34 Gardens of the Blue Ridge
A 53 Lamb Nurseries

VIOLETS
A 29 Far North Gardens
A 38 Griffey's Nursery
A 69 Orchid Gardens

VITEX
A 95 Terrapin Springs Farm

VRIESEAS
A 21 Cornelison Bromeliads
A 88 Shelldance Nursery

PAGE SOURCE

WALNUTS
A 13 Burnt Ridge Nursery
A 29 Fernald's Hickory Hill Nursery
A 32 Fowler Nurseries, Inc.
A 36 John H. Gordon, Jr., Grower
A 38 Grimo Nut Nursery
A 61 Meta Horticultural Labs
A 64 Mountain Mist Nursery
A 67 Nolin River Nut Tree Nursery
A 83 Saginaw Valley Nut Nursery
A 84 St. Lawrence Nurseries
A 89 Skyblue Nurseries
A 105 Wiley's Nut Grove
A 106 Windy Ridge Nursery

WATER LILIES
A 34 The Garden Source, Ltd.
A 50 Kester's Wild Game Food Nurseries
A 56 Lilypons Water Gardens
A 64 Moore Water Gardens
A 72 Paradise Water Gardens
A 84 Santa Barbara Water Gardens
A 85 S. Scherer & Sons
A 89 Slocum Water Gardens
A 95 Tilley's Nursery/The WaterWorks
A 97 William Tricker, Inc.
A 99 Van Ness Water Gardens
A 101 Water Lily World
A 102 Water Ways Nursery
A 102 Waterford Gardens
A 104 Wicklein's Aquatic Farm & Nursery, Inc.

WATERMELONS
A 3 Alston Seed Growers
A 13 D.V. Burrell Seed Growers Co.
A 76 Porter & Son
A 83 SPB Sales
A 98 Otis Twilley Seed Co.
A 105 Willhite Seed Co.

WILD RICE
A 50 Kester's Wild Game Food Nurseries

WILDFLOWERS
See Also - Specific Plants
See Also - Specific Regions

WILDFLOWERS, AUSTRALIAN
A 13 Bushland Flora (Australian Seed Specialists)
A 46 International Seed Supplies
A 70 D. Orriell - Seed Exporters
A 89 Anthony J. Skittone

WILDFLOWERS, BRITISH
A 18 John Chambers
A 38 Grianan Gardens

WILDFLOWERS, CALIFORNIAN
A 3 Alpine Plants
A 53 Larner Seeds
A 63 Moon Mountain Wildflowers
A 72 Theodore Payne Foundation
A 91 Specialty Seeds
A 98 Twin Peaks Seeds

WILDFLOWERS, HIMALAYAN
A 52 P. Kohli & Co.

WILDFLOWERS, MANY REGIONS
A 3 Alpina Research & Montane Garden
A 4 Angel Seed Company
A 5 Applewood Seed Company
A 11 Botanic Garden Seed Co.

PAGE SOURCE

WILDFLOWERS, MANY REGIONS
A 17 Carter Seeds
A 18 John Chambers
A 26 E & H Products
A 36 Goodwin Creek Gardens
A 39 Halcyon Gardens
A 40 Harris Seeds
A 46 International Growers Exchange
A 47 Island Seed Mail Order
A 60 Maver Rare Perennials
A 63 Moon Mountain Wildflowers
A 65 Native Seeds, Inc.
A 71 Owl Ridge Alpines
A 73 Peaceful Valley Farm Supply
A 77 The Primrose Path
A 81 Richters
A 81 Clyde Robin Seed Co.
A 87 Seeds Blum
A 89 Siskiyou Rare Plant Nursery
A 91 Southwestern Native Seeds
A 100 Vermont Bean Seed Co.
A 100 Vermont Wildflower Farm
A 102 We-Du Nurseries

WILDFLOWERS, MIDWESTERN U.S.
A 33 Garden Perennials
A 52 LaFayette Home Nursery, Inc.
A 56 Little Valley Farm
A 62 Midwest Wildflowers
A 63 Moon Mountain Wildflowers
A 66 Natural Gardens
A 69 Orchid Gardens
A 76 Prairie Moon Nursery
A 76 Prairie Nursery
A 77 Prairie Ridge Nursery/CRM Ecosystems, Inc.
A 82 Rocknoll Nursery
A 104 The Wildflower Source
A 106 Windrift Prairie Shop

WILDFLOWERS, NEW ZEALAND
A 90 Southern Seeds

WILDFLOWERS, NORTH AMERICAN
A 11 Botanic Garden Seed Co.
A 12 Joseph Brown, Native Seeds
A 62 Midwest Wildflowers
A 63 Moon Mountain Wildflowers
A 65 Native Gardens
A 65 Native Seeds, Inc.
A 71 Painted Meadows Seed Co.
A 72 Passiflora
A 87 Shady Oaks Nursery
A 93 Sunlight Gardens
A 99 K. Van Bourgondien & Sons, Inc.
A 100 Vermont Wildflower Farm
A 104 The Wildflower Source

WILDFLOWERS, NORTHEASTERN U.S.
A 2 Allen, Sterling & Lothrop
A 20 Conley's Garden Center
A 21 Cooper's Garden
A 63 Moon Mountain Wildflowers
A 65 Native Seeds, Inc.
A 66 Natural Gardens
A 71 Painted Meadows Seed Co.
A 77 Putney Nursery, Inc.
A 87 Select Seeds
A 93 Sunlight Gardens
A 100 Vesey's Seeds Ltd.
A 101 Wyrttun Ward
A 104 Wildginger Woodlands

PAGE SOURCE

WILDFLOWERS, NORTHWESTERN U.S.
A 1 Abundant Life Seed Foundation
A 33 Frosty Hollow Nursery
A 45 Ed Hume Seeds, Inc.
A 59 Maplethorpe
A 63 Moon Mountain Wildflowers
A 68 Northplan/Mountain Seed
A 89 Skyline Nursery

WILDFLOWERS, PRAIRIE
A 27 Echinational Plant Products
A 37 Green Horizons
A 52 LaFayette Home Nursery, Inc.
A 63 Moon Mountain Wildflowers
A 65 Native Seeds, Inc.
A 76 Prairie Moon Nursery
A 77 Prairie Ridge Nursery/CRM Ecosystems, Inc.

WILDFLOWERS, ROCKY MOUNTAIN
A 42 High Altitude Gardens
A 64 Mountain West Seeds
A 68 Northplan/Mountain Seed
A 75 Plants of the Southwest
A 90 Solar Green, Ltd.

WILDFLOWERS, SOUTH AFRICAN
A 9 Bio-Quest International
A 14 C 'n C Protea
A 83 Rust-En-Vrede Nursery
A 89 Anthony J. Skittone

WILDFLOWERS, SOUTHEASTERN U.S.
A 7 Vernon Barnes & Son Nursery
A 8 Beersheba Wildflower Garden
A 34 Gardens of the Blue Ridge
A 47 Izard Ozark Natives
A 65 Native Gardens
A 66 Natural Gardens
A 67 Niche Gardens
A 72 Passiflora
A 93 Sunlight Gardens
A 102 We-Du Nurseries
A 106 Woodlanders, Inc.

WILDFLOWERS, SOUTHWESTERN U.S.
A 9 Bernardo Beach Native Plant Farm
A 19 Christa's Cactus
A 23 The Nursery at the Dallas Nature Center
A 37 Green Horizons
A 43 Horizon Seeds
A 57 The Lowrey Nursery
A 75 Plants of the Southwest
A 91 Southwestern Native Seeds
A 102 Weddle Native Gardens, Inc.

WILDLIFE FOOD PLANTS
A 16 Carino Nurseries
A 17 Cascade Forestry Service
A 26 Dutch Mountain Nursery
A 35 Glendale Enterprises
A 50 Kester's Wild Game Food Nurseries
A 54 Lawyer Nursery, Inc.
A 57 The Lowrey Nursery
A 65 Native Seed Foundation
A 66 Natural Gardens
A 68 Northplan/Mountain Seed
A 68 Northwoods Nursery
A 75 Plants of the Wild
A 76 Prairie Nursery
A 77 Prairie Ridge Nursery/CRM Ecosystems, Inc.
A 88 R. H. Shumway Seedsman
A 91 Southmeadow Fruit Gardens

PAGE SOURCE

WOODLAND PLANTS
See Also - Shade Plants
A 3 Alpina Research & Montane Garden
A 3 Alpine Plants
A 10 Boehlke's Woodland Gardens
A 11 The Bovees Nursery
A 16 Canyon Creek Nursery
A 19 Choice Edibles
A 26 Eastern Plant Specialties
A 29 Fancy Fronds
A 29 Far North Gardens
A 31 Foliage Gardens
A 31 Forestfarm
A 33 Frosty Hollow Nursery
A 35 Draig Goch Seed Co.
A 36 Gossler Farms Nursery
A 53 Larner Seeds
A 56 Little Valley Farm
A 59 Maplethorpe
A 60 Maver Rare Perennials
A 62 Milaeger's Gardens
A 65 Native Seed Foundation
A 66 Natural Gardens
A 66 Nature's Garden Nursery
A 69 Orchid Gardens
A 73 Peter Pauls Nurseries
A 74 Piedmont Gardens
A 75 Plants of the Wild
A 76 Prairie Moon Nursery
A 77 Prairie Ridge Nursery/CRM Ecosystems, Inc.
A 81 Rice Creek Gardens
A 87 Shady Oaks Nursery
A 89 Siskiyou Rare Plant Nursery
A 93 Sunlight Gardens
A 95 Thompson & Morgan
A 96 Tradewinds Nursery
A 99 Vandenberg
A 101 Wyrttun Ward
A 102 We-Du Nurseries
A 104 The Wildflower Source
A 104 Wildginger Woodlands
A 104 The Wildwood Flower

YAM PLANTS
A 53 Lagomarsino Seeds
A 59 Margrave Plant Co.

YEWS
A 32 Foxborough Nursery
A 100 Vineland Nurseries
A 102 Waynesboro Nurseries

YUCCA
A 6 Aztekakti/Desertland Nursery
A 14 The Cactus Patch
A 20 Colvos Creek Nursery & Landscaping
A 106 Winter Country Cacti

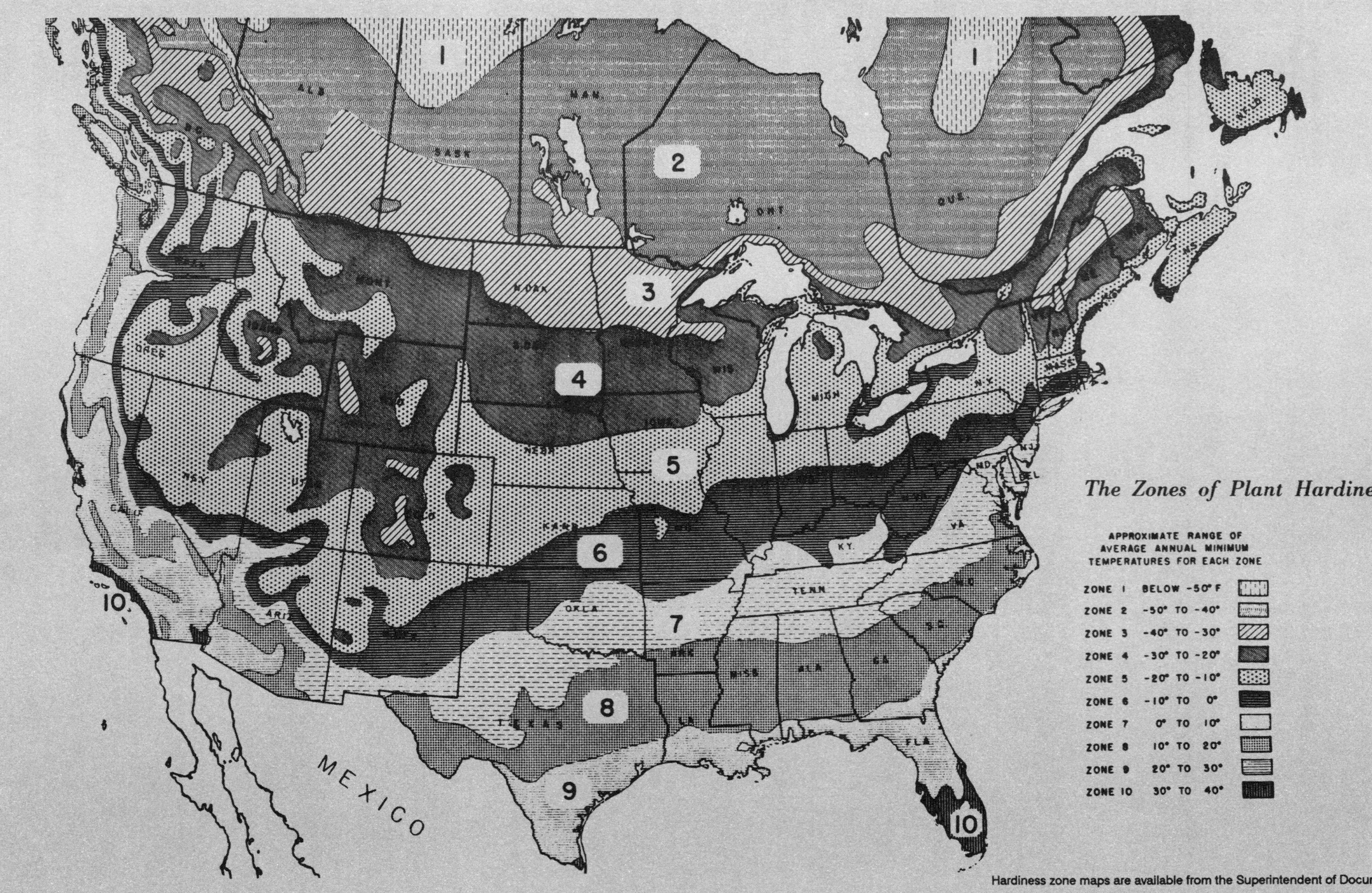

Hardiness zone maps are available from the Superintendent of Documents, U. S. Government Printing Office, Washington, DC 20402. Send $.25, and ask for Misc. Pub. No. 814.

ALABAMA

PAGE	CITY/ZIP	N=NURSERY G=GARDEN MO=MAIL ORDER ONLY	SOURCE
A 79	Birmingham 35206	N G	Steve Ray's Bamboo Gardens
A 59	Chunchula 36521	N G	Magnolia Nursery & Display Garden
A 58	Dothan 36303	N	Ma-Dot-Cha Hobby Nursery
A 33	Killeen 35645	N	Garden of the Enchanted Rainbow
A 40	Mobile 36608	N	Hatten's Nursery
A 25	Semmes 36575	MO	Bill Dodd's Rare Plants
A 9	Theodore 36582		Belle Fontaine Nursery

ALBERTA, CANADA

PAGE	CITY/ZIP	N=NURSERY G=GARDEN MO=MAIL ORDER ONLY	SOURCE
A 8	Beaverlodge T0H 0C0	MO	Beaverlodge Nursery
A 2	Bowden T0M 0K0	N	Alberta Nurseries & Seed Company
A 86	Edmonton T5L 4K1	N	Seed Centre Ltd.
A 106	Hythe T0H 2C0	N G	Windy Ridge Nursery

ARIZONA

PAGE	CITY/ZIP	N=NURSERY G=GARDEN MO=MAIL ORDER ONLY	SOURCE
A 26	Chino Valley 86323	N	Earthstar Herb Gardens
A 98	Chino Valley 86323	N G	21st Century Gardens
A 19	Coolidge 85228	N G	Christa's Cactus
A 10	Cortaro 85652	N	Boojum Unlimited
A 88	Phoenix 85051	N G	Shepard Iris Garden
A 66	Tucson 85745	G MO	Native Seeds/SEARCH
A 91	Tucson 85703	MO	Southwestern Native Seeds
A 98	Tucson 85705	N G	Tucson Succulents

ARKANSAS

PAGE	CITY/ZIP	N=NURSERY G=GARDEN MO=MAIL ORDER ONLY	SOURCE
A 4	Fayetteville 72703	MO	Ames' Orchard and Nursery
A 32	Little Rock 72205	N G	Fox Orchids, Inc.
A 6	Morrilton 72110	N G	Atkinson's Greenhouse
A 47	Mountain View 72560	MO	Izard Ozark Natives
A 11	Mountainburg 72946	MO	Boston Mountain Nurseries
A 42	Pettigrew 72752	N G	Highlander Nursery

AUSTRALIA

PAGE	CITY/ZIP	N=NURSERY G=GARDEN MO=MAIL ORDER ONLY	SOURCE
A 13	Hillarys 6025	N	Bushland Flora (Australian Seed Specialists)
A 70	Mt. Yokine, WA 6060	N	D. Orriell - Seed Exporters
A 46	Nowra, NSW 2541	N	International Seed Supplies
A 67	Woogenilup 6324	N	Nindethana Seed Service

BRITISH COLUMBIA, CANADA

PAGE	CITY/ZIP	N=NURSERY G=GARDEN MO=MAIL ORDER ONLY	SOURCE
A 94	Agassiz V0M 1A0	N	Tansy Farm
A 23	Chilliwack V2P 3T2	MO	Dacha Barinka
A 103	Nelson V1L 5P5	N G	West Kootenay Herb Nursery
A 3	Surrey V3S 4N8	N	Alpenflora Gardens
A 84	Vancouver V6K 1P1	N	Sanctuary Seeds/Folklore Herb Co.
A 103	Vancouver V4R 4G7	N	Western Biologicals Ltd.
A 14	Victoria V8X 3X4	N G	The Butchart Gardens
A 47	Victoria V8X 3X8	MO	Island Seed Mail Order
A 18	West Vancouver V7V 3P2	N	Charles Island Gardens

CALIFORNIA

PAGE	CITY/ZIP	N=NURSERY G=GARDEN MO=MAIL ORDER ONLY	SOURCE
A 68	Altadena 91001	N	Nuccio's Nurseries
A 28	Anaheim 92817-7538	MO	Evergreen Y. H. Enterprises
A 107	Arroyo Grande 93420	N G	Young's Mesa Nursery
A 63	Atascadero 93423	MO	Mohns, Inc.
A 14	Bakersfield 93312	N G	Cactus by Mueller
A 98	Belmont 94002	MO	Tsang & Ma
A 105	Berkeley 94708	MO	Nancy Wilson Species & Miniature Narcissus
A 26	Bermuda Dunes 92201	MO	E & H Products
A 68	Bodega 94922	MO	North Coast Rhododendron Nursery
A 53	Bolinas 94924-0407	N G	Larner Seeds

(continued next page)

PAGE	CITY/ZIP	N=NURSERY	G=GARDEN	MO=MAIL ORDER ONLY	SOURCE
CALIFORNIA (continued)					
A 56	Bolinas 94914	N	G		Living Tree Centre
A 96	Calpella 95418	N	G		Tradewinds Nursery
A 14	Camarillo 93010-6041	N			C 'n C Protea
A 71	Campbell 95009-0972	N	G		Pacific Coast Hybridizers
A 19	Carlotta 95528			MO	Choice Edibles
A 9	Carlsbad 92009-4843	N	G		Bird Rock Tropicals
A 37	Carmel 93922	N			Greener 'N' Ever Tree Farm & Nursery
A 1	Carpinteria 90313	N	G		Abbey Gardens
A 70	Carpinteria 93013	N	G		Orchids Royale
A 92	Carpinteria 93013	N	G		Stewart Orchids
A 81	Castro Valley 94546				Clyde Robin Seed Co.
A 71	Chula Vista 92010	N	G		Pacific Tree Farms
A 96	Chula Vista 92010	N	G		Tiny Petals Nursery
A 63	Clearlake Oaks 95423	N	G		Moonshine Gardens
A 51	Clements 95227	N	G		King's Mums
A 70	Coarsegold 93614	N	G		Orchid Species Specialists
A 97	Coarsegold 93614				Tropical Imports
A 5	Covelo 95428			MO	Apple Hill Orchards
A 14	Cupertino 95014-1138	N	G		Cactus Gem Nursery
A 82	Diamond Springs 95619	N	G		Rose Acres
A 54	Dixon 95620				Le Marche Seeds International
A 91	Encinitas 92024	N	G		Stallings Exotic Nursery
A 86	Escondido 92025	N	G		Seaborn Del Dios Nursery
A 98	Eureka 95501			MO	Twin Peaks Seeds
A 103	Eureka 95501	N	G		Westgate Garden Nursery
A 77	Fallbrook 92028				Protea Farms of California
A 88	Felton 95018	N	G		Shepherd's Garden Seeds
A 15	Fremont 94536				California Nursery Co.
A 32	Fremont 94539	N			Four Winds Growers
A 42	Fresno 93711	N	G		Hill 'n dale
A 41	Ft. Bragg 95437		G	MO	Heritage Rose Gardens
A 78	Ft. Bragg 95437	N	G		Rainman Succulent Nursery
A 97	Ft. Bragg 95437				Trillium Lane Nursery
A 72	Fulton 95434	N			Panda Products
A 49	Galt 95632	N			K & L Cactus Nursery
A 38	Garberville 95440	N	G		Greenmantle Nursery
A 78	Gardena 90249	N	G		Rainforest Flora, Inc.
A 86	Geyserville 95441				Sea God Nurseries
A 107	Gilroy 95020	N	G		Wright Iris Nursery
A 26	Goleta 93116	N	G		Dos Pueblos Orchid Co.
A 38	Goleta 93116			MO	Greenwood Nursery
A 4	Grass Valley 95945				The Angraecum House
A 40	Graton 95444	N			Harmony Farm Supply
A 90	Healdsburg 95448	N	G		Sonoma Antique Apple Nursery
A 83	Igo 96047	N	G		Jim & Irene Russ Quality Plants
A 65	Inverness 94937	N			Mushroompeople
A 104	Kenwood 95452	N			Wildwood Farm
A 9	La Crescenta 91214	N			Bentley's Botanical Gardens
A 78	La Habra 90633-0721	N	G		Rainbow Gardens Nursery & Bookshop
A 58	Lemon Grove 92045	N	G		McDaniel's Miniature Roses
A 100	Lincoln 95648	N	G		Violets Collectible
A 101	Lincoln 95648				Wapumne Native Plant Nursery
A 74	Lincoln Acres 92047				The Plant Kingdom
A 31	Livermore 94550	N	G		Fordyce Orchids
A 14	Lodi 95242	N	G		Cactus by Dodie
A 91	Lompoc 93436			MO	Specialty Seeds
A 23	Los Angeles 90041	N			Cycad Gardens
A 93	Los Angeles 90048			MO	Succulenta
A 101	Los Angeles 90064			MO	Vireya Specialties Nursery
A 101	Los Angeles 90049				W. K. Quality Bromeliads
A 69	Los Osos 93402	N	G		The Orchid House
A 79	Malibu 90265				R. J. Rands Orchids
A 108	Malibu 90265	N			Zuma Canyon Orchids
A 88	Marina 93933	N			Shein's Cactus
A 29	McKinleyville 95521	N			Fairyland Begonia & Lily Garden
A 86	Morgan Hill 95037	N	G		Schulz Cactus Gardens
A 63	Morro Bay 93442-0034	N	G		Moon Mountain Wildflowers
A 73	Nevada City 95959	N			Peaceful Valley Farm Supply

(continued next page)

PAGE	CITY/ZIP	N=NURSERY	G=GARDEN	MO=MAIL ORDER ONLY	SOURCE
CALIFORNIA (continued)					
A 32	Newcastle 95658	N	G		Fowler Nurseries, Inc.
A 44	North Hollywood 91607	N	G		Spencer M. Howard Orchid Imports
A 107	North Hollywood 91601	N	G		Guy Wrinkle Exotic Plants
A 49	Northridge 91324	N			KSA Jojoba
A 89	Northridge 91325	N	G		Singers' Growing Things
A 52	Ojai 93023				Kusa Research Foundation
A 21	Orange 92669	N	G		Country Bloomers Nursery
A 16	Oroville 95965	N			Canyon Creek Nursery
A 7	Oxnard 93030	N	G		Barbara's World of Flowers
A 88	Pacifica 94044	N			Shelldance Nursery
A 8	Pasadena 91107	N	G		Beahm Epiphyllum Gardens
A 28	Pauma Valley 92061				F W H Seed Exchange
A 19	Perris 92370	N	G		Circle 'N' Ranch
A 44	Placerville 95667	N	G		Hortica Gardens
A 60	Redding 96001	N	G		Maxim's Greenwood Gardens
A 80	Redlands 92373	N	G		Rhapis Palm Growers
A 44	Redwood City 94064			MO	J. L. Hudson, Seedsman
A 80	Redwood City 94064			MO	Redwood City Seed Co.
A 74	Reseda 91335	N			The Plant Shop's Botanical Gardens
A 15	Riverside 92504			MO	Cal Dixie Iris Gardens
A 30	Roseville 95678	N	G		Fiddyment Farms
A 39	Sacramento 95816	N			Robert B. Hamm
A 53	Sacramento 95824	N			Lagomarsino Seeds
A 62	Sacramento 95828	N	G		Mighty Minis
A 33	Salinas 93907			MO	G & G Gardens and Growers
A 28	San Diego 92117				Evon Orchids
A 5	San Francisco 94117	N			Arbor & Espalier
A 38	San Francisco 94114			MO	Grianan Gardens
A 89	San Francisco 94132	N			Anthony J. Skittone
A 93	San Gabriel 91775			MO	Sunnyslope Gardens
A 60	San Jose 95125	N	G		Maryott's Gardens
A 92	San Jose 95133	N	G		Stocking Rose Nursery
A 83	San Luis Obispo 93401	N	G		SLO Gardens
A 3	San Marcos 92069			MO	Altman Specialty Plants
A 21	San Marcos 92069			MO	Cordon Bleu Farms
A 59	Santa Ana 92705	N			Marilynn's Garden
A 9	Santa Barbara 93150-5752	N			Bio-Quest International
A 84	Santa Barbara 93111	N	G		Santa Barbara Orchid Estate
A 84	Santa Barbara 93160-6520			MO	Santa Barbara Seeds
A 84	Santa Barbara 93140	N	G		Santa Barbara Water Gardens
A 51	Santa Clara 95051-3012			MO	Kitazawa Seed Co.
A 4	Santa Cruz 95062				Antonelli Brothers
A 8	Santa Cruz 95060			MO	Bay View Gardens
A 53	Santa Margarita 93453	N	G		Las Pilitas Nursery
A 3	Santa Rosa 95404	N	G		Alpine Valley Gardens
A 7	Sebastopol 95472	N	G		A Bamboo Shoot
A 7	Sebastopol 95472	N	G		Bamboo Sourcery
A 63	Sebastopol 95472	N	G		Miniature Plant Kingdom
A 81	Sebastopol 95472			MO	Robinett Bulb Farm
A 90	Sebastopol 95472	N	G		Sonoma Horticultural Nursery
A 107	Solvang 93463	N	G		Zaca Vista Nursery
A 5	Somis 93066			MO	Armstrong Roses
A 28	Soquel 95076	N	G		John Ewing Orchids, Inc.
A 58	South San Francisco 94080	N	G		Rod McLellan Co.
A 50	Stockton 95208	N	G		Keith Keppel
A 56	Stockton 95201	N			Lockhart Seeds
A 94	Studio City 91604	N	G		Sunswept Laboratories
A 72	Sun Valley 91352	N	G		Theodore Payne Foundation
A 3	Tahoe Vista 95732	N			Alpine Plants
A 27	Tustin 92681	N			Endangered Species
A 99	Upland 91786-1199	N	G		Van Ness Water Gardens
A 90	Ventura 93004	N			South Seas Nursery
A 87	Visalia 93277	N	G		Sequoia Nursery - Moore Miniature Roses
A 15	Vista 92083	N	G		California Epi Center
A 17	Vista 92083	N			Carter Seeds
A 28	Vista 92083	N	G		Exotica Seed Co. & Rare Fruit Nursery
A 33	Vista 92084	N	G		G & B Orchid Laboratory
A 38	Vista 92084	N	G		Grigsby Cactus Gardens

(continued next page)

J 4 GEOGRAPHICAL INDEX

N=NURSERY G=GARDEN MO=MAIL ORDER ONLY

PAGE	CITY/ZIP	N	G	MO	SOURCE
CALIFORNIA (continued)					
A 50	Vista 92083	N	G		Kartuz Greenhouses
A 66	Vista 92084	N	G		New Leaf
A 72	Vista 92084			MO	The PanTree
A 94	Vista 92084	N			Taylor's Herb Gardens
A 18	Walnut Creek 94596		G	MO	Cherry Lane Gardens of Glenn Corlew
A 76	Walnut Creek 94596	N			Pollen Bank
A 25	Watsonville 95076	N	G		Desert Theater
A 82	Watsonville 95076-0398	N	G		Roses of Yesterday & Today
A 103	Westley 95387	N	G		Westside Exotics Palm Nursery
A 11	Willits 95490	N	G		Bountiful Gardens
A 21	Wilton 95693	N	G		Cottage Gardens
A 48	Woodacre 94973			MO	Johnson Seeds
A 74	Yorba Linda 92686	N	G		Pixie Treasures Miniature Rose Nursery
A 61	Yucca Valley 92284-9404	N	G		Mesa Flora Nursery
COLORADO					
A 106	Aspen 81612				Wilton's Organic Seed Potatoes
A 20	Avon 81620	N			Colorado Alpines, Inc.
A 57	Boulder 80306	N	G		Long's Gardens
A 42	Denver 80218	N	G		High Country Rosarium
A 80	Denver 80221			MO	Recor Tree Seed
A 100	Englewood 80110	N			The Violet Showcase
A 5	Golden 80002			MO	Applewood Seed Company
A 106	Littleton 80123				Winter Country Cacti
A 11	Niwot 80544	N	G		Boulder Valley Orchids
A 102	Palisade 81526	N	G		Weddle Native Gardens, Inc.
A 13	Rocky Ford 81067-0150	N			D.V. Burrell Seed Growers Co.
CONNECTICUT					
A 56	Danielson 06239	N	G		Logee's Greenhouses
A 27	Deep River 06417	N			Ericaceae
A 13	Eastford 06242	N	G		Buell's Greenhouse, Inc.
A 47	Easton 06612	N	G		J & L Orchids
A 93	Elmwood 06110-0058			MO	Sunrise Oriental Seed Co.
A 12	Gaylordsville 06755-0005	N	G		Lee Bristol Nursery
A 99	Litchfield 06759			MO	Van Engelen Inc.
A 103	Litchfield 06759-0050	N	G		White Flower Farm
A 14	Oxford 06483-1598	N	G		Butterbrooke Farm
A 17	Oxford 06483-1224	N			Catnip Acres Farm
A 54	Salisbury 06068	N	G		Lauray of Salisbury
A 87	Stamford 06903	N			Shanti Bithi Nursery
A 22	Sterling 06377	N			Country Girl Greenhouses
A 87	Union 06076	N	G		Select Seeds
A 74	Waterbury 06706	N	G		Piedmont Gardens
A 36	Westport 06880			MO	Grace's Gardens
A 20	Wethersfield 06109	N	G		Comstock, Ferre & Co.
A 93	Woodbury 06798			MO	Suni's Violets
ENGLAND					
A 52	Ashtead, Surrey KT21 1NN				L. Kreeger
A 11	Aylesbury, Bucks. HP22 4QB	N	G		S & N Brackley
A 91	Bedford MK42 8ND	N	G	MO	Southwest Seeds
A 6	Bridgewater,Somerset TA5 1JE			MO	B & T Associates
A 9	Bristol BS18 4JL	N			Blackmore & Langdon
A 45	Chatham, Kent ME5 9QT	N			Brenda Hyatt
A 2	Hassocks, W. Sussex BN6 9NB	N			Allwood Bros. (Hassocks) Ltd.
A 44	Hayle, Cornwall TR27 4BE			MO	C. W. Hosking - Exotic Seed Importer
A 94	Isles of Scilly TR21 0JY	N	G		A.P. & E.V. Tabraham
A 18	Kettering, Northants NN15 5AJ	N			John Chambers
A 107	King's Lynn, Norfolk PE33 0QH	N			Roy Young, Seedsman
A 17	Slough, Berks. SL3 8BE			MO	Chadwell Himalayan Seed
A 17	Swanley, Kent BR8 7NU			MO	Richard G. M. Cawthorne
A 94	Torquay, Devon TQ2 7QJ			MO	Sutton Seeds, Ltd.
A 18	Ulverston, Cumbria LA12 7PB			MO	Chiltern Seeds
FLORIDA					
A 18	Alachua 32615	N	G		Chestnut Hill Nursery, Inc.
A 6	Apopka 32712	N	G		BDK Nursery

(continued next page)

PAGE	CITY/ZIP	N=NURSERY	G=GARDEN	MO=MAIL ORDER ONLY	SOURCE
FLORIDA (continued)					
A 69	Arcadia 33821	N	G		The Orchid Center
A 20	Auburndale 33823			MO	Color Farm Growers
A 2	Boynton Beach 33435	N	G		Alberts & Merkel Bros., Inc.
A 12	Brandon 33511			MO	John Brudy Exotics
A 47	Cantonment 32533	N	G		J & M Tropicals, Inc.
A 37	Crystal River 32629	N			Greenleaf Orchids
A 35	DeFuniak Springs 32433	N	G		Glendale Enterprises
A 96	Fort Myers 33902			MO	Tomato Growers Supply Company
A 46	Ft. Lauderdale 33315				Idle Hours Orchids
A 58	Ft. Myers 33905	N	G		Madcap Orchids
A 106	Gainesville 32605-3237	N			Wimberlyway Gardens
A 30	Gulf Hammock 32639	N			The Fig Tree Nursery
A 33	Hollywood 33020	N	G		Garden of Delights
A 29	Homestead 33031	N	G		Fennell's Orchid Jungle
A 55	Homestead 33031	N	G		W. O. Lessard Nursery
A 31	Jacksonville 32225	N	G		Fort Caroline Orchids
A 73	Largo 33543			MO	The Pepper Gal
A 90	Loxahatchee 33470	N			South Florida Seed Supply
A 84	Madison 32340	N	G		Salter Tree Farm
A 41	Miami 33186	N	G		Heliconia Haus
A 43	Miami 33173	N	G		Jerry Horne - Rare Plants
A 44	Miami 33173	N			Huan Bui Orchids, Inc.
A 49	Miami 33187-1112	N	G		Jones & Scully
A 54	Miami 33187	N	G		Laurel Orchids
A 54	Miami 33184	N			Lee's Botanical Gardens
A 70	Miami 33187	N	G		Orgel's Orchids
A 76	Miami 33187	N	G		Possum Trot Tropical Fruit Nursery
A 80	Miami 33156				Joseph R. Redlinger Orchids
A 21	North Ft. Myers 33903	N			Cornelison Bromeliads
A 79	Oneco 33558	N			Reasoner's
A 24	Sanford 32771	N	G		Daylily World
A 51	Sanford 32771	N			Kilgore Seed Company
A 15	Sebring 33871	N	G		Caladium World
A 93	Sebring 33870			MO	Sunshine Caladium Farms
A 93	Tampa 33636-1610	N	G		Sunset Nursery, Inc.
A 47	Weirsdale 32695	N			Ivies of the World
A 57	West Palm Beach 33415			MO	Paul P. Lowe
A 59	Windemere 32786	N			Ann Mann's Orchids
A 89	Winter Haven 33880-6099	N	G		Slocum Water Gardens
GEORGIA					
A 74	Albany 31703			MO	Piedmont Plant Company
A 34	Atlanta 30341	N	G		The Garden Source, Ltd.
A 40	Atlanta 30302-4274	N			Hastings
A 54	Ball Ground 30107	N	G		Lawson's Nursery
A 73	Bishop 30621	N	G		Piccadilly Farm
A 47	Brooks 30205	N	G		Ison's Nursery
A 27	Decatur 30031	N	G		Eco-Gardens
A 66	Duluth 30136			MO	New Frontiers
A 48	Ellijay 30540	N	G		Johnson Nursery
A 98	Fayetteville 30214				Turnipseed Nursery Farms
A 38	Griffin 30223			MO	Greenlife Gardens Greenhouses
A 97	Lavonia 30553	N	G		Transplant Nursery
A 106	Marietta 30007-0513	N	G		World Insectivorous Plants
A 33	Molena 30258	N			Fruitwood Nursery
A 97	Ochlochnee 31773-0042	N			Travis' Violets
A 101	Omega 31775			MO	Mary Walker Bulb Company
A 43	Stone Mountain 30083			MO	Holiday Seeds
A 95	Thomasville 31799-0007	N	G		Thomasville Nurseries
A 95	Tifton 31793			MO	Terrapin Springs Farm
A 98	TyTy 31795	N	G		TyTy Plantation
A 50	Valdosta 31601-4235	N	G		Karleens Achimenes
A 49	Watkinsville 30677				Justice Gardens
A 82	Winston 30187	N	G		Rocky Waters Farm
GERMANY					
A 48	D 2000 Hamburg 56	N			Klaus R. Jelitto
A 51	Erzhausen/Darmstadt D-6106			MO	Gerhard Koehres Cactus & Succulent Nursery

PAGE	CITY/ZIP	N=NURSERY	G=GARDEN	MO=MAIL ORDER ONLY	SOURCE
HAWAII					
A 73	Aiea 96701				Pearl Harbor Orchids
A 29	Haiku, Maui 96708	N	G		Farnsworth Orchids
A 60	Hilo 96720			MO	Mauna Kea Orchids
A 19	Honokaa 96727	N	G		Cloud Forest Orchids
A 28	Honolulu 96816	N			Exotics Hawaii, Inc.
A 50	Honolulu 96816	N	G		Kawamoto Orchid Nursery
A 78	Honolulu 96814	N	G		Rainforest Plantes et Fleurs, Inc.
A 37	Kaaawa 96730	N	G		Green Plant Research
A 98	Kailua 96734			MO	Tropicals Unlimited
A 105	Kaneohe 96744	N	G		Wilk Orchid Specialties
A 77	Kula, Maui 96790	N	G		Protea Gardens of Maui
A 103	Pahoa 96778	N	G		Ken West Orchids
IDAHO					
A 87	Boise 83706			MO	Seeds Blum
A 42	Ketchum 83340	N	G		High Altitude Gardens
A 90	Moore 83255			MO	Solar Green, Ltd.
A 68	Moscow 83843	N			Northplan/Mountain Seed
A 65	Moyie Springs 83845			MO	Native Seed Foundation
ILLINOIS					
A 87	Batavia 60510-2999	N	G		Shady Hill Gardens
A 75	Belleville 62221	N	G		Plant Villa
A 13	Bloomington 61701				Burgess Seed & Plant Co.
A 32	Bloomington 61701				Four Seasons Nursery
A 71	Bloomington 61701	N		MO	Richard Owen Nursery
A 46	Champaign 61820	N			Illinois Foundation Seeds, Inc.
A 5	Chapin 62628			MO	Applesource
A 58	Chicago 60660			MO	McClure & Zimmerman
A 68	Dundee 60118-0025	N	G		Oak Hill Gardens
A 7	Elmhurst 60126			MO	Fred Bach Epiphyllums
A 88	Elmwood 61529	N			Shissler Seed Company
A 104	Fox Lake 60020			MO	The Wildflower Source
A 51	Hampshire 60193	N			Arnold J. Klehm Grower, Inc.
A 52	Lafayette 61449			MO	LaFayette Home Nursery, Inc.
A 29	Monmouth 61462	N	G		Fernald's Hickory Hill Nursery
A 46	Monticello 61856				Illini Iris
A 106	Oregon 61061	N			Windrift Prairie Shop
A 11	Peoria 61656			MO	Breck's
A 91	Peoria 61656			MO	Spring Hill Nurseries Co.
A 62	Rockton 61072			MO	Midwest Wildflowers
A 9	San Jose 62682				Blue Dahlia Gardens
A 51	South Barrington 60010	N	G		Klehm Nursery
A 77	Trilla 62469	N			Prairie State Commodities
A 70	Villa Park 60181	N	G		Orchids by Hausermann, Inc.
INDIA					
A 52	Srinagar, Kashmir 190009			MO	P. Kohli & Co.
INDIANA					
A 24	Crawfordsville 47933	N	G		Davidson-Wilson Greenhouses
A 43	Evansville 47711	N	G		Holly Hills, Inc.
A 1	Huntingburg 47542	N			Ahrens Strawberry Nursery
A 52	Middlebury 46540	N	G		Krider Nurseries
A 82	New Salisbury 47161	N	G		Rocky Meadow Orchard & Nursery
A 62	Ossian 46777	N	G		Miller's Manor Gardens
A 46	Winamac 46996	N	G		Iris Acres
IOWA					
A 17	Cascade 52033			MO	Cascade Forestry Service
A 89	Charles City 50616	N			Smith Nursery Co.
A 24	Council Bluffs 51502	N			DeGiorgi Company, Inc.
A 81	Farmington 52626	N			Rider Nurseries
A 46	Hamburg 51640-0208				Inter-State Nurseries
A 41	Johnston 50131			MO	Heard Gardens, Ltd.
A 30	Shenandoah 51602			MO	Henry Field Seed & Nursery Co.
A 60	Shenandoah 51603	N			Earl May Seed & Nursery Co.

PAGE	CITY/ZIP	N=NURSERY G=GARDEN MO=MAIL ORDER ONLY	SOURCE
KANSAS			
A 22	Bunker Hill 67626-9701	N G	Cross Seed Company
A 44	Burlington 66839-0187	N G	Huff's Garden Mums
A 28	Lansing 66043	N	Essie's Violets
A 21	Lyons 67554	N	Cook's Geranium Nursery
A 14	Radium 67571	N G MO	The Cactus Patch
A 21	Sedgwick 67135	N G	Country Cottage
A 58	Wichita 67207	N	McKinney's Glasshouse
KENTUCKY			
A 23	Louisville 40222	MO	Dabney Herbs
A 65	Louisville 40228	MO	Nationwide Seed & Supply
A 61	Meta 41501	N	Meta Horticultural Labs
A 73	Tomkinsville 42167	N G	Pick's Ginseng
A 67	Upton 42784	N G	Nolin River Nut Tree Nursery
LOUISIANA			
A 3	Baton Rouge 70821	N	Amaryllis, Inc.
A 37	Folsom 70437	N G	Green Valley Orchids
A 10	New Orleans 70114	MO	Arthur Boe Distributor
A 22	New Orleans 70184-4458	N G	Creole Orchids
A 57	Opelousas 70570	N	Louisiana Nursery
A 88	Sibley 71073	N	Sherwood's Greenhouses
A 48	Terrytown/Gretna 70056	N G	Jeannette's Jesneriads
MAINE			
A 48	Albion 04910	MO	Johnny's Selected Seeds
A 103	Biddeford 04005	N G	Whistling Wings Farm, Inc.
A 20	Boothbay Harbor 04538	N G	Conley's Garden Center
A 61	Camden 04843	N G	Merry Gardens
A 64	Dixmont 04932	N	Moose Tubers
A 98	East Lebanon 04027	N G	Valente Gardens
A 2	Falmouth 04105	N	Allen, Sterling & Lothrop
A 24	Litchfield 04350	N G	Daystar
A 74	New Gloucester 04260	N G	Pinetree Garden Seeds
A 64	St. Francis 04774	MO	Moosebell Flower, Fruit & Tree Co.
A 29	Waterville 04901	MO	Fedco Seeds
MANITOBA, CANADA			
A 58	Brandon R7A 6A6	MO	McFayden Seeds
A 64	Morden R0G 1J0	N	Morden Nurseries, Ltd
A 94	Winnepeg R3C 3P6	N	T & T Seeds, Ltd.
MARYLAND			
A 10	Baldwin 21013	N G	Kurt Bluemel, Inc.
A 53	Baltimore 21230	N	D. Landreth Seed Company
A 61	Baltimore 21231		Meyer Seed Co.
A 81	Baltimore 21228	MO	Roberts' Gesneriads
A 104	Baltimore 21234	N	Wicklein's Aquatic Farm & Nursery, Inc.
A 41	Brookville 20833	N	Heritage Rosarium
A 22	Crownsville 21032	N MO	Crownsville Nursery
A 102	Damascus 20872	N G	Webber Gardens
A 65	Dayton 21036	MO	Native Seeds, Inc.
A 49	Edgewood 21040	N G	Jungle-Gems, Inc.
A 24	Frederick 21701		Dan's Garden Shop
A 82	Galena 21635	N G	Rosehill Farm
A 50	Kensington 20895	N G	Kensington Orchids
A 56	Lilypons 21717-0010	N G	Lilypons Water Gardens
A 13	Owings Mills 21117	N G MO	Bundles of Bulbs
A 10	Riderwood 21139	MO	Boordy Nursery
A 2	Salisbury 21801	N	Allen Company
A 12	Salisbury 21801	N	Brittingham Plant Farms
A 79	Salisbury 21801	MO	Rayner Bros.
A 32	Street 21154	N G	Foxborough Nursery
A 17	Westminster 21157	N	Carroll Gardens
MASSACHUSETTS			
A 40	Barre 01005	N G	Hartman's Herb Farm
A 93	Barre 01005	N	Sunshine Orchids International

(continued next page)

PAGE	CITY/ZIP	N=NURSERY G=GARDEN MO=MAIL ORDER ONLY			SOURCE
MASSACHUSETTS (continued)					
A 57	Cambridge 02140	N			John D. Lyon, Inc.
A 86	Carlisle 01741	N	G		Seawright Gardens
A 37	Conway 01341			MO	Greenleaf Seeds
A 12	East Sandwich 02537	N	G		Briarwood Gardens
A 16	Falmouth 02540	N			Cape Cod Violetry
A 61	Ipswich 01938	N			Messelaar Bulb Co.
A 46	Lynnfield 01940	N	G		Innis Violets
A 101	Middleboro 02346	N			Wyrttun Ward
A 35	Northfield 01360	N	G		Gladside Gardens
A 93	Reading 01867			MO	Sunnyvale Cactus Nursery
A 96	Rehoboth 02769-1395	N	G		Tranquil Lake Nursery
A 22	Rowley 01969	N			Cricket Hill Herb Farm Ltd.
A 67	Rowley 01969	N	G		Nor'East Miniature Roses
A 86	Sandwich 02563-1023			MO	F. W. Schumacher Co.
A 68	South Deerfield 01373	N	G		Nourse Farms, Inc.
A 24	South Hamilton 01982	N			Peter De Jager Bulb Co.
A 97	Southampton 01073	N	G		Tripple Brook Farm
A 1	Swansea 02777	N	G		A & P Orchids
A 72	Whitman 02382				Paradise Water Gardens
A 2	Wilmington 01887	N			Arthur Eames Allgrove
MICHIGAN					
A 26	Augusta 49012				Dutch Mountain Nursery
A 24	Bellevue 49021	N			Corwin Davis Nursery
A 83	Birch Run 48415			MO	Saginaw Valley Nut Nursery
A 78	Burton 48529				Rakestraw's Perennial Gardens
A 22	Chesaning 48616	N	G		Country View Gardens
A 71	Clarkston 48016	N	G		Owl Ridge Alpines
A 12	Clifford 48727	N			Elizabeth Buck African Violets
A 60	Detroit 48221				Mary's African Violets
A 52	Dowagiac 49047	N	G		Krohne Plant Farms
A 102	Fennville 49408	N			Wavecrest Nursery & Landscaping Co.
A 19	Free Soil 49411-9752	N			Cold Stream Farm
A 27	Galesburg 49053	N	G		Ensata Gardens
A 4	Garden City 48135-0100			MO	Angel Seed Company
A 40	Grand Junction 49056	N			Hartmann's Plantation, Inc.
A 61	Grand Rapids 49550				Michigan Bulb Co.
A 31	Hartford 49057	N			Dean Foster Nurseries
A 99	Holland 49424	N	G		Veldheer Tulip Gardens
A 27	Hopkins 49328	N	G		Englerth Gardens
A 88	Imlay City 48444	N			Siegers Seed Co.
A 69	Kalamazoo 49007-3077	N	G		Oikos
A 53	Lake Odessa 48849	N	G		Lake Odessa Greenhouse
A 38	Lakeside 49116	N	G		Grootendorst Nurseries
A 91	Lakeside 49116	N			Southmeadow Fruit Gardens
A 29	Livonia 48154			MO	Far North Gardens
A 46	Livonia 48152-0248			MO	International Growers Exchange
A 60	Livonia 48154	N			Marvelous Minis
A 69	Niles 49120	N	G		Oakwood Daffodils
A 32	Parma 49269				Fox Hill Farm
A 37	Romulus 48174	N			Great Lakes Orchids
A 27	Stevensville 49127				Emlong Nurseries
A 99	Three Oaks 49128	N			Valley Creek Nursery
A 79	Vulcan 49892			MO	Reath's Nursery
A 59	Ypsilanti 48197	N			Makielski Berry Farm & Nursery
MINNESOTA					
A 28	Albert Lea 56007	N			Fairway Enterprises
A 14	Cokato 55321	N	G		Busse Gardens
A 85	Edina 55435	N	G		Savory's Greenhouse
A 10	Faribault 55021	N	G		Borbeleta Gardens
A 29	Faribault 55021	N			Farmer Seed & Nursery
A 4	Forest Lake 55025	N	G		Anderson Iris Gardens
A 69	Grand Rapids 55744	N	G		Orchid Gardens
A 59	Hastings 55033	N	G		Maroushek Gardens
A 26	Hutchinson 55350				Dooley Gardens
A 81	Minneapolis 55432	N	G		Rice Creek Gardens
A 81	Minneapolis 55430	N	G		Riverdale Iris Gardens

(continued next page)

PAGE	CITY/ZIP	N=NURSERY	G=GARDEN	MO=MAIL ORDER ONLY	SOURCE
MINNESOTA (continued)					
A 87	Northfield 55057-0175		G		Shannon Gardens of Oak Brook Farm
A 16	Pequot Lakes 56472	N	G		Camelot North
A 21	Roseville 55113	N	G		Cooper's Garden
A 11	St. Cloud 56302			MO	Brand Peony Farm
A 66	St. Paul 55118	N	G		The New Peony Farm
A 89	St. Paul 55118-0061			MO	Skyblue Nurseries
A 87	Waseca 56093			MO	Shady Oaks Nursery
A 76	Winona 55987	N	G		Prairie Moon Nursery
MISSISSIPPI					
A 81	Biloxi 39532	N	G		Riverbend Orchids
A 12	Olive Branch 38654	N	G		Brussel's Bonsai Nursery
MISSOURI					
A 1	California 65018		G	MO	Adamgrove
A 39	Desloge 63601	N	G		Hahn's Rainbow Iris Garden
A 96	Fayette 65248	N			Tomara African Violets
A 20	Gower 64454	N	G		Comanche Acres Iris Gardens
A 41	Kansas City 64110	N	G		Herb Gathering Inc.
A 55	Kansas City 64133	N	G		Lenington-Long Gardens
A 62	Kansas City 64106	N			Midwest Seed Growers, Inc.
A 78	Lee's Summit 64063	N			Rainwater Violets
A 7	Louisiana 63353-0050			MO	Bakker of Holland
A 92	Louisiana 63353-0010	N			Stark Bro's Nurseries & Orchards Co.
A 62	New Melle 63365			MO	Midwest Cactus
A 49	Overland 63114	N			Judy's Violets
A 105	Ozark 65721	N			Wilson's Greenhouse
A 104	Sarcoxie 64862-0338	N	G		Gilbert H. Wild & Son, Inc.
A 2	Waynesville 65583	N	G		Alice's Violet Room
MONTANA					
A 63	Bigfork 59911			MO	Mo's Greenhouse
A 47	Bozeman 59715	N	G		Iris Gardens
A 99	Helena 59601	N	G		Valley Nursery
A 3	Kalispell 59901	N	G	MO	Alpen Gardens
A 57	Kalispell 59901	N	G		Lost Prairie Herb Farm
A 54	Plains 59859	N			Lawyer Nursery, Inc.
NEBRASKA					
A 50	Arlington 68002-0398	N	G		Kent's Flowers
A 36	Bayard 69334		G	MO	Grandview Iris Gardens
A 32	Ft. Calhoun 68023			MO	The Fragrant Path
A 42	Lexington 68850-9304	N	G		Hildenbrandt's Iris Gardens
A 30	Lincoln 68504				Fleming's Flower Fields
A 68	Norfolk 68701	N			North Pine Iris Gardens
A 59	Ponca 68770	N	G		Maple Tree Gardens
A 33	Wayne 68787	N			Garden Perennials
A 46	Wayne 68787	N	G		Iris Country
A 31	Wynot 68792	N	G		Flowerland
NEW HAMPSHIRE					
A 57	Nashua 03062		G	MO	Lowe's own-root Roses
NEW JERSEY					
A 26	Adelphia 07710			MO	Dutch Gardens, Inc.
A 67	Atlantic Highlands 07716	N	G		North American Wildflowers
A 74	Cinnaminson 08077	N	G		Plant Factory
A 29	Clarksboro 08020			MO	Fern Hill Farm
A 26	Colonia 07067	N	G		Eastern Plant Specialties
A 97	Franklinville 08322	N	G		Triple Oaks Nursery
A 78	Hillsdale 07642			MO	Quality Dutch Bulbs
A 95	Jackson 08527	N			Thompson & Morgan
A 30	Linwood 08221-1398	N	G		Fischer Greenhouses
A 23	Marlboro 07746	N	G		The Cummins Garden
A 96	Metuchen 08840			MO	The Tomato Seed Company, Inc.
A 9	Pompton Lakes 07442			MO	Black Copper Kits
A 103	Port Murray 07865	N	G		Well-Sweep Herb Farm
A 27	Robbinsville 08691	N	G		Edelweiss Gardens

(continued next page)

PAGE	CITY/ZIP	N=NURSERY	G=GARDEN	MO=MAIL ORDER ONLY	SOURCE
NEW JERSEY (continued)					
A 102	Saddle River 07458	N	G		Waterford Gardens
A 54	Sewell 08080-0007	N	G		Orol Ledden & Sons
A 42	Voorhees 08043	N	G		Hillhouse Nursery
NEW MEXICO					
A 66	Albuquerque 87114		G	MO	New Mexico Desert Garden
A 9	Belen 87002	N	G		Bisnaga Cactus Nursery
A 61	Belen 87002	N	G		Mesa Garden
A 66	Belen 87002	N	G		New Mexico Cactus Research
A 79	Cerrillos 87010				Rancho de la Flor de Lis
A 75	Chaparral 88021		G		Pleasure Iris Gardens
A 25	Deming 88030	N	G		Desert Nursery
A 83	Roswell 88201	N	G		Roswell Seed Co.
A 75	Santa Fe 87501	N	G		Plants of the Southwest
A 9	Veguita 87062	N	G		Bernardo Beach Native Plant Farm
NEW YORK					
A 21	Albany 12210	N			The Cottage Herb Farm Shop
A 99	Babylon 11702	N			K. Van Bourgondien & Sons, Inc.
A 86	Bayville 11709				Sea Breeze Orchids
A 11	Brooklyn 11201			MO	Botanic Garden Seed Co.
A 92	Buffalo 14240		G	MO	Stokes Seed Company
A 62	Canandaigua 14424	N	G		J. E. Miller Nurseries, Inc.
A 73	Canandaigua 14424	N	G		Peter Pauls Nurseries
A 91	Canandaigua 14424	N	G		Square Root Nursery
A 56	Cato 13033	N	G		Lloyd's African Violets
A 99	Chester 10918	N			Vandenberg
A 58	Clinton Corners 12514	N			MB Farm Miniature Roses
A 50	Dansville 14437	N	G		Kelly Nurseries of Dansville, Inc.
A 83	Dix Hills 11746	N	G		Roslyn Nursery
A 57	Dolgeville 13329-0249	N	G		Lyndon Lyon Greenhouses, Inc.
A 55	East Moriches 11940	N			Henry Leuthardt Nurseries, Inc.
A 22	East Rochester 14445	N			Crosman Seed Corp.
A 84	Freedom 14065			MO	Sandhurst Seeds
A 55	Geneva 14456	N	G		Legg Dahlia Gardens
A 66	Geneva 14456				New York State Fruit Testing Coop. Assn.
A 86	Glen Head 11545	N	G		Seagulls Landing Orchids
A 87	Hall 14463-0250	N			Seedway, Inc.
A 35	High Falls 12440	N			Gloria Dei
A 36	N. Tonawanda 14120	N	G		John H. Gordon, Jr., Grower
A 85	New York 10005			MO	John Scheepers, Inc.
A 35	Newfield 14867			MO	Draig Goch Seed Co.
A 85	Northport 11768	N			S. Scherer & Sons
A 92	Pomona 10970	N	G		Stonehurst Rare Plants
A 84	Potsdam 13676	N	G		St. Lawrence Nurseries
A 18	Red Creek 13143	N	G		Chestnuts a Reality
A 40	Rochester 14624			MO	Harris Seeds
A 85	Saratoga Springs 12866	N	G		Saxton Gardens
A 8	Schenectady 12301			MO	Belche Herb Company
A 66	Schenectady 12309			MO	E. B. Nauman, Nurseryman
A 31	Setauket 11733-3038	N			Floyd Cove Nursery
A 73	Shrub Oak 10588				Peekskill Nurseries
A 16	South Salem 10590	N			Carlson's Gardens
A 104	Webster 14580			MO	Wildginger Woodlands
A 10	Williamstown 13493	N	G		Blue Star Lab
A 71	Woodstock 12498			MO	Ozark National Seed Order
NEW ZEALAND					
A 90	Canterbury 8173	N	G		Southern Seeds
NORTH CAROLINA					
A 3	Asheville 28805			MO	Alpina Research & Montane Garden
A 60	Asheville 28850	N	G		Maver Rare Perennials
A 11	Brown Summit 27214-9744	N	G		Breckinridge Orchids
A 15	Chapel Hill 27514	N	G		Camellia Forest Nursery
A 67	Chapel Hill 27514	N	G		Niche Gardens
A 100	Charlotte 28217	N	G		The Vine and the Branch
A 48	Dunn 28334	N	G		Jernigan Gardens

(continued next page)

PAGE	CITY/ZIP	N=NURSERY G=GARDEN MO=MAIL ORDER ONLY			SOURCE
NORTH CAROLINA (continued)					
A 26	Fairview 28730	N	G		Donnelly's Nursery
A 95	Fairview 28730	N	G		Tiki Nursery
A 43	Fletcher 28732	N	G		Holbrook Farm & Nursery
A 107	Garner 27529	N			Wyatt-Quarles Seed Co.
A 72	Germanton 27019	N	G		Passiflora
A 79	Godwin 28344	N	G		Rasland Farm
A 63	Hillsborough 27278	N	G		Montrose Nursery
A 55	Kannapolis 28081	N	G		Lenette Greenhouses
A 84	Leicester 28748	N	G		Sandy Mush Herb Nursery
A 101	Leicester 28748	N	G		Washington Evergreen Nursery
A 3	Littleton 27850			MO	Alston Seed Growers
A 102	Marion 28752	N	G		We-Du Nurseries
A 38	Marshall 28753	N	G		Griffey's Nursery
A 34	Pineola 28662	N	G		Gardens of the Blue Ridge
A 71	Pisgah Forest 28768-0365	N	G		Owens Orchids
A 104	Pittsboro 27312	N			The Wildwood Flower
A 76	Princeton 27569	N	G		Powell's Gardens
A 45	Raleigh 27607	N			Hungry Plants
A 55	Rocky Point 28457	N			Lewis Strawberry Nursery
A 16	State Road 28676	N			Cardinal Nursery
A 53	Warrensville 28693	N	G		Lamtree Farm
NOVA SCOTIA, CANADA					
A 79	Truro B2N 2P6	N			Rawlinson Garden Seed
A 25	Windsor B0N 2T0				Howard N. Dill
OHIO					
A 20	Athens 45701	N	G		Companion Plants
A 104	Chardon 44024	N	G		Wildwood Gardens
A 43	Chesterland 44026	N	G		Homestead Division of Sunnybrook Farms
A 93	Chesterland 44026	N	G		Sunnybrook Farms Nursery
A 64	Cincinnati 45226			MO	Mowbray Gardens
A 4	Dayton 45402			MO	American Bamboo Company
A 42	Gallipolis 45631	N			Highland Succulents
A 34	Geneva 44041				Louis Gerardi Nursery
A 35	Geneva 44041	N			Girard Nurseries
A 82	Hillsboro 45133	N			Rocknoll Nursery
A 97	Independence 44131	N	G		William Tricker, Inc.
A 10	Madison 44057	N			Bluestone Perennials
A 105	Mansfield 44907-3024	N	G		Wiley's Nut Grove
A 34	Mentor 44061-0388			MO	Garden Place
A 56	New Philadelphia 44663	N			Liberty Seed Company
A 61	North Lima 44452	N	G		Mellinger's Inc.
A 68	Novelty 44072			MO	Novelty Nurseries
A 43	Painesville 44077	N	G		Historical Roses
A 34	Perry 44081	N			Gilson Gardens
A 9	Seville 44273	N	G		Bittersweet Farm
A 35	Stewart 45778-0097	N	G		Glasshouse Works
A 16	Toledo 43611	N			Carol's Violets & Gifts
A 83	Wauseon 43567			MO	Rupp Seeds, Inc.
OKLAHOMA					
A 84	Collinsville 74021	N	G		Sand Ridge Greenhouse
A 51	Lawton 73506	N	G		Kinder Canna Farm
A 61	Oklahoma City 73157	N	G		Mid-America Iris Gardens
A 60	Tulsa 74127	N	G		Marvin's Cactus
A 21	Turpin 73950	N			Corns
ONTARIO, CANADA					
A 39	Barrie L4M 4S4	N			Growin'house
A 45	Bright's Grove N0N 1C0	N	G		Huronview Nurseries & Garden Centre
A 52	Carlisle L0R 1H0	N	G		V. Kraus Nurseries, Ltd.
A 24	Dundas L9H 6M1	N			William Dam Seeds
A 26	Georgetown L7G 4A2				Dominion Seed House
A 81	Goodwood L0C 1A0	N	G		Richters
A 97	Hamilton L8R 1J4	N			Tregunno Seeds
A 75	Keswick L4P 3E9	N			Plants 'n' Things
A 51	Komoka N0L 1R0	N	G		Kilworth Flowers

(continued next page)

PAGE	CITY/ZIP	N=NURSERY	G=GARDEN	MO=MAIL ORDER ONLY	SOURCE
ONTARIO, CANADA (continued)					
A 36	Marlbank K0K 2L0			MO	Golden Bough Tree Farm
A 10	Maynooth K0L 2S0			MO	Blueberry Hill
A 19	Mississauga L5J 2Y4	N	G		Clargreen Gardens Ltd.
A 106	Mississauga L5A 2K1	N	G		Woodland Nurseries
A 38	Niagara on the Lake L0S 1J0	N	G		Grimo Nut Nursery
A 58	Norwich N0J 1P0		G		McMillen's Iris Garden
A 73	Paris N3L 3E1	N			Phipps African Violets
A 74	Pickering L1V 1A6	N			Pickering Nurseries Inc.
A 74	Pickering L1V 2R4	N	G		Pine Ridge Garden Gallery
A 58	Port Burwell N0J 1T0	N	G		McConnell Nurseries, Inc.
A 31	Port Stanley N0L 2A0	N			Floridel Gardens
A 64	Port Stanley N0L 2A0	N	G		Moore Water Gardens
A 92	St. Catharines L2R 6R6			MO	Stokes Seed Company
A 34	Thornhill L3T 4A5	N			Gardenimport, Inc.
A 23	Toronto M4P 2M1	N			C. A. Cruickshank, Ltd.
A 63	Toronto M8W 1T9	N			Miree's Gesneriads
A 8	Trout Creek P0H 2L0			MO	Beckers Seed Potatoes
A 100	Vineland Station L0R 2E0	N	G		Vineland Nurseries
A 72	Virgil L0S 1T0	N	G		Carl Pallek & Son Nursery
A 44	Waterdown L0R 2H0				Hortico, Inc.
A 69	Whitby L1N 5R5	N	G		Orchid Haven
OREGON					
A 67	Albany 97321	N	G		Nichols Garden Nursery, Inc.
A 19	Aurora 97002	N	G		Coenosium Gardens
A 70	Aurora 97002			MO	Oregon Bulb Farms
A 66	Beaverton 97007			MO	Nature's Garden Nursery
A 70	Beaverton 97007	N			Oregon Miniature Roses
A 91	Boring 97009	N	G		Stanley & Sons Nursery, Inc.
A 41	Brooks 97305				Marc Henny Nursery
A 94	Canby 97013	N	G		Swan Island Dahlias
A 15	Central Point 97502	N			Callahan Seeds
A 57	Cloverdale 97112	N	G		Loucks Nursery
A 72	Corvallis 97333	N	G		Peace Seeds
A 80	Corvallis 97330	N			Redlo Cacti
A 17	Days Creek 97429				Casa Yerba Gardens
A 77	Eddyville 97343	N	G		Qualitree Nursery
A 91	Estacada 97023	N	G		Squaw Mountain Gardens
A 25	Eugene 97404	N	G		Del's Japanese Maples
A 38	Eugene 97401-1794	N	G		Greer Gardens
A 43	Eugene 97404	N			Hookland's Dahlias
A 31	Forest Grove 97116	N	G		Flora Lan Nursery
A 63	Hubbard 97032		G	MO	Grant Mitsch Novelty Daffodils
A 18	Junction City 97448			MO	Chambers Nursery
A 39	Junction City 97448	N	G		Hall Rhododendrons
A 59	Lake Oswego 97035			MO	Maplewood Seed Company
A 95	Lorane 97451	N	G		Territorial Seed Co.
A 48	Medford 97501		G	MO	Jackson & Perkins Co.
A 89	Medford 97501	N	G		Siskiyou Rare Plant Nursery
A 68	Molalla 97038	N	G		Northwoods Nursery
A 18	Newberg 97132	N	G		Chehalem Gardens
A 83	Newberg 97132	N			S & H Organic Acres
A 40	Philomath 97370	N			Hass Nursery
A 11	Portland 97219	N	G		The Bovees Nursery
A 34	Roseburg 97470	N			Garden Valley Dahlias
A 36	Salem 97304	N	G		Russell Graham, Purveyor of Plants
A 56	Salem 97303	N			Lon's Oregon Grapes
A 59	Salem 97301	N	G		Maplethorpe
A 85	Salem 97303			MO	Schreiner's Gardens
A 104	Salem 97304			MO	Whitman Farms
A 39	Scotts Mills 97375		G		Dr. Joseph C. Halinar
A 101	Scotts Mills 97375	N			Walden - West
A 97	Sheridan 97378	N			Trans Pacific Nursery
A 16	Sherwood 97140	N	G		Caprice Farm
A 80	Sherwood 97140	N	G		Red's Rhodies & Alpine Gardens
A 21	Silverton 97381				Cooley's Gardens
A 36	Springfield 97478-9663	N	G		Gossler Farms Nursery
A 54	Springfield 97478	N	G		Laurie's Garden

(continued next page)

PAGE	CITY/ZIP	N=NURSERY	G=GARDEN	MO=MAIL ORDER ONLY	SOURCE
OREGON (continued)					
A 87	Troutdale 97060	N	G		Shackleton's Dahlias
A 64	Veneta 97487	N			Mountain Mist Nursery
A 68	West Linn 97068	N	G		Northwest Biological Enterprises
A 92	West Linn 97068	N	G		Stubbs Shrubs
A 31	Williams 97544	N	G		Forestfarm
A 36	Williams 97544	N	G		Goodwin Creek Gardens
A 96	Williams 97544	N			Tolowa Nursery
A 49	Wilsonville 97070	N			Justice Miniature Roses
A 82	Wilsonville 97070			MO	Roses by Fred Edmunds
A 4	Woodburn 97071	N	G		Angelwood Nursery
PENNSYLVANIA					
A 17	Allison Park 15101			MO	Cedar Ridge Nurseries
A 4	Ambler 19002	N			Anything Grows Greenhouse
A 34	Ambler 19002			MO	Gary's Perennials
A 1	Aspers 17304	N	G		Adams County Nursery, Inc.
A 13	Aspers 17304	N	G		Bull Valley Rhododendron Nursery
A 25	Bodines 17722	N			Dionysos' Barn
A 39	Carrolltown 15722				Hanchar Nursery
A 95	Coopersburg 18036	N	G		Tilley's Nursery/The WaterWorks
A 7	Easton 18042	N	G		The Banana Tree
A 34	Georgetown 15043			MO	Georgetown Greenhouse & Nursery
A 39	Gibsonia 15044			MO	Halcyon Gardens
A 53	Hanover 17331			MO	Lakeland Nursery Sales
A 96	Huntingdon Valley 19006	N	G		Tinari Greenhouses
A 16	Indiana 15701				Carino Nurseries
A 65	Indiana 15710-0340	N	G		Musser Forests Inc.
A 71	Kingston 18704-0865			MO	Painted Meadows Seed Co.
A 41	Loretto 15940	N	G		Hickory Hill Gardens
A 92	McKnightstown 17343			MO	Stillpoint Gardens
A 28	Meadville 16335	N			Ernst Crownvetch Farms
A 82	Mechanicsburg 17055	N	G		The Rosemary House
A 98	Media 19063	N	G		Upper Bank Nurseries
A 64	North East 16428	N			Mums by Paschke
A 94	Orefield 18069			MO	Ter-El Nursery
A 28	Philadelphia 19147-0436	N			Exotic Blossoms (TM) Topiary Sculptures
A 60	Philadelphia 19111	N	G		Matsu-Momiji Nursery
A 5	Reedsville 17084	N			Appalachian Wildflower Nursery
A 30	Sagamore 16250	N			Flickingers' Nursery
A 77	Scottdale 15683	N	G		The Primrose Path
A 98	Trevose 19047			MO	Otis Twilley Seed Co.
A 13	Warminster 18974	N	G		W. Atlee Burpee Company
A 99	Warrington 18976	N	G		Varga's Nursery
A 5	Waynesboro 17268	N	G		Appalachian Gardens
A 52	Wellsville 17365	N	G		Michael & Janet Kristick
A 89	Wexford 15090	N			Soergel Greenhouses
A 73	Wynnewood 19096	N			Penn Valley Orchids
PRINCE EDWARD ISLAND, CANADA					
A 100	Charlottetown C0A 1P0	N	G		Vesey's Seeds Ltd.
QUEBEC, CANADA					
A 69	Ste Foy G2E 3L9	N	G		Orchibec
RHODE ISLAND					
A 61	Wyoming 02898	N			Meadowbrook Herb Garden
SASKATCHEWAN, CANADA					
A 43	Parkside S0J 2A0	N	G		Honeywood Lilies
A 26	Saskatoon S7K 3S9	N			Early's Farm & Garden Centre, Inc.
A 53	Saskatoon S7K 3J6	N	G		Lakeshore Tree Farms, Ltd.
A 81	Saskatoon S7K 3J8	N	G		Riverside Gardens
SOUTH AFRICA					
A 83	Constantia 7848			MO	Rust-En-Vrede Nursery
A 67	Rondebosch,Cape Town 7700			MO	Nooitgedag Disa Nursery
A 77	Sloanpark 2152	N			Protea Seed & Nursery Suppliers
A 72	Somerset West, Cape 7130	N		MO	Parsley's Cape Seeds

(continued next page)

PAGE	CITY/ZIP	N=NURSERY G=GARDEN MO=MAIL ORDER ONLY	SOURCE
SOUTH AFRICA (continued)			
A 16	Stellenbosch, Cape 7609	MO	Cape Seed & Bulb
SOUTH CAROLINA			
A 106	Aiken 29801	N G	Woodlanders, Inc.
A 82	Cross Hill 29332-0560	N G	The Rose Garden & Mini Rose Nursery
A 88	Graniteville 29829	N	R. H. Shumway Seedsman
A 77	Greenville 29607	MO	Prentiss Court Ground Covers
A 72	Greenwood 29648-0046	N G	Park Seed Company, Inc.
A 102	Hodges 29695-0001	MO	Wayside Gardens
A 19	Myrtle Beach 29577	N G	Coastal Gardens & Nursery
A 17	Newberry 29108	N G	Carter & Holmes, Inc.
SOUTH DAKOTA			
A 27	Vermillion 57069	G MO	Echinational Plant Products
A 39	Yankton 57078	N	Gurney Seed & Nursery Co.
SWITZERLAND			
A 86	Meyrin, Geneve CH 1217	N	Seedalp
TENNESSEE			
A 8	Beersheba Springs 37305		Beersheba Wildflower Garden
A 42	Cookeville 38501	N G	Hidden Springs Nursery - Edible Landscaping
A 69	Corryton 37721	N G	Oakes Daylilies
A 32	Dresden 38225	N G	Fred's Plant Farm
A 59	Gleason 38229	MO	Margrave Plant Co.
A 65	Greenback 37742	N G	Native Gardens
A 2	Knoxville 37901	MO	Alfrey -- Peter Pepper Seeds
A 8	Knoxville 37938	N	Beaver Creek Nursery
A 93	Loudon 37774	N G	Sunlight Gardens
A 7	McMinnville 37110	MO	Vernon Barnes & Son Nursery
A 23	McMinnville 37110-0471	MO	Cumberland Valley Nurseries, Inc.
A 64	McMinnville 37110	N	Mt. Leo Nursery
A 85	McMinnville 37110	N G	Savage Farms Nursery
A 83	Nash 75569	MO	SPB Sales
A 66	Oak Ridge 37830	MO	Natural Gardens
A 56	Red Boiling Springs 37150	N G	Long Hungry Creek Nursery
A 71	Ripley 38063	N G	Owen Farms
A 8	Signal Mountain 37377	N G	Bee Rock Herb Farm
TEXAS			
A 78	Alamo 78516	N	Quality Cactus
A 92	Azle 76020	MO	Ed Storms, Inc.
A 90	Beaumont 77702	N	Southern Exposure
A 4	Brenham 77833	N G	Antique Rose Emporium
A 75	Brenham 77833	MO	Pleasant Hill African Violets
A 105	Bryan 77802	N G	Wilson's Violet Haven
A 6	Burleson 76028	N G	Artistic Plants
A 79	College Station 77840	N G	Ray's African Violets
A 57	Conroe 77385	N G	The Lowrey Nursery
A 24	Corpus Christi 78411	N	Dane Company
A 23	Dallas 75249	N G	The Nursery at the Dallas Nature Center
A 44	Dallas 75381-0082	MO	Horticultural Enterprises
A 62	Dallas 75208	MO	Mini-Roses
A 101	Dallas 75219	N G	Volkman Bros. Greenhouses
A 106	DeLeon 76444	N	Womack Nursery Co.
A 6	El Paso 79927	N G	Aztekakti/Desertland Nursery
A 80	Gregory 78359	N G	Rhapis Gardens
A 43	Hereford 79045	MO	Horizon Seeds
A 45	Hico 76457	N G	Huggins Farm Irises
A 1	Houston 77026	N	Air Expose
A 33	Houston 77034		Lorine Friedrich
A 76	Houston 77282-0014	N G	The Plumeria People
A 101	Houston 77093	N G	Water Lily World
A 107	Ingram 78025	N	Y. O. Ranch Cactus Co.
A 48	Joshua 76058		J-Lot Gardens
A 37	Kerrville 78028	N	Green Horizons
A 34	Laredo 78043	N G	Garden World
A 10	Lavernia 78121	N G	Bonsai Farm

(continued next page)

PAGE	CITY/ZIP	N=NURSERY	G=GARDEN	MO=MAIL ORDER ONLY	SOURCE
TEXAS (continued)					
A 7	Nacogdoches 75961	N			Barnee's Garden
A 12	Omaha 75571			MO	Brown's Omaha Plant Farms, Inc.
A 105	Poolville 76076			MO	Willhite Seed Co.
A 44	San Antonio 78233				Hortense's African Violets
A 76	Stephensville 76401-0104	N	G		Porter & Son
A 62	Texarkana 75502	N			Miller-Bowie County Farmers Assn.
A 4	The Woodlands 77380			MO	American Daylily & Perennials
A 49	Victoria 77904	N	G		JoS Violets
A 107	Waller 77484	N	G		Yucca Do Nursery
UTAH					
A 70	Bountiful 84010	N	G		Orchids Bountiful
A 64	Logan 84321	N			Mountain Valley Seeds & Nursery
A 63	Roy 84067				Mission Bell Gardens
A 46	Salt Lake City 84119	N	G		Intermountain Cactus
A 6	Santa Clara 84765				Australflora of Utah
A 79	Sunset 84015	N	G		Randy's Iris Garden
VERMONT					
A 100	Charlotte 05445	N	G		Vermont Wildflower Farm
A 100	Fair Haven 05743	N	G		Vermont Bean Seed Co.
A 20	Londonderry 05148	N	G		The Cook's Garden
A 77	Putney 05346				Putney Nursery, Inc.
A 54	West Danville 05873-0044	N	G		Le Jardin du Gourmet
A 37	White River Junction 05001	N	G		Green Mountain African Violets
VIRGINIA					
A 27	Afton 22920	N			Edible Landscaping
A 50	Charlottesville 22903			MO	Kalmia Farm
A 12	Christiansburg 24073			MO	Brookfield Nursery & Tree Plantation
A 100	Fisherville 22939	N	G		Andre Viette Farm & Nursery
A 67	Gainesville 22065	N	G		Nicholls Gardens
A 23	Gloucester 23061	N	G		The Daffodil Mart
A 12	Gloucester Point 23062			MO	Joseph Brown, Native Seeds
A 102	Lovettsville 22080	N	G		Water Ways Nursery
A 47	McLean 22101		G	MO	The Iris Pond
A 90	Newport News 23606	N	G		Solomon Daylilies
A 90	North Garden 22959		G		Southern Exposure Seed Exchange
A 6	Radford 24141		G		Avonbank Iris Gardens
A 39	Spotsylvania 22553	N			Hager Nurseries, Inc.
A 102	Waynesboro 22980				Waynesboro Nurseries
WASHINGTON					
A 8	Auburn 98002	N	G		The Beall Orchid Company
A 31	Bellevue 98005	N	G		Foliage Gardens
A 37	Bellevue 98007	N			The Greenery
A 101	Bothell 98011	N	G		Wanda's Hide-a-Way
A 71	Bow 98232	N	G		Pacific Berry Works
A 44	Bremerton 98310	N			Horsley Rhododendron Nursery
A 104	Brinnon 98320	N	G		Whitney Gardens
A 12	Buckley 98321	N	G		Buckley Nursery
A 18	Chehalis 98532	N	G		Chehalis Rare Plant Nursery
A 73	Chelan 98816			MO	Perennial Seed Exchange
A 47	College Place 99324	N	G		Iris Test Gardens
A 7	Edmonds 98020			MO	Bailey's
A 41	Elma 98541	N	G		Heaths and Heathers
A 41	Fall City 98024	N	G		The Herbfarm
A 36	Issaquah 98027	N			Grand Ridge Nursery
A 52	Kalama 98625	N	G		Kordonowy's Dahlias
A 45	Kent 98035			MO	Ed Hume Seeds, Inc.
A 51	Kirkland 98033	N	G		Kirkland Iris Garden
A 96	La Conner 98257	N			Tillinghast Seed Co.
A 33	Langley 98260			MO	Frosty Hollow Nursery
A 45	Montesano 98563	N	G		Hughes Nursery
A 78	Morton 98356	N	G		Raintree Nursery
A 6	Mt. Vernon 98273				B & B Laboratories
A 89	Mt. Vernon 98273	N	G		Skagit African Violets
A 8	Northport 99157-0411	N			Bear Creek Nursery

(continued next page)

PAGE	CITY/ZIP	N=NURSERY G=GARDEN	MO=MAIL ORDER ONLY	SOURCE
WASHINGTON (continued)				
A 33	Olympia 98507		MO	Fungi Perfecti
A 13	Onalaska 98570	N G		Burnt Ridge Nursery
A 1	Port Townsend 98368	N G		Abundant Life Seed Foundation
A 6	Port Townsend 98368	N G		B & D Lilies
A 80	Port Townsend 98368	N		Rex Bulb Farms
A 88	Roy 98580	N		Silvaseed Company, Inc.
A 20	Seattle 98101		MO	Colvos Creek Nursery & Landscaping
A 29	Seattle 98119	N G		Fancy Fronds
A 80	Seattle 98112		MO	Red Barn Dahlias
A 86	Seattle 98198	N G		Sea-Tac Gardens
A 89	Sequim 98382	N		Skyline Nursery
A 40	Shelton 98584	N G		Harstine Island Nursery
A 22	Snohomish 98290	N G		Cricklewood Nursery
A 53	Spokane 99202	N		Lamb Nurseries
A 23	Sumner 98390	N G		Dahlias by Phil Traff
A 26	Sumner 98390			Dunford Farms
A 20	Tacoma 98446	N G		Connell's Dahlias
A 75	Tekoa 99033	N G		Plants of the Wild
A 36	Tonasket 98855	N G		Good Seed Co.
A 2	Vancouver 98685	N G		Aitken's Salmon Creek Garden
A 22	Walla Walla 99362			C. Criscola Iris Garden
A 32	Walla Walla 99362	N G		French Iris Gardens
A 99	Wenatchee 98801	N G		VanWell Nursery, Inc.
A 7	Woodinville 98072			Baker & Chantry Orchids
A 94	Woodinville 98072		MO	The Sweetbriar
WEST VIRGINIA				
A 107	Berkeley Springs 25411	N G		Wrenwood of Berkeley Springs
WISCONSIN				
A 40	Bayfield 54814	N G		Hauser's Superior View Farm
A 22	Crivitz 54114	N		The Country Garden
A 48	Dousman 53118			Johnson Seed Company
A 19	East Troy 53120			Clifford's Perennial & Vine
A 30	Elkhorn 53121	N G		Flora Favours
A 10	Germantown 53022		MO	Boehlke's Woodland Gardens
A 30	Madison 53713	N		Flad's Glads
A 3	Monroe 53566	N G		Alpine Gardens & Calico Shop
A 77	Mt. Horeb 53572	N G		Prairie Ridge Nursery/CRM Ecosystems, Inc.
A 50	Omro 54963	N		Kester's Wild Game Food Nurseries
A 30	Peshtigo 54157	N G		Field and Forest Products, Inc.
A 102	Plainfield 54966	N G		The Waushara Gardens
A 62	Racine 53402-2498	N G		Milaeger's Gardens
A 49	Randolph 53957	N		J. W. Jung Seed Co.
A 56	Richland Center 53581		MO	Little Valley Farm
A 76	Tilleda 54978	N G		Pony Creek Nursery
A 76	Westfield 53964	N G		Prairie Nursery
A 48	Wilson 54027	N G		Jasperson's Hersey Nursery
WYOMING				
A 64	Cheyenne 82003	N		Mountain West Seeds

PRODUCT SOURCES INDEX K 1

PAGE	STATE	CITY	SHOP?	SOURCE
ADD-IT FERTILIZER INJECTOR (TM)				
B 31	CA	Santee	Yes	Trickle Soak Systems
AFRICAN VIOLET SUPPLIES				
B 15	AR	Camden		House of Violets
A 62	CA	Sacramento	Yes	Mighty Minis
A 107	CA	Solvang	Yes	Zaca Vista Nursery
B 24	CA	Ventura	Yes	Phologistics
A 100	CO	Englewood	Yes	The Violet Showcase
A 93	CT	Woodbury		Suni's Violets
B 32	FL	Gainesville	Yes	The Violet House
B 8	FL	Merritt Island	Yes	DoDe's Gardens, Inc.
A 97	GA	Ochlochnee	Yes	Travis' Violets
B 9	IN	Jeffersonville		Earlee, Inc.
A 48	LA	Terrytown/Gretna	Yes	Jeannette's Jesneriads
A 16	MA	Falmouth	Yes	Cape Cod Violetry
A 46	MA	Lynnfield	Yes	Innis Violets
B 16	MI	Detroit		Indoor Gardening Supplies
A 60	MI	Detroit		Mary's African Violets
A 78	MO	Lee's Summit	Yes	Rainwater Violets
A 49	MO	Overland	Yes	Judy's Violets
A 2	MO	Waynesville	Yes	Alice's Violet Room
A 74	NJ	Cinnaminson	Yes	Plant Factory
A 30	NJ	Linwood	Yes	Fischer Greenhouses
A 16	OH	Toledo	Yes	Carol's Violets & Gifts
A 39	ON	Barrie	Yes	Growin'house
A 75	ON	Keswick	Yes	Plants 'n' Things
A 73	ON	Paris	Yes	Phipps African Violets
A 96	PA	Huntingdon Valley	Yes	Tinari Greenhouses
A 75	TX	Brenham		Pleasant Hill African Violets
A 105	TX	Bryan	Yes	Wilson's Violet Haven
A 101	TX	Dallas	Yes	Volkman Bros. Greenhouses
A 49	TX	Victoria	Yes	JoS Violets
A 30	WI	Elkhorn	Yes	Flora Favours
ANIMAL REPELLENTS				
See Also - Live Traps				
B 22	MN	Park Rapids	Yes	North Star Evergreens
A 53	PA	Hanover		Lakeland Nursery Sales
ARBORS				
B 4	MA	Bolton	Yes	Bow House, Inc.
B 18	PA	Point Pleasant	Yes	Kinsman Company, Inc.
B 11	TN	Memphis	Yes	The Garden Concepts Collection
B 29	WI	Delafield	Yes	Sun Designs
AUGER FOR PLANTING				
B 6	WI	Menasha		Chesnutt Corp.
AUTOMATIC VENT OPENERS				
See Also - Greenhouse Ventilators				
B 30	CA	Huntington Beach	Yes	Superior Autovents
B 20	CT	Stamford		Memory Metals, Inc.
B 4	MA	Salem		Bramen Company, Inc.
B 13	NH	Epping	Yes	Greenhouse Builders Supply
B 8	TN	Knoxville	Yes	Dalen Products, Inc.
AUTOMATOR (R)				
B 8	TN	Knoxville	Yes	Dalen Products, Inc.

PAGE	STATE	CITY	SHOP?	SOURCE
BAT GUANO				
B 22	AR	Fayetteville	Yes	Nitron Industries, Inc.
B 1	IN	Indianapolis	Yes	Alternative Garden Supply, Inc.
B 8	OR	Eugene	Yes	Down to Earth Distributors
B 16	WA	Wenatchee	Yes	I. F. M.
B 9	WI	Manitowoc		The Dramm Company
BED & BREAKFAST				
A 92	PA	McKnightstown		Stillpoint Gardens
A 77	PA	Scottdale	Yes	The Primrose Path
A 12	VA	Christiansburg		Brookfield Nursery & Tree Plantation
BEES AND BEEKEEPING SUPPLIES				
B 5	NC	Moravian Falls	Yes	Brushy Mountain Bee Farm, Inc.
A 83	NM	Roswell	Yes	Roswell Seed Co.
B 26	OH	Medina	Yes	A. I. Root Company
B 30	OR	Albany		Tecnu Enterprises, Inc.
B 30	PA	Eighty Four	Yes	Sunstream Bee Supply
BIRD FEEDERS AND FOOD				
B 26	CA	Sebastopol	Yes	Reed Bros.
A 40	GA	Atlanta	Yes	Hastings
B 8	IL	Moline		John Deere Catalog
B 9	IN	Jeffersonville		Earlee, Inc.
B 4	MA	Framingham		Bird 'n Hand
B 22	MA	Topsfield	Yes	Walter Nicke Company
B 16	MA	Waltham		Hyde Bird Feeder Co.
A 2	ME	Falmouth	Yes	Allen, Sterling & Lothrop
A 102	MI	Fennville	Yes	Wavecrest Nursery & Landscaping Co.
B 9	NH	Penacook	Yes	Duncraft, Inc.
B 6	OH	Waterville	Yes	Carruth Studio
B 24	VA	Madison	Yes	The Plow & Hearth
A 50	WI	Omro	Yes	Kester's Wild Game Food Nurseries
BIRD HOUSES				
B 7	CA	Long Beach		J Collard
B 21	CA	San Anselmo		The Natural Gardening Company
B 26	CA	Sebastopol	Yes	Reed Bros.
B 1	IL	Galesburg		Alsto's Handy Helpers
B 16	MA	Waltham		Hyde Bird Feeder Co.
B 21	MN	Grand Rapids	Yes	Mr. Birdhouse
B 2	NC	Greensboro		Autumn Innovations
B 5	NC	Moravian Falls	Yes	Brushy Mountain Bee Farm, Inc.
B 9	NH	Penacook	Yes	Duncraft, Inc.
B 19	OK	Oklahoma City		MAC Industries
B 18	PA	Point Pleasant	Yes	Kinsman Company, Inc.
BIRD NETTING				
B 17	MN	Minneapolis	Yes	InterNet, Inc.
A 53	PA	Hanover		Lakeland Nursery Sales
B 8	TN	Knoxville	Yes	Dalen Products, Inc.
BIRD REPELLENTS				
B 28	CA	Emeryville	Yes	Seabright Enterprises
A 13	CO	Rocky Ford	Yes	D.V. Burrell Seed Growers Co.
A 40	MI	Grand Junction	Yes	Hartmann's Plantation, Inc.
B 8	TN	Knoxville	Yes	Dalen Products, Inc.
B 23	WA	Seattle	Yes	Organic Pest Management
BIRDBATHS				
B 1	CA	Pt. Arena		American Sundials, Inc.
B 9	NH	Penacook	Yes	Duncraft, Inc.
B 11	NY	Long Island City	Yes	Florentine Craftsmen, Inc.
B 6	OH	Waterville	Yes	Carruth Studio
B 10	RI	Newport	Yes	Erkins Studios, Inc.
BONSAI POTS AND SUPPLIES				
A 3	CA	San Marcos		Altman Specialty Plants
A 87	CT	Stamford	Yes	Shanti Bithi Nursery

(continued next page)

PAGE	STATE	CITY	SHOP?	SOURCE
BONSAI POTS AND SUPPLIES (continued)				
B 4	FL	Hollywood		Bonsai Creations
B 25	IL	Rock Island		Pot Lock
B 7	MA	Andover		Country House Floral Supply
B 24	MA	Sudbury	Yes	John Palmer Bonsai
B 4	MD	Baltimore	Yes	Bonsai Associates, Inc.
A 12	MS	Olive Branch	Yes	Brussel's Bonsai Nursery
B 16	NY	Rochester		International Bonsai Containers
A 19	ON	Mississauga	Yes	Clargreen Gardens Ltd.
A 60	PA	Philadelphia	Yes	Matsu-Momiji Nursery
A 6	TX	Burleson	Yes	Artistic Plants
A 10	TX	Lavernia	Yes	Bonsai Farm
B 14	WA	Kent	Yes	Heritage Arts
BONSAI TOOLS				
B 4	FL	Hollywood		Bonsai Creations
B 24	MA	Sudbury	Yes	John Palmer Bonsai
B 4	MD	Baltimore	Yes	Bonsai Associates, Inc.
A 12	MS	Olive Branch	Yes	Brussel's Bonsai Nursery
B 16	NY	Rochester		International Bonsai Containers
A 60	PA	Philadelphia	Yes	Matsu-Momiji Nursery
A 6	TX	Burleson	Yes	Artistic Plants
A 10	TX	Lavernia	Yes	Bonsai Farm
B 14	WA	Kent	Yes	Heritage Arts
B 28	WA	Mt. Vernon	Yes	Skagit Gardens
BOOK CLUBS				
B 11	NY	New York		The Garden Book Club
B 23	PA	Emmaus		Organic Gardening Book Club
BOOKS, AFRICAN VIOLETS				
A 107	CA	Solvang	Yes	Zaca Vista Nursery
BOOKS, ALPINE AND ROCK GARDENS				
A 89	OR	Medford	Yes	Siskiyou Rare Plant Nursery
BOOKS, BONSAI				
B 12	CA	Rancho Palos Verdes	Yes	V. L. T. Gardner
A 87	CT	Stamford	Yes	Shanti Bithi Nursery
B 4	FL	Hollywood		Bonsai Creations
B 24	MA	Sudbury	Yes	John Palmer Bonsai
B 4	MD	Baltimore	Yes	Bonsai Associates, Inc.
A 12	MS	Olive Branch	Yes	Brussel's Bonsai Nursery
B 4	NJ	Englishtown	Yes	The Book Tree
B 34	NJ	Hopewell	Yes	Elisabeth Woodburn
B 16	NY	Rochester		International Bonsai Containers
B 17	OR	Portland	Yes	International Specialized Book Services, Inc.
A 6	TX	Burleson	Yes	Artistic Plants
A 10	TX	Lavernia	Yes	Bonsai Farm
B 14	WA	Kent	Yes	Heritage Arts
BOOKS, BROMELIADS				
A 78	CA	La Habra	Yes	Rainbow Gardens Nursery & Bookshop
B 12	CA	Rancho Palos Verdes	Yes	V. L. T. Gardner
B 18	CA	San Marino		Myron Kimnach
B 4	NJ	Englishtown	Yes	The Book Tree
B 34	NJ	Hopewell	Yes	Elisabeth Woodburn
B 17	OR	Portland	Yes	International Specialized Book Services, Inc.
BOOKS, BULBS				
A 58	IL	Chicago		McClure & Zimmerman
BOOKS, CACTI & SUCCULENTS				
A 1	CA	Carpinteria	Yes	Abbey Gardens
B 5	CA	Concord	Yes	Brooks Books
A 14	CA	Cupertino	Yes	Cactus Gem Nursery
A 49	CA	Galt	Yes	K & L Cactus Nursery
A 9	CA	La Crescenta	Yes	Bentley's Botanical Gardens
A 78	CA	La Habra	Yes	Rainbow Gardens Nursery & Bookshop

(continued next page)

PAGE	STATE	CITY	SHOP?	SOURCE
BOOKS, CACTI & SUCCULENTS (continued)				
A 14	CA	Lodi	Yes	Cactus by Dodie
A 89	CA	Northridge	Yes	Singers' Growing Things
A 3	CA	San Marcos		Altman Specialty Plants
B 18	CA	San Marino		Myron Kimnach
B 18	OR	Newburg	Yes	The Ken-L-Questor
BOOKS, CALIFORNIA NATIVE PLANTS				
A 72	CA	Sun Valley	Yes	Theodore Payne Foundation
BOOKS, CARNIVOROUS PLANTS				
A 106	GA	Marietta	Yes	World Insectivorous Plants
BOOKS, CONIFERS				
A 19	OR	Aurora	Yes	Coenosium Gardens
BOOKS, FERNS				
A 78	CA	La Habra	Yes	Rainbow Gardens Nursery & Bookshop
B 18	CA	San Marino		Myron Kimnach
BOOKS, FLOWER ARRANGING				
B 3	PA	Greeley	Yes	Dorothy Biddle Service
BOOKS, GESNERIADS				
A 13	CT	Eastford	Yes	Buell's Greenhouse, Inc.
BOOKS, HERBS				
A 17	CT	Oxford	Yes	Catnip Acres Farm
A 23	KY	Louisville		Dabney Herbs
B 33	MA	Lincoln	Yes	Wilkerson Books
A 22	MA	Rowley	Yes	Cricket Hill Herb Farm Ltd.
A 93	OH	Chesterland	Yes	Sunnybrook Farms Nursery
A 82	PA	Mechanicsburg	Yes	The Rosemary House
A 8	TN	Signal Mountain	Yes	Bee Rock Herb Farm
A 41	WA	Fall City	Yes	The Herbfarm
B 34	WI	Oregon	Yes	Wood Violet Books
BOOKS, LANDSCAPE ARCHITECTURE				
B 12	CA	Rancho Palos Verdes	Yes	V. L. T. Gardner
B 33	MA	Lincoln	Yes	Wilkerson Books
B 18	NH	Exeter		Landscape Books
B 34	NJ	Hopewell	Yes	Elisabeth Woodburn
BOOKS, LILIES				
B 18	OR	Newburg	Yes	The Ken-L-Questor
BOOKS, MUSHROOMS				
A 103	BC	Vancouver	Yes	Western Biologicals Ltd.
A 65	CA	Inverness	Yes	Mushroompeople
B 18	OR	Newburg	Yes	The Ken-L-Questor
BOOKS, NEW				
See Also - Specific Subjects				
B 8	Au	Rose Bay, NSW		Direct Book Service
A 84	BC	Vancouver	Yes	Sanctuary Seeds/Folklore Herb Co.
B 5	CA	Berkeley	Yes	Builders Booksource
B 5	CA	Concord	Yes	Brooks Books
B 1	CA	Davis	Yes	agAccess
B 28	CA	Mill Valley	Yes	Smith & Hawken
B 3	CA	Palo Alto	Yes	Bell's Book Store
B 12	CA	Rancho Palos Verdes	Yes	V. L. T. Gardner
B 23	CA	San Francisco		Ortho Information Services
A 89	CA	San Francisco	Yes	Anthony J. Skittone
A 27	CA	Tustin	Yes	Endangered Species
A 11	CA	Willits	Yes	Bountiful Gardens
A 93	CT	Elmwood		Sunrise Oriental Seed Co.
B 19	En	Kew, Surrey	Yes	Lloyds' of Kew
B 14	En	London		Hatchard's
A 27	GA	Decatur	Yes	Eco-Gardens

(continued next page)

PAGE	STATE	CITY	SHOP?	SOURCE
BOOKS, NEW (continued)				
A 87	ID	Boise		Seeds Blum
A 42	ID	Ketchum	Yes	High Altitude Gardens
B 6	MA	West Newton		The Clapper Co.
A 74	ME	New Gloucester	Yes	Pinetree Garden Seeds
A 29	ME	Waterville		Fedco Seeds
B 4	NJ	Englishtown	Yes	The Book Tree
B 34	NJ	Hopewell	Yes	Elisabeth Woodburn
B 11	NY	New York		The Garden Book Club
B 28	Ne	Auckland		South Pacific Books, Ltd.
A 61	OH	North Lima	Yes	Mellinger's Inc.
A 26	ON	Georgetown		Dominion Seed House
A 81	ON	Goodwood	Yes	Richters
A 67	OR	Albany	Yes	Nichols Garden Nursery, Inc.
A 38	OR	Eugene	Yes	Greer Gardens
A 95	OR	Lorane	Yes	Territorial Seed Co.
B 17	OR	Portland	Yes	International Specialized Book Services, Inc.
B 23	PA	Emmaus		Organic Gardening Book Club
A 106	SC	Aiken	Yes	Woodlanders, Inc.
B 15	So	Newlands, Cape Town	Yes	Honigklip Nurseries & Book Sales
B 21	VA	New Castle	Yes	Necessary Trading Co.
A 90	VA	North Garden		Southern Exposure Seed Exchange
B 30	WA	Centralia		Jane Sutley Horticultural Books
A 78	WA	Morton	Yes	Raintree Nursery
A 1	WA	Port Townsend	Yes	Abundant Life Seed Foundation
B 6	WI	Deer Park	Yes	Capability's Books & Videos
B 34	WI	Oregon	Yes	Wood Violet Books
BOOKS, OLD GARDEN ROSES				
B 3	CA	Palo Alto	Yes	Bell's Book Store
BOOKS, ORCHIDS				
A 32	AR	Little Rock	Yes	Fox Orchids, Inc.
A 92	CA	Carpinteria	Yes	Stewart Orchids
B 12	CA	Rancho Palos Verdes	Yes	V. L. T. Gardner
B 23	CA	San Francisco		Ortho Information Services
A 58	CA	South San Francisco	Yes	Rod McLellan Co.
A 29	FL	Homestead	Yes	Fennell's Orchid Jungle
B 20	FL	Jacksonville		McQuerry Orchid Books
A 68	IL	Dundee	Yes	Oak Hill Gardens
A 70	IL	Villa Park	Yes	Orchids by Hausermann, Inc.
A 50	MD	Kensington	Yes	Kensington Orchids
B 31	MI	Lowell		Twin Oaks Books
B 4	NJ	Englishtown	Yes	The Book Tree
B 34	NJ	Hopewell	Yes	Elisabeth Woodburn
A 45	ON	Bright's Grove	Yes	Huronview Nurseries & Garden Centre
A 51	ON	Komoka	Yes	Kilworth Flowers
B 17	OR	Portland	Yes	International Specialized Book Services, Inc.
A 70	UT	Bountiful	Yes	Orchids Bountiful
BOOKS, USED AND OUT-OF-PRINT				
See Also - Specific Subjects				
B 33	AL	Ft. Payne		Gary Wayner - Bookseller
B 17	CA	Berkeley		Ian Jackson
B 5	CA	Concord	Yes	Brooks Books
B 3	CA	Palo Alto	Yes	Bell's Book Store
B 12	CA	Rancho Palos Verdes	Yes	V. L. T. Gardner
B 18	CA	San Marino		Myron Kimnach
B 28	CT	Morris		Robert Shuhi - Books
B 20	CT	New Preston		Timothy Mawson
B 19	En	Kew, Surrey	Yes	Lloyds' of Kew
B 14	En	London		Hatchard's
B 17	En	Redhill, Surrey	Yes	Ivelet Books
B 1	IL	Brookfield	Yes	The American Botanist
B 27	MA	Lanesboro	Yes	Savoy Books
B 33	MA	Lincoln	Yes	Wilkerson Books
B 34	ME	Hampden	Yes	Gary W. Woolson, Bookseller
B 28	NH	Bedford		Edward F. Smiley, Bookseller
B 18	NH	Exeter		Landscape Books

(continued next page)

PAGE	STATE	CITY	SHOP?	SOURCE
BOOKS, USED AND OUT-OF-PRINT (continued)				
B 16	NH	Westmoreland	Yes	Hurley Books
B 4	NJ	Englishtown	Yes	The Book Tree
B 34	NJ	Hopewell	Yes	Elisabeth Woodburn
B 9	NY	Boiceville		Editions
B 5	NY	Lansingburgh	Yes	Warren F. Broderick - Books
B 25	ON	Rockton	Yes	Pomona Book Exchange
B 3	OR	Gold Hill		Beth L. Bibby Books
B 18	OR	Newburg	Yes	The Ken-L-Questor
B 3	OR	Portland		Carol Barnett - Books
B 2	RI	Newport	Yes	Anchor & Dolphin Books
B 15	So	Newlands, Cape Town	Yes	Honigklip Nurseries & Book Sales
B 30	WA	Centralia		Jane Sutley Horticultural Books
B 34	WI	Oregon	Yes	Wood Violet Books
B 12	Wa	Hawarden, Clwyd	Yes	Gladstone & Campbell
B 4	Wa	Nr. Presteign		Mary Bland
BOOKS, VEGETABLE & FRUIT GROWING				
A 90	CA	Healdsburg	Yes	Sonoma Antique Apple Nursery
A 54	GA	Ball Ground	Yes	Lawson's Nursery
A 84	NY	Potsdam	Yes	St. Lawrence Nurseries
B 25	ON	Rockton	Yes	Pomona Book Exchange
A 36	WA	Tonasket	Yes	Good Seed Co.
BOOKS, WATER GARDENS				
A 99	CA	Upland	Yes	Van Ness Water Gardens
A 89	FL	Winter Haven	Yes	Slocum Water Gardens
A 72	MA	Whitman		Paradise Water Gardens
A 56	MD	Lilypons	Yes	Lilypons Water Gardens
A 102	NJ	Saddle River	Yes	Waterford Gardens
A 97	OH	Independence	Yes	William Tricker, Inc.
A 64	ON	Port Stanley	Yes	Moore Water Gardens
A 95	PA	Coopersburg	Yes	Tilley's Nursery/The WaterWorks
BOOKS, WILDFLOWERS				
A 62	IL	Rockton		Midwest Wildflowers
A 72	NC	Germanton	Yes	Passiflora
A 37	TX	Kerrville	Yes	Green Horizons
BOOT SCRAPER				
B 9	NV	Silver City	Yes	Dressler & Co.
BRIDGES				
B 21	CA	Bayside	Yes	Nampara Gardens
B 4	MA	Bolton	Yes	Bow House, Inc.
B 15	NY	Canastota	Yes	Hermitage Gardens
B 11	TN	Memphis	Yes	The Garden Concepts Collection
B 29	WI	Delafield	Yes	Sun Designs
CACTUS JUICE (R)				
B 6	IL	Deerfield		Clarel Laboratories, Inc.
CANNING SUPPLIES				
A 58	MB	Brandon		McFayden Seeds
A 48	ME	Albion		Johnny's Selected Seeds
B 3	ON	St. Thomas	Yes	Berry-Hill Limited
B 8	OR	Eugene	Yes	Down to Earth Distributors
A 39	SD	Yankton	Yes	Gurney Seed & Nursery Co.
A 96	WA	La Conner	Yes	Tillinghast Seed Co.
B 21	WY	Cody		Modern Farm
CARTS				
B 26	CA	Point Arena		Peter Reimuller's Cart Warehouse
B 14	CT	Unionville		Hayes Equipment Co.
B 8	FL	Miami	Yes	Day-Dex Co.
B 1	IL	Galesburg		Alsto's Handy Helpers
B 8	IL	Moline		John Deere Catalog
B 25	IL	Rockford		RAM Log Splitters
B 29	KS	Stanley		The Stanley Forge Co., Inc.

(continued next page)

PAGE	STATE	CITY	SHOP?	SOURCE
CARTS (continued)				
B 10	MA	Woburn	Yes	FXG Corporation
B 7	MO	St. Joseph	Yes	Composting Fast & Easy
B 3	NC	Matthews		BCS Mosa, Inc.
B 12	NY	Troy		Garden Way Manufacturing Co.
B 15	OR	Salem		Homestead Carts
B 13	TX	Littlefield		The Greener Thumb
B 7	VT	Charlotte		Country Home Products, Inc.
B 22	WI	Stoughton	Yes	Norwood Engineering, Inc.
B 21	WY	Cody		Modern Farm
CIDER AND WINE PRESSES				
B 14	KS	Paola	Yes	Happy Valley Ranch
B 17	NH	Jaffrey		Jaffrey Mfg. Co.
B 3	ON	St. Thomas	Yes	Berry-Hill Limited
A 39	SD	Yankton	Yes	Gurney Seed & Nursery Co.
CLOGS				
B 20	CA	Guerneville	Yes	Emi Meade, Importer
COLDFRAMES				
B 8	TN	Knoxville	Yes	Dalen Products, Inc.
COMPOSTING EQUIPMENT				
B 22	AR	Fayetteville	Yes	Nitron Industries, Inc.
B 19	IA	Charles City	Yes	McDermott Garden Products
B 26	MN	Eden Prairie	Yes	Ringer Research
B 7	MO	St. Joseph	Yes	Composting Fast & Easy
B 18	PA	Point Pleasant	Yes	Kinsman Company, Inc.
B 13	TX	Littlefield		The Greener Thumb
B 21	VA	New Castle	Yes	Necessary Trading Co.
B 12	VT	Burlington	Yes	Gardener's Supply Company
COMPUTEMP (R)				
B 26	NE	Columbus	Yes	Rodco Products Co., Inc.
COMPUTER PROGRAMS				
B 1	CA	Davis	Yes	agAccess
B 23	CA	San Francisco		Ortho Information Services
B 9	FL	Daytona Beach		Economy Label Sales Co., Inc.
B 7	MD	Arnold		Computer/Management Services
B 7	MD	Silver Spring	Yes	CompuGarden, Inc.
A 34	PA	Georgetown		Georgetown Greenhouse & Nursery
B 6	WI	Deer Park	Yes	Capability's Books & Videos
CONSERVATORIES				
B 20	CT	Wilton		Machin Designs (USA) Inc.
B 10	MD	Columbia	Yes	Everlight Greenhouses, Inc.
B 1	NJ	Cranbury	Yes	Amdega Conservatories
COOKBOOKS				
A 28	CA	Anaheim		Evergreen Y. H. Enterprises
A 98	CA	Belmont		Tsang & Ma
A 54	CA	Dixon		Le Marche Seeds International
A 90	CA	Healdsburg	Yes	Sonoma Antique Apple Nursery
A 93	CT	Elmwood		Sunrise Oriental Seed Co.
A 54	GA	Ball Ground	Yes	Lawson's Nursery
A 1	IN	Huntingburg	Yes	Ahrens Strawberry Nursery
B 14	KS	Paola	Yes	Happy Valley Ranch
A 41	MO	Kansas City	Yes	Herb Gathering Inc.
A 83	OR	Newberg	Yes	S & H Organic Acres
A 50	VA	Charlottesville		Kalmia Farm
A 71	WA	Bow	Yes	Pacific Berry Works
CYROFLEX (R)				
B 13	NH	Epping	Yes	Greenhouse Builders Supply
DOG AND CAT PEST CONTROLS				
B 9	CA	Oakland		EcoSafe Laboratories, Inc.

(continued next page)

PAGE	STATE	CITY	SHOP?	SOURCE
DOG AND CAT PEST CONTROLS (continued)				
A 23	KY	Louisville		Dabney Herbs
B 4	NY	Yorkville	Yes	Bonide Chemical Co., Inc.
B 23	OH	Hartville	Yes	Ohio Earth Food, Inc.
B 8	OR	Eugene	Yes	Down to Earth Distributors
B 21	VA	New Castle	Yes	Necessary Trading Co.
A 41	WA	Fall City	Yes	The Herbfarm
B 23	WA	Seattle	Yes	Organic Pest Management
B 16	WA	Wenatchee	Yes	I. F. M.
DRIP IRRIGATION SUPPLIES				
B 22	AR	Fayetteville	Yes	Nitron Industries, Inc.
B 26	CA	Chatsworth		Raindrip, Inc.
A 40	CA	Graton	Yes	Harmony Farm Supply
B 28	CA	Huntington Beach	Yes	Spot Systems Div., Wisdom Ind.
B 11	CA	Redway	Yes	Full Circle Garden Products
B 31	CA	San Francisco	Yes	The Urban Farmer Store
B 9	CA	Van Nuys	Yes	Drip Irrigation Garden
B 21	FL	Palmetto		Moss Products, Inc.
A 40	MI	Grand Junction	Yes	Hartmann's Plantation, Inc.
B 24	MO	Grover	Yes	Plastic Plumbing Products, Inc.
B 29	MO	North Kansas City		Stuppy Greenhouse Manufacturing, Inc.
B 17	NY	Niagara Falls		Irrigro
B 16	ON	St. Catharines	Yes	International Irrigation Systems
B 29	TX	Lubbock	Yes	Submatic Irrigation Systems
A 76	TX	Stephensville	Yes	Porter & Son
B 28	WA	Mt. Vernon	Yes	Skagit Gardens
B 9	WI	Manitowoc		The Dramm Company
DRIP IRRIGATION SYSTEMS				
B 26	CA	Chatsworth		Raindrip, Inc.
B 28	CA	Huntington Beach	Yes	Spot Systems Div., Wisdom Ind.
B 31	CA	San Francisco	Yes	The Urban Farmer Store
B 31	CA	Santee	Yes	Trickle Soak Systems
B 9	CA	Van Nuys	Yes	Drip Irrigation Garden
B 16	CO	Colorado Springs	Yes	Hydro-Gardens of Denver
B 21	FL	Palmetto		Moss Products, Inc.
B 21	IN	Sunman		Natural Gardening Research Center
B 24	MO	Grover	Yes	Plastic Plumbing Products, Inc.
B 17	NY	Niagara Falls		Irrigro
B 16	ON	St. Catharines	Yes	International Irrigation Systems
A 13	PA	Warminster	Yes	W. Atlee Burpee Company
EARTHWORMS				
B 5	GA	Bronwood		Bronwood Worm Gardens
B 3	GA	Dawson		Beatrice Farms
B 6	GA	Plains		Carter Fishworm Farm
B 6	MA	Buzzards Bay		Cape Cod Worm Farm
EASY WEEDER (TM)				
B 33	NY	Rochester	Yes	Warnico/USA, Inc.
ELECTRIC CHAIR-CART				
B 9	NJ	Sewell		Electric Mobility Corp
EMPLOYMENT SERVICES				
B 11	FL	Deland		Florapersonnel
FELCO PRUNERS (R)				
B 14	NJ	Old Tappan		Harlane Company, Inc.
FERTILIZERS				
A 9	CA	La Crescenta	Yes	Bentley's Botanical Gardens
B 11	CA	Redway	Yes	Full Circle Garden Products
B 30	CO	Boulder		Swallowtail Corporation
B 32	FL	Gainesville	Yes	The Violet House
B 22	FL	Miami		OFE International, Inc.
B 31	FL	Orlando	Yes	Tropical Plant Products, Inc.
A 51	FL	Sanford	Yes	Kilgore Seed Company

(continued next page)

PAGE	STATE	CITY	SHOP?	SOURCE
FERTILIZERS (continued)				
A 59	FL	Windemere	Yes	Ann Mann's Orchids
B 6	IL	Deerfield		Clarel Laboratories, Inc.
B 11	IL	Schaumburg	Yes	Florist Products, Inc.
A 40	MI	Grand Junction	Yes	Hartmann's Plantation, Inc.
A 11	NC	Brown Summit	Yes	Breckinridge Orchids
B 13	NC	Matthews		Gro-n-Energy
A 54	NJ	Sewell	Yes	Orol Ledden & Sons
A 83	NM	Roswell	Yes	Roswell Seed Co.
B 24	NY	Buffalo		Plant Collectibles
A 97	ON	Hamilton	Yes	Tregunno Seeds
B 1	OR	Junction City	Yes	Agrilite
A 26	SK	Saskatoon	Yes	Early's Farm & Garden Centre, Inc.
A 10	TX	Lavernia	Yes	Bonsai Farm
A 39	VA	Spotsylvania	Yes	Hager Nurseries, Inc.
A 104	WA	Brinnon	Yes	Whitney Gardens
FERTILIZERS, ORGANIC				
B 22	AR	Fayetteville	Yes	Nitron Industries, Inc.
B 1	CA	Fresno	Yes	Actagro
A 40	CA	Graton	Yes	Harmony Farm Supply
A 73	CA	Nevada City	Yes	Peaceful Valley Farm Supply
B 11	CA	Redway	Yes	Full Circle Garden Products
A 11	CA	Willits	Yes	Bountiful Gardens
B 9	IL	Mendota	Yes	EnP Inc.
B 9	IN	Jeffersonville		Earlee, Inc.
B 21	IN	Sunman		Natural Gardening Research Center
B 22	ME	Waldoboro		North American Kelp
B 24	MN	Duluth		Plant Magic Products, Inc.
B 26	MN	Eden Prairie	Yes	Ringer Research
B 23	OH	Hartville	Yes	Ohio Earth Food, Inc.
A 81	ON	Goodwood	Yes	Richters
B 8	OR	Eugene	Yes	Down to Earth Distributors
B 23	SC	West Columbia	Yes	Organic Farm & Garden Supply
B 33	TX	Houston		Spray-N-Grow
B 13	TX	Littlefield		The Greener Thumb
B 21	VA	New Castle	Yes	Necessary Trading Co.
B 22	VT	Newbury	Yes	North Country Organics
B 13	WA	Puyallup	Yes	Green Earth Organics
B 23	WA	Seattle	Yes	Organic Pest Management
B 16	WA	Wenatchee	Yes	I. F. M.
B 9	WI	Manitowoc		The Dramm Company
FISH, GARDEN PONDS				
A 99	CA	Upland	Yes	Van Ness Water Gardens
A 104	MD	Baltimore	Yes	Wicklein's Aquatic Farm & Nursery, Inc.
A 56	MD	Lilypons	Yes	Lilypons Water Gardens
A 102	NJ	Saddle River	Yes	Waterford Gardens
A 97	OH	Independence	Yes	William Tricker, Inc.
A 95	PA	Coopersburg	Yes	Tilley's Nursery/The WaterWorks
FLORALIGHT (TM)				
B 10	ON	Willowdale		Floralight Gardens Canada, Inc.
FLOWER ARRANGING SUPPLIES				
B 18	CA	Corona del Mar		The Keth Company
B 6	IL	Deerfield		Clarel Laboratories, Inc.
B 7	MA	Andover		Country House Floral Supply
A 2	MA	Wilmington	Yes	Arthur Eames Allgrove
A 19	ON	Mississauga	Yes	Clargreen Gardens Ltd.
B 3	PA	Greeley	Yes	Dorothy Biddle Service
B 10	VA	Rustburg		Floral Accents
FORESTRY EQUIPMENT/SUPPLIES				
A 37	CA	Carmel	Yes	Greener 'N' Ever Tree Farm & Nursery
B 22	MN	Burnsville	Yes	Northern Hydraulics, Inc.
B 22	MN	Park Rapids	Yes	North Star Evergreens
B 18	OH	Piqua		C. M. Leonard, Inc.

PAGE	STATE	CITY	SHOP?	SOURCE
FOUNTAINS				
A 84	CA	Santa Barbara	Yes	Santa Barbara Water Gardens
B 19	CT	Wilton		Kenneth Lynch & Sons, Inc.
B 25	NY	Bronxville		Pompeian Studios
B 15	NY	Canastota	Yes	Hermitage Gardens
B 11	NY	Long Island City	Yes	Florentine Craftsmen, Inc.
A 85	NY	Northport	Yes	S. Scherer & Sons
A 64	ON	Port Stanley	Yes	Moore Water Gardens
A 95	PA	Coopersburg	Yes	Tilley's Nursery/The WaterWorks
B 10	RI	Newport	Yes	Erkins Studios, Inc.
B 29	SC	Spartanburg	Yes	Strassacker Bronze, Inc.
B 27	VA	Hillsboro	Yes	Royal Tidewater Collection, Inc.
B 7	VT	Bristol	Yes	Robert Compton, Ltd.
FRUIT BOXES				
B 16	MN	Osseo		Hubbard Folding Box Co.
GARDEN BENCHES, METAL				
B 24	DC	Washington	Yes	Park Place
B 19	FL	Live Oak		The Live Oak Railroad Co.
B 33	NE	Broken Bow		Wikco Industries, Inc.
B 10	RI	Newport	Yes	Erkins Studios, Inc.
B 6	SC	Charleston	Yes	Charleston Battery Bench, Inc.
B 32	VT	Randolph	Yes	Vermont Castings
GARDEN BENCHES, STONE				
B 2	MA	Boston		Ascot Designs
B 6	OH	Waterville	Yes	Carruth Studio
B 10	RI	Newport	Yes	Erkins Studios, Inc.
GARDEN BENCHES, WOOD				
B 21	CA	Bayside	Yes	Nampara Gardens
B 2	CA	Fairfax	Yes	ANZA Architectural Wood Products
B 8	CA	Fort Bragg	Yes	Cypress Street Center
B 28	CA	Mill Valley	Yes	Smith & Hawken
B 26	CA	Sebastopol	Yes	Reed Bros.
B 34	GA	Savannah		Woodventure, Inc.
B 8	IL	Moline		John Deere Catalog
B 32	MA	Walpole		Walpole Woodworkers
B 6	MA	West Newton		The Clapper Co.
B 7	MD	Germantown	Yes	Country Casual
B 34	NY	High Falls	Yes	Wood Classics, Inc.
B 33	NY	Willsboro		Willsboro Wood Products
B 8	PA	Carlisle	Yes	Cumberland Woodcraft
B 13	SK	Saskatoon		Green Hand Tools
B 24	VA	Madison	Yes	The Plow & Hearth
B 33	VA	Salem	Yes	Winterthur Museum & Gardens
GARDEN CLOTHING				
See Also - Gloves				
B 20	CA	Guerneville	Yes	Emi Meade, Importer
B 30	CA	Santa Barbara		There's Always the Garden
B 34	ME	Berwick		Womanswork
B 22	MN	Burnsville	Yes	Northern Hydraulics, Inc.
B 25	NH	Wilton	Yes	Putnam's
GARDEN DIARIES				
B 25	CA	Burlingame		Putterin Press
B 14	CA	Los Angeles		The Growing Company
B 12	NC	Stanfield		Goodly Publishing
GARDEN FURNITURE				
See Also - Specific Type				
B 28	AL	Birmingham		Southern Statuary and Stone
B 21	CA	Bayside	Yes	Nampara Gardens
B 8	CA	Fort Bragg	Yes	Cypress Street Center
B 7	CA	Long Beach		J Collard
B 12	CA	San Francisco		Gardener's Eden
B 18	CA	San Francisco	Yes	Sue Fisher King

(continued next page)

PAGE	STATE	CITY	SHOP?	SOURCE
GARDEN FURNITURE (continued)				
B 26	CA	Sebastopol	Yes	Reed Bros.
A 103	CT	Litchfield	Yes	White Flower Farm
B 19	CT	Wilton		Kenneth Lynch & Sons, Inc.
B 20	CT	Wilton		Machin Designs (USA) Inc.
B 24	DC	Washington	Yes	Park Place
B 34	GA	Savannah		Woodventure, Inc.
B 1	IL	Galesburg		Alsto's Handy Helpers
B 32	MA	Walpole		Walpole Woodworkers
B 6	MA	West Newton		The Clapper Co.
B 7	MD	Germantown	Yes	Country Casual
B 2	NC	Greensboro		Autumn Innovations
B 5	NC	Moravian Falls	Yes	Brushy Mountain Bee Farm, Inc.
B 34	NY	High Falls	Yes	Wood Classics, Inc.
B 11	NY	Long Island City	Yes	Florentine Craftsmen, Inc.
B 33	NY	Willsboro		Willsboro Wood Products
B 17	OH	Cleveland	Yes	David Kay Garden & Gift Catalogue, Inc.
B 6	SC	Charleston	Yes	Charleston Battery Bench, Inc.
B 11	TN	Memphis	Yes	The Garden Concepts Collection
B 33	TX	Kemp		Westwind Mfg. Co.
B 24	VA	Madison	Yes	The Plow & Hearth
GARDEN MARKERS				
See Also - Plant Labels				
B 17	CA	Aptos		International Nursery Labels
B 10	CA	Cloverdale		Evergreen Garden Plant Labels
B 31	DE	Wilmington		F. R. Unruh
B 9	FL	Daytona Beach		Economy Label Sales Co., Inc.
B 24	MI	Paw Paw		Paw Paw Everlast Label Co.
B 14	NJ	Old Tappan		Harlane Company, Inc.
B 10	OH	Holland		Eon Industries
A 8	TN	Signal Mountain	Yes	Bee Rock Herb Farm
B 6	WA	Mt. Vernon	Yes	Charley's Greenhouse Supply
GARDEN ORNAMENTS				
See Also - Specific Type				
B 28	AL	Birmingham		Southern Statuary and Stone
B 21	CA	Bayside	Yes	Nampara Gardens
B 12	CA	Coloma	Yes	Gardenworks
B 7	CA	Long Beach		J Collard
B 28	CA	Mill Valley	Yes	Smith & Hawken
B 6	CA	Pasadena		Cindy's Bows
B 12	CA	San Francisco		Gardener's Eden
B 18	CA	San Francisco	Yes	Sue Fisher King
B 26	CA	Sebastopol	Yes	Reed Bros.
B 19	CT	Wilton		Kenneth Lynch & Sons, Inc.
B 24	DC	Washington	Yes	Park Place
B 2	FL	Orlando	Yes	Autumn Forge
B 8	IL	Moline		John Deere Catalog
B 2	MA	Boston		Ascot Designs
B 6	MA	West Newton		The Clapper Co.
B 15	ME	Yarmouth	Yes	Heritage Lanterns
B 27	NJ	Roosevelt	Yes	Sculpture Cast Editions
B 25	NY	Bronxville		Pompeian Studios
B 11	NY	Long Island City	Yes	Florentine Craftsmen, Inc.
B 17	OH	Cleveland	Yes	David Kay Garden & Gift Catalogue, Inc.
B 6	OH	Waterville	Yes	Carruth Studio
B 15	OK	Bixby		Heritage Sundial
B 8	PA	Carlisle	Yes	Cumberland Woodcraft
A 28	PA	Philadelphia	Yes	Exotic Blossoms (TM) Topiary Sculptures
B 14	PA	Pleasant Gap	Yes	Philip Hawk & Company
B 10	RI	Newport	Yes	Erkins Studios, Inc.
B 29	SC	Spartanburg	Yes	Strassacker Bronze, Inc.
B 11	TN	Memphis	Yes	The Garden Concepts Collection
B 32	TX	Fredericksburg	Yes	Vintage Wood Works
B 19	VA	Arlington	Yes	Mrs. McGregor's Garden Shop
B 27	VA	Hillsboro	Yes	Royal Tidewater Collection, Inc.
B 33	VA	Salem	Yes	Winterthur Museum & Gardens
B 7	VT	Bristol	Yes	Robert Compton, Ltd.

PAGE	STATE	CITY	SHOP?	SOURCE
GARDEN PLANS				
B 9	MA	Waltham	Yes	Laura D. Eisener, Landscape Design
B 7	MD	Silver Spring	Yes	CompuGarden, Inc.
B 15	PA	Bernville	Yes	Historical Landscapes
A 82	PA	Mechanicsburg	Yes	The Rosemary House
GARDEN STRUCTURES				
B 4	MA	Bolton	Yes	Bow House, Inc.
GARDEN STRUCTURES, PLANS				
B 15	PA	Bernville	Yes	Historical Landscapes
B 29	WI	Delafield	Yes	Sun Designs
GAZEBOS				
B 18	CA	San Francisco	Yes	Sue Fisher King
B 4	MA	Bolton	Yes	Bow House, Inc.
B 8	PA	Carlisle	Yes	Cumberland Woodcraft
B 32	PA	Elverson		Vixen Hill Gazebos
B 8	PA	Philadelphia		Jim Dalton Garden House Co.
B 32	TX	Fredericksburg	Yes	Vintage Wood Works
B 33	TX	Kemp		Westwind Mfg. Co.
B 29	WI	Delafield	Yes	Sun Designs
GIFTS FOR GARDENERS				
B 25	CA	Burlingame		Putterin Press
B 7	CA	Long Beach		J Collard
B 14	CA	Los Angeles		The Growing Company
B 28	CA	Mill Valley	Yes	Smith & Hawken
B 6	CA	Pasadena		Cindy's Bows
B 6	CA	Pasadena		Cindy's Bows
B 12	CA	San Francisco		Gardener's Eden
B 30	CA	Santa Barbara		There's Always the Garden
A 5	IL	Chapin		Applesource
B 11	IL	Schaumburg	Yes	Florist Products, Inc.
A 16	MA	Falmouth	Yes	Cape Cod Violetry
B 16	MN	Osseo		Hubbard Folding Box Co.
B 26	NE	Columbus	Yes	Rodco Products Co., Inc.
A 11	NY	Brooklyn		Botanic Garden Seed Co.
B 17	OH	Cleveland	Yes	David Kay Garden & Gift Catalogue, Inc.
A 9	OH	Seville	Yes	Bittersweet Farm
A 81	ON	Goodwood	Yes	Richters
A 39	PA	Gibsonia		Halcyon Gardens
A 82	PA	Mechanicsburg	Yes	The Rosemary House
B 19	VA	Arlington	Yes	Mrs. McGregor's Garden Shop
B 24	VA	Madison	Yes	The Plow & Hearth
B 33	VA	Salem	Yes	Winterthur Museum & Gardens
A 41	WA	Fall City	Yes	The Herbfarm
GLOVES				
B 7	CA	Long Beach		J Collard
B 28	CA	Mill Valley	Yes	Smith & Hawken
B 21	CA	San Anselmo		The Natural Gardening Company
B 34	ME	Berwick		Womanswork
B 25	NH	Wilton	Yes	Putnam's
A 11	NY	Brooklyn		Botanic Garden Seed Co.
GOPHER (TM)				
B 6	WI	Menasha		Chesnutt Corp.
GOT-CHA (TM)				
B 30	ID	Boise		Thurston Distributing, Inc.
GRAFTING SUPPLIES				
A 71	CA	Chula Vista	Yes	Pacific Tree Farms
A 82	IN	New Salisbury	Yes	Rocky Meadow Orchard & Nursery
A 106	TX	DeLeon	Yes	Womack Nursery Co.
B 9	WI	Manitowoc		The Dramm Company

PAGE	STATE	CITY	SHOP?	SOURCE
GRANNY'S BLOOMERS (R)				
B 6	IL	Deerfield		Clarel Laboratories, Inc.
GREENHOUSE ACCESSORIES				
B 12	AL	Mobile	Yes	Gothic Arch Greenhouses
B 27	CA	Camarillo	Yes	Santa Barbara Greenhouses
B 30	CA	Huntington Beach	Yes	Superior Autovents
B 4	FL	Jacksonville	Yes	Bloomin' Greenhouse, Inc.
B 22	FL	Miami		OFE International, Inc.
B 29	IL	Elmhurst		Suncraft, Inc.
B 1	IN	Indianapolis	Yes	Alternative Garden Supply, Inc.
B 17	MD	Laurel		Janco Greenhouses
B 31	NC	Goldsboro	Yes	Turner Greenhouses
B 26	NE	Columbus	Yes	Rodco Products Co., Inc.
B 29	NY	Commack		Sun System Greenhouses
B 8	OH	Medina	Yes	Cropking Greenhouses
B 1	OR	Junction City	Yes	Agrilite
B 29	OR	Portland	Yes	Sturdi-Built Mfg. Co.
B 30	TX	Ft. Worth	Yes	Texas Greenhouse Co.
B 32	VA	Charlottesville	Yes	Victory Garden Supply Co.
B 6	WA	Mt. Vernon	Yes	Charley's Greenhouse Supply
B 28	WA	Mt. Vernon	Yes	Skagit Gardens
B 30	WA	Seattle	Yes	Sunglo Solar Greenhouses
GREENHOUSE CONTROLS				
B 27	CA	Camarillo	Yes	Santa Barbara Greenhouses
B 23	CA	Cotati	Yes	Pacific Coast Greenhouse Mfg. Co.
B 17	MD	Laurel		Janco Greenhouses
B 29	MO	North Kansas City		Stuppy Greenhouse Manufacturing, Inc.
B 13	NH	Epping	Yes	Greenhouse Builders Supply
B 27	NJ	Princeton	Yes	Science Associates
B 8	OH	Medina	Yes	Cropking Greenhouses
GREENHOUSE EQUIPMENT				
B 9	CA	Van Nuys	Yes	Drip Irrigation Garden
B 16	CO	Colorado Springs	Yes	Hydro-Gardens of Denver
B 13	FL	Princeton		Greenhouse Specialties Co.
B 31	NC	Goldsboro	Yes	Turner Greenhouses
B 29	OR	Portland	Yes	Sturdi-Built Mfg. Co.
B 13	TX	Littlefield		The Greener Thumb
GREENHOUSE GRO (R)				
B 23	OH	St. Marys	Yes	Organic Research Laboratories
GREENHOUSE HEATERS				
B 12	AL	Mobile	Yes	Gothic Arch Greenhouses
B 4	FL	Jacksonville	Yes	Bloomin' Greenhouse, Inc.
B 13	FL	Princeton		Greenhouse Specialties Co.
B 29	IL	Elmhurst		Suncraft, Inc.
B 13	NH	Epping	Yes	Greenhouse Builders Supply
B 8	OH	Medina	Yes	Cropking Greenhouses
GREENHOUSE MATERIALS				
B 13	FL	Princeton		Greenhouse Specialties Co.
B 29	IL	Elmhurst		Suncraft, Inc.
B 22	ND	Neche	Yes	Northern Greenhouse Sales
B 13	NH	Epping	Yes	Greenhouse Builders Supply
B 32	NY	New York		Vegetable Factory, Inc.
B 6	WA	Mt. Vernon	Yes	Charley's Greenhouse Supply
B 2	WI	Hammond	Yes	Arctic Glass & Window Outlet
GREENHOUSE SUPPLIES				
B 12	AL	Mobile	Yes	Gothic Arch Greenhouses
A 103	BC	Vancouver	Yes	Western Biologicals Ltd.
B 23	CA	Cotati	Yes	Pacific Coast Greenhouse Mfg. Co.
B 10	FL	Ft. Lauderdale	Yes	Environmental Concepts
B 11	IL	Schaumburg	Yes	Florist Products, Inc.
B 29	MO	North Kansas City		Stuppy Greenhouse Manufacturing, Inc.
B 13	NC	Matthews		Gro-n-Energy

(continued next page)

PAGE	STATE	CITY	SHOP?	SOURCE
GREENHOUSE SUPPLIES (continued)				
B 1	OR	Junction City	Yes	Agrilite
A 34	PA	Georgetown		Georgetown Greenhouse & Nursery
B 4	PA	New Brighton		Brighton By-Products Co., Inc.
A 17	SC	Newberry	Yes	Carter & Holmes, Inc.
GREENHOUSE VENTILATORS				
B 12	AL	Mobile	Yes	Gothic Arch Greenhouses
B 13	FL	Princeton		Greenhouse Specialties Co.
B 17	MD	Laurel		Janco Greenhouses
B 13	ME	South Berwick	Yes	Gro-Tek
B 13	NH	Epping	Yes	Greenhouse Builders Supply
B 32	VA	Charlottesville	Yes	Victory Garden Supply Co.
GREENHOUSE WINDOWS				
B 29	NY	Commack		Sun System Greenhouses
B 19	NY	Melville		Lord & Burnham
B 2	WI	Hammond	Yes	Arctic Glass & Window Outlet
GREENHOUSES				
B 12	AL	Mobile	Yes	Gothic Arch Greenhouses
B 22	AR	Fayetteville	Yes	Nitron Industries, Inc.
B 27	CA	Camarillo	Yes	Santa Barbara Greenhouses
B 23	CA	Cotati	Yes	Pacific Coast Greenhouse Mfg. Co.
B 16	CO	Colorado Springs	Yes	Hydro-Gardens of Denver
B 4	FL	Jacksonville	Yes	Bloomin' Greenhouse, Inc.
B 29	IL	Elmhurst		Suncraft, Inc.
B 11	IL	Schaumburg	Yes	Florist Products, Inc.
B 10	MD	Columbia	Yes	Everlight Greenhouses, Inc.
B 17	MD	Laurel		Janco Greenhouses
B 29	MO	North Kansas City		Stuppy Greenhouse Manufacturing, Inc.
B 31	NC	Goldsboro	Yes	Turner Greenhouses
B 13	NH	Epping	Yes	Greenhouse Builders Supply
B 29	NY	Commack		Sun System Greenhouses
B 11	NY	Farmingdale		Four Seasons Greenhouses
B 19	NY	Melville		Lord & Burnham
B 32	NY	New York		Vegetable Factory, Inc.
B 8	OH	Medina	Yes	Cropking Greenhouses
B 3	ON	St. Thomas	Yes	Berry-Hill Limited
B 29	OR	Portland	Yes	Sturdi-Built Mfg. Co.
A 53	PA	Hanover		Lakeland Nursery Sales
B 30	TX	Ft. Worth	Yes	Texas Greenhouse Co.
B 32	VA	Charlottesville	Yes	Victory Garden Supply Co.
B 12	VT	Burlington	Yes	Gardener's Supply Company
B 6	WA	Mt. Vernon	Yes	Charley's Greenhouse Supply
B 30	WA	Seattle	Yes	Sunglo Solar Greenhouses
GROWING SUPPLIES, GENERAL				
See Also - Indoor Growing Supplies				
See Also - Propagation Supplies				
A 86	AB	Edmonton	Yes	Seed Centre Ltd.
B 18	CA	Atlanta		Kinsmen Corp.
A 14	CA	Lodi	Yes	Cactus by Dodie
B 11	CA	Redway	Yes	Full Circle Garden Products
A 13	CO	Rocky Ford	Yes	D.V. Burrell Seed Growers Co.
A 96	FL	Fort Myers		Tomato Growers Supply Company
B 32	FL	Gainesville	Yes	The Violet House
B 22	FL	Miami		OFE International, Inc.
A 48	GA	Ellijay	Yes	Johnson Nursery
A 42	ID	Ketchum	Yes	High Altitude Gardens
B 1	IL	Galesburg		Alsto's Handy Helpers
A 23	KY	Louisville		Dabney Herbs
A 58	MB	Brandon		McFayden Seeds
A 61	MD	Baltimore		Meyer Seed Co.
A 24	MD	Frederick		Dan's Garden Shop
A 48	ME	Albion		Johnny's Selected Seeds
A 2	ME	Falmouth	Yes	Allen, Sterling & Lothrop
A 31	MI	Hartford	Yes	Dean Foster Nurseries
B 26	MN	Eden Prairie	Yes	Ringer Research

(continued next page)

PAGE	STATE	CITY	SHOP?	SOURCE
GROWING SUPPLIES, GENERAL (continued)				
B 22	MN	Park Rapids	Yes	North Star Evergreens
B 14	MN	St. Paul	Yes	Harvest Glow Systems
B 13	NC	Matthews		Gro-n-Energy
B 5	NH	Peterborough	Yes	Brookstone Co.
A 54	NJ	Sewell	Yes	Orol Ledden & Sons
A 83	NM	Roswell	Yes	Roswell Seed Co.
B 24	NY	Buffalo		Plant Collectibles
A 40	NY	Rochester		Harris Seeds
B 4	NY	Yorkville	Yes	Bonide Chemical Co., Inc.
B 8	OH	Medina	Yes	Cropking Greenhouses
A 56	OH	New Philadelphia	Yes	Liberty Seed Company
A 61	OH	North Lima	Yes	Mellinger's Inc.
B 18	OH	Piqua		C. M. Leonard, Inc.
A 26	ON	Georgetown		Dominion Seed House
A 97	ON	Hamilton	Yes	Tregunno Seeds
A 23	ON	Toronto	Yes	C. A. Cruickshank, Ltd.
A 67	OR	Albany	Yes	Nichols Garden Nursery, Inc.
A 95	OR	Lorane	Yes	Territorial Seed Co.
B 4	PA	New Brighton		Brighton By-Products Co., Inc.
B 18	PA	Point Pleasant	Yes	Kinsman Company, Inc.
A 98	PA	Trevose		Otis Twilley Seed Co.
A 13	PA	Warminster	Yes	W. Atlee Burpee Company
A 100	PE	Charlottetown	Yes	Vesey's Seeds Ltd.
A 72	SC	Greenwood	Yes	Park Seed Company, Inc.
B 23	SC	West Columbia	Yes	Organic Farm & Garden Supply
A 39	SD	Yankton	Yes	Gurney Seed & Nursery Co.
A 26	SK	Saskatoon	Yes	Early's Farm & Garden Centre, Inc.
A 76	TX	Stephensville	Yes	Porter & Son
B 24	VA	Madison	Yes	The Plow & Hearth
A 90	VA	North Garden		Southern Exposure Seed Exchange
B 12	VT	Burlington	Yes	Gardener's Supply Company
A 100	VT	Fair Haven	Yes	Vermont Bean Seed Co.
B 28	WA	Mt. Vernon	Yes	Skagit Gardens
B 13	WA	Puyallup	Yes	Green Earth Organics
A 49	WI	Randolph	Yes	J. W. Jung Seed Co.
A 76	WI	Tilleda	Yes	Pony Creek Nursery
GROWTH STIMULANTS				
B 31	FL	Bradenton	Yes	Tropexotic Growers, Inc.
B 4	KS	Topeka		Brady-Brooke Farms
B 29	TX	Houston		Spray-N-Grow
HAMMOCKS				
B 8	IL	Moline		John Deere Catalog
B 21	WY	Cody		Modern Farm
HANDLES, REPLACEMENT				
B 23	AR	Eureka Springs	Yes	Ozark Handle & Hardware
HANGING BASKETS				
B 22	FL	Miami		OFE International, Inc.
B 31	FL	Orlando	Yes	Tropical Plant Products, Inc.
B 24	NY	Buffalo		Plant Collectibles
A 9	OH	Seville	Yes	Bittersweet Farm
HISTORICAL REPRODUCTIONS, ORNAMENTAL				
See Also - Specific Type				
B 18	CA	San Francisco	Yes	Sue Fisher King
B 19	FL	Live Oak		The Live Oak Railroad Co.
B 2	MA	Boston		Ascot Designs
B 25	NY	Bronxville		Pompeian Studios
B 11	NY	Long Island City	Yes	Florentine Craftsmen, Inc.
B 8	PA	Carlisle	Yes	Cumberland Woodcraft
A 28	PA	Philadelphia	Yes	Exotic Blossoms (TM) Topiary Sculptures
B 11	TN	Memphis	Yes	The Garden Concepts Collection
HONEYDEW (TM)				
B 3	CA	Berry Creek	Yes	Bio-Control Co.

PAGE	STATE	CITY	SHOP?	SOURCE
HORTICULTURAL RESEARCH				
A 32	WA	Walla Walla	Yes	French Iris Gardens
HORTICULTURAL TOURS				
B 27	CA	Santa Barbara		Santa Barbara Orchid Garden & Library
B 7	En	London		Cox & Kings Travel
B 21	En	London		Raoul Moxley Travel
A 29	FL	Homestead	Yes	Fennell's Orchid Jungle
B 3	FL	Miami		Leona Bee Tours & Travel
B 28	MA	Cambridge		Serendipity Garden Tours
B 19	VT	Burlington		Limewalk Tours
HORTOPAPER (R)				
B 1	CA	Fresno	Yes	Actagro
HUMIDIFIERS				
B 23	CA	Cotati	Yes	Pacific Coast Greenhouse Mfg. Co.
B 20	CA	San Francisco		Don Mattern
B 29	RI	Pawtucket	Yes	Standard Humidifier
HUSKY-FIBER (R)				
A 59	FL	Windemere	Yes	Ann Mann's Orchids
HYDRION (R) PAPERS				
B 21	NY	Brooklyn		Micro Essential Laboratory, Inc.
HYDROPONIC SUPPLIES				
B 11	CA	Redway	Yes	Full Circle Garden Products
B 2	CA	San Rafael	Yes	Applied Hydroponics
B 16	CO	Colorado Springs	Yes	Hydro-Gardens of Denver
B 8	OH	Medina	Yes	Cropking Greenhouses
A 19	ON	Mississauga	Yes	Clargreen Gardens Ltd.
B 2	PQ	Montreal	Yes	Applied Hydroponics of Canada
HYDROPONIC SYSTEMS				
B 19	CA	Anaheim	Yes	Living Green, Inc.
B 11	CA	Redway	Yes	Full Circle Garden Products
B 2	CA	San Rafael	Yes	Applied Hydroponics
B 16	CO	Colorado Springs	Yes	Hydro-Gardens of Denver
B 4	FL	Jacksonville	Yes	Bloomin' Greenhouse, Inc.
B 8	OH	Medina	Yes	Cropking Greenhouses
B 2	PQ	Montreal	Yes	Applied Hydroponics of Canada
B 13	WI	Sheboygan	Yes	Green Thumb Hygro-Gardens
INDOOR GROWING SUPPLIES				
See Also - Growing Supplies, General				
See Also - Propagation Supplies				
B 19	CA	Anaheim	Yes	Living Green, Inc.
B 11	CA	Redway	Yes	Full Circle Garden Products
B 2	CA	San Rafael	Yes	Applied Hydroponics
A 58	CA	South San Francisco	Yes	Rod McLellan Co.
B 30	CO	Boulder		Swallowtail Corporation
B 10	FL	Ft. Lauderdale	Yes	Environmental Concepts
B 32	FL	Gainesville	Yes	The Violet House
B 8	FL	Merritt Island	Yes	DoDe's Gardens, Inc.
B 31	FL	Orlando	Yes	Tropical Plant Products, Inc.
B 11	IL	Schaumburg	Yes	Florist Products, Inc.
A 24	IN	Crawfordsville	Yes	Davidson-Wilson Greenhouses
B 1	IN	Indianapolis	Yes	Alternative Garden Supply, Inc.
A 58	KS	Wichita	Yes	McKinney's Glasshouse
A 24	MD	Frederick		Dan's Garden Shop
B 13	ME	South Berwick	Yes	Gro-Tek
B 16	MI	Detroit		Indoor Gardening Supplies
B 24	NY	Buffalo		Plant Collectibles
B 4	NY	Yorkville	Yes	Bonide Chemical Co., Inc.
B 1	OR	Junction City	Yes	Agrilite
B 21	OR	Medford	Yes	Nature's Control
A 39	PA	Gibsonia		Halcyon Gardens
B 3	PA	Greeley	Yes	Dorothy Biddle Service

(continued next page)

PAGE	STATE	CITY	SHOP?	SOURCE
INDOOR GROWING SUPPLIES (continued)				
B 2	PQ	Montreal	Yes	Applied Hydroponics of Canada
B 6	WA	Mt. Vernon	Yes	Charley's Greenhouse Supply
INSECT CONTROLS, ORGANIC				
B 28	CA	Arroyo Grande		Spalding Laboratories
B 3	CA	Berry Creek	Yes	Bio-Control Co.
B 9	CA	Oakland		EcoSafe Laboratories, Inc.
B 11	CA	Redway	Yes	Full Circle Garden Products
B 3	CA	Santa Paula		Bio-Resources
A 11	CA	Willits	Yes	Bountiful Gardens
B 10	CO	Broomfield		Evans BioControl, Inc.
B 26	CO	Palisade		Rocky Mountain Insectary
B 22	FL	Miami		OFE International, Inc.
A 51	FL	Sanford	Yes	Kilgore Seed Company
B 9	IN	Jeffersonville		Earlee, Inc.
B 21	IN	Sunman		Natural Gardening Research Center
B 26	MN	Eden Prairie	Yes	Ringer Research
A 54	NJ	Sewell	Yes	Orol Ledden & Sons
B 4	NY	Yorkville	Yes	Bonide Chemical Co., Inc.
B 23	OH	Hartville	Yes	Ohio Earth Food, Inc.
B 8	OR	Eugene	Yes	Down to Earth Distributors
B 21	OR	Medford	Yes	Nature's Control
B 3	PA	Chambersburg	Yes	BioLogic
B 21	VA	New Castle	Yes	Necessary Trading Co.
A 90	VA	North Garden		Southern Exposure Seed Exchange
A 78	WA	Morton	Yes	Raintree Nursery
B 13	WA	Puyallup	Yes	Green Earth Organics
B 23	WA	Seattle	Yes	Organic Pest Management
B 16	WA	Wenatchee	Yes	I. F. M.
INSECT TRAPS				
B 28	CA	Emeryville	Yes	Seabright Enterprises
B 21	IN	Sunman		Natural Gardening Research Center
B 12	MI	Vestaburg	Yes	Great Lakes IPM
B 8	OR	Eugene	Yes	Down to Earth Distributors
B 21	OR	Medford	Yes	Nature's Control
B 23	WA	Seattle	Yes	Organic Pest Management
INSECTS, BENEFICIAL				
B 28	CA	Arroyo Grande		Spalding Laboratories
B 3	CA	Berry Creek	Yes	Bio-Control Co.
B 11	CA	Corona	Yes	Foothill Agricultural Research, Inc.
B 33	CA	Gridley	Yes	West Coast Ladybug Sales
B 11	CA	Rough & Ready		Fountain Sierra Bug Company
B 31	CA	Sacramento		Unique Insect Control
B 3	CA	Santa Paula		Bio-Resources
B 16	CO	Colorado Springs	Yes	Hydro-Gardens of Denver
B 26	CO	Palisade		Rocky Mountain Insectary
B 1	IN	Indianapolis	Yes	Alternative Garden Supply, Inc.
B 21	IN	Sunman		Natural Gardening Research Center
A 65	KY	Louisville		Nationwide Seed & Supply
B 21	OR	Medford	Yes	Nature's Control
B 3	PA	Chambersburg	Yes	BioLogic
B 23	SC	West Columbia	Yes	Organic Farm & Garden Supply
B 21	VA	New Castle	Yes	Necessary Trading Co.
B 23	WA	Seattle	Yes	Organic Pest Management
B 16	WA	Wenatchee	Yes	I. F. M.
A 76	WI	Tilleda	Yes	Pony Creek Nursery
INSTRUCTIONAL MATERIALS				
B 32	CA	Soquel		VT Productions
B 20	CT	Southport		The Matrix Group
B 10	En	Uxbridge, Middlesex	Yes	Floracolour
B 27	IL	Chicago		Jack Schmidling Productions
B 14	VA	Seaford		Harper Horticultural Slide Library
B 32	WA	Seattle		Videodiscovery, Inc.

PAGE	STATE	CITY	SHOP?	SOURCE
IRRIGATION SUPPLIES				
See Also - Drip Irrigation				
See Also - Mist Irrigation				
B 26	CA	Chatsworth		Raindrip, Inc.
B 31	CA	San Francisco	Yes	The Urban Farmer Store
B 1	IL	Galesburg		Alsto's Handy Helpers
B 13	ME	South Berwick	Yes	Gro-Tek
B 4	PA	New Brighton		Brighton By-Products Co., Inc.
B 12	VT	Burlington	Yes	Gardener's Supply Company
JUNGLE JUICE (R)				
B 6	IL	Deerfield		Clarel Laboratories, Inc.
KEEP 'EM BLOOMIN' (R)				
B 6	IL	Deerfield		Clarel Laboratories, Inc.
LANTERNS, STONE				
A 87	CT	Stamford	Yes	Shanti Bithi Nursery
B 14	PA	Pleasant Gap	Yes	Philip Hawk & Company
LASCOLITE (R)				
B 13	NH	Epping	Yes	Greenhouse Builders Supply
LEXIMULCH (TM)				
B 19	IN	Indianapolis		Lexigrow
LIGHT FIXTURES				
B 24	DC	Washington	Yes	Park Place
B 19	FL	Live Oak		The Live Oak Railroad Co.
B 16	ID	Sandpoint	Yes	Idaho Wood Industries, Inc.
B 15	ME	Yarmouth	Yes	Heritage Lanterns
B 12	NJ	Vincentown		Genie House
B 1	OR	Junction City	Yes	Agrilite
B 14	PA	Hanover		Hanover Lantern
B 25	PA	Pittsburgh		Popovitch & Associates, Inc.
B 29	SC	Spartanburg	Yes	Strassacker Bronze, Inc.
LIGHTING SYSTEMS				
B 33	CA	Burbank	Yes	Wendelighting
B 6	MA	West Newton		The Clapper Co.
A 78	MO	Lee's Summit	Yes	Rainwater Violets
A 85	NY	Northport	Yes	S. Scherer & Sons
B 1	OR	Junction City	Yes	Agrilite
B 14	PA	Hanover		Hanover Lantern
LIL SUCKER (TM)				
B 30	OR	Albany		Tecnu Enterprises, Inc.
LIVE TRAPS, ANIMALS				
See Also - Animal Repellents				
B 28	CA	Emeryville	Yes	Seabright Enterprises
B 27	IA	Garrison		Safe-N-Sound Live Traps
B 3	ON	St. Thomas	Yes	Berry-Hill Limited
B 21	VA	New Castle	Yes	Necessary Trading Co.
B 23	WA	Seattle	Yes	Organic Pest Management
LOG SPLITTERS				
B 25	IL	Rockford		RAM Log Splitters
B 10	MA	Woburn	Yes	FXG Corporation
B 33	NE	Broken Bow		Wikco Industries, Inc.
B 20	OH	London	Yes	Mainline of North America
LOW-E SUPER-INSULATED GLASS (TM)				
B 2	WI	Hammond	Yes	Arctic Glass & Window Outlet
LUWASA HYDROCULTURE (R)				
B 2	PQ	Montreal	Yes	Applied Hydroponics of Canada

PAGE	STATE	CITY	SHOP?	SOURCE
METERS AND INSTRUMENTS				
B 23	AR	Eureka Springs	Yes	Ozark Handle & Hardware
B 16	CO	Colorado Springs	Yes	Hydro-Gardens of Denver
B 10	FL	Ft. Lauderdale	Yes	Environmental Concepts
B 16	MI	Detroit		Indoor Gardening Supplies
B 26	NE	Columbus	Yes	Rodco Products Co., Inc.
B 14	NJ	Old Tappan		Harlane Company, Inc.
B 27	NJ	Princeton	Yes	Science Associates
B 23	OH	Hartville	Yes	Ohio Earth Food, Inc.
B 31	WA	Enumclaw	Yes	Trade-Wind Instruments
MIST IRRIGATION SUPPLIES				
B 28	CA	Huntington Beach	Yes	Spot Systems Div., Wisdom Ind.
B 9	CA	Van Nuys	Yes	Drip Irrigation Garden
B 21	FL	Palmetto		Moss Products, Inc.
B 24	MO	Grover	Yes	Plastic Plumbing Products, Inc.
B 2	NY	Huntington		Aquamonitor
B 29	TX	Lubbock	Yes	Submatic Irrigation Systems
B 28	WA	Mt. Vernon	Yes	Skagit Gardens
B 9	WI	Manitowoc		The Dramm Company
MIST IRRIGATION SYSTEMS				
B 28	CA	Huntington Beach	Yes	Spot Systems Div., Wisdom Ind.
B 21	FL	Palmetto		Moss Products, Inc.
B 24	MO	Grover	Yes	Plastic Plumbing Products, Inc.
B 2	NY	Huntington		Aquamonitor
B 6	WA	Mt. Vernon	Yes	Charley's Greenhouse Supply
B 9	WI	Manitowoc		The Dramm Company
MOONSHINE (R)				
B 6	IL	Deerfield		Clarel Laboratories, Inc.
MULCHES, FABRIC				
B 19	IN	Indianapolis		Lexigrow
B 4	PA	New Brighton		Brighton By-Products Co., Inc.
MULCHES, PAPER				
B 1	CA	Fresno	Yes	Actagro
B 4	MA	Salem		Bramen Company, Inc.
MULCHES, PLASTIC				
B 22	AR	Fayetteville	Yes	Nitron Industries, Inc.
B 8	TN	Knoxville	Yes	Dalen Products, Inc.
MUSHROOM GROWING SUPPLIES				
A 65	CA	Inverness	Yes	Mushroompeople
A 33	WA	Olympia		Fungi Perfecti
NOLO BAIT (TM)				
B 10	CO	Broomfield		Evans BioControl, Inc.
ORCHID SUPPLIES				
A 32	AR	Little Rock	Yes	Fox Orchids, Inc.
A 92	CA	Carpinteria	Yes	Stewart Orchids
B 7	CA	Lincoln	Yes	Critter Creek Laboratory & Orchids
A 84	CA	Santa Barbara	Yes	Santa Barbara Orchid Estate
A 28	CA	Soquel	Yes	John Ewing Orchids, Inc.
A 58	CA	South San Francisco	Yes	Rod McLellan Co.
A 33	CA	Vista	Yes	G & B Orchid Laboratory
A 11	CO	Niwot	Yes	Boulder Valley Orchids
A 47	FL	Cantonment	Yes	J & M Tropicals, Inc.
A 58	FL	Ft. Myers	Yes	Madcap Orchids
A 29	FL	Homestead	Yes	Fennell's Orchid Jungle
B 22	FL	Miami		OFE International, Inc.
B 31	FL	Orlando	Yes	Tropical Plant Products, Inc.
A 59	FL	Windemere	Yes	Ann Mann's Orchids
A 70	IL	Villa Park	Yes	Orchids by Hausermann, Inc.
B 7	MD	Arnold		Computer/Management Services
A 50	MD	Kensington	Yes	Kensington Orchids

(continued next page)

PAGE	STATE	CITY	SHOP?	SOURCE
ORCHID SUPPLIES (continued)				
A 81	MS	Biloxi	Yes	Riverbend Orchids
A 11	NC	Brown Summit	Yes	Breckinridge Orchids
A 86	NY	Glen Head	Yes	Seagulls Landing Orchids
A 45	ON	Bright's Grove	Yes	Huronview Nurseries & Garden Centre
A 51	ON	Komoka	Yes	Kilworth Flowers
A 19	ON	Mississauga	Yes	Clargreen Gardens Ltd.
A 31	ON	Port Stanley	Yes	Floridel Gardens
A 17	SC	Newberry	Yes	Carter & Holmes, Inc.
A 70	UT	Bountiful	Yes	Orchids Bountiful
ORCHIDS EXOTICA (R)				
B 6	IL	Deerfield		Clarel Laboratories, Inc.
ORGANIC GARDEN PRODUCTS				
B 1	CA	Fresno	Yes	Actagro
A 73	CA	Nevada City	Yes	Peaceful Valley Farm Supply
B 10	CO	Broomfield		Evans BioControl, Inc.
B 9	IL	Mendota	Yes	EnP Inc.
B 9	IN	Jeffersonville		Earlee, Inc.
B 21	IN	Sunman		Natural Gardening Research Center
B 4	KS	Topeka		Brady-Brooke Farms
A 74	ME	New Gloucester	Yes	Pinetree Garden Seeds
B 13	ME	South Berwick	Yes	Gro-Tek
A 29	ME	Waterville		Fedco Seeds
B 24	MN	Duluth		Plant Magic Products, Inc.
B 26	MN	Eden Prairie	Yes	Ringer Research
A 54	NJ	Sewell	Yes	Orol Ledden & Sons
B 4	NY	Yorkville	Yes	Bonide Chemical Co., Inc.
B 23	OH	Hartville	Yes	Ohio Earth Food, Inc.
B 8	OR	Eugene	Yes	Down to Earth Distributors
B 23	SC	West Columbia	Yes	Organic Farm & Garden Supply
B 12	VT	Burlington	Yes	Gardener's Supply Company
B 22	VT	Newbury	Yes	North Country Organics
B 13	WA	Puyallup	Yes	Green Earth Organics
B 23	WA	Seattle	Yes	Organic Pest Management
PATIO CARTS				
B 8	CA	Fort Bragg	Yes	Cypress Street Center
B 26	CA	Sebastopol	Yes	Reed Bros.
B 34	GA	Savannah		Woodventure, Inc.
B 33	WI	Janesville	Yes	Wisconsin Wagon Co.
PAVING MATERIALS				
B 2	MA	Boston		Ascot Designs
PEST CONTROLS, ORGANIC				
B 22	AR	Fayetteville	Yes	Nitron Industries, Inc.
B 28	CA	Emeryville	Yes	Seabright Enterprises
A 73	CA	Nevada City	Yes	Peaceful Valley Farm Supply
B 9	CA	Oakland		EcoSafe Laboratories, Inc.
B 10	CO	Broomfield		Evans BioControl, Inc.
B 30	ID	Boise		Thurston Distributing, Inc.
B 9	IN	Jeffersonville		Earlee, Inc.
B 21	IN	Sunman		Natural Gardening Research Center
B 12	MI	Vestaburg	Yes	Great Lakes IPM
B 26	MN	Eden Prairie	Yes	Ringer Research
B 22	MN	Park Rapids	Yes	North Star Evergreens
A 57	MT	Kalispell	Yes	Lost Prairie Herb Farm
B 4	NY	Yorkville	Yes	Bonide Chemical Co., Inc.
B 23	OH	Hartville	Yes	Ohio Earth Food, Inc.
A 81	ON	Goodwood	Yes	Richters
B 1	OR	Junction City	Yes	Agrilite
B 21	OR	Medford	Yes	Nature's Control
B 23	SC	West Columbia	Yes	Organic Farm & Garden Supply
B 13	TX	Littlefield		The Greener Thumb
B 21	VA	New Castle	Yes	Necessary Trading Co.
B 13	WA	Puyallup	Yes	Green Earth Organics
B 16	WA	Wenatchee	Yes	I. F. M.

(continued next page)

PAGE	STATE	CITY	SHOP?	SOURCE
PEST CONTROLS, ORGANIC (continued)				
A 102	WI	Plainfield	Yes	The Waushara Gardens
PET DOORS				
B 24	CA	Torrance	Yes	Patio Pacific, Inc.
PHOTOGRAPHS, HORTICULTURAL				
B 32	CA	Soquel		VT Productions
B 10	En	Uxbridge, Middlesex	Yes	Floracolour
B 9	MA	Waltham	Yes	Laura D. Eisener, Landscape Design
B 30	NY	Mamaroneck		Talisman Cove Productions
A 17	PA	Allison Park		Cedar Ridge Nurseries
A 92	TX	Azle		Ed Storms, Inc.
B 14	VA	Seaford		Harper Horticultural Slide Library
B 32	WA	Seattle		Videodiscovery, Inc.
PLANT HANGERS				
B 2	FL	Orlando	Yes	Autumn Forge
B 22	MA	Topsfield	Yes	Walter Nicke Company
PLANT LABELS				
See Also - Garden Markers				
B 17	CA	Aptos		International Nursery Labels
B 10	CA	Cloverdale		Evergreen Garden Plant Labels
A 14	CA	Lodi	Yes	Cactus by Dodie
B 9	FL	Daytona Beach		Economy Label Sales Co., Inc.
B 32	FL	Gainesville	Yes	The Violet House
B 22	FL	Miami		OFE International, Inc.
A 24	MD	Frederick		Dan's Garden Shop
B 24	MI	Paw Paw		Paw Paw Everlast Label Co.
B 24	NY	Buffalo		Plant Collectibles
B 10	OH	Holland		Eon Industries
A 39	OR	Junction City	Yes	Hall Rhododendrons
A 10	TX	Lavernia	Yes	Bonsai Farm
A 39	VA	Spotsylvania	Yes	Hager Nurseries, Inc.
PLANT LIGHTS				
B 2	CA	San Rafael	Yes	Applied Hydroponics
A 100	CO	Englewood	Yes	The Violet Showcase
B 32	CT	Greenwich		Verilux, Inc.
B 16	MI	Detroit		Indoor Gardening Supplies
B 14	MN	St. Paul	Yes	Harvest Glow Systems
B 25	NY	New York		Public Service Lamp Corp.
B 1	OR	Junction City	Yes	Agrilite
B 2	PQ	Montreal	Yes	Applied Hydroponics of Canada
PLANT MAGIC (TM)				
B 24	MN	Duluth		Plant Magic Products, Inc.
PLANT SEARCH SERVICE				
B 22	ME	Troy		North Star Seed & Plant Search
PLANT STANDS				
B 13	CA	Lancaster	Yes	The Green House
A 100	CO	Englewood	Yes	The Violet Showcase
B 8	FL	Merritt Island	Yes	DoDe's Gardens, Inc.
A 97	GA	Ochlochnee	Yes	Travis' Violets
B 11	IL	Schaumburg	Yes	Florist Products, Inc.
B 20	MA	Marion	Yes	Marion Designs
B 16	MI	Detroit		Indoor Gardening Supplies
B 14	MI	Livonia		H. P. Supplies, Inc.
A 30	NJ	Linwood	Yes	Fischer Greenhouses
A 39	ON	Barrie	Yes	Growin'house
A 75	ON	Keswick	Yes	Plants 'n' Things
B 10	ON	Willowdale		Floralight Gardens Canada, Inc.
A 96	PA	Huntingdon Valley	Yes	Tinari Greenhouses
B 2	PQ	Montreal	Yes	Applied Hydroponics of Canada
B 11	TN	Memphis	Yes	The Garden Concepts Collection
A 101	TX	Dallas	Yes	Volkman Bros. Greenhouses

PAGE	STATE	CITY	SHOP?	SOURCE
PLANT SUPPORTS				
B 10	CA	Cloverdale		Evergreen Garden Plant Labels
A 2	En	Hassocks, W. Sussex	Yes	Allwood Bros. (Hassocks) Ltd.
B 22	MA	Topsfield	Yes	Walter Nicke Company
PLANTERS				
B 2	CA	Fairfax	Yes	ANZA Architectural Wood Products
B 6	CA	Pasadena		Cindy's Bows
B 18	CA	San Francisco	Yes	Sue Fisher King
B 27	CA	San Luis Obispo		San Luis Plastic Products
B 26	CA	Sebastopol	Yes	Reed Bros.
B 19	IA	Charles City	Yes	McDermott Garden Products
B 2	MA	Boston		Ascot Designs
B 7	MD	Germantown	Yes	Country Casual
B 26	ME	Georgetown		Joe Reed, Woodsmith
B 14	MN	St. Paul	Yes	Harvest Glow Systems
B 19	NY	Rochester	Yes	Living Wall Gardening Co.
B 17	OH	Cleveland	Yes	David Kay Garden & Gift Catalogue, Inc.
B 6	OH	Waterville	Yes	Carruth Studio
A 28	PA	Philadelphia	Yes	Exotic Blossoms (TM) Topiary Sculptures
B 10	RI	Newport	Yes	Erkins Studios, Inc.
B 11	TN	Memphis	Yes	The Garden Concepts Collection
B 19	VA	Arlington	Yes	Mrs. McGregor's Garden Shop
PLANTERS, HYDROPONIC				
B 19	CA	Anaheim	Yes	Living Green, Inc.
B 14	MN	St. Paul	Yes	Harvest Glow Systems
PLANTERS, SELF-WATERING				
B 15	AR	Camden		House of Violets
B 32	FL	Gainesville	Yes	The Violet House
B 14	MN	St. Paul	Yes	Harvest Glow Systems
PLAY STRUCTURES				
B 7	WI	Sun Prairie		Creative Playgrounds, Ltd.
POISON OAK/IVY CLEANSER				
B 30	OR	Albany		Tecnu Enterprises, Inc.
POLARPANE INSULATED GLASS (TM)				
B 2	WI	Hammond	Yes	Arctic Glass & Window Outlet
POLYETHYLENE, WOVEN				
B 23	AR	Eureka Springs	Yes	Ozark Handle & Hardware
B 22	ND	Neche	Yes	Northern Greenhouse Sales
B 8	TN	Knoxville	Yes	Dalen Products, Inc.
PONDS AND POOLS				
A 84	CA	Santa Barbara	Yes	Santa Barbara Water Gardens
A 99	CA	Upland	Yes	Van Ness Water Gardens
B 19	CT	Wilton		Kenneth Lynch & Sons, Inc.
A 104	MD	Baltimore	Yes	Wicklein's Aquatic Farm & Nursery, Inc.
A 56	MD	Lilypons	Yes	Lilypons Water Gardens
A 102	NJ	Saddle River	Yes	Waterford Gardens
B 15	NY	Canastota	Yes	Hermitage Gardens
A 85	NY	Northport	Yes	S. Scherer & Sons
A 97	OH	Independence	Yes	William Tricker, Inc.
A 64	ON	Port Stanley	Yes	Moore Water Gardens
A 95	PA	Coopersburg	Yes	Tilley's Nursery/The WaterWorks
POTPOURRI SUPPLIES				
A 40	MA	Barre	Yes	Hartman's Herb Farm
A 79	NC	Godwin	Yes	Rasland Farm
The Rosemary House				
A 8	TN	Signal Mountain	Yes	Bee Rock Herb Farm
POTS				
A 49	CA	Galt	Yes	K & L Cactus Nursery
A 14	CA	Lodi	Yes	Cactus by Dodie

(continued next page)

PAGE	STATE	CITY	SHOP?	SOURCE
POTS (continued)				
B 18	CA	San Francisco	Yes	Sue Fisher King
B 32	FL	Gainesville	Yes	The Violet House
B 22	FL	Miami		OFE International, Inc.
B 31	FL	Orlando	Yes	Tropical Plant Products, Inc.
B 22	MA	Topsfield	Yes	Walter Nicke Company
A 24	MD	Frederick		Dan's Garden Shop
A 11	NC	Brown Summit	Yes	Breckinridge Orchids
B 13	NC	Matthews		Gro-n-Energy
B 24	NY	Buffalo		Plant Collectibles
A 49	TX	Victoria	Yes	JoS Violets
A 36	WA	Issaquah	Yes	Grand Ridge Nursery
B 28	WA	Mt. Vernon	Yes	Skagit Gardens
POTTING BENCHES				
B 20	MA	Marion	Yes	Marion Designs
PROPAGATION SUPPLIES				
See Also - Growing Supplies, General				
See Also - Indoor Growing Supplies				
B 11	IL	Schaumburg	Yes	Florist Products, Inc.
B 4	MA	Salem		Bramen Company, Inc.
B 22	MA	Topsfield	Yes	Walter Nicke Company
A 24	MD	Frederick		Dan's Garden Shop
B 13	ME	South Berwick	Yes	Gro-Tek
B 16	MI	Detroit		Indoor Gardening Supplies
B 13	NC	Matthews		Gro-n-Energy
B 24	NY	Buffalo		Plant Collectibles
B 2	NY	Huntington		Aquamonitor
A 56	OH	New Philadelphia	Yes	Liberty Seed Company
A 61	OH	North Lima	Yes	Mellinger's Inc.
B 4	PA	New Brighton		Brighton By-Products Co., Inc.
A 72	SC	Greenwood	Yes	Park Seed Company, Inc.
A 10	TX	Lavernia	Yes	Bonsai Farm
B 12	VT	Burlington	Yes	Gardener's Supply Company
A 88	WA	Roy	Yes	Silvaseed Company, Inc.
PUMPS, WATER POWERED				
B 26	VA	Lowesville		The Ram Company
RAINMATIC (TM) WATER TIMER				
A 26	NJ	Colonia	Yes	Eastern Plant Specialties
RATCHET-CUT (R)				
B 1	CT	Plantsville	Yes	American Standard Co.
REPAIR/REPLACEMENT SUPPLIES				
B 23	AR	Eureka Springs	Yes	Ozark Handle & Hardware
B 26	CA	Point Arena		Peter Reimuller's Cart Warehouse
ROLCUT (R)				
B 4	MA	Salem		Bramen Company, Inc.
ROOTS 'N' ALL (TM)				
B 33	NY	Rochester	Yes	Warnico/USA, Inc.
ROSE GROWING SUPPLIES				
B 14	NJ	Old Tappan		Harlane Company, Inc.
B 4	NY	Yorkville	Yes	Bonide Chemical Co., Inc.
B 26	OH	Van Wert		Rose Tender
ROSE-GRO (R)				
B 23	OH	St. Marys	Yes	Organic Research Laboratories
ROW COVERS				
A 40	CA	Graton	Yes	Harmony Farm Supply
A 29	ME	Waterville		Fedco Seeds
A 56	OH	New Philadelphia	Yes	Liberty Seed Company
A 100	PE	Charlottetown	Yes	Vesey's Seeds Ltd.

(continued next page)

PAGE	STATE	CITY	SHOP?	SOURCE
ROW COVERS (continued)				
B 8	TN	Knoxville	Yes	Dalen Products, Inc.
A 90	VA	North Garden		Southern Exposure Seed Exchange
B 12	VT	Burlington	Yes	Gardener's Supply Company
B 13	WA	Puyallup	Yes	Green Earth Organics
B 16	WA	Wenatchee	Yes	I. F. M.
SCANMASK (R)				
B 3	PA	Chambersburg	Yes	BioLogic
SEAWEED FERTILIZERS				
B 9	IL	Mendota	Yes	EnP Inc.
B 4	MA	Salem		Bramen Company, Inc.
B 22	ME	Waldoboro		North American Kelp
B 22	VT	Newbury	Yes	North Country Organics
SEED SEARCH SERVICE				
B 22	ME	Troy		North Star Seed & Plant Search
SEED STARTER PLUS (R)				
B 23	OH	St. Marys	Yes	Organic Research Laboratories
SHADE CLOTH				
B 12	AL	Mobile	Yes	Gothic Arch Greenhouses
B 16	CO	Colorado Springs	Yes	Hydro-Gardens of Denver
B 8	FL	Miami	Yes	Day-Dex Co.
B 34	GA	Cornelia	Yes	Yonah Manufacturing Co.
B 13	ME	South Berwick	Yes	Gro-Tek
B 29	MO	North Kansas City		Stuppy Greenhouse Manufacturing, Inc.
B 8	OH	Medina	Yes	Cropking Greenhouses
B 28	WA	Mt. Vernon	Yes	Skagit Gardens
SHREDDERS				
B 28	CA	Mill Valley	Yes	Smith & Hawken
B 3	NC	Matthews		BCS Mosa, Inc.
B 12	NY	Troy		Garden Way Manufacturing Co.
B 17	PA	Lititz	Yes	Kemp Company
B 2	PA	Parker Ford		Amerind-MacKissic
B 18	PA	Point Pleasant	Yes	Kinsman Company, Inc.
B 27	PA	Pottstown		The Scotchmen
B 20	SC	Charleston	Yes	Meridian Equipment Corporation
SICKLE-BAR MOWER				
B 18	MN	St. Paul	Yes	Kinco Manufacturing
B 3	NC	Matthews		BCS Mosa, Inc.
B 12	NY	Troy		Garden Way Manufacturing Co.
B 20	OH	London	Yes	Mainline of North America
SNAIL BARRIERS				
B 21	CA	San Anselmo		The Natural Gardening Company
SOIL AMENDMENTS				
B 22	AR	Fayetteville	Yes	Nitron Industries, Inc.
B 18	CA	Atlanta		Kinsmen Corp.
A 58	CA	South San Francisco	Yes	Rod McLellan Co.
B 9	IL	Mendota	Yes	EnP Inc.
B 9	IN	Jeffersonville		Earlee, Inc.
B 4	KS	Topeka		Brady-Brooke Farms
A 48	ME	Albion		Johnny's Selected Seeds
B 22	ME	Waldoboro		North American Kelp
B 26	MN	Eden Prairie	Yes	Ringer Research
A 83	NM	Roswell	Yes	Roswell Seed Co.
B 4	NY	Yorkville	Yes	Bonide Chemical Co., Inc.
B 23	OH	St. Marys	Yes	Organic Research Laboratories
B 23	SC	West Columbia	Yes	Organic Farm & Garden Supply
B 22	VT	Newbury	Yes	North Country Organics
B 13	WA	Puyallup	Yes	Green Earth Organics

PAGE	STATE	CITY	SHOP?	SOURCE
SOIL TESTING				
B 11	CA	Freedom	Yes	Freedom Soil Lab
B 23	OH	Hartville	Yes	Ohio Earth Food, Inc.
B 16	WA	Wenatchee	Yes	I. F. M.
A 102	WI	Plainfield	Yes	The Waushara Gardens
B 18	WY	Laramie		LaRamie Soils Service
SOIL TESTING PRODUCTS				
A 51	FL	Sanford	Yes	Kilgore Seed Company
B 1	IN	Indianapolis	Yes	Alternative Garden Supply, Inc.
B 21	NY	Brooklyn		Micro Essential Laboratory, Inc.
B 23	OH	Hartville	Yes	Ohio Earth Food, Inc.
A 34	ON	Thornhill	Yes	Gardenimport, Inc.
A 83	TN	Nash		SPB Sales
SOLAR STRUCTURES (R)				
B 32	NY	New York		Vegetable Factory, Inc.
SPRAY-N-GROW (TM)				
B 29	TX	Houston		Spray-N-Grow
SPRAYERS				
A 37	CA	Carmel	Yes	Greener 'N' Ever Tree Farm & Nursery
B 9	CA	Van Nuys	Yes	Drip Irrigation Garden
B 16	IL	Chicago		H. D. Hudson Mfg. Co.
B 1	IN	Indianapolis	Yes	Alternative Garden Supply, Inc.
B 22	MN	Park Rapids	Yes	North Star Evergreens
B 24	NC	Arden		PeCo Inc.
B 3	NC	Matthews		BCS Mosa, Inc.
A 97	ON	Hamilton	Yes	Tregunno Seeds
B 20	PA	Huntingdon Valley	Yes	Mantis Manufacturing Co.
B 2	PA	Parker Ford		Amerind-MacKissic
B 27	PA	Pottstown		The Scotchmen
B 13	TN	Memphis	Yes	Greenleaf Technologies
B 13	TX	Littlefield		The Greener Thumb
B 9	WI	Manitowoc		The Dramm Company
B 21	WY	Cody		Modern Farm
SPRINKLERS				
See Also - Irrigation Supplies				
A 40	CA	Graton	Yes	Harmony Farm Supply
B 28	CA	Huntington Beach	Yes	Spot Systems Div., Wisdom Ind.
B 9	CA	Van Nuys	Yes	Drip Irrigation Garden
B 21	FL	Palmetto		Moss Products, Inc.
B 26	OH	Van Wert		Rose Tender
A 95	OR	Lorane	Yes	Territorial Seed Co.
B 13	SK	Saskatoon		Green Hand Tools
B 5	TX	Hereford	Yes	C & C Products
B 29	TX	Lubbock	Yes	Submatic Irrigation Systems
B 9	WI	Manitowoc		The Dramm Company
STATUES				
B 28	AL	Birmingham		Southern Statuary and Stone
B 6	CA	Pasadena		Cindy's Bows
B 19	CT	Wilton		Kenneth Lynch & Sons, Inc.
B 27	NJ	Roosevelt	Yes	Sculpture Cast Editions
B 25	NY	Bronxville		Pompeian Studios
B 11	NY	Long Island City	Yes	Florentine Craftsmen, Inc.
B 6	OH	Waterville	Yes	Carruth Studio
B 10	RI	Newport	Yes	Erkins Studios, Inc.
B 29	SC	Spartanburg	Yes	Strassacker Bronze, Inc.
B 27	VA	Hillsboro	Yes	Royal Tidewater Collection, Inc.
B 33	VA	Salem	Yes	Winterthur Museum & Gardens
STORAGE BUILDINGS				
B 32	MA	Walpole		Walpole Woodworkers
B 29	WI	Delafield	Yes	Sun Designs

PAGE	STATE	CITY	SHOP?	SOURCE
SUN-PORCH (R)				
B 32	NY	New York		Vegetable Factory, Inc.
SUNBEAM STRUCTURES (R)				
B 32	NY	New York		Vegetable Factory, Inc.
SUNBIRD TILLERS (TM)				
B 29	OH	Millersburg	Yes	Sunbird Products, Inc.
SUNDIALS				
B 1	CA	Pt. Arena		American Sundials, Inc.
B 19	CT	Wilton		Kenneth Lynch & Sons, Inc.
B 2	FL	Orlando	Yes	Autumn Forge
B 26	IL	Chicago		Replogle Globes, Inc.
B 2	MA	Boston		Ascot Designs
B 2	NC	Greensboro		Autumn Innovations
B 9	NH	Penacook	Yes	Duncraft, Inc.
B 11	NY	Long Island City	Yes	Florentine Craftsmen, Inc.
B 15	OK	Bixby		Heritage Sundial
B 10	RI	Newport	Yes	Erkins Studios, Inc.
B 27	VA	Hillsboro	Yes	Royal Tidewater Collection, Inc.
B 24	VA	Madison	Yes	The Plow & Hearth
B 21	WY	Cody		Modern Farm
SUPERTHRIVE (TM)				
B 31	FL	Bradenton	Yes	Tropexotic Growers, Inc.
SUPPLIES, WATER GARDENS				
See Also - Fish, Garden Ponds				
See Also - Ponds and Pools				
A 99	CA	Upland	Yes	Van Ness Water Gardens
A 89	FL	Winter Haven	Yes	Slocum Water Gardens
A 72	MA	Whitman		Paradise Water Gardens
A 104	MD	Baltimore	Yes	Wicklein's Aquatic Farm & Nursery, Inc.
A 56	MD	Lilypons	Yes	Lilypons Water Gardens
A 102	NJ	Saddle River	Yes	Waterford Gardens
B 15	NY	Canastota	Yes	Hermitage Gardens
A 97	OH	Independence	Yes	William Tricker, Inc.
A 64	ON	Port Stanley	Yes	Moore Water Gardens
A 95	PA	Coopersburg	Yes	Tilley's Nursery/The WaterWorks
SUSSEX TRUGS				
B 2	NC	Greensboro		Autumn Innovations
SWINGS AND GLIDERS				
B 21	CA	Bayside	Yes	Nampara Gardens
B 24	DC	Washington	Yes	Park Place
B 34	GA	Savannah		Woodventure, Inc.
B 32	MA	Walpole		Walpole Woodworkers
B 6	MA	West Newton		The Clapper Co.
B 7	MD	Germantown	Yes	Country Casual
B 5	NC	Moravian Falls	Yes	Brushy Mountain Bee Farm, Inc.
B 34	NY	High Falls	Yes	Wood Classics, Inc.
B 33	TX	Kemp		Westwind Mfg. Co.
B 24	VA	Madison	Yes	The Plow & Hearth
TERRARIUMS				
A 62	CA	Sacramento	Yes	Mighty Minis
A 58	KS	Wichita	Yes	McKinney's Glasshouse
A 9	NJ	Pompton Lakes		Black Copper Kits
THERMOFOR (R)				
B 4	MA	Salem		Bramen Company, Inc.
TIER BENCHES				
B 8	FL	Miami	Yes	Day-Dex Co.
TILLERS				
B 9	IN	Jeffersonville		Earlee, Inc.

(continued next page)

PAGE	STATE	CITY	SHOP?	SOURCE
TILLERS (continued)				
B 3	NC	Matthews		BCS Mosa, Inc.
B 12	NY	Troy		Garden Way Manufacturing Co.
B 20	OH	London	Yes	Mainline of North America
B 2	OH	London	Yes	Mainline of North America
B 29	OH	Millersburg	Yes	Sunbird Products, Inc.
B 20	PA	Huntingdon Valley	Yes	Mantis Manufacturing Co.
TISSUE CULTURE, CUSTOM				
A 45	NC	Raleigh	Yes	Hungry Plants
TISSUE CULTURE, ORCHIDS				
A 103	BC	Vancouver	Yes	Western Biologicals Ltd.
B 8	CA	Saskatoon, SK	Yes	Custom Orchid Propagation
B 23	NY	Burdett		Orchis Laboratories
TOMAHAWK (R)				
B 12	NY	Troy		Garden Way Manufacturing Co.
TOOL HANDLES				
B 23	AR	Eureka Springs	Yes	Ozark Handle & Hardware
TOOLS				
A 86	AB	Edmonton	Yes	Seed Centre Ltd.
B 7	CA	Long Beach		J Collard
B 28	CA	Mill Valley	Yes	Smith & Hawken
A 73	CA	Nevada City	Yes	Peaceful Valley Farm Supply
B 21	CA	San Anselmo		The Natural Gardening Company
A 30	IA	Shenandoah		Henry Field Seed & Nursery Co.
B 1	IL	Galesburg		Alsto's Handy Helpers
B 8	IL	Moline		John Deere Catalog
B 25	IL	Rockford		RAM Log Splitters
A 74	ME	New Gloucester	Yes	Pinetree Garden Seeds
B 5	NH	Peterborough	Yes	Brookstone Co.
A 61	OH	North Lima	Yes	Mellinger's Inc.
B 3	ON	St. Thomas	Yes	Berry-Hill Limited
A 34	ON	Thornhill	Yes	Gardenimport, Inc.
B 18	PA	Point Pleasant	Yes	Kinsman Company, Inc.
A 13	PA	Warminster	Yes	W. Atlee Burpee Company
B 12	VT	Burlington	Yes	Gardener's Supply Company
B 21	WY	Cody		Modern Farm
TOOLS, HAND				
B 21	CA	San Anselmo		The Natural Gardening Company
B 12	CA	San Francisco		Gardener's Eden
A 103	CT	Litchfield	Yes	White Flower Farm
B 1	CT	Plantsville	Yes	American Standard Co.
B 1	IL	Galesburg		Alsto's Handy Helpers
B 8	IL	Moline		John Deere Catalog
B 1	IN	Indianapolis	Yes	Alternative Garden Supply, Inc.
B 22	MA	Topsfield	Yes	Walter Nicke Company
B 6	MA	West Newton		The Clapper Co.
A 61	MD	Baltimore		Meyer Seed Co.
B 22	MN	Park Rapids	Yes	North Star Evergreens
B 5	NH	Peterborough	Yes	Brookstone Co.
A 11	NY	Brooklyn		Botanic Garden Seed Co.
B 33	NY	Rochester	Yes	Warnico/USA, Inc.
A 43	OH	Chesterland	Yes	Homestead Division of Sunnybrook Farms
B 17	OH	Cleveland	Yes	David Kay Garden & Gift Catalogue, Inc.
B 18	OH	Piqua		C. M. Leonard, Inc.
B 18	PA	Point Pleasant	Yes	Kinsman Company, Inc.
B 20	SC	Charleston	Yes	Meridian Equipment Corporation
B 13	SK	Saskatoon		Green Hand Tools
B 13	TX	Littlefield		The Greener Thumb
B 19	VA	Arlington	Yes	Mrs. McGregor's Garden Shop
B 24	VA	Madison	Yes	The Plow & Hearth
B 6	WA	Mt. Vernon	Yes	Charley's Greenhouse Supply
B 6	WI	Menasha		Chesnutt Corp.

PAGE	STATE	CITY	SHOP?	SOURCE
TOOLS, PRUNING				
A 37	CA	Carmel	Yes	Greener 'N' Ever Tree Farm & Nursery
A 5	CA	Somis		Armstrong Roses
B 1	CT	Plantsville	Yes	American Standard Co.
B 14	KS	Paola	Yes	Happy Valley Ranch
B 7	MA	Andover		Country House Floral Supply
B 4	MA	Salem		Bramen Company, Inc.
B 22	MA	Topsfield	Yes	Walter Nicke Company
B 6	MA	West Newton		The Clapper Co.
B 22	MN	Park Rapids	Yes	North Star Evergreens
B 14	NJ	Old Tappan		Harlane Company, Inc.
B 18	OH	Piqua		C. M. Leonard, Inc.
B 20	SC	Charleston	Yes	Meridian Equipment Corporation
B 13	SK	Saskatoon		Green Hand Tools
A 83	TN	Nash		SPB Sales
A 106	TX	DeLeon	Yes	Womack Nursery Co.
B 13	TX	Littlefield		The Greener Thumb
B 28	WA	Mt. Vernon	Yes	Skagit Gardens
A 8	WA	Northport	Yes	Bear Creek Nursery
A 22	WA	Snohomish	Yes	Cricklewood Nursery
TOPIARY FRAMES				
B 12	CA	Coloma	Yes	Gardenworks
B 19	CT	Wilton		Kenneth Lynch & Sons, Inc.
B 31	FL	Tampa		Topiary, Inc.
B 32	OR	Portland		Vine Arts
A 28	PA	Philadelphia	Yes	Exotic Blossoms (TM) Topiary Sculptures
TRAKE (TM)				
A 5	PA	Waynesboro	Yes	Appalachian Gardens
TROY-BILT (R)				
B 12	NY	Troy		Garden Way Manufacturing Co.
TRUBLOOM (R)				
B 32	CT	Greenwich		Verilux, Inc.
ULTRA VIOLETS (R)				
B 23	OH	St. Marys	Yes	Organic Research Laboratories
VIDEO CASSETTES				
B 26	CA	Chatsworth		Raindrip, Inc.
B 18	CA	Hollywood	Yes	Kohan-Matlick Productions
B 12	CA	Rancho Palos Verdes	Yes	V. L. T. Gardner
B 23	CA	San Francisco		One Up Productions
B 23	CA	San Francisco		Ortho Information Services
B 20	CT	Southport		The Matrix Group
B 27	IL	Chicago		Jack Schmidling Productions
B 5	NC	Moravian Falls	Yes	Brushy Mountain Bee Farm, Inc.
B 16	NY	Rochester		International Bonsai Containers
A 70	OR	Aurora		Oregon Bulb Farms
A 31	WA	Bellevue	Yes	Foliage Gardens
A 45	WA	Kent		Ed Hume Seeds, Inc.
B 6	WI	Deer Park	Yes	Capability's Books & Videos
VIDEODISCS				
B 32	CA	Soquel		VT Productions
B 20	CT	Southport		The Matrix Group
B 32	WA	Seattle		Videodiscovery, Inc.
VIRUS TESTING				
B 7	CA	Lincoln	Yes	Critter Creek Laboratory & Orchids
B 23	NY	Burdett		Orchis Laboratories
VITA-GRO LIQUID PLANTFOOD (R)				
B 30	CO	Boulder		Swallowtail Corporation
VITALOAM II (R)				
B 23	OH	St. Marys	Yes	Organic Research Laboratories

PAGE	STATE	CITY	SHOP?	SOURCE
WATER PURIFIERS				
B 28	CA	San Marcos		Spiral Filtration
B 24	CA	Ventura	Yes	Phologistics
WEATHER INSTRUMENTS				
B 11	IL	Schaumburg	Yes	Florist Products, Inc.
B 26	NE	Columbus	Yes	Rodco Products Co., Inc.
B 27	NJ	Princeton	Yes	Science Associates
B 18	OH	Piqua		C. M. Leonard, Inc.
B 31	WA	Enumclaw	Yes	Trade-Wind Instruments
B 6	WA	Mt. Vernon	Yes	Charley's Greenhouse Supply
B 21	WY	Cody		Modern Farm
WEATHER SHIELD WINDOWS (R)				
B 2	WI	Hammond	Yes	Arctic Glass & Window Outlet
WEATHERVANES				
B 19	CT	Wilton		Kenneth Lynch & Sons, Inc.
B 2	FL	Orlando	Yes	Autumn Forge
B 8	IL	Moline		John Deere Catalog
B 27	NJ	Princeton	Yes	Science Associates
B 11	NY	Long Island City	Yes	Florentine Craftsmen, Inc.
B 3	ON	St. Thomas	Yes	Berry-Hill Limited
B 20	SC	Charleston	Yes	Meridian Equipment Corporation
B 21	WY	Cody		Modern Farm
WEEDERS, GAS/ELECTRIC				
B 7	VT	Charlotte		Country Home Products, Inc.
WEEDERS, HAND				
B 22	MA	Topsfield	Yes	Walter Nicke Company
WHEELBARROWS				
B 33	WI	Janesville	Yes	Wisconsin Wagon Co.
WINDOW BOXES				
B 19	VA	Arlington	Yes	Mrs. McGregor's Garden Shop
WONDERLITE (R)				
B 25	NY	New York		Public Service Lamp Corp.
B 2	PQ	Montreal	Yes	Applied Hydroponics of Canada
WORM CASTINGS				
B 3	GA	Dawson		Beatrice Farms
B 6	GA	Plains		Carter Fishworm Farm
B 1	IN	Indianapolis	Yes	Alternative Garden Supply, Inc.
B 21	IN	Sunman		Natural Gardening Research Center
B 6	MA	Buzzards Bay		Cape Cod Worm Farm
B 24	MN	Duluth		Plant Magic Products, Inc.
B 8	OR	Eugene	Yes	Down to Earth Distributors
B 13	WA	Puyallup	Yes	Green Earth Organics

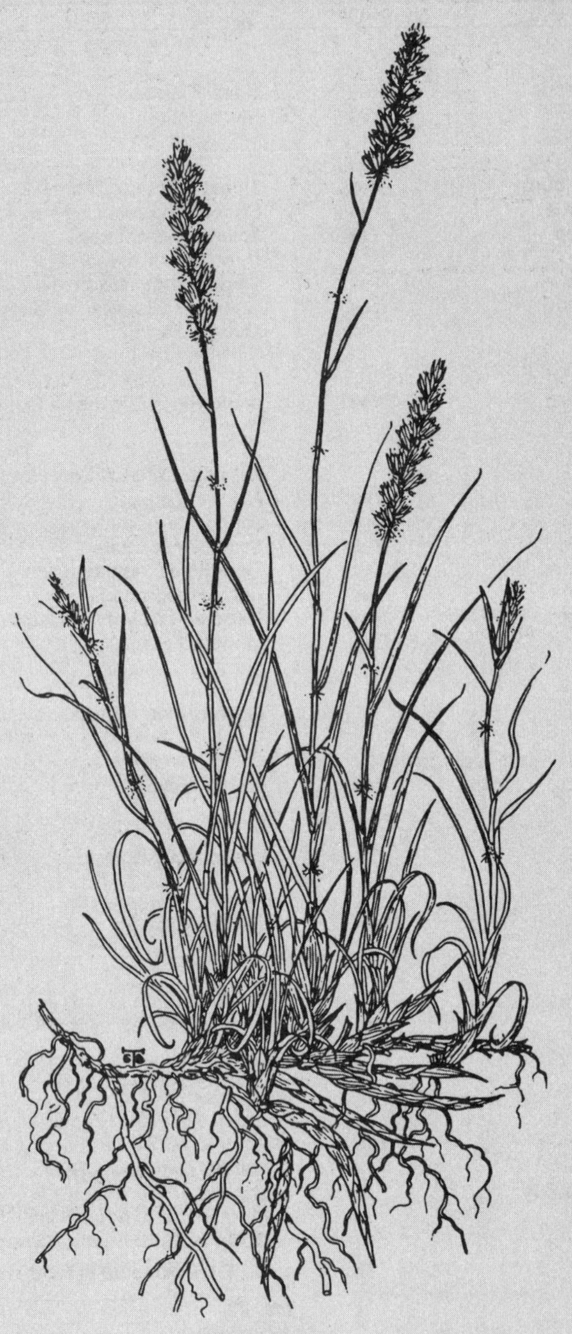

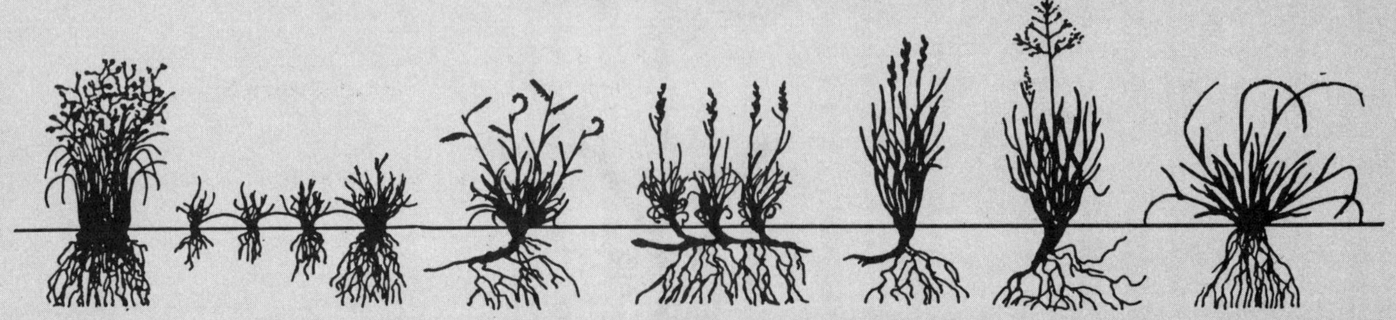

PAGE SOCIETY

AFRICAN VIOLETS
D 1 African Violet Society of America, Inc.
D 1 African Violet Society of Canada
D 17 Saintpaulia International

ALOES
D 1 Aloe, Cactus & Succulent Society of Zimbabwe

ALPINE PLANTS
D 1 Alpine Garden Club of British Columbia
D 1 Alpine Garden Society
D 4 American Rock Garden Society
D 17 Scottish Rock Garden Club
D 19 Vancouver Island Rock & Alpine Garden Society

AMARYLLIDS
D 3 American Plant Life Society

AQUATIC PLANTS
D 20 Water Lily Society

AROIDS
D 11 International Aroid Society

ASCLEPIADS
D 11 International Asclepiad Society

AZALEAS
D 4 American Rhododendron Society
D 5 Azalea Society of America

BAMBOO
D 1 American Bamboo Society

BEGONIAS
D 1 American Begonia Society
D 6 British Columbia Fuchsia & Begonia Society

BONSAI
D 1 American Bonsai Society
D 5 Bonsai Canada
D 5 Bonsai Clubs International
D 19 The Toronto Bonsai Society

BOXWOOD
D 2 American Boxwood Society

PAGE SOCIETY

BROMELIADS
D 6 Bromeliad Society, Inc.
D 6 Bromeliad Study Group of Northern California

BULBOUS PLANTS
D 3 American Plant Life Society
D 11 Indigenous Bulb Growers Assn. of South Africa

BULBS, SOUTH AFRICAN
D 11 Indigenous Bulb Growers Assn. of South Africa

CACTUS
D 1 Aloe, Cactus & Succulent Society of Zimbabwe
D 6 The British Cactus & Succulent Society
D 6 Cactus & Succulent Society of America
D 11 International Cactus & Succulent Society
D 19 The Toronto Cactus & Succulent Club

CAMELLIAS
D 2 American Camellia Society
D 11 International Camellia Society
D 14 New Zealand Camellia Society

CARNIVOROUS PLANTS
D 11 International Carnivorous Plant Society

CHRYSANTHEMUMS
D 7 Canadian Chrysanthemum & Dahlia Society
D 13 National Chrysanthemum Society (UK)
D 13 National Chrysanthemum Society, Inc. (USA)

CITRUS
D 11 Indoor Citrus & Rare Fruit Society

CLEMATIS
D 12 The International Clematis Society

CONIFERS
D 2 American Conifer Society

CRABAPPLES
D 12 International Ornamental Crabapple Society

CRYPTANTHUS
D 8 The Cryptanthus Society

CYCADS
D 8 The Cycad Society

PAGE SOCIETY

CYCLAMEN
D 8 Cyclamen Society

DAFFODILS
D 2 American Daffodil Society, Inc.
D 8 The Daffodil Society (UK)

DAHLIAS
D 2 American Dahlia Society
D 7 Canadian Chrysanthemum & Dahlia Society
D 16 Puget Sound Dahlia Association

DAYLILIES
D 2 American Hemerocallis Society

DELPHINIUMS
D 8 The Delphinium Society

EPIPHYLLUMS
D 8 Epiphyllum Society of America

FERNS
D 2 American Fern Society
D 12 International Tropical Fern Society
D 12 Los Angeles International Fern Society

FIGS
D 9 Friends of the Fig

FRUIT
D 4 American Pomological Society
D 9 Friends of the Trees
D 10 Home Orchard Society
D 11 Indoor Citrus & Rare Fruit Society
D 12 International Dwarf Fruit Tree Association
D 15 North American Fruit Explorers
D 17 Rare Fruit Council International, Inc.
D 20 Vinifera Wine Growers Association

FRUIT, NEW VARIETIES
D 4 American Pomological Society
D 15 North American Fruit Explorers

FRUIT, SUB-TROPICAL
D 7 California Rare Fruit Growers, Inc.
D 11 Indoor Citrus & Rare Fruit Society

FUCHSIAS
D 2 American Fuchsia Society
D 4 Australian Fuchsia Society
D 6 British Columbia Fuchsia & Begonia Society
D 6 British Fuchsia Society
D 13 National Fuchsia Society
D 14 New Zealand Fuchsia Society
D 18 South African Fuchsia Society

PAGE SOCIETY

GARDEN HISTORY
D 4 Australian Garden History Society
D 9 Garden History Society
D 18 Southern Garden History Association

GARDENIAS
D 9 Gardenia Society of America

GENERAL INTEREST
D 3 American Horticultural Society
D 7 California Horticultural Society
D 10 Horticultural Society of New York
D 13 Massachusetts Horticultural Association
D 13 Minnesota State Horticultural Society
D 16 Northwest Horticultural Society
D 16 The Pennsylvania Horticultural Society
D 18 Southern California Horticultural Institute
D 19 Texas Horticultural Society
D 20 Western Horticultural Society

GERANIUMS
D 5 Australian Geranium Society
D 6 British & European Geranium Society
D 6 British Pelargonium & Geranium Society
D 7 Canadian Geranium & Pelargonium Society
D 12 International Geranium Society

GERANIUMS, SPECIES
D 6 British Pelargonium & Geranium Society

GESNERIADS
D 2 American Gloxinia & Gesneriad Society, Inc.
D 9 Gesneriad Hybridizers Association
D 9 Gesneriad Society International
D 19 Toronto Gesneriad Society

GINGERS
D 2 American Ginger Society

GLADIOLUS
D 7 Canadian Gladiolus Society
D 15 North American Gladiolus Council

GLOXINIAS
D 2 American Gloxinia & Gesneriad Society, Inc.

GOURDS
D 2 American Gourd Society

GREENHOUSE GARDENING
D 10 Hobby Greenhouse Association
D 11 The Indoor Gardening Society of Canada

HEATHERS
D 10 The Heather Society
D 15 North American Heather Society

PAGE SOCIETY

HELICONIA
D 10 Heliconia Society International

HERBS
D 10 Herb Research Foundation
D 10 Herb Society of America

HIBISCUS
D 3 American Hibiscus Society
D 5 Australian Hibiscus Society

HOLLY
D 10 Holly Society of America

HOSTAS
D 3 American Hosta Society

HOUSEPLANTS
D 10 Hobby Greenhouse Association
D 11 Indoor Gardening Society of America
D 11 The Indoor Gardening Society of Canada
D 12 Light Gardening Society of America
D 16 Peperomia Society International
D 19 The Terrarium Association

HOYAS
D 10 The Hoya Society International

HYDROPONIC GROWING
D 11 Hydroponic Society of America
D 11 Hydroponic Society of Victoria

INDOOR GARDENING
D 11 Indoor Gardening Society of America
D 11 The Indoor Gardening Society of Canada

IRIS
D 3 American Iris Society
D 4 Aril Society International
D 6 British Iris Society
D 7 Canadian Iris Society
D 18 The Society for Japanese Irises
D 18 Society for Louisiana Irises
D 18 Society for Pacific Coast Native Iris
D 19 Species Iris Group of North America

IVY
D 3 American Ivy Society
D 6 The British Ivy Society

LILACS
D 12 International Lilac Society

LILIES
D 7 Canadian Prairie Lily Society
D 15 North American Lily Society, Inc.

PAGE SOCIETY

LILIES
D 16 Ontario Regional Lily Society
D 16 Pacific Northwest Lily Society

MAGNOLIAS
D 3 American Magnolia Society

MARIGOLDS
D 13 Marigold Society of America, Inc.

NATIVE PLANTS
D 1 Alaska Native Plant Society
D 4 Arizona Native Plant Society
D 4 Arkansas Native Plant Society
D 6 Botanical Club of Wisconsin
D 6 Botanical Society of South Africa
D 7 California Native Plant Society
D 8 Colorado Native Plant Society
D 9 Georgia Botanical Society
D 10 Hawaiian Botanical Society
D 11 Idaho Native Plant Society - Pahvoe Chapter
D 13 Louisiana Native Plant Society
D 13 Michigan Botanical Club
D 13 Minnesota Native Plant Society
D 13 Mississippi Native Plant Society
D 13 Missouri Native Plant Society
D 14 Native Plant Society of New Mexico
D 14 Native Plant Society of Oregon
D 14 Native Plant Society of Texas
D 14 New Jersey Native Plant Society
D 15 Northern Nevada Native Plant Society
D 16 Ohio Native Plant Society
D 16 Pennsylvania Native Plant Society
D 18 The Society for Growing Australian Plants
D 18 Southern California Botanists
D 19 Southern Illinois Native Plant Society
D 19 Tallgrass Prairie Alliance
D 19 Tennessee Native Plant Society
D 19 Utah Native Plant Society
D 20 Washington Native Plant Society
D 20 Wyoming Native Plant Society

NERINES
D 14 Nerine Society

NUTS, HARDY
D 15 Northern Nut Growers Association

OLEANDERS
D 12 International Oleander Society

ORCHIDS
D 3 American Orchid Society
D 7 Canadian Orchid Society
D 8 Cymbidium Society of America
D 16 Orchid Correspondence Club
(continued next page)

PAGE SOCIETY

ORCHIDS (continued)
D 16 Pacific Orchid Society
D 17 Saskatchewan Orchid Society
D 20 Victoria Orchid Society

ORGANIC GARDENING
D 5 Bio-Dynamic Farming & Gardening Assn.
D 5 Bio-Integral Resource Center (BIRC)
D 7 Canadian Organic Growers
D 8 Alan Chadwick Society
D 17 Seattle Tilth Association

PALMS
D 12 The International Palm Society

PELARGONIUMS
D 6 British Pelargonium & Geranium Society
D 7 Canadian Geranium & Pelargonium Society

PENSTEMONS
D 3 American Penstemon Society

PEONIES
D 3 American Peony Society

PEPERMOMIAS
D 16 Peperomia Society International

PERENNIALS
D 8 Cottage Garden Society
D 9 Hardy Plant Society (UK)
D 9 Hardy Plant Society of Oregon

PEST MANAGEMENT, NON-TOXIC
D 5 Bio-Integral Resource Center (BIRC)

PLUMERIAS
D 16 The Plumeria Society of America, Inc.

POINSETTIAS
D 4 American Poinsettia Society

POTATOES
D 19 Tubers

PRIMROSES
D 4 American Primrose Society
D 13 National Auricula & Primula Society

PUMPKINS, GIANT
D 20 World Pumpkin Confederation

RHODODENDRONS
D 4 American Rhododendron Society
D 5 Australian Rhododendron Society
D 17 Rhododendron Society of Canada

PAGE SOCIETY

RHODODENDRONS
D 17 Rhododendron Species Foundation

ROCK GARDENS
D 1 Alpine Garden Society
D 4 American Rock Garden Society
D 17 Scottish Rock Garden Club
D 19 Vancouver Island Rock & Alpine Garden Society

ROSES
D 4 American Rose Society
D 7 Canadian Rose Society
D 9 Federation of International Rose Exhibitors
D 10 Heritage Roses Group
D 17 Rose Hybridizers Association
D 17 Royal National Rose Society

SELF-SUFFICIENCY
D 9 Friends of the Trees

SEMPERVIVUMS
D 18 Sempervivum Fanciers Association
D 18 The Sempervivum Society

SOLANACEAE
D 18 Solanaceae Enthusiasts

SUCCULENTS
D 1 Aloe, Cactus & Succulent Society of Zimbabwe
D 6 The British Cactus & Succulent Society
D 6 Cactus & Succulent Society of America
D 11 International Cactus & Succulent Society
D 19 The Toronto Cactus & Succulent Club

SWEET PEAS
D 14 National Sweet Pea Society

VEGETABLE GARDENING
D 14 National Gardening Association
D 17 Seed Savers Exchange

WATER LILIES
D 20 Water Lily Society

WILDFLOWERS
D 1 Alabama Wildflower Society
D 8 The Canadian Wildflower Society
D 12 Kansas Wildflower Society
D 14 New England Wild Flower Society
D 15 North Carolina Wild Flower Preservation Soc.
D 20 Virginia Wildflower Preservation Society

WINE GRAPES
D 20 Vinifera Wine Growers Association

MAGAZINE INDEX M 1

PAGE	MAGAZINE	* = AVAILABLE TO MEMBERS ONLY	ISSUER
D 1	ABStracts	*	American Bonsai Society
C 1	ACGA Journal	*	American Community Gardening Association
D 3	A.O.S. Awards Quarterly	*	American Orchid Society
D 9	ARS Rosaceae	*	Federation of International Rose Exhibitors
C 1	ASTA Newsletter	*	American Seed Trade Association
E 1	Actinidia Enthusiasts Newsletter		Friends of the Trees
D 1	African Violet Magazine	*	African Violet Society of America, Inc.
D 1	Alpine Gardening	*	Alpine Garden Society
E 1	Amaranth Today		Rodale Press, Inc.
D 2	American Fern Journal	*	American Fern Society
C 1	American Forests	*	American Forestry Association
D 3	American Horticulturist	*	American Horticultural Society
D 3	American Horticulturist News	*	American Horticultural Society
D 3	American Hosta Society Bulletin	*	American Hosta Society
D 3	American Orchid Society Bulletin	*	American Orchid Society
D 4	The American Rose Magazine	*	American Rose Society
D 13	Amerigold Newsletter	*	Marigold Society of America, Inc.
D 14	Annual	*	National Sweet Pea Society
D 15	Annual Report	*	Northern Nut Growers Association
C 1	Arboriculture Consultant	*	American Society of Consulting Arborists
E 1	Arnoldia		Harvard Univ., The Arnold Arboretum
D 11	Aroideana	*	International Aroid Society
D 4	Australian Garden Journal	*	Australian Garden History Society
E 1	Australian Orchid Review		See Magazine Section
D 18	Australian Plants	*	The Society for Growing Australian Plants
E 1	The Avant Gardener		Horticultural Data Processors
D 5	The Azalean	*	Azalea Society of America
E 1	Baer's Garden Newsletter		John Baer's Sons
D 1	The Begonian	*	American Begonia Society
E 1	Bev Dobson's Rose Letter		Beverly R. Dobson
D 5	Bio-Dynamics	*	Bio-Dynamic Farming & Gardening Assn.
E 1	Blair & Ketchum's Country Journal		Historical Times, Inc.
D 5	Bonsai Clubs International	*	Bonsai Clubs International
D 1	Bonsai Journal	*	American Bonsai Society
D 2	The Boxwood Bulletin	*	American Boxwood Society
D 6	Bradleya		British Cactus & Succulent Society
D 6	British Cactus and Succulents Journal	*	The British Cactus & Succulent Society
D 6	The Bromeliad Hobbyist	*	Bromeliad Study Group of Northern California
D 1	Bulletin	*	Aloe, Cactus & Succulent Society of Zimbabwe
C 1	Bulletin	*	American Assn. of Botanical Gardens
D 2	Bulletin	*	American Conifer Society
D 2	Bulletin	*	American Dahlia Society
D 3	Bulletin	*	American Iris Society
D 3	Bulletin	*	American Peony Society
D 4	Bulletin	*	American Rock Garden Society

MAGAZINE INDEX M 2

PAGE	MAGAZINE	* = AVAILABLE TO MEMBERS ONLY	ISSUER
D 7	Bulletin	*	California Native Plant Society
D 8	Bulletin	*	The Daffodil Society (UK)
C 2	Bulletin	*	Garden Writers Association of America
D 10	Bulletin	*	The Heather Society
D 14	Bulletin	*	National Sweet Pea Society
D 14	Bulletin	*	Native Plant Society of Oregon
D 15	Bulletin	*	North American Gladiolus Council
D 16	Bulletin	*	Northwest Fuchsia Society
D 16	Bulletin	*	Pacific Northwest Lily Society
D 16	Bulletin	*	Puget Sound Dahlia Association
D 17	Bulletin	*	Rhododendron Society of Canada
D 20	Bulletin	*	Virginia Wildflower Preservation Society
E 1	Bulletin of American Garden History		Ellen Richards Samuels
D 3	Bulletin of the Amer. Penstemon Society	*	American Penstemon Society
D 9	Bulletin of the Hardy Plant Society	*	Hardy Plant Society (UK)
D 13	Bulletin/Panorama	*	National Chrysanthemum Society (UK)
E 1	The Bu$iness of Herbs		Portia Meares
D 7	COGnition	*	Canadian Organic Growers
D 6	C.S.S.A. Newsletter	*	Cactus & Succulent Society of America
E 1	Cactus & Succulent Journal		Abbey Garden Press
D 2	The Camellia Journal	*	American Camellia Society
D 7	Canadian Gladiolus Annual		Canadian Gladiolus Society
E 2	Canadian Horticultural History		Royal Botanical Gardens (CCHHS)
D 7	The Canadian Orchid Journal	*	Canadian Orchid Society
D 7	Canadian Rose Annual	*	Canadian Rose Society
D 11	Carnivorous Plant Newsletter	*	International Carnivorous Plant Society
D 1	Chatter	*	African Violet Society of Canada
E 2	Chestnutworks		Chestnut Growers Exchange
D 13	The Chrysanthemum	*	National Chrysanthemum Society, Inc. (USA)
D 5	Common Sense Pest Control	*	Bio-Integral Resource Center (BIRC)
C 4	Conservogram	*	Soil & Water Conservation Society
D 12	Crab Gab	*	International Ornamental Crabapple Society
D 18	Crossosoma	*	Southern California Botanists
D 9	Crosswords	*	Gesneriad Hybridizers Association
E 2	The Cultivar		UCSC Agroecology Program
D 8	The Cycad Newsletter	*	The Cycad Society
D 8	Cyclamen Journal	*	Cyclamen Society
D 2	The Daffodil Journal	*	American Daffodil Society, Inc.
D 2	Daylily Journal	*	American Hemerocallis Society
D 8	Delphinium Year Book	*	The Delphinium Society
E 2	Desert Plants		Boyce Thompson Southwestern Arboretum
D 20	Douglasia	*	Washington Native Plant Society
E 2	Dwarf Conifer Notes		Theophrastus
D 8	Epiphyllum Society Bulletin	*	Epiphyllum Society of America
E 2	Euphorbia Journal		Strawberry Press
D 1	Excelsa	*	Aloe, Cactus & Succulent Society of Zimbabwe
D 2	Fiddlehead Forum	*	American Fern Society
D 9	The Fig Leaflet	*	Friends of the Fig
E 2	Fine Gardening		The Taunton Press
E 2	Flower & Garden		Modern Handcraft, Inc.

PAGE	MAGAZINE	* = AVAILABLE TO MEMBERS ONLY	ISSUER
E 2	The Four Seasons		East Bay Regional Park District
D 7	Fremontia	*	California Native Plant Society
D 9	Friends of the Trees Yearbook	*	Friends of the Trees
D 7	The Fruit Gardener	*	California Rare Fruit Growers, Inc.
D 4	Fruit Varieties Journal	*	American Pomological Society
D 13	Fuchsia Fan	*	National Fuchsia Society
C 2	GCA Bulletin	*	The Garden Club of America
C 2	G.G.A. Newsletter	*	Garden Centers of America
D 10	Garden		Horticultural Society of New York
D 17	The Garden		The Royal Horticultural Society
E 2	Garden Design		American Society of Landscape Architects
D 9	Garden History	*	Garden History Society
C 3	The Gardener	*	Men's Garden Clubs of America, Inc.
E 2	Gardener's Index		Compudex Press
D 9	Gardenia Quarterly	*	Gardenia Society of America
E 2	Gardening Newsletter by Bob Flagg		Morningside Associates
D 6	Gazette	*	British & European Geranium Society
D 16	The Gazette	*	Peperomia Society International
D 12	Geraniums Around the World	*	International Geranium Society
D 9	Gesneriad Saintpaulia News	*	Gesneriad Society International
D 2	The Gloxinian	*	American Gloxinia & Gesneriad Society, Inc.
C 3	Going & Growing	*	National Junior Horticulture Association
D 2	The Gourd	*	American Gourd Society
D 16	The Green Scene		The Pennsylvania Horticultural Society
E 3	Greener Gardening, Easier		E. Dexter Davis, Horticulturist
E 3	Growing from Seed		Thompson & Morgan
E 3	Gurney's Gardening News		Gurney Seed & Nursery Company
D 10	HSI Bulletin	*	Heliconia Society International
D 10	HSNY Newsletter	*	Horticultural Society of New York
E 3	Harrowsmith		Camden House Publishing
C 3	Harvests Newsletter		The Lawn Institute
D 15	Heather News	*	North American Heather Society
E 3	Helping Each Other		Judy Huber
E 3	The Herb Quarterly		Uphill Press, Inc.
E 3	The Herb, Spice and Medicinal Plant Digest		University of Massachusetts
E 3	The Herbal Kitchen		Diane Lea Mathews
D 10	Herbalgram	*	Herb Research Foundation
D 10	The Herbarist	*	Herb Society of America
D 3	Herbertia	*	American Plant Life Society
D 10	Heritage Rose Letter	*	Heritage Roses Group
D 5	The Hibiscus	*	Australian Hibiscus Society
E 3	Himalayan Plant Journal		Primulaceae Books
D 10	Hobby Greenhouse	*	Hobby Greenhouse Association
D 10	Holly Society Journal	*	Holly Society of America
C 4	Horticultural Societies Newsletter	*	Ontario Horticultural Association
E 3	Horticulture		See Magazine Section
E 3	HortIdeas		Greg & Pat Williams
E 3	Hortline		Tom's World Horticulture Consulting
E 3	Hortus		See Magazine Section
D 18	Houseleeks	*	The Sempervivum Society

MAGAZINE INDEX M 4

PAGE	MAGAZINE	* = AVAILABLE TO MEMBERS ONLY	ISSUER
E 3	Houseplant Forum		HortiCom Inc.
D 10	The Hoyan	*	The Hoya Society International
D 11	IBSA Bulletin	*	Indigenous Bulb Growers Assn. of South Africa
E 4	The IPM Practitioner		Bio-Integral Resource Center
E 4	Indian Orchid Journal		Ganesh Mani Pradhan & Udai C. Pradhan
D 11	Indoor Garden	*	Indoor Gardening Society of America
D 11	Inside Green	*	The Indoor Gardening Society of Canada
E 4	International Bonsai		Intl. Bonsai Arboretum
D 11	International Camellia Journal	*	International Camellia Society
D 6	The Iris Year Book	*	British Iris Society
C 3	Irrigation News	*	The Irrigation Association
D 3	The Ivy Journal	*	American Ivy Society
E 1	John E. Bryan Gardening Newsletter		John E. Bryan Inc.
D 1	Journal	*	American Bamboo Society
D 4	Journal	*	American Rhododendron Society
D 5	Journal	*	Australian Geranium Society
D 6	Journal	*	The British Ivy Society
D 8	Journal	*	The Cryptanthus Society
C 2	Journal of Arboriculture	*	International Society of Arboriculture
E 4	Journal of Garden History		Taylor & Francis, Inc.
C 4	Journal of Soil & Water Conservation	*	Soil & Water Conservation Society
D 6	Journal of the Bromeliad Society	*	Bromeliad Society, Inc.
C 1	Journal of Therapeutic Horticulture	*	American Horticultural Therapy Association
D 12	Kansas Wildflower Society Newsletter	*	Kansas Wildflower Society
E 4	The Kew Magazine		See Magazine Section
D 12	LAIFS Journal	*	Los Angeles International Fern Society
C 1	Landscape Architecture	*	American Society of Landscape Architects
E 4	Lindleyana		American Orchid Society
E 4	Living off the Land, Subtropic Newsletter		Geraventure
D 3	Magnolia, Jnl. of the AMS	*	American Magnolia Society
D 15	Menzelia	*	Northern Nevada Native Plant Society
D 11	Mid-Year Newsletter	*	International Camellia Society
D 13	Minnesota Horticulturist	*	Minnesota State Horticultural Society
D 13	Mississippi N. P. S. Newsletter	*	Mississippi Native Plant Society
D 1	Monthly Bulletin	*	Alpine Garden Club of British Columbia
D 2	Monthly Bulletin	*	American Fuchsia Society
D 18	Monthly Bulletin	*	Southern California Horticultural Institute
D 12	Monthly Fern Lesson	*	Los Angeles International Fern Society
D 16	Na Okika O Hawaii/Hawaiian Orchid Journal	*	Pacific Orchid Society
C 2	The National Future Farmer	*	Future Farmers of America
C 3	The National Gardener	*	National Council of State Garden Clubs, Inc.
D 14	National Gardening	*	National Gardening Association
D 12	Nerium News	*	International Oleander Society
E 4	The New England Gardener		New England Horticultural Services, Inc.
C 4	The New Farm	*	Regenerative Agriculture Association
D 14	New Zealand Camellia Bulletin	*	New Zealand Camellia Society
D 9	News Letter	*	Hardy Plant Society (UK)
D 14	News Letter	*	New Zealand Fuchsia Society
D 1	Newsletter	*	Alaska Native Plant Society
C 1	Newsletter	*	American Assn. of Botanical Gardens & Arboreta

PAGE	MAGAZINE	* = AVAILABLE TO MEMBERS ONLY	ISSUER
D 1	Newsletter	*	American Bamboo Society
D 3	Newsletter	*	American Hosta Society
D 7	Newsletter	*	California Horticultural Society
D 7	Newsletter	*	Canadian Iris Society
D 7	Newsletter	*	Canadian Prairie Lily Society
D 8	Newsletter	*	Colorado Native Plant Society
D 8	Newsletter	*	Cottage Garden Society
C 2	Newsletter	*	Future Farmers of America
C 2	Newsletter	*	The Garden Club of America
D 9	Newsletter	*	Garden History Society
D 9	Newsletter	*	Hardy Plant Society of Oregon
D 11	Newsletter	*	Hydroponic Society of America
D 11	Newsletter	*	Hydroponic Society of Victoria
D 12	Newsletter	*	The International Clematis Society
D 12	Newsletter	*	International Lilac Society
D 14	Newsletter	*	Native Plant Society of New Mexico
D 14	Newsletter	*	New England Wild Flower Society
D 15	Newsletter	*	North Carolina Wild Flower Preservation Soc.
D 15	Newsletter	*	Northern Nevada Native Plant Society
D 16	Newsletter	*	Ontario Regional Lily Society
C 4	Newsletter	*	Perennial Plant Association
D 16	Newsletter	*	The Plumeria Society of America, Inc.
D 17	Newsletter	*	Rare Fruit Council International, Inc.
D 17	Newsletter	*	Saskatchewan Orchid Society
C 4	Newsletter	*	Seedpeople Network
D 18	Newsletter	*	Society for Louisiana Irises
D 18	Newsletter	*	Southern Garden History Association
D 19	Newsletter	*	Tennessee Native Plant Society
D 19	Newsletter	*	Vancouver Island Rock & Alpine Garden Society
D 20	Newsletter	*	World Pumpkin Confederation
D 15	Nutshell	*	Northern Nut Growers Association
D 6	Occasional Papers	*	The British Ivy Society
D 20	Occasional Papers	*	Washington Native Plant Society
D 16	On the Fringe	*	Ohio Native Plant Society
D 8	The Orchid Advocate	*	Cymbidium Society of America
E 4	The Orchid Digest		See Magazine Section
D 16	The Orchid Information Exchange	*	Orchid Correspondence Club
E 4	The Orchid Review		The Orchid Review, Ltd. (U.K.)
D 16	PHS News	*	The Pennsylvania Horticultural Society
E 4	Pacific Horticulture		Pacific Horticultural Foundation
D 6	Pelargonium News	*	British Pelargonium & Geranium Society
E 4	Permaculture with Native Plants		Curtin Mitchell
E 4	Plant Lore		See Magazine Section
D 4	Plant Press	*	Arizona Native Plant Society
E 4	Plants & Gardens		Brooklyn Botanical Garden
E 5	The Plantsman		N. P. Publishing
D 10	Pome News	*	Home Orchard Society
15	Pomona	*	North American Fruit Explorers
D 4	Primroses	*	American Primrose Society
D 12	Principes	*	The International Palm Society

MAGAZINE INDEX M 6

PAGE	MAGAZINE	* = AVAILABLE TO MEMBERS ONLY	ISSUER
D 2	Pteridologia		American Fern Society
D 15	Quarterly Bulletin	*	North American Lily Society, Inc.
D 11	Quarterly Newsletter	*	Indoor Citrus & Rare Fruit Society
D 17	RSF Newsletter	*	Rhododendron Species Foundation
D 18	The Review	*	The Society for Japanese Irises
D 5	The Rhododendron	*	Australian Rhododendron Society
D 17	The Rock Garden	*	Scottish Rock Garden Club
E 5	Rodale's Organic Gardening		Rodale Press, Inc.
D 7	The Rosarian	*	Canadian Rose Society
D 17	The Rose	*	Royal National Rose Society
D 17	Rose Hybridizers Association Newsletter	*	Rose Hybridizers Association
E 5	Rosy Outlook Magazine		"Rosy" McKenney
D 19	SIGNA	*	Species Iris Group of North America
D 18	SPCNI Almanac	*	Society for Pacific Coast Native Iris
D 11	Sage Notes	*	Idaho Native Plant Society - Pahvoe Chapter
D 17	Sea-Tilth	*	Seattle Tilth Association
D 3	The Seed Pod	*	American Hibiscus Society
D 19	Sego Lily	*	Utah Native Plant Society
D 18	Sempervivum Fanciers Assn. Newsletter	*	Sempervivum Fanciers Association
D 18	Solanaceae Quarterly	*	Solanaceae Enthusiasts
D 18	The South African Fuchsia Fanfare	*	South African Fuchsia Society
E 5	Southern Herbs		Eve Elliott
E 5	Southern Living		See Magazine Section
E 5	Sunset Magazine		Lane Publishing Co.
D 19	Tallgrass Prairie Alliance	*	Tallgrass Prairie Alliance
D 19	Tallgrass Prairie News	*	Tallgrass Prairie Alliance
D 19	Tater Talk	*	Tubers
D 19	The Texas Gardener	*	Texas Horticultural Society
D 14	Texas Native Plant Society News	*	Native Plant Society of Texas
D 6	Veld & Flora	*	Botanical Society of South Africa
D 20	Vinifera Wine Growers Journal	*	Vinifera Wine Growers Association
D 20	WNPS Newsletter	*	Wyoming Native Plant Society
D 20	Water Lily Journal	*	Water Lily Society
E 5	The Weekend Garden Journal		Jim Bennett
E 5	Westscape		Rick Hassett
D 14	Wild Flower Notes	*	New England Wild Flower Society
D 8	Wildflower	*	The Canadian Wildflower Society
D 17	Winter Yearbook	*	Seed Savers Exchange
D 6	Year Book	*	British & European Geranium Society
D 10	Year Book	*	The Heather Society
D 13	Year Book	*	National Chrysanthemum Society (UK)
D 4	Yearbook	*	Aril Society International
D 5	Yearbook	*	Bonsai Canada
D 6	Yearbook	*	British Pelargonium & Geranium Society
D 13	Yearbook	*	National Auricula &Primula Society
D 17	Yearbook	*	Rare Fruit Council International, Inc.
D 19	Yearbook	*	Texas Horticultural Society
D 2	Zingiber	*	American Ginger Society

Practical Matters

This section contains a number of practical forms which I hope you will find useful. All can be removed or photocopied for your use. As a matter of "good formsmanship" and to be sure you get what you request, be sure to carefully print or type your name and address.

• **I Found You in Gardening by Mail 2** – A catalog and information request form. This form is intended for you to use to request catalogs, to request information from societies and magazines or to ask companies if they can supply specific items on your "want list".

The best use of the form is to photocopy it once, print or type in your name and address, and then photocopy it again as many times as you like. You can then check off the appropriate boxes for each specific request. If you don't use this form, please mention **Gardening by Mail.**

• **Record of Catalog and Information Requests.** This form is meant to remain in the book so that you can keep a record of the requests you have sent and if you have received a reply.

• **Reader Feedback.** We are eager to hear your opinions on and suggestions for **Gardening by Mail.** Please use this form to tell us what you like and don't like about the book, any improvements you'd like to see, what your needs are and how you use the book – so we can make this book more and more the "perfect" gardeners' resource.

We also urge you to send suggestions for new listings. If your suggestions meet the requirements for listing in the book (see the Request for Listing in Next Edition form), we may include them in our quarterly updates.

• **Request for Listing in Next Edition or Update of Current Listing.** If you feel your company, society, publication or library should be listed in the next edition of this book, please let us know about you by filling in and sending us this form as soon as possible. The information requested on the form is the **minimum** we need to know about you. We also include new sources in our quarterly updates.

Companies and organizations already listed in this edition can use this form to update their listing. We will include updated information in our quarterly updates. All information will be verified before publication of the next edition.

• **Order Form.** Use this form to order **Gardening by Mail** if you can't find it in your local book stores. Tusker Press only accepts **prepaid** orders.

• **Updates to Gardening by Mail.** Use this form to order quarterly updates to **Gardening by Mail.** These updates include all changes, corrections and deletions that we know about after the first printing of this edition. We will also include new sources and "late breaking" information.

Updates are **cumulative** – so you only need to order the most recent or future updates to stay current.

• **Last Minute Changes and Corrections.** At each printing of **Gardening by Mail,** we will include the most recent information we have. The first printing of this book does not include this section. See **Updates to Gardening by Mail** above.

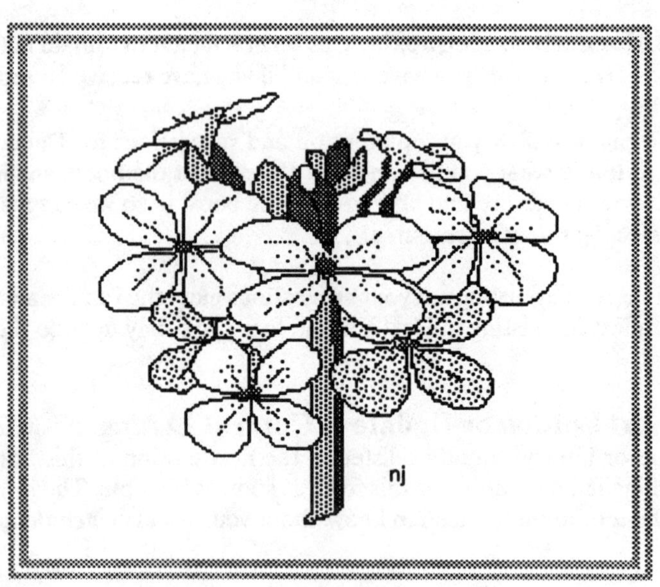
nj

I Found You in Gardening by Mail 2: A Source Book

Catalog and Information Request Form

Date: ______________________________

Dear: ______________________________

[ ] Please send me your free catalog.

[ ] I enclose a long self-addressed envelope with $ ______________ postage.

[ ] Please send me your catalog, for which I enclose $ ______________ .

[ ] You did not provide the price of your catalog, please send me one or advise me of the cost.

[ ] Please send me information on joining your society.

[ ] I'd like to subscribe to your periodical, please tell me your current rates.

[ ] Please let me know if you have: ______________________________

____

[ ] Other information I need: ______________________________

____

My name and address are:

Name: ______________________________

Address: ______________________________

City and State: ______________________________

Country: ______________________________ Postal Code: ______________

Phone Number: (Daytime): ______________________ (Evenings): ______________

Gardening by Mail 2: A Sourcebook
Published by Tusker Press, P.O. Box 1338, Sebastopol, CA 95473

Record of Catalog Orders and Requests

Company/Organization	Date of Request	Received

Record of Catalog Orders and Requests

Company/Organization	Date of Request	Received

Reader Feedback

Please tell us what suggestions you have for improving **Gardening by Mail.**

What I Like About **Gardening by Mail**

What I Don't Like About **Gardening by Mail**

Suggestions for Improvements to the Next Edition

[ ] Please let me know when the next edition of **Gardening by Mail** is Published.

Name:

Mailing Address:

City: State/Province:

Country: Postal Code:

Send this form to:

Please continue on back.

Tusker Press, Reader Feedback
P.O. Box 1338, Sebastopol, CA 95473

You should include in the next edition (plant and product sources, societies, magazines, etc.)

Name: ______________________________

Address: ______________________________

City, State, Country and Postal Code: ______________________________

Proprietor: ______________________ Telephone: (______)__________

Specialty: ______________________________

Name: ______________________________

Address: ______________________________

City, State, Country and Postal Code: ______________________________

Proprietor: ______________________ Telephone: (______)__________

Specialty: ______________________________

Name: ______________________________

Address: ______________________________

City, State, Country and Postal Code: ______________________________

Proprietor: ______________________ Telephone: (______)__________

Specialty: ______________________________

How I found out about **Gardening by Mail**: ______________________________

I am a: [ ] Home Gardener [ ] Professional/Commercial Horticulturist [ ] Both

[ ] New to Gardening [ ] Experienced [ ] Very Experienced

I Use **Gardening by Mail** for:

- [ ] Mail Orders
- [ ] Finding Local Sources
- [ ] Visiting Display Gardens
- [ ] Reference when Traveling
- [ ] Finding Plants by Climate Zone
- [ ] Finding Products/Services
- [ ] Finding Gardening Books
- [ ] Finding Magazines
- [ ] Finding Societies
- [ ] Finding Libraries
- [ ] Making Professional Contacts
- [ ] Buying Plants/Products for resale
- [ ] Selling Plants/Products to retailers
- [ ] Mailing List for Prospects
- [ ] Finding Unusual Plants or Products for Customers
- [ ] Fnding Sources of Educational Material
- [ ] Other uses: ______________________________

____

Request for Listing in Next Edition Of Gardening By Mail or Update of Current Listing

If you would like to be listed in the next edition of **Gardening By Mail**, please return this form by December 31, 1988 **with** your current catalog, sample periodical or literature. **We also list new sources in our quarterly updates.**

Current listees: Please use this form to notify us of any changes. **Changes will be included in our quarterly updates.**

To be listed in **Gardening by Mail**:

Seed Companies, Nurseries, Other Plant Suppliers, and Garden Suppliers must sell direct by mail order to buyers in the U.S. and/or Canada and **must enclose their most recent catalog with this request.**

Plant and Horicultural Societies must welcome members from the U.S. and/or Canada and **must include a current issue of their periodical with this request.**

Libraries must allow members of their sponsoring organizations and/or the public to use their facilities for reference.

Questionnaires will be sent to those who return this form. Those listed in the current edition will automatically receive a questionnaire, but must meet the above conditions AND send catalog or literature to be listed again.

Questionnaires vary by type of company or organization. Please specify your **primary** category:

[ ] Seed Company

[ ] Nursery

[ ] Garden Suppliers: Category ______________________________

[ ] Trade, Professional or Umbrella Organization

[ ] Plant or Horticultural Society

[ ] Horticultural Library

[ ] Gardening/Horticultural Magazine or Newsletter

[ ] Other (be specific and indicate why you should be listed): ______________

Final selection of those listed is at the discretion of the author.

Please type or print – if we can't read it, we can't use it.

[ ] Request for Listing [ ] Current Listing Update (provide current listing name, and new name, if changed).

Name of Business or Organization: ______________________________

Proprietor/Manager: ______________________________

Who Should Receive Questionnaire: ______________________________

Mailing Address: ______________________________

City and State: ______________________________

Country: ______________________ Postal Code: ______________

Phone Number(s): ______________________________

Please send this form to:

Please continue on back. →

Tusker Press, Database Department
P.O. Box 1338, Sebastopol, CA 95473

[ ] We have added Tusker Press to our mailing list.

[ ] We have provided the name of an individual who will promptly complete and return your future Questionnaires.

The following information is the **minimum** Tusker Press needs to know now:

The price of our catalog is: [ ] $ ________________ [ ] Long SASE [ ] Free

[ ] Minimum retail order is: $ ________________

[ ] Telephone orders accepted with credit cards – $ ________ minimum.

[ ] We sell wholesale AS WELL AS retail.

[ ] We ship to ( ) USA ( ) Canada ( ) Overseas

[ ] We ship live/perishible materials in the months: ________________

[ ] We sell MAIL ORDER ONLY (no nursery or shop/sales location).

[ ] We also sell at this Sales Address: ________________

[ ] We have a Display Garden or many plants/products on display at sales location.

The eight most important plants/products that we sell are::

____

____

____

____

____

____

____

____

Comments/Other Information:

____

____

____

____

____

Order Form for Gardening by Mail 2

If you are unable to find **Gardening by Mail 2** in your local bookstore, you can use this form to order it from Tusker Press.

Price per copy, prepaid in U.S. Dollars:

$19.50 postpaid, book post (California, Canada and Overseas)

$18.50 postpaid, book post (United States **except** California)

All orders will be sent Book Post. If First Class, Airmail or U.P.S. delivery is desired, payment must be by credit card so we can add appropriate delivery charges to the cost of your order.

Please send me ______________ copies of **Gardening by Mail 2: A Source Book at $**______________ per copy.

Total Order: $______________

Payment Method: [ ] Check or money order in U.S. Dollars enclosed [ ] Master Card [ ] Visa

Card #: ______________________________ Expiration Date: ______________

Name as it Appears on Card ______________________________

Billing Address: ______________________________

Card Holder's Signature: ______________________________

Ship Via: [ ] Surface Mail, Book Post [ ] First Class Mail [ ] U.P.S. [ ] Airmail

Ship To: ______________________________

Name: ______________________________

Mailing Address: ______________________________

Street Address (if U.P.S.): ______________________________

City and State: ______________________________

Country: ______________________________ Postal Code: ______________

Daytime Phone Number: ( ) ______________________________

Please allow six to eight weeks for delivery.

Send this form to:

Tusker Press, Order Department
P.O. Box 1338, Sebastopol, CA 95473
Library orders or orders for resale, please request our terms of business.

Updates to Gardening by Mail 2

A word about the Update division of Tusker Press: over the past few years that we have been collecting information about horticultural sources, we have learned one sobering lesson: things change – and rapidly. As fast as we gather information, our listees are changing their names, addresses, ownership, going out of business or ceasing to fill mail orders. We try to keep current and we're constantly on the lookout for changes – but it's like trying to catch sand in a hairnet.

In addition, we are continually finding new and exciting sources of plants and supplies, new societies, libraries, magazines and books which we'd like to share with our readers.

Tusker Press issues quarterly updates to **Gardening by Mail** which include new sources and any name and address changes that **we know about** for the listings in the book. **The updates are cumulative, so you only need to order the most recent update to be current.**

To order updates, send **U.S.$ 1.00 for each update desired** to Tusker Press, at the address below, and check the updates you wish.

Please send me ____________ update(s) to **Gardening by Mail** *as checked below* (updates are cumulative, so order **only** recent or future issues):

[ ] January 1988 [ ] April 1988 [ ] July 1988 [ ] October 1988 [ ] January **1989** [ ] April **1989**

I enclose a check or money order for U.S. $__________________________.

Name: ____

Mailing Address: ____

City: ______________________________ State/Province: ______________

Country: ______________________________ Postal Code: ______________

[ ] Please let me know when you publish a new edition of **Gardening by Mail.**

Have you sent us a Reader Feedback form? We'd appreciate it very much.

Send this form to:

Tusker Press, Update Division
P.O. Box 1338, Sebastopol, CA 95473